ALBUMS

THE STORIES BEHIND
50 YEARS
OF GREAT RECORDINGS

Thunder Bay Press
An imprint of the Advantage Publishers Group
5880 Oberlin Drive, San Diego, CA 92121-4794
www.thunderbaybooks.com

ISBN-10: 1-59223-295-7
ISBN-13: 978-1-59223-295-6

Library of Congress Cataloging in Publication Data available upon request.

COMMISSIONING EDITOR: MARK BREND
MANAGING EDITOR / RESEARCHER: THOMAS JEROME
EDITORS: SIMON SMITH & TONY BACON
DESIGN: MAIN ARTERY
PRODUCTION: PHIL RICHARDSON

Origination by Global Graphics (Czech Republic) & DL Repro Ltd. (England)
Printed by Colorprint Offset Ltd. (Hong Kong)

ALBUMS

THE STORIES BEHIND
50 YEARS
OF GREAT RECORDINGS

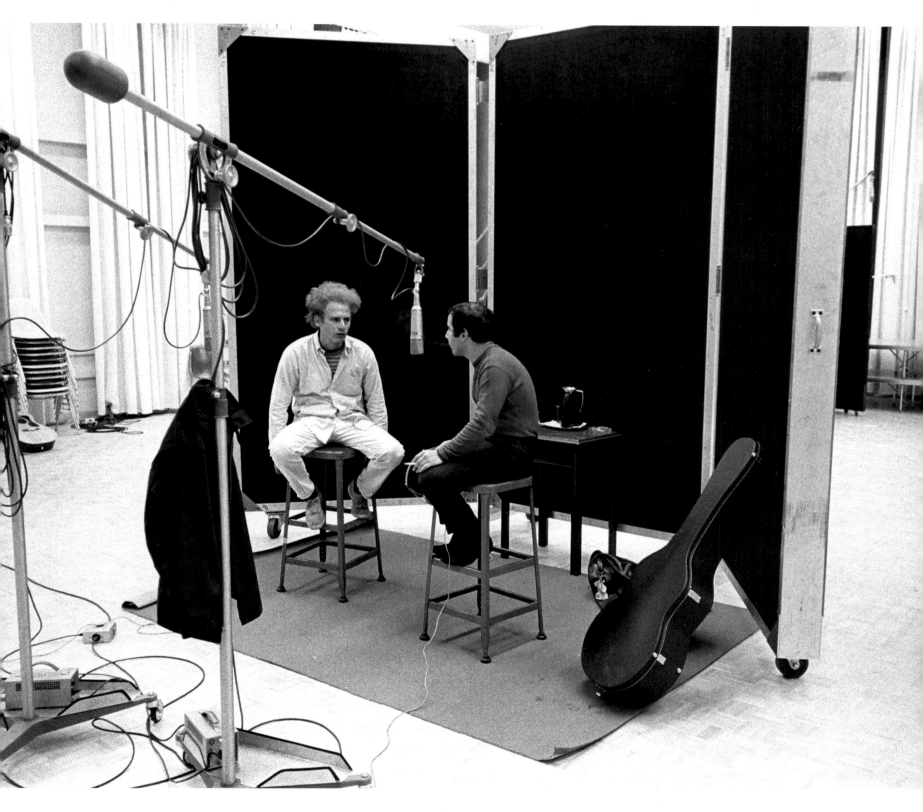

Thunder Bay
P·R·E·S·S
San Diego, California

A revolution in sound

Of all the ingenious methods for playing recorded music in the home devised since Thomas Edison's tin-foil cylinder, none has matched the affection earned by the 12-inch long-playing vinyl record.

And yet the LP was not the result of clever market research or revolutionary technological advance: it came from dogged efforts to improve on what was already available. The only thing new about it was that it worked.

From 1900 until 1948, records were either 10 inches or 12 inches in diameter, made of a brittle material called shellac, usually played at 78rpm, and of no more than three or four minutes' duration a side. Classical music, which tends to require longer playing time, was presented in sets of disks in cardboard sleeves or binders, known as "albums." From the 1940s popular artists also had collections of their single songs released in the same way.

RCA Victor marketed a 33⅓rpm long-playing record as early as 1932, made from a vinyl compound, but it proved incapable of withstanding the pounding it received from the heavy pickups used on the old 78 players. It was also only capable of running for eight minutes a side: hardly long playing at all.

In 1939 the giant broadcaster CBS bought the American Record Corporation. American owned the Columbia Records name, and CBS set about turning its new acquisition against its arch rival, RCA. Columbia's new boss, Ted Wallerstein, had been responsible for canceling the LP project at RCA but now revived it as a weapon for his new company. He realized that

what was needed was a whole long-playing system. It wasn't simply a matter of improving the record: he determined that what was required was a complete renewal of the sound reproduction chain.

World War II interrupted progress, but it began again straight afterward. Wallerstein decided he needed to set a target for the new record's duration. After timing numerous classical works he came up with 17 minutes a side, calculating that 90 per cent of all such music would fit on the two sides of the disk.

By 1947 the engineers, led by a young man called William Bachman, had devised a new system that involved much narrower microgrooves on the new records – there were 300 per inch, compared with 85 per inch on 78s – and new equipment for formulating, pressing, and playing back the new vinyl compound.

Interestingly, there was discussion at the time about whether to produce a smaller, shorter-play version aimed at the pop market, but CBS decided it had spent enough and pressed ahead with the classically biased product. There would also be 10-inch albums for pop recordings. Launch date was set for autumn 1948, player production was contracted out – CBS had no real interest in making playing equipment – and plans were made to bring in other record companies to share in the revolution. The important thing was to establish the format and get in early with what we would now call the 'software.'

In June 1948 there was a press launch, by which time duration was up to 22 minutes a side. About 100 titles were made available within a fortnight, initially using turntables that plugged into existing radio sets. These cost $29.95, quickly reduced to $9.95, and came bundled with three of the new LPs.

At the launch Wallerstein stood next to two piles of records containing the same 325 tracks: the pile of 78s was 8 feet tall; the pile of LPs was only 15 inches. Listeners, however, had mixed views on the sound quality. Just like early CDs, early LPs did not always impress with their sound: they were inclined to be hard and wiry, and there were problems with 'wow' and pre-echo, where loud passages intrude on neighboring grooves and can thus be heard faintly in advance.

Though the new system was a hit with what we now call 'early adopters' – technology enthusiasts – it took a while to take off. For classical fans the economic argument was powerful. Classical LPs were priced at $4.85 and promised to be indestructible; five-disk shellac albums of the same music cost $7.25.

The first classical album was Beethoven's *Violin Concerto*, Nathan Milstein soloing with Bruno Walter and the New York Philharmonic. Columbia's first pop LP was *The Voice of Frank Sinatra*. Originally issued in 1946, as an album of four 78s, its eight songs were now placed on a single 10-inch LP disk. A year before the launch of the new format Columbia had assigned a man secretly to assemble suitable eight-song packages to be the first releases. The first real hit, however, was the cast album of the Broadway musical *South Pacific*, recorded and in the shops in just four days in 1949.

RCA, meanwhile, had been mysteriously quiet since rejecting the Columbia system. Then, in March 1949, it launched its response: the 7-inch, 45rpm microgroove record. This was sold on convenience – the records would fit upright on your bookshelves – and sound quality: it was claimed that the grooves were all contained within the 'quality zone.' Interestingly, RCA's format seems to have been the only one that had ever been scientifically worked out. Mathematics showed that the optimum performance occurs when the inner groove is half the diameter of the outer groove: hence a 7-inch disk with a label 3½ inches in diameter.

The obvious problem with the 7-inch disk was that it didn't last any longer than the old 78, so it was marketed with a $24.95 autochanger – later reduced to $12.95 – that could play 10 disks in a sitting. RCA insisted this would make it just as suitable for classical music as Columbia's 12-inch disk. Classical purists, however, felt the company had lost interest in them in its pursuit of pop.

A brief but bitter war of speeds followed, which temporarily brought to an end the post-war boom in the record industry. People would not buy when there was such uncertainty – a lesson the record and consumer electronics industries have consistently failed to learn. Gradually, though, the CBS system gained ground. In the latter part of 1949 it was adopted by more and more record companies later including Capitol.

Finally, RCA announced the launch of its own LPs, but it did not intend to throw away its investment in the 45rpm disk. It now launched a ferocious and costly advertising campaign to insist that the 7-inch single record was the natural vehicle for pop music. Pop buyers liked the 7-inch, and soon even Columbia was producing singles for its pop acts. By 1954 RCA could proudly say that more than half of all the records produced in the U.S.A. were in its 45rpm format.

In the meantime, of course, record-player manufacturers had learned to produce multiformat machines, capable of supporting all speeds and diameters and the two different needle dimensions for both standard 78s and the new microgroove records.

The stories behind 50 years of great recordings

■ *Gene Vincent & His Blue Caps at Capitol Studios, Hollywood, in 1956. Left to right: Cliff Gallup, Gene Vincent, Willie Williams, Dickie Harrell, and Jack Neal.*

1955

In The Wee Small Hours
Frank Sinatra

Capitol W581 (U.S.A.) / CAPS1008 (U.K.)
Released April 1955

The year 1955 was remarkable both in the career of Francis Albert Sinatra and in the development of the album.

Not only did Sinatra successfully take on the role of tormented heroin-addicted card dealer Frankie Machine in *The Man With The Golden Arm* but he released an album, *In The Wee Small Hours*, which showed the world the enormous potential of the 12-inch format.

It was his first to be conceived from the off as a full-length, 12-inch album, and, unlike previous collections, was designed to be listened to in the order laid down. Just reading through the titles tells a story, and, with eight songs on each side now available to him thanks to the new long-player (LP) format, he had double the space in which to tell that story.

Sinatra had been making the painful transition from teen idol – with a following consisting almost exclusively of bobby-soxers – to an entertainer of much greater stature. As a solo performer between 1943 and 1952 he had clocked up an amazing 86 hits during his time on the Columbia label, and alongside his recording success there were appearances in popular movies such as *Anchors Aweigh* and *On The Town*. But by the mid 1950s, as his personal life ran into difficulties, so his musical fortunes were beginning to fade. *In The Wee Small Hours*, however, was to prove to be the album that turned his career around and was the first of many hit albums and singles to come.

In so many ways the album bears the imprint of the second Mrs Sinatra, high-flying actress Ava Gardner, from whom he'd split in late 1953 amid much rancor. The pair's affair had, for a couple of years, run parallel to his first marriage to Nancy, but when that ended things got worse rather than better. Sinatra had wanted a child, but Gardner had twice ended pregnancies, telling him: "We don't have the ability to live together like any normal married couple." This was hard coming on top of the bad publicity that leaving his family had attracted, and his attempts to rekindle the relationship, including a journey to Africa where she was filming, proved fruitless.

The combination of two strong, successful characters hadn't been the recipe for long-term success – according to legend, Gardner dumped him via an MGM press release – and in its aftermath Sinatra had embraced the high-rolling Las Vegas lifestyle with a vengeance. Breakfasting at five in the afternoon, he now lived a nocturnal life, making the newly written title song by David Mann and Bob Hilliard a particularly appropriate one. The cover, too, depicts late-night desolation particularly effectively, showing a solitary Sinatra smoking a cigarette under a streetlight's baleful glow.

He entered KHJ Studios in Hollywood in the company of arranger-conductor Nelson Riddle and pianist Bill Miller on February 8th 1955 for the first of five sessions – the others were on February 16th and 17th and March 1st and 4th. With a musical recipe of less-is-more, he had a firm vision of what he wanted to achieve, using a basic rhythm section of guitar and celesta that built on Miller's piano and was augmented by Riddle's strings at appropriate moments.

Riddle had followed in Sinatra's footsteps by joining Tommy Dorsey's band as trombonist in 1944, albeit three years after Sinatra had gone solo,

Continued on next page

1955

before settling in California after national service and moving into arranging. Riddle and Sinatra brought out the best in each other, and it was no surprise that Riddle served as musical director on most of the singer's popular television specials. The relationship with Riddle – otherwise best known for his work with Nat King Cole on songs such as 'Unforgettable,' 'Somewhere Along The Way,' and 'Ballerina' – had only begun in 1953 but was to be a mutually beneficial teaming for the individuals concerned, and Riddle succeeded Axel Stordahl as Sinatra's arranger of choice.

The material on this album, as with all Sinatra's Capitol releases, was selected by the singer and his A&R man, Voyle Gilmore, who also gets a production credit. Then Sinatra and Riddle would work out how to give it the kind of treatment they wanted. "My father was paramount when it came to that," son Christopher Riddle told Spencer Leigh in 2003, "and Frank became more and more comfortable with my father's decisions because he understood that my father was making things that slotted in with him perfectly. He was creating wonderful orchestrations, which would enhance him and make him sound better than anything he could come up with. Frank would say to my dad, 'Make it sound like this' or 'Make it sound like that' or whatever. Sometimes Nelson would be saying in the arrangement, 'Hello, Frank, I remembered what you said and here is my little musical rejoinder.'"

The sessions would begin at eight in the evening and extend until well past midnight. Part of this was down to Sinatra's notorious perfectionism, cutting his vocal short 27 times in a single song to correct either himself or the orchestra. Yet he seemed able to re-establish the mood the instant he began to sing again.

In 1963 Sinatra would explain to *Playboy* magazine that he was ideally suited to singing sad songs: "Being an 18-karat manic depressive and having lived a life of violent emotional contradictions I have an over-acute capacity for sadness as well as elation." He also stated that: "When I sing, I believe, I'm honest," and the honesty shines through, especially here in Hoagy Carmichael's 'I Get Along Without You Very Well,' a song that epitomizes the mood of the entire album and highlights Sinatra's vocal prowess.

Track three on Side One, 'Glad to Be Unhappy,' the first of three Rodgers & Hart tunes, showcased a voice now deeper and more ravaged than the light tenor of early days, and it would be this, plus Sinatra's mastery of phrasing, that gave standards, such as Duke Ellington's 'Mood Indigo' and Arlen & Harburg's 'Last Night When We Were Young,' an added dimension. 'Can't We Be Friends?' by the husband and wife team of Paul James (James Paul Warburg) and Kay Swift tells an all too familiar tale: "She didn't mean it, / I should have seen it, / But now it's too late."

The first side ends with 'When Your Lover Has Gone,' penned by Edgar Swan, a number Sinatra had originally recorded back in 1944 with Axel Stordahl handling the orchestration. With a decade of life lived since then, Sinatra's vocal performance effortlessly surpasses the earlier version – and

Continued on next page

1955

legend has it that he broke down in the studio and cried after concluding the master take. It is certainly a fitting point to remove the stylus and pause for thought.

Side two kicks off with Cole Porter's 'What Is This Thing Called Love?' – a question Sinatra must have spent much time considering. Riddle's clarinet theme here is arguably as persuasively haunting as Porter's original melody.

With track 11, Alec Wilder's 'I'll Be Around,' the possibility of a brighter future is at least hinted at. Two Broadway show tunes by the masters, Rodgers & Hart, help bring the album to its conclusion: 'It Never Entered My Mind' (from the 1940 show *Higher And Higher*) has been described by one critic as "perhaps the definitive musical evocation of loneliness," while 'Dancing On The Ceiling,' from 1930's *Evergreen*, again sees Sinatra daring to hope.

The final track of any album is, inevitably, the one the listener is left with, and for track 16 Sinatra returned to a song he'd written with Sol Parker and Hank Sanicola back in 1941, 'This Love Of Mine.' It is the only Sinatra writing credit on the label, and it gave him and his fans a message of hope in the belief that "This love of mine goes on and on." If Ava Gardner was listening, and there was little doubt she was, the message was that he intended to put her in the past. He'd sung out his blues and was ready to move on.

> ## "BOB [HILLIARD] AND I HAD WRITTEN THE SONG AND HAPPENED TO BE IN NEW YORK EN ROUTE TO VISIT A PUBLISHER. AS WE WERE WALKING ALONG THE STREET, BOB SAID, 'HEY, THERE'S SINATRA AND NELSON RIDDLE.' SURE ENOUGH, THEY WERE WALKING AHEAD OF US, SO WE CALLED OUT TO THEM AND SHOWED THEM THE SONG. FRANK LIKED IT, AND ASKED, 'IS IT PUBLISHED YET? WE'LL USE IT ON THE ALBUM WE'RE WORKING ON RIGHT NOW.'"
> DAVE MANN, CO-WRITER (WITH HILLIARD) OF 'IN THE WEE SMALL HOURS.'

In The Wee Small Hours reached Number Two in the *Billboard* charts, proving that, while the album was sophisticated enough to appeal to jazz fans, Sinatra still commanded as big a popular audience as ever. Most importantly, it achieved its objective in winning Sinatra the attention and affection of the male half of the species, who, prior to this release, would have considered him an irredeemable teen idol. As it stands, bar-room crooners all the way through to Tom Waits have listened and learned, while in a bizarre gender reversal Carly Simon covered the title track in 1993 for the movie *Sleepless In Seattle*.

Time is a healer, they say, and Frank Sinatra's recording career bears out the saying. A year after these sessions he was busy waxing another very different masterpiece in *Songs For Swinging Lovers*. He'd spent 1955 making no fewer than five movies and, as he ended the year back in harness at The Sands, the Las Vegas hotel he co-owned, he started the new year of 1956 on an upbeat note.

It's hard to believe the man who steamed into 'You Make Me Feel So Young' was the same who'd ripped the heart out of his audience with 'I Get Along Without You Very Well,' but the evidence was there for all to hear.

Sinatra would cannily continue the pattern of alternating slow, sad albums and up-tempo swingers to the end of the decade, augmenting them where appropriate with Christmas albums, compilations, and soundtracks. Interestingly, however, it would be his 1958 release, *Frank Sinatra Sings For Only The Lonely* – which reunited him with Nelson Riddle – that bore comparison with *In The Wee Small Hours*, in the eyes of the critics and the

singer himself. When aficionados laud Sinatra's output in the 1950s, it is usually these two albums plus *Songs For Swinging Lovers* on which they base their argument. The fact that artists such as Linda Ronstadt brought Riddle out of retirement three decades later to try to achieve the same effect that he had with Sinatra – and as he had with Peggy Lee, Dean Martin, Dinah Shore, and others – says it all.

Sinatra recordings were the yardstick by which all other vocalists would be judged when it came to dealing with the American Popular Songbook. Sarah Vaughan, Ella Fitzgerald, and Tony Bennett have all put up worthy challenges, but it is easy to state a case for Sinatra offering the definitive performance of each and every song *In The Wee Small Hours* contains. One critic summed it up, accurately, as "an album so desolate you feel like you're in a basement bar in Manhattan on a rainy, miserable night and you can smell the bourbon and Lucky Strikes."

Rita Kirwan of *Music* magazine was one of the favored few to witness the sessions back in 1955, and her account of the end of one night's proceedings – appropriately in the wee small hours of the morning – gives an evocative flavor: "Sinatra takes a gulp of the lukewarm coffee remaining in the cup most recently handed to him, and then he lifts the inevitable hat from his head a little, and plops it right back, almost as if he'd wanted to relieve pressure from the hat band. The studio empties fast; just music stands and chairs remain. Sinatra flops on to one of the chairs, crosses his legs and hums a fragment of one of the songs he's been recording. He waves to the night janitor now straightening up the studio and says, 'Jeez. What crazy working hours we got. We both should've been plumbers, huh?'" If you want your waterworks testing, then this is the album.

Liberace At The Hollywood Bowl **Liberace**

Columbia CL 600 (U.S.A) / Philips BBL 7159 (U.K.)
Released March 1955 (U.S.A.) / January 1958 (U.K.)

An American of Polish-Italian descent, pianist Liberace was a self-made legend, and his performance at the Hollywood Bowl was pure wish fulfillment.

Four years earlier, to the very night, he'd performed to an empty auditorium, having saved enough money to rent the Bowl on an off night. This time around he fully lived out his dream, with his brother George conducting the orchestra, before a wildly enthusiastic, standing-room-only crowd of some 20,000.

Liberace At The Hollywood Bowl, as released in 1955, is an edited version of the first half of the concert; *Hollywood Bowl Encore*, an edited version of the second half, was released three months later. (A four-record boxed set of 78s from the Hollywood Bowl Concerts is particularly collectable.) A double CD set issued in 2002, 15 years after Liberace's death, includes all of the music performed that night in original sequence. He had yet to incorporate 'I'll Be Seeing You' into the act as his finale, but the music – as glitzy and exotic as the wardrobe he preferred – displays all the musical frills and trills for which he became famous throughout the world.

The material ranges from classics to popular tunes and includes standards such as 'Stardust' and 'As Time Goes By' as well as a humorous version of 'Chopsticks.' His style, epitomized by the candelabra on the grand piano and aped by the likes of Elton John, would last longer than the music, but *Liberace At The Hollywood Bowl* is probably the album to have. It's just a pity they didn't film it.

Tamboo
Les Baxter, His Orchestra And Chorus

Capitol T-655 (U.S.A.) / LC6807 (U.K.)
Released June 1955

The long career of pianist, saxophonist, conductor, composer, and arranger Les Baxter encompassed swing, jazz, and movie soundtracks, but it is as the founding father of the 1950s genre exotica that he is best remembered.

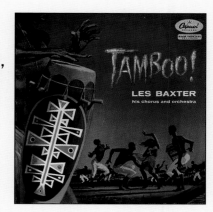

Like all genres, exotica resists easy definition. In its portrayal of various imagined traditional forms of music from 'exotic' parts of the world – predominantly Polynesian, Afro-Caribbean, and Hawaiian – it betrayed a debt to Hollywood stereotypes of the time, all rustling grass skirts and whooping Tarzan cries. Crucially, it has no roots in any real non-Western musical tradition, but it is an imagining of what such music might sound like. Its chord progressions and grooves owe something to jazz, but it lacks that genre's sense of artistic gravity. Sometimes it was meant to serve as light background music, at other times it was overtly showy and attention grabbing. Perhaps it is best to think of exotica as a fantastic country, part Hawaii, part Africa, part West Coast technological paradise, populated by seasoned musicians who had already worked extensively in jazz, light classical, soundtrack music, and pop, being served endless cocktails by many dusky maidens. And in their midst was Les Baxter.

It all started in 1951, when Baxter released *Le Sacre Du Sauvage*, later reissued in expanded form as *Ritual Of The Savage*, both on Capitol. As *Variety* magazine put it: "Les Baxter . . . has started a whole new trend on wax with his quasi-exotic sounds." It included what would become exotica's theme song, 'Quiet Village,' later a hit for Martin Denny. *Le Sacre Du Sauvage* was the first of a long run of albums for Capitol that lasted until 1962, including such evocative period pieces as *Skins! Bongo Party With Les Baxter*, *The Primitive And The Passionate*, and *Jungle Jazz*. *Tamboo* was one of these, appearing in 1955. Like all Baxter's work it conjured up a fantasy world, an alternative to the harsher urban sounds of the newly emerging rock'n'roll.

Exotica petered out in the early 1960s, and Baxter spent the rest of his career composing soundtracks for b-movies. He died in 1996, living just long enough to see his music rediscovered by a new generation of musicians and enthusiasts, and many of his albums reissued.

1956

Rock Around The Clock (Original Soundtrack)

Decca DL 8225 (U.S.A.) / Brunswick LAT 8117 (U.K.)
Released March 1956

The Girl Can't Help It (Original Soundtrack)

Key Cat # (U.S.A.) / Capitol EAP 1-823 (U.K.)
Released December 1956

When it became clear that rock'n'roll was no passing fad, Hollywood moved quickly to cash in.

Producer Sam Katzman, a veteran of many years' service on second features for Columbia, signed Bill Haley and named the singer's first movie *Rock Around The Clock* after his trademark hit. Its unexciting storyline – failed manager discovers rock'n'roll, "like hillbilly with a beat," and steers

band, The Comets, to stardom – and bargain-basement production values were masked by the excitement of the music. (Perhaps the movie's greatest legacy is the portrayal of black act The Platters as the equals of their white counterparts in a society still inclined to buy 'vanilla' cover versions.)

The movie's success swiftly inspired a follow-up, *Don't Knock The Rock*. Little Richard co-starred in the latter, and it was one of his hits that titled *The Girl Can't Help It*. Directed by Frank Tashlin, this appeared in late 1956 and boasted appearances by Gene Vincent, Eddie Cochran, and Fats Domino alongside the 'Georgia Peach.' Julie London's 'Cry Me A River' is probably the standout track of a movie that, with a budget permitting the casting of blonde bombshell Jayne Mansfield as the heroine, Edmond O'Brien as her gangster boyfriend, and Tom Ewell as the agent charged with making Mansfield a star. It proved rock'n'roll could inspire a major movie and not just cheap

exploitation features, and it was also one of the first rock movies to be shot in color, a luxury afforded to few bar Elvis Presley until well into the following decade. Indeed, the footage of Gene Vincent playing 'Be Bop A Lula' is the only known color footage of the man and his – largely – original Blue Caps in existence (the guitarist featured here is not Cliff Gallup).

The soundtrack veers from the sublime Eddie Cochran – bizarrely portraying an example of how you don't need talent to succeed in rock'n'roll – to Ray Anthony, the man who dubbed Edmond O'Brien singing 'Rock Around The Rock Pile.'

Having opened the rock-movie era, Sam Katzman more or less brought down the curtain with 1961's *Twist Around The Clock*, leaving a gap in the market to be to be filled by more imaginative movie-makers later in that decade.

The Platters **The Platters**

King/Federal 549 (U.S.A.) / Parlophone PMD 1058 (U.K.)
Released May 1956

With sales of over 50 million records, The Platters are the bestselling black doo-wop band of all time, and this album contains their first singles.

Coached by Buck Ram, a white lawyer in his 40s, they proved right his assertion that mixing orchestral arrangements with an R&B beat was a recipe for success. They'd been releasing singles since 1953, but the first two million-sellers were 'Only You,' released in 1955, and the chart-topping 'The Great Pretender,' released in early 1956. Pioneering DJ Alan Freed, a champion of black music, arranged for The Platters to appear in the movie *Rock Around The Clock*, and across-the-board success was the result. This album consists of material cut for King/Federal prior to that breakthrough and clearly shows their gospel roots, and it became the first by a rock'n'roll group to make the U.S. Top Ten.

Tony Williams' high lead voice was the band's secret weapon. The line-up was completed by Zola Taylor, Paul Robi, Herb Reed – who continues to lead

a line-up today – and David Lynch. The album opens with an earlier version of 'Only You (And You Alone),' but also contains a number of less successful singles, 'Give Thanks,' 'Tell The World,' 'Shake It Up Mambo,' and 'I'll Cry When You're Gone.' Other selections range from the onomatopoeic 'Voo-Vee-Ah-Bee' to a doo-wop take on movie theme 'Roses Of Picardy.' The Platters' inclusion on the soundtrack of *American Graffiti* and induction into the Rock'n'Roll Hall Of Fame in 1990 was well-deserved recognition. This is where that long-running story started.

Calypso **Harry Belafonte**

RCA Victor 1248 (U.S.A.) / RD 27107 (U.K.)
Released June 1956

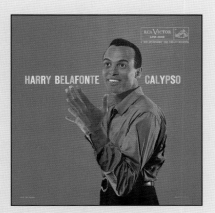

Harold George Belafonte made 1957 the year of the 'Calypso Boom,' and this, his third album, was the catalyst. It was also the first LP ever to be certified a million-seller.

Belafonte, an actor of West Indian parentage, had trained alongside such classmates as Marlon Brando, Walter Matthau, and Tony Curtis, but broadened his options to include music when he figured he'd not be able to emulate their successes. His musical journey gathered momentum when he signed a recording contract with RCA in the early 1950s, and his first two albums, eclectic reflections of global folk music, were both successes, with the second, *Belafonte*, a chart topper.

But it was a meeting with Irving Burgie – an American with a Barbadian mother who performed West Indian songs as Lord Burgess and His Serenaders – that turned Belafonte on to calypso in particular. The album *Calypso* was the result, though the project initially found "significant resistance" among the RCA hierarchy. So he took his plan directly to company president, George Merek, who gave him the green light to proceed. He was rewarded with an unprecedented 31 weeks at the top of the U.S. charts. (It would not be until 1962 and *West Side Story* that *Calypso*'s run at Number One would be bettered.)

Burgie was credited with the majority of the songs, which had been well rehearsed before Belafonte entered the studio with The Tony Scott Orchestra, conductor Norman Luboff, and guitarist Millard Thomas. Ironically, then, it was the one piece of improvisation, 'Day O,' that would give the album its opening signature track and inspire a plethora of imitators. This number is accompanied by a 'version,' entitled 'Star O,' on Side Two, but the album, described as "a cross section of folk music from Jamaica, Trinidad, and other islands," is by no means full of soundalike filler. 'I Do Adore Her' and 'Come Back Liza' are evocative ballads, while 'Man Smart (Woman Smarter),' later covered by artists as diverse as The Carpenters and Robert Palmer, could be termed the first feminist folk song. 'Jamaica Farewell' was the hit single selected by RCA, but when future actor Alan Arkin's folk group, The Tarriers, reached Number Four with a cover of 'Day O' – retitled 'The Banana Boat Song' – Belafonte's version was issued and peaked just one place below its competitor despite being second off the blocks.

Boosted by this, *Calypso* stayed on the *Billboard* chart for 99 weeks, and inspired many folk singers and groups to pick up their acoustic guitars – most notable among which were The Kingston Trio, named after the capital city of Jamaica. Indeed, the following decade found at least one song of West Indian origin in every self-respecting folk act's repertoire. Little wonder the album gets a five-star rating at the *All Music Guide* website, which believes it remains "a record of inestimable influence" today.

Resisting the impulse to record a follow-up album immediately, Belafonte instead spaced out his calypso albums, releasing them at five-year intervals in 1961, 1966, and 1971.

As well as singing stardom, Belafonte's later career embraced movies and television, though his more recent activities, since an appearance on 1985's U.S.A. For Africa all-star single, have been in the political world.

From Studio To Turntable

From the crude wax disks of the 1940s to the virtually limitless sound-manipulation properties of modern-day digital audio, recording technology has made enormous strides over the last half-century. Many of today's listeners will have been born too late to recognize the sound of a needle descending on to vinyl, and have no other point of reference than affordable, near-perfect sound.

The various studio enhancements have had a profound impact on the record business as a whole, altering the manner in which musicians perform in the studio and the way composers craft new songs. But what effect did all this have on the music world? There are those who claim that the evolution in music-making machinery has enhanced the creative process, while digital detractors blame sampling, sequencing, and other button-pushing activities for the general decline in studio ingenuity.

Perhaps the most heated debate concerns the impact of technology on the long-playing, vinyl album, introduced during the late 1940s and all but replaced by the Compact Disk some 40 years later. Supporters cite the durability and high-fidelity of the digital medium, not to mention the longer running times of the average CD release. Analog romantics, on the other hand, often prefer a warm piece of old vinyl to a shrill digitally mastered reissue, and mourn the loss of the double-sided track line-up of the turntable era.

In order to understand our place in music history in the early 21st century, it's helpful to start by returning to a time when recording methods were very different.

State-of-the-art record making in 1945 – which involved cutting a groove along a wax disk using a magnetically driven needle – was light-years ahead of the earliest days of sound reproduction, when musicians would gather around a large funnel-shaped horn and create acoustic vibrations that formed grooves on a turning cylinder.

In the mid 1920s the condenser microphone, manufactured by the Neumann company, ushered in the era of electrical recording. For the first time vocalists could sing at normal volume, rather than bellowing over a wailing orchestra. Even so, making records during the 1930s and 1940s was a far from leisurely process. The sound produced by studio performers was simultaneously printed on to a rotating wax disk – known as the master – from which copies could later be cut. Once the recording was under way, there was no turning back. Any mistake would ruin the disk and force the group to start again with a fresh master.

The medium would soon change, and in dramatic fashion. While stationed in Britain during World War II, Lieutenant Jack Mullin, a trained electronics engineer, became intrigued by the lifelike quality of the classical-music radio being broadcast from Germany. After the war ended he made a remarkable discovery: the broadcasts were not live, they just sounded that way. Some years earlier the Germans had devised an ingenious method for recording and reproducing sound using a roll of magnetic tape that was spooled between two reels on a machine called a magnetophon. Mullin immediately requested a demonstration. "I really flipped – I couldn't tell from the sound whether it was live or a playback."

A year later Mullin and business partner Bill Palmer played a sample recording to executives of NBC, who were immediately struck by the high quality of the sound. By 1948 the Ampex Corporation had introduced its Model 200, the first in a long line of industry-standard tape-recording units. It was Bing Crosby who saw the enormous potential of the new apparatus. Crosby had earlier almost single-handedly changed the practice of vocal recording from operatic to intimate by moving closer to the mike. He now became the first popular artist to utilize the new Ampex recorder.

Continued on page 17

1956

Sings The Rodgers & Hart Songbook Vol. 1
Ella Fitzgerald

Verve MGV 4002-2 (U.S.A.) / HMV CLP 1116 & 1117 (U.K.)
Released August 1956 (U.S.A.) / May 1957 (U.K.)

Part of her 'Songbook' series of recordings of the late 1950s – others include George and Ira Gershwin and Cole Porter – Ella Fitzgerald here turns her attention to the songs of Rodgers & Hart.

She entered the newly opened Capitol Records Studio A in Hollywood with producer Norman Granz on August 27th 1956 and emerged four days later with a classic. Lorenz Hart's sophisticated and witty lyrics were natural partners for Richard Rodgers' music throughout a 24-year partnership that produced 40-plus shows and movie scores. Yet, just as with Fitzgerald's versions of Cole Porter songs, it is as if these were written just for her. As Deena Rosenberg commented in the liner notes: "When songs from the musical theater are taken outside the theater, each performer can choose whether to imitate the original version or to evolve a more personal one. Ella's interpretation . . . leaves the listener with the feeling that there is little more to say."

Perfect pitch and diction, not to mention a vocal range of more than two octaves, were the Fitzgerald hallmarks, as may be heard here on 'The Lady Is A Tramp,' 'Where Or When,' and over a dozen more. Buddy Bergman's orchestral arrangements are noticeably sweeter than those employed on the two-volume *Cole Porter Songbook* project or, indeed, Nelson Riddle's Gershwin treatments, but somehow this adds to the charm.

Ira Gershwin once commented in awe: "I never knew how good our songs were until I heard Ella Fitzgerald sing them." Rodgers & Hart would doubtless agree.

Memorial Album **Hank Williams**

MGM E-202 (U.S.A.) / D137 (U.K.)
Released September 1956 (U.K.)

***Memorial Album* is one of several releases that cashed in on the passing of country giant Hank Williams, who died in the back of a Cadillac driving him to a gig on New Year's Day 1953, nine months short of his 30th birthday.**

Newspapers of the time quaintly described him as a "star hillbilly singer," but the songs he wrote and sang in his brief life proved instrumental in bringing hillbilly music into the mainstream. And, while the scant 8-track selection on *Memorial Album* is hardly representative of his work, no one could deny the quality of the material here.

The rough and ready 'Cold Cold Heart' and 'Hey Good Lookin'' were 1951 country chart toppers, while 'Half As Much' made Number Two the following year. Most telling, though, is the number of cover versions of his songs recorded during his lifetime and which attest to Williams' immediate influence. Tony Bennett, then in the spring of his career, cut 'Cold Cold Heart,' Joni James recorded 'Your Cheatin' Heart,' and Frankie Laine tried 'Kaw-Liga' for size. All feature on *Memorial Album* in their original form. Half a century later, and with Williams as influential as ever, now on a new alt.country generation personified by the likes of Ryan Adams, the covers keep on coming.

A colorful personal life, alcohol, and prescription drugs proved a fatal combination, but Hank Williams shook up the world of country music and the reverberations continue, thanks to the raw emotion of tracks like these.

Ellington At Newport **Duke Ellington**

Columbia (U.S.A.) / Philips BBL 7152 (U.K.)
Released November? 1956

Pre-war jazz giant, Duke Ellington, took the opportunity to prove that class is permanent when he and his band were invited to play the third *Newport Jazz Festival* **in 1956.**

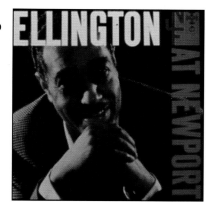

Having suffered the onslaught of rock'n'roll and the post-war financial pressures that made touring with big bands an impossibility, Ellington and band were at a low ebb when they opened the Saturday evening entertainment on July 7th.

With the program running late, they took the stage again at midnight with the prospect of losing most of the audience – but, after playing a specially commissioned 'Newport Jazz Festival Suite,' Ellington threw caution to the wind and gave tenor saxophone player Paul Gonsalves his head on 'Diminuendo and Crescendo in Blue,' a number from some 20 years previously. "Just get out there and blow your tail off," he advised, and, as the crowd applauded wildly, the set and the band's fortunes were transformed by a 27-chorus improvisation. Four encores and a cover story from *Time* magazine later, Duke Ellington and his band faced a far rosier future.

"The event marked not only the turning point in one concert," reported the magazine, "it confirmed a turning point in a career." Historian Mark Tucker depicted it as "a high point in his performing career comparable in some ways to the opening at London's Palladium in 1933 and the Carnegie Hall debut in 1943." In 1999 Columbia released *The Complete Ellington At Newport*, a double-CD set including the renowned concert in its entirety – and in stereo – as well as the studio recreations issued on the original *Ellington At Newport* album. The release was supervised by original producer George Avakian.

Continued from page 15

The arrival of the tape machine coincided with yet another astonishing studio breakthrough. In 1947 the Neumann company once again made history with the introduction of its famous U47 condenser microphone (the first mike capable of both direct and omni-directional recording), which was distributed by the Telefunken Company (hence its nickname of Telly). It was followed in 1949 by the slightly modified M49. Both offered stunning range and clarity, and helped usher in the golden age of vocal sound. (As a measure of their quality, they remain among the most respected – and expensive – vocal microphones on the vintage market.)

These technological advances represented a major turning point for the industry at the close of the 1940s. To recording engineers, magnetic tape was a blessing. Reel-to-reel tape machines could be stopped and restarted quickly and easily in the event of a mistake. Engineers could also edit together several different takes of the same song by cutting out the best sections of the tape using a razor blade, then sticking them back together to form a final master. The continuity that tape provided helped keep the momentum going during a session.

The Echo Revolution

In the early days of record-making, engineers would mike up a large room or concert hall to give a recording its proper ambience. However, with the introduction of the vocal microphone (and, later, separate recording tracks), singers were often isolated in an enclosed space known as a vocal booth in order to provide some degree of sound separation. For many vocalists, the results were simply too 'dry,' hence the need to replenish some of the ambience removed during the isolation process.

In 1947 the Chicago-based engineer Bill Putnam achieved an echo-laden sound on 'Peg-O-My-Heart' by Jerry Murad and his group, The Harmonicats, by recording part of the song in the marbled restroom at the nearby Civic Opera House. 'Peg-O-My-Heart' went on to become the first ever million-selling hit. Putnam later refined the concept by building a series of echo chambers – isolated reverberant rooms – made of reflective plaster. He then fed individual recording signals directly from the console to the room through a basic loudspeaker, which would be returned with a lone microphone.

By the early 1950s echo chambers had become the leading source of studio-sound enhancement. Over the years engineers refined the art of chamber construction, adding rounded corners (made from plaster-coated chicken wire), making the rooms asymmetrical, or pointing the speakers against the wall instead of facing the microphone for a rolling-reverb effect. No two echo chambers sounded alike, simply because each one was individually built, and many engineers still maintain that the best echo chambers were unparalleled as a reverb source, even by today's standards.

It was the guitarist and inventor Les Paul who, during the early 1950s, helped define the sound of the echo chamber. While experimenting in his home studio in 1949, Paul discovered tape echo, whereby a signal from one tape head was fed to a second machine running at a slower speed then returned to the original. Tape echo neatly replicated the actual reflections found in reverberant rooms, but Paul took the invention one step further. Using his own echo chamber, constructed underground adjacent to his New Jersey home, Paul tried sending a recorded signal to the echo chamber by way of the tape-delay unit. By inserting a multisecond delay between the original dry signal and the returned chamber signal, Paul created an entirely unique reverb effect that would become the toast of the studio industry.

The tape delay was just one of many groundbreaking devices that emerged from Paul's garage during this time. His most notable brainwave made it possible to record individual parts one after the other, using an Ampex 300 tape machine outfitted with a second playback head. Paul's invention – which he called "sound on sound" – gave birth to the era of multitrack recording, and, in time, would change the course of popular music.

Meanwhile, recording researchers continued to break new ground. The first mechanical rival to the echo chambers came from Germany's EMT corporation, which introduced the first plate reverb systems. The EMT 140 model in particular, introduced in 1957, immediately became a viable form of studio sound enhancement. A plate reverb consisted of a long thin sheath of sheet metal that was housed in a protective wooden enclosure. Sound would be fed into a driver at one end of the plate, and the resulting reverberation would be picked up at the other and sent back to the recording console. The plate could also be dampened

Continued on page 19

1956

Elvis Presley Elvis Presley

RCA LPM1254 (US) / HMV CLP1093 (UK)
Released March 1956

Elvis Elvis Presley

RCA LPM1382 (U.S.A.) / HMV CLP1105 (U.K.)
Released October 1956

While the impact of Elvis Presley is nearly always measured in singles, it was a landmark day when, on January 10th 1956, he walked into the RCA Victor recording studios in Nashville to begin his first album-recording session for his new employers.

While success at Sun had come out of the blue, a $40,000 transfer fee now sat on his shoulders. Would the young man who'd only turned 21 a couple of days earlier still be able to deliver?

His first two days in the studio provided the answer in the shape of five tracks, three of which – 'Money Honey,' 'I'm Counting On You,' and 'I Got A Woman' – would grace his first album *Elvis Presley*, released just two months later. One of the others recorded at these sessions was the Number One single 'Heartbreak Hotel,' which, as was the custom in those days, was not included on the album. Five of the 12 tracks had been recorded at Sun Studios, so they only needed to be topped up by seven more to complete a historic LP.

Presley was backed not only by his familiar rhythm section of Scotty Moore, Bill Black, and D.J. Fontana but also by vocal group The Jordanaires. Those seasoned sessioneers were unimpressed by the raw newcomer, but his pledge that, "If one of these songs goes big, I want you to record with me all the time," proved their passport to fame and fortune. The relatively untutored Presley also caused the studio staff problems, his hard-strummed guitar tending to bleed into the vocal microphone because

he played the guitar high on his chest. The solution was to use a felt pick that muted the sound somewhat.

The cover of the album has itself become iconic and much-imitated, most notably by The Clash with *London Calling* (1979). Earliest pressings had the name Elvis in light pink (it darkened on later examples). Presley was in green across the bottom, the name framing a monochrome photograph by William S. 'Popsie' Randolph of the guitar-strumming singer in full cry.

Several of the songs on the album would have been familiar through original versions by Ray Charles ('I Got A Woman'), Little Richard ('Tutti Frutti'), The Drifters ('Money Honey'), and Rodgers & Hart ('Blue Moon'). Interestingly, 'Blue Moon,' 'I Love You Because,' and 'I'll Never Let You Go,' ballads all, were songs well-established in the Presley repertoire that had been recorded at Sun but were considered unsuitable for release by Sam Phillips, the Sun Records supremo who discovered Presley. However, their inclusion here results in a more varied LP, emphasizing the broad base of his musical roots.

The album opens with 'Blue Suede Shoes,' a song Presley's former Sun stablemate Carl Perkins, who

composed it, had taken into the U.S. Top Five. Unfortunately for Perkins, his involvement in a near-fatal car crash slowed his progress, and he had to watch the rival version become a hit – but was doubtless consoled by the royalties.

Presley's own musical career would soon be slowed up, too, for while movies would prove amazing vehicles in which to promote the star, his output would lose the edge that had made it such vital listening for millions of teenagers the world over. Needless to say, his screen test with Paramount Studios, undertaken shortly after the album sessions, led to an immediate three-picture deal. Shooting of the first, *Love Me Tender*, would begin in late August, just before the sessions for second album *Elvis*.

This was committed to tape during the first three days of September at Radio Recorders in Hollywood, though one track, 'So Glad You're Mine,' which opens Side Two, was held over from the RCA Studio sessions earlier in the year. The sleeve is known to exist in at least 11 different versions, because of the advertisements for different RCA albums alongside an essay on the star.

Again, no room was found for the Number One single 'Don't Be Cruel' b/w 'Hound Dog,' while there had been a session in between albums one and two to produce music for *Love Me Tender*. This had, however, seen Presley recording with session men, much to his annoyance, so when he reconvened with Moore, Black, Fontana, and The Jordanaires – whose Gordon Stoker also contributed piano – the assembled cast had a point to prove. Thirteen tracks were waxed in the three-day session, which not unnaturally resulted in a more cohesive whole than its two-stage

Continued on page 20

Continued from page 17

through a movable pad, which allowed the engineer to control the length of the decay. Plate reverbs also had company in the form of spring reverb units, which mimicked natural reverb by attaching feeds to either end of a generous expanse of wrapped spring coil.

■ *(Left to right) Elvis Presley, Bill Black, Scotty Moore, and Sam Phillips.*

Sam Phillips And Sun Records

Before the 1950s audio limitations were such that it would have been nearly impossible to distinguish the sound of one studio from the next. Tape recording, however, opened doors unimaginable just a few years earlier. By the start of the decade studio owners had begun to take advantage of the improved technology, using emerging sound-sculpting tools such as echo and delay to create exciting new records. Such haphazard creativity helped bolster the reputation of a select few studios during this time and, in turn, helped fortify the careers of some soon-to-be legendary recording artists.

It would be wrong to assume that Elvis Presley knew exactly what he was doing when he began his long career in 1954 with 'You're a Heartbreaker,' 'I'm Left, You're Right, She's Gone,' and the various other cinder blocks of rock'n'roll. In fact, it was how little he knew that ushered in the most explosive period in pop history.

Not that it was all left to chance: Presley had the look and the style, an intuitive sense of timing, and, when it came to selecting songs, impeccably good taste. All that was needed was to get the goods down on tape. That was easier said than done, however. In order to complete the equation, it would be necessary for Elvis and his regular collaborators, Scotty Moore and Bill Black – whom Elvis had met at Sun Studios in Memphis – to hook up with a forward-thinking studio technician who'd be willing to break a few rules. That person turned out to be Sun's own Sam Phillips.

A former audio engineer at a Memphis radio station, Phillips opened his one-man studio operation, Sun Records, at 706 Union Avenue in the winter of 1950. Originally outfitted with a 16-inch acetate disk cutter, the studio later upgraded with a pair of Ampex tape units.

"The sound of Sun was determined by its limitations," notes Ernst Jorgensen, longtime Presley archivist. "Sam had a very small space, and as a result there were no drums – just room enough for acoustic guitar, electric, and bass. So in order to make it sound fuller, he created this embellishment – and that became

Continued on page 21

1956

predecessor. Engineer Thorne Nagar was influential in guiding the still-inexperienced band through the recording process, and, though no producer was credited for either album, the powers behind the throne were undoubtedly RCA executives Steve Sholes and Chet Atkins.

The Little Richard songbook was on this occasion raided no fewer than three times – for the opener 'Rip It Up' as well as 'Long Tall Sally' and 'Ready Teddy' – while Otis Blackwell contributed 'Paralyzed.' Jerry Leiber and Mike Stoller, the white songwriting and production team that had penned tracks for several classic black vocal groups, followed up 'Hound Dog,' their Number One for Presley, with 'Love Me,' which reached Number Two as a single in its own right.

But perhaps the track for which the album will most often be associated in many people's minds is the one that has been most lampooned over the years: 'Old Shep.' Presley first performed the song at the Mississippi-Alabama Fair at ten years of age, and he clearly enjoyed the memory. Furthermore, his piano playing on the track was his first recorded performance on that instrument.

Released in mid October, *Elvis* entered the U.S. pop chart at Number Seven, an impressive debut that would only be beaten four years later by *GI Blues* and remains his second highest *Billboard* LP-chart entry. One month later it hit the top, staying there for five weeks – as against its predecessor's ten – and making many a Christmas-present list. Once deposed by Nat King Cole it hung around at Number Two for another 11 weeks, ten of them consecutive, so it's no surprise that *Elvis* was certified three million copies sold in 1960.

These two chart-topping albums in the space of seven months – not to mention a rush of singles and EPs – confirmed that Elvis Presley and rock'n'roll were no mere flashes in the pan.

'S Wonderful **Ray Conniff**

Columbia 925 (U.S.A.) / CBS 24 (U.K.)
Released December 1956

Massachusetts-born Conniff, a seasoned back-room boy who came good as a performer thanks to Columbia A&R svengali Mitch Miller, found a hit formula with this album.

It was a formula he reproduced more than 30 times in the dozen years that followed, to the undying delight of fans of easy listening.

He began arranging as a youngster in 1933, and went on to work with the likes of Artie Shaw before the war and Harry James after. In fact, he had first arranged this album's Gershwin-penned title track while working with Shaw, and he had also arranged the hit version of 'September Song' reprised here, for James.

Having joined Columbia in 1954 and worked on hits by stars such as Guy Mitchell, Rosemary Clooney, Johnny Mathis, and Marty Robbins, Conniff was eventually given his own album by Miller. Orchestral versions of such popular standards as 'Begin The Beguine,' 'Stardust,' and 'I Get A Kick Out Of You' effectively updated the pre-war big band sound for the 1950s, a distinctive innovation being the use of wordless vocals delivered by a male-female chorus. This blend was often imitated, but never eclipsed.

After this album's spring 1957 chart success, peaking just outside the U.S. Top Ten, better-performing follow-ups *'S Marvelous* and *'S Awful Nice*

led eventually to 'proper' singing on 1960's *It's The Talk Of The Town*, while Conniff's version of 'Lara's Theme,' from the hit movie *Dr Zhivago*, made the U.S. Top Ten singles in 1965. His music also found favor in the U.S.S.R., where he recorded in 1974 with a local choir supplying vocals. This, however, is the album that started it all – wordlessly.

Finger-Style Guitar **Chet Atkins**

RCA Victor LPM1383 (U.S.A.) / Not issued in U.K.
Released September 1956

Inspired by the thumb-and-finger-picking style of Merle Travis, Chet Atkins developed his own variation while trying to copy the records, and in doing so made history.

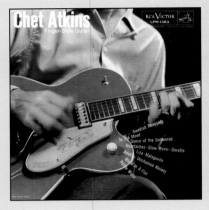

One of the major architects of country music's Nashville Sound, Atkins has been said to be the most recorded solo instrumentalist in history. Signed to RCA Victor in 1947 as a singer and guitarist, Atkins also helped to promote the careers of Hank Williams and Elvis Presley, but his own albums of instrumental music were highly influential in their own right on aspiring guitarists. Albums cut with the likes of Mark Knopfler attest to this.

This 1956 offering is an album of two very different sides: a rhythm section supports Atkins on the first side, cutting such well-known numbers such as 'In The Mood;' while the second side has the likes of 'Gavotte in D' and 'Waltz in A-Flat' performed solo in a more classical style. (Not to say that he was averse to using the studio here, as Side Two's 'Unchained Melody' features a delayed, overdubbed chorus.)

Each year, until his death in 2001, Atkins was proud to see fans, guitar enthusiasts, and students from across the nation and overseas meet in Nashville for a four-day convention. "I was kind of an innovator and I could pull it off very well," he admitted. "I can see that now. At the time I thought I was terrible, but that kept me improving and trying to learn to play better." This album remains a primer for Mark Knopfler and his fellow Atkins-ites.

1957

Around The World In 80 Days
(Original Soundtrack)

Decca 79046 (U.S.A.) / Brunswick LAT 8185 (U.K.)
Released April 1957

Just as Hollywood enlivened the post-war cultural landscape, so movie soundtracks dominated the popular music charts, despite the mounting challenge of rock'n'roll.

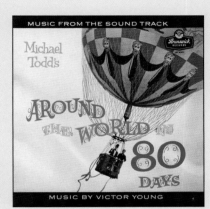

The U.S. Top Five had featured hits from *My Fair Lady*, *The Eddy Duchin Story*, *The King And I*, and *High Society* the previous year, and in July 1957 it was time for Victor Young's score for *Around The World In 80 Days* to take its place there. Sadly, Young himself was not around to witness this feat, having unexpectedly passed away in November 1956 at the age of 56.

While such numbers as 'Invitation To A Bull Fight' and 'India Country Side' really only work in the context of the film, there is a real song – and a classic at that – in the title track, which inspired covers from artists as celebrated as Frank Sinatra, Bing Crosby, The Maguire Sisters, and, most successfully in chart terms, orchestral maestro Mantovani. Interestingly, a single pairing Victor Young's instrumental version with Crosby's vocal reached a peak of Number 13 in the same week this album topped the chart.

A tug of war between Decca and RCA-Victor that delayed release for some six weeks (producer Mike Todd favoring RCA) failed to dent the soundtrack's commercial potential, and though it was knocked off the top by yet another soundtrack – that of Elvis Presley's second movie, *Loving You* – it would regain the summit for another nine weeks before once again deferring to The King, this time with *Elvis' Christmas Album*.

Only three soundtracks would achieve pole position in the U.S.A. in 1958, an indication that the balance of pop power was changing. But, just as the movie starring Shirley MacLaine and David Niven remains a classic, so the soundtrack retains its charm.

■ *Beale Street, Memphis, in the 1950s, home of Sam Phillips's legendary Sun Studios*

Continued from page 19

the *sound.*" That sound was the product of tape echo. "It wasn't necessarily that Sam had this vision of how everything should work," says Jorgensen, "it was just what he had and how he made it work. If you listen to some of the early Sun ballads, you can hear him changing that echo effect – trying to find the right balance."

On vocals, tape echo nicely replicated the actual reflections found in small rooms or echo chambers. When applied to Moore's strident guitar lines, Black's bass, and Presley's briskly strummed acoustic, the combined 'slapback' effect was something else altogether. "Elvis's acoustic – which was always miked up on its own right up to the beginning of the 1960s – had this breezy and melodic sound," says Jorgensen, "but at the same time, you've got this incredibly percussive thing going all the way through on account of Bill's slap-bass playing. I've had to argue with people who insist that there's real percussion going on in there! When, in fact, it's just the combination of the playing and the echo."

By 1955 Phillips had fully mastered the sounds that would soon reverberate around the world. "Sam was a very different type of producer – mainly because he didn't work with big 'professional' artists," continues Jorgensen. "Time wasn't really a factor. As a result, Elvis had the luxury of being able to let things happen – to create the songs spontaneously."

Moving to Multitrack

Studio technology continued its rapid development through the 1950s. Working in conjunction with Les Paul and David Sarser early in the decade, Ampex brought multitrack recording into the marketplace with the introduction of its revolutionary 3-track tape machine. By 1955 Ampex had patented Sel-Sync, a mechanism that made it possible for an overdubbed part to be easily synchronized with a previous track.

Though most of the major studios bucked the multitrack trend, the more adventurous independent labels were intrigued. One such company was New York-based Atlantic Records, whose visionary young engineer, Tom Dowd, saw multitrack as a powerful tool and a most worthy investment. In the early 1950s Dowd began recording jazz sessions using both a mono machine and a 2-track recorder for back-up. This allowed Atlantic to compile a backlog of stereo material well before stereo had even hit the mass market. "When stereo came in," said Dowd years later, "while everyone else was making fake stereo, we already had the real thing."

Atlantic didn't stop there. In 1957 the label acquired (at considerable expense) an Ampex 8-track machine, making it the first in the business to have such recording capability.

Recording artists still went about the business of making records as they had for years, arriving well-rehearsed and cutting upward of ten songs or more in a matter of hours. The real difference was in the dramatically improved fidelity of the new equipment. Recording engineers quickly came of age, learning how to place the microphones around the room in order to capture the best dynamics of a studio performance.

The results of their efforts were stunning. Scratchy 78s from the 1940s were replaced by such albums as Sinatra's *Songs For Swingin' Lovers*, with a sound that was almost like being inside Capitol's Studio A during the actual performance. The life-like quality of the vinyl LP lit a fire under the careers of crooners like Ella Fitzgerald, Nat 'King' Cole, Johnny Mathis, and many others, creating a pop-vocal explosion that would last well into the 1960s.

The advanced sound quality of the LP set the stage for an unprecedented hi-fi boom. Acoustic Research developed its famed AR-1 speaker, which, in tandem with the Dynakit power amplifier, became one of the top sellers in home audio. Variable-groove recording made its debut, increasing the music capacity of the LP. The mastering process evolved: multiple 'mother' positive disks, cut from the original negative master, were used to make 'stampers,' each one capable of producing copies of an LP, further streamlining the production process.

The record industry was more than happy to cash in on the audiophile market. Since recording artists were typically capable of recording an entire album's worth of material in a single day, labels could expect multiple products by a hit performer during the course of a year. By the mid 1950s, album sales were brisk.

1957

The Tommy Steele Story Tommy Steele

Not issued in U.S.A. / Decca LF 1288 (U.K.)
Released June 1957

It didn't take long for Britain's first home-grown rock'n'roll star to steer into the middle of the road. Tommy Steele, a former seaman, had encountered American music on his travels, and, just as he entered his 20s, manager John Kennedy aimed him at the teen rock'n'roll market.

His first single, 'Rock With The Caveman,' saw him backed –

uncredited – by top British jazzman Ronnie Scott. However, it was when he reached Number One in the U.K. with 'Singing The Blues' in early 1957 that he became a household name. Immediately following this plans were announced for a movie – the low-budget, semi-factual *The Tommy Steele Story* (aka *Rock Around The World*) – based on the life story of the former Tommy Hicks. The album of the same name hit the top in July.

The movie, shot in black and white and running to a scant 82 minutes, also featured jazzman Humphrey Lyttleton, The Chas McDevitt Skiffle Group, The Tommy Steele Calypso Band, and Chris O'Brien's Caribbeans, and took the story from Steele's supposed discovery in a coffee bar to the (then) present. Two tracks, 'Butterfingers' and 'Water Water,' became Top Ten singles, while this album and a book were perfectly timed tie-ins. But by the end of the year he was courting future wife Anne Donati and appearing in Christmas pantomime, leaving the British rock'n'roll stage to the likes of Cliff Richard and his fellow Larry Parnes protégé Marty Wilde.

Steele did score another Number One with the soundtrack to *The Duke Wore Jeans*, but by 1959 and *Tommy The Toreador* – with its novelty hit 'Little White Bull' – the world of musicals that has sustained his career ever since was already beckoning. Yet, despite the brevity of his rock'n'roll career, Steele did serve as a prototyoe for early British rockers.

Here's Little Richard Little Richard

Specialty 2100 (U.S.A.) / London HA-O 2055 (U.K.)
Released July 1957

Jerry Lee Lewis Jerry Lee Lewis

Sun 1230 (U.S.A.) / London HAS 2138 (U.K.)
Released December 1957

Rock And Rollin' With Fats Domino Fats Domino

Imperial 9004 (U.S.A.) / London HA-P 2041 (U.K.)
Released November 1955 / March 1957

While the electric guitar rather than the piano has generally been considered rock'n'roll's primary instrument, in their own very different ways, Little Richard, Jerry Lee Lewis, and Fats Domino all sought to overturn the stereotype.

Richard Wayne Penniman, otherwise known as Little Richard, grew up one of 13 children and emerged as an unashamed attention-seeker. Bursting on to the charts in 1956 with 'Tutti Frutti,' he appeared in such rock exploitation movies as *Don't Knock The Rock*, *The Girl Can't Help It*, and *Mister Rock'n'Roll* before quitting music to enroll in a Seventh Day Adventist college. This divide between rock and religion has continued to dog the God-fearing piano-thumper, as he has retired and returned many times during his career. His first album, *Here's Little Richard*, remains, however, a classic of its kind, produced by Bumps Blackwell in New Orleans and containing two bona fide U.S. Top Ten hits in 'Long Tall Sally' and 'Jenny, Jenny.'

made his name and inspired the 1989 movie, *Great Balls Of Fire*, was essentially the 18 months from early 1957 to mid 1958, of which this album is a snapshot.

If Lewis blazed brightly but briefly, New Orleans native Antoine 'Fats' Domino's first LP, *Rock And Rollin' With Fats Domino* – originally released as *Carry On Rockin'* – took its time to chart, being the third of his albums to grace the Billboard listings in 1957 once retitled and reissued. The catalyst was a string of his singles, and 'Ain't That A Shame' from this album not only made the Top Ten back home but gave him his third U.K. hit. He received sterling support from drummer Cornelius Coleman and guitarist Walter Nelson, but it was Domino's bejeweled fingers caressing those trademark piano triplets, combined with his rich, slightly melancholy vocal, that provided the hooks.

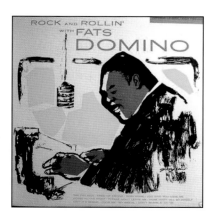

Purists say Domino cut his crucial material prior to his commercial breakthrough, which, by that reckoning, makes this album the last of the best. And even when the hits dried up – and with at least 22 million-selling singles there were many – Domino continued to tour into the 1990s to a loyal worldwide audience.

Jerry Lee Lewis, The Killer, was another artist from the Sun Records' stable from which Elvis had prematurely bolted. But, within a year of his eponymous debut album, Lewis's career was already on the slide thanks to publicity surrounding his bigamous marriage to a 13 year-old second cousin. Prior to that, his impact, thanks to television appearances on the *Steve Allen Show*, had been of Presley-esque proportions, surmounting the piano – often literally – to push debut single 'Whole Lotta Shakin' Goin' On' to the U.S. Number Three spot in the summer of 1957.

His second album, *Volume 2*, made the U.K. Top 20, but the impact was already waning. He would rise again later in the 1960s as a country singer, with a more world-weary, less physical stance than the wildman heard in the decade that gave birth to rock'n'roll. The amazingly short period that

Things Are Swingin' Peggy Lee

Capitol 1049 (U.S.A.) / T1049 (U.K.)
Released October 1958 (U.S.A.) / January 1959 (U.K.)

This was the fourth U.S. Top 20 album for Peggy Lee and it ranks alongside similarly themed albums released by Capitol label mates Frank Sinatra (*Songs For Swingin' Lovers*) and Dean Martin (*This Time I'm Swingin'*).

Lee – born Norma Delores Egstrom in Jamestown, North Dakota, in 1920 – had enjoyed two decades in the business before her definitive version of 'Fever,' previously a hit for Little Willie John, brought worldwide renown in 1958. Lee added her own lyrics to the first couple of verses and supplied the arrangement. The album exhibits the classic, warm 1950s-era Capitol stereo sound with the exception of 'You Don't Know' and 'Fever,' both recorded in mono because of technical problems.

As well as 'It's a Wonderful World,' 'It's Been A Long, Long Time,' 'Life Is For Livin',' and 'Fever,' the album includes two self-penned numbers: the title track and 'It's A Good, Good Night,' both of which compare well with the aforementioned tunes.

Peggy Lee's last hit record came in 1969, when 'Is That All There Is?' made it to the U.S. Top 40, but her albums still sell in healthy numbers. The following year saw her star in the show *Side By Side By Sondheim*, which she clearly enjoyed – and, being a musical institution, she was able to pick and choose her projects. By the time of her death in 2002, her continued popularity had long been assured, and her passing was mourned by millions throughout the world.

1958

South Pacific (Original Soundtrack)

RCA Victor 1032 (U.S.A.) / RB16065 (U.K.)
Released March 1958

West Side Story (Original Soundtrack)

Columbia 2070 (U.S.A.) / CBS 4676061 (U.K.)
Released October 1961

These two movie soundtracks topped the U.S. charts nearly four years apart, confirming the enduring appeal of the American musical.

Interestingly, the original Broadway cast album of *West Side Story* had been released simultaneously with the *South Pacific* soundtrack, but only when the show became a movie itself did the cash registers start ringing. *South Pacific* was the work of Richard Rodgers and Oscar Hammerstein II, the most successful partnership in the history of Broadway musicals. Composer Rodgers and librettist Hammerstein had both worked successfully with others, but the impact of this and their other hit shows – *Carousel*, *The King And I*, and *The Sound Of Music*, for example – was such that few now think of one without the other.

The pair of New Yorkers had scored their first hit with *Oklahoma!* in 1943, and *South Pacific* – based on a novel, *Tales Of The South Pacific*, by James A. Michener – opened on Broadway six years later with the largest advance ticket sales ever registered. The tale of a U.S. Navy nurse and a suave French planter thrown together in wartime made such an impact that it won the Pulitzer Prize for Drama – the first musical ever to achieve the honor. The main protagonists' slow-starting romance is paralleled by a tragic inter-racial liaison between a young American lieutenant and an island girl, which ends in the former's death, so adding an extra dimension to the story.

The role of Frenchman Emile de Becque had been written by Rodgers specifically for opera star Ezio Pinza, who starred opposite Mary Martin in the Broadway production, but in the movie it is played by Rossano Brazzi. Mitzi Gaynor beat Doris Day, Elizabeth Taylor, and Audrey Hepburn to the role of Nellie Forbush, the woman who falls for him on 'Some Enchanted Evening.' On the soundtrack only Gaynor did her own singing, the remainder of the cast being voiced by others, with opera singer Giorgio Tozzi singing the male lead. The orchestra was conducted by longtime Rodgers & Hammerstein associate Alfred Newman. Movie-goers enjoyed the bonus of 'My Girl Back Home,' a number cut from the stage production for time reasons but restored to the score here. Extensive location shooting led to the decision to record the soundtrack at the 20th Century-Fox sound stage in Hollywood before shooting began. This meant that, while performers could lip-synch to the recording, it did lead to some rather wooden performances.

South Pacific had followed the successful *Oklahoma!* on to the big screen, and its setting on the Hawaiian island of Kauai, combined with the new Todd-AO 65mm process, which offered previously unseen clarity, made it an immediate winner. Director Joshua Logan's casting was panned by critics, however, who also slated the movie for its length (170 minutes) and the over-use of colored filters. But songs such as 'Bali Ha'i,' 'I'm Gonna Wash That Man Right Out Of My Hair,' and 'Happy Talk' – which became an unlikely U.K. Number One in 1982 in the hands of Captain Sensible from punk band The Damned – certainly stand the test of time. Besides, the public voted with their wallets and made it Number One. And when it did so, the original cast recording, having already notched up an incredible 208 chart weeks, followed it up to Number Two to make an amazing double. In Britain, the soundtrack topped the charts in May 1958, clocking up 313 weeks on the listings.

The appeal of *West Side Story* lies in the way it integrates song, dance, and narrative, showing how the movie musical could still be relevant in a new decade. The combination of young, thrusting lyricist Stephen Sondheim and seasoned composer Leonard Bernstein was perfect. The music was almost entirely a joint venture, with only the themes of 'Maria' and 'Cool' pre-dating their collaboration. Work began in autumn 1955 and was completed in the summer of 1957, Bernstein having taken a six-month sabbatical in the middle to work on *Candide*.

By updating Shakespeare's *Romeo And Juliet* and transplanting it to a big-city New York setting, Sondheim and Bernstein were eventually rewarded, despite the relatively moderate success of the original stage show, with a movie soundtrack album that broke all records with a 54-week residency at Number One in the U.S. and 175 chart weeks in Britain, where it also made the top spot. The movie itself received 11 Academy Award nominations and won ten Oscars – only two other movies, *Ben-Hur* (1959) and *Titanic* (1997), have earned more – including Best Picture, Best Supporting Actor (George Chakaris), Best Supporting Actress (Rita Moreno), and Best Direction (Robert Wise and Jerome Robbins). Robbins had also choreographed the work for the stage show, and co-director Wise would go on to mastermind another big-budget musical, *The Sound Of Music*, in 1965.

All the voices bar that of Russ Tamblyn (Riff) were dubbed by other singers, notably Marni Nixon (Maria), Jim Bryan (Tony), and Betty Ward (Anita). Individual songs, such as 'Maria' and 'Tonight,' picked up pop covers from artists as diverse as P.J. Proby, Johnny Mathis, and Shirley Bassey, while some six years later, at the height of the Vietnam War, British rock group The Nice used 'America' as the soundtrack to torching the Stars and Stripes on stage, much to Bernstein's displeasure.

It was the fact that the gangs represented racial groupings – The Jets white teenagers and The Sharks Puerto Ricans – that gave *West Side Story* an added contemporary dimension. Natalie Wood didn't convince everybody as Latina heroine Maria who falls for Tony, but it emerged as a powerful modern parable that would show the way for the likes of Bob Fosse's *Sweet Charity* and *Cabaret*.

The belated success of *West Side Story* certainly proved the power of the big screen to change people's perceptions. "Suddenly everyone could hum everything," said a bemused Sondheim of a show many critics had initially decried for not possessing memorable melodies. The *joie de vivre* seen here would inspire the likes of *Fame* in the following decade.

■ *Main picture: Russ Tamblyn (Riff) in* West Side Story. *Left: Mitzi Gaynor washes that man right out of her hair in* South Pacific.

1958

Johnny's Greatest Hits Johnny Mathis

Columbia 8634 (U.S.A.) / Fontana 1STP (U.K.)
Released March 1958

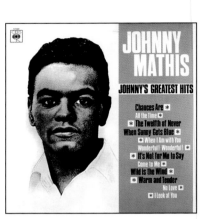

Fans of Johnny Mathis clearly couldn't get enough of the suave San Franciscan, and this, the first greatest-hits album of the pop era, proved it.

The brainchild of Columbia Records A&R director, Mitch Miller, it gave new life to such hit singles as 'It's Not For Me To Say,' 'Chances Are,' and 'The Twelfth Of Never,' and, crucially, bought Mathis time to record a new album. The music owes much to the work of arranger Ray Conniff, a big-selling orchestra leader in his own right, whose work on the likes of 'Wonderful! Wonderful!' and 'When Sunny Gets Blue' had been accomplished with a maximum of ten musicians in a de-consecrated church in New York.

The result was a Number One album that stayed on the *Billboard* listings for just two and a half months short of 500 weeks – a record for longevity it would take something of the magnitude of Pink Floyd's 1973 release, *Dark Side Of The Moon*, to eclipse. By the time Mathis topped the U.S. albums chart again in 1959 with a collection of standards and show tunes, Columbia had already released *More Johnny's Greatest Hits*, which attained a highly respectable Number Two. He'd go on to register 26 Top 40 albums by the end of the 1970s – at which point his chart career began to slow up, though he continues to record new material and release albums to this day – including three more greatest-hits-style compilations. A profitable format was born.

One Dozen Berrys Chuck Berry

Chess LP-1432 (U.S.A.) / London HAM 2132 (U.K.)
Released March 1958

While primarily considered a singles artist, Chuck Berry also turned out albums on a regular basis.

His sole U.S. Top Ten LP came as late as 1973 with the all-star *London Sessions*. His other two Top 40 albums were a live set and a hits collection, underlining the fact that his self-contained three-minute story-songs, powered by trademark Gibson guitar riffing, were ideal for being spread over two sides of seven-inch plastic.

Indeed, this, his second full-length Chess album – and the first to be released in the U.K. – contains a number of tracks previously issued as singles, both a- and b-sides. These were 'Oh Baby Doll' b/w 'La Juanda' (June 1957), 'Rock And Roll Music' b/w 'Blue Feeling' (September 1957), and the million-selling 'Sweet Little Sixteen' b/w 'Reelin' And Rockin'' (January 1958). 'La Juanda' appears in a different mix from the single release, while, in a labor-saving tactic, 'Blue Feeling' is on the album twice, in its original form and at half speed, entitled 'Low Feeling.'

Berry would record at Chess Studios in Chicago in batches between concert dates, having taken the decision to discard his touring band in favor of picking up local backing musicians from town to town. The resulting transportation and wage savings meant he could afford to fly, but a valuable by-product was that, by giving Berry the opportunity to rehearse with new musicians, he was given the musical inspiration for new compositions. Other songs, he later admitted in his autobiography, were attempts to clone his successes, as with 'Oh Baby Doll,' which was a self-confessed rewrite of early hit 'School Day.'

The visual content of his writing was striking. 'Reelin' And Rockin'' was inspired by seeing bluesman Big Joe Turner through the window of a Chicago club to which Berry, then 16, was too young to be admitted. 'Sweet Little Sixteen,' on the other hand, was his retelling of an occasion, backstage at a gig at the Ottawa Coliseum, when he observed a young female fan intent on getting the autograph of Paul Anka. Berry's observational qualities and ability to sum up the spirit of youth in a few well-turned words or phrases are his much-imitated calling cards.

One Dozen Berrys contained the new songs 'Guitar Boogie,' 'In-Go,' 'Rock At The Philharmonic,' 'It Don't Take But A Few Minutes,' and 'How You've Changed.' Life would change for him a couple of years later, after a conviction for transporting a minor across a state line for immoral purposes led to him spending 1962 and 1963 in prison.

But even if Leonard Chess hadn't stockpiled material to release in order to keep Berry's name fresh in record buyers' minds, his influence would still have been undiminished. As proof, tracks on this album alone attracted covers by, among others, The Beach Boys, The Beatles, and The Rolling Stones – not a bad fan club.

Sam Cooke **Sam Cooke**

Keen A-2001 (U.S.A.) / HMV CLP1261 (U.K.)
Released March 1958

Sam Cooke was one of the most important early figures in the creation and development of what we now know as soul music, and Otis Redding and Marvin Gaye were among his earliest disciples.

Sam Cooke, the singer's first totally secular album, was cut for Bob Keene's Keen label and not for Specialty, with whom Cooke had been signed as a gospel artist. His aim was to flee his musical roots and cross over into the popular market, but this was blocked by Specialty, as it would lose him the following he had won while singer with The Soul Stirrers. The minister's son had created waves since replacing R.H. Harris as their lead singer, but label boss Art Rupe was opposed to his first ventures away from gospel under the name of Dale Cook.

Orchestra leader Bumps Blackwell, who gets a credit on the sleeve, was instrumental in the switch. He struck a deal with Rupe to forego any future royalties for his work with Little Richard – Blackwell had production credits on many of Richard's biggest early hits – in order to take Cooke away and sign to Keen. He'd been impressed by a Soul Stirrers' gospel show at the Shrine Auditorium in Los Angeles and had seen the potential immediately. "My initial impression was 'This cat should be pop,'" he told Cooke's biographer Daniel Wolff. "That was just too much voice to be in such a limited market."

After initial attempts to cut pop material at J&M Studio in New Orleans proved unsuccessful, the scene shifted to Los Angeles in 1957. Blackwell wisely attempted to meld blues chord structures with teen-centered lyrics "because white girls are buying records these days." White vocal trio The Pied Pipers were recruited to add background sweetening, and an early result, 'You Send Me,' sold 1.7 million copies when backed with

'Summertime' on a January 1957 single. It topped the U.S. chart and made the U.K. Top 30.

Cooke's eponymous album, released that March, was arguably overloaded with familiar ballads, such as 'Ol' Man River,' 'Moonlight In Vermont,' and 'Danny Boy,' not to mention interpretations of such jazz standards as 'Ain't Misbehavin'' and 'That Lucky Old Sun,' but, nevertheless, it reached Number 16 in March 1958.

In the light of his being forced to record material he felt inappropriate, as well as an ill-starred Copacabana concert in which he was obliged to dress in a suit with tails, Cooke decided to rebel against Blackwell's aim to capture a white audience. They split after a second Keen album, *Encore*, and, by early 1960, Cooke was recording for RCA – who paid a $100,000 transfer fee – with producers Hugo and Luigi.

But Cooke's complicated private life, which included losing his first wife in an auto accident in 1959, led to his fatal shooting in 1964 after an unsavory motel incident with sexual overtones. Some 200,000 fans paid their respects at two memorial services, but the true legacy of Sam Cooke was in those he inspired. Otis Redding, another soul legend to meet an untimely end, covered 'Shake' and used it to make the breakthrough to a white audience on his own terms that Cooke would surely have achieved had he lived. 'You Send Me' alone has been covered by artists as diverse as Steve Miller, Rod Stewart, and Aretha Franklin, while The Rolling Stones, Bryan Ferry, and Cat Stevens are others to dip into his songbook.

1959

Kind Of Blue **Miles Davis**

C.B.S. 8163 (US) / CBS62066 (UK)
Released August 1959

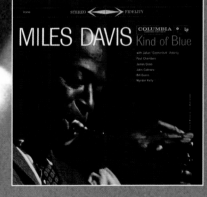

■ *Main Picture: A rare smile from Miles Davis. Left: Alto-sax player 'Cannonball' Adderley. Right: Davis takes a breather as John Coltrane (left), Adderley, and pianist Bill Evans play on.*

Kind Of Blue is one of the best albums of Miles Davis's career and one of the most important records in the history of jazz. But more than this, it has been for many the gateway to the world of jazz.

It exists on the edge of jazz the way the Statue of Liberty stands before the promise of New York City and the U.S.A. itself, holding a beacon up to the musically hungry, offering solace to fatigued ears, hearts, and minds. For 40 years it has sold largely by word-of-mouth, finding a home even in record collections that are otherwise jazz-free. Its appeal is international, and in the last decade it has

actually increased its sales rate, now past five million.

Like many famous albums, *Kind Of Blue* has a legend attached: that its five tracks were cut in two days and improvised on the spot. This is not quite true, but not far off. Recording began on March 2nd 1959 at Columbia's 30th Street Studio in New York. Now demolished, the studio was a big space, a hundred feet square with high ceilings; it could hold a symphony orchestra and classical recordings were often made there. Engineers and musicians valued its reverberant sound, resulting from the natural wooden surfaces. The five musicians who assembled there were a jazz supergroup: Miles Davis on trumpet, Julian 'Cannonball' Adderley on alto sax, John Coltrane on tenor sax, Bill Evans on piano – replaced on one track by Wynton Kelly – Paul Chambers on upright bass, and Jimmy Cobb on drums. The producer was Irving Townsend.

The first session ran from 2.30pm to 5.30pm, followed by a second from 7.00pm until 11.00pm. *Kind Of Blue* is marked by restraint and a brooding thoughtfulness. Davis was exploring a new style, 'modal jazz,' which used scales other than the common major and minor. The emphasis was to be on the improvisation of lines of single notes. Solos became more important and could be longer. Tempos got slower to accommodate this melodic soloing. The complex chords and rapid changes of earlier jazz were to be simplified. Davis told the *Jazz Review* in 1958: "Guys give me tunes and they're full of chords. I can't play them . . . I think a movement in jazz is beginning away from the conventional string of chords, and a return to emphasis on melodic rather than harmonic variation. There will be fewer chords but infinite possibilities as to what to do with them."

Bill Evans's sleevenotes made a fashionable connection with a type of Japanese art in which the artist must paint spontaneously. This fixed the notion that the whole album had been created from nothing and chimed with the Beat Generation's interest in Zen. In fact, 'All Blues' and 'So What' had been played live a couple of times. Though all the music is credited to Miles Davis this has been disputed: it has been argued that Bill Evans sketched out 'Blue In Green' and co-wrote 'Flamenco Sketches.' But composition in this sense only means basic ideas and structure. Where the players did have written directions they amounted to no more than a few notes and scales on paper. Davis wanted spontaneity in the playing. He didn't want to rehearse the tunes. On occasion, instructions as to who was to solo next were given during the recording itself. So, in this sense, the legend of *Kind Of Blue*'s spontaneous creation has a kind of truth.

The March 2nd session started with 'Freddie Freeloader,' a 12-bar blues-based structure to ease the musicians in, and the only track with Wynton Kelly playing piano instead of Evans. They did three aborted takes before the fourth and final run through nailed it. The recording was done on a state-of-the-art 3-track tape. A small amount of echo was added to the mix in addition to the studio's natural reverb, which can be heard in the middle of the stereo image if you listen on headphones.

The second track to be recorded is the album's most famous, 'So What,' named after a favorite dismissive term of Davis's. 'So What' gives the album its beguiling introduction, with an atmospheric passage for piano and bass in a free rhythm. Unexpectedly, this colorful section gives way to a two-chord riff, one that musically sounds like the 'So What' of the title. There is a neat call-and-answer idea between the bass and the other instruments. Miles Davis said the inspiration for the music came from two sources. One was the African folk rhythms and timings he had recently heard when watching the Ballet Africaine perform. The second was American church music, recalled from childhood when he lived on his grandfather's farm: "I added some other kind of sound I remembered from being back in Arkansas, when we were walking home from church and they were playing these bad gospels. That feeling is what I was trying to get close to . . . six years old, walking with my cousin along that dark Arkansas road." A complete fourth take did the business. The first day's recording was completed with the delicate ten-bar sequence of 'Blue In Green.' The solos are provided by trumpet, piano, and tenor saxophone, with Adderley sitting out.

Kind Of Blue's second session took place on the afternoon of Wednesday April 22nd. The first track recorded that afternoon was 'Flamenco Sketches.' The bass pattern had been played by Evans in a song called 'Peace Piece' on the album *Everybody Digs Bill Evans* earlier that year. The five scales that form the basis of 'Flamenco Sketches' had been worked out

Continued on next page

on the morning of the first session in March, when Evans went to Davis's apartment. It got its name because one of the scales – the Phrygian – has a Spanish flavor and is often heard in flamenco music. The first take was complete and became the only one that wasn't used from the entire sessions. (It has been added to the most recent CD edition of the album.) The finished second take took another five more tries, culminating in a complete take six. The Spanish feel of 'Flamenco Sketches' later bore fruit in Davis's 1964 album, *Sketches Of Spain*. After the concentrated effort of 'Flamenco Sketches,' the ensemble recorded the bouncy 'All Blues.'

The album was released on August 17th 1959, with a cover shot of Davis taken at the Apollo Theater that further cemented the importance of the trumpeter as an African-American hero. The album sold steadily, and within about a year student jazz bands were doing covers of its tunes. It found a crossover audience and influenced many musicians throughout the 1960s.

During the 1990s it was discovered that a motor problem on the recording machine had caused the tape to run a fraction slower than it should have during the March session. Consequently, the playback was slightly faster than actual time, and for over 30 years the world had heard three of *Kind Of Blue*'s tracks not as they were played. The current CD version has the tracks at the right speed and pitch. If you don't know *Kind Of Blue*, take the advice of San Francisco columnist C. H. Garrigues: "Buy it and play it, quietly, around midnight . . ."

1959

Elvis' Golden Records **Elvis Presley**

RCA LPM 1707 (U.S.A.) / RB 16069 (U.K.)
Released April 1958

50,000,000 Elvis Fans Can't Be Wrong: Elvis' Golden Records Vol.2
Elvis Presley

RCA LPM 2075 (U.S.A.) / RD 27159 (U.K.)
Released December 1959

Fourteen million-selling singles, seven of which were chart toppers, made _Elvis' Golden Records_ a greatest-hits compilation by anyone's definition.

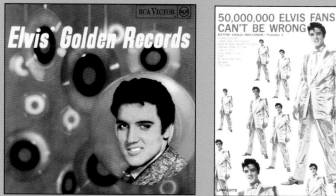

Eschewing the early Sun releases, the album kicks off with the seminal 'Heartbreak Hotel' and ends with 'Jailhouse Rock,' which had topped the U.S. charts earlier in 1958. Other Number Ones include 'I Want You I Need You I Love You,' 'Don't Be Cruel,' 'Hound Dog,' 'Too Much,' and 'All Shook Up.'

Maybe the Christmas album that had preceded it had made fans feel they were buying less essential material, as _Elvis' Golden Records_ entered _Billboard_'s album listings at a modest Number Nine. It rose only six places further, though it enjoyed a further 23 chart weeks after the singer's death in 1977 to add to an initial 40, and has five times gone platinum. (Curiously, British release was on RCA's classical imprint, Red Seal.)

'Wear My Ring Around Your Neck' was a result of Elvis's last studio session before being drafted into the U.S. Army, but he managed to sneak into the studio again in Nashville in June to provide more product to be released as singles. It was clear, however, that the goose was laying fewer golden eggs, and an album of b-sides and EP tracks, _For LP Fans Only_, was cobbled together as a spring 1959 stopgap.

The second volume of _Golden Records_, _50,000,000 Elvis Fans Can't Be Wrong_, emerged just in time for Christmas 1959, and boasted an eye-catching image of Presley in a gold lamé suit. It is, inevitably, a slighter collection than its predecessor, with just five singles released since early 1958 with their b-sides padding out the tracklist. The movie theme 'King Creole' (unreleased as a single in the U.S. but a big British hit) is a surprise omission, but the singles, including two Number One hits – 'Don't' and 'A Big Hunk O'Love' – were all genuine million-sellers. 'Hunk' and its b-side, 'My Wish Come True,' would be the last of the June 1958 Nashville recordings to make it to single, manager Colonel Tom Parker putting the brakes on and hoping thereby to create a demand for new product to coincide with Elvis's March 1960 demobilization.

Reflecting the fact, perhaps, that Presleymania had subsided somewhat during his years in the Army, this second hits collection peaked at a modest Number 31 and would take until 1966 to exceed a million dollars' sales; _Golden Records_, on the other hand, was so certified in 1961. In Britain, however, it reached Number Four in mid 1960, thus setting the pattern of greater European chart success than in Presley's native country that would continue until his death. Subsequent compilation albums have proved even more of a moneymaking phenomenon, and still rarely a year passes without a 'new' title charting in Britain and/or the U.S.A., while 2002's _Elv1s 30 #1 Hits_ topped the U.K. charts on the 25th anniversary of his passing.

The Birth Of Stereo

Record companies seemed to have learned from the 'war of the speeds' debacle, at least in the short term. So when stereo came along, a standard was agreed before marketing began.

Attempts to provide a spacial dimension to sound were, of course, nothing new. In 1881, in Paris, Clément Ader, an eccentric inventor and pioneer of aviation, demonstrated a system called the Théâtrophone, which transmitted the sound from a series of microphones in front of the stage at the Paris Opéra to listeners at the International Electrical Exhibition. Because listeners used two earpieces and because the microphones were spaced, a kind of stereophony was the result. Ader went on to market the system commercially as a wired predecessor of wireless.

In the 1920s new understanding of the mechanisms of hearing brought the first two-eared hearing aids and, as a spin-off, further experimentation with multichannel sound. But what we know today as stereo was really invented, and patented, by the EMI engineer Alan Blumlein in 1931. Frustrated by the way sound failed to follow the characters on the movie screen, he began thinking of practical ways of adding a directional element to recorded sound. He also tried to persuade his EMI bosses that stereo – or 'binaural,' as he called it – would breathe life into the good but flat recordings then being made.

> "EVERYONE SAT DOWN, SCRATCHED THEIR COLLECTIVE HEADS, AND ASKED, 'WHAT SHALL WE CALL THIS NEW SOUND?' FINALLY OUR PR PEOPLE TOOK THE HINT WHEN WE SAID IT REPRESENTED A LIFE-LIKE EXPERIENCE, AND SETTLED ON 'LIVING STEREO.'"
> *PRODUCER JACK PFEIFFER ON RCA'S 1950S TECHNOLOGY*

In his patent he created a theoretical stereo recording chain, from microphone placement to disk cutting, but was not able to carry it all out in practice before being moved by EMI first to television and then to war work. Nonetheless, right through 1932 and 1933, EMI allowed him to build microphones, circuitry, and a stereo disk-cutting lathe and experiment with them.

In 1934 his whole kit was moved to EMI's new studios at Abbey Road, in London. In the room later made famous by The Beatles, Blumlein made his first stereo music recording, two tracks by Ray Noble's Dance Band. Finally, on January 19th 1934, Blumlein recorded a rehearsal of Mozart's 'Symphony No. 41,' conducted by Sir Thomas Beecham. Then he moved on to his real interest, stereo movie soundtracks, which he pursued until ordered to move on to EMI's electronic television system, then still locked in battle with John Logie Baird's mechanical system.

Blumlein's original stereo patent expired in 1947, five years after his death in an airplane crash while testing an airborne radar system. It was extended for five years, and then expired altogether. EMI never used his work commercially, not taking an interest in stereo again until its arch-rival Decca came up with a system in 1955.

In the meantime, Bell Laboratories in the U.S.A. had in 1931 begun working with the great conductor Leopold Stokowski, who was unhappy with the recorded sound he was getting with his Philadelphia Orchestra. A new cutting lathe was developed and then, in March 1932, two years before Blumlein's experiments, a stereo recording of Scriabin's 'Poem Of Fire' was produced, using two separate grooves on the same wax disk. Two styli and cartridges were required to play it back.

This was obviously not the way forward, however, though public demonstrations of stereo continued throughout the 1930s and work on multichannel sound didn't stop. Disney, with *Fantasia*, and the new Cinerama and Cinemascope

Continued on page 38

1959

Exotica Vol. 1 **Martin Denny**

Liberty 3034 (U.S.A.) / London SAHW 6062 (U.K.)
Released April 1959

Exotica Vol. 2 **Martin Denny**

Liberty LST 7034 (U.S.A.) / London SAHW 6076 (U.K.)
Released July 1959

While the name Martin Denny means little in Britain, the classically trained pianist's musical recipe, an "exotic fruit salad," titillated America's taste-buds to such an extent that 1959 saw him score a Number One album in *Exotica* and a Number Two single in lead track 'Quiet Village.'

A job as a bar pianist in Hawaii in 1954 led to Denny forming a quartet, and the response to his music, which contained Polynesian and Asian influences – as *Mojo* magazine put it in 1995: "Hawaiian melodies, Latin rhythms and all-American sentiments" – was immediate and positive.

Les Baxter – another pianist, arranger, and composer, who had been working in a similar field for most of the decade, and who is the true founding father of the genre that became known as exotica – contributed three tracks, 'Quiet Village,' 'Stone God,' and 'The Love Dance.'

The record, cut at Honolulu's Webley Edwards studio, cost well under a thousand dollars to make. Since spoof bird calls, improvised by musicians Arthur Lyman (vibes), Augie Colon (percussion), and John Kramer (double bass), had proved a surprise hit in concert, they reprised these in the studio, while frog noises were generated by Denny using a grooved percussion instrument. The album was recorded twice: the 1956 mono version featuring Arthur Lyman, and the stereo his replacement, Julius Wechter.

Denny's early releases were lavished with near-unanimous critical acclaim. The *Seatle Times* proclaimed Denny, somewhat ironically, to be "just what the doctor ordered to banish the Presleys and [Rick] Nelsons from teenagers affections." The *San Francisco Examiner*, meanwhile, heaped praise on "the most exciting group of musicians I have ever heard."

In the wake of this initial success Denny recorded no fewer than 36 further albums of "exotic mood music" for Liberty, rejoicing in such titles as *Primitiva*, *Hypnotique*, and *Romantica*. Many featured model Sandy Warner on the cover, underlining the genre's label as "bachelor-pad music," while the mid 1960s saw Denny's work percolate into ballet as well as being used as background music in locations as disparate as restaurants and massage parlors.

In the 1990s Creation Records' Rev-Ola subsidiary put Denny's music back on the market in digital form, bolstering his cult status, while the Scamp label combined the first two volumes of *Exotica* on a 1997 CD.

In just a few years Buddy Holly inspired the formation of countless groups and provided them with songs to cover – and in the case of The Hollies a name. The Beatles' earliest recordings included a demo of 'That'll Be The Day,' and The Rolling Stones' first Top Ten hit was a version of 'Not Fade Away.' 'It's So Easy' certainly sounds like an anticipation of Merseybeat. Later movies and stage musicals have put Holly's music before the public again and supported a stream of compilations.

Have 'Twangy' Guitar Will Travel
Duane Eddy

Jamie LP 3000 (U.S.A.) / London HAW2160 (U.K.)
Released June 1959

In the late 1950s Duane Eddy's instrumental hits helped put the electric guitar at the very heart of popular music.

Eddy's trademark was 'twangy' guitar motifs and melodies played on the lower strings. The combination of metal strings, low pitched notes, and undistorted amplification created his signature sound, along with studio reverb and echo. The idea of making the electric guitar the focus of a recording was itself revolutionary.
Eddy once said: "My background was more country than pop. There are two types of guitar players, the players who have developed their skills to a point where they can play anything in any style, and me. I can't do that . . . I found a sound, the so-called twangy guitar sound, and I stayed with it."

Between 1958 and 1963 his releases were often in the Top 40. Among the most famous are 'Rebel Rouser' and 'Peter Gunn,' the latter a television series theme on which his guitar is joined by growling sax. 'Peter Gunn' was covered in 1986 by U.K. group Art Of Noise, an update that earned them a Grammy. One way or another, the Eddy sound was emulated by Eddie Cochran, The Ventures, The Shadows, and other instrumental groups. It fell from favor when The Beatles put the emphasis back on vocals, and amplifier distortion replaced twang as the definitive rock sound. One of the greatest homages to his work is the playing of Vic Flick on the James Bond soundtracks from 1962 onward.

The Buddy Holly Story **Buddy Holly**

Coral 57279 (U.S.A.) / 9105 (U.K.)
Released May 1959

Released three months after Holly's death in a plane crash on February 3rd 1959, T*he Buddy Holly Story* was an early example of the posthumous album achieving huge sales on the wave of public sympathy that follows a performer's untimely death. (Hank Williams's *Memorial Album*, 1955, was another.)

This was the first album of Holly material released after his death, and it stayed on the charts for three years.
The crash at Clear Lake, Iowa, was later put into song by Don McLean as 'the day the music died' in his tribute song, 'American Pie.'

Buddy Holly's professional career lasted little more than two years. Born in Lubbock, Texas, in 1936, Holly recorded his first demos in 1954 and 1955, followed by others in Nashville in a rockabilly style as a solo artist for Decca. His first single was issued in July 1956. After his Decca contract was terminated because of a lack of commercial success, he went to Clovis, New Mexico, and met producer Norman Petty. With his new group, The Crickets, Holly re-recorded 'That'll Be The Day,' which became a Top Three single on both sides of the Atlantic in 1957, the first of a sequence of million-sellers. By late 1958 Holly was second only to Elvis in popularity.

Of the 12 tracks, 11 are mono, and the album lasts a mere 26 minutes. It opens appropriately with 'Raining In My Heart,' with its evocative pizzicato strings. 'Early In The Morning' is a gruffer, more forceful vocal than you expect from Holly. 'Peggy Sue' is memorable for its fast, distant drumming and Holly's trademark 'hiccup' vocal. The guitar solo required someone other than Holly – who, in order to maintain the rhythm, was unable to stop strumming to flick the pick-up switch – to kneel down in front of him to change the setting on his Stratocaster at the start and end of the solo, thus creating a striking change in tone and volume. Other hits from 1957 and 1958 were 'Maybe Baby,' 'Everyday,' with its slapped thigh rhythm and musical chimes, the rocking 'Rave On' and 'Think It Over,' the sarcastic 'That'll Be The Day,' with its famous blues guitar intro, the Latin-influenced 'Heartbeat,' and the high energy of 'Oh Boy!'

The album ends with Holly's first single of 1959, a cover of Paul Anka's 'It Really Doesn't Matter Anymore.' Its bittersweet resignation at the end of a relationship was inevitably heard after Holly's death as a deeper world-weariness, as though he were singing about parting from life. (Otis Redding's 'Dock Of The Bay' and Jimi Hendrix's 'Voodoo Chile' are two later singles whose lyrics were similarly recontextualized by their performers' deaths.) This track is in stereo and shows an expansion of Holly's original sound with smooth strings and harp glissandos.

Continued from page 36

systems explored multichannel systems in movies, for example, and in the early 1950s record companies began recording in stereo, but without a feasible stereo disk-playing system the commercial possibilities remained limited.

Research continued, and, in 1952, experimenter and audio engineer Amory Cook released binaural disks in which two entirely separate grooves were cut for left and right channels. Enthusiasts needed a record deck with two pickup cartridges alongside each other. It was extremely difficult to place the needles in the grooves accurately enough to get both channels to start together.

In 1957 three more refined systems were placed before the U.S. record industry: Decca's 'vertical-lateral' system, a system offered by Columbia, and a third devised by Westrex, manufacturers of record-cutting lathes.

Both Blumlein's and Keller's stereo experiments in the 1930s had used the side-to-side and up-and-down movements of the stylus in the groove to provide two channels. However, both had also – independently of one another – devised a much better system, in which the two channels were recorded on opposite sides of the V-shaped groove, though neither seems to have been able to make this '45/45 system' – so called because each channel is at that angle to the disk surface – work at the time, not least because of having to use shellac. The Westrex system – apparently devised in ignorance of Blumlein's patents (which had languished in EMI's vaults before expiring) as well as Keller's work – was another such 45/45 system. It had the great advantage of nominal compatibility with mono: two channels playing the same sound in phase produce a sideways movement that is reproduced on mono equipment as the two channels added together to make one sound.

For once the industry agreed on a common system – and the best system – and started planning a controlled transition to stereo, though not without the odd hiccup. A small company called Audio Fidelity sent some tapes to Westrex to have a master cut "for test purposes." One side contained various sound effects, with test tones, and the other was taken from a stereo tape recording of The Dukes Of Dixieland. To the annoyance of the entire industry, Audio Fidelity immediately put the disk on sale, purely so that it could claim to be the first. At that stage there was not even a commercially available stereo cartridge to play the record – but nonetheless it sold well.

Within a year of Westrex's first demonstration of the system, every significant company was offering stereo records. But the buyers were less enthusiastic. They needed something to convince them to make the expensive transition to stereo. For classical listeners, that came in the shape of Decca's record of Wagner's *Das Rheingold*, the beginning of the first complete recording of The Ring Cycle, and a tour de force of stereo sound and effects, produced by John Culshaw in London.

Meanwhile, the sensation for pop listeners was bandleader Enoch Light's *Persuasive Percussion*, which made great use of ping-pong directional effects. However, it would be a while before stereo settled down as a great boon for classical listeners and a new wave of hi-fi enthusiasts. By 1968 all classical records were being released in stereo.

For pop listeners, playing singles on small record-players, it was largely irrelevant, at least until the late 1960s and the rise of the album market. In 1969 EMI took the controversial decision to release The Beatles' *Abbey Road* LP in stereo only. This forced people at the very least to change their record-player cartridges, since, despite their theoretical compatibility, mono cartridges and styli very quickly destroyed stereo records.

1959

Film Encores **Mantovani**

London 1700 (U.S.A.) / SKL 4002 (U.K.)
Released April 1959

The dapper, Venice-born Annunzio Paolo Mantovani was one of the most successful orchestra leaders in history, with a career spanning six decades.

The son of a violinist who played at Milan's La Scala opera house under Toscanini, he followed his father's instrumental example, came to London at the age of 16, and, four years later, was conducting the Hotel Metropole's orchestra. Al Bowlly was just one of the famous singers with whom he worked. He scored U.S. hits in 1935 and 1936 with 'Red Sails In The Sunset' and 'Serenade In The Night.' After a spell as a musical director in London's West End, Mantovani turned his attention to the U.S.A. again in the 1950s.

His trademark 'cascading' strings sound, concocted with the assistance of arranger Ronnie Binge, was unveiled in 1950, when he revived the pre-World War I song 'Charmaine' to million-selling effect. This proved the key to further success, and, though he'd reprised his theatrical past with success for 1955's *Song Hits From Theatreland*, which took him into the *Billboard* Top Ten for the first time, the release that took him to the very top in July 1959 was this specially recorded movie-theme collection.

Decca Records, pioneers in the new technique of stereo recording, allowed Mantovani to choose the repertoire, and his selections clearly struck a chord with the public. *High Noon*, *My Foolish Heart*, *Intermezzo*, and *Three Coins In The Fountain* were all represented by their title themes, while 'Over The Rainbow' from *The Wizard Of Oz* and 1955 chart topper 'Unchained Melody' from *Unchained* were numbers everyone could sing.

Surprisingly, given his past singles success, none of the tracks were spun off as hits in their own right. But follow-up albums in very much the same vein, such as *Songs To Remember* (1960), kept the pot boiling, even if critics claimed any one album was indistinguishable from any other. The new medium of television helped Mantovani maintain his popularity, and his flamboyance at the podium was matched by a tendency to hold notes longer than his competitors. The former violinist is also said to have been the first million-selling stereo recording artist but, said his son Kenneth, he never regarded himself as a pop star. "He went off to work and played records – he had his job to do – but then came home just like any other father."

Mantovani's 40-piece orchestra continued to sell records worldwide despite ever-changing fads and fashions, fighting off competition from many similarly configured orchestras, notably that of Percy Faith. Though he was never to repeat the Number One success of *Film Encores*, the similarly titled *Continental Encores* gave Mantovani a U.K. chart album – the first of 11 – in the same year, 1959. Fifty-one albums charted in the U.S.A., mostly in the Top 50, and all – bar the score to 1964 Broadway hit *Kismet* – were instrumental. He died in Tunbridge Wells, Kent, in 1980, but his music and his orchestra play on.

1960

String Along **The Kingston Trio**

Capitol 1407 (U.S.A. & U.K.)
Released July 1960

Joan Baez Joan Baez

Vanguard VSD2077 (U.S.A.) / Fontana STFL6002 (U.K.)
Released October 1960

Folk was the youthful sound of the pre-beat early 1960s, and the Kingston Trio and Joan Baez were leading exponents.

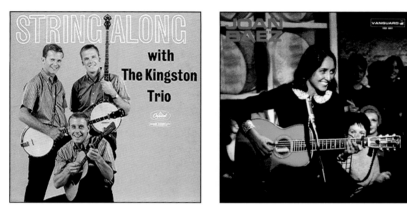

String Along was The Trio's fifth studio album, and all had reached Number One. The three San Franciscan students – Dave Guard, Nick Reynolds, and Bob Shane – had moved on somewhat from their first album, which had been released just over two years earlier, by introducing 12-string guitar and exotic percussion to the mix, which led to comparisons with The Everly Brothers.

One song on the album, 'Bad Man's Blunder,' was recorded as an act of charity for one for the song's writers, Cisco Houston, who was hospitalized and facing large medical bills. Released as a single, it only made Number 37 and is even today classed by *Billboard* as a novelty number. The second single, 'Everglade,' fared even worse, peaking at Number 60, a far cry from their chart-topping days of 1958 when 'Tom Dooley' ruled the roost. Though they'd enjoy four more Top 40 entries in 1962 and 1963, The Trio's days as a chart act were numbered, something Guard's replacement by John Stewart could not reverse.

Joan Baez had hitched a lift on the Kingston Trio's coat-tails, along with Peter, Paul, and Mary, Judy Collins, and others. She enjoyed her first break in 1958 when performing as guest of Bob Gibson at the first *Newport Folk Festival*.

Signed by Vanguard Records, apparently because co-founder and producer Maynard Soloman was an idealist like herself, she released her first, eponymous album in November 1960, but would later gain in notoriety thanks to a personal association with Bob Dylan and a link with the protest movement, particularly her work in mobilizing public opinion against U.S. involvement in the Vietnam War. Her breakthrough in Britain came in 1965 when she played the Royal Albert Hall, and her fifth album, issued hard on the heels of single 'We Shall Overcome,' breached the Top Three, while *Joan Baez* finally made it into the UK chart at Number Nine.

This first album, which Baez recorded at the age of 19, was cut in a New York hotel bedroom and relied upon traditional folk standards – many, like 'Silver Dagger' and 'Mary Hamilton,' from Scotland – and included such staples as 'House Of The Rising Sun,' the spiritual 'All My Trials,' and the Spanish political song, 'El Preso Numero Nuevo.' Simplicity and sincerity were the keywords, both musically and lyrically, and Solomon had to work hard to convince Baez to employ another musician, guitarist Fred Hellerman, to fill out her sound.

Baez would record 16 more albums for Vanguard before signing with A&M in the 1970s. If she'd made the move to a major label earlier or become Dylan's labelmate on CBS she might have done even better even quicker, but by giving folk the kind of sex appeal the likes of The Kingston Trio lacked she did the genre a great service.

1960

Unforgettable **Dinah Washington**

Mercury 20572 (U.S.A.) / MMC14048 (U.K.)
Released February 1960

The trade papers called her 'Queen Of The Jukeboxes,' while she herself preferred 'Queen of the Blues.' What's certain is that Dinah Washington brought her bluesy delivery to the jazz world until her untimely death at the age of just 39, three years after this release.

Born Ruth Lee Jones in Tuscaloosa, Alabama, in 1924, Washington lived life to the full, marrying no fewer than seven times and showing a partiality to drink, but this became part of the appeal of a performer who demanded fans accept her just as she was. It certainly gave her the emotional armory to invest every song on this ballad-heavy album with the necessary gravitas. As one critic put it: "Nearly all the tunes are ballads, and they're all about loneliness, about women wronged, and yet always hoping for that good man to come to whom they can offer their great gift: complete devotion." 'Unforgettable' itself is, of course, the Nat King Cole classic, and it's a measure of Washington's self-belief that she thought she could put her own stamp on such a song.

Washington had first crossed to the pop chart in 1950 with a sensual reading of 'I Wanna Be Loved,' and her audience grew from the black record-buying public to a much wider market. 'What A Difference A Day Makes' and duets with fellow Mercury artist Brook Benton opened up new vistas, but it was the likes of *Unforgettable*'s 'This Bitter Earth' – her fifth R&B singles chart topper – that exemplified a bleaker setting for her talents.

In 1964 the 21-year-old Aretha Franklin was moved to record a tribute to Washington. Also titled 'Unforgettable,' it was a timely reminder of a sadly missed singer.

It's Everly Time **The Everly Brothers**

WB WS 1381 (U.S.A.) / Warner Bros WS8012 (U.K.)
Released April 1960

One of the great male duos in popular music, the Everly Brothers' voices match as though a singer is harmonizing with himself. Their presence loomed large in popular music between the death of Buddy Holly and 'Love Me Do.'

Signed in 1956 to Cadence, their first success came with 'Bye Bye Love' (1957), which started a run of hits: 'Wake Up Little Susie,' 'All I Have To Do Is Dream,' 'Claudette,' 'Bird Song,' 'Till I Kissed You,' and 'Walk Right Back.' Their harmony vocals and acoustic guitars were country in origin, but guitarist Chet Atkins helped with arrangements to give The Everlys a stronger beat.

In 1960 The Everlys signed the first million-dollar music industry contract, with Warner Brothers. Shortly after, 'Cathy's Clown' went to Number One in the U.S.A. (five weeks) and the U.K. (nine weeks). *It's Everly Time* was recorded in March 1960 at RCA's Nashville Sound Studio B. The follow-up to 'Cathy's Clown,' 'So Sad,' is a strong meditative opener. The husband-and-wife team of Felice and Boudleaux Bryant, who wrote hits for Roy Orbison, provided five of the tracks, of which 'Sleepless Nights' shows off their skills to great effect, with its impressively unpredictable chord sequence sinking through various keys.

The Everlys were a huge influence on many 1960s' acts, such as The Beatles, The Hollies, The Searchers, and Simon and Garfunkel. Graham Nash recalled: "I remember going to a school dance and listening to The Everly Brothers do 'Bye Bye Love.' It paralyzed me. I had to stop what I was doing, which was walking across the dance floor. And I stopped because I was so shocked musically . . . something inside of me said, 'I want to make people feel what I feel at this moment.'"

The Sound Of Fury **Billy Fury**

Not issued in U.S.A. / Decca LF1329 (U.K.)
Released May 1960

This ten-inch debut album by the Liverpudlian Fury was cut in just two sessions at Decca's West Hampstead studio in London in January and April 1960.

The album mimicked the legendary Sun Sound better than any other British rock'n'roller, and would subsequently be hailed as the first great U.K. rockabilly album. Boasting material penned under Fury's pseudonym, Wilbur Wilberforce, it was an album that its producer Jack Good regarded as 'remarkable.' Good got two bass players in to achieve an authentic slap bass sound: Alan Weighell played the note on electric bass and Bill Stark just slapped his upright. Piano player Reg Guest was the band leader; a group of singers called The Four Jays – later to become a Brian Epstein beat group, The Fourmost – played The Jordanaires; and Joe Brown provided lead guitar. Brown recalled: "I got 26 shillings for the whole session, and it was done in virtually one take, most of it – two takes at the most. We went in with chord sheets and down it went in a couple of hours. Whole album."

On this album Fury's reference point was Eddie Cochran, whom Brown had backed on his U.K. appearances, with touches of Presley ('Since You've Been Gone'), but he achieved some kind of originality with the ballad 'You Don't Know.' Lead track, 'That's Love,' was put out as a single in the U.K. in the month of the album's release, peaking one rung lower than *The Sound Of Fury*, which reached Number 18.

While superficially derivative, *The Sound Of Fury* was influential because the likes of Johnny Kidd And The Pirates, Joe Brown's band The Bruvvers, and Sounds Incorporated all used it as a blueprint to create British rock'n'roll.

Time Out **The Dave Brubeck Quartet**

Columbia CL1397 (U.S.A.) / Fontana TFL5085 (U.K.)
Released June 1960

Time Out is rightly regarded as an all-time great jazz album. Recorded in the same studio as Miles Davis's *Kind Of Blue*, it achieved a similar crossover success.

With a delightful balance of the cerebral and the expressive, *Time Out* is an album for people who think they don't like jazz.

IIn 1954, the year he joined Columbia, Brubeck was already famous enough to make the cover of *Time*. The concept behind *Time Out* was to experiment with unusual time signatures such as 9/8 and 5/4. The Quartet comprised Brubeck on piano, Paul Desmond on alto saxophone, Eugene Wright on bass, and Joe Morello on drums. The seven tracks were recorded on June 25th, July 1st, and August 18th 1959. Among them was 'Take Five,' where the group manage to give the most extraordinarily relaxed lilt to a 5/4 beat. The melody was written by Desmond, whose lazy, purring lines are beautifully articulated, while Brubeck keeps things simple with the accompaniment so the others won't get lost.

Amazingly, 'Take Five' became a pop hit in 1961, reaching Number 25 in the U.S.A. and spending almost ten weeks in the U.K. Top 20. The LP had unprecedented sales for a jazz record. Brubeck had managed to promote jazz to a middle-class white audience that had previously missed it. It was also a big hit with a college audience who saw themselves as too hip for rock'n'roll or Bobby Vee. *Time Out* was the natural soundtrack to 'heavy' conversations about French poetry, existentialism, Marx, Kerouac, and the Bomb. Its successor, *Time Further Out*, is also worth a listen.

1960

The Eddie Cochran Memorial Album
Eddie Cochran

Not issued in U.S.A. / London HAG 2267 (U.K.)
Released September 1960

Singer-guitarist Eddie Cochran was one of the early rock'n'roll greats, and one of the first U.S. artists to tour extensively in Britain.

Tragically he met his end, aged just 21, in a car crash near Chippenham, in south-west England, in April 1960. This resulted in a wave of public sympathy that propelled the poignantly titled 'Three Steps To Heaven' to Number One in Britain, though it failed to chart in his country of origin.

The shamelessly titled *Eddie Cochran Memorial Album* was issued later that year by his British label, Decca/London, and reached Number Nine in the U.K. (It would re-chart in 1963, peaking at Number 11.) As well as the posthumous chart topper it contained Eddie's previous four British hits – 'Summertime Blues,' 'C'Mon Everybody,' 'Somethin' Else,' and a cover of Ray Charles' 'Hallelujah I Love her So,' with which he opened his shows. DJ John Peel later rated seeing Cochran perform this as one of the earliest highlights of his own personal musical journey, while the Joe Meek-produced Heinz hit, 'Just Like Eddie,' celebrated Cochran's life in song.

It was Cochran's guitar work that proved most influential at the time on the likes of George Harrison, notably the latter's adoption of the semi-acoustic Gretsch and employing such tricks as using an unwound third string to assist note bending. Since then Cochran's songs have attracted covers from The Who, Blue Cheer, The Sex Pistols, and The Faces among many others. The Rolling Stones used his '20 Flight Rock' as their stage intro music in the early 1980s. In the same decade 'C'Mon Everybody' received advertising's ultimate accolade, the Levi's television commercial. So Eddie Cochran's music truly is his memorial.

1961

Hey, Lets Twist! (Original Soundtrack)

Roulette 25168 (U.S.A.) / Columbia DB4803 (U.K.)
Released November 1961

Among the last of the pre-Beatles rock-exploitation movies, *Hey, Lets Twist!* was named for the latest dance craze.

Shot in black and white, it was set in the Peppermint Lounge, the New York venue on West 45th Street where middle-aged trendsetters let their hair down. Fueled by press and television interest, the Twist – which had enjoyed a first flourishing in August 1960 in the hands of Chubby Checker – was temporarily back in the news, and a movie resulted.

Joey Dee And The Starliters were the house band at the Peppermint Lounge, and they scored a U.S. chart-topping single with the movie-featured 'Peppermint Twist,' written by Dee and his producer, Henry Glover. Singers Jo-Ann Campbell ('Let's Do My Twist') and Teddy Randazzo ('It's A Pity To Say Goodnight') also participated in the movie, the soundtrack of which reached Number 18 in the U.S.A. in March 1962. Yet, such was the rapid fall off of public interest that the title track, released as a single in January, could barely scrape into the Top 20. (Britain remained relatively immune, Dee's dance disk stalling three places short of the Top 30.)

Dee, born Joseph DiNicola, chose to continue in the movie world, and the CD reissue of *Hey, Lets Twist!* teamed this with the soundtrack of *Two Tickets To Paris*, his other movie of note, from October 1962. Henceforth, the only interest in his Starliters was the membership of three Young Rascals-to-be and, briefly, one James Marshall Hendrix.

The Shadows **The Shadows**

Columbia 1374 (U.S.A.) / 33SX 1374 (U.K.)
Released September 1961

The Shadows were the U.K.'s most successful instrumental group of all time, with numerous hits between 1960 and the beginning of the 21st century. This debut album was heavily influenced by Duane Eddy, and helped popularize the electric guitar.

The instrumental single had a higher profile in the early 1960s than at any period since, with records such as 'Stranger On The Shore' (by jazz clarinettist Acker Bilk) and 'Telstar' (by The Tornados) reaching Number One. Popular music was making use of new technology, and The Shadows' success was partly down to their exploration of the novel sounds that could be created. The electric guitar was newly established in the rock quartet line-up of two guitars, bass, and drums, and was the hippest instrument in the world – as evidenced by its role in the James Bond movies and many television themes of the day.

The Shadows originated with Hank Marvin and Bruce Welch playing skiffle in a London coffee bar. Marvin had taken up the guitar in 1957 at 16. As The Drifters they became Cliff Richard's backing group. One of the enduring figures of the British popular-music scene, Richard has topped the U.K. singles chart more often than any other artist bar Elvis and The Beatles – though, despite a couple of U.S. chart hits, he has never achieved sustained success in the U.S.A.

The group started recording as The Shadows in 1960. Jerry Lordan's tune, 'Apache' (July 1960), became their first U.K. Number One, and it topped the *New Musical Express* (U.K.) poll for best British instrumental of the year. Marvin's tone was cool and mostly clean. He played one of the first Fender Stratocasters imported into the U.K., using melodies on the lower strings as Eddy did but also higher lead breaks. His sound was shaped by echo, early examples of string-bending, and vibrato from the Strat's tremolo arm. For a generation of players inspired by Marvin's lead playing on tracks like 'Shadoogie' and 'Nivram,' he was the first British guitar hero. The 1999 EMI CD remaster of this album includes mono and stereo mixes of the 14 tracks.

The Soul Of Ike And Tina Turner
Ike And Tina Turner

Sue P-2001 (U.S.A.) / Kent K519 (U.K.)
Released October 1961

While the stormy relationship between Ike and Tina Turner has been chronicled and dissected in book and movie form, there's little doubt that Ike coaxed some amazing vocal performances out of his sometime wife. This album, which was not released in Britain until 1984, contains many early examples.

Tina's act combined sex and religion, inspiring worship and lust from a mainly male audience. "I styled her that way," Ike said. "I made it happen. The lights came down on her, there was no spotlight on me."

With the recording of 'A Fool In Love,' which, as *Billboard*'s review accurately reported, had "a touch of gospel style in the screaming passages," the Turners hit a groove they would retread relentlessly until Phil Spector got involved with production in the mid 1960s. The exuberant 'I Idolize You' from this album also scored, and was teamed on a single with the teen-slanted 'Letter From Tina,' while 'It's Gonna Work Out Fine,' 'Poor Fool,' and 'Tra-La-La-La-La' were further examples of Ike's successful formula. Legend has it Tina was only offered a shot at 'A Fool In Love' when a session singer failed to show. If so, it was a happy accident indeed.

Spector's input opened up a whole new world for Tina, and would inevitably weaken Ike's hold on her. The 1980s and 1990s saw her reap the rewards that decades of hard work had prepared her for, but *The Soul Of Ike And Tina Turner*, an early entry on a formidable resume, remains something she can be proud of.

1962

Jazz Samba Stan Getz, Charlie Byrd

Verve 8432 (U.S.A.) / Verve SULP 9013 (U.K.)
Released September 1962

The combination of jazz guitarist Charlie Byrd, tenor saxophonist Stan Getz, and a new type of Brazilian rhythmic music, brought back by Byrd from a tour of South America, catapulted artists and genre on to the charts in 1963.

The bossa nova craze helped Getz become one of the most successful jazzmen ever to cross over to the mainstream, thanks to four Top 40 LPs within a couple of years. This album of instrumentals, produced by Creed Taylor, was the first. While Getz's existing fans may have been dismayed at the saxophonist 'selling out' to commercialism, no one dared argue that he had not paid his fair share of dues, having served in the bands of such respected leaders as Jack Teagarden, Stan Kenton, Benny Goodman, Tommy Dorsey, and Woody Herman.

Getz first became interested in bossa nova in December 1961, when Byrd played him an LP by João Gilberto. Getz saw in the music an excitement and immediacy that was missing from contemporary jazz. He asked Byrd to put together and rehearse a rhythm section for a prospective jazz-samba album, and to call him in when the band was ready.

On February 13th 1962 Getz flew to Washington, D.C., to cut the album. The recording studio was, in fact, a church hall. Two drummers, Bill Reichenbach and Buddy Deppenschmidt, were employed at the sessions in imitation of Brazilian polyrhythmic jazz groups. The other musicians were bassist Keter Betts and Byrd's brother Gene, on bass and guitar respectively. The sextet cut the seven songs on *Jazz Samba* in three hours, after which Getz flew straight back to New York for dinner.

> ### "I JUST THOUGHT IT WAS PRETTY MUSIC. I NEVER THOUGHT IT WOULD BE A HIT."
> #### *STAN GETZ*

Having chosen not to rehearse with Byrd and his band before the sessions, Getz relied on his finely honed improvisational ability, and nowhere is this more in evidence than on the opening track, 'Desafinado,' co-written by Brazilian father of the bossa nova, Antonio Carlos Jobim. This reached the U.S. Top 20 when released as a single, while Getz would make the Top Five in 1964 with 'The Girl From Ipanema,' for which he teamed up with singer Astrud Gilberto. (Their 1964 LP *Getz/Gilberto* won a Grammy Award.) But this U.S. Number One album, which reached Number 15 in the U.K., was the start of it all.

Green Onions Booker T. And The MGs

Stax 701 (U.S.A.) / London HAK 8182 (U.K.)
Released October 1962 (U.S.A.) / July 1964 (U.K.)

Here, one of the 1960s' greatest studio session groups grabs the spotlight for once, instead of backing more famous acts, such as Otis Redding and Wilson Pickett.

Renowned for their disciplined but gritty style, The MGs were the house band of the Stax label, based in Memphis – hence MGs: Memphis Group – with an equivalent role to The Funk Brothers over at Motown in Detroit. The quartet's line-up was Booker T. Jones (organ), Steve Cropper (guitar), Al Jackson (drums), and Lewis Steinberg (bass).

The album originated when the group recorded 'Behave Yourself' and 'Green Onions' after a studio session with rockabilly star Billy Lee Riley in June 1962. The remaining ten tracks were cut that August and included Ray Charles's 'I Got A Woman,' 'Twist And Shout,' 'Stranger On The Shore,' Smokey Robinson's 'One Who Really Loves You,' and 'Mo' Onions,' an attempt to re-write the title track. 'Green Onions' wasn't first choice as a single but when it got airplay it was released and became a Top Three U.S. million-seller, with Booker only 16 at the time. The album, produced by Jim Stewart, followed three months later. In the U.K., where the group had a cult following, it came out in mono on the London label in 1964 and nearly reached the Top Ten.

Reissued by Atlantic in 1966 – again in mono – it finally came out in stereo in late 1969. Despite the album's success, Booker T. carried on music studies at Indiana University until 1966.

▪ *Main picture: Booker T. And The MGs' Steve Cropper at Stax Studios. Below: a set of publicity shots of the group from the mid 1960s.*

Al Jackson, JR

Booker T

Donald "Duck" Dunn

Steve Cropper

1962

Modern Sounds In Country And Western Music
Ray Charles

ABC-Paramount 410 (US) / HMV CLP 1580 (UK)
Released April 1962

Having dominated black music in the late 1950s, pianist-vocalist Ray Charles delighted in breaking musical boundaries, and never more so than with this hugely popular excursion into country.

Charles had already passed through several distinct musical incarnations, starting with the night-club style of the late 1940s, through to the classic R&B Atlantic material of the 1950s, before he signed for ABC-Paramount in 1959. He was one of the few artists of the period who demanded – and got – total control over his recorded material, as well as retaining ownership of the masters. The freedom this gave him was reflected in the eclectic nature of his output, which has influenced several succeeding generations of artists.

Each phase of his work has its own special appeal, but it was during the 1960s that Charles was at his boldest and most prolific, and enjoyed his greatest commercial success. He'd already explored the jazz sphere, with 1961's *Genius + Soul = Jazz*, on which he'd been assisted by members of Count Basie's band. That album reached U.S. Number Four and emboldened him to try a daring incursion into country music. This, however, did not meet with the approval of ABC president Sam Clark. "He felt I was making a mistake," said Charles later, "but I felt if I lost any fans he would gain as many as I would lose." The result was the bestselling album of his career. It was *Billboard*'s Number One for 14 straight weeks and remained on the pop chart for three weeks short of two years.

Charles had long enjoyed country music, having listened to the *Grand Ole Opry* on the radio during his youth in Greenville, South Carolina, and gigged with a country band, The Florida Playboys, in Tampa in 1947 as a sideline alongside his main job with Charlie Brantley's Honeydrippers.

Producer Sid Feller took the helm in the studio – though, like Sam Clark, he had taken some convincing. "I hadn't known what the hell he was talking about, but hell, it worked – he loved the simple, plaintive lyrics, and thought giving the music a lush treatment would make it different."

Having mixed the sacred and the profane in gospel and R&B in the 1950s, Charles was now playing country with what was effectively a big band. (Ironically, in the 1980s he would to all intents and purposes become a country singer by recruiting steel guitars and the like to his arrangements.) Repertoire sources ranged widely: the Webb Pierce-Everly Brothers classic 'Bye Bye Love,' Big Bill Broonzy's arrangement of 'Careless Love,' and Hank Williams's 'You Win Again' and 'Hey Good Lookin'' were highlights. Other writers included Eddy Arnold, Floyd Tillman, and Jimmie Davis, a prolific singer-songwriter – he co-wrote 'You Are My Sunshine' – and sometime Louisiana governor.

Perhaps the greatest performance was on Don Gibson's 'I Can't Stop Loving You,' an unusual choice in that Gibson's own version had sold a million just four years earlier, albeit as a b-side. It was hidden away as second-to-last track, reflecting Sid Feller's low opinion of it. But when Tab Hunter recorded a soundalike version for single release, Charles's hand was forced, and it became first of an unusually large number of singles to be taken from the album, boosting sales to unexpected heights. The song reached Number One, and the follow-up, the Cindy Walker–Eddy Arnold-penned 'You Don't Know Me,' stalled just one place short.

Two sessions – in New York and Los Angeles – was all it took to complete the album in February 1962. Big-band arrangements on the half-dozen New York tracks were essayed by Gerald Wilson and Gil Fuller, while strings on the Los Angeles cuts were by Marty Paich – whose son David would emerge two and a half decades later as leader of AOR supergroup Toto. The songs were recorded live in the studio, six or seven a day at a total cost of $22,000.

This was all the more remarkable given Charles's turbulent private life, which included a heroin habit that was making him distinctly unreliable as a performer. Indeed, he'd escaped a drug bust in Indianapolis on a technicality just before the sessions for this album started. He had money to indulge such foolishness, Ray Charles Enterprises having grossed a staggering $1.5 million in 1961.

A follow-up was expected, and, having been recorded on east and west coasts exactly like its predecessor, *Modern Sounds In Country And Western Music Volume Two* was duly released in late 1962. It visited near-identical song sources, reached Number Two during a 67-week chart stay and yielded Top Ten hit singles in 'You Are My Sunshine' and 'Take These Chains From My Heart.' In Britain the album hit Number Six, a position he would never again surpass.

Other related albums include *Crying Time* and *Country And Western Meets Rhythm and Blues*, both recorded in 1965. Ray Charles was nothing if not prolific, and *Modern Sounds* – ABC's first million-seller – was just one of six of his albums to make the U.S. Top 40 in 1962. (That said, three were compilations of his Atlantic material designed to cash in on his success.)

While *Modern Sounds* turned a whole lot of newcomers on to the Ray Charles phenomenon, Charles's loyal fans stayed with him no matter which musical route he took. Jazz magazine *Downbeat* voted him best male singer five years in a row from 1961, even though he was straying into other fields, while *Billboard*'s chart records show he was the ninth bestselling artist in the U.S.A. in the 1960s – a decade where musical fads and fashions came and went with breathtaking rapidity.

In a sense, it didn't matter what style he chose: Ray Charles's innate character shone through. "Some people say my style comes from the church-singing in gospel choirs," he said, "some people say it's jazz, but really I just sing about life." With earnings at $1.6 million in 1962, life was rich indeed.

Spinning Gold

When partners Stan Ross and Dave Gold signed the $175-a-month lease agreement on a property located at the corner of Santa Monica and Vine in the fall of 1950, they had no idea that their start-up enterprise would one day become a major piece of pop-music lore.

"It was an old building that had been previously used by a dentist," says Gold. "Given the equipment we were using at the time, making records was like pulling teeth."

It didn't happen overnight, but by the turn of 1960s the disparate elements combined to make Gold Star Recording Studios the most sought-after independent facility in Hollywood. Over the next decade Gold Star's 23-feet by 35-feet recording-room would play host to a diverse crowd of characters, from Sonny & Cher ('I Got You Babe') and The Beach Boys ('Good Vibrations'), to rockers The Who ('I Can See For Miles') and Iron Butterfly ('Inna Gada Da Vida').

In Dave Gold the studio had a master technician who built from scratch many of the studio's best pieces of machinery. Gold's twin echo chambers – perfected near the end of the 1950s – produced some of the finest recording effects in all of pop music. Ross and his cousin Larry Levine, who signed on in 1952, were pioneers in the engineering trade, and their miking and mixing techniques became the backbone for scores of hit records over a 30-year period. Rounding out the essential ingredients was Gold Star's inimitable house band, dubbed The Wrecking Crew,

Continued on page 49

The Freewheelin' Bob Dylan Bob Dylan

Columbia CL 1986 (U.S.A.) / CBS62193 (U.K.)
Released May 1963

Dylan's second album, *The Freewheelin' Bob Dylan*, introduced protest lyrics into the consciousness of the pop audience. Blues and folk artists had always used songs to comment on the injustices of politics, war, and society but, for mainstream record buyers, Dylan's angry invective was a revelation.

In 1958, against a background of bobby-soxers and rock'n'rollers, a huge folk boom had swept the U.S.A. after The Kingston Trio's ground-breaking Number One single 'Tom Dooley.' Many of the hits generated in its wake, however, were sanitized and bowdlerized before they reached the mass market. Dylan's vision of folk music had little truck with this comfortably commercial niche.

On September 29th 1961 the *New York Times* music critic Robert Shelton raved over a Dylan gig at Gerdes Folk City, describing him as "a cross between a choirboy and a beatnik" who was "bursting at the seams with talent." Shortly afterward, Dylan was signed to Columbia by revered A&R man John Hammond, who had previously discovered Billie Holiday and would subsequently nurture Bruce Springsteen. Dylan was quickly tagged 'Hammond's folly' because few Columbia executives could see much commercial potential in this raspy-voiced troubadour, whose eponymous 1962 debut album consisted largely of folk-blues covers, giving little indication of what was to come.

Recording for *Freewheelin'* started in April 1962 at Columbia's Studio A in New York City, and carried on sporadically for a year, during which dozens of tracks were recorded and discarded while Dylan was finding his own voice as a writer. Musically, *Freewheelin'* remained firmly in the same style as the debut – one man and his finger-pickin' guitar – but the youth of America had never heard anything resembling the lyrics of tracks like 'A Hard Rain's A-Gonna Fall,' a vision of impending apocalypse conjured through metaphorical images of trees dripping blood, dead oceans, and empty diamond-studded highways.

It's indicative of just how far Dylan's lyrics stood apart from mainstream pop that, on the same day as the final *Freewheelin'* session, Jan & Dean recorded 'Surf City' in Los Angeles, a vibrant teen anthem celebrating the joys of the Californian lifestyle with "two girls for every boy." Significantly, at the start of 'Bob Dylan's Blues' Dylan referred sarcastically to this yawning gulf, observing: "Tin Pan Alley – that's where most of the folk songs come from nowadays." *Freewheelin'* also included the achingly beautiful lament for love gone wrong that is 'Don't Think Twice, It's All Right,' but it was the uncompromising protests – 'Masters Of War' and 'Blowin' In The Wind' – that spoke loudest to Americans terrified by the Cold War and disgusted by the treatment of racial minorities in their land of the free.

Freewheelin' stalled at Number 22 in the *Billboard* albums chart because, for the moment, Dylan's audience consisted largely of young radical intellectuals. This was a relatively small but disproportionately influential cohort, some of whom – Phil Ochs, Tim Rose, and Barry McGuire to name a few – would themselves become protest songwriters and spread the word. By 1965, however, when The Byrds turned his 'Mr Tambourine Man' into an international pop hit, Dylan began to be regarded as a spokesman for his generation.

In just a few years Buddy Holly inspired the formation of countless groups and provided them with songs to cover – and in the case of The Hollies a name. The Beatles' earliest recordings included a demo of 'That'll Be The Day,' and The Rolling Stones' first Top Ten hit was a version of 'Not Fade Away.' 'It's So Easy' certainly sounds like an anticipation of Merseybeat. Later movies and stage musicals have put Holly's music before the public again and supported a stream of compilations.

Have 'Twangy' Guitar Will Travel
Duane Eddy

Jamie LP 3000 (U.S.A.) / London HAW2160 (U.K.)
Released June 1959

In the late 1950s Duane Eddy's instrumental hits helped put the electric guitar at the very heart of popular music.

Eddy's trademark was 'twangy' guitar motifs and melodies played on the lower strings. The combination of metal strings, low pitched notes, and undistorted amplification created his signature sound, along with studio reverb and echo. The idea of making the electric guitar the focus of a recording was itself revolutionary.

Eddy once said: "My background was more country than pop. There are two types of guitar players, the players who have developed their skills to a point where they can play anything in any style, and me. I can't do that . . . I found a sound, the so-called twangy guitar sound, and I stayed with it."

Between 1958 and 1963 his releases were often in the Top 40. Among the most famous are 'Rebel Rouser' and 'Peter Gunn,' the latter a television series theme on which his guitar is joined by growling sax. 'Peter Gunn' was covered in 1986 by U.K. group Art Of Noise, an update that earned them a Grammy. One way or another, the Eddy sound was emulated by Eddie Cochran, The Ventures, The Shadows, and other instrumental groups. It fell from favor when The Beatles put the emphasis back on vocals, and amplifier distortion replaced twang as the definitive rock sound. One of the greatest homages to his work is the playing of Vic Flick on the James Bond soundtracks from 1962 onward.

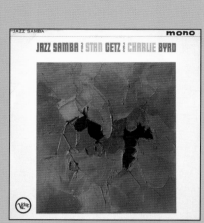

In The Wind Peter, Paul & Mary

Warner Bros 1507 (U.S.A.) / Warner Bros WM8142 (U.K.)
Released October 1963

**Having helped introduce
American youth to folk music,
Peter Yarrow, Paul Stuckey, and
Mary Travers did another service
with their third album by
including three songs by the
then cult folkie Bob Dylan.**

Granted, there was a certain amount
of nepotism involved, as the trio and
Dylan shared a manager, Albert
Grossman, but titling their album
after a song of his nailed their colors
firmly to the Zimmerman mast and
undoubtedly gave their stablemate – whose first album had signally failed to
chart – much-needed exposure.

Both 'Blowin' In The Wind' and 'Don't Think Twice, It's Alright,' which
reached Numbers Two and Nine as U.S. singles before the realease of *In
The Wind*, also appear on Dylan's 1963 LP *The Freewheelin' Bob Dylan*,
though the Peter, Paul & Mary album track, 'Quit Your Low Down Ways,'
would wait until 1991 to be anthologized by its author on a retrospective
box set.

In Britain, where they toured before Dylan, *In The Wind* would prove the trio's
most successful album, peaking at Number 11 in 1964 in the wake of the
title track's Number 13 success. Back home, it took only two weeks to hit
the top, displacing their debut album, which had just reassumed the
Number One slot. Dylan found such lofty heights harder to reach, and only
when *Planet Waves* reached pole position in 1974 could he look down on all
comers. By that time the winsome Peter, Paul & Mary were three years into
their solo careers – though they have subsequently re-formed.

Continued from page 47

a rotating cast of session players that included drummer Hal Blaine, bassist Carole
Kaye, guitarists Glen Campbell and Billy Strange, and many others.

It was a combination of ingenuity and technical know-how that kept Gold Star in the
black during the early years. When a deal on a recording console fell through, Gold
simply got out the toolbox and went to work. "As a last resort, I got some old
chassis together, a bunch of tubes, and turned it into a four-input unit," says Gold.
"It was pretty crude, but it worked. And that's what we used for several years."

"All the Columbia records made in New York during that time had the most
wonderful echo sound," says Ross. "It was because they had these beautiful echo
chambers there. I used to love to hear that on a recording – so right away, that was
something we wanted to have on our own productions."

It would take some doing before the Gold Star crew hit on a winning formula. "We
started by using this long hallway that we had off the original Studio A," says Gold.
"We opened the door on one end and put a microphone at the other end. Then
we'd just put the singer down there. It wasn't very much, but it did the job for the
time being."

Gold then embarked on a string of echo experiments, most of them less than
extraordinary. "I tried using springs, which were OK for instruments but never really
sounded good with vocals. We then constructed this long 4-by-4 crawlspace that ran
above the hallway. We painted the walls in order to make it more reflective – it's a
wonder we didn't die in the process. But that didn't work either. During this one
session, we tried putting this female singer in the bathroom – which wasn't half
bad, except the song was called 'Well of Loneliness,' and we couldn't stop cracking
up!"

By 1956 it was decided that a proper echo chamber was the only way to go. "I did
a bunch of research, and finally came up with something that looked like it might
work," says Gold, who formulated a cement-plaster concoction especially for the
walls of the chamber (its ingredients remain a secret). "We built these two
trapezoid-shaped rooms right behind Studio A," says Gold, "with isolation walls and
a cement slab that separated them from everything else in the building. And then
we put up that concrete mixture, about 2 inches thick. The thing is, when you were
building echo chambers, it was always hit or miss – there were certain things you
had to do in there but there were never any guarantees it would sound good once
you were finished." To Gold's amazement, his new chambers sounded good – really
good. "At that point all we had to do was figure out the right kind of mike and
speaker to use – which turned out to be an RCA ribbon mike and a 12-inch speaker
powered by a ten-watt amp. But really, just about anything would've worked in
there."

In 1958 – the year The Champs cut the chart-topping 'Tequila' at Gold Star – a
ramshackle group of teens known as The Teddy Bears pulled into Gold's place for
the purpose of recording some sides for the fledgling Dore Records label. Leading
the pack was 18-year-old Bronx native Harvey Phillip Spector, a recent graduate of
local Fairfax High School. "Phil came to Gold Star because he'd heard I was a
Fairfax alumnus," says Ross. "He may have gone to a few other places as well at
the time, but I don't think too many people really wanted to deal with him – he was
a pretty unusual character."

Intended as a b-side, the Spector-penned 'To Know Him is To Love Him' became an
out-of-the-blue Number One hit. Unable to repeat that success, Spector returned to
New York, ostensibly to become a court stenographer. Within two years he was
back in the business, determined to parlay his lone credit as a hit-maker into a
successful career in record production. It worked, and by 1961 Spector had
compiled an enviable string of hits, most notably Curtis Lee's 'Pretty Little Angel
Eyes' and The Paris Sisters' ethereal 'I Love How You Love Me.' Just 21, Spector
had fame, money, and the respect of the entire industry.

Near the end of 1962 Spector flew to Los Angeles to cut 'He's a Rebel' for The
Crystals. "And it was from that session that he realized he could capture this one
particular sound he'd been hearing in his head at Gold Star," says Levine. "Who
knows why that was – it's just something that happened while he was there."

In order to achieve his sound, Spector loaded up Gold Star's recording-room with
multiple bassists, guitarists, and percussionists, then pumped everything through
the studio's echo chambers, with the echo return on full. Spector called his peculiar
brand of musical cacophony the 'Wall Of Sound.'

Continued on page 51

1963

Live At The Apollo James Brown

King 826 (U.S.A.) / London HA8184 (U.K.)
Released June 1963

This frenzied, sweat-drenched aural-sex workout catapulted James Brown to the forefront of the rapidly evolving 1960s' soul scene, paving the way for the birth of funk.

Ray Charles, whose 1955 smash 'I Got A Woman' is often cited as the first song to be labeled 'soul,' has described the genre as "the fusion of gospel and blues." Certainly, the word 'soul' was common currency among black American musicians from the early 1950s, cropping up in the titles of jazz instrumentals, in gospel band names – such as Sam Cooke's early combo The Soul Stirrers – or as rock'n'roll song titles – Little Richard's 'Ooh! My Soul,' for example.

By the time James Brown, a regular fixture in the 1950s' R&B charts, started scoring Top 40 pop chart success in the early 1960s, the term was being widely applied to more pop-oriented R&B acts, such as Little Anthony & The Imperials, The Clovers, and The Coasters. However, despite his chart hits, Brown felt he was still not reaching the widest possible audience. Inspired by a Top 20 placing in 1960 for Ray Charles's live album, *In Person*, Brown decided that an in-concert release could reveal the power of his super-charged stage shows to an audience that only knew him through his studio recordings.

Unfortunately, Brown was contracted to King Records of Cincinnati, run by Syd Nathan, a formerly shrewd entrepreneur who was losing his touch. With soul album sales generally low, Nathan figured that if an act was performing regularly, there would be no demand for a recorded version, and refused to fund it.

Furious, Brown put $5,700 of his own money up to finance the recording at the end of a week's residency in the legendary Harlem Apollo. The day was bitterly cold, so Brown's crew perked the audience up with free coffee, and, from start to finish the gig was dynamite. Brown's musical director, Bobby Byrd, has recalled: "There was tension, you know, we were nervous about recording and all. But the minute we hit the stage – magic!" Brown and his tightly drilled band pounded out the hits – 'I'll Go Crazy,' 'Please Please Please,' 'Night Train,' and the rest – while the engineers caught their manic live urgency on tape.

Even so, on release, Nathan's continuing reluctance was evidenced by an initial pressing of a mere 5,000 copies. There was like-for-like competition in the market place with Little Stevie Wonder's live album, *12 Year Old Genius*, but within days R&B radio DJs were playing the entire Apollo album end to end, and King Records was obliged to order the first of many re-pressings.

In a staggering 66 weeks on the pop LP chart, it peaked at Number Two, held off the Number One slot by an album that was its polar opposite, Andy Williams's *Days Of Wine And Roses*.

Live At The Apollo not only earned James Brown the title of the 'Hardest-Working Man In Showbusiness' but proved that in-concert albums could be very good for business indeed, attracting a vast new audience to an already established artist.

A Christmas Gift For You From Phil Spector
Phil Spector

Philles PHLP 4005 (U.S.A.) / London HAU8141 (U.K.)
Released November 1963

Before Phil Spector became a producer, the key factors for hit records were melody, words, arrangement, and performance; after Spector, the unique sonic landscape of a record was often equally important.

One of many contenders for the title of 'First Rock Concept Album,' *A Christmas Gift For You* is also considered the first bona fide rock'n'roll Christmas album.

Spector learned his craft as an apprentice to Jerry Leiber and Mike Stoller, one of the greatest songwriting and production teams of the 1950s. His first solo production, 'To Know Him Is To Love Him,' for his own band The

Continued from page 49

Teddy Bears, went to Number One in the U.S.A. in 1958, after which there was no stopping him. By the age of 20 he was head of A&R for Atlantic Records in Los Angeles, and two years later he started his own label, Philles, almost immediately scoring another Number One with The Crystals' 'He's A Rebel.'

A ruthless manipulator, Spector didn't let The Crystals sing on the tracks issued under their name. That job went to Darlene Love, lead vocalist of another band of Spector protégées, The Blossoms. "When Phil told me he was planning a rock'n'roll Christmas album," Love recalls, "I thought he was crazy. Nobody had done anything like that before." Rock'n'rollers had, of course, made Christmas albums, but their raw style was invariably toned down to fit what was perceived as the Spirit of Christmas. Spector's innovation was that this would unmistakably be rock'n'roll music.

By the time recording started in mid 1963, Spector had become known for his Wall Of Sound production technique, which he had developed at the Gold Star Studios in Los Angeles. Indeed, the specific qualities of that studio were essential to the effect he created. First of all, Gold Star boasted superb echo chambers, which, when fully open, produced a vast cavernous wash of reverb and sympathetic harmonic vibrations. Secondly, the walls of the recording-room were painted with a lead-based paint, which caused any noise to ring around in the air. Finally, the facilities were relatively primitive, with no means of equalization or compression.

All of this suited Spector ideally. His technique was the opposite of everything that sophisticated studios strove to achieve. While they recorded every instrument clearly and separately, Spector would cram Gold Star's little 22-by-32-foot room with upward of 30 musicians, none of whom were isolated from each other by sound baffles. He would then let the resulting sounds intermingle freely into a huge sonic soup. Individual instruments might be swamped to the point of inaudibility, but the overall sound is massive.

That Wall Of Sound when paired with appropriately seasonal sound effects and applied to such numbers as 'Frosty The Snowman' and 'White Christmas' – sung by Spector's stable of hitmakers, including Darlene Love, Bob B. Soxx And The Blue Jeans, The Crystals, and The Ronettes – resulted in a timelessly exciting Christmas album.

Shortly after its release, however, President John F. Kennedy was assassinated and the U.S.A. was plunged into mourning. Out of respect Spector re-called the album from the shops, so it didn't even have a chance to chart, despite which its reputation has grown over the years.

The song that would become the prototype for all Wall projects was 'Zip-A-Dee-Doo-Dah,' a hit for Bob B. Soxx & The Blue Jeans (featuring Spector mainstay Darlene Love). "We'd been working on it for around three hours, and he kept boosting the levels, till it finally reached the point where everything was pinning," says Levine. "It was my first session with Phil, I really didn't have the nerve to say anything to him at first. Finally I couldn't take it any more, so I just shut down all the mikes at once! Phil accepted that graciously – he started screaming at me! I told him I had no option but to do that. So slowly I started bringing the mikes back up one at a time, balancing them as I was going along. I got to the last microphone, which was Billy Strange's guitar, and Phil jumps up and says, 'That's it – that's the sound – let's record!' I told him I didn't have the guitar mike up yet, but that was what he wanted. So we went with it. And it was the most incredible recording experience I'd ever had." Incredibly, Levine and Spector mixed the entire spectacle to a single track of an Ampeg 3-track machine.

There's no doubt that Spector knew exactly what he was doing when he created the Wall – but in all likelihood it wouldn't have been quite the same without the elements that existed at Gold Star. Though many tried to replicate the sound, few even came close.

Homemade Mixers

Most of the best professional studios in existence today utilize the same type of equipment made by a handful of famous-name audio manufacturers – the way it's been for many years. This was not the case at the start of the 1960s, when record labels typically had their own research and development staff construct customized mixing consoles from scratch, each one specifically designed to match the particular nuances of the recording-rooms as well as the needs of the engineers who operated them. Such gadgetry helped give a studio its 'signature' sound.

"Every place had a hand-made console," recalls studio session guitarist Al Gorgoni. "That was a big part of it. The sound was homemade! And the resident engineer really knew the board, all of its little functions, and you could really hear that on the finished product as well. Unfortunately, house engineers have become a thing of the past."

"What differs from how things are manufactured today," remarks producer Jim Reeves, a former engineer with CBS Records, "is that, in the designing stage of these consoles, the recording engineers actually sat with the design staff and communicated what those demands in the modern recording process were. As a result, the consoles were specifically designed to make sense for us 'users.'"

In 1960 most studio mixing consoles utilized the same basic design (largely attributed to Universal Audio's Bill Putnam), which included anywhere from six to ten microphone inputs, a handful of channel faders, 'send' and 'return' functions for adding echo, and so forth. Many engineers, however, frequently saw fit to augment the console's functions based on their own particular needs.

When Atlantic Records moved into roomier facilities on New York's West 60th Street in 1959, house engineer Tom Dowd took the opportunity to toss out his old mixing console and began building his own revamped unit that would include a revolutionary new concept: sliding faders. "The equipment most places were using in those days consisted of hand-me-down stuff from broadcast facilities, including consoles that had these big fat 3-inch knobs," says Dowd. "The problem was that you couldn't get two or three under your hands. It wasn't just inaccurate, it was plain stupid. Eventually I found a manufacturer who was making slide wires – faders were linear instead of cylindrical and traveled five inches up and down. Because of the narrow width of these things, I could fit them into a board half as wide. Which enabled me to put a whole group of faders in two hands, which is what I'd wanted to do all along. Finally, I could play the faders like you could play a piano."

Above all, mixing consoles that were built in-house as opposed to on an assembly line were made to last. "All the consoles I used at Columbia were completely dependable," says Roy Halee, ex-Columbia engineer for Simon & Garfunkel and many others. "With the idea being that with 50 or more musicians, you can't afford breakdowns. And they never did – not once."

1963

Please Please Me **The Beatles**

Not issued in U.S.A. / Parlophone 46435 (U.K.)
Released March 1963

**With their second Parlophone
single, 'Please Please Me,'
closing in on the top of what
was then known as 'The Hit
Parade' in the U.K., producer
George Martin hastily scheduled
recording time for The Beatles'
first LP.**

Years of constant gigging had made
The Beatles a solid live act, but it
wasn't until February 11th 1963 that
Martin and the rest of the staff at
London's EMI Recording Studios
realized just how good they really were. By the end of that day, *Please
Please Me* – the album that would launch British Beatlemania – was ready
for release.

Beginning at 10am with the tricky two-part vocal harmony of
'There's a Place,' the group proceeded to knock out 11
more songs in under 12 hours, among them 'Baby It's
You,' 'Misery,' 'Chains,' and 'Anna,' leading up to the
grand finale, John Lennon's historic rendering of Bert
Berns's 'Twist and Shout,' completed in a single take
just after 10pm. It mattered little that Lennon was
nursing a bad cold and spent the day downing
throat lozenges in order to keep up the pace. "I
don't know how they do it," remarked producer
Martin near the end of the marathon session.
"We've been recording all day, but the longer we
go on, the better they get."

Though EMI already had in its possession a 4-track
recorder, Martin and crew – engineers Norman Smith
and Richard Langham – cut the entirety of *Please Please
Me* live to 2-track (a McCartney double-track vocal on 'A
Taste of Honey' and a harmonica add-on to 'There's a Place'
would be patched in later). The band set up in a configuration
that would change little over the following years. Harrison's and
Lennon's Vox AC30 guitar amplifiers were placed gingerly atop
folding chairs, and situated perilously close to Ringo Starr's kit.
Neumann vocal and instrument microphones, fastened atop a set of
rolling stands, stood nearby, with cables strewn across the parquet
floor, and little or no baffling dividing the individual players.

"The first album was basically just an effort to capture the feeling
of their stage act, which they'd really mastered by then," says
Langham. "There were just two mikes on Ringo's drums,
with very little baffling, maybe just a low drum screen,
and that was about it, really. It was very typical of the
method used for artist's tests or commercial tests."

If anything, the wide-open arrangement gives
Please Please Me a sense of urgency that's
still palpable over 40 years on. Lennon and
McCartney's locked harmonies verge on
distortion; Starr's snare drum, aided by
the ample leakage, resonates loudly
throughout EMI's massive Studio 2. In
short, The Beatles sound like a band
on a mission.

"You listen to 'I Saw Her Standing There,' or anything on that first album,"
remarks EMI engineer Richard Lush, "and you hear the drums going all over
the vocal mike, there are things like limiters going on and off, as soon as
the music stop the drums comes up. It's so unlike anything you'd hear
today. But it just adds to the overall excitement of the recording. Face it –
when something like 'Twist and Shout' comes on that's live or has a bit of
vibe to it, your ears always prick up."

The 12 Year Old Genius **Little Stevie Wonder**

Tamla 240 (U.S.A.) / Oriole PS40050 (U.K.)
Released July 1963

**Having failed to make a mark
with first album, *Tribute To Ray
Charles*, Stevie Wonder was
recorded live, and like James
Brown at the Apollo, Wonder's
in-concert charisma put him on
the musical map.**

It wasn't such a gamble, given his
show-stopping performances on the
Motortown Revue tours, at which
Wonder – born Steveland Morris –
performed out front with vocals and

harmonica rather than, as later, ensconced behind keyboards. Suffice to say that 'Little' Stevie – he dropped the diminutive in 1964 – did not seem out of place beside the more mature talents of Marvin Gaye, The Supremes, The Miracles, and Mary Wells.

The album's blues-based opening song, 'Fingertips,' recorded at the Regal in Chicago, was label boss Berry Gordy's choice as a single, and repaid his faith by selling a million. Split over two sides, it topped the U.S. charts six weeks after release. *The 12 Year Old Genius* followed suit a fortnight later, deposing Andy Williams in August 1963 and becoming not only the first live chart topper but the first of Stevie's three U.S. Number One albums – though he'd have to wait 11 years for the next.

> ## "I LISTENED TO EVERYTHING I COULD HEAR. MUSIC WAS MY COMMUNICATION TO THE WORLD. DIFFERENT LANGUAGES, VOICES, SINGERS – I HEARD EVERYTHING."
> ### STEVIE WONDER

Material ranges from more chantalong material, such as 'La La La La La,' through the self-penned 'Drown In My Own Tears' and Ray Charles's 'Hallelujah I Love her So,' to the more sophisticated 'Masquerade Is Over,' one of several tracks first heard earlier that year on *The Jazz Soul Of Little Stevie*. And, while the result was impressive, Wonder found the title 'genius' hard to live with. Happily, he overcame the child-prodigy tag – he is still the youngest singer to top the U.S. albums chart – to sustain a 40-year-plus recording and performing career.

Call Me/That's The Way Love Is **Bobby Bland**

Duke 77 (U.S.A.) / Vocalion 8034 (U.K.)
Released September 1963

Hedging its bets by being named after both sides of what was then his biggest pop hit, this album was a long-awaited pop album-chart breakthrough for Robert Calvin Bland, whose journey to *Billboard*'s listing included a stint as driver and valet to B.B. King.

Bobby 'Blue' Bland hedged his bets, straddling blues, gospel, and soul, but perhaps not moving with the times in the same way as the likes of Marvin Gaye. Hence his core audience, right through to the 1990s, was a black one.

As was usual for black-music albums of the time, this was a collection based on successful singles. 'Call Me,' with its staccato trumpets, is, against type, Latin in flavor, and it reached Number 22 in the pop chart, while 'That's The Way Love Is,' a R&B chart topper in its own right, hit Number 33 as the b-side.

The songs were written by a combination of trumpeter-arranger Joe Scott – the man who helped shape Bland's musical style after he signed for Duke Records in 1955 – his manager Don Robey, and one Deadric Malone, creator of the majority of tracks here. *Black Music* magazine suggested Malone was in fact a *nom de plume* of Robey. Certainly, the duo/triumvirate steered Bland's career until the parting of the ways in the late 1960s brought a dip in fortunes.

Over in Belfast, Northern Ireland, one man who was clearly listening to Bobby Bland was Van Morrison, whose hero-worship is such that he has invited Bland to open for him on a number of occasions.

The Ventures In Space **The Ventures**

Dolton 8027 (U.S.A.) / Liberty LBY1189 (U.K.)
Released December 1963

The Ventures were the most successful instrumental group of the 1960s. When they weren't covering others' hits, they wrote tunes such as 'Fear,' that now seem like the soundtracks of long-lost b-movies.

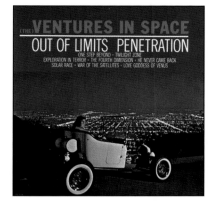

The group formed in Seattle in 1959 by Bob Bogle and Don Wilson. They were joined by Nokie Edwards – who at first played bass then switched to lead guitar when Bogle took up bass himself – and drummer Howie Johnson. Their 1960 debut single, as The Versatones, was on their own Blue Horizon label. They quickly learned how to arrange music to fit their style, and became very prolific. The first hit was 'Walk Don't Run,' and they had four hit albums in 1961. During the 1960s they released 33 albums that charted, more than half of them reaching the Top 40, and selling a million LPs in 1963 alone, the year that *In Space* was first released (1970s reissue pictured).

The main characteristic of The Ventures' music is the guitar instrumental, often powered by a galloping shuffle from the rhythm section. Guitar techniques taken from Duane Eddy and other rock'n'rollers are spiced with primitive string-bending, effects such as echo, reverb, and tremolo, and many tracks feature unconventional chord changes and juxtapositions. Some tracks – 'Moon Child,' for example – are reminiscent of The Tornados' 'Telstar' and British instrumental outfit The Shadows, though in comparison with the latter The Ventures have a more garage sound and a liking for unusual instrumentation. (This tendency had been evident on their 1962 hit, 'The 2,000 Pound Bee,' where the guitar is put through a fuzzbox, an effect virtually unknown at the time.)

The Ventures survived the British Invasion of the mid 1960s by finding a new market in Japan, where they went on to sell over 30 million albums. Their influence can be heard in the playing of guitarists such as Jerry Garcia (Grateful Dead) and Jorma Kaukonen (Jefferson Airplane), and elements of their music can be heard from Quicksilver Messenger Service's *Happy Trails* to more recent albums by the likes of Liverpool band The Coral.

The Beatles At Abbey Road

The former EMI engineer Richard Langham still remembers the first few hints of early Beatlemania invading the all-business environment at EMI's Studio 2 at 3 Abbey Road, London SW8.

"It was a freezing cold day," says Langham. "We were outside getting all The Beatles' gear out of the van to bring into the studio. I noticed these bits of paper falling out of the backs of the amplifiers – they were all these little folded notes that the girls had thrown on to the stage that they'd read and then tossed into their amps! I knew right then that this was going to be a very interesting time."

Up to the late 1950s EMI's Abbey Road premises – a nine-bedroom Victorian residence transformed into a three-room record-making facility in 1931 – had been the exclusive domain of classical and jazz artists, such as pianist Fats Waller and violinist Yehudi Menuhin. Though a few teen pop hits by British heart-throb Cliff Richard helped boost EMI's profit margin as the 1960s approached, few could have predicted the long-term impact on corporate earnings that began with the June 1962 audition by four working-class youths from Liverpool.

Much of the credit for the kinetic feel of the early Beatles albums goes to first engineer Norman Smith, who decided right from the start that the band would fare much better by working as they did on stage, without the constraints of imposing baffling screens. Against the advice of EMI heads, Smith turned Studio 2 into one large, open recording space. His hunch was correct, and any leakage merely added to the overall energy of the recordings.

"The whole thing about The Beatles' records is that they've got excitement," says former EMI engineer Richard Lush. "You put on a record like 'Twist and Shout' – I mean, the vocal performance on that song is just staggering, especially when you bear in mind that John had already been there for 12 hours, singing his guts out live to 2-track. It's absolutely amazing."

Amazing, yes – but in 1963 The Beatles, like many other professional outfits of the time, had spent their formative years playing several shows a day, five, six, seven days a week. By the time they made their debut inside a professional studio, they had the stamina, the energy, and, most of all, the expertise to make a great-sounding recording – often without the aid of overdubs or edits.

"Both John and Paul could step up to that vocal mike and nail those takes again and again," says Lush. "You put on *Anthology* and hear all the various takes and false starts – each time they come back, they're always right there, they just never hit a bum note. That kind of precision comes from working together constantly – to be able to instinctually pull it off without fail."

Within two years of the band's initial audition, four Beatles albums had topped the *Billboard* chart – each one conceived at 3 Abbey Road. The former gneral manager of Abbey Road, Ken Townsend, has observed: "Let's face it, there's a certain kind of spontaneity that occurs when you aren't multitracking everything. The Beatles' first few years proved that."

■ *John Lennon and Paul McCartney at work in Abbey Road Studios with producer George Martin. Between May 1963 and 1965 The Beatles – and, to a lesser extent, The Rolling Stones – held a strangehold over the U.K. albums chart. During that period The Beatles spent a total of 83 weeks at Number One with albums including* Please, Please Me, With The Beatles, *and* A Hard Day's Night.

1964

All Summer Long **The Beach Boys**

Capitol S+/T 2110 (U.S.A. & U.K.)
Released July 1964

Beach Boys Concert **The Beach Boys**

Capitol S+/T 2198 (U.S.A. & U.K.)
Released November 1964

The Beach Boys' albums of the early 1960s demonstrate the group's swift progression from idealistic, surf-obsessed rock'n'roll to music of the depth and magnitude of *Pet Sounds*.

As with all the group's work, the unifying thread here is the combination of the three Wilson brothers' voices with those of their cousin, Mike Love, and neighbor, Al Jardine, to create one of the finest vocal harmony groups of all time. The Beach Boys worked at a prodigious rate throughout the 1960s, producing two or three albums per year while touring solidly. Their debut, *Surfin' Safari* (1962), and *Surfin' U.S.A.* (1963), are fairly one-dimensional, feelgood tributes to sand, sea, and beautiful girls; *Surfer Girl* and *Little Deuce Coupe* (both 1963) show the first signs of Brian Wilson's capacity for delicate, melancholic songs, notably *Surfer Girl*'s 'In My Room.'

All Summer Long was recorded in April and May 1961 at Western Recorders in Hollywood. The album is the first on which Brian Wilson took complete control of The Beach Boys' sound; he fired his overbearing father, Murray, the group's manager, during the opening session.

All Summer Long contains some of the strongest and most memorable songs of The Beach Boys' early career, among them 'Little Honda,' 'Wendy,' and 'I Get Around,' which became the group's first U.S. Number One hit single and reached Number Seven in the U.K. Of the less well-known tracks, 'Girls On The Beach' is one of Wilson's finest pre-*Pet Sounds* ballads, while the wistful title track now reads like a farewell to the sun and surf that dominated the group's first phase. The album itself peaked at Number Four in the U.S.A. It was not issued in the U.K. until the following summer, where it failed to chart.

"PEOPLE BEGAN TO REALIZE THE POTENTIAL IMPACT OF THE GROUP AND GIVE CONSIDERATION TO THE BEACH BOYS AS A MAJOR ATTRACTION."

CONCERT PROMOTER FRED VAILS

Shortly after the release of *All Summer Long*, and with the album still riding high in the U.S. *Billboard* chart, The Beach Boys played two shows at the Civic Auditorium in Sacramento, California, on August 1st, both of which were recorded. Assisted by the engineer Chuck Britz, Brian pieced together the best of both performances the following month for the live set *Beach Boys Concert*. Ever the perfectionist, he also re-recorded some of the group's vocals. The album features renditions of a number of earlier Beach Boys hits, alongside covers of 'Johnny B. Goode' and 'Monster Mash.'

Beach Boys Concert reached Number One in the U.S.A. in December, a feat unmatched by any of the group's albums apart from the 1974 compilation *Endless Summer*. The album also marked the end of Brian Wilson's role as a touring member of the group. In late 1964, after suffering the first of several mental breakdowns, Wilson would retire from live performance and concentrate his efforts exclusively on studio work.

Muddy Waters: Folk Singer Muddy Waters

Chess 1483 (U.S.A.) / Pye International NPL 28040 (U.K.)
Released April 1964

The legendary blues singer and guitarist Muddy Waters began his recording career in the early 1940s, when Alan Lomax tracked him down in Mississippi for the Library Of Congress Archive Of Folk Song.

Waters's international profile began to rise in the mid 1960s, as the Chicago-blues style he had pioneered in the 1940s and 1950s became the primary influence on a wave of British R&B groups. However, on *Folk Singer* Waters capitalized on the growing popularity of folk by reverting to a stripped-down, live acoustic setup, predating the idea of the 'MTV Unplugged' album by two decades.

Muddy Waters: Folk Singer was recorded in September 1963 at Tel Mar Studios in Chicago. Alongside Waters on the album are Buddy Guy on second acoustic guitar, Clifton James on drums, and Willy Dixon, who also produced the sessions, on bass. Most of the songs are Waters's own compositions, performed in a style reminiscent of his very first Chess recordings in the late 1940s. The album also includes a version of Dixon's chain-gang song, 'My Captain,' and a reading of John Lee 'Sonny Boy' Williamson's 'Good Morning Little School Girl.'

A 1999 reissue of the album adds two 1964 sessions featuring a larger ensemble of backing musicians, among them James Cotton on harmonica and J.T. Brown on tenor saxophone and clarinet. These more electrified recordings illustrate the two sides of Waters's music in the mid 1960s.

1965

A Love Supreme
John Coltrane

Impulse! A77 (U.S.A.) / MCA DMCL 1648 (U.K.)
Released February 1965

One of the most important jazz recordings of all time, the influence of *A Love Supreme* extends way beyond the world of jazz to rock and fusion musicians, including Carlos Santana.

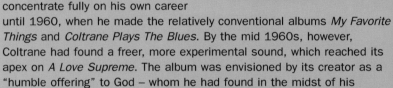

Saxophonist John Coltrane made his name as a sideman with, among others, Miles Davis, on whose epochal *Kind Of Blue* he had played in 1959. Coltrane didn't begin to concentrate fully on his own career until 1960, when he made the relatively conventional albums *My Favorite Things* and *Coltrane Plays The Blues*. By the mid 1960s, however, Coltrane had found a freer, more experimental sound, which reached its apex on *A Love Supreme*. The album was envisioned by its creator as a "humble offering" to God – whom he had found in the midst of his

lengthy battle with heroin addiction – and is divided into four distinct parts: 'Acknowledgement,' 'Resolution,' 'Pursuance, and 'Psalm.' Expanding deliriously on these four central themes, Coltrane's passionate tenor saxophone work is, of course, the focal point, but the music is held together by the exemplary rhythm playing of drummer Elvin Jones, bassist Jimmy Garrison, and pianist McCoy Tyner. As was typical of jazz albums of the time, *A Love Supreme* was recorded live in one session, on December 9th 1964, with producer Bob Thiele at Van Gelder Studio, New Jersey. The LP's sleevenotes contain a lengthy piece written in thanks to The Lord by Coltrane.

His most fully realized artistic statement, *A Love Supreme* is also the bestselling album in Coltrane's catalog, eventually selling over a million copies worldwide. Coltrane's life and music would become more turbulent in the years that followed, and his album releases grew more and more chaotic before his death in 1967 from liver cancer. In the last year of his life Coltrane's band featured his wife, Alice, who would go on to make a number of acclaimed albums of her own, including 1970's richly orchestrated *Universal Consciousness*.

A Love Supreme has been reissued in several slightly different forms since Coltrane's passing. Most notable is the 2002 Deluxe Edition, a two-CD set combining previously unheard recordings with a newly remastered version of the album itself, sourced from tapes discovered in the late 1990s in the vaults of EMI in London.

The Sound Of Music (Original Soundtrack)

RCA Victor 2005 (US) / 90368 (UK)
Released March 1965

When it opened in March 1965, the movie version of *The Sound Of Music* became the highest-grossing movie to date in the U.S.A., and would, a year later, be named Best Picture at the Academy Awards.

The movie was adapted from the 1959 Broadway musical of the same name, the last of many collaborative efforts by Rodgers & Hammerstein. The musical, in its turn, was based on a book by Howard Lindsay and Russel Crouse, which drew heavily on the autobiography of Maria Von Trapp.

Columbia had already issued an original-cast recording from the Broadway production five years earlier, when RCA Victor decided to issue an album of songs from the movie version. Though this recording of the stage show had

been highly successful, and could be found in many record collections across the U.S.A., it didn't stop the new version selling well. *The Sound Of Music* reached Number One in the U.S.A. and the U.K., and remained on the albums charts on both sides of the Atlantic for several years. Between 1965 and 1969 the soundtrack album spent a total of 70 weeks at the top of the U.K. charts, and has sold over 11 million copies since its original release.

The original 1959 stage cast had featured the then 45-year-old singer Mary Martin – at whose request Richard Rodgers and Glendenning Hammerstein had written the show – in the role of the 21-year-old Maria. By the time the movie version went into production Martin was 50 and deemed too old to be considered for the lead. Instead, Maria would be played by Julie Andrews, who had recently won an Oscar for her performance in the title role of another piece of sentimental musical cinema, *Mary Poppins* (1964). Andrews's performances, both on screen and on the soundtrack, are exemplary throughout. However, some of the other actors' voices are dubbed over by stronger singers – though both Christopher Plummer (Captain Von Trapp) and Peggy Wood (Mother Abbess) are credited on the sleeve, neither's voice is actually heard on record.

As well as the change of lead actress, the movie version of *The Sound Of Music* cut some of the less upbeat songs from the stage production, such as 'How Can Love Survive?' and 'No Way To Stop It.' Of the songs that remain, however, many have become popular standards, including the title track as well as 'Do-Re-Mi,'

'Climb Every Mountain,' 'My Favorite Things,' and 'Edelweiss.' The movie version also adds a new song, 'I Have Confidence,' with both words and music having been written by Rodgers after Hammerstein's death in 1960.

The Sound Of Music remains one of the most successful soundtrack albums of all time, surpassed only by the likes of *Saturday Night Fever* (1977) and *The Bodyguard* (1992).

Look At Us **Sonny & Cher**

ToAtco LP 33-177 (U.S.A.) / Atlantic ATL 5036 (U.K.)
Released August 1965

**To all intents and purposes, the
album that put Salvatore 'Sonny'
Bono and his teenage bride
Cherilyn 'Cher' Lapierre on the
map in the summer of 1965 was
little more than a vehicle for the
duo's massively successful first
hit single, 'I Got You Babe' – but
what a single it was.**

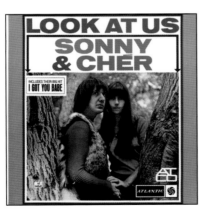

Written by Bono – a proven composer
who had co-written The Searchers'
'Needles and Pins' – the Number One
smash showed just how much Bono
had learned during his long apprenticeship with Phil Spector. Like most of
Spector's works, the Bono-produced *Look at Us* – which peaked at Number
Two on the *Billboard* chart and also sported the Bono-penned follow-up 'Just
You' – was recorded at the famed Gold Star Recording Studios, which in
1965 still only used three tracks, with an array of Spector regulars,
including guitarist Barney Kessel, drummer Hal Blaine, and bassist Lyle Ritz.

A unique sound-balancing method devised by engineer and Gold Star co-
owner Stan Ross ensured that Harold Batiste's majestic arrangement of 'I
Got You Babe' got the attention it deserved. "We had this deal with KHJ, the
local station, to play the acetates of the new songs just after they'd been
cut," says Ross. "I'd sit there in the studio and listen to the broadcast over
the speakers we had in there. When I'd cut the master, my EQ adjustments
would be based on what I'd heard coming back over the airwaves! That way
I knew exactly how it would sound over every other station in the country
from that point forward. It was that simple."

What Now My Love?
Herb Alpert And The Tijuana Brass

A&M 3265 (U.S.A. & U.K.)
Released April 1965

**Herb Alpert was one of popular
music's first renaissance men.
As well as being one of the
biggest-selling instrumental pop
performers of all time, he is the
founder, and 'A,' of A&M – 'M' is
business partner Jerry Moss –
the record label that has over
time been home to many
successful artists.**

Alpert began his musical career as a
songwriter, collaborating with Lou
Adler on the Sam Cooke hit
'Wonderful World.' After setting up A&M in 1962 he had an immediate U.S.
Top Ten hit with his single 'The Lonely Bull.' During the 1960s Alpert had a
run of 11 Top 20 albums in the U.S.A., of which *What Now My Love?* was
the most successful, spending nine weeks at Number One. *What Now My
Love?* captures the trumpet-playing Alpert and his band – which included
pianist Lou Pagani and guitarist John Pisano – at their peak, mixing original
pieces with interpretations of contemporary pop and Broadway hits, all set
in a style dubbed 'Ameriachi' by music critics.

It was through the success of Alpert's own recordings that A&M was able to
develop a roster of impressive, emerging stars. Among the label's signings
in the late 1960s were The Carpenters, Humble Pie, Cat Stevens, and Burt
Bacharach. A&M grew vastly in stature over the next two decades, until
1990, when Alpert and Moss sold the label to Polygram for $500 million.
The duo have since founded a new label, Almo Sounds, which continues to
issue Alpert's work as well as material by other artists, including Garbage.

The Paul Butterfield Blues Band
The Paul Butterfield Blues Band

Elektra EKL/EKS 7294 (U.S.A. & U.K.)
Released October 1965

**One of the most gifted
harmonica players of his
generation, Paul Butterfield led
the U.S.A.'s first great white
blues band.**

Born in Chicago in 1942, Butterfield
started performing in local blues
clubs in the late 1950s. In 1963 he
recruited Howlin' Wolf's rhythm
section – drummer Sam Lay and
bassist Jerome Arnold – and guitarist
Elvin Bishop, and completed the
classic line-up of his unusually
racially integrated Blues Band the following year with the addition of slide
guitarist Mike Bloomfield.

After signing to Elektra, the group entered the studio with producer Paul
Rothschild during the summer of 1965 to cut the 11 songs on their debut
album . The material is mostly made up of ragged reinterpretations of
classic Chicago blues, from Willie Dixon's 'Mellow Down Easy' to Muddy
Waters's 'I Got My Mojo Working.' Butterfield's harmonica dominates, but
the twin-guitar interplay of Bloomfield and Bishop proved equally influential.
Having witnessed a blistering performance by the group at the 1965
Newport Folk Festival, Bob Dylan was so impressed that he recruited
Bloomfield for his own set later the same evening.

The Paul Butterfield Blues Band was not a huge commercial success on its
release in 1965, but it paved the way for numerous other white blues
groups of the mid to late 1960s.

1965

Bringing It All Back Home **Bob Dylan**

Columbia CL 2328 (U.S.A.) / CBS 62515 (U.K.)
Released March 1965

Highway 61 Revisited **Bob Dylan**

Columbia CL 2389 (U.S.A.) / CBS 62572 (U.K.)
Released August 1965

A brand new and enduring musical genre, folk rock, sprang into being partly as a result of Bob Dylan's fifth album, *Bringing It All Back Home*. As with most such revolutionary moments there was no master plan. It happened because it had to.

With his early acoustic albums Dylan had revolutionized the early-1960s folk scene simply by writing his own songs. Chart-topping albums and singles by The Kingston Trio, The Highwaymen, and The Rooftop Singers testify to the massive popularity of folk music at the time, but all of these acts covered traditional songs. The scene generated very little in the way of original material until Dylan came along, at which point the floodgates opened and every sensitive teenager who could pick three chords on a battered acoustic guitar suddenly became a folksy singer-songwriter. Dylan was also seen as the inventor of protest music, so the eyes of the music community were firmly fixed on him, watching his every move.

However, when he went into Columbia's New York studios on January 13th 1965 to begin recording sessions for *Bringing It All Back Home*, he was not planning to invent a new electric-folk style. One entire side of the album, in fact, remained firmly in his acoustic, solo-troubadour mode.

There were, however, certain songs that he felt were not going to work without additional instrumentation. "I had this thing called 'Subterranean Homesick Blues,'" he explained later. "It just didn't sound right by myself." Maybe that's because its rapid-fire, semi-rapped lyric bears more than a passing resemblance to Chuck Berry's 'Too Much Monkey Business,' a rock'n'roll classic that Dylan would have known well.

The popular notion that Dylan was a Greenwich Village folkie who made a shocking volte-face into rock'n'roll is one that has long muddied the waters around his next move. Dylan grew up in the 1950s listening to rock'n'roll, particularly enjoying Buddy Holly, The Everly Brothers, and Elvis Presley, of whom he has said: "When I first heard Elvis' voice I just knew that I wasn't going to work for anybody; and nobody was going to be my boss . . ." On June 5th 1959 when he left Hibbing High School, Minnesota, the school yearbook noted that he intended "to follow Little Richard," and one of his first paid jobs was a brief stint as pianist in teen idol Bobby Vee's band. So his decision to bring in rock players for 'Subterranean Homesick Blues' was more a return to his roots than a radical restructuring of folk idioms.

Continued on next page

As a guitarist, Dylan chose Bruce Langhorne, whom he'd worked with in 1962, during rarely mentioned unreleased electric sessions for the album *The Freewheelin' Bob Dylan*. Dylan's producer, Tom Wilson, chose the rest of the band, including John Sebastian, later to form The Lovin' Spoonful, and John Hammond Jr, who has subsequently become a highly regarded bluesman.

> ## "I'VE WRITTEN SOME SONGS THAT I LOOK AT, AND THEY JUST GIVE ME A SENSE OF AWE. STUFF LIKE 'IT'S ALRIGHT MA,' JUST THE ALLITERATION IN THAT BLOWS ME AWAY."
>
> *BOB DYLAN*

Photographer Daniel Kramer, who attended the sessions, vividly recalls the excitement and elation when 'Maggie's Farm' was first played back: "There was no question about it – it swung, it was happy, it was good music, and, most of all, it was Dylan." The rock instrumentation also worked a treat for another up-tempo Chuck Berry-style workout, 'Outlaw Blues,' and for the hilariously surreal 'On The Road Again.' The guitars are also plugged in, but appropriately more mellow, for two of Dylan's most memorable love songs, 'She Belongs To Me' and 'Love Minus Zero/No Limit.'

The album gave him his first Top Ten entry, and 'Subterranean Homesick Blues' sneaked into the Top 40 singles chart, but, even more significantly, one of the album's acoustic tracks, 'Mr Tambourine Man,' went to Number One in June in an electrified version by The Byrds. Folk rock had arrived, and the overwhelming mass of white American teens embraced it immediately, soaking up similarly styled hits from Simon & Garfunkel, The Turtles, and Barry McGuire.

Unfortunately, to the folk fraternity who had previously adored him, amplified folk was a crime against nature. When Dylan debuted his new electric band at the *Newport Folk Festival* on July 25th he was booed off the stage, and similar demonstrations of dismay and anger greeted him wherever he toured for the rest of the year.

He was, nevertheless, not about to turn back. *Highway 61 Revisited* followed just six months after *Bringing It All Back Home*, and this time the electricity crackled and fizzed from every groove.

Guitarist Mike Bloomfield once claimed that the sessions were chaotic because "no one had any idea what the music was supposed to sound like." Neither Dylan nor producer Tom Wilson, according to Bloomfield, directed the musicians: "It was a matter of pure chance." More likely it was a matter of choosing the right musicians to start with, then giving them their creative head.

The opening swagger and swirl of Al Kooper's organ and Paul Griffin's piano on 'Like A Rolling Stone' left no doubt that in a few short months Dylan had made a quantum leap and was now the king of a hill built by his own hand. Snarling and sneering his way through the vitriolic lyric, Dylan had never before sounded so sure of himself. He was certainly confident enough to release it as a six minute single against the advice of Columbia Records, who insisted that radio wouldn't play anything over three minutes in length. It went Top Five on both sides of the Atlantic.

Bloomfield's stinging lead guitar kicks 'Tombstone Blues' into a higher rock'n'roll gear than Dylan had

ever previously managed, but the album's real strength is not its style but its content. Such songs as 'It Takes A Lot To Laugh, It Takes A Train To Cry,' and 'Ballad Of A Thin Man' are beautifully understated, with every instrument perfectly complementing Dylan's straggling melodies. The lyrics, too, had leaped ahead, with virtually every line of 'Desolation Row' elegantly conjuring word pictures that combine into a dark and surreal movie playing in the back of the listener's head.

Arguably, *Highway 61 Revisited* also marks the dividing line between rock'n'roll and rock. Here was a music too cerebral to be pop, too bluesy and ballsy to be folk rock, and, most significantly, it was also too sophisticated to be rock'n'roll.

Even 40 years after its release this is a hard album to fault. The worst that can be said is that it stands responsible for countless crimes against songwriting committed by legions of inferior artists who misguidedly imagined themselves to be the next Bob Dylan.

1966

Blonde On Blonde Bob Dylan

Columbia 841 (US) / CBS S+/66012 (UK)
Released May 1966

The first double album in rock, *Blonde On Blonde* stands as the culmination of a period of intense activity for Dylan, having been released within a year of his equally highly regarded *Bringing It All Back Home* and *Highway 61 Revisited*.

After a hectic period that had seen the inauguration of his new electric sound, Dylan decamped to Columbia Music Row Studios in Nashville, Tennessee, to begin work on his seventh studio album. This was one of the first instances of a rock musician recording in the home of country music with Nashville musicians, though Dylan

did bring with him organist Al Kooper and guitarist Robbie Robertson of The Band. The other musicians at the *Blonde On Blonde* sessions were guitarist and bandleader Charlie McCoy, drummer Kenny Buttrey, bassist Henry Strzelecki, Wayne Moss on guitar, and Hargus 'Pig' Robbins on piano, all veterans of the Nashville scene. The sessions were produced by Bob Johnston and were completed in eight days in February and March 1966.

Dylan himself turned up four hours late for the first day of recording – St Valentine's Day 1966 – with the lyrics to the song with which he wished to begin still not finished. The Nashville players had to wait several more hours as he continued to write. They were eventually called down to the studio in the middle of the night, at which point Dylan presented them with a brief fragment of 'Sad-Eyed Lady Of The Lowlands.' Without the luxury of a rehearsal, the band went straight into the recording of what would end up as an 11-minute epic. More used to playing on two-minute country tracks, the band looked at one another in disbelief

as Dylan unfolded verse after verse. In a recent interview with Dylan-historian Howard Sounes, drummer Buttrey remarked: "It went on and on . . . We'd never heard anything like this before."

Many at the time assumed that this epic song, which closed the album, was about Joan Baez, but the sad-eyed lady in question was, in fact, Dylan's new wife Sara. Notoriously guarded about his private life, Dylan went to great lengths to keep the marriage a secret, even going so far as to hide Sara in a walk-in closet when a pair of DJs came to interview him backstage at a gig in Vancouver, BC. Sara would later inspire a less cheerful song cycle on *Blood On The Tracks* (1975), often referred to as Dylan's 'divorce album.'

Dylan worked through the rest of the *Blonde On Blonde* material in much the same way over the next few days. Each song was recorded live, mostly in one or two takes. Dylan rarely played the band more than a verse or two before the red light came on. Despite this, the Nashville musicians' playing on *Blonde On Blonde* is exemplary, lending the album a more fluid, expansive quality than the harsh folk rock of the previous year's *Highway 61*. In return, Dylan credited the players by name on the record's sleeve, which at the time was highly unusual. Their appearance on the album also raised the profile of country music considerably within the rock audience and helped pave the way for future country-rock crossovers.

As with 'Sad-Eyed Lady,' Dylan would often finish writing the songs on the day of recording. He arrived at the studio one morning with the freshly written, cinematic lyrics to 'Stuck Inside Of Mobile With The Memphis Blues Again' on headed hotel notepaper. Among the other key tracks on the album are 'Just Like A Woman' and 'Leopard-Skin Pill-Box Hat,' both believed to be about the model Edie Sedgwick, and the delicate 'I Want You.'

Perhaps the most infamous song on *Blonde On Blonde* is 'Rainy Day Women # 12 & 35.' Deciding that he couldn't do it justice with "a bunch of straight people," Dylan insisted that, in the words of the song, "everybody must get stoned" before the recording began. Somewhat reticent to begin with, the inebriated musicians swapped instruments and, with the addition of trombonist Wayne 'Doc' Butler, cut the song in the sloppy marching-band style that Bob wanted. The end result is the most off-kilter piece in the Dylan canon.

Blonde On Blonde was mixed in Los Angeles in mid March 1966 by Dylan and Bob Johnston. By this stage it had become clear that there was much more material than would fit on a traditional LP, thus giving birth to the first double-album set in rock music. Numerous other artists have since followed Dylan's lead, often with mixed results; most lack the consistency and focus of *Blonde On Blonde*. Among the other late-1960s' double-vinyl releases that succeeded Dylan's magnum opus are Frank Zappa's *Freak Out* (1966), Donovan's *A Gift From A Flower To A Garden*, Captain Beefheart's *Trout Mask Replica* (both 1967), and *Electric Ladyland* by Jimi Hendrix (1968). Two more achievements: Blonde On Blonde's 'Sad-Eyed Lady Of The Lowlands' was the first song to fill an entire side of vinyl and was then the longest popular song on record.

Blonde On Blonde was released in May 1966 while Dylan was in the midst of his controversial first electric tour of the U.K., and the album reached the Top Ten in both the U.S.A. and Britain. Two months later Dylan was injured in a mysterious motorcycle accident, after which he became somewhat reclusive, bringing to an end the most frenetic period of his career. His next release, the country-tinged *John Wesley Harding*, would not emerge for another 18 months.

Blonde On Blonde appeared in a strange disparity of mixes on its

release around the world. As was the case at the time, the mono mix took precedence, but, strangely, the stereo version of the album featured shortened versions of several of the songs. One song, '4th Time Around,' added a harmonium part missing on the mono version. The original U.K. release of the album was mistakenly cut from an early master and included odd fragments of music at the end of several of the songs. In 1968 the mono versions of the album were dropped, eventually to be replaced in 1970 by yet another new stereo mix, which altered the lengths of eight of the 14 tracks.

About The Sleeve

Not only was *Blonde On Blonde* the first rock double album, it was also the first to be issued in a gatefold sleeve. The artwork was designed by Josephine DiDonato, who has also produced album sleeves for Wynton Marsalis, Tony Bennett, and Harry Connick Jr.

The front and back covers of the LP are made up of an iconic portrait of Dylan in a double-breasted brown suede jacket and black-and-white checked scarf, photographed by Jerry Schatzberg. The sleeve opens to reveal a collage of smaller, monochrome images, again taken by Schatzberg. The layout of these images has changed since *Blonde On Blonde* was first released in 1966. There were originally nine images spread across the two sides of the inner sleeve; most were of Dylan himself but there were also shots of the actress Claudia Cardinale, an unidentified woman – seen whispering in Dylan's ear – and a self-portrait by the photographer. After objections from Cardinale over the inclusion of her photograph, a replacement sleeve was issued in the U.S.A., removing the images of both Cardinale and the unknown woman. The U.K. edition retains the original artwork.

After *Blonde On Blonde*, the gatefold-sleeve album became more commonplace for both single and double albums, most notably The Beatles' *Sgt Pepper's Lonely Hearts Club Band*.

Tale Of The Tape

The success of stereo records destroyed the nascent home-tape market, except for those who needed a recording capability. But tape didn't die.

The vinyl LP record achieved remarkable levels of fidelity – plenty of people still prefer its sound to that of CD – but it was not a portable medium for music. The single was better, but it was still no fun to lug a portable record-player and a box of records with you to the beach or a picnic. And then there was the problem of in-car entertainment. In 1955 Dr Peter Goldmark, head of CBS's research laboratories and overseer of the LP project, had created the Highway Hi-Fi system, but it used special 16rpm records. Then, in 1960, several U.S. car manufacturers adopted the RCA Auto Victrola, an in-car autochanger stacked with 14 singles. It lasted only a couple of years.

The time was right for another look at tape. There had been some developments over the years. In 1959, the 4-track format doubled playing time, but that didn't solve the fundamental problem with tape, which was consumer resistance to its awkwardness. RCA, perhaps fulfilling the promise it had made at the time of the LP rpm debacle, came up with an idea to tackle that. Called simply the Sound Tape Cartridge, it was uncannily like a larger version of the later Philips Compact Cassette. It placed two spools of ¼-inch tape in a seven-inch by five-inch plastic box normally running at 3¾ inches per second to provide 30 minutes of playing time. Like Compact Cassette, the tape format was 4-track, allowing stereo on each side. RCA duly produced a portable machine and a library of pre-recorded titles for it.

Unfortunately, the system was chronically unreliable and disappeared within a couple of years. A system by 3M, in which tape was reeled out of a cartridge into the player and then wound back at the end, proved another dead end. But then the background music industry had the brilliant idea of creating a cartridge in which the tape was pulled out of a central spool and then fed back in a continuous loop. The Fidelipac system of 1962 was a 2-track development of that concept, initially used for broadcast, and then adapted for in-car use. A 4-track version followed, doubling the playback time. It was marketed by a former used-car salesman, Earl 'Madman' Muntz. This was a Californian success in the early 1960s, particularly among the Hollywood crowd – Frank Sinatra, James Garner, and Peter Lawford were among those who had Muntz Fidelipac players. In 1964 pre-recorded tapes began to appear, as well as the first home players.

But then Bill Lear, creator of the Learjet business aircraft, announced his own Stereo-8 system. He had previously installed Muntz's machines on his airplanes, now he changed the design of the cartridge (apparently to circumvent any patents on the Muntz system). He also fitted a new playback head to the player, with eight tracks of sound across the ¼-inch tape providing four selections of stereo music. When each selection finished, the loop tape was in position to play it again, but the playback head now moved across to the next pair of tracks and played those. In that way it would instead automatically switch to the next pair of playback heads and so play different music.

What made the Stereo-8 system succeed was not so much down to its inherent qualities as Lear's business abilities. The system wasn't perfect, and Lear's great mistake was to place the pinch wheel, the essential moving part in any tape system, inside the cartridge rather than leaving it in the player; this meant it had to be cheap, which made it unreliable. Despite this, he persuaded RCA to provide music and Ford to fit the machines as options on its 1966 models. It was an immediate and lasting success, spawning home models and rising to take a quarter of the U.S. home-music market by the mid 1970s. Elsewhere, however, it was much less successful. Player manufacturers began to lose interest after 1975, and large-scale production of tapes ended in 1983.

The system also had some bizarre musical side-effects. Ideally the format required four musical selections of identical lengths: the maximum was 20 minutes. In order to achieve this equality, albums were given different running orders. In some cases, songs were faded out and in again to cross the join. (Notoriously, the 8-track version of *Sgt Pepper* not only had the tracks in the wrong order it had a crudely edited special version of 'Sgt Pepper's Lonely Hearts Club Band (Reprise)' with the last ten seconds repeated to make that selection the right length.)

1966

Sounds Of Silence **Simon & Garfunkel**

Columbia CS9269 (U.S.A.) / CBS 62690 (U.K.)
Released January 1966

Unknown to the record-buying public, Simon & Garfunkel's first hit album came into being solely because of studio trickery and the vision of a producer.

In June 1965, when Bob Dylan ran late for a *Highway 61 Revisited* recording date, producer Tom Wilson found himself with a studio full of musicians twiddling their thumbs. "We had no idea what we were going to work on," remembers guitarist Vinnie Bell. "There were no artists . . . and we had no music. They just played a demo of these two guys singing." The two guys were Paul Simon and Art Garfunkel, a folksy acoustic New York duo, who had broken up when their debut album stiffed. The track, 'The Sound Of Silence,' wasn't actually a demo, it came from that failed album, *Wednesday Morning, 3am*. Wilson got the studio crew to add electric instruments to the track, and the result was so successful that it was released as a single that, with folk rock emerging as a new genre, promptly shot to Number One.

Simon & Garfunkel quickly reunited and were given a month in which to cobble together a cash-in album. As Garfunkel recalls: "We were under the influence of big business. We had this Number One single, and it was a case of business trying to make the music conform to the situation."

Astonishingly, the pressure-cooked duo came up with a genuinely memorable album that includes not just the classic title track, but another Simon-composed cornerstone of the genre, 'I Am A Rock.'

The Monkees **The Monkees**

Colgems COS-101 (U.S.A.) / RCA SF-7844 (U.K.)
Released October 1966

The Monkees were the first manufactured pop group, but it's worth remembering that the system used to record music under The Monkees moniker had long been standard practice in the music industry.

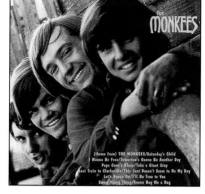

Such teen idols as Frankie Avalon, Bobby Vee, and Bobby Vinton, were routinely fitted up with songs by Brill Building tunesmiths and then presented with a backing track recorded by session men to which they would add their vocals. There was never any pretence that such Motown groups as The Four Tops or The Supremes played on or wrote the songs they sang, but The Monkees' svengali, Don Kirshner, realized that in order to launch The Monkees as a viable American alternative to The Beatles, they had to appear to be a credible rock band. And that's where the lies had to start.

Inspired by the success of The Beatles' movie, *A Hard Day's Night*, Kirshner, of the successful Aldon Music publishing company in New York, conceived a scheme to manufacture an equally lovable pop band, and felt that a weekly television show in the wacky Beatles'-movie style was the ideal means of delivery.

Having recruited four handsome boys via trade-magazine adverts, Kirshner hired professional writers, including Neil Diamond, and teams such as Tommy Boyce and Bobby Hart, Carole King and Gerry Goffin, to knock out enough songs for a debut album. The crack Los Angeles session-player mafia, known as The Wrecking Crew, was employed to create backing tracks to which The Monkees added vocals, and then mimed to on television.

The formula worked, the album sold four million copies, and The Monkees were trapped into living Kirshner's lie for some while to come. Tempting as it is to dismiss The Monkees as pop trash, such songs as 'Last Train To Clarkesville' and 'Take A Giant Step' are hard to resist, and the two songs on the album with composer credits for Monkee Mike Nesmith – 'Papa Gene's Blues' and 'Sweet Young Thing' – revealed that here was a *bona fide* talent in waiting.

Eventually, of course, The Monkees turned on Kirshner, demanded the right to compose their own songs and play on their records, and promptly saw their career flush itself down the drain. Kirshner, having learned his lesson, next transformed the popular *Archie* comic-book characters into a television cartoon band called The Archies and had another huge international smash with 'Sugar Sugar' – and, being cartoons, they never insisted on writing their own songs.

Collecting 8-track tapes and equipment has become a contemporary obsession in the U.S.A., and enthusiasts have come up with various reasons for the format's death: the most likely culprit, though, was a European invader, the Philips Compact Cassette.

When it was introduced in 1963 the Compact Cassette was intended to be a simple, sturdy, reliable, and low-fidelity home-and-office recording medium. No one seems to have foreseen its success as a carrier for music. It used narrow ⅛-inch ferric tape moving at a slow 1⅞ inches per second. But it did permit 30 minutes of recording (later 45 then 60 minutes) on each side of the tape, it was portable, and its efficient design meant it had sufficiently low power requirements to permit battery use. As so often, convenience was about to win out over sound quality.

In 1965 Philips freely licensed its new technology to rival manufacturers of tapes and machines, who agreed to abide by its technical specifications. By 1966 pre-recorded cassettes had begun to appear on the market, but the real breakthrough for cassette's acceptance as a serious music medium was the arrival of Dolby B, a noise reduction system, available on new machines from 1970 onward. The Dolby system and Dolby-processed tapes soon became near-universal. Together with improved tape formulations and more sophisticated player mechanics, they ensured a long life for cassette. The arrival, in 1979, of the portable playback-only cassette machine, better known as the Sony Walkman, took its fortunes to new heights. (It also accustomed the population at large for the first time to the appealing new sensation of listening on headphones, a pleasure previously little known outside hi-fi circles.)

Cassette reached its peak in the late 1980s, when it dominated the market for recorded music, though in due course it was to be crushed by CD almost everywhere. Philips itself stopped making pre-recorded cassettes in 2000. Since then recordable CD has effectively finished it off in the West, though it remains important in some parts of the world, notably the Indian sub-continent.

Not everyone was satisfied with trying to extract high-quality sound from a medium so inherently limited as the cassette, however. In 1976, Sony introduced Elcaset, a new system using standard ¼-inch tape, running at 3¾ inches per second in a larger and more precisely engineered cassette. Several Japanese manufacturers took up the standard, but no pre-recorded tapes were available and the system rapidly foundered. The machines were capable of excellent results but standard cassette was much improved by the time of their introduction. In any case, by 1977 Sony was already working on a digital-disk system, and audio enthusiasts were inclined to wait for that. In 1980 the remains of the Elcaset production run were unceremoniously auctioned off to a company in Finland, where the system lived on for a few years.

1966

Revolver **The Beatles**

Capitol 2576 (U.S.A.) / Parlophone PMC/PCS 7009 (U.K.)
Released August 1966

With *Revolver* The Beatles moved toward using the studio as an instrument in itself, rather than merely a room in which recording takes place.

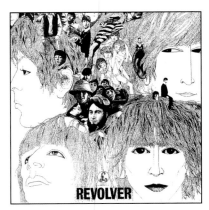

Because of this, as well as a new sophistication in the band's songwriting, these 14 tracks advanced the boundaries of what was considered possible in popular music. Only three years earlier The Beatles were playing Merseybeat; now they were mixing up Indian and blues influences. *Revolver*, and in particular the track 'Tomorrow Never Knows,' helped create and popularize the taste for psychedelic music that would soon become a defining trait of the hippie movement.

With George Martin once more at the producer's helm, the recording sessions started early in April and lasted until June. *Revolver* featured an intriguing mix of up-tempo numbers, melodious ballads, and songs that defied categorization. *Revolver* gave Harrison his best opportunity thus far to shine in his own right – his seminal slashed chords on 'Taxman' sounded harsher and more angular in 1966 than they do now. Instead of stealing from Chuck Berry, the lead-guitar break has an Indian influence in its phrasing. The lyric theme of 'Taxman' had a wide appeal. The British Labour Party was re-elected in March 1966, and the government introduced a new, high, top rate of tax. 'Doctor Robert' has a similar blues-rock feel. Many of *Revolver*'s songs have unexpected twists in them: 'I Want To Tell You' is a Harrison song that fades in with its dissonant piano playing a deliberate wrong note for several bars.

'Good Day Sunshine' offered two rollicking pianos and two drum kits, and a second verse that unpredictably terminates early in a piano solo. 'And Your Bird Can Sing,' where Lennon takes the lead vocal, is the best rocker on the album, with carefully plotted harmonized guitar breaks and a steadier beat. (For the comical chaos of some Beatles sessions, seek out the version on *Anthology 2*.) Less predictable because of its

asymmetrical phrasing is 'She Said She Said,' with its static background and a lyric that mixes metaphysics ('I know what it's like to be dead') with recollections of childhood, which was a central theme of British psychedelia. 'Got To Get You Into My Life' is a fine soul tune, complete with brass section and an adventurous melody, and this was probably influenced by the many mid-1960s' chart hits written for the Motown label by Holland-Dozier-Holland.

Of the ballads, 'Eleanor Rigby' is the standout, creating in just over two minutes an unforgettable glimpse of old age and loneliness, a world normally avoided in the lyrics of popular song. McCartney sings over an octet of four violins, two violas, and two cellos. 'Here, There and Everywhere' is a more traditional love song. Apparently inspired by an early listen to The Beach Boys' *Pet Sounds*, it doesn't quite emulate the less-predictable movement of Brian Wilson's chord patterns, and consequently its tenderness comes over as sentimental in a way that *Pet Sounds* avoids. The piano figure on the somewhat bitter 'For No One' sounds as if influenced by The Beach Boys, whose work at the time often featured eighth-note piano chords.

Revolver also has one of the most popular children's pop songs of all time, 'Yellow Submarine,' sung by Ringo Starr to a battery of sound effects, such as breaking surf, clinking glasses, a brass band, engine-room clatters, and mock-nautical orders. Dylan's 'Rainy Day Women # 12 and 35' has been cited as an influence, but so is the 1950s' BBC radio comedy series

The Goon Show. 'Yellow Submarine' has an appropriately jaunty verse tune and an effective lower vocal harmony line to buttress the chorus. Lennon's adult counterpart is 'I'm Only Sleeping,' a narcoleptic acoustic strum with one of his typical narrow-range melodies, some fluid shifts in song structure, tape-speeded vocals, and serpentine flickers of two 'backward' guitars.

For millions of young people *Revolver* also opened a door on Indian music and the 'mystic' East. It was musically courageous for a band in The Beatles' position to put 'Love You To' on a rock album in 1966, dominated as it is by Indian instruments and open imitation of Indian music. But exotic as it was, Harrison's homage to the culture he was coming to revere couldn't compete with the impact of the album's closing track, 'Tomorrow Never Knows,' one of the most revolutionary statements ever made in popular music. The first song to be worked on, 'Tomorrow Never Knows' was

inspired by Lennon's considerable LSD intake and his reading of *The Psychedelic Experience* by Tomothy Leary, Ralph Metzner, and Richard Alpert, which itself alluded to the *Tibetan Book Of The Dead*. The lyric of the song summarized what was to become the core tenet of the counterculture, that belief in the power of reason, which had dominated Western science and philosophy for two centuries, was inadequate to explain or penetrate the mystery of existence.

As rockets put U.S. and Soviet astronauts into outer space, 'Tomorrow Never Knows' pointed to a new frontier: inner space. The mind had to be turned off, transcended, in order for reality and the self to be fathomed. This would be a revolution in human consciousness, from which would evolve a utopia of enlightened beings.

Work on the song – originally entitled 'The Void' – started on April 6th with the basic rhythm tracks.

Musically, 'Tomorrow' ambitiously attempts to approximate this new vision of reality. Starting with sitar, it opens out a soundscape that breaks with Western musical tradition in abandoning musical progression. The drum pattern and virtually a single chord sustain the track, along with five tape loops – a 'seagull' effect (McCartney laughing); an orchestral chord of B-flat major; a Mellotron flute; another Mellotron oscillating a string tone from B-flat to C; and an ascending sitar phrase – all subjected to tape-speeding and other effects. Lennon's lead vocal was put through a Leslie cabinet. The Beatles had managed to get a piece of essentially avant-garde music across to millions, but, being who they were, couldn't resist the facetious bit of piano at the end. Here was the start of the psychedelic 1960s, which in many ways is what people have come to think of as the 1960s.

'She Said She Said' was the last song to be recorded, on June 21st 1966. The sessions also produced

'Paperback Writer,' their 12th British single, recorded on April 13th and 14th along with its b-side, 'Rain.'

Two days after finishing *Revolver* The Beatles were back on the road playing in Germany on the 24th. The U.S. version omits 'And Your Bird Can Sing,' 'I'm Only Sleeping,' and 'Doctor Robert,' all of which had been included on *Yesterday And Today*, a U.S.-only Beatles LP released two months before *Revolver*.

It was common practice in the 1960s for the tracklistings of albums to differ on either side of the Atlantic. The Beatles are the best example of this; the original U.K. versions of each of the group's albums up to and including *Revolver* were altered for their U.S. issue, often to take in non-album singles (which tended not to feature on the U.K. editions). Much of The Rolling Stones' output of the time was given the same treatment, notably *Out Of Our Heads* (1965) and *Aftermath* (1966).

1966

Otis Blue **Otis Redding**

Atlantic SD33284 (U.S.A.) / 587036 (U.K.)
Released February 1966

In the mid 1960s Otis Redding's popularity rivaled that of James Brown. Nicknamed 'Mr Pitiful' for his plaintive phrasing, and drawing on blues, pop, and gospel, Redding's soul appeal crossed racial boundaries, as was evident during his seminal set at the 1967 Monterey Pop festival.

The bulk of *Otis Blue* was recorded on July 27th 1965 at the Stax studios in Memphis, backed by Booker T. And The MGs and The Memphis Horns. Ten of the 11 tracks were laid down between 10am on the 27th and 8am the following morning, with an eight-hour intermission for the musicians to play a club gig! One other song had been recorded the previous April. Wayne Jackson of The Memphis Horns: "Otis would come into a session, get his guitar out and start singing his song – he'd walk round the studio and sing it to Duck [Dunn, bass] until Duck was in the groove, sing it to the drummer, come round to me and Andrew [Love, the saxophonist] and sing us the horn parts. Once everybody was in the groove then Otis would go to the microphone . . . and we'd start recording. He was the most charismatic of all the people we worked with, the most exciting to be around."

Otis Blue is a warm, confident record, with three Sam Cooke tunes, including 'Wonderful World,' and The Temptations' 'My Girl,' showing the grittier R&B feel of Stax. Two Redding originals – 'Respect' and 'I've Been Loving You Too Long' – were subsequently covered by Aretha Franklin and Tina Turner.

In December 1967, three days after cutting what was to be his biggest hit, 'Dock Of The Bay,' Redding died in a plane crash, aged just 26.

Blues Breakers With Eric Clapton **John Mayall**

London LL3492 (mono) LL492 (stereo) (U.S.A.) / Deram LK 4804 (U.K.)
Released July 1966

Nicknamed 'The *Beano* Album,' after the comic that Eric Clapton is reading on the sleeve, this record advanced rock guitar from the twangy sound that had dominated the early 1960s, establishing Eric Clapton as the new guitar supremo and accelerating the British blues boom.

Clapton joined Mayall after having left The Yardbirds in March 1965. He'd wanted to continue playing straight blues, and was not happy with The Yardbirds' new more chart-friendly direction. Mayall said: "I'd known about Eric, of course, before he joined . . . but when I heard the b-side to 'For Your Love' ['Got To Hurry'], I knew he was the guitarist for the band. And he didn't take much persuading."

Clapton joined a line-up that included Mayall on vocals, keyboards, and harmonica, John McVie on bass – later the 'Mac' of Fleetwood Mac – and Hughie Flint on drums. Flint commented: "It was frustrating in the Blues Breakers before Eric came in because we couldn't really get the Chicago sound that John wanted. As soon as Eric came in, the band completely transformed . . . We were able to play all the blues standards by people like Buddy Guy and Freddie King – just the music that John loved . . . When Eric came in, all of us were a bit overawed by the way he played guitar. I'd never heard a blues guitarist like this outside of the Americans." The press thought the same. *Melody Maker* (U.K.) said: "No British musicians have sounded like this on record."

The album included Clapton's first vocal (Robert Johnson's 'Ramblin' on My Mind'), and covers of famous blues numbers, such as Freddie King's

'Hideaway' and Otis Rush's 'All Your Love.' On Ray Charles's 'What I'd Say' the band throw in The Beatles' 'Day Tripper' riff for good measure.

Clapton plugged a Gibson Les Paul – then, incredibly, out of production – into a Marshall JTM 45 amplifier, and horrified the engineers by recording at high volume. Clapton went after a Les Paul after seeing one on the cover of the album *Freddie King Sings The Blues*. He first used this set-up for the Mayall single 'I'm Your Witchdoctor' b/w 'Telephone Blues,' produced by Jimmy Page, who acknowledged that Clapton was the first to combine the Les Paul with Marshall amplification, a guitar tone that would come to define heavy rock. By the end of the 1960s the Les Paul would be widely regarded as the premier rock guitar.

Clapton said: "I suppose my aim was to get some kind of thickness that would be a combination of the way all of the musicians I heard played, plus the sustain of a slide guitar . . . When they tried to set up the recording, I wouldn't let them put the microphone anywhere near my amplifier." The lead breaks are typified by stinging distortion on the edge of feedback and vibrato, effortless sustain, wild and subtle string-bending, and a precocious command of the Chicago electric blues idiom. Some of the playing contains the blueprint for Cream's approach to the blues. The effect of the record is summed up by Queen's Brian May: "He was what turned me away from The Shadows style and sent me back to listening to B.B. King, Bo Diddley, and all those people. I didn't realize the depth or emotion there was in the music until I saw Eric Clapton. That somehow made it accessible for me." May was only one of thousands who started investigating the blues originals.

1966

Aftermath
The Rolling Stones

London PS476 (U.S.A.) / Decca SKL 4786 (U.K.)
Released April 1966

The Rolling Stones' fourth album, *Aftermath,* **was the first on which singer Mick Jagger and guitarist Keith Richards wrote every song.**

Well into the mid 1950s, the roles of songwriter and performer had been almost entirely separate in popular music. Songs were composed by so-called 'Tin Pan Alley' tunesmiths – such as Irving Berlin, Harold Arlen, and Cole Porter – and sung by specialist singers like Frank Sinatra, Ella Fitzgerald, and Bing Crosby. The distinction between the two jobs was, however, much less pronounced in folk and blues circles, where a Woody Guthrie or a Leadbelly would habitually write and perform his own songs. As rock'n'roll evolved, emerging young artists – notably Chuck Berry, Buddy Holly, and Bob Dylan – drew their inspiration from blues, folk, and country music, and so considered it perfectly normal to write their own material. Thus, the boundaries between folk, blues, and popular music became increasingly blurred.

With the arrival of The Beatles and their in-house writing team of Lennon & McCartney, the floodgates burst wide open, and The Stones were in the vanguard of innumerable British bands that decided to follow The Fab Four's lead. Mick Jagger has admitted that their first attempt at composition was "a horrible song," adding: "It was pop, and we didn't record it, because it was crap." To their surprise, Jagger & Richards found that their earliest songs – 'As Tears Go By,' written for Marianne Faithfull, is an obvious example – didn't match their personalities. "We were these two rebellious band members and we would write nice little tunes, but sentimental stuff."

By the end of 1965, however, they'd got the hang of it, and set to work on their first entirely self-composed album. Recording started at the end of a grueling U.S. tour with a five day session, between December 6th and 10th, at the RCA Studios, Los Angeles. From the outset it was obvious that this would be the first real Rolling Stones album. With the solitary exception of a sprawling semi-jam, 'Goin' Home,' The Stones' original incarnation as R&B wannabes was swept aside. Gone were the regurgitated hymns to American cars, bars, and boardwalks, replaced by songs about suburban housewives on tranquillizers, brain-dead dolly birds, and the corrupted values of modern life. And if these songs, shot through with misogynistic, narcissistic, and sneering lyrics, revealed The Stones as being far from lovable 'mop-tops,' at least they now had their own identity.

Though Jagger & Richards were writing the songs, Brian Jones gave the album much of its musical appeal. The baroque dulcimer in 'Lady Jane,' the sitar in 'Mother's Little Helper,' the marimbas on 'Under My Thumb,' these are all Jones's contributions, and they lift the tracks out of the riff-rock ruts they might otherwise have sunk into.

The release of *Aftermath* affected the band in three important ways: first, it brought them a new level of respect, placing them on a par with The Beatles, The Who, and The Kinks; second, generating their own material gave Jagger & Richards full creative control of the band's musical direction; and, finally, it earned them songwriting royalties that, before very long, would prove very lucrative.

1966

Andrew Loog Oldham

For much of the 1960s The Rolling Stones' career was nurtured by Andrew Loog Oldham, who acted as the group's manager and producer. He quickly established the group as the bad boys of the mid-1960s' British music scene, providing a direct contrast to The Beatles' clean-cut image.

A former publicist, Oldham produced all of The Rolling Stones' albums from the group's 1964 debut, *The Rolling Stones* (called *England's Newest Hit Makers* in the U.S.A.), up to *Between The Buttons* (1967). He also formed The Andrew Loog Oldham Orchestra, issuing a series of albums of symphonic renditions of contemporary groups' songs. His reinterpretation of The Stones' 'The Last Time' was later sampled by The Verve, and formed the backbone of the group's 1997 British hit single 'Bittersweet Symphony.'

In 1965 Oldham founded Immediate, one of the best known British independent record labels of the 1960s. The company was initially highly successful, issuing albums by artists including The Small Faces and The Nice, but was bankrupt by the end of the decade. By this stage Oldham had also been relieved of his duties with The Rolling Stones.

Oldham continued to work sporadically as both producer and manager of other acts through the 1970s, but never again reached the level of success he had achieved with The Rolling Stones.

1966

Pet Sounds
The Beach Boys

Capitol ST2458 (U.S.A.) / MS2197 (U.K.)
Released May 1966

Pet Sounds, a new high in studio creativity in the mid 1960s, became possible after December 23rd 1964, when Brian Wilson suffered a severe mental breakdown on a flight to Houston, leading him to retire from touring and become a studio-based artist.

With their latest single, 'Dance, Dance, Dance,' easily making the U.S. Top Ten, December had been an intensely busy month for The Beach Boys. They had been shuttling across the U.S.A. between recording sessions, live gigs, and television appearances, most of the pressure falling squarely on the shoulders of the band's presiding genius Brian Wilson. Not only was he a performing band member but also their songwriter, arranger, and producer. As Brian's brother Carl noted: "He never did like touring, ever. He didn't like flying, or being away from home, or anything."

Adding to his mental anguish was the fact that earlier that month he had married Marilyn Rovell of Californian girl group The Honeys, but the relationship was already fraught with tension because Wilson was convinced that his new bride was having an affair with his band's lead vocalist, Mike Love. Brian, a 22-year-old survivor of parental abuse, found such burdens intolerable, and he had lately turned to marijuana in search of an escape from his torments.

So, two days before Christmas The Beach Boys boarded a plane in Los Angeles, heading for a gig in

Houston, but, before it landed, Brian had snapped. He charged up and down the aisle, screaming abuse at staff, passengers, and the other Beach Boys until his brothers wrestled him to the floor and, reluctantly, had him sedated.

Brian began seeing a psychiatrist and concluded that the best way to deal with his unbearable workload was to stop playing in the band. "It was bound to happen," reckoned Carl philosophically. "He just said, 'I don't want to tour. I want to stay home. I want to make good music.'" From that moment on the studio was Brian Wilson's home. He became increasingly aware that a recording studio could be as much of a creative tool as any musical instrument, and Pet Sounds became the embodiment of that philosophy.

Hand in hand with this realization came another change in Wilson's world view. In the spring of 1965 he took LSD for the first time, and told Marilyn that the experience had been a spiritual confrontation with God. Now the stage was set. Though it would ultimately wreak havoc with his already parlous mental state, the perceptual changes triggered in Wilson by the drug would directly contribute to his creativity over the coming months.

Despite the fact that no firm plan – or even title – for the new album had yet entered Wilson's head, the earliest recording to appear on what was to become Pet Sounds took place on July 12th 1965 at Wilson's favorite studio, Western Recorders in Hollywood. Beach Boy Al Jardine had brought Wilson a somewhat gloomy Caribbean folk song, 'The Wreck Of The John B.' In the space of one day Wilson refashioned it as 'Sloop John B,' using the finest West Coast session players available – including The Wrecking Crew, who played on Phil Spector's biggest hits. Wilson pushed the tempo up and introduced an optimistic glockenspiel backing. "All we had to do was show up and sing," recalled Jardine.

As instrumentalists, the other Beach Boys were beginning to find themselves effectively – and infuriatingly – redundant, but Wilson applied the same rigorous standards to himself. He was a perfectly capable bass guitarist, but, for recording sessions, he used legendary session bassist Carol Kaye. "Sure, I could play bass," Wilson has explained, "but I could see the bigger picture if I left that to someone else so I could stay in the control booth and produce the session." However, even with Kaye on board, virtually every bass note was written by Wilson, and he had the final say on every aspect of the production. He was in total control and this would be the blueprint for every track on Pet Sounds.

Wilson's right-hand man at the console was Chuck Britz, who helped make the most of Wilson's increasingly complex compositions. "Chuck Britz," Wilson later observed, "taught me how to concentrate on what I was listening to . . . how to get my soul right into the music." It was Britz who masterminded the magnificent reverberation heard on 'Good Vibrations' and other Beach Boys classics. Western Recorders' live echo chamber had been haphazardly constructed from cinder block, but produced one of the finest reverb effects of the time. "Something about those cement blocks seemed to be able to expand the sound even more than usual," recalled Britz. "It was so warm – Brian's voice, in particular, sounded great in that chamber."

It was around this time that advertising copywriter Tony Asher dropped by the studio and was introduced to Wilson. The pair threw some ideas around, and Wilson – never a sophisticated lyricist – was sufficiently impressed by the young wordsmith to file his name mentally for future reference.

The instrumental parts for another Pet Sounds track, 'You Still Believe In Me,' were recorded on November 1st, under the title 'In My Childhood.' Neither this nor 'Sloop John B' were, however, recorded as part of any album. They were simply tracks.

Everything changed on December 6th, the date of the U.S. release of The Beatles' new album, Rubber Soul. In Wilson's own words: "When

Continued on next page

I heard *Rubber Soul*, I said, 'I have to top that.' Then I did *Pet Sounds* and McCartney said, 'I'll top that with *Sgt Pepper*.'"

Wilson had noticed that every track on *Rubber Soul* seemed to have been recorded with the same care and attention normally lavished on a single. Until this time pop albums were regarded by the music industry as a way to cash in on hit singles. Rock'n'roll was regarded as a passing phase, so an album tended to consist of nine formulaic tracks quickly recorded to fill up the space between two or three carefully created singles. Wilson now decided that his next album would meet and even exceed the quality levels set by *Rubber Soul*, so that the entire album would stand as a coherent and creative whole.

Within days Wilson was back in Western Recorders finishing off 'Sloop John B.' After trying out every member of the band on lead vocals, he decided to do it himself, much to Jardine's dismay, and paid guitarist Billy Strange $500 to add a distinctive 12-string guitar backing.

For most of January 1966 The Beach Boys were touring the Far East, leaving Brian in Los Angeles, where he took full advantage of their absence to push ahead. On January 18th he entered Western to work on the instrumental track 'Let's Go Away For A While.' *Pet Sounds* was officially under way.

Wilson had also now begun working with Tony Asher as a lyricist, sometimes presenting him with complete instrumental tracks, sometimes just with melodies or even fragments of melodies. "The general tenor of the lyrics was always his," says Asher, "and the actual choice of words was usually mine. I was really just his interpreter."

"THE MUSIC OF *PET SOUNDS* WAS CREATED SOLELY FOR THE PURPOSE OF MAKING PEOPLE FEEL GOOD. I WANTED TO CREATE MUSIC THAT PEOPLE WOULD FEEL WOULD GET TO THEIR FEELINGS MORE."
BRIAN WILSON

By the 22nd Wilson had shifted to Gold Star Studios and moved on to another new song, 'Wouldn't It Be Nice.' Mark Linett, who later produced the stereo and 5.1 Surround Sound versions of *Pet Sounds*, points out that the richness of sound on tracks made at Gold Star came, to some extent, from the relatively small size of the studio. "You hear these huge records that Brian and Phil Spector made and you think it must be an enormous space," he explains. "Well, no, it's a very small space, because that allowed the coincident information to be useful. If you were in a huge room like Studio 1 at Western, the bounceback from instruments to the other mikes would have been objectionable, whereas in a small room, it added another dimension." The depth of sound on the album is all the more remarkable given that Wilson mixed it in mono. (His reluctance towards working in stereo was due in no small part to the fact that he was deaf in one ear.)

Returning to Western on the 24th Wilson laid down tracks for the haunting ballad 'You Still Believe In Me.' In his ongoing efforts to find new sounds he devised a piano introduction that required sessioneer Larry Knechtel to play the keyboard while another musician clambered inside the piano and plucked the strings to make them ring out.

The Beach Boys' Far Eastern tour ended with a gig in Hawaii on the 29th, after which they took a well-earned rest while Wilson ploughed on with the new album. The collaboration with Asher was proving fruitful. Listening to Wilson speak about his high-school crush on a girl called Carol Mountain, Asher had written a lyric titled 'Carol, I Know,' but Wilson mis-heard the phrase and sang it as the much more poignant 'Caroline, No.' One of the pair's loveliest songs, recording of 'Caroline, No' was started on January 31st.

Suitably refreshed after their break, the other Beach Boys joined Wilson in Western Studios on February 9th. As Asher has pointed out, they were "hoping for and expecting more of what had been hits for them all along." Instead they were confronted by a radically more sophisticated style and

Continued on next page

sound, which didn't seem to require any input from them other than their voices. "We were a surfing group when we left the country," observed Al Jardine, "and now basically we came back to this new music."

Asher has confirmed that the band were unenthusiastic about the new songs and couldn't understand why their proven hit-making formula needed changing. "There was resistance," Wilson revealed. "There was a little bit of inter-group struggle. It was resolved in that they figured it was a showcase for Brian Wilson, but it was The Beach Boys. In other words, they gave in."

Wilson was back in Western on the 11th without the other Beach Boys, working on what he has described as "one of the sweetest, most loving songs that I ever sang," 'Don't Talk (Put Your Head On My Shoulder).'

During a session on the 14th, Wilson made his first use of an electro-theremin in the backing for 'I Just Wasn't Made For These Times.' Played by another session musician, Paul Tanner, the instrument was a variation on an earlier device invented in the 1920s by Russian scientist Leon Theremin. Both instruments emit the same eerie sound, half-way between a violin and a soprano voice, but the original theremin was apallingly difficult to master, because pitch and volume were varied by the performer's hands moving around in a magnetic field generated by the instrument. Accurate production of notes was much simpler on the electro-theremin which used a slider control for pitch and an amplifier for volume.

The following day saw the entire band rendezvous at the petting paddock in San Diego Zoo to shoot the album's cover. The best that can be said of the result is that it has a certain naive charm, and it ties in with the title, which Wilson says was chosen "because we specialized in certain sounds. It was our best – the songs were our 'Pet Sounds.'"

Later the same day they reassembled at Western and recorded 'That's Not Me,' a song whose lyric deals with Wilson's rationale for giving up touring. The track is remarkable for being the only one on *Pet Sounds* to feature the band playing its own instruments, though even here they were augmented by session players.

With the album sessions in full swing, Wilson now set to work on 'Good Vibrations,' but this classic single would not be completed in time to be included on the album.

Much of the next month and a half was occupied by the band adding its vocals under Brian's supervision. Recalling this long and painstaking process, Mike Love has stated: "If there was a hint of a sharp or flat, we would have to do it again until it was right." Frequently, Wilson would stop the group to pick up on some tiny error which no one else had even noticed. Even at this point, however, there were three new songs still to be recorded, 'Here Today,' 'I'm Waiting For The Day,' and, taking pride of place, 'God Only Knows.'

After a couple of days of Brian working on backing tracks without the band, they joined him in Columbia Studio A on March 10th. "When I walked in on 'God Only Knows,'" remembers Beach Boy Bruce Johnston, "I realized that something wonderful was happening." The song wasn't completed until a month later, when Carl Wilson recorded his transcendently beautiful lead vocal, widely regarded as his finest moment with the band. With 'God Only Knows' in the can, *Pet Sounds* was effectively complete.

Pet Sounds was released on May 16th, but, though now recognized as a landmark album, it stalled at Number Ten in the US chart because Capitol Records simply didn't get behind it. "They didn't promote *Pet Sounds*," reasons Johnston, "because they said it wasn't commercial and people wouldn't understand it."

The British audience liked it better, sending it to Number Two, and unswerving British devotion to *Pet Sounds* has seen it re-evaluated over the years, often topping critics' polls as the best album of all time. In Paul McCartney's own words: "It blew me out of the water," and there's no question that it set a new benchmark that The Beatles now felt they would have to top. Speaking of *Pet Sounds* some years later, The Beatles' producer George Martin observed that: "It gives you an elation that is beyond logic." And that, surely, is the point at which music intersects with magic.

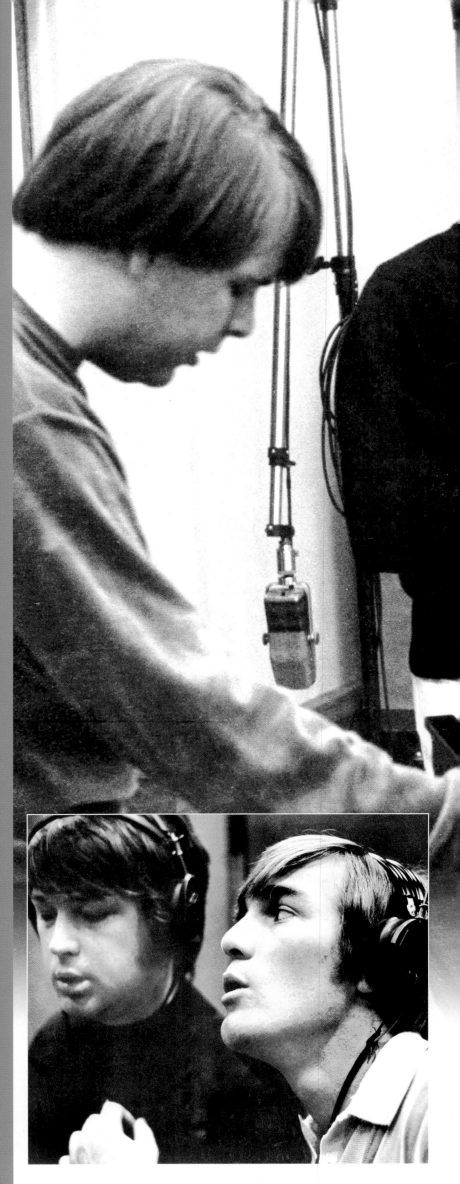

1967

I Never Loved A Man (The Way I Loved You)
Aretha Franklin

Atlantic 8139 (U.S.A.) / 587/588 085 (U.K.)
Released March 1967

Recorded in a handful of sessions between Muscle Shoals, Alabama, and Manhattan during the winter of 1967, Aretha Franklin's premier Atlantic album – which eventually settled at Number Two in the U.S.A. on its way to selling over a million copies – helped bring soul music to a worldwide audience.

A showcase for top songwriters – including King Curtis ('Save Me') and Chips Moman ('Do Right Woman, Do Right Man') – *I Never Loved A Man* also included a pair of fine originals in 'Baby, Baby, Baby' and 'Don't Let Me Lose This Dream.' But it was the cover of Otis Redding's 'Respect' that gave Franklin her first Number One single and brought her the richly deserved title of 'Queen of Soul.'

Few people had ever heard of the 25-year-old pianist-vocalist before her March 1967 soul breakout. Signed by Columbia in 1960, Franklin spent six frustrating years as a Dinah Washington-style pop balladeer until Atlantic's Jerry Wexler saw in her the makings of a world-class artist who'd simply been playing for the wrong team. Shortly after he recruited Franklin in late 1966 the pair headed for Alabama, where a revelatory one-off session at FAME Studios produced the stunning title track, written by Franklin's friend Ronnie Shannon. Rush-released as a single in late February, 'I Never Loved a Man' immediately shot up the charts, leaving Wexler and Franklin just weeks to polish off the remainder of the album at Atlantic's New York studios.

Over the next eight years Wexler would go on to cut an additional 14 albums with Franklin, his most valued client of all. "In this business, it's so important to be able to work on the music only when it's needed – because if it ain't broke, don't fix it," says Wexler. "With Aretha, there was never any second-guessing. In the studio, she was nothing short of miraculous."

Surrealistic Pillow **Jefferson Airplane**

RCA Victor LSP-3766 (U.S.A.) RD/SF 7889 (U.K.)
Released March 1967

On November 15th 1965, with an unprecedented $25,000 advance, Jefferson Airplane became the first West Coast hippy band to be signed up by a major record label, RCA, the home of Elvis Presley.

They were launched as a "San Francisco sextet singing in the folk-rock vein," but their debut album, *Jefferson Airplane Takes Off*, didn't trouble the charts.

Surrealistic Pillow – so named by Jerry Garcia of The Grateful Dead, who produced it – was their second effort, recorded over 13 days during November 1966. This one amped up The Airplane's quirky 'folksydelia' with rockier riffs, but the principal change was the arrival of the band's new vocalist Grace Slick. And with her came two songs, 'White Rabbit" and 'Somebody To Love,' written for her previous band, The Great Society. 'White Rabbit,' perhaps the quintessential Haight-Ashbury hit, was inspired by Slick's observation that virtually every great children's story – from *Peter Pan* though *The Wonderful Wizard Of Oz* to *Alice's Adventures In Wonderland* – involved children ingesting strange substances then having fantastical dream-like adventures.

"I TOOK ACID AND LISTENED TO MILES DAVIS'S *SKETCHES OF SPAIN* FOR ABOUT 24 HOURS STRAIGHT."

GRACE SLICK ON THE INSPIRATION BEHIND 'WHITE RABBIT'

The band's other major songwriter, Marty Balin, also contributed several powerful tracks, while guitarist Jorma Kaukonen provided the shimmering acoustic solo piece, 'Embryonic Journey,' but it was Slick's songs that would provide the two hits that would establish The Airplane as a major chart force. The album peaked at Number Three that spring, and was declared gold on July 24th, opening the floodgates for Frisco's hippy bands.

The Elektra Records Story

In the mid 1960s, Elektra Records radically expanded the horizons of rock by insisting on excellence and innovation in every aspect of its operations.

While a college student at St John's, Annapolis, Maryland, company founder Jac Holzman had more interest in electronics, radio, and tape recorders than in his scheduled classes. Inspired by a classical concert he had attended, Holzman decided to start his own record company, and, on October 10th 1950, he named it Elektra Records.

Elektra's first release, *New Songs*, by contemporary classical composer John Gruen, was a commercial disaster. Holzman relocated to Greenwich Village, opened a record store to generate cash, and recorded a second album, the memorably titled *Jean Ritchie Singing The Traditional Songs Of Her Kentucky Mountain Family*. This garnered critical acclaim and sold enough copies to put Elektra on a firmer footing.

Adding blues to its folk-based catalog in 1954, Elektra moved to bigger offices. Always politically active, Holzman boldly signed singer-guitarist Josh White to Elektra when White's former label, Decca, dumped him because he had been blacklisted during Senator Joe McCarthy's Communist witch-hunt. The early-1960s' folk boom boosted Elektra's fortunes, and Holzman's earlier reservations about rock music were swept away when, on July 25th 1965, he watched Bob Dylan go electric at *Newport Folk Festival.* "Dylan and folk music and Elektra were never the same again," he has said.

Determined to get behind the new, politically aware, intellectually challenging form of rock that was emerging, Holzman first signed Los Angeles-based Love – "Five guys of all colors, black, white, and psychedelic – that was a real first. My heart skipped a beat. I had found my band!" – and then The Doors.

Suddenly, without compromising its principles, little Elektra was scoring hit singles and competing in the same arena as giants Columbia, Capitol, and RCA. Entering its golden age, Elektra signed a string of ground-breaking acts, each of which explored the outer fringes of rock. To name just three: The Holy Modal Rounders, who invented psychedelic folk; Ars Nova, who took the combination of baroque and rock to its logical conclusion; and The Stooges, who were hammering out punk years before its time.

The label's big, blocky 'E' logo became a hallmark of quality, not just for Elektra's choice of artists but for exquisite sound reproduction and imaginative sleeve designs. Holzman's unswerving commitment to quality also meant that when album sales began to overtake singles in the late 1960s, his label was perfectly placed to reap the benefits, because knocking off quick hits had never been a feature of Elektra's recording policy.

Throughout this period Elektra also continued to record cutting-edge singer-songwriters, including Tim Buckley and Phil Ochs, while its classically oriented sister label, Nonesuch, scored a totally unexpected international smash with Joshua Rifkin's recordings of piano rags by Scott Joplin.

By the start of the 1970s, however, Holzman was wearying of the business and had moved to Hawaii. Elektra was merged, first with David Geffen's Asylum Records, then with Warner Brothers, thus forming WEA (Warner/Elektra/Asylum). Under new management the label continued to sign quality artists and achieved higher sales figures than ever, but the Holzman fingerprint was gone and Elektra's unique identity was lost for ever.

The Doors The Doors

EKS-74007 (U.S.A. / U.K.)
Released January 1967

The Doors' debut album broke new ground by fusing elements of theatre, poetry, and psychology into a hard rock format.

The Doors was recorded over six days in August 1966 at Sunset Sound, Los Angeles. Much of the album's impact comes from the exotic blending of Ray Manzarek's keyboards (splicing New Orleans stride and classical discipline) with Robbie Krieger's swooping fretwork (sometimes bluesy, sometimes evoking Indian ragas), while drummer John Densmore employed every percussion trick in the book to illustrate Jim Morrison's story-songs without ever skipping a beat. The real jolt, however, was Morrison's intimidating and surreal lyrics, exploring areas formerly taboo, even in rock.

'Light My Fire,' the Krieger-composed hit single, gave the band superstar status. But the key track is 'The End,' which had been recorded by the light of a single candle. This brooding, hallucinatory, gothic nightmare set to music was wholly new in its musical structure and oedipal lyrics.

In a world where the most outrageous of mainstream rock bands could achieve notoriety simply by turning their amplifiers up or introducing sexual or socio-political themes into their lyrics, The Doors' music was remarkably sophisticated, and Morrison's lyrics, probing the murkier depths of the human psyche, were downright shocking.

1967

Forever Changes **Love**

EKS 74013 (U.S.A. / U.K.)
Released November 1967

Frequently hailed as a classic of psychedelia, Love's third album, *Forever Changes*, is actually that much rarer artifact: an album that exists in its own category.

As the first rock band signed to the previously folk-dominated Elektra Records, the Los Angeles-based Love had a lot to prove. Initially touted as the 'new Byrds,' their eponymous 1966 debut album certainly ploughed a similar folk-rock furrow, but by the time of its successor, *Da Capo*, they were clearly heading in another, more idiosyncratic direction.

At the heart of the band was Arthur Lee, whom Elektra Records' president, Jac Holzman, has called "one of the few geniuses I have met." Born in Memphis, Lee had grown up with eclectic musical tastes that embraced soul, R&B, folk rock, and MOR. He seemed equally at home rocking out with his friend Jimi Hendrix or chilling out to the smooth sounds of Nat 'King' Cole, and elements of both are clearly audible in *Forever Changes*.

Recording began at Sunset Sound, Los Angeles, in June 1967, but, by that point, the band was falling apart. There had been personnel changes, much internal bickering, and escalating hard-drug problems. Things were so bad that Elektra Records' producer Bruce Botnick, who was to co-produce the album with Neil Young, decided to dispense with the services of all the band members except Lee, and brought in the Los Angeles crack team of session players, The Wrecking Crew, to create the instrumental backings.

The first two tracks to be recorded – 'The Daily Planet' and 'Andmoreagain' – were completed with Lee arranging, playing, and singing, while the other band members merely watched from the sidelines. Horrified by the ease with which they had been replaced, they demanded their old jobs back. "The band was so shocked," remembers Botnick, "that it caused them to forget about their problems and become a band again."

When the sessions resumed on August 11th, Lee had usurped Young, and the rest of the band had replaced The Wrecking Crew. Precisely what happened next remains a matter of whose version you'd most like to believe – virtually all of the participants have offered dramatically different scenarios, and, given how stoned they apparently were during the sessions, their recollections can hardly be relied upon.

What is irrefutable is that Lee wrote most of the songs, though the band's other guitarist-vocalist, Bryan MacLean, composed the best-remembered track, 'Alone Again Or,' as well as the haunting 'Old Man.' The other major contributor to the album's unique sonic palette was David Angel, an orchestral arranger who had previously worked with Andy Williams and Herb Alpert's Tijuana Brass.

Angel's input is evident from the opening track, the lovely 'Alone Again Or,' where shimmering strings and mariachi horns, courtesy of members of The Los Angeles Philharmonic Orchestra, brilliantly intensify the drama of the band's delicately finger-picked acoustic-guitar patterns. In a way, the track represents the whole album in microcosm. The musical elements – acoustic guitars, strings, horns, understated bass and drums – are all here. Having

been blown away by the guitar pyrotechnics of his now internationally acclaimed old associate Hendrix, Lee had astutely decided there was no point in trying to compete. Instead, *Forever Changes* would be largely acoustic and focused on well-constructed songs rather than on instrumental virtuosity. Lyrically, too, the mood of other-worldly strangeness in MacLean's song sets listeners up for Lee's similar – if noticeably weirder – approach throughout the subsequent tracks. However, Lee's obsessive need to control every aspect of the album is demonstrated in the mixing of 'Alone Again Or,' because, lacking confidence in MacLean's singing, Lee turned down the composer's lead vocal, burying it under his own harmony part.

Lee was the principal element that ensured *Forever Changes* would stand apart from the general run of West Coast psychedelia at the time. Unlike the rainbow-eyed battalions of hippie bands promoting love, peace, and brotherhood, Lee saw the world as a dark, dangerous place on the brink of self-destruction. "When I did that album," he has said, "I thought I was going to die."

At just 22 years old he was convinced that he would not live beyond 26, and the album brims over with dire portents of the apocalypse he believed was imminent. 'The Daily Planet,' for example, is a damning indictment of the tedium of modern life generally and, very specifically, of the part played by toy guns in conditioning children for war. The title of the song 'The Red Telephone' refers to the hotline linking The White House to The Kremlin, to be used only on the brink of nuclear attack. And, in 'A House Is Not A Motel,' he asserts: "By the time that I'm through singing / The bells from the schools of wars will be ringing." Given all of this, it should be an intensely depressing album, but the sheer beauty of the music conspires – at least at first – to sugar the bitter pill of Lee's lyrics. As a result, when the lyrics do finally seep through after repeated listens, their impact is significantly greater.

The innovations on *Forever Changes* are too many to document here, but a few examples will serve to give a flavor: 'The Good Humor Man He Sees Everything Like This' employs cut-up tapes of horn parts to simulate the sound of a needle jumping in a vinyl groove; 'Maybe The People Would Be The Times Or Between Clark And Hilldale' features an ingenious lyrical device of holding back the final word of the verse and then using it as the first word of the next; the otherwise tightly constructed 'Live And Let Live' ends with a guitar solo that deliberately falls apart.

When recording finished in September Love had fashioned an album as innovative as *Sgt Pepper* or *Are You Experienced?*, but with an entirely different mood and musical landscape. So different, indeed, that the world wasn't quite ready for it. On release, *Forever Changes* staggered to Number 154 on the *Billboard* album chart before disappearing back below the horizon. Only the passage of time and the persistence of critical acclaim has elevated it to the status of an all-time classic – but it still hasn't gone gold.

Resurgent interest in Love – and *Forever Changes* in particular – peaked in 2003 when, several months after the 25th anniversary of its original release, Lee began performing the album in its entirety with his new band and an eight-piece Scandinavian string and horn section. *Forever Changes Concert* captures one such performance, taped at the Royal Festival Hall in London on January 13th 2003. Lee was one of several artists to revisit a past masterwork in a live setting: Beach Boys founder Brian Wilson performed *Pet Sounds* in full on his 2000–1 tour, while David Bowie reworked his landmark *Low* (1977) on stage in 2002.

1967

Disraeli Gears **Cream**

Atco SD33232 (U.S.A.) / Reaction 594003 (U.K.)
Released November 1967

Eric Clapton, Jack Bruce, and Ginger Baker were dubbed rock's first 'supergroup,' choosing the name Cream in ironic acknowledgment of the fact. Their second album, *Disraeli Gears*, with its classic psychedelic sleeve, mixes heavy blues with rock riffery.

Disraeli Gears was recorded on 8-track in ten days at Atlantic Studios in New York with Tom Dowd producing. 'Sunshine Of Your Love' has a classic and memorable riff, and songs such as 'World Of Pain,' 'Dance The Night Away,' and 'We're Going Wrong' have pretty chord sequences and a delicate touch. The heavy riffing and Baker's distinctive drumming – Keith Moon meets the whirling dervishes – are juxtaposed with poetic lyrics sung in a relaxed if moody style, a contrast heightened by the mix itself. Singeribassist Jack Bruce said: "I had this idea that you could have very heavy, wild instrumental stuff but a gentle, lyrical vocal . . . very rhythmic backing, very smooth voices on top. It would've been easy to scream something, but then it's one-dimensional."

Clapton's fuzzy front pickup on 'Swlabr' is one of the definitive tones in rock guitar, and 'Tales Of Brave Ulysses' a fine early deployment of the wah-wah pedal. The album influenced legions of guitarists. Eddie Van Halen said: "I started out playing blues; I learned from the *Blues Breakers* album. Then I learnt [some of the Cream solos] note-for-note." And Buddy Guy: "My favorite is 'Strange Brew.' I was really impressed by the tone [Clapton] was getting, plus the way he was playing." *Disraeli Gears* gives ample evidence of a creative partnership, the potential of which was perhaps never fully realized at the time. An expanded remastered version of the album was released in 2004.

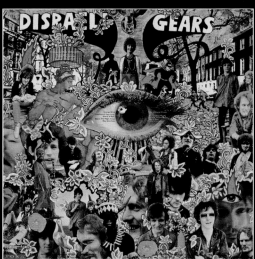

■ **Above: Ginger Baker (left), Jack Bruce (center), and Eric Clapton pose with local children in Battersea Park, London, during the summer of 1967. Pictures from this photo session were used on the psychedelic collaged sleeve of Disraeli Gears, which was designed by Martin Sharp. The design was subtly different on the U.S. (left) and U.K. (right) editions of the album (back covers pictured). Sharp's design was adapted again for the 1997 retrospective collection, Those Were The Days.**

The Velvet Underground & Nico
The Velvet Underground

Verve V6 5008 (U.S.A.) / S+/VLP9184 (U.K.)
Released March 1967

White Light/White Heat
The Velvet Underground

Verve V6-5046 (U.S.A.) / S+/VLP9201 (U.K.)
Released December 1967

On release, *The Velvet Underground And Nico* barely limped into the *Billboard* chart at Number 197 before promptly disappearing without trace, but it is now acknowledged as one of the most influential albums of all time.

The Velvets, whose music can now be seen as New York's brutally realist street-wise riposte to San Francisco's hippy dreams, was launched largely from a platform provided by their association with the 1960s' most celebrated pop artist, Andy Warhol. As an outrageous quartet they had become New York's hottest rock ticket during 1966, but, by the time they started recording their debut album, they had been joined by Warhol's protégée, the striking blonde German actress, model, and chanteuse, Nico.

■ *Above: The Velvet Underground with Nico (left). Right: the line-up for the band's second album, by which time the German singer had departed.*

Keen to establish Nico as next in his line of 'superstars,' Warhol financed the album, securing three days at a studio on Broadway, at a cost of $2,500. In return, the band would feature Nico as a vocalist and credit Warhol as producer, though he rarely showed his face at the studio. Lou Reed, the band's principal songwriter, found Nico's presence hard to take – and there were, undeniably, solid musical reasons for not wanting her in the band. A perforated ear-drum made her deaf in one ear and, as a result, she would often lose control of her vocals. Multi-instrumentalist John Cale recalls: "We'd hear her go off-key or hit the wrong pitch. We would sit there and snigger."

According to drummer Mo Tucker time was so limited that most of the tracks were recorded live with virtually no overdubs. "We went in the studio for just eight hours to do it, and all the gigs we'd done just paid off. It wasn't a case of 'Let's do it again; let's overdub here.' What you hear is exactly what we played, mistakes and all."

It could be said that this was exactly what the music required. Held together by Tucker's rudimentary pounding drum patterns, The Velvets incorporated lashings of feedback, distortion, and screeching electrified viola into songs whose chord progressions were primitive in the extreme. To invest more time and effort into capturing their crazed cacophonies in perfect hi-fi would have been to miss the point.

The recording of Reed's epic 'Heroin' is a good example of how poor recording facilities served to enhance the visceral intent of the material. "The guys couldn't have their amps up loud in the studio," recalls Tucker, "so I couldn't hear anything. When we got to the part where you speed up, it became this mountain of drum noise. I couldn't hear shit. So I just stopped and, being a little wacky, they just kept going." And that's the version that ended up on the album.

As well as the minimalist, and often discordant, sonic assault of the music, what set Velvet Underground songs apart from the mainstream was Lou Reed's unblinkingly nihilistic lyrics. Then as now, variations on teen romantic themes provided the words for most chart hits. Though folk rock had broadened the scope to cover socio-political issues, and the San Francisco bands were exploring free love and dope-related ideas, nothing prepared the public for Reed's tales of sado-masochism, alienated junkies, and teenage girls turning blue.

The completed album was first rejected by Atlantic Records (who didn't want drug songs), then by Elektra (who hated the violas), before producer Tom Wilson secured them a deal with MGM's jazz subsidiary, Verve, which was trying to revamp

itself for the psychedelic era. According to Cale, however, Wilson insisted on re-recording some tracks in California, resulting in marked disparities in sound quality across the album.

When the album hit the streets it was embraced by the more adventurous record critics of the day but, despite being dressed up in its famed Warhol banana cover, rejected by the public, who were not yet ready to move on from pop, protest, and psychedelia. Verve's commitment to the band wavered, and the label now put its promotional efforts into its other major signing, The Mothers Of Invention. Ironically, as Reed has pointed out, "that was one of the reasons why we could do what we wanted."

With Nico now out of the band, what they wanted for their second album, *White Light/White Heat*, was to go beyond the limits of the first one. "It was a very rabid record," explains Cale. "The first one had some gentility, some beauty. The second one was consciously anti-beauty." Cale also notes that the chaotic nature of their lives on the road is reflected in the album. "We decided to go in and turn all the instruments up and fuck the engineer."

The album's centerpiece is, unquestionably, the relentlessly churning 17-minute 'Sister Ray.' There already existed a vogue for lengthy album tracks, which tended to be excuses for bands to show off their ensemble improvisational skills, but in The Velvets' hands that notion went out the window. Instead, Reed sets up a simple, dirty guitar riff that gets increasingly basic as the track evolves, while the rest of the band fights for attention. "When Cale came surging through the wall of sound on his first solo," explained Sterling Morrison, "all of a sudden, the organ is way louder than me or Lou. I couldn't turn up; I was already maxed out. At one point, I was down at the bridge pickup on my Stratocaster, so I decided to get a little more oomph on the neck pickup. So I switched to that, which was good." On purely musical merits, 'Sister Ray' is hard to justify, but as an organically evolving, living, gasping sonic monster, it remains unsurpassed in the annals of rock.

'Sister Ray' alone would justify the album's place in rock history, but *White Light/White Heat* also includes Cale's horrific spoken-word tale, 'The Gift,' and the indescribably nightmarish 'Lady Godiva's Operation,' plus a trio of more conventionally excellent rock workouts.

Despite the poor performance of both albums on release, their influence has been enormous, with bands as diverse as R.E.M., Nirvana, and The Strokes having cited them as inspiration.

Songs Of Leonard Cohen **Leonard Cohen**

Columbia 9533 (U.S.A.) / CBS 63241 (U.K.)
Released December 1967

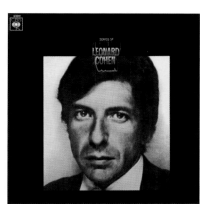

Already in his 30s, Cohen was a successful poet and novelist and well known in his native Canada before the release of this debut album thrust him into the international spotlight.

Where Dylan's greatest lyrics achieve much of their dazzling effect by being inscrutable, surreal, stream of consciousness, Cohen's most enduring songs are usually easy to understand. The only smoke and mirrors element with Cohen was how he pulled off the clever trick of writing almost exclusively about love and sex, while making it feel like the stuff of arcane metaphysics.

The religious allusions of 'Sisters Of Mercy,' for example, make it seem much more than a song about a night in the company of two mini-skirted girls, which is what it actually is. "I suppose I always wanted to be a pop singer," he said many years later while talking about this album, going on to explain that he'd rather be the kind of writer whose songs "were sung by the women washing their clothes" than be considered an intellectual.

None of this, however, detracts from Cohen's achievements on this album, evoking powerful emotions with a limited vocal range, a finger-picking guitar accompaniment, and the ability to spin an engaging yarn. In 'Suzanne,' for instance, her "place by the river" is brought vividly to the mind's eye with judicious details about "tea and oranges that come all the way from China." Cohen felt that producer John Simon's over-dubbed strings, choirs, and percussion marred his songs, but their timeless ability to stir the heart isn't undermined.

Exploring The Possibilities Of The Studio

1967

The summer of 1967 – the 'Summer Of Love' – officially got under way at midnight on June 1st, when radio stations across the U.S.A. were given the go-ahead to begin broadcasting *Sgt Pepper's Lonely Hearts Club Band*, The Beatles' long-awaited psychedelic masterpiece and the band's first full-length release since *Revolver* nine months earlier.

An album packed with swirling guitars, panning vocals, crossfades, odd sound effects, and a fade-out finale nearly as long as the band's first single, *Sgt Pepper* represented a major departure from conventional rock recording. Though its hallucinogenic imagery and trippy sitars haven't aged all that gracefully, nearly 40 years on it remains one of only a handful of undisputed landmark rock recordings.

Above all, the arrival of *Sgt Pepper* signaled a complete transformation for The Beatles, a band that had long exhibited remarkable studio economy, writing and recording almost non-stop while issuing upward of three albums per year. By 1967, however, the rules of in-studio etiquette were being rewritten as the era of multitrack recording fully took hold. While bands still cut their rhythm tracks as a live unit, more often than not vocals, percussion, lead guitar, and other instrumentation were added as carefully conceived overdubs. After spending an unprecedented four months inside EMI's Studio 2 at work on *Revolver*, The Beatles allowed themselves a half-year assembling the bits and pieces that would become *Sgt Pepper*, along with the February 1967 double a-side single 'Penny Lane' / 'Strawberry Fields.'

In 1967 The Beatles were still working exclusively with 4-track machines, so EMI's staff had grown accustomed to taping such complex pieces as 'Strawberry Fields' and 'All You Need Is Love' using virtually the same machinery as in the early days – though this did, on occasion, cause a few headaches, as former EMI engineer Richard Lush recalls: "I remember the night we did 'All You Need Is Love,' which was being recorded and broadcast live to hundreds of millions of people. We had two tape machines there, one playing the backing track for the song, the other recording the live vocals, orchestra, and the rest. I remember George Martin saying, 'Just make sure you record on the right machine, otherwise it's going to be very quiet in here!' You've never seen two guys run to a pub as fast as [engineer] Geoff Emerick and I did the second that show ended."

It wasn't until mid 1968, in fact, that the group finally doubled its capacity with the 8-track taping of 'Hey Jude,' albeit at neighboring Trident Studios. Not that the problems came to an end once EMI finally secured its first 8-track unit during the making of *The Beatles* (better known as *The White Album*) in mid 1968. "The machine we got from 3M was a bit of a disaster, because it didn't have a bloody clock on it," recalls Lush. "They'd be out there recording five takes of a song and ask to hear it back – except you didn't know where to look! We ended up having to make all these little marks on the tape, but the problem was you never knew which chorus you were on, and of course there were a couple of things that got [accidentally] wiped along the way."

Coincidentally or not, the beginning of the 8-track era at Abbey Road marked the beginning of the end for The Beatles, whose disintegration can be traced to *The White Album* sessions when, ironically, improved technology made it possible for the four members to work individually for the first time.

"Great things were still happening, obviously," says Lush. "You listen to John's demos from the time – things like 'Happiness Is A Warm Gun' and 'Glass Onion' – and you hear the work that the band did to the songs in the final product. But there was less

Continued on page 94

Sgt Pepper's Lonely Hearts Club Band **The Beatles**

Capitol 2653 (U.S.A.) / Parlophone PCS 7027 (U.K.)
Released June 1967

Whatever else *Sgt Pepper* may or may not be, it unquestionably established in the minds of the record-buying public a blueprint for what a truly great album should be.

It was not the first concept album, it was not the first psychedelic album, it may not even be the best album The Beatles ever made, but it did set the benchmark by which all subsequent albums were judged for decades after.

It was Paul McCartney's ongoing love-hate relationship with The Beatles' mega-success that provided the background to his invention of an imaginary band. Already, in 1965, in an effort to establish whether or not Beatles songs were hits just because of the band's fame McCartney had written the single 'Woman' for pop duo Peter & Gordon under the pseudonym Bernard Webb, and only revealed that he was the composer after it became a hit. And by 1967 The Beatles were even more successful, so when he dreamed up Sgt Pepper's band it should have

been no surprise to anyone because, as he said: "it would be nice to lose our identities, to submerge ourselves in the persona of a fake group."

As their producer George Martin remembers it: "Paul came in with this song, 'Sgt Pepper,' and he was kind of identifying it with The Beatles themselves. We recorded the song, and then the idea came to make it into the concept for the whole album."

Concept albums had been around for some years, beginning with LPs unified by having a single theme – dreams, weather, travel – running through all of the songs, and continuing with the likes of 1965's *Beach Boys' Party!* album, which pretended to be a party at which The Beach Boys just happened to be in attendance with their instruments. The arrival of psychedelia, however, gave such albums a shot in the arm, and The Beatles were among the first to recognize the potential of setting an entire album inside its own parallel vision of reality.

The first Beatles album that could be called psychedelic was *Revolver*, but *Sgt Pepper* would take several giant steps further. To achieve McCartney's vision, they effectively took over Abbey Road's main studio for an unprecedented 129 days, during which, as staff engineer Peter Vince recalls: "We actually sat around a lot of the time doing nothing, waiting for them to come up with ideas. But you had to be there because suddenly they'd get the idea and want to go straight for it. They were the innovators of working through the night and very long hours. Prior to them, everyone went home at 10pm."

Viewed with a critical eye, the album might be said to offer only three songs that can be regarded as truly imaginative leaps forward, those being 'Lucy In The Sky With Diamonds,' 'She's Leaving Home,' and 'A Day In The Life.'

This trio is the creative core on which the album's gigantic reputation rests. There's also a brace of universally popular singalongs, 'With A Little Help From My Friends' and 'When I'm Sixty-Four.' Both are very much in McCartney's irresistibly tuneful but irrefutably lightweight tradition, though much enhanced by Martin's clever arrangements and production wizardry.

Crucially for justifying the album's now legendary status, even the less groundbreaking songs – 'Fixing A Hole,' 'Good Morning Good Morning,' 'Getting Better,' 'Being For The Benefit Of Mr Kite,' and 'Lovely Rita' – are rendered magical and fascinating by careful attention to detail, intelligent use of sound effects, and convincingly dynamic performances. This leaves the conceptual bookends – two versions of the title song – and one of Harrison's by now obligatory Indian-flavored tracks, 'Within You Without You.'

So, that's *Sgt Pepper's Lonely Hearts Club Band* neatly summarized, but the whole has become so much more than the sum of those parts. Over the years, every track has been subjected to relentless analysis, scrutiny, deconstruction, and dismemberment, to such an extent that we now know, for example, that 'When I'm Sixty-Four' had actually been written by McCartney back in the days when The Beatles played The Cavern Club in Liverpool. Lyrically and musically it's his tribute to his 64-year-old father, Jim, who had played in dance bands during the war. "It was a pastiche," notes George Martin, "a kind of send-up of the old stuff. Paul always had that sneaking regard for the old rooty-tooty music."

We know, too, that 'A Day In The Life,' Lennon's principal contribution to *Sgt Pepper*, came about through the accidental proximity of a copy of a newspaper. "I was reading the *Daily Mail* one day and noticed two stories,"

Continued on page 96

Continued from page 92

group effort – and it's through interaction that real ideas develop. Because nine times out of ten, it's one bloke sitting in a room, and it's his view on it all. There's something that occurs when you introduce an idea to different people . . . and that was such an important element for The Beatles."

The trend toward a more leisurely use of recording time went hand in hand with the increasingly sophisticated perception of rock music that arrived in 1967. The year of *Sgt Pepper* also saw the world's first successful rock-concert extravaganza – the *Monterey International Pop Festival* – as well as the birth of Jann Wenner's *Rolling Stone* magazine, which ushered in the era of serious rock criticism. With such acts as Jimi Hendrix and Frank Zappa's Mothers of Invention pushing the creative envelope, rock'n'roll was no longer considered the exclusive domain of the teeny bopper but a mature, complex genre. And, as record executives were beginning to find out, it was one with tremendous financial potential.

All of these factors gave rise to the methodical approach to record-making that would define the waning years of the 1960s and beyond. (Not surprisingly, it also had a profound impact on the number of albums produced each year: after releasing a total of 14 U.S. albums during the period from 1964 to 1967, the industry's leading maker of product, The Beatles, offered just one collection, *The White Album*, in 1968.)

In the wake of *Sgt Pepper*, pop artists around the world unleashed albums that used conventional instrumentation and studio gadgetry in unconventional ways. On their November 1967 second effort, *Again*, Los Angeles rockers The Buffalo Springfield – the first major group to sport a three-guitar line-up – unveiled a staggering array of acoustic and electric-guitar tracks, leads, and colorations that would help shape an entire nation of studio accompaniment in the years that followed. Up the coast in San Francisco, Moby Grape, yet another three-guitar

Continued on page 96

■ *Main picture: The Beatles perform 'All You Need Is Love' as part of* **Our World,** *the first ever satellite-linked television broadcast, at Abbey Road Studios on June 25th 1967, three weeks after the release of* **Sgt Pepper.** *Below: (left to right) manager Brian Epstein, producer George Martin, and engineer Richard Lush look on from the control room.*

Continued from page 94

outfit, delivered their self-titled Columbia debut, a brilliant collection of expertly crafted songs and choice guitar work. In sharp contrast to the silly self-consciousness of the era, The Who's late-December release, *The Who Sell Out*, celebrated the charmingly crass commercialism that was and still is pop radio, featuring original radio jingles and capped by 'I Can See For Miles,' the band's first foray into the U.S. Top Ten.

Not to be outdone were The Grateful Dead, the most notorious band among 1967's psychedelic crowd. Signing with Warner Brothers in 1967, the band insisted on a clause that allowed them as much studio time as they felt necessary to complete a recording project. The unfettered access gave The Dead the opportunity to learn first hand the machinations of a modern studio, but it was an expensive lesson.

In 1968 the band issued *Anthem Of The Sun*, an ambitious mix of live and studio tracks – most averaging around ten minutes in length – that featured experimental sound montages and quirky instrumentation. The Grateful Dead continued their overdubbing exploits on their next effort, *Aoxomoxoa*, this time with the help of a 16-track machine. With neither album selling well outside of the group's San Franciscan fan base, The Dead's total tab for *Anthem Of The Sun* and *Aoxomoxoa* reached nearly $200,000. By that time psychedelia, The Grateful Dead's natural musical home, was already a waning force. New arrivals like The Beatles' *White Album* and The Rolling Stones' *Beggars Banquet* signaled the coming of a more acoustic, song-based pop format. By the end of 1969 the message from Warner Brothers' top brass was unequivocal: the band's next album had better be cheap – and good.

Standing on the sidelines during this period of technological upheaval was Bob Dylan, who'd spent the greater part of 1967 holed up in Woodstock, New York, following a motorcycle accident a year earlier. For Dylan, the overly meticulous trend in record-making was anathema. A noted technophobe, Dylan frequently recorded entire albums in a week or less, and had little use for conventional studio methods. "A Dylan session was completely different," remarks Columbia engineer Frank Laico. "For one thing, Dylan wanted everyone close together – in fact, he wanted to be on top of the drums, which was unique! That was OK – in fact, I never liked it in later years when the bands would be spread apart, to the point that the different players were situated in separate rooms. What's the point?"

"I didn't know how to record the way other people were recording and I didn't want to," Dylan later observed. "The Beatles had just released *Sgt Pepper*, which I didn't like at all. I thought it was a very indulgent album, though the songs on it were real good. I didn't think all that production was necessary because The Beatles had never done that before."

When he eventually returned to the studio to schedule a series of recording sessions in the waning days of 1967, Dylan knew exactly what he wanted: an album that was the diametric opposite of the industry's accepted standard of the time. "Every artist in the world was in the studio trying to make the biggest-sounding record they possibly could," recalled Dylan's producer, Bob Johnston. "So what does Dylan do? He comes to Nashville and tells me he wants to record with a bass, drum, and guitar."

It took Dylan and his Nashville cats all of three days to nail down *John Wesley Harding* (1968), a collection of sparse, acoustic songs that was as majestic for its simplicity as any multitrack manifesto. "We went in and knocked 'em out like demos," remembers session drummer Kenny Buttrey. "It seemed to be the rougher the better. Dylan would hear a mistake and laugh a little bit to himself as if to say, 'Great man, that's just great. Just what I'm looking for.' . . . He knew everything and knew exactly what he wanted."

Coming just months after *Sgt Pepper*, *John Wesley Harding* signaled an entirely new direction in pop music – and, for many, a complete repudiation of obsessive multitracking. Following Dylan's lead, over the next several years groups such as The Grateful Dead, The Band, and Crosby, Stills, Nash & Young helped launch a spirited back-to-basics trend, and, by the start of the 1970s, an unprecedented revolution in acoustic-based music.

Continued from page 93

he explained. "One was about the Guinness heir who killed himself in a car. On the next page was a story about 4,000 holes in the streets of Blackburn. Paul contributed the beautiful little lick 'I'd love to turn you on.'" It's common knowledge, too, that a Victorian circus poster provided the lyrics for 'Being For The Benefit Of Mr Kite;' that 'Lovely Rita' was inspired by a real encounter with a female traffic warden; and that Lennon regarded 'Good Morning Good Morning' as "a throwaway, a piece of garbage."

What isn't always appreciated, however, is the context in which *Sgt Pepper* was being made. While The Beatles were undeniably in the vanguard of psychedelia, they were certainly not blazing that path alone. To name just a couple of others, there were The Byrds in Los Angeles, Jefferson Airplane in San Francisco, both of whom were pushing back the frontiers musically, and there's no doubt that McCartney in particular kept himself well abreast of what those transatlantic innovators were up to.

However, back in London, Pink Floyd were actually in Abbey Road Studios working on their debut album, *Piper At The Gates Of Dawn*, at precisely the same time as The Beatles were making *Sgt Pepper*.

On learning that they were next door, Paul, George, and Ringo dropped in to say hello, and Floyd's co-manager, Andrew King, remembers the visit. "The Beatles came through to have a look at us. McCartney, dressed in a loud, yellow-checked overcoat, was very friendly and encouraging, but we also went through and saw them mixing 'Lovely Rita.' We didn't stay long, though, because the atmosphere was, well, it was a very bad vibe in there." King's partner, Peter Jenner, has noted: "I'm sure The Beatles were copying what we were doing, just as we were copying what we were hearing down the corridor."

Elsewhere in Abbey Road, The Pretty Things were in the early stages of recording tracks for their rock-opera, *S.F. Sorrow*. "There really was no sense of competition," states Pretties' guitarist Dick Taylor. "Lennon was always very supportive, and I seem to remember we borrowed Ringo's snare drum at one point. We all shared an interest in experimenting with sound and it wasn't about rivalry."

One major advantage that The Beatles had over bands such as Pink Floyd or The Pretty Things was the size of their budget. Depending on whose figures you choose to accept, recording *Sgt Pepper* cost between $60,000 and $240,000 (between £25,000 and £100,000 at 1967 rates of exchange), either of which were staggering amounts in those days. And, naturally, the most extravagant album in rock history to date would have to be clad in the most extravagant cover.

On March 30th The Beatles came together in artist Peter Blake's Chelsea studio to have their picture taken for the cover. Work on the revolutionary design, an ambitious life-sized collage of The Beatles' heroes, had been going on for some time before their presence in the studio was required. Brian Epstein's personal assistant, Wendy Hanson, had spent an entire week doing nothing but obtaining clearances from celebrities who were to be included. "I spent many hours and pounds on calls to the States. Fred Astaire was very sweet; Shirley Temple wanted to hear the record first; I got on famously with Marlon Brando, but Mae West wanted to know what she would be doing in a Lonely Hearts' Club."

Even though Blake only charged a surprisingly reasonable £200 for his work – cheap for an artist of his stature – he has commented: "The Beatles were at their absolute peak. If we decided to do something, they could go to EMI and say, 'This is what we want to do.' If they said 'No,' then EMI wouldn't get the record. They were very powerful, so it meant that we could break through lots of barriers."

Part of the cover's impact derives from the fact that it is a gatefold sleeve, but Blake claims that this was a pragmatic rather than an artistic decision. "It was going to be a double album," he says. "It ended up as only one record, but it was a double-sleeve. They thought that there would be more material but there wasn't enough for two records, so then we compiled this sheet of things you could cut out, the Sergeant's stripes and the like, for inclusion in one of the pockets."

Released on June 1st 1967, *Sgt Pepper* soared to Number One in the albums chart two days later, a slot it held for 22 weeks, selling so well that it even turned up in the singles chart at Number 21.

band's mentally ill leader, Syd Barrett. "Working with Syd was sheer hell," says EMI engineer Norman Smith. "I don't think I left a single Floyd session without a splitting headache. Syd never seemed to have any enthusiasm for anything. He would be singing a song and I'd call him into the control room to give a few instructions, then he'd go back out and not even sing the first part the same, let alone the bit I'd been talking about."

Andrew King seemed to see a different side to Barrett. "It was the most intensely creative time of Syd's life. He was not like a dominant band leader so much as he was Hale-Bopp [comet] and they were dragged along in the tail. I remember watching him mixing on a 4-track desk and he played it like it was an instrument."

Whichever version is true, *Piper At The Gates Of Dawn* – its name drawn from a chapter title in Kenneth Grahame's book *The Wind In The Willows* – was destined to prove a one-off, a completely unique listening experience. Barrett's songs are peopled by dwarves,

Piper At The Gates Of Dawn Pink Floyd

Not issued in the U.S.A. / Columbia SCX 6157 (U.K.)
Released August 1967

At the same time as The Beatles were recording *Sgt Pepper*, their Abbey Road neighbors, Pink Floyd, were in the process of recording their first album, *Piper At The Gates Of Dawn*.

Riding on the success of their first major hit single, 'See Emily Play,' the band had moved into Studio 3 at Abbey Road to work on the album, which would prove to be the first and last flowering of the genius of the

scarecrows, fairies, and weird felines, drifting through fantastical landscapes conjured up by a veritable sonic kaleidoscope of strange electronic noises, stuttering guitar rhythms and curiously looping drum patterns.

Peter Jenner has, however, pointed out that the carefully constructed songs on the album bear very little resemblance to what Pink Floyd did on stage, because: "If we'd put out what we were playing live, it wouldn't have sold at all." Jenner states that only the extended spacey instrumental, 'Interstellar Overdrive,' resembled a live Floyd track. "They played it twice," he says, "one version recorded straight on top of the other. They double-tracked the whole track. Why? Well it sounds pretty weird doesn't it? That big sound and all those hammering drums."

Their Satanic Majesties Request
The Rolling Stones

London 2 (U.S.A.) / Decca TXS103 (U.K.)
Released December 1967

Nudged along by *Sgt Pepper* and *Piper At The Gates Of Dawn*, even The Rolling Stones decided to go trippy on their next album, *Their Satanic Majesties Request*, but the results were, to say the least, patchy.

The best tracks were lavishly produced, convincingly weird-sounding songs about cosmic journeys, alienation, and the future, with more than a hint of Pink Floyd in their ever-shifting electronic landscapes, but guitarist Keith Richards has since admitted: "I liked a few songs, like '2,000 Light Years,' 'Citadel,' and 'She's A Rainbow' but, basically, I thought the album was a load of crap."

A harsh judgment, perhaps, but it certainly didn't feel like a real Stones album. Not even its $25,000 (£10,000) state-of-the-art three-dimensional cover image – clearly intended to out-weird *Sgt Pepper* – could dispel the uncomfortable feeling that The Stones had merely seen a bandwagon passing and were struggling to clamber aboard.

1968

Greatest Hits **Diana Ross And The Supremes**

Motown 663 (U.S.A.) / STML 11063 (U.K.)
Released January 1968

The Four Tops Greatest Hits **The Four Tops**

Motown 662 (U.S.A.) / STML 11061 (U.K.)
Released January 1968

The Hollies Greatest Hits **The Hollies**

Epic 32061 (U.S.A.) / Parlophone PCS 7057 (U.K.)
Released August 1968

**Record-players in the 1960s had mechanical devices for stacking
45s above the turntable. After the first had played, the arm would
swing back out from the run-off groove, the next 45 dropped on
to the previous disk, and the needle lowered on to the run-in edge
to play it.**

Mostly it worked, though by the fourth
or fifth single the needle often looked
like it was on a roller-coaster, as 45s
were not perfectly flat; sometimes
the needle fell off and hit the edge of
the turntable with a ghastly noise.

But there was another way to hear a
run of favorite singles: the greatest-
hits album.

Here was a winning concept that
pleased everyone. The listener got all
the hits on a single LP if they didn't
buy them first time out on singles, and those who already had copies got a
new pressing to replace crackling 45s – and the record companies had no
qualms about persuading the public to purchase the same song twice.
These albums also brought these songs to an audience too young to buy
the singles on their first release. And, as some acts in that chart-focused
decade never made memorable albums, it is the greatest-hits compilation
that best represents their music. Nowhere is this truer than with Motown.

As much as any white rock or pop acts, the team of writers, sessioneers,
and performers in Detroit helped Motown typify the sounds of the 1960s. In
its golden era the label permanently occupied large areas of the Top 20.
Berry Gordy's shrewd business sense meant it wasn't long before Motown
capitalized on the greatest-hits concept, with U.S.-released collections by
Marvin Gaye (1964 and 1967), Mary Wells (1964), The
Miracles (1965), The Marvelettes (1966), and The
Temptations (1966). Those by The Four Tops and
The Supremes were issued in the U.K. on the Tamla
Motown label in 1968 and both went to Number One.

sell out big venues several nights consecutively, notably the Royal Albert Hall in London. Like The Supremes, it was Holland-Dozier-Holland who were the driving force behind their success, and when the songwriting trio left Motown in 1968 The Tops suffered.

The greatest-hits format was used by many labels. The Rolling Stones put out *Big Hits: High Tide And Green Grass* in 1966, and The Hollies had a career-boost with their U.K.-only collection in 1968. All bar one of the tracks on The Hollies' album – among them 'Just One Look,' 'Bus Stop,' and 'Carrie Anne' – had been U.K. Top Ten hits over a five-year period, and featured the vocal harmonies of Allan Clarke and Graham Nash, the latter of whom later formed a supergroup trio with David Crosby and Stephen Stills. The U.S. edition of *The Hollies Greatest Hits*, issued in 1973, adds the 1969 hit 'He Ain't Heavy, He's My Brother.'

There were also greatest-hits miscellanies that drew on a range of artists on a single label. Motown issued no fewer than 11 volumes of *16 Big Hits* between 1963 and 1969 before replacing it with the 'Motown Chartbusters' series. Numbers One to Five (1970–1) make a brilliant introduction to the label, while numbers Three and Four, with their metallic colors, are among the most effective sleeve-art designs of their era.

For much of the 1960s The Supremes were Motown's flagship act, rivaling The Beatles, The Beach Boys, and Elvis in popularity. Initially overshadowed by The Marvelettes, everything changed when they hooked up with songwriting team Holland-Dozier-Holland for their first Number One, the foot-stamping 'Where Did Our Love Go.' Ten of the 12 tracks on Diana Ross And The Supremes' *Greatest Hits* were U.S. Number Ones, and the entire record was written by Holland-Dozier-Holland. By 1967 The Supremes were charting with the lyrically daring 'Love Child' and 'Reflections,' a track musically sophisticated enough to rival Brian Wilson.

The Supremes now tend to be assessed in the light of Diana Ross's subsequent solo career, but that shouldn't detract from their impact at the time. The popularity of Motown with white audiences may be said to have helped to shift racial attitudes in the U.S.A. and the U.K. However, in November 1968 The Supremes found themselves on a British Royal Command Performance bill with The Black And White Minstrels, a popular British television cabaret act of the time that featured blacked-up white men and white women. Ross protested and added a brief eulogy for Martin Luther King – who had been assassinated in April that year – that was edited out of the television broadcast. The next day she found herself answering press criticism of her 'controversial' behavior.

When 'Baby I Need Your Loving' hit the charts in 1964 The Four Tops had been together for ten years. It was 'I Can't Help Myself' (1965) where they really started to sound like a 'Hitsville' act, and by the mid 1960s they were able to

1968

At Folsom Prison
Johnny Cash

Columbia CS-9639 (U.S.A.) / CBS 63308 (U.K.)
Released March 1968

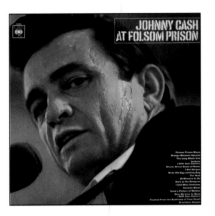

By January 1968 the U.S.A. was experiencing a major wave of social and political upheaval. The war in Vietnam had boiled over, hastening the demise of President Lyndon Johnson's administration and creating a firestorm of political tension throughout the country.

As rock music increasingly became the voice of dissent, Nashville, the acknowledged seat of social conservatism in music, stood in sharp contrast with its tales of drinking, divorce, and redneck mayhem.

Few knew about the raucous side of life better than Johnny Cash, who'd had his share of booze, pills, and bruises during his first dozen years in the business. Not surprisingly, some of Cash's most ardent fans were the U.S.A.'s most dangerous criminals, and for years Cash had performed free concerts at high-security prisons throughout California. Cash was still on the jail trail in 1967 when he approached his label, Columbia, with the idea of cutting a live date from inside one such correctional facility. After convincing label heads that a concert before convicts was worth a shot, on January 13th 1968 producer Bob Johnston procured a pair of 4-track recorders and headed out to Folsom Prison, the hardball correctional facility located 100 miles east of San Francisco. There he was joined by Cash along with backing band The Tennessee Three – guitarist Luther Perkins, bassist Marshall Grant, and drummer W.S. Holland – plus vocalists The Statler Brothers, as well as Cash's wife-to-be, June Carter.

It would be a gig like no other. Performing before a crowd of 2,000 potentially violent inmates inside a thunderously reverberant prison cafeteria with armed guards taking aim from the catwalks overhead, Cash, clad in characteristic black, never lets up, delivering classic renditions of 'Jackson' (a duet with Carter), '25 Minutes To Go' (a darkly humorous tale of a convict's final moments before his execution), as well as the ballad 'Green, Green Grass Of Home' with unparalleled conviction. But the clincher was 'Folsom Prison Blues,' originally a hit for Cash on the C&W chart in 1956, early in his career. To this day, the knowing cheer that follows the line "I shot a man in Reno, just to watch him die" remains one of the most eerie moments in live recording.

Issued on March 1st – the same day Cash and Carter were wed – *At Folsom Prison* became an instant success, going gold by year's end and achieving multiplatinum status in 2003. On the heels of the crossover smash hit of the re-released 'Folsom Prison Blues' single – a C&W chart Number One and Number 32 in the pop chart – record companies by the score began hauling tape machines in and out of correctional facilities in order to capitalize on the trend. Among the many artists who went from working the bar crowd to the behind-bars crowd were Big Mama Thornton, B.B. King, and, of course, The Man In Black himself, who repeated his feat a year later with the million-selling 'A Boy Named Sue,' recorded live at San Quentin Prison, California.

Sweetheart Of The Rodeo **The Byrds**

Columbia CS 9670 (U.S.A.) / CBS 63353 (U.K.)
Released August 1968

Having pioneered the psychedelic movement in music in 1966 with their album *Fifth Dimension*, The Byrds – along with Bob Dylan and The Band – were among the first to react against it.

Sweetheart Of The Rodeo marked a return to the folksy roots of American music, to simple melodies, sweet close-harmony vocals, and comprehensible lyrics – much like Dylan's *John Wesley Harding* and The Band's *Music From Big Pink* (both also 1968).

When The Byrds assembled to begin recording in Nashville during March 1968 they were in a state of disarray, having lately replaced two founder members – drummer Michael Clarke and singer-songwriter David Crosby – with Kevin Kelley and Gram Parsons. It was Parsons, with his roots in country and soul, who was most responsible for The Byrds' whole-hearted plunge into music formerly associated with rednecks and truck drivers.

As well as guitarist Clarence White, who would later join The Byrds full-time, the band was augmented in Nashville by a squad of the finest session players money could buy, including John Hartford on banjo, Earl Ball on piano, Roy Huskey on bass, and, most significantly, Lloyd Green and Jaydee Maness on pedal-steel guitars. It was the prominence of the slippery quicksilver swooping and soaring of those guitars that made *Sweetheart* sound unlike any album previously marketed at rock fans. With hindsight, of course, it's easy to see country rock as a logical development for a band whose bass player, Chris Hillman, had earned his chops in bluegrass bands, and whose leader, Roger McGuinn, had served his time as a Greenwich Village folkie. At the time, however, it didn't seem that way. Country was seen as a reactionary right-wing music, whereas rock tended to be left wing and radical, so a switch from one to the other was not just a bold move, it was potentially career-busting.

What saved the project was the sincerity The Byrds brought to the album, playing it absolutely straight – except perhaps for McGuinn's exaggerated dopey-hick vocal on 'The Christian Life' – and picking a selection of great songs that straddled folk, soul, and country, alongside a couple of fine Parsons originals and two recent Dylan songs.

A certain amount of mystery still shrouds McGuinn's decision to remove Parsons's lead vocals from several cuts, replacing them with his own. Parsons's former producer, Lee Hazlewood, started the problems by threatening to sue because he still had him under contract, but there's also little doubt that McGuinn was unhappy to have Parsons's voice dominating the album. For one thing, though Parsons's singing was always deeply emotional, it wasn't always strictly in tune; for another, The Byrds had been McGuinn's band from the start, and he wasn't about to accept being relegated to the role of back-up singer.

Though critics received the album warmly, the public's confusion about the new direction meant that *Sweetheart* was not a big seller. Nevertheless, a year later The Beatles would be singing 'Get Back,' and country rock would emerge as a powerful new force in the early 1970s when The Eagles took The Byrds' new direction to its logical conclusion.

The Circle Game **Tom Rush**

Elektra EKL 4018 (mono) / EKS 74018 (stereo) (U.S.A. & U.K.)
Released May 1968

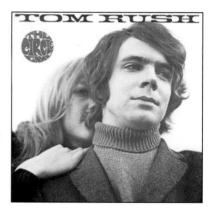

Tom Rush started his career as one of many acoustic singer-songwriters thrown up by the folk boom of the early 1960s.

And, like many of those performers, he, too, later went 'electric,' with a 1966 album, *Take a Little Walk With Me*, which had one electric side (mainly cover versions of old 1950s' rock'n'roll songs) and one acoustic side.

Rush's next album, *The Circle Game*, didn't appear for another two years, by the standards of the time an unusually long gap between releases. With its subtle orchestrations, impeccable musicianship, and consistently strong material, *The Circle Game* marked a step forward, not only for Rush but the singer-songwriter movement in general. Rush's unaffected, almost casual vocal delivery and the pervading atmosphere of confessional intimacy was a forerunner of later, more popular albums by the likes of Jackson Browne, James Taylor, and Joni Mitchell. Indeed, Rush did much to bring these three artists to public attention by covering songs of theirs on *The Circle Game*

before any of them had released albums of their own. Rush modestly disavows any special foresight on his part, saying in *Rolling Stone* magazine in 1975: "If I hadn't done it, those people would have gotten recorded anyway. They were just too good to go unnoticed."

Rush himself contributed just two songs to *The Circle Game*: the first, a neat guitar instrumental called 'Rockport Sunday,' segues into the album's closing song, 'No Regrets.' The most enduring of Rush's compositions, it was later a hit single for both The Walker Brothers and Midge Ure.

1968

Days Of Future Passed **Moody Blues**

London 18012 (U.S.A.) / Deram SML 707 (U.K.)
Released January 1968

The Who Sell Out **The Who**

Decca DL4950 (U.S.A.) / Track 613002 (U.K.)
Released January 1968

Ogden's Nut Gone Flake **The Small Faces**

Immediate Z1252008 (U.S.A.) / IMSP 012 (U.K.)
Released June 1968

The Kinks Are The Village Green Preservation Society **The Kinks**

Reprise 6327 (U.S.A.) / Pye NSPL 18233 (U.K.)
Released November 1968

S.F. Sorrow **The Pretty Things**

Rare Earth 506 (U.S.A.) / Columbia SCX6306 (U.K.)
Released December 1968

The Beatles' *Sgt Pepper* raised the stakes for rock groups who wanted to be seen as important in the grander scheme of things.

As the counter-culture got into its stride, a number of bands began to realize that LPs could be more than a miscellany of ten songs. One answer to this was the so-called concept album. The concept album could satisfy creative ambition, garner publicity, and sell records, all at once. A number of such albums appeared in 1968, as bands tried to catch up with The Beatles, though how substantial or convincing the concept was varied from record to record.

The Moody Blues were best known for their hit 'Go Now,' but with the departure of vocalist Denny Laine they needed a new musical direction.

Their record company, Decca, asked them to record Dvořak's *New World Symphony* with an orchestra for a demonstration record to show off the label's new 'Deramic' sound. Instead, the band ended up writing *Days Of Future Passed*, a song-sequence that went from dawn to midnight. Kitted out in a boldly colored pop-art sleeve, it launched The Moodies' career as an albums band and managed several hits, notably the wildly romantic 'Nights In White Satin.' *Days* was well-recorded for its time, though much of the orchestration is MOR, with the 'morning music' resembling the busy-busy scores once featured on travel documentaries. 'Dawn Is A Feeling' is the highlight of the first side. Side Two is more engaging, having 'Nights' and 'Tuesday Afternoon,' the latter a U.S. hit and glorious Mellotron-driven pop for the 'Summer Of Love.'

Between 1964 and 1968 The Who released singles that were among the hardest rock of the time, musically powerful and lyrically adventurous, as Pete Townshend showed himself to be a courageous chronicler of the teenage experience. *The Who Sell Out* is a sequence of songs linked by Radio London jingles and pastiche commercials, as heard on 1960s' British pirate radio. It had one hit single, 'I Can See For Miles' – the band's first U.S. Top Ten hit – and several songs that anticipated the themes and procedures of The Who's 1969 rock-opera, *Tommy*.

A few months later in the year The Small Faces released *Ogden's Nut Gone Flake*, its famous circular sleeve based on an Edwardian tobacco tin. Side One was a miscellany of songs that included the hit 'Lazy Sunday' and the powerful 'Afterglow.' The second side was comprised of six songs that told the story of Happiness Stan, the boy who searched for the missing half of the moon. Between tracks there were short spoken links by British comedian Stanley Unwin, renowned for his ability to re-order the English language into hilarious but strangely comprehensible gobbledygook.

Like The Who, by 1968 The Kinks were looking for a new direction after enjoying a run of hits that included such classic songs as 'You Really Got Me' and 'Waterloo Sunset.' The Kinks were sidelined musically in 1967–8 when beat-pop gave way to heavy blues and psychedelia, so they adjusted by becoming an albums band. *The Kinks Are The Village Green Preservation Society* looked back on and celebrated the culture of a pre-1960s England that was already receding fast. Failing to chart in either the U.S.A. or the U.K., the LP was described by singer-songwriter

■ *Main picture: The Pretty Things. Far left: The Moody Blues. Above left: The Small Faces. Below left: The Kinks.*

Ray Davies as "the most acclaimed flop of all time," but it has since established itself as an enduringly eccentric evocation of British life.

Another important concept album of the same period is The Pretty Things' *S.F. Sorrow*. It is now recognized as the first rock-opera, but, as guitarist Dick Taylor remembers, when recording began, that wasn't the plan.

"We'd recorded two tracks, 'Bracelets Of Fingers' and 'I See You' before the concept came up." From the start, though, it had been about experimentation: "I'd bought a bagpipe chanter in a junkshop, which turned out to be in the right key for the tooty bits in 'Bracelets Of Fingers.'"

Once the rock-opera concept emerged, vocalist Phil May supplied a plot based on a short story he'd written about World War II, featuring a central character who was an amalgam of May himself and his foster father, Charlie.

The songs follow this composite, S.F. Sorrow, from birth to death, with love, work, war, and burning airship disasters in between, and the story-telling element lent itself naturally to the inclusion of unusual sounds to represent events in Sorrow's life. "Our basic principle," says Taylor, "was that if it made a noise we would bring it to the studio, and find a way to incorporate it into a track." The pegs and strings from an old upright piano, for example, were scavenged to create a home-made zither which provided eerie twanging sounds on 'Death.'

The rock-opera idea was so new that EMI found it difficult to market the album, but the press recognized it as a milestone. A few months later, however, The Who stole much of The Pretties' thunder when they unveiled *Tommy*.

NBC Special
Elvis Presley

RCA LSP4088 (U.S.A.) / RCA RD8011 (U.K.)
Released December 1968

The erstwhile King Of Rock'n'Roll rode out the British Invasion, psychedelia, and all of the other movements in 1960s pop by starring in a series of lame movies.

In the process he came to bear an increasing resemblance to the bland performers he had swept away in 1956, becoming more safe MOR entertainer than focus of teenage rebellion. But in 1968 he slimmed down, poured himself into a black leather suit, and re-launched himself as a rock star, stepping out in front of an audience for the first time in years on a live televised concert, and he rarely looked or sounded better.

The combination of nerves and excitement re-created in Presley the fizzing kinetic energy of his youth. He delivered a masterful performance throughout, particularly during the section with guitarist Scotty Moore and drummer DJ Fontana, who had worked with him on his seminal material in the 1950s. The three old friends sat close to the studio audience in a television producer's contrivance of an improvised jam session, Elvis strumming electric guitar, irrepressible and in great voice.

Recorded at NBC Studios and Western Recorders, Burbank, California, in June 1968 but not broadcast or released until December of that year, the *NBC Special* album – later reissued as *TV Special* – rejuvenated Presley, propelling him into the second great phase of his career. The following year he recorded his best studio album since the 1950s, *From Elvis in Memphis*, and scored with the classic hit singles 'Suspicious Minds' and 'In The Ghetto.'

Presley would never hit these heights again. Soon he was drawn into a money-spinning routine of Las Vegas cabaret seasons, precipitating a slow decline and that tragic early death.

1968

1968

Astral Weeks
Van Morrison

Warner Bros WS1768 (U.S.A.) / K46024 (U.K.)
Released November 1968

Astral Weeks is frequently cited as one of the great albums of popular music, as well as a highpoint of Van Morrison's career. Like Miles Davis's Kind Of Blue, the spontaneity and speed of its recording is part of its legend.

Van Morrison came to fame as the singer with Northern Irish band Them on hits such as 'Baby Please Don't Go' and 'Here Comes The Night.' After going solo Morrison had a hit with 'Brown-Eyed Girl.' Warner Brothers signed him in early 1968, and Astral Weeks was his first release on the label. Morrison was provided with a select group of jazz musicians, including guitarist Jay Berliner, Richard Davis on double bass – who had worked with Miles Davis – and Modern Jazz Quartet drummer Connie Kay, plus horn player John Payne, and percussionist Warren Smith Jr. Lewis Merenstein produced, and Louis Fallon took care of some aspects of the arrangements.

The first session was held at Century Sound Studios on West 52nd Street in New York on September 25th 1968. Work began at 7pm, and the musicians made rapid progress – for the jazz musicians the chord sequences were straightforward and repetitive. Arriving around 9pm meant Berliner missed being on 'Cyprus Avenue' and 'Madame George.' The first session also saw 'Beside You' and 'Astral Weeks' completed; 'Beside You' had previously been recorded for the Bang label.

The following morning there was an aborted session, so the remaining songs were recorded on October 15th. 'Slim Slow Slider' ran to over 13 minutes as an improvisation but was trimmed back to 3 minutes 20 seconds for the record. The first four songs were grouped by producer Lewis Merenstein under the phrase 'In The Beginning,' and the second side was titled 'Afterwards,' thus hinting at some sort of hidden narrative to the songs.

It is unfortunate that the words were not printed on the sleeve, since they are more like extended poems than lyrics, full of images and phrases that tease and provoke the imagination. The tunes are love songs dominated by nostalgia for youth, love, and the desire for rebirth. Such numbers as 'Cyprus Avenue' are located in personal memories of childhood, but most people will have similar memories attached to wherever they grew up, giving this song, as with many others on the album, a universal appeal. Much of the lyrical content was written by instinct: Morrison described 'Madame George' as "just a stream-of-consciousness thing, as is 'Cyprus Avenue.' Both those songs came right out. I didn't even think about what I was writing. There are some things that you write that just come out all at once, and there's other things that you think about and consider where you'll put each bit."

Morrison described Astral Weeks as "probably the most spiritually lyrical album I've ever done." 'Madame George' includes a significant reference to "child-like vision," and the album's very title suggests the spiritual dimension, 'astral' being a term that came from the counter-culture's metaphysical lexicon, most commonly associated with the phrases 'astral projection,' an out-of-body experience, and 'astral plane,' a Theosophical concept of a dimension beyond the material world ruled by emotion and imagination. The duration of an 'astral week' could not be measured by earthly clocks, and its quality would transcend the mundane.

The music is introspective, relatively free-form, and atmospheric, with diluted elements of folk, blues, gospel, and rock. The songs themselves depart from the obvious demarcations of verses, choruses, and bridges, to stretch out past the five-minute mark in five of the eight tracks. The music uses an instrumentation that would have struck its audience as unusual and sophisticated. There is light percussion instead of the expected big beat and the double bass lends a jazzy feel. Other sounds include vibraphone, strings, flute, acoustic guitars, soprano saxophone, and, on 'Cyprus Avenue,' a harpsichord.

It seems that much of the time the players were allowed to come up with their own parts. This gives the performances a certain spontaneity at the same time as it makes the tracks ramble. Guitarist Jay Berliner said: "I played a lot of classical guitar on those sessions and it was very unusual to play classical guitar in that context. What stood out in my mind was the fact that he allowed us to stretch out. We were used to playing to charts, but Van just played us the songs on his guitar and then told us to go ahead and play exactly what we felt." This means that though the album was recorded very quickly, the songs were not literally improvised.

If the album has a weakness it is the vocal melodies. After only a couple of tracks it is evident that Morrison's tunes are largely taken from a small number of vocal tricks and phrases. Essentially, he sings much the same melody throughout: it is certainly distinctive, but could tend to monotony once this is noticed. (The exception is 'The Way Young Lovers Do,' which does achieve greater melodic distinction.) Morrison's lack of vibrato can also seem rather out of place and somewhat harsh at times for the material, particularly at the end of 'Beside You.'

Astral Weeks didn't sell well on first release – a figure of 20,000 has been mentioned – and Morrison understood he needed to record something thereafter that would have more immediacy and a wider appeal, which resulted in the R&B of Moondance (1970). Nevertheless, Astral Weeks continues to find new listeners and remains a record that, in its own way, suggested new expressive possibilities for the album.

Electric Ladyland
Jimi Hendrix

Reprise 2R6307 (U.S.A.) / Track 2657001 (U.K.)
Released October 1968

Jimi Hendrix's third studio album was a double vinyl, and the last he recorded with The Experience. One of the all-time great rock albums, *Electric Ladyland* mixes blues, rock, psychedelia, soul, jazz, and proto-funk in highly imaginative ways. It topped the U.S. chart and provided four hit singles.

As a double, with the extended nature of some of the individual songs, *Electric Ladyland* demonstrated Hendrix's desire to expand his music beyond the restrictive verse-chorus limits of the single. Some early tracks were cut in London, others at the Record Plant in New York in spring of 1968. His restless ambition led to protracted sessions and many re-recordings in pursuit of his vision. Manager Chas Chandler perceived this as self-indulgence and lack of focus, and he quit.

Hangers-on in the studio – 'electric lady' was a Hendrix term for groupie – didn't help. Relationships between the band members – especially between Hendrix and bassist Noel Redding – were at an all-time low, to the extent that some of the bass parts were not played by Redding at all, and his one song on the album, 'Little Miss Strange,' is almost as dwarfed by its surroundings as is 'Sloop John B' on *Pet Sounds*. Engineer Eddie Kramer helped Hendrix by supplying effects such as phasing and varispeeding of the tape. Guest musicians included Buddy Miles and Al Kooper, as well as Chris Wood, Dave Mason, and Stevie Winwood of Traffic.

Here was a rock record where there seemed to be no boundaries: on 'Burning Of The Midnight Lamp' Hendrix pitted harpsichord against wah-wah Fender Stratocaster; 'Rainy Day' was a one-chord jazz-inspired vamp where Hendrix dueled with saxophone player Freddie Smith as though modal jazz was back in fashion. While the cover of Earl King's 'Come On' nodded to the traditional excitement of blues rock, '1983 (A Merman I Should Turn To Be)' and 'Moon, Turn The Tides . . . Gently Gently Away' were impressionistic science-fiction epics that demanded headphones so you could get lost in their watery world. (It is astonishing to think that Hendrix drew such sounds from a Fender Stratocaster, the same model of guitar Buddy Holly was strumming on 'Peggy Sue' only ten years earlier.) 'Have You Ever Been

To Electric Ladyland?' has the light soul feel of Curtis Mayfield, while by contrast 'Crosstown Traffic' is blistering full-on rock. Like Muhammad Ali, Hendrix could float like a butterfly and sting like a bee. 'House Burning Down' makes extraordinary use of foxtrot rhythm and has an outro with one of Hendrix's most far-out pieces of guitar. It is followed by an audacious and authoritative re-imagining of a Dylan song, 'All Along The Watchtower,' a song that, like 'House Burning Down,' reflected the incendiary atmosphere of the U.S.A. in 1968. The apocalyptic imagery in 'Watchtower' matched the spirit of the year.

There are two arrangements of 'Voodoo Chile,' which had developed from the band playing Muddy Waters's 'Catfish Blues.' One is a slow blues jam, the other an up-tempo rock arrangement that evolved over eight takes and closed the record. This 'Slight Return' version gave Hendrix a posthumous U.K. Number One in 1970.

1968

About The U.K. Sleeve

The gatefold sleeve of the U.K. release of *Electric Ladyland* featured 19 naked women against a dark background. Apparently, the group photos used on the U.S. cover didn't make it to the U.K. in time, leaving the record company's art department to come up with something.

It was every male teenage rock fan's fantasy, but Hendrix himself commented: "I wouldn't have put this picture on the sleeve myself but it wasn't my decision. It's mostly all bullshit." Though Hendrix may not have liked it, it was publicity and it fed the sexual aura about him – it even had to be displayed in record stores in a brown-paper wrapper, as if it was a pornographic magazine. However, as the women were from a variety of racial groups, a cosmopolitan, multiracial world – albeit one of sex – was evoked. Maybe that message could be said to have redeemed, at least in part, its sexism at a time when racial barriers were still strong.

1969

In The Court Of The Crimson King
King Crimson

Atlantic SD8245 (U.S.A.) / Island ILPS 9111 (U.K.)
Released October 1969

In The Court Of The Crimson King was a milestone in the development of the progressive rock that enjoyed considerable success between 1969 and 1975.

'Prog,' as it later became known, was a kind of displacement-activity response to the apparent failure of the 1960s counter-culture: by 1969 the revolution may have been lost, but it could be carried on by artistic means through a music that challenged The Establishment. Philosophical lyrics, complex music, and performer virtuosity all suggested an assault on the citadels of high culture – in the case of *In The Court Of The Crimson King* the sleeve itself featured a 'high art' reference in adapting a picture by the visionary poet and artist William Blake.

King Crimson has had many line-ups over the years. The musicians playing on this album were Robert Fripp (guitar), Mike Giles (drums), Ian McDonald (keyboards), and Greg Lake (bass, later of Emerson, Lake & Palmer). They had made their live debut at the Speakeasy Club in London on April 9th 1969, went on to a residency at the Marquee, and played The Rolling Stones' historic July 5th free concert in London's Hyde Park. By the time *In The Court of The Crimson King* was released, there was a stir about the band, and the album made the U.S. Top 30 and the U.K. Top Five.

In Fripp they had an experimental and cerebral guitarist, and they set themselves against the prevailing back-to-roots and heavy-blues/hard-rock trends, combining folk, classical, jazz, and rock influences into a unique fusion. The songs were multisectioned and often grandiose. The album's highpoint was the scampering guitar-sax riffing on the apocalyptic '21st-Century Schizoid Man,' while such Mellotron ballads as 'I Talk With The Wind' could have featured on a Moody Blues album. The pioneering music here led to the likes of ELP, Genesis, and Yes finding an audience.

Trout Mask Replica
Captain Beefheart And His Magic Band

Straight Records/ Reprise RS 2027 (U.S.A.) / STS1053 (U.K.)
Released November 1969

Uncle Meat
Frank Zappa And The Mothers Of Invention

Bizarre 2024 (U.S.A.) / Transatlantic TRA 197 (U.K.)
Released April 1969 (U.S.A.) / September 1969 (U.K.)

One of the most idiosyncratic albums ever released, *Trout Mask Replica* has been cited as a defining influence on innumerable avant-garde rock acts, but in fact sounds like nothing else ever recorded.

 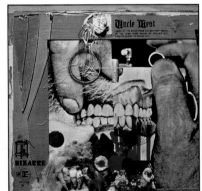

Having made the comparatively straightforward, blues-based *Safe As Milk* and the somewhat more challenging *Strictly Personal*, Captain Beefheart (born Don Van Vliet) signed to his high-school friend Frank Zappa's Straight Records, and promptly wrote, apparently in just nine hours, the 28 songs that would become *Trout Mask Replica*. He then spent the best part of a year perfecting the arrangements of these songs in a rented house in Woodland Hills, California, with what is generally considered to be the seminal line-up of his Magic Band: drummer John 'Drumbo' French, guitarists Bill 'Zoot Horn Rollo' Harkleroad and Jeff 'Antennae Jimmy Semens' Cotton, bassist Mark 'Rockette Morton' Boston, and bass clarinetist Victor 'The Mascara Snake' Fleming.

After this lengthy rehearsal process, the band was able to record the 78-minute double album in one four-and-a-half-hour session. The result is a dense, sprawling work, blending primitive blues and garage rock with the free jazz of Ornette Coleman. The complex rhythms and atonal, dueling guitar lines, as well as Beefheart's gruff vocals and surreal lyrical imagery, proved off-putting to most listeners, though the album reached the Top 30 in the U.K., and has since become a cult favorite.

Earlier that same year, Zappa himself had issued a complex double album with his own band, The Mothers Of Invention. *Uncle Meat* blends the experimental rock of his earlier releases – notably *We're Only In It For The Money* – with the more kinetic side of contemporary composer Steve Reich. The album's focal point is the six-part epic 'King Kong,' a template for much of the jazz rock of the future. Several months later, Zappa released the more concise *Hot Rats*, which featured the unmistakable vocal talents of Captain Beefheart on the track 'Willie The Pimp.'

The Velvet Underground
The Velvet Underground

MGM 4617 (U.S.A.) / CS 8108 (U.K.)
Released March 1969

Having horrified the ruling hippy cadre with their decadent and hedonistic debut album and reduced rock to a minimalist onslaught with their second, The Velvets did a complete volte-face on their third offering.

The naked aggression that had been one of their distinguishing features was now replaced by resignation and despair. The stories in Lou Reed's songs still originated in the gutters of the Big Apple, but the music was delicate, pretty, and restrained. This was largely because John Cale, who had been tussling with Reed for control of the band, had been maneuvered out in late 1968. With Cale's experimental, avant-garde tendencies excised, Reed's songwriting became the core of The Velvets, whose other members were relegated to sidemen rather than the partners they had previously seemed to be.

Reed found Cale's replacement, Doug Yule, easier to dominate, and it is Yule's voice, sounding not unlike a sweeter version of Reed's, that gives much of this album its character. The up-tempo tracks, 'What Goes On' and 'Beginning To See The Light,' though excellent, are comparatively lightweight. The real passion comes through on the slow introspective songs like 'Pale Blue Eyes' – where a threat of violence lurks beneath the song's placid surface – or the despairing 'Jesus,' in which Reed petitions heaven for salvation from a corrupted life.

"Some people might call it Muzak," said Reed at the time, "but I think it can function on both that and the intellectual or artistic levels at the same time." The passage of time has certainly borne out his words.

1969

Crosby, Stills & Nash Crosby, Stills & Nash

Atlantic SD8229 (U.S.A.) / 588189 (U.K.)
Released May 1969

Déjà Vu Crosby, Stills, Nash & Young

Atlantic SD7200 (U.S.A.) / 2401001 (U.K.)
Released March 1970

Through the 1960s, power in the music industry gradually moved from managers, promoters, producers, and songwriters, to the performers themselves.

Many followed The Beatles' example and wrote their own material, and by 1968 a small number of musicians were venerated as rock equivalents of the virtuosos of classical music. If one rock superstar made a band great, the logic ran, surely four superstars would make a group four times greater. Thus was born that triumph of faith over human nature, the supergroup.

In fact, the majority of supergroups comprised of members of other successful bands usually turned out less than the sum of their joint reputations, often staying together – as with Eric Clapton's Blind Faith – for only one album of middling achievement. In Humble Pie's case, the combination was Steve Marriott (ex-Small Faces) and Peter Frampton (ex-Herd) along with Jerry Shirley and Greg Ridley (ex-Spooky Tooth). Their first two albums were strongly influenced by The Band, but the fourth, *Rock On* (1970), was a bestseller. Playing more aggressive rock, for a while, at least, they almost lived up to expectations.

Stephen Stills had an early taste of the supergroup when he played on *Super Session*, a project arranged by keyboard player Al Kooper, where Stills shared guitar duties with Mike Bloomfield of The Paul Butterfield Blues Band. Previously Stills had been a member of Buffalo Springfield along with Neil Young. In 1969, David Crosby (ex-Byrds), Graham Nash (ex-Hollies) sang together with Stills at a party in Los Angeles. Genuinely surprised by how well their voices blended, they got together and recorded *Crosby Stills & Nash*, which made the U.S. Top 30 and U.K. Top Ten. As well as the hit single 'Marrakesh Express,' the album includes the multisectioned 'Suite:

Judy Blue Eyes,' written for Judy Collins, and Crosby's 'Long Time Gone,' inspired by the assassination of Robert F. Kennedy; 'Lady of The Islands' was about Joni Mitchell, and 'Guinevere' was written for Crosby's girlfriend Christine. *Crosby, Stills & Nash* is a classic album of acoustic guitars and vocal harmonizing, with 'Wooden Ships' evoking the Woodstock Nation-era perfectly.

The following year the trio became a quartet with the addition of Neil Young, and they cut *Déjà Vu*, which yielded several hit singles in the U.S.A. An intoxicating mixture of folk rock, open-tuned balladry, and spiky electric workouts, it made CSN&Y the quintessential hippie spokesmen, and it was thought they might become that elusive thing, an 'American Beatles.' However, internal band relationships were soon strained, and with four such accomplished songwriters there was bound to be tension as each contested space for their songs.

Graham Nash looked back on the achievement: "In our first year together, we spent probably eleven months together, 24 hours a day . . . with just a couple of guitars [we] would sit people down and say, 'Listen to this,' and . . . rip off these ten songs, do them brilliantly, and floor people . . . Musically, we ate, drank, and slept together every night. I was with Joni, and that was flowering. Stephen was with Judy Collins, and that was flowering. David was with Christine, and that was flowering. Within a year, it had all changed. My relationship with Joni had turned sour, Stephen had stopped going with Judy, and David's girlfriend Christine had been killed. We were knocked for a loop. We were all romantic people, and our love-lives were in shambles. Then bring in Neil and plug into his insanity, and it's amazing *Déjà Vu* ever got recorded."

Cloud Nine The Temptations

Gordy 939 (U.S.A.) / Motown STML 11109 (U.K.)
Released September 1969

By 1968 Motown was fighting to keep its finger on the pulse.

The U.S.A. was experiencing civil unrest to a soundtrack of acid rock, socially aware pop, and Sly Stone's bad-ass funk. If the label was to remain "the sound of young America" it had to get hip to what was happening. Enter the psychedelic funk and hard rhythms of The Temptations' *Cloud Nine*.

Signed in 1961, The Temptations didn't break into the charts until 'The Way You Do The Things You Do' in 1964, notching up 14 Top Ten singles and 32 Top Ten R&B hits in the U.S.A. over the next eight years. Melvin Franklin provided the bass vocal, the middle range was handled by Paul and Otis Williams, and melodies were usually sung by David Ruffin or Eddie Kendricks. By the time of *Cloud Nine*, however, Ruffin had been replaced by Dennis Edwards.

Producer Norman Whitfield was attuned to rhythm. He said: "When we first did [*Cloud Nine*] with The Temptations, I started studying African rhythms on my own, and I wanted to know how to make a song have as much impact without using a regular 2/4 or 4/4 backbeat. And it turned out to be very successful." He updated the Motown sound with adventurous productions and songs built with a few basic chords and riffs.

One day in 1968 Whitfield came into the studio declaring he wanted to do something fresh and set the musicians jamming. The result was 'Cloud Nine,' with its prominent groove and wah-wah guitar. Lyrically, too, this drugs song was a change from the band's usual themes. *Cloud Nine* led to further recordings by The Temptations in a similar vein, such as 'Psychedelic Shack,' 'Papa Was A Rolling Stone,' and 'Ball Of Confusion.' In the 1970s the album proved a major influence on the development of disco.

■ *Main Picture: (Left to Right) David Crosby, Graham Nash, and Stephen Stills. Left: (Left to Right) Nash, Crosby, Neil Young, and Stills.*

1969

Dusty In Memphis
Dusty Springfield

Atlantic SD8214 (U.S.A.) / Philips SBL7889 (U.K.)
Released March 1969

**The highpoint of Dusty Springfield's career,
Dusty In Memphis is an album of
sophisticated and sexy 'blue-eyed' soul and pop
that matched one of the best singers the U.K. has
ever produced with a classic U.S. session team.**

The 14 hits she had scored thus far, starting in 1963 with 'I Only Want To Be
With You,' were often big Phil Spector-style orchestrations that were perfect
settings for her husky voice. But she had a passion for Motown and R&B, so
it seemed entirely appropriate that she should go to Memphis in September
1968 to record. The experience was not a happy one, however, as there were
disagreements about the songs and working methods in the studio, so she
ended up adding the vocals later at Atlantic Studios in New York.

She later said: "I hated it at first . . . because I couldn't be Aretha Franklin.
If only people like [co-producer] Jerry Wexler could realize what a deflating
thing it is to say 'Otis Redding stood there' or 'that's where Aretha sang.'
Whatever you do, it's not going to be good enough. Added to the natural
critic in me, it was a paralyzing experience. I was someone who had come
from thundering drums and Phil Spector, and I wanted to fill every space. I
didn't understand that the sparseness gave it an atmosphere. When I got
free of that I finally liked it, but it took me a long time. I wouldn't play it for
a year."

She might have thought it wasn't good enough, but 'Son Of A Preacher Man'
is a standout track by any standards, one of her finest vocals, and a
deserved hit. Recent CD issues of the album include extra tracks from the
sessions. Unfortunately it wasn't a chart success on its release, and
signaled the beginning of Springfield's commercial decline.

The Gilded Palace Of Sin
The Flying Burrito Brothers

A&M SP 4175 (U.S.A.) / AMLS 931 (U.K.)
Released April 1969

When Gram Parsons quit The Byrds after their country-rock classic, *Sweetheart Of The Rodeo*, he set about founding The Flying Burrito Brothers, and was soon joined by another disillusioned Byrd, bassist Chris Hillman.

The Gilded Palace Of Sin, however, proved to be much more than just a successor to *Sweetheart*. Whereas The Byrds had retained much of the traditional elegance of country music, The Burritos dragged it kicking and screaming into the rock age, letting rip with distorted steel guitars and studio effects right there alongside the mandolins and honky-tonk pianos.

> "IN THE BURRITOS, WHEN GRAM WAS A COHERENT GUY, WE HAD THIS WONDERFUL VISION. WE WERE SHARING THE HOUSE TOGETHER, HAD BOTH COME OFF A COUPLE OF UNPLEASANT RELATIONSHIPS, AND TOOK SOLACE IN EACH OTHER AS FRIENDS. BUT WE ALSO WROTE SOME GREAT SONGS."
>
> *CHRIS HILLMAN ON HIS RELATIONSHIP WITH GRAM PARSONS*

Parsons and Hillman hit their songwriting peaks with this album, and it is Parsons's impassioned, soulful performances on the tracks 'Hot Burrito No. 1' and 'Hot Burrito No. 2' that are the bedrock of his huge reputation. But the album's real and lasting achievement lies in its fusing of country performance techniques with rock attitude and amplification, thus kicking open the doors of the Nashville establishment for every inspired young cowboy who felt that the people's music had stagnated. Its impact was not felt so much in sales as in the slew of young acts who followed in its wake, from The Eagles to The Nitty Gritty Dirt Band, Commander Cody, and The Ozark Mountain Daredevils.

Back To Basics

At the start of 1969 Paul McCartney had undertaken his 'back-to-the-egg' campaign in a desperate attempt to keep The Beatles from falling apart.

Coming on the heels of the raw-but-revelatory double disk *The Beatles* (aka *The White Album*), McCartney's 'Get Back' project called for a series of completely live tracking sessions reminiscent of the band's earliest studio dates. By that point, however, McCartney's bandmates had little use for anything of the kind, as was later revealed on the dysfunctional *Let It Be* movie and album, released post-breakup in the spring of 1970. Instead, *Abbey Road*, the album that resulted from these sessions and the group's final recorded work, would be unlike anything previously attempted by the band, an entire collection of songs built around an intricate framework of guitar colorations and carefully constructed vocal harmonies, all rampantly overdubbed. Perhaps more than any other Beatles album, *Abbey Road* celebrated studio technology.

Despite their striking differences, the sessions for *Let It Be* and *Abbey Road* were very close in time, with the group setting down a rhythm track for John Lennon's 'She's So Heavy' at Trident Studios in London only weeks after the legendary January 30th 1969 rooftop concert. By then The Beatles were a group teetering on the brink of collapse; that they summoned the strength to return to the sanctity of Abbey Road that summer certainly surprised producer George Martin, who thought he'd seen the last of them.

Utilizing both Studio 2 and Studio 3 the group gradually put together its most polished and intricate work over eight consecutive weeks in July and August. As always, there were new sounds. For Ringo Starr, it was the deadened tom-tom tones (the result of a new set of calf-head skins acquired just prior to the *Abbey Road* sessions) that gave 'Come Together' its distinctive thud. Meanwhile, George Harrison, an early proponent of electronic music, turned his bandmates on to the sounds of the original Moog synthesizer, a prominent component of 'Here Comes The Sun' and 'Maxwell's Silver Hammer.'

Though it wasn't John Lennon's cup of tea – "We put out something slick to preserve the myth," he later claimed – *Abbey Road*'s ornate Side Two neatly predicted the gussied-up production values that would come to define 1970s guitar rock. It mattered little that the outgoing band could only muster a handful of completed songs; to this day, the side-long medley that is the album's crowning achievement sounds like a carefully constructed set of overtures rather than what it really was: a hodgepodge of discarded Lennon & McCartney bits and pieces.

On August 20th 1969 – almost seven years to the day that the band's lead-off single 'Love Me Do' was recorded – The Beatles convened inside Studio 2's control-room to preview a final mix of 'She's So Heavy,' then went their separate ways. "It felt comfortable being back there with George Martin," Ringo remembered years later. "We knew the place; we felt at home. It was like, 'Here we are again, lads.'"

Without a doubt, the most compelling statistic in Fab Four folklore is the sheer speed with which Lennon, McCartney, Harrison, and Starr arrived, conquered, compiled, and then fled, shedding their stylistic skin with each and every album, often many times in a single year. Though they both benefited from and helped inspire the enormous technological advances in the world of recording, The Beatles made their mark largely on the strength of studio ingenuity rather than studio machinery. The day the group called it quits, studios around the globe were already busy installing machines capable of recording upward of 32 individual tracks. The Beatles never made it beyond eight.

"It seems that whenever you get that kind of economy, things do tend to happen in a more creative manner," remarks Beatles historian Mark Lewisohn. "Even in later years, when The Beatles were in the vanguard of a more relaxed and stretched form of recording, there was still an undercurrent of economy in the their work. And I truly believe that they benefited from it."

1969

Led Zeppelin
Led Zeppelin

Atlantic SD8216 (U.S.A.) / 588171 (U.K.)
Released April 1969

Led Zeppelin II
Led Zeppelin

Atlantic SD8236 (U.S.A.) / 588198 (U.K.)
Released October 1969

These two albums simultaneously took heavy blues to its ultimate expression and wrote much of the rule book for heavy rock in the 1970s.

Led Zeppelin's debut is a record where many aspects of 1960s music cross-pollinated and bloomed. The immediate sources are late Yardbirds (courtesy of Page), blues (from Cream, Hendrix, British blues), a little touch of art rock, and a real understanding of the greater possibilities the album format offered over the 45rpm single.

'Good Times Bad Times' blasted off Zeppelin's recorded career with a double-punch E-chord, a chorus of pure power-pop, and a Jimmy Page guitar solo played on a Telecaster through a Leslie speaker, a one-man blizzard of notes, all in a mere 3 minutes 43 seconds. Likewise, nothing could be further from the turgid clichés of Zeppelin-inspired heavy metal than 'Communication Breakdown,' a taut two-minute blast of power that evoked the energy of The Who's 'I Can't Explain' and The Kinks' 'All Day And All Of The Night.' It is impeccably played garage rock, a sonic onslaught punctuated by another mad Page solo careering off the splash of Bonham's cymbal white-noise. By contrast, the English folk-guitar of Bert Jansch, Davey Graham, and John Renbourn led to 'Black Mountainside,' a DADGAD-tuned instrumental based on Jansch's 'Black Waterside,' itself a traditional tune.

Unlike many of their later imitators, Zeppelin benefited from the wide-ranging musical tastes of its members. Bonham and Plant had played blues and R&B; Plant had recorded pop material for CBS on a couple of singles that sounded not unlike Long John Baldry; and both liked the West Coast rock scene of Moby Grape, Love, and Buffalo Springfield. Jones enjoyed jazz and classical, and shared Bonham's fondness for Motown and Stax, which would have a significant effect on the Zeppelin groove. The fact that Page and Jones were experienced sessioneers-arrangers gave them an ear for detail that made *Led Zeppelin* remarkably polished for a debut. Zeppelin were a band of virtuosos who knew how to be a team.

Scrutiny of Led Zeppelin's body of work led to the discovery of all manner of specific 'steals' and alleged similarities between their songs and those of others. Leaving aside obvious blues debts – now settled legally – many such claims stem from a basic misunderstanding about the inevitability with which ideas in popular music will be recycled. When *Led Zeppelin* was released, eyebrows were raised by the fact that the earlier Jeff Beck album *Truth* – which featured Rod Stewart on vocals – also had a version of Willie Dixon's 'You Shook Me.' It was said Page and Plant had stolen their thunder – but, evidently their thunder wasn't loud enough. (And, as Plant has pointed out, there were hundreds of bands in the U.K. at the time covering the song.) In the Zeppelin version everyone except Bonham gets a solo – Plant on harmonica, Jones on the organ, and finally Page on backward-reverb guitar that allows him to pile up chiming lead over Bonham's drum barrage. Other bands may have played this song but not with Zeppelin's dramatic sense – which made them immediately successful live. Similarly, 'I Can't Quit You Baby,' another Dixon song, had been covered by John Mayall, whose version is at once more authentic but anemic by comparison. (Zeppelin's studio cut is bettered by a live version taped at the Royal Albert Hall, London, on January 9th 1970, where the band play with amazing ferocity.)

Sources and influences are one thing, but the true measure of Led Zeppelin is how far they transcended those influences. Zeppelin had more imagination than most bands, more structure than Hendrix or Cream, better songs and a wider range of styles than Free, and more punch than anyone – with the possible exception of The Who. Even the acoustic track 'Babe I'm Gonna Leave You' – a traditional song also recorded by Joan Baez – is played powerfully. The descending finger-picking could be the intro to something by Simon & Garfunkel, but there's no mistaking the band on the crashing choruses.

The band's ambition was signaled by the epics that close each side of the vinyl. Side One ends with 'Dazed and Confused,' developed from The Yardbirds' 'I'm Confused.' In the middle section Jones and Bonham play call-and-answer, while Page conjures eerie sounds from the guitar with a violin bow and a wah-wah. The whole track is an artful orchestration of dynamics and ensemble playing. Side Two closes with 'How Many More Times.' A fusion of Albert King's 'How Many More Years' and 'The Hunter' – the latter written by members of Booker T. And The MGs – it boasts the hardest riff on the album.

For *Led Zeppelin II* the band found themselves in the unenviable position of having to write and record a follow-up while criss-crossing the U.S.A. on an exhausting tour. Playing to increasingly large audiences, within six months they were a headline act. Riffs and ideas began to emerge from their on-stage improvisations. Their power and dynamics drew an increasingly frenzied response. Stoned audiences got up and danced. This probably focused the musical direction of *Led Zeppelin II*, as the blues element of the first album was evened out with hard rock riffs.

'Whole Lotta Love' was their first undisputed classic and a strong contender for the track that 'invented' heavy metal. It is a musical jackhammer that melded lyrics from Willie Dixon's 'You Need Love' with a gargantuan three-note riff, and the result is undeniably raw and exciting. In the middle section Page and engineer Eddie Kramer pushed technology to the limits, creating a soundscape of simulated sex best appreciated on headphones. Page used a Theremin for some high-pitched wails. A thunderous snare roll from Bonham leads the band into Page's guitar solo, its phrases crunchingly punctuated by the rhythm section.

There are more electrifying riffs to be found on 'Heartbreaker,' with its frenetic guitar break, 'Living Loving Maid,' the start and finish of 'Moby Dick' (a drum solo), and the bulk of 'Bring It On Home.' On 'Ramble On' and 'What Is And What Should Never Be' explosive choruses detonate more delicate verses that evoked Tolkein and West Coast rock respectively. Zeppelin understood the power of dynamic contrast. There is even a beautiful ballad in 'Thank You,' with tumbling cascades of 12-string guitar and a slow Hammond fade. *Led Zeppelin II* is an album to which you can go berserk or – and this is rare for a hard rock album – you could just sit down and listen. Either way it is rewarding.

Building on the success of the first album (which made Number Ten in the U.S.A. and Number Six in the U.K.) *Led Zeppelin II* topped the charts on both sides of the Atlantic.

1969

Tommy **The Who**

Decca DL7205 (U.S.A.) / Track 613013/4 (U.K.)
Released May 1969

Quadrophenia **The Who**

MCA 210004 (U.S.A.) / Track 2657013 (U.K.)
Released November 1973

Tommy and *Quadrophenia* stretched the notion of what the rock album could be and are among the best attempts to use the LP for a group of inter-related songs. *Tommy* not only to saved The Who's career but gave them commercial success and critical standing.

By 1968 the band were creatively and financially in a fix, their troubles exacerbated by the costly habit of smashing equipment. Between 1964 and 1967 The Who had charted with a sequence of superb, bold singles, such as 'My Generation' and 'The Kids Are Alright,' but the failure of the barnstorming 'I Can See For Miles' to fulfill Townshend's expectations in the U.K. charts shocked him – though it did become their first U.S. Top Ten hit. With the onset of heavy blues rock and psychedelia, a gulf between chart pop and album rock opened up. To maintain credibility The Who needed to make a play for the latter audience. The likes of The Beatles' *Sgt Pepper*, The Pretty Things' *S.F. Sorrow*, and The Small Faces' *Ogden's Nut Gone Flake* seemed to point one way forward, and The Who's manager, Kit Lambert, repeatedly pushed the idea of a rock-opera at Townshend until it took hold.

Townshend was primed to write something like *Tommy* because he had a group of themes in his head that needed expression: childhood memories, psychedelic trips, how a rock band relates to its audience, reflections on the counter-culture, and the spiritual teachings of Meher Baba. He had already written multisectioned songs, but he wanted *Tommy* to be a multilayered entity: it would rock and it would roll, and appeal to a young audience; it would be something The Who could reproduce in concert; it was to be a spiritual parable. He later said: "I wanted it to have a rock-singles

level and a bigger concept level. I wanted it to appeal as a fairy-story to young people and to be intellectually entertaining. But I also wanted it to have a spiritual message, too." *Tommy* ranged from popular culture and the hippy world – pinball, LSD, inner space, guru figures – to references to Britain during World War II and to 1950s holiday camps. Townshend told the *New Musical Express* (U.K.) that *Tommy* "can be taken as one of three things – a spiritual symbol, the life of a pop star, or a rock'n'roll album."

By May 1968 Townshend had imagined the character of a "deaf, dumb, and blind kid," the antithetical figure for a society in thrall to sensory overload. The writing and recording process was held up by tours, so the songs assembled themselves like a jigsaw puzzle. Some – 'We're Not Gonna Take It' and 'Sensation,' for example – were composed before *Tommy* was conceived. One of its strongest songs, 'Pinball Wizard,' arose almost by accident because Townshend knew that Nik Cohn, an influential rock critic and author, was a pinball enthusiast. There was never a clear narrative. Townshend's versions of the story, as told to journalists, were often contradictory as he changed his mind and groped toward artistic coherence. The band got on with recording their parts with no idea what the story was about, but trusting that Townshend knew what he was doing. Entwistle came up with two important contributions to the drama in 'Fiddle About' and 'Cousin Kevin,' and Keith Moon had the basic idea for 'Tommy's Holiday Camp.'

Tommy was billed as the first rock-opera – though it would be more accurate to say rock cantata. This claim was symptomatic of how rock was defining itself as a more serious form of creativity than disposable pop. One way to do this was to imitate classical forms within a rock context – which is what, to a degree, *Tommy* does – so there is some attempt to repeat themes, hence the inclusion of an 'Overture,' and the way 'Christmas' anticipates 'See Me, Feel Me.'

The recording went on through the autumn and winter of 1968 at IBC in London. Multitrack machines now made it easier for groups with only four members to build up a layered sound. Townshend resisted the idea, briefly entertained, of orchestrating parts of *Tommy*, and the band confined themselves to instruments they could play or sounds they could make in the studio. Entwistle added French horn, there are backward tapes on 'Amazing Journey,' buried sitar on 'Cousin Kevin,' and fairground barrel-organ for 'Tommy's Holiday Camp.' Throughout, Townshend's acoustic-guitar playing is as important as his electric. Many songs went through repeated re-recordings until he was happy with them. Kit Lambert pushed the band through the inevitable moments of despair to complete the 24 tracks, and the fact that *Tommy* did eventually hit the record shops was a minor triumph in itself. The album was a U.K. Number Two and U.S. Number Four, staying on the U.S. charts for 47 weeks. Its triple gatefold sleeve was impressive, the lattice-work sky depicting the theme of inner space. As the first album of its kind it had considerable novelty value.

Unfortunately, the album's mix didn't do justice to the band's power. This has been partly remedied by the 1996 CD reissue which went back to the original 8-track tapes – an unusual step, as CD remastering of classic albums is normally from quarter-inch stereo masters which do not permit any remixing at all.

For a time *Tommy* rejuvenated and dominated The Who's live act – especially for Daltrey, who, with his fringed jacket and long curly hair, was able to project the character of Tommy – though eventually it was trimmed back to a few key tracks, such as 'Pinball Wizard,' with its prime power-chording and mike-swinging abandon, 'See Me, Feel Me,' 'I'm Free,' and 'Listening To You.' They used its material to great effect at *Woodstock* in the summer of 1969, and live versions of many of the album's songs can be heard on *The Who Live At The Isle Of Wight* and the extended reissue of *Live At Leeds*.

Thereafter, *Tommy* became something of a parasite, sucking some of The Who's vitality, as a variety of re-workings drained the band's time and energy. The first was Lou Reizner's 1972 orchestral version, with guest

■ *The Who at IBC Studios, London. Main Picture: Bassist John Entwistle (left), Roger Daltrey, and producer Kit Lambert look on as Pete Townshend plays the Hammond organ. Above left: Daltrey. Right: Entwistle pauses for thought while Townshend (right, and inset) re-strings his guitar.*

singers and The London Symphony Orchestra and Chamber Choir. This often gains in richness over the original *Tommy* what it loses in punch. Here, Ritchie Havens's version of 'Eyesight To The Blind' is a career highpoint; Steve Winwood, Sandy Denny, Maggie Bell, and Ringo Starr all perform their tracks superbly; and there is an exhilarating combination of voices on '1921.' Rod Stewart's 'Pinball Wizard' is surely preferable to Elton John's, which came only a few years later when, in August 1975, Ken Russell's movie version of *Tommy* was released, complete with new soundtrack. London's West End saw a stage version in 1979; in 1989 another star-studded version was filmed in Los Angeles and released as a video, *Live Tommy*; while in the 1990s surviving members of The Who did a new concert version, and there was also a Broadway stage musical.

The drawback of Tommy's success was that it obliged Townshend and The Who to better it. The first project intended to follow it up was called *Lifehouse*, but this collapsed for many reasons, leaving a bunch of superb songs to be released as *Who's Next* and its satellite singles. The real successor was *Quadrophenia* (1973), as under-rated as *Tommy* is over-rated, a more consistent and powerful set of songs.

Quadrophenia was a play on the concept of schizophrenia. The central character, a mod called Jimmy, manifested four characters, equivalent to the four members of The Who. On the cover their faces are placed in the mirrors on his scooter. The story loosely takes Jimmy through a process of progressive disillusionment. He argues with his parents, loses his job, ruins his best suit, smashes up his scooter, watches the band he loves get too successful, quarrels with his girlfriend, and sees the 'ace face' he had looked up to working as a menial bell-boy at a seaside hotel in Brighton. He takes pills on a train to the coast from London's Waterloo Station and has a spiritual experience of sorts on a rock in the sea, stripped psychologically to "the bare bones of what I am." The lavish packaging sketched all this with several thousand words of monologue and a number of black-and-white photographs.

Revealingly, *Quadrophenia* is dedicated "to the kids of Goldhawk Road, Carpenders Park, Forest Hill, Stevenage New Town and to all the people we

Continued on page 121

1969

Continued from page 119

played to at the Marquee and Brighton Aquarium in the summer of '65." It's full of nostalgia for the days when The Who were a mod band, and views that period through the lens of the later-1960s desire for transcendence. The problem is that, conceptually at least, the album is unable to reconcile its bleak vision of Jimmy's life and times with its apparent desire to go back and re-live it. The Who's history as a band and the individual members are mixed up with the story in such a way as to make its nostalgia also narcissistic. In one of the cover photographs this narcissism is allowed to violate time: Jimmy (supposedly in 1965) is outside the Hammersmith Odeon watching The Who (1970s vintage) making their way to a limo. In this respect, the snatch of 'The Kids Are Alright' faintly echoing at the end of 'Helpless Dancer' is poignant and symptomatic.

Whatever these problems, the music was consistently good. Townshend brought the band only rough demos, allowing more input during the recording. Some of the 8-track demos carried over on to the 16-track master. Entwistle wrote and overdubbed 50 horn parts. Each band member had a theme, gathered in the opening track 'I Am The Sea:' 'Helpless Dancer' (Daltrey's theme), 'Is It Me?' (Entwistle's theme), 'Bell Boy' (Moon's theme), and 'Love Reign O'er Me' (Townshend's theme). Lyrically, there is plenty about a rock band growing older and away from its audience, making *Quadrophenia* itself a meditation on the line "Hope I die before I get old" from 'My Generation.' The sea and the beach provided a unifying imagery. Townshend said: "It's more a series of impressions. Of memories. You see a kid on a rock in the middle of the sea, and this whole thing explains how he got there." The music evokes this superbly.

There are 17 tracks, including several instrumentals. Synthesizers were again used here, as they had been on The Who's earlier album, 1971's musically innovative *Who's Next*. The Who managed to sustain the intensity throughout. Side Three's sequence of '5.15,' 'Sea and Sand,' 'Drowned,' and 'Bell Boy' is among the finest material they ever recorded. There were impressive sound effects and links, such as the sound of rain and storm, a radio broadcast, or Townshend walking along shingle. It was initially thought the album would be released in quadraphonic sound but that never materialized. Many people complained that the album is not mixed as well as it could be. Daltrey was allegedly unhappy with how his vocals sat in the music, and this opened up conflict between him and Townshend. (Two days of rehearsals before a tour due to start on October 28th 1973 in Stoke ended in a punch-up between the two that left Townshend unconscious.)

Where the album faltered in The Who's intentions was that it failed to find much space in their live set. They started off with the noble intention of replicating the whole thing live with backing tapes, a huge undertaking. But the tapes didn't work properly, throwing the band off, and they felt constrained at having to play to fixed structures and tempos. Consequently, much of the album was soon dropped from concerts, leaving only such gems as '5.15,' 'Bell Boy,' and 'Drowned' remaining in their sets into the mid 1970s.

In the U.S.A. the album went gold in one day, becoming the highest-charting Who album at Number Two, and *Quadrophenia* later became a movie. Despite this, the mod imagery of the story had a limited understanding beyond the U.K. As rock critic and biographer of the band Dave Marsh has pointed out, mod defied translation, being "the only important aspect of 1960s British pop culture not adopted by Americans." It also became a milestone that indicated The Who would not be able to escape from or improve on their 1960s heritage.

■ *A still from the 1979 movie version of* **Quadrophenia,** *which starred The Police frontman and future solo performer Sting (center). The GS on the fairing of his motorbike stands for his real name, Gordon Sumner.*

1970

On Her Majesty's Secret Service (Original Soundtrack)
John Barry

EMI 90618 (U.S.A) / United Artists UAS29020 (U.K.)
Released January 1970

In their quest for new markets record companies discovered that people would buy the music soundtrack to movies they had enjoyed. No franchise has been more successful in this respect than the James Bond movies.

These appeared as albums in their own right with impressive movie-poster sleeves, and have been trawled for many Bond greatest-hits compilations. In the Bond movies the music was a crucial part of the glamour, doing much to establish the erotic, action-packed world of Ian Fleming's secret agent. The magic of the movies may wane with maturity but the music doesn't, and the man responsible for formulating the Bond-music style in the 1960s was John Barry.

Barry knew from the age of nine that he wanted to be a composer. Helping his father run a cinema had exposed Barry to countless movie soundtracks, though he was initially drawn to classical music. However, his discovery of swing jazz broadened his horizons, and he took up the trumpet. This combined knowledge of brass instrumentation and the syncopation of jazz became crucial for his work as a composer.

By the late 1950s Barry was working on British television series, such as *Six-Five Special* and *Oh Boy!*, playing in his band, The John Barry Seven. By the early 1960s he was scoring movies – *From Russia With Love* (1963) and *Zulu* (1964) are early examples – and he has since gone on to compose for over 60 movies, becoming the most successful British movie composer ever. Rarely has any soundtrack music achieved the level of identification with its subject as Barry's has with the Bond movies – not to mention the hit single theme songs. In the 1990s his popularity once again soared, and the influence of Barryesque harmony, themes, and instrumentation could be heard in mainstream pop. He gave concerts of his music and released solo albums, such as *The Beyondness Of Things* (1998).

The soundtracks of *From Russia With Love*, *Goldfinger*, and *Thunderball* are saturated with the Cold War atmosphere of the pre-psychedelic 1960s. Barry always found the right singer for the title songs: Shirley Bassey's strident 'Goldfinger' and breathy 'Diamonds Are Forever,' Tom Jones's hormonal 'Thunderball,' and Louis Armstrong's touching 'We Have All The Time In The World' from *On Her Majesty's Secret Service*. Many of the songs – the latter, for example – were penned with Burt Bacharach's lyricist Hal David.

On Her Majesty's Secret Service, like every John Barry Bond soundtrack, repays close attention to detail. Trumpets blare, timpani boom, snare drums crack and rattle, strings soar and counterpoint the brass – usually on angular intervals – and such exotic instruments as the cimbalom evoke far-flung corners of the world. The chord sequences are often unusual, outside the norms of popular music, and each tends to be a mini-essay on the use of dissonance to achieve a sexy, violent atmosphere. Even 'Do You Know How Christmas Trees Are Grown?' – which features a children's choir – has some unexpected chord changes in it. Just as Bond had all the latest gadgets, so did Barry: he gave the electric guitar and electric bass prominent roles in his orchestra, and the title track of *On Her Majesty's Secret Service* is a lovely slice of 1960s pop with pioneering use of synthesizer.

Bridge Over Troubled Water
Simon & Garfunkel

Columbia CK-9914 (U.S.A.) / CBS 63699 (U.K.)
Released January 1970

The first major album release of the 1970s was also one of the decade's most important – *Bridge Over Troubled Water* was a mammoth achievement on nearly every level.

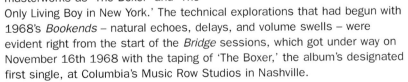

The album owed as much to the production wizardry of longtime Simon & Garfunkel associate Roy Halee as the song contributions of Paul Simon, who outdid himself with, in addition to the towering title track, such pop masterworks as 'The Boxer' and 'The Only Living Boy in New York.' The technical explorations that had begun with 1968's *Bookends* – natural echoes, delays, and volume swells – were evident right from the start of the *Bridge* sessions, which got under way on November 16th 1968 with the taping of 'The Boxer,' the album's designated first single, at Columbia's Music Row Studios in Nashville.

Session man Fred Carter Jr, who was detailed to handle guitar duties, spontaneously devised the song's beautifully cascading intro – which, ironically, was almost assigned to another instrument altogether. "I came up with this thing and played it to Paul," says Carter, "and he said, 'I love it . . . but I think it needs to be played on a concertina.' So there was some dude from Italy doing his first tour of the U.S.A., who just happened to be Italy's greatest classical concertina player. So Paul brings him in with an interpreter, and we sat there all day and went over the lick, and they wrote it out for the guy, who then played it. And afterward Paul says, 'Naw, that's not it.' And he dismissed the guy and he walks out in bewilderment, and we went right back to where we were, and got it in about the third take."

When Garfunkel accepted an offer to appear in the Mike Nichols movie *Catch-22*, work on *Bridge* effectively ground to a halt for the better part of a year. But, after reconvening at Columbia's Studio B in New York in the late fall of 1969, Halee, Simon, and Garfunkel took little more than three weeks to complete the bulk of the album, during which time Garfunkel cut his now-famous title-track vocal and numerous other sonic journeys were attempted – for example, drums were overdubbed using an open elevator shaft for reverb; vocals were taped in a nearby chapel; random instruments and entire orchestral sections were 'flown in' at will. All of these imaginative leaps would ultimately test the limits of Columbia's 1969 recording capability, forcing Halee to wire up multiple machines in order to handle the multitude of tracks, as well as the patience of boss Clive Davis, who at one point wondered aloud if all of these "extras" were really necessary.

> "WHEN THE TWO OF THEM WERE SINGING LIVE, SOMETHING WOULD HAPPEN IN THE SOUND FIELD BETWEEN THEIR VOICES THAT WAS MAGICAL. THE MINUTE YOU'D PUT [SOMETHING] BETWEEN THEM, IT WENT AWAY. SO I'D ALWAYS INSIST, 'YOU GOTTA DO IT LIVE.'"
>
> *PRODUCER ROY HALEE ON WORKING WITH SIMON & GARFUNKEL*

By the time *Bridge Over Troubled Water* was finished so too, to all intents and purposes, was the career of Simon & Garfunkel. Regardless, *Bridge* would become their crowning achievement, scoring a multitude of Grammys and topping albums charts the world over. In the U.K. the album charted for more than 300 weeks, 41 of them at Number One.

Tea For The Tillerman **Cat Stevens**

Columbia CK-9914 (U.S.A.) / CBS 63699 (U.K.)
Released January 1970

Cat Stevens was one of the most popular and prolific British singer-songwriters of the 1970s. *Tea For The Tillerman* was his breakthrough album.

Born in London in 1947 to a Greek father and a Swedish mother, Stevens was a teen-pop idol in the late 1960s, but was forced to take a sabbatical from the music business after contracting tuberculosis in 1968. When he returned two years later it was with a more mature sound in the James Taylor mold. *Mona Bone Jakon* (1970) was a minor U.K. hit, but it was *Tea For The Tillerman*, released just five months later, that first brought Stevens widespread international success.

Produced by former Yardbird Paul Samwell-Smith, *Tea For The Tillerman* doesn't deviate much from the gentle folk-pop sound of its predecessor, but it does have a more confident and optimistic feel, which undoubtedly gave it a wider popular appeal. The album peaked at Number 20 in the U.K. and Number Eight on the U.S. *Billboard* chart in early 1971, and includes several of Steven's most famous songs, notably 'Father And Son' and 'Wild World.'

Stevens recorded seven further international hit albums during the 1970s, among them *Teaser And The Firecat* (1971) and *Buddah And The Chocolate Box* (1974). He retired from music in 1979, however, after becoming a Muslim and changing his name to Yusuf Islam.

1970

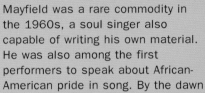

Curtis **Curtis Mayfield**

Curtom 8005 (U.S.A.) / Buddah 2318 015 (U.K.)
Released September 1970 (U.S.A.) / February 1971 (U.K.)

Curtis Mayfield had enjoyed considerable success in the early and mid 1960s as lead vocalist and songwriter in The Impressions, whose hits included 'Gypsy Woman' (1962) and 'People Get Ready' (1965).

Mayfield was a rare commodity in the 1960s, a soul singer also capable of writing his own material. He was also among the first performers to speak about African-American pride in song. By the dawn of the 1970s, alongside Marvin Gaye and Stevie Wonder, he was one of a peerless triumvirate of soul-music auteurs, innovating not just with the social consciousness of their lyrics but also by integrating funk and psychedelia into their music.

Still only 28, Mayfield had left The Impressions in 1970 to pursue a solo career. *Curtis*, his solo debut, was issued on his own Curtom label, also home to, among others, the remaining members of The Impressions as well as The Staple Singers.

Curtis remains Mayfield's defining statement, though it would be surpassed commercially by his soundtrack to the 'blaxploitation' movie *Superfly* (1972). *Curtis* has latterly become known as the '*Sgt Pepper* Of Soul,' though it confounded some critics on its original release, with *Rolling Stone* magazine hoping that Mayfield was "just in a slump" and would "soon be writing tunes with real life in them again." Both statements are somewhat puzzling, given the power of songs like 'Miss Black America' and 'Give It Up' and Mayfield's mastery of such a wide sonic palette. *Curtis* reached Number 19 in the U.S.A. on release, while the single '(Don't Worry) If There's A Hell Below We're All Going To Go' peaked at Number Three, though neither album nor single charted in the U.K.

Loaded **The Velvet Underground**

Cotillion SD9034 (U.S.A.) / Atlantic 2400111 (U.K.)
Released September 1970

Loaded saw the ever-changing Velvet Underground mutate yet again, but it also brought their golden era to an end.

Recorded under difficult circumstances during the summer of 1970, the album was a triumph of creativity over adversity. The band was simultaneously holding down an exhausting ten-week residency at Max's Kansas City, drummer Mo Tucker was taking time out to look after her newborn daughter, and guitarist Sterling Morrison was studying part-time at college.

Yet, from the breezy harmony vocals and chiming guitars of the opener, 'Who Loves The Sun?' *Loaded* overturned all expectations. Their first three albums, though stylistically different, all shared a disturbing emotional intensity that was assumed to be the band's defining characteristic, but now they sounded like they were having fun. If the lyric of the album's first acknowledged classic, 'Sweet Jane,' wallows in sordid details of New

York's decadent sub-culture, the track's simple, churning guitar riff is positively celebratory, as is 'Rock & Roll,' Reed's hymn to the delights of pop radio.

In late August, on the last night of their Max's Kansas City residency, Reed quit. He'd simply had enough. For the next two years he lived with his parents in Freeport, Long Island, working as a $40-a-week typist in his father's accountancy firm. Bassist Doug Yule, assisted by producer Geoffrey Haslam, brought the album to completion and, as with every Velvet Underground album, it was largely ignored by the record buying public at the time. Fortunately, given the glorious '20/20 vision' of hindsight, *Loaded* now stands revealed as a classic.

John Barleycom Must Die **Traffic**

United Artists 5500 (U.S.A.) / Island Records 9116 (U.K.)
Released July 1970

While most of the psychedelic and progressive rock of the late 1960s and early 1970s was dominated by the sound of the electric guitar, Traffic ploughed a more individualistic furrow, one built around the expressive playing of organist-guitarist Steve Winwood and flautist-saxophonist Chris Wood.

Winwood had begun his musical career in 1964 at the age of 15 as keyboard player and vocalist in The Spencer Davis Group, before forming Traffic with Wood, guitarist Dave Mason, and drummer Jim Capaldi. Traffic's early work betrayed a deep love for The Beatles' *Revolver*, but over time the group began to develop a sound all of their own, drawing on folk, jazz, and R&B. Mason quit the group in 1969, leading to the temporary dissolution of Traffic, and Winwood, now 22, originally intended *John Barleycorn Must Die* to be his solo debut, planning to play all the instruments on it himself. He began recording the album with producer Guy Stevens in February 1970, but soon realized he needed to replace Stevens with Island Records head Chris Blackwell and bring his erstwhile Traffic collaborators back into the fold – though, in truth, Capaldi's and Wood's contributions often seem like mere backdrops to Winwood's multitracked keyboard parts and impressive, soulful vocals.

John Barleycorn Must Die contains six expansive songs that sit apart from Traffic's late-1960s material, sounding closer in mood to the jazz rock of Santana or Tim Buckley. Nonetheless, the album was Traffic's most successful commercially, reaching the Top 20 both in the U.S.A. – where it went gold – and the U.K.

Fire and Water **Free**

A&M 4268 (U.S.A.) / Island ILPS 9120 (U.K.)
Released July 1970

Fire and Water is a definitive slice of blues-based hard rock. Formed in the shadow of Cream and the British blues boom, Free cut seven albums in their short, turbulent career (1968–73).

Simon Kirke was a solid drummer, Andy Fraser's bass work was adventurous in the best tradition of Jack Bruce, and the late Paul Kossoff remains unequalled as a master of 'one-note-says-it-all' lead guitar. In Paul Rodgers Free had a voice of striking assurance for someone so young. His delivery seemed effortless, rasping one moment and purring the next.

Partly as a result of Rodgers's blues-inflected tunes, much of Free's music is imbued with an obscure sorrow for woman lost or woman found and then lost. Lyrically, at least, their most famous song, 'All Right Now,' is atypical, and its enduring popularity obscures other fine songs in their canon. The brooding 'Fire And Water' and the loping menace of 'Mr Big' show how Free thrust the space in their music to the fore. They didn't go for Wall Of Sound-type onslaught or mass overdubs, preferring to walk the space like a tightrope.

There's tension, too, between the macho thump of the rockers and the vulnerability of the ballads. It's deceptive music because it sinks in slowly, and when hooked you can't say exactly why. Hard rock gets harder, heavier, and happier than Free, but it doesn't get any more bruised than 'Don't Say You Love Me.'

1970

Bitches Brew Miles Davies

Columbia 26 (U.S.A.) / CBS 66236 (U.K.)
Released May 1970

The late 1960s was a period of great transition for Miles Davis. With *Miles In The Sky* and *Filles De Kilimanjaro* he had begun to turn to electric instrumentation, while the line-up of his touring band, no longer a traditional quintet, seemed in a constant state of flux.

Just as importantly, though, Davis and his producer Teo Macero were in the midst of devising a whole new way of making albums, essentially a precursor to the sampling and sequencing methods used so prominently from the 1980s onward. Macero would record the band live in the studio and then, under Davis's direction, piece together whole new compositions by cutting up and splicing together pieces of tape. This method was used to great effect on the album *In A Silent Way*, recorded in early 1969, which also marked the first time Davis used three electric-piano players and guitarist John McLaughlin on record.

Bitches Brew took both processes a step further. While *In A Silent Way* had made use of rock instrumentation, Davis's next recordings drew more explicitly on the sound and feel of hard rock and funk. Following sessions for *A Tribute To Jack Johnson* – which would not be released until 1971 – Davis and his band recorded the six expansive pieces that would make up *Bitches Brew* over three days in August 1969. The caliber of the band was high, and many of the players Davis assembled had already enjoyed or would go on to achieve success in their own right. The musicians included McLaughlin, saxophonist Wayne Shorter, bass clarinet player Bernie Maupin, the aforementioned trio of keyboardists (Joe Zawinul, Chick Corea, and Larry Young), two bassists (Dave Holland and Harvey Brooks), two drummers Jack DeJohnette and Lenny White), and Jumma Santos and Don Alias on percussion.

Much of the lengthy material on *Bitches Brew* was recorded in short sections to be pieced together later. The epic title track, built around staccato bass, over-lapping, discordant electric pianos, and hypnotic funk drumming, was originally conceived as a five-part suite, though only three parts made the final cut. A fourth section was retitled 'John McLaughlin' and also included on the album. Davis's trumpet is often drowned in extreme echo, adding to the dark, foreboding feel of the track. The equally moody and chaotic opener, 'Pharaoh's Dance,' required 19 edits when Davis and Macero began post-production; several two-bar fragments are looped to disorientating effect, while further use was made of echo and reverb. With its melodic Fender Rhodes electric piano and obvious Latin feel, 'Spanish Key' is as close as *Bitches Brew* gets to light relief, though the choppy guitar lines and frantic horn solos never truly allow the listener to settle. 'Miles Runs The Voodoo Down' betrays more than a hint of the influence of Jimi Hendrix before the album closes with a version of Shorter's 'Sanctuary,' almost unrecognizable from the version Davis had recorded in the 1950s, as included on the compilation *Circle In the Round*.

Though there was some resistance from jazz purists at the time, *Bitches Brew* was an instant critical and commercial success, becoming Davis's only album to reach the *Billboard* Top 40 and the first to achieve gold. As well as casting a huge shadow on much of the jazz that followed – in a way comparable, perhaps, only to The Beatles' impact on popular music – *Bitches Brew* also had a profound impact on rock and funk musicians, from Carlos Santana to the influential Krautrock group Can.

Abraxas **Santana**

Columbia 30130 (U.S.A.) / CBS 64087 (U.K.)
Released September 1970

Emerging in the late 1960s from the Bay Area scene that also gave birth to Jefferson Airplane and The Grateful Dead, Santana reached their creative peak with _Abraxas_, a successful fusion of Latin rhythms and psychedelic guitar playing.

Named for their guitarist, The Santana Blues Band, as it was originally known, developed a strong live reputation before cutting its eponymous Columbia debut in 1969. Santana entered the studio to record their sophomore album in April of the following year, just as Columbia was gearing up for the release of Miles Davis's epochal _Bitches Brew_. The band shared Davis's pioneering spirit in its desire to fuse what were then considered disparate musical styles to create a wholly new sound, and there would also be a striking similarity between the sleeves of _Abraxas_ and _Bitches Brew_.

As with its predecessor, _Abraxas_ featured Mexican-born Carlos Santana alongside keyboardist Gregg Rolie, bassist David Brown, drummer Bob Livingstone, and percussionists Marcus Malone and Jose 'Chepito' Areas, whose conga and timbales work give it a distinct Latin flavor. Drawing on rock, blues, jazz, and salsa, the album features probably the best known recording of Santana's career, a cover of Fleetwood Mac's 'Black Magic Woman,' which peaked at Number Four on the U.S. singles chart. _Abraxas_ topped the _Billboard_ chart immediately on its release, and soon provided a second hit single, a frenetic rendition of Tito Puente's 'Oye Como Va.' Santana consolidated its success the following year with _Santana III,_ after which the original line-up split, leaving Santana to follow a more jazz-based aesthetic for subsequent, less commercially successful releases.

1970

Woodstock **Various Artists**

Cotillion CT3-500 (U.S.A.) / Atlantic 2663001 (U.K.)
Released August 1970

The *Woodstock* triple album stands as a glorious audio celebration of the crowning moment of 1960s hippiedom, when half a million young people came together on Yasgur's Farm in upstate New York for a weekend of peace, love, and music. Maybe.

Viewed from another perspective, this lavishly produced, sprawling three-album set might be seen as

the beginning of the cynical and ruthless exploitation of stoned-out traditional hippies by stoned-out capitalist hippies. It's often conveniently forgotten that *Woodstock* was set up to be a massive money-making enterprise, and only became a free festival after the fences were trampled down. Part of that enterprise was the movie and this companion live album, the combined effect of which was to turn *Woodstock* into the most mythologized rock concert of all time.

The original vinyl is, undeniably, nicely packaged in a full-color, triple-fold-out sleeve, but is it a great album? In truth, probably not. The recording quality is entirely acceptable, but many of the performances are sloppy or lackluster. With its stage announcements, mini-interviews, and crowd chants it works well as a documentary of the event but, for the most part, the studio versions of most of the songs featured here are superior. Nevertheless, buoyed up by the burgeoning *Woodstock* myth, the album went gold two weeks after release and dollar signs began appearing in the eyes of record executives around the globe as it dawned on them that a triple album recorded live over a period of three days was sitting at Number One on the albums chart.

Compared with the costs of putting a superstar band into a studio for six months – which was beginning to become the norm – recording a live album was astonishingly cheap and the profits could be enormous. There had been successful live albums in the past – *James Brown Live At The Apollo* and

the double *Live Dead* by The Grateful Dead being notable examples – but there were no successful triple live albums until *Woodstock*. What *Woodstock* said to the marketing departments was that if a live concert could be adequately 'eventized' – built up in the public's imagination – then there were huge profits to be made from recording it.

Woodstock Two, naturally, was released soon after, and 1971 brought a three-LP set entitled *The First Great Rock Festivals Of The Seventies*, featuring live recordings from the *Atlanta Pop Festival* and *The Isle Of Wight*. Before long, no self-respecting festival could consider itself complete without an attendant album of 'classic' live performances. A nicely boxed set, *The Last Days Of The Fillmore*, appeared in 1972, but most of what appeared was shoddily produced until 1978, when The Band's superb guest-star-studded movie-album tie-in *The Last Waltz* was released.

The respective merits of such albums is, however, not the central issue. The real point is that the *Woodstock* triple spawned an entirely new and lucrative marketing phenomenon that, in essence, was built around the realization that concert souvenirs could be sold to people who hadn't actually been there.

■ **Main picture: to save time between performances, there were two circular stages at Woodstock, one of which could be set up while the other was in use and then pulled into place when needed. Right: Janis Joplin on stage at the festival, on August 16th 1969.**

Workingman's Dead The Grateful Dead

Warner Bros. WS-1869 (U.S.A. & U.K.)
Released June 1970

American Beauty The Grateful Dead

Warner Bros. WS-1869 (U.S.A. & U.K.)
Released December 1970

They recorded just three studio albums in their final 15 years, but back in 1970 The Grateful Dead somehow managed to assemble their two best works all within the space of five months.

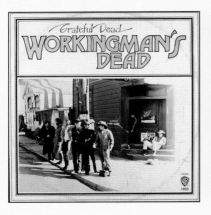

Workingman's Dead, the group's first studio release since 1969's *Aoxomoxoa*, marked the beginning of a new, more efficient era for The Grateful Dead, and with good reason. In trouble with the law following a marijuana bust in New Orleans and in debt to Warner Brothers to the tune of nearly $200,000 for studio excesses incurred during the band's previous two albums – *Anthem Of The Sun* and *Aoxomoxoa* – The Dead had no choice but to make their next album on the cheap.

This led chief songsmith Jerry Garcia and lyricist Robert Hunter to reach back to their folk roots and come up with a collection of tight, melodic songs with a simple, acoustic framework. By the end of 1969 the set included the slow blues 'Black Peter,' the countrified 'High Time,' and the epic 'Uncle John's Band,' the latter a nod to the three-part harmonizing of colleagues Crosby, Stills & Nash. To make the imminent recording process as smooth as possible, the band diligently began rehearsing the new tunes. "Jerry and I worked out the two acoustic-guitar parts well beforehand, in hotel rooms, in the practise studio, whenever we got the chance," Bob Weir recalls. "Each of us came up with some part that contrasted with what the other was playing. One of us would play the root chords, and the other would invert the chords up the neck. We really had it down by the time we went in to cut the album." In February 1970 the band entered San Francisco's Pacific High

Recording, the studio operated by Alembic, the Dead-associated musical-instrument manufacturer. Unlike the group's previous efforts, *Workingman's Dead* was the product of a band that knew exactly what needed to be done right from the start – and the simplicity of the arrangements made the going that much easier. "We were set up in what looked like a little crescent around the drums," Weir recalls, "almost elbow to elbow. It was pretty tight. There's a lot of live leakage because of that, but that was fine."

On the strength of FM-friendly cuts 'Uncle John's Band' and 'Casey Jones,' *Workingman's Dead*, issued in early June 1970, made it all the way into the *Billboard* Top 25, becoming the group's first bona fide hit album. But there was more to come. Even before the release of *Workingman's Dead* a whole new crop of Hunter-Garcia songs began popping up on the group's set lists. 'Attics of My Life,' 'Till The Morning Comes,' and 'Candyman' sported captivating Garcia melodies and tight, meticulously arranged three-part harmonies, while 'Friend of The Devil' and 'Ripple' continued the bluegrass spirit of *Workingman's Dead*.

By midsummer the band was back in the studio, ready to crank out its second album in the space of a year. For the making of *American Beauty* they chose a new location, Wally Heider's in San Francisco, and a new producer, 20-year-old Steve Barncard, who'd recorded Garcia's famous pedal-steel

overdub for the Crosby, Stills, Nash & Young hit 'Teach Your Children' some months earlier.

At Barncard's suggestion the band set up in Heider's upper-level Studio C, birthplace of classic recordings by the likes of Creedence Clearwater Revival, Jefferson Airplane, and CSN&Y. Even with drummer Bill Kreutzmann perched just a few feet away, Barncard insisted on cutting the band's acoustic guitars live. "That was so important – especially when there would be any interplay between the two acoustic guitars," Barncard recalls. "The reason those rhythm tracks are so tight is because they were set up really close together, just sitting in these plastic chairs facing each other, with very little obstruction. I may have had a few small baffles around the drums, but that was it. When they were recording, they liked to be able to look at each other's fingers, pick up on accents, and so forth. The interplay was a very big part of those sessions. One of the reasons it was such a fun record to make was that the band got the basic arrangements together well ahead of time. They were just completely prepared and professional in their approach. I'll never forget hearing the sound of Phil, Jerry, and Bob's second vocal pass on 'Attics of My Life' coming through the monitors. It was as pure a recording process as you could get."

David Grisman overdubbed mandolin parts on 'Ripple' and 'Friend of The Devil,' and guitarist Dave Nelson supplied some quick string work on the Phil Lesh album opener 'Box of Rain.' "Phil had given me the chord chart the previous night," Nelson recalls. "It was just a ton of what seemed like totally random chords thrown together. Every line was similar to the last, but not quite [the same]. I took that piece of paper to the session the next day. I ran my Telecaster straight into the board, they put on the track, and I just read it straight off the chart – solo break and all. I had no idea what I was doing or what it was sounding like, but there it was."

Workingman's Dead was still selling well by the time *American Beauty* entered the charts that fall, and, by Christmas, The Grateful Dead had their second Top 30 album of the year. Both would eventually become million-sellers.

1970

Paranoid Black Sabbath

Warners 1887 (U.S.A.) / Vertigo 6360011 (U.K.)
Released September 1970

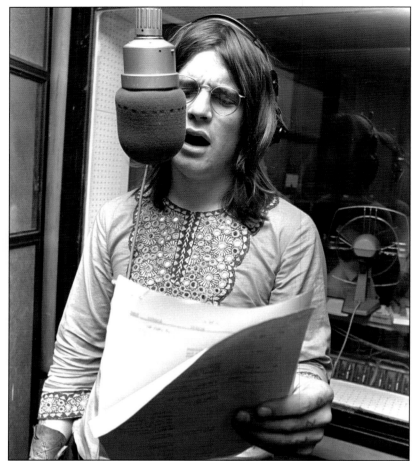

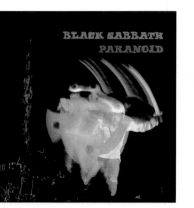

Who first conjured heavy metal out of the pit? The metal bands with huge libidos borrow from Led Zeppelin and the flashy neo-progressives look up to Deep Purple, but the prophets of doom are the spawn of Black Sabbath.

The sound of Sabbath was defined by Tony Iommi's guitar – an ultra-fuzzy proto-grunge that sounded like it had just crawled out of the primeval soup and was trying with its one brain cell to go back. Iommi doubled up his riffs but kept the parts simple, while Ozzy Osbourne seemed to sing as if chained up somewhere down the corridor. The Birmingham, UK, outfit wrote the odd tearjerker ballad – 'Changes,' for example – but their real calling was to express downer sentiments evoked by pentatonic riffs fit to make a television evangelist's head revolve.

Sabbath took the Book Of Rock and handed it on with 90 percent of its pages missing: blues, psychedelia, hippie mysticism, soul basslines, folk, rock'n'roll – you name it, Sabbath dumped it. And they were asexual, immune to the erotic pulse that dated back to Elvis's gyrations. Sabbath was for boys "worried about girls," "not interested in girls," or whose idea of a sex-guru was author Dennis Wheatley. Sabbath's hit 'Paranoid,' with its distinctive riff, has Ozzy finishing with his woman because she couldn't help him with his "mind." 'Iron Man' is the ultimate detuned riff, and 'War Pigs' compares generals with witches – thus cementing the military-occult axis that would become the mainstay of heavy metal. Sabbath were 'No Futurist's' before British punk bands like The Pistols ever shook a safety pin, and their continued influence is evident in the likes of Metallica.

■ *Black Sabbath recording* Paranoid *at Parr Street Studios, Liverpool, England. Main picture (left to right): Bill Ward, Ozzy Osbourne, 'Geezer' Butler, and Tony Iommi. Below: Ward at the drums, and Osborune at the piano.*

After The Gold Rush **Neil Young**

Reprise RSLP 6383 (U.S.A. & U.K.)
Released September 1970

Harvest **Neil Young**

Reprise MS 2032 (U.S.A.) / Reprise K/K4 54005 (U.K.)
Released March 1972

After successful spells in Buffalo Springfield and alongside Crosby, Stills & Nash, Neil Young established himself as one of the most influential songwriters of his generation with *After The Gold Rush*.

Having spent much of the previous year on tour or in the studio with CSN&Y, in early summer 1970 Young regrouped with his regular backing band, Crazy Horse, which was comprised of guitarist Danny Whitten, bassist Billy Talbot, and drummer Ralph Molina. He also recruited the then-unknown 17-year-old guitarist-pianist Nils Lofgren in an effort to move away from the hard-rock sound of his previous solo release, *Everybody Knows This Is Nowhere*.

Young's early solo work tended toward the lavish. The multilayered arrangement of his 'Expecting To Fly' – from the Buffalo Springfield album *Again* – was a three-and-a-half minute sound fantasy punctuated by abrupt stereo pans, subtle edits, and keyboard parts that were felt rather than heard. By the time he came to make *After The Gold Rush*, though, Young had settled on a simpler, sparser sound. He had also set up a basic studio in the basement of his new home in the Topanga Canyon hills of Los Angeles, which he soundproofed with lead and pine milled from the trees in his backyard. A modest collection of gear included a Scully 8-track, a small mixer, and a handful of mikes.

"There was a shitload of room on those recordings," Young told writer Jimmy McDonough, "because there wasn't anything else goin' on. The song was it . . . and everything else was supporting it."

The songs in question, inspired largely by the Dean Stockwell-Herb Berman screenplay that gave the album its title, stick in the main to the country-folk that had served him so well on CSNY's *Déjà Vu*, with even the rockier tracks underpinned by Lofgren's stately piano playing. Perhaps the most important of the album's ten originals is 'Only Love Can Break Your Heart,' the single that first brought Young mainstream attention, while another key track is the cautiously optimistic 'Don't Let It Bring You Down.' More infamous, however, is 'Southern Man,' the scathing attack on racism and bigotry in the Deep South of the U.S.A. that prompted Lynyrd Skynyrd to reply in 1974 with 'Sweet Home Alabama.'

Though not entirely successful with the critics – *Rolling Stone* magazine's Langdon Winner concluded that "most of this music was simply not ready to be recorded" – *After The Gold Rush* struck an immediate chord with the disillusion felt by many after the death of the 1960s dream. By Christmas, it had become Young's first Top 10 hit album, and remained on the U.S. chart for over a year on its way to selling two million copies.

Young built on the success of *After The Gold Rush* two years later with the lighter *Harvest*, which became the biggest-selling album of his career. Perhaps surprisingly, given its commercial success, *Harvest* contains a strange disparity of styles, from the country-edged 'Out On The Weekend' and 'Heart Of Gold' – the only U.S. Number One hit single of his career – to the ragged rock of 'Old Man' and 'Words (Between The Lines Of Age).' It also includes two songs recorded with The London Symphony Orchestra, and the stark anti-heroin ballad 'The Needle And The Damage Done.'

1970

Apple STCH 639 (U.S.A. & U.K.)
Released June 1970

All Things Must Pass introduced the rock world to the mixed pleasures of the studio triple album. Box sets had previously been the reserve of classical labels releasing operas, choral works, and symphony cycles, works whose length necessitated three or more 12-inch LPs.

By contrast, in the 1950s and early 1960s single-oriented pop struggled to get to grips with even a single album. Record companies often threw LPs together by combining a couple of hits with eight tracks of indifferent 'filler' until the artistic ambition of rock led groups to make albums where all the tracks counted, and eventually to stretch themselves across four sides of vinyl. But six?

For Harrison, a triple album was a personal statement in the context of The Beatles' post-split politics. As a musician his input had not always been fully appreciated, and it had always been a bone of contention that he lacked an outlet for his songs in the band, owing to the songwriting dominance of those other two guys. Consequently he had a large backlog of songs – 'Wah-Wah,' for example, a track on this album, actually dated back to early 1969, and was written at the time of Harrison's temporary walk-out (captured on film during the making of *Let It Be*) after yet another studio row between Lennon and McCartney – and now was the time to release them.

At its best, *All Things Must Pass* balances the emotional uplift of 1960s pop with spiritual concerns, keeping its feet on the floor even when its head is in the clouds. This is exemplified in the swooning rush and barbed lyric of

■ *A year after the release of* All Things Must Pass, *George Harrison organized* The Concert For Bangladesh, *the first major charity rock-music event. Responding to the plight of refugees during the 1971 Bangladeshi struggle for independence from West Pakistan, Harrison arranged two nights of all-star performances at Madison Square Garden, New York. Among the guests were Bob Dylan (center) and Leon Russell (right), pictured below with Harrison, as well as Ringo Starr, Badfinger, and Eric Clapton.*

Awaiting On You All,' as well as the famous 'My Sweet Lord,' surely one of the greatest religious songs of the past 50 years. The infamous legal action, in which Harrison was judged to have plagiarized The Chiffons' 'He's So Fine,' may or may not have been a victory for copyright law but was a moral and artistic injustice. For, whatever the similarities of melodic phrase and harmony, 'He's So Fine' is mere candyfloss compared with the thumping majesty, the fabulous key-change, and slide-guitar breaks of Harrison's enlightened fusion of Christianity and Hinduism.

Harrison's muse can be melancholic, as on a song like 'Let It Roll,' but the album also has 'If Not For You,' the beautiful 'I'd Have You Anytime' – co-written with Bob Dylan – and the sunny 'What Is Life,' with its huge sound and driving beat. In the sleevenotes to the remaster of 2001, Harrison wrote that he would have liked "to liberate some of the songs from the big production," which he now thought "a bit over the top." (Some will be thankful he didn't, for *All Things Must Pass* is perhaps the last great example of Phil Spector's Wall Of Sound production.) Harrison explained: 'Some of the sessions were very long in the preparation of the sound and the arrangements had at times various percussion players, sometimes two or three; two drummers, four or five acoustic guitars, two pianos, and even two basses on one of the tracks. The songs were played over and over again until the arrangements were sorted out so that the engineer in the control-room could get the sound with Phil Spector. Many of the tracks were virtually live." A number of guests were featured, including Ringo Starr, Eric Clapton, Peter Frampton, members of Delaney and Bonnie, Badfinger, and Procol Harum.

In 1971–2 Harrison enjoyed the greatest commercial success of any of the ex-Beatles. This was all the more remarkable given the cost of production of the triple album. Perhaps it could have been better shorter, perhaps the all-star jams were expendable, but *All Things Must Pass* stands as Harrison's monument.

Taproot Manuscript Neil Diamond

Universal 73092 (U.S.A.) / Universal UNLS 117 (U.K.)
Released October 1970

This extraordinary album, which Diamond described as "an attempt to convey my passion for the folk music of that black continent," pre-dated Paul Simon's African-inspired *Graceland* project by over 15 years.

'African Trilogy,' which makes up one half of *Taproot Manuscript*, was acknowledged on release as "a stunning example of pop crossbreeding" by *Time* magazine, but because its creator had written hits for The Monkees and spent most of his subsequent career in sequined shirts crooning to moist housewives, it has been ignored by the rock cognoscenti.

"The 'Trilogy' took 18 months to write," Diamond has said, "but it gave me far more satisfaction than anything I'd done before." It was also a nightmare for everyone else involved in it at Western Sound in Los Angeles. Engineer Armin Steiner described Diamond as the "most incredible mass of self-torture I have ever seen," and tales of his endless bickering over Marty Paich's lovely orchestral arrangements are legendary. The end result, however, was an impressive six-song suite based on African themes, featuring ambitious use of sound effects, exotic instruments, and vocal textures unheard of in popular music at the time. Undeniably much more pop-oriented than Simon's *Graceland*, it nevertheless explored similar issues, with lyrics touching on poverty, natural disasters, and the effects of Christianity on indigenous African cultures.

The album, which went gold two months after release, includes not just a classic Number One hit in 'Cracklin' Rosie' but also 'Done Too Soon,' which sounds uncannily like the inspiration for Billy Joel's 1989 smash hit 'We Didn't Start The Fire.'

Vanity Lables

During the 1960s and 1970s there was a fashion for successful pop and rock groups to form their own 'vanity' record labels, often in association with a major-label parent company, through which they would issue their own music as well as records by other artists.

This trend was started by Frank Sinatra, who in 1961 set up the highly successful Reprise label, initially to issue his own *Sinatra Swings* – the title of which had to be changed from *Swing Along With Me* after his paymasters at Capitol claimed it was too similar to the earlier *Come Swing With Me*. Much of Sinatra's subsequent recorded output, which began to head in a more jazz-based direction, was issued on Reprise. In its infancy, the label also issued albums by Sammy Davis Jr, Dean Martin, and Bing Crosby. Warner Brothers bought a majority shareholding in 1963, but the label has continued as a separate entity since.

In 1967, in the week that 'Good Vibrations' went gold, The Beach Boys launched Brother Records. The label issued all of the group's albums and singles from *Smiley Smile* onward, though their records also bore the imprint of the group's parent label at the time, Capitol. When The Beach Boys signed with Reprise in 1970 the group's albums were credited to Brother/Reprise. Brother Records also issued an album by The Flame, a group produced by Dennis Wilson.

Many bands started their own labels for financial reasons, so that they could invest their earnings in a company and limit the amount of tax they would have to pay. This was particularly true of The Beatles, who formed Apple Records in 1968. Two years earlier George Harrison had sung "It's one for you, 19 for me" in the song 'Taxman,' drawing attention to the fact that the Labour government had introduced stiff taxation for big earners, taxing them at 95 per cent on their higher-level income.

The first release on Apple was John Lennon and Yoko Ono's controversial *Two Virgins* album, which Apple's parent companies – Capitol in the U.S.A. and EMI in the U.K. – refused to distribute because of its 'obscene' cover, on which Lennon and Ono appeared naked. Apple issued all of the group's albums from *The Beatles* (aka *The White Album*) onward, many of the four Beatles' early solo projects, and albums and singles by other artists, including the popular singer Mary Hopkin. Apple began to dwindle in the mid 1970s, but re-emerged in the 1990s with the launch of The Beatles' *Anthology* series.

In 1969, shortly after issuing the symphonic rock concept album *On The Threshold Of A Dream*, The Moody Blues founded Threshold Recordings. The label's first release was the group's own *To Our Children's Children's Children* later the same year. They also opened a chain of record-stores under the name Threshold.

In 1974, after recording five globally successful albums, Led Zeppelin created their Swan Song label. As well as issuing the group's albums after *Physical Graffiti* in 1975, the label was also home to a number of other groups, including Bad Company and The Pretty Things, and helped fund the cult comedy movie *Monty Python And The Holy Grail* (1975).

1970

Sweet Baby James James Taylor

Warner Brothers 1843 (U.S.A.) / K46043 (U.K.)
Released February 1970

James Taylor was one of the first of a new breed of West Coast singer-songwriters to achieve widespread commercial success.

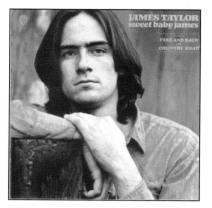

Sweet Baby James is thought by many to be Taylor's first album, but he had in fact recorded a lesser-known, eponymous debut for The Beatles' Apple label in 1968, which featured Paul McCartney on bass. While *James Taylor* limped to Number 62 on the U.S. *Billboard* albums chart, its follow-up faired much better, reaching the Top Ten on both sides of the Atlantic. Two of its gentle, folk-rock songs were U.S. hit singles, 'Fire And Rain' and 'Country Road,' which featured backing vocals from Joni Mitchell. Taylor repaid the favor by appearing on Mitchell's landmark *Blue*, issued the following year. He also contributed to Carole King's *Tapestry*.

Taylor's own career continued to go from strength to strength throughout the 1970s and beyond. All but one of his 12 subsequent album releases of the next 30 years achieved gold or platinum status in the U.S.A.

1971

Blue Joni Mitchell

Reprise 2038 (U.S.A.) / K44128 (U.K.)
Released August 1971

In May and June 1971 they locked the doors to the A&M Studios in Los Angeles as Joni Mitchell bared her soul to record her fourth LP, an album she has described as "probably the purest emotional record I will ever make in my life."

Stephen Stills and James Taylor made contributions, and Mitchell brought a new sophistication to the singer-songwriter idiom, both musically and lyrically, as she mulled over adult relationships. For young women struggling with moody boyfriends the world over she became a wise older sister who knew how they felt. Her vocals were instantly recognizable: a slow, wide vibrato, with unpredictable swoops in the phrasing. So was her guitar work, owing to unusual tunings that gave unique chords, as evident on the likes of 'This Flight Tonight.' She once observed: "For some reason, once I got the open tunings I began to get the harmonic sophistication that my musical fountain inside was excited by. Once I got some interesting chords to play with, my writing began to come."

She had already written hits in 'Big Yellow Taxi' and 'Woodstock,' but she was moving away from her folk beginnings into a more crossover style. For the upbeat 'Carey' she employed light percussion and bass, two guitars, and her own multitracked backing vocals, but generally the record has a sparse sound. 'My Old Man,' 'Blue,' and 'Little Green' have not much more than voice with piano or guitar. The lyrics are haunted by journeys and lovers, none more so than 'The Last Time I Saw Richard,' which closes the record with a narrative that juxtaposes different outlooks on life and where they lead.

Tapestry **Carole King**

ODE 77009 (U.S.A.) / A&M AMLH2025 (U.K.)
Released February 1971

Tapestry established Carole King as the first superstar female singer-songwriter. Joni Mitchell, Janis Ian, Laura Nyro, and others had preceded her and blazed a trail, but none had achieved the kind of sales figures and chart accomplishments that King would with this album.

Since starting in the music business in 1959 King had, together with her Brill Building lyric-writing husband Gerry Goffin, composed over 100 Top 40 hits, including eight Number One singles, for the likes of Little Eva, The Drifters, and The Monkees, but she was not regarded as a singer-songwriter because those songs had been written for other artists.

Encouraged by her friend James Taylor, King had taken her first step as a solo songwriter in 1970 with the album *Writer*, but only because the success of The Beatles and Bob Dylan had encouraged so many artists to write their own songs that she was finding it hard to make a living. *Writer* had sold a miserable 6,000 copies, but with *Tapestry*, recorded at A&M Studios in Hollywood, the decision to make a stripped-back, piano-based album that sounded like her demos for other artists, proved absolutely right for the time. Listeners weary of the excesses of psychedelia and progressive rock were attracted to the clarity and directness of King's melodies, and in her lyrics they heard comforting echoes of their own thoughts about love and life in the early 1970s.

'Will You Love Me Tomorrow,' written for The Shirelles a full decade earlier, was miraculously transformed by King's new treatment. The girl-group version had seemed fraught with all the insecurities and double standards of the traditional boy-girl relationships of that earlier era, whereas King's own version comes across as a mature, clear-headed appraisal of the uncertainties of any relationship in any era. Her determination to survive and move on from a failed relationship in 'It's Too Late' and her promise of life-long loyalty in 'You've Got A Friend' were philosophical touchstones for a newly liberated sisterhood of women.

Even so, King never sought to ingratiate herself with the hardline feminists. She was a model of the new woman – hard working, financially independent, the equal of any man she encountered in the music business – but she took her role as a mother as seriously as her career. She frequently stated that she had never encountered sexual discrimination in her working life, and she was happy to acknowledge that she had called the album after a piece of tapestry she had been working on as relaxation between takes.

On June 19th 1971 Tapestry hit Number One on the *Billboard* albums chart for the first of a staggering 15 weeks on its way to notching up 10 million sales in two years. At the Grammys, King collected Best Album, Best Song, Best Record, and Best Female Vocalist, and the album went on to spend 302 weeks on the charts, securing it the distinction of being the longest-charting album ever by a female solo artist.

In short, King's achievements with *Tapestry* paved the way for every Tori Amos, Alanis Morrisette, and Avril Lavigne to follow in its wake.

■ *Sessions for Carole King's **Tapestry**. Above: King at the mixing desk in A&M Studios, Hollywood, with producer Lou Adler. Opposite: James Taylor and Joni Mitchell add their backing vocals.*

1971

Stoney End **Barbra Streisand**

Columbia PCQ-30378 (U.S.A.) / CBS 64269 (U.K.)
Released February 1971

Already an emerging Broadway star, Barbra Streisand became one of the most commercially successful singers of the early 1960s with *The Barbra Streisand Album* (1962), an album of torch songs and standards that stood apart from the prevailing trend for rock'n'roll.

The singer spent much of the rest of the decade working on stage and screen, winning an Academy Award for her role in the movie adaptation of the musical *Funny Girl*, in which she had also starred on Broadway.

With her movie career on the wane, Streisand made her first attempt at a return to the pop market in 1969 with *What About Today?*, which drowned great songs by Lennon & McCartney, Bacharach, and others in insipid, Las Vegas-style arrangements. Needless to say, the album sold poorly. On *Stoney End*, however, Streisand made a more successful attempt at lending her powerful voice to the popular music of the time.

The title track, perhaps surprisingly, is a straight version of a song by the eclectic late-1960s singer-songwriter Laura Nyro, which provided Streisand with a U.S. Top Ten hit in early 1971. The rest of the album sits closer to Joni Mitchell – whose 'I Don't Know Where I Stand' Streisand covers – than the show tunes for which she was best known. It also includes songwriting contributions from Gordon Lightfoot and Randy Newman, who plays piano on several tracks. *Stoney End* reached Number Ten in the U.S.A. and laid the foundations for a career resurgence that culminated with starring roles in the movie musicals *The Way We Were* (1973) and *A Star Is Born* (1976).

Sticky Fingers **The Rolling Stones**

Rolling Stones COC59100 (U.S.A. / U.K.)
Released April 1971

The first album on The Stones' own label, Rolling Stones Records, *Sticky Fingers* found the band digging ever deeper into rootsy veins of Americana, with bohemian, good-vibes producer Jimmy Miller at the helm.

The hit single 'Brown Sugar' defines the sloppy-rock groove of the entire proceedings, but guitarist Keith Richards's increasing use of the open-G tuning he had learned from Ry Cooder adds much swampy ambience and a country feel.

In some ways, it's a grab-bag of tracks recorded over the preceding two years, some using the band's newly acquired mobile recording studio parked outside Mick Jagger's country home, Stargroves, others at their favorite London studio, Olympic, and still more in Muscle Shoals, Alabama, in search of authentic Southern accents. Despite this, the album sounds remarkably coherent, with tracks seeming almost to merge into each other.

The album's extraordinary sleeve, however, probably attracted more attention than its music. Shot by Andy Warhol, who had previously devised the peelable banana cover for The Velvet Underground, this one featured a grainy black-and-white close-up of a jeans-clad groin into which a fully functioning metal zipper was inserted. The Stones were presumably sniggering up their sleeves at the thought of countless female fans enjoying the vicarious little thrill of unzipping what they assumed to be Jagger's jeans, unaware that the groin in the photograph belonged to gay icon Joe Dallesandro. As a sales-boosting gimmick it was a stroke of genius but, in practice, the zipper played havoc with the cover of whichever album it was shelved beside.

■ *The Rolling Stones maintain their modesty with the help of a copy each of their* Sticky Fingers *LP, the sleeve artwork for which was designed by Andy Warhol.*

Who's Next **The Who**

Decca DL79182 (U.S.A.) / Track 2408102 (U.K.)
Released September 1971

The Who's finest single album, *Who's Next* was a landmark in its innovative use of synthesizers and sequencers in rock. It is also one of the finest examples in rock history of artistic victory snatched from the jaws of defeat.

The success of *Tommy* had left The Who, and Pete Townshend in particular, with the challenge of where to go next. Immersed in spiritual ideas and the afterglow of counter-culture idealism, Townshend spent months working on a project called *Lifehouse*, intended to be the ultimate concert experience and companion rock album. It was a grand science-fiction narrative on themes of spiritual identity and a quest for transcendence shared between band and audience. Overburdened and overworked, Townshend had a nervous breakdown, and the project collapsed under the weight of its own ambition. But something had to be salvaged from the wreckage. From the fragments of *Lifehouse*, and songs already recorded, came not only *Who's Next* but a run of marvelous singles, such as 'Join Together' and 'Relay,' released in its wake.

Who's Next caught The Who at their peak, doing full justice to their power. 'Baba O'Reilly' and 'Won't Get Fooled Again' became anthems to rival anything from their chart heyday in the 1960s. Both feature explosive power-chording from Townshend, Moon's whirlwind drumming, Entwistle's melodic bass, and Daltrey's commanding vocals, as well as an underlay of sequencer – and in the case of 'Baba O'Reilly' a violin break. Every one of the nine tracks is a gem, from the muscular spirituality of 'Bargain,' the moving 'The Song Is Over,' and the black humor of 'My Wife,' to the romantic resolve of 'Getting In Tune,' the agit rock of 'Going Mobile,' and the majestic vocal harmonies and dynamic climax of 'Behind Blue Eyes.'

■ *Above: The Who on the British TV show* Top Of The Pops *in 1971.*

Pictures At An Exhibition
Emerson, Lake & Palmer

Manticore 66666 (U.S.A.) / Island HELP 1 (U.K.)
Released December 1971

As its political and social influence waned with the end of the 1960s, rock compensated by taking itself more seriously. It wanted to be seen to be Art, and this led to a skirmish with the frock-coated world of classical music.

The Who had already messed about with Edvard Grieg's 'Hall Of The Mountain King' and parodied 'Land Of Hope And Glory.' When Deep Purple recorded their *Concerto For Group And Orchestra* in 1970 at the Royal Albert Hall with The London Philharmonic, the rebels were not just at the gates, it seemed they were in the palace. ELP went one better. In the immortal words of Peter Sellers, they started "muckin' abaht with the classics." The result was *Pictures At An Exhibition*, recorded live at Newcastle City Hall in March 1971.

In ELP Keith Emerson's keyboards took the place of guitar in the standard power trio, with Greg Lake on bass and vocals, and Carl Palmer on drums. Emerson performed with the flamboyance and theatrics of Hendrix, while the band pursued elaborate and hard-hitting pieces. Composed by Modest Mussorgsky as a set of piano pieces, *Pictures At An Exhibition* had received many orchestral treatments, most successfully by Ravel. The point about 'prog' going 'classical' was that the bands couldn't lose: impressed by technique, half the audience considered the band a cut above the average for tackling it (and themselves a cut above the average rock fan for listening to it); the other half thought it was a rebel wheeze, like taking a spray-can to a Constable painting. ELP gave *Pictures* a thorough rock mugging and threw in B. Bumble & The Stinger's 1960s hit 'Nut Rocker' for good measure. In a continuation of this theme, later in the 1970s they had a singles hit with a version of Aaron Copland's 'Fanfare For The Common Man.'

Electric Warrior
T.Rex

Reprise 6466 (U.S.A.) / Fly HiFly6 (U.K.)
Released September 1971

The first LP Marc Bolan made with the four-piece band T. Rex, *Electric Warrior* is the album that opened the door for glam rock, pre-dating Bowie's *Ziggy Stardust* by a year.

Periodically, rock renews itself by returning to its 12-bar roots. Despite his four mostly acoustic albums cut as the two-man Tyrannosaurus Rex, Bolan had always been a fan of rock'n'roll. By 1970 he had returned to electric guitar, reaching a new audience with the album *T. Rex* and his first big hit 'Ride A White Swan.' His songwriting began to filter the raw excitement of rock'n'roll through an eclectic post-Hendrix, post-Dylan sensibility, which took T. Rex beyond the 1950s pastiche of Sha Na Na or the *Grease* soundtrack. Bolan's lyrics mixed up his earlier Tolkeinesque wizards-and-elves imagery with such elements of Americana as DJ Alan Freed, Fender guitars, the *Dr Strange* comics, and Cadillacs. His distinctive woodland warble floated over Chuck Berry-derived riffs, with funky congas, and dappled English strings courtesy of producer Tony Visconti.

Electric Warrior contains two hit singles – the classic boogie 'Get It On' (aka 'Bang A Gong' in the U.S.A.) and 'Jeepster' – alongside gentle ballads 'Girl' and the reincarnation song, 'Cosmic Dancer,' with its spooky backward lead guitars, the chugging 'Mambo Sun,' and the doo-wop-derived 'Monolith,' which was 'Duke Of Earl' meets Arthur C. Clarke. (Bolan can be heard on the tapes joking with Visconti that the take should be titled 'Duke Of Monolith.') Against prevailing denim trends, Bolan dressed up in satin and Lurex, and, in the wake of *Warrior*, toured to scenes of 'T. Rexstasy' reminiscent of Beatlemania.

1971

What's Going On
Marvin Gaye

Tamla Motown TS 310 (U.S.A.) / STML11190 (U.K.)
Released May 1971 (U.S.A.) / September 1971 (U.K.)

A star in the sunset of Motown's golden Detroit era, *What's Going On* is the most significant album that the label released.

What's Going On strikes a creative balance between Gaye's personal and public concerns, and is where the label almost exclusively associated with hit singles belatedly discovered the album as an artistic entity in its own right. It gave Marvin Gaye a road back from the wilderness in which he'd found himself following the death of singing partner Tammi Terrell. *What's Going On* revitalized Gaye's music, satisfying on the one hand his long-held ambition as a singer to perform more sophisticated material, and on the other his generous impulse to respond to the plight of his brother Frankie and the thousands like him serving in Vietnam, and to the social upheaval in the U.S.A. at the close of the 1960s.

It might have been Gaye's vision and voice, but both in the writing and the playing *What's Going On* is a team effort. By 1970 Gaye had the reputation at Motown of being difficult to work with. David Van DePitte was assigned as producer and arranged the orchestral parts, but found that Gaye hadn't finished the songs and kept taking time off. Recording sessions for the title track

were on June 1st, with vocals overdubbed on July 6th, 7th, and 10th, and strings on September 21st 1970. The basic tracks for the remaining songs were recorded on March 17th, 19th, and 20th, with overdubs on March 24th, 26th–30th 1971. Obie Benson of The Four Tops was called in to help finish songs, and the LP became the last hurrah for Motown's session players, with Funk Brothers veterans James Jamerson and Bob Babbitt (bass), Joe Messina and Robert White (guitars), Earl Van Dyke (piano), and Jack Ashford (percussion) actually getting credits on the sleeve for once, instead of being unnamed session players. Jamerson's bass lines are frequently astonishing in both their rhythm and jazz inflections. Jamerson hardly ever talked about a day's recording when he got home, but after cutting 'What's Going On' he reputedly told his wife the track was a masterpiece.

In contrast to the anguished vocals that were *de rigueur* for most male singers at Motown, and which Gaye had used on such hits as 'I Heard It Through The Grapevine,' here he tried singing in a more relaxed way. He said: "I felt like I'd finally learned how to sing. I'd been studying the microphone for a dozen years, and suddenly I saw what I'd been doing wrong. I'd been singing too loud, especially on those Whitfield songs. It was all so easy. One night I was listening to a record by Lester Young, the horn player, and it came to me. Relax, just relax." He also multitracked his voice, blurring the distinction between lead and backing vocal, so that many of the songs have multiple vocal lines weaving in and out of each other. (The idea for this came from the happy accident of a playback when he heard two of his vocal tracks at once instead of one.)

Unfortunately, when Motown's boardroom first heard the final tapes they rejected the album, and Gaye had to deliver them an ultimatum to get it released. He commented: "[Motown] didn't like it, didn't understand it, and didn't trust it. Management said the songs were too long, too formless, and would get lost on a public looking for easy three-minute stories. For months they wouldn't release it. My attitude had to be firm. Basically I said, 'Put it out or I'll never record for you again.' Berry Gordy eventually said, 'Marvin, we learn from everything. That's what life's all about. I don't think you're right, but if you really want to do it, do it. And if it doesn't work you'll learn something; and if it does I'll learn something.' The album was called *What's Going On*. I learned something." Gaye's confidence was vindicated, for *What's Going On* became Motown's biggest selling album to date, yielding three hit singles – the title track, 'Mercy Mercy Me,' and 'Inner City Blues.'

In strictly musical terms it is a cohesive album. This is partly because of the linking of one track to another so that the music unfolds continuously, with the occasional jolt of a sudden tempo and key change as one groove runs straight into the next. Other factors are the recycling of vocal phrases and the re-using of chord progressions on more than one song. The bridge of 'What's Going On' becomes the intro of 'What's Happening Brother,' and the main progression of the former crops up again in 'Mercy Mercy Me.' The

music has far more of a jazz feel than was usual with Motown, the overall sound an ambient groove. There were innovative production touches, the heavily reverbed congas, for example – used most effectively on the droning melancholy of 'Inner City Blues' – with strings, brass, and celeste adding lushness and sparkle to the album.

Written and conceived in a generous and humane spirit, the lyrics touch on many issues of the day, making the record a State Of The Union address from a President Of Soul: the Vietnam War, poverty and crime in the inner cities, drugs, unemployment, ecology, all were handled with a poignant grace, along with Gaye's ever-faithfuls, love and religion. Gaye told Smokey Robinson: "God is writing this album. God is working through me." Sensual and spiritual, only occasionally does the record slip into sentimentality, on 'Save The Children,' for instance.

In 2001 Motown issued an exemplary 'deluxe' edition with two separate mixes, one from Detroit in April 1971 which is 'drier,' the other prepared in May in Los Angeles and used for the LP release. It also contains a live performance of much of the album from a concert at the Kennedy Center in Washington on May 1st 1972. Three decades later, *What's Going On* still retains its freshness and humanity.

1971

There's A Riot Goin' On Sly & The Family Stone

Epic 30986 (U.S.A.) / EPC/40 64613 (U.K.)
Released November 1971

"One of the most drugged-sounding albums yet to be released," according to a *New Musical Express* (U.K.) review at the time, Sly Stone's dark, political masterpiece would prove inspirational to countless musicians of disparate genres, from 1970s disco to hip-hop in the 1990s.

Having studied music and composition at university and worked as a DJ in the early 1960s, Sylvester Stewart formed The Family Stone in 1966, rechristening himself Sly Stone in the process. The band had early hits with the kinetic, funky 'Dance To The Music,' 'Everyday People' – which topped the pop and R&B charts – and its parent album, *Stand*, before bridging the gap between black and white audiences with a triumphant performance at *Woodstock*. Subsequent single releases, 'Thank You (Falettin Me Be Mice Elf Again)' and 'Family Affair,' also reached Number One in the U.S.A.

'Family Affair' was also the first single to be drawn from Stone's epic masterwork, *There's A Riot Goin' On*. Where the bulk of the band's previous offerings had been in tune with the optimism of the late 1960s, *There's A Riot Goin' On* took *Stand*'s 'Don't Call Me Nigger, Whitey' as a starting point. Stone's songs became overtly political in nature, a cynical commentary on the decline of U.S. values and civilization. Given its lyrical content, the album's iconic sleeve – a stark image of the Stars and Stripes – could not be more fitting.

Musically, while retaining the commercial edge that had served his band so well in recent years, Stone began to delve further into his melting pot of taut funk, psychedelic soul, rock, and blues. Perhaps the biggest influence on the record's sound was Stone's prodigious intake of cocaine, which is surely responsible for its bleak, hazy overtones. His propensity for repeatedly overdubbing his band's performances with his own often sloppy playing also led to the master tapes becoming warped in places. Where it is left untouched, the playing of The Family Stone – arguably the first fully racially integrated band – is exceptional, in particular Greg Errico's staccato drum breaks and Larry Graham's peerless bass work. Stone also makes early use of a drum machine on some tracks, including 'Family Affair.'

Despite its somewhat claustrophobic tone and uncompromising lyrical agenda, *There's A Riot Goin' On* kept Sly And The Family Stone's run of success going, topping the U.S. albums chart and also making the U.K. Top 40. As well as 'Family Affair,' the album also spawned 'Runnin' Away,' perhaps the most perfect pop moment in Stone's career. The rest of *Riot* is built around two lengthy, thematically similar, jazzy funk songs, 'Africa Talks To You (The Asphalt Jungle)' and 'Thank You For Talkin' To Me Africa,' a slowed-down remake of the earlier single 'Thank You (Falettin Me Be Mice Elf Again).'

Stone would never again hit the commercial and artistic peaks of *There's A Riot Goin' On*, falling into a desperate period of drug dependency and eventual bankruptcy by the late 1970s.

Maggot Brain **Funkadelic**

Westbound 2007 (U.S.A.) / 6310 200 (U.K.)
Released August 1971

Throughout the 1970s, funk pioneer George Clinton led two of the genre's most important groups, Parliament and Funkadelic.

Though the membership of both overlapped, Clinton used Parliament as an outlet for his more groove-orientated, upbeat material, while Funkadelic's recordings had more of a social and political conscience.

After working as a songwriter for Motown in the 1960s, Clinton formed Funkadelic in 1969 and recorded the group's eponymous debut the following year. Funkadelic issued *Free Your Mind And Your Ass Will Follow* in early 1971 before starting work on *Maggot Brain*. Like *There's A Riot Goin' On* by Sly And The Family Stone, which was released in November 1971, *Maggot Brain* betrays the influence of late-

1960s rock groups, notably The Jimi Hendrix Experience and MC5. The epic, instrumental title track opens the album with a cry of "Mother Earth is pregnant for the third time, y'all have knocked her up." Underpinned by a simple acoustic-guitar figure, the song is dominated by Eddie Hazel's slow, drawn-out electric guitar solo, apparently inspired by Clinton's instructions to "play like your momma just died." Lyrically, the song encourages the listener to rise up above his or her troubles or risk drowning among the maggots of the earth. Elsewhere, there is a gospel influence on 'Can You Get To That,' while the drums on 'Super Stupid' are heavily distorted, giving them a detached, electronic edge.

Maggot Brain ends with 'Wars Of Armageddon,' an expansive, full-band jam, on which Clinton, keyboardist Bernie Worrell, and Funkadelic's three guitarists battle for control. *Maggot Brain* failed to chart on release in either the U.S.A. or the U.K., but is now regarded as one of the finest funk records of the era.

Clinton continued to record at a prodigious rate throughout the 1970s, and retained the socio-political edge to his work with Funkadelic even as his contemporaries moved towards more throwaway, hedonistic material in the latter part of the decade. In 1978 Funkadelic issued one of their best-loved and most commercially successful albums, *One Nation Under A Groove*, which features an updated version of 'Maggot Brain.' The title track was a hit when issued as a single on both sides of the Atlantic.

1971

[Untitled] IV
Led Zeppelin

Atlantic SD7208 (U.S.A.) / 2401012 (U.K.)
Released November 1971

After the bafflement in the music press over the acoustic leanings of their third album, Led Zeppelin came back to remind the world that no one could rock their audience like they could.

The biggest-selling hard-rock album ever, Zeppelin's fourth brought the band's acoustic and electric, mystical and erotic aspects into perfect balance. These eight tracks have the strength of rain-washed granite.

IV, as it has become known, was recorded using The Rolling Stones' mobile facility at Headley Grange, a large Victorian house in Hampshire, U.K., and in London, during the winter of 1970–1. The band's genius for dynamics and strange 'look-Ma-no-time-signature' riffs drives 'Black Dog,' and 'Rock and Roll' blasts like a supercharged V8 running on jet fuel. 'Misty Mountain Hop' matches a concrete-demolishing riff with tales of hippy days in the park, and 'Four Sticks' pits stratospheric singing and churning drums with innovative synthesizers. 'Going To California' set romantic disillusionment to delicate acoustic guitar and mandolin. 'When The Levee Breaks' took Memphis Minnie's 1929 blues and rewrote it to enormous proportions, lifting off from Bonham's much-sampled battering intro. (This classic drum sound was achieved with ambient miking in Headley Grange's hall and an echo unit.)

At the album's heart are 'The Battle Of Evermore' and 'Stairway To Heaven.' Page had picked up a mandolin one night during a holiday he and Plant were enjoying in a cottage in Wales, and wrote 'Evermore' with the first shapes his fingers found. Despite the absence of electric instruments, the song still has an extraordinary intensity and haunting atmosphere, as it pictures the eternal battle between good and evil with images drawn from J.R.R. Tolkein's *The Lord Of The Rings*, at the time a cult book among the hippies. It is also one of the few Zeppelin songs to feature a guest musician, the late Sandy Denny, then ex-singer with British folk outfit Fairport Convention. The balance between Plant's voice and hers is superb.

To feel the full effect of 'Stairway To Heaven' always listen to 'The Battle of Evermore' first. One of rock radio's most played tracks, 'Stairway To Heaven' is neither the pompous anthem ridiculed by fashionable prejudice nor the backward-message-infested Satanism of twisted imaginations. 'Stairway' sustains the mystic pastoralism of 'The Battle of Evermore,' with its idealized English country landscape – reminiscent of the paintings of Samuel Palmer – inhabited by the mysterious figures of the May Queen, the piper, and a Celtic goddess promising spiritual wisdom and redemption. The inspiration came partly from Plant's reading of Lewis Spence's *The Magical Arts In Celtic Britain*. 'Stairway' is a tautly constructed eight-minute masterpiece of arrangement, carefully building from acoustic guitar and recorders to multiple electric guitars and Zeppelin at full throttle, and the lone-voice ending. Every individual's performance is exemplary, with Bonham's drum entry giving the song a spine-tingling lift-off, and Page supplying one of the rock's most expressive solos over Jones's Motown-inspired bass line.

Fittingly, the use of 'runic' symbols to name the album, the absence of words from the sleeve, the juxtaposition of urban destruction with the hermit's mountain-top light of wisdom, gave the vinyl album a mystique no CD could match – a perfect package for music that remains timelessly potent.

Hunky Dory David Bowie

RCA AFL-1 4623 (U.S.A.) / SF/PK 8244 (U.K.)
Released December 1971

The Rise And Fall Of Ziggy Stardust And The Spiders From Mars
David Bowie

RCA AFL-1 4702 (U.S.A.) / SF/PK 8267 (U.K.)
Released June 1972

The first classic Bowie release, *Hunky Dory* marked the start of an impressive run of high-quality albums throughout the 1970s; the following year's *Ziggy Stardust*, meanwhile, is the first of his character-based concept albums and the best-loved release of his career.

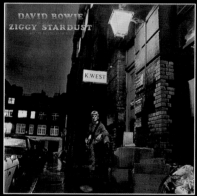

Having begun his career in the mid 1960s as Davy Jones, the rechristened David Bowie first hit his stride, artistically and commercially, with the single 'Space Oddity,' which was given a wider exposure when used to accompany television pictures of the first moon landing in 1969. In spite of this, its parent album, *Man Of Words, Man Of Music* – later retitled *Space Oddity* – and the follow-up, *The Man Who Sold The World*, both failed to chart. The latter had a surprisingly hard, almost heavy-metal sound, but when it came to recording *Hunky Dory* Bowie had returned, for the most part, to the acoustic guitar-based, singer-songwriter sound of his earlier work. What elevated the album above his late-1960s material, 'Space Oddity' aside, was Bowie's newly developed and highly ambitious capacity for bridging the gap between highbrow and lowbrow art forms, taking classic pop and peppering it with cabaret stylings and sexually ambiguous lyrics.

Hunky Dory includes several songs that have since become touchstones in the Bowie canon, notably the euphoric 'Changes' and 'Life On Mars' – originally composed with Sinatra in mind – a pair of peerless piano-led pop singles. The other key ingredient of the success of the album was the first appearance of Bowie's mythical backing group, The Spiders From Mars, who add an early glam feel to the likes of 'Andy

Warhol' and 'Queen Bitch.' The album also features Rick Wakeman, who would soon join Yes, on piano.

Though *Hunky Dory* failed to make a big impact on the charts on its release, its success was buoyed by the first issue of 'Changes' as a single – it would reach Number One in the U.K. when reissued alongside 'Space Oddity' in 1975 – and the controversy sparked by Bowie's proclamation in *Melody Maker* (U.K.) that he was bisexual. Bowie had already started work on his next album by the time *Hunky Dory* saw release in December 1971. In fact, he had issued embryonic versions of two songs – 'Moonage Daydream' and 'Hang On To Yourself' – from *Ziggy Stardust* under the pseudonym Arnold Corns six months previously. He had begun to conceive the idea of a concept album for which he would 'become' the title character, an amalgam of Bowie's good friend (Z)Iggy Pop, cult 1960s performer The Legendary Stardust Cowboy, Vince Taylor (the 'French Elvis'), and various aspects of Japanese culture, which gave Ziggy his distinctive shock of red hair.

While the Ziggy character was integral to Bowie's mainstream breakthrough, it is the quality of the music found on *Ziggy Stardust* that cemented its status as one of the most important British records of the time. Like *Hunky Dory* the

album was produced by Ken Scott, who had previously worked as an engineer on The Beatles' *Magical Mystery Tour* and *The Beatles* (aka *The White Album*). With Wakeman now devoting his time to Yes, The Spiders also have a larger role to play on this album; virtually all of the material is built on the four-piece rock-band dynamic, with occasional flourishes of strings and piano. The album begins with one of Bowie's strongest songs, the apocalyptic 'Five Years,' which is followed by the more upbeat 'Soul Love' and 'Moonage Daydream.' However, the key musical ingredient of the album's success, is 'Starman,' which reached the U.K. Top Ten on its release as a single. As the album progresses, guitarist Mick Ronson – who was also responsible for the impressive string arrangements – is given more of a chance to shine, on the heavier 'Suffragette City,' the proto-punk 'Hang On To Yourself,' and the title track. *Ziggy Stardust* closes with perhaps its finest moment, the slow-burning 'Rock'n'Roll Suicide.'

Bowie spent much of 1972 and the first half of the following year performing – in character – the songs from *Ziggy Stardust* to a devoted fan base, many of whom had begun to attend his concerts in Ziggy-inspired costume. On July 3rd 1973 he shocked a packed audience at London's Hammersmith Odeon with the words: "Not only is this the last show of the tour, it's the last show that we'll ever do." The performance was filmed by noted documentary-maker D.A. Pennebaker and released as a home video in 1982. What Bowie in fact meant with his stark on-stage declaration was that it would be the last appearance by Ziggy Stardust And The Spiders From Mars. His career was only just beginning, with *Ziggy Stardust*'s impressive follow-up, *Aladdin Sane*, already in stores, and true international success soon to come.

1972

Pink Moon Nick Drake

Island SMAS-9318 (U.K.) / ILPS 9184 (U.K.)
Released February 1972

Though ignored in his lifetime, Nick Drake has since become one of the best loved singer-songwriters of the 1970s.

Drake's work has a somber majesty quite apart from his contemporaries. His first two albums, *Five Leaves Left* (1969) and *Bryter Layter* (1970), both have a distinct melancholy, but are brightened by Robert Kirby's baroque string arrangements and a number of impressive guest musicians, including John Cale, formerly of The Velvet Underground. Island Records and Drake himself had high hopes for both LPs, but neither registered with the listening public – total sales of all Drake's albums during his lifetime, in fact, reached less than 5,000 copies.

Thoroughly dejected after pouring his heart and soul into those first two albums, Drake retreated to Island head Chris Blackwell's Spanish villa to write the songs that would become *Pink Moon*. He recorded the album in two late-night sessions in October 1971 with his friend John Wood, a veteran of the late-1960s English folk scene. On both occasions Drake arrived at the studio after midnight, sang a handful of songs, and left. With the exception of the title track, which includes a brief piano motif, all of the recordings feature just Drake's fragile vocal and nimble, close-miked guitar playing, performed mostly in one take. The resulting album is less than half an hour of haunting, delicate music comparable to nothing except, perhaps, Robert Johnson's sparse delta blues. Like its predecessors, *Pink Moon* sold poorly on release, and would prove to be Drake's last album proper.

On November 25th 1974 he died after an overdose of sleeping pills. However, Drake's profile began to rise after his death, and numerous performers started to acknowledge a debt to his work. Interest had grown sufficiently by 1986 for Hannibal Records to issue a collection of unreleased recordings, *Time Of No Reply*, and a boxed set of that and his three full albums, *Fruit Tree*. In 2002 he was given further exposure when the title track from *Pink Moon* was used as the soundtrack to a car commercial.

Sail Away Randy Newman

Reprise 2064 (U.S.A.) / K44185 (U.K.)
Released June 1972

Born into a musical family – two of his uncles wrote movie scores – Newman made his recording debut with the flop single 'Golden Gridiron Boy' in 1962.

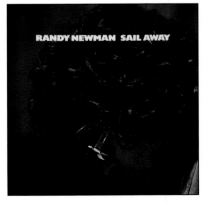

He didn't make another record of his own for several years, instead finding work as a staff songwriter and arranger, first for Liberty Records and then Warners. In the mid-to-late 1960s the likes of Dusty Springfield, Peggy Lee, Alan Price, and Gene Pitney had hits with Newman's songs, but his own albums *Randy Newman*

Creates Something Under The Sun (1968) and *12 Songs* (1970) sold poorly despite strong reviews.

Sail Away was the first of Newman's albums to achieve any commercial success of note, though he remained a cult figure for most of the 1970s. Part of the reason for this was his subtle, acerbic wit, which confounded most listeners; his limited vocal abilities also put pop audiences off his songs unless somebody else was singing them. The majority of Newman's songs were written in character, including *Sail Away*'s title track, on which he adopted the persona of a slave-trader in Africa.

Musically, the album finds a common ground between the rich orchestrations of *Something Under The Sun* and the stripped-back blues rock of *12 Songs*. Among the strongest tracks on the album are the sardonic 'Political Science' and 'You Can Leave Your Hat On,' later a hit for both Joe Cocker and Tom Jones. *Sail Away* ends with the bitter anti-religious rant 'God's Song (That's Why I Love Mankind).' The album failed to chart on release, but is now regarded as a cult classic.

'Hot Hits' And 'Top Of The Pops' Compilations

In the late 1960s through to the mid 1970s some of the biggest-selling compilation albums in the U.K. did not feature any original artists at all.

Two competing budget-priced series, 'Top of The Pops' – named after the long-running BBC television chart show – and 'Hot Hits' spawned dozens of releases, each full of the hits of the day performed in the style of the original versions by faceless session men. Or at least, that was the idea. All too often the results were a bland and unintentionally comic mixture of awkwardly mimicked vocal inflections and tired instrumental impersonations. Nonetheless, the albums sold in their millions, and even scored high chart positions until it was decided that they didn't qualify on account of their low price.

There were no credits on the albums, so you never knew who had heroically attempted singing first in the style of Engelbert Humperdinck and then Donny Osmond. But in later years, long after the albums had been rendered obsolete by cheap compilations of original hits by the real artists, pop historians discovered that artists of the caliber of David Bowie and Elton John had served time on pop's cover-version production line before they, too, had hits of their own that would be perfunctorily rendered down by their former colleagues.

Nuggets Various Artists

Elektra 7E-2006 (U.S.A. & U.K.)
Released September 1972

Released at a time when rock music was taking itself increasingly seriously, the *Nuggets* compilation was a reminder of more innocent times.

Compiled by Lenny Kaye, later of The Patti Smith Group, *Nuggets* collected 27 classic U.S. garage-rock tracks from the mid 1960s, when countless U.S. teenagers had enthusiastically bashed out imitations of then current British-invasion bands such as The Beatles, The Rolling Stones, and The Yardbirds. The recording careers of most of these teenagers went no further than a locally released single – all of the ambition, frustration, and energy of youth condensed into three minutes. A few, including The Electric Prunes, The Standells, and The 13th Floor Elevators, all of whom feature on

Nuggets, sustained careers for several years, releasing albums, having hits, and even, in the case of The Electric Prunes, touring internationally.

It is a telling comment on how fast music was developing that, by the time *Nuggets* appeared in 1972, a mere four to six years since the singles featured had originally been released, it seemed like a monument to a bygone age. *Nuggets* has been reissued several times since, culminating with a greatly expanded four-CD boxed set in 1998. Several of the songs featured on the original vinyl-double are now acknowledged classics of their time, including 'I Had Too Much To Dream Last Night' by The Electric Prunes and 'You're Gonna Miss Me' by The 13th Floor Elevators. The *Nuggets* concept itself has proved influential, with several similar series of other psychedelic garage-rock compilations following in its wake, including *Pebbles* and *Rubble*.

■ *The Electric Prunes, one of the higher-profile acts featured on* Nuggets.

Machine Head **Deep Purple**

Warners 2607 (U.S.A.) / Purple TPSA 7504 (U.K.)
Released April 1972

**Machine Head captured the
British heavy-rock group Deep
Purple at their creative peak,
and includes the group's best-
loved song, 'Smoke On The
Water.'**

The first of many incarnations of
Deep Purple was formed in 1967 by
guitarist Richie Blackmore, drummer
Ian Paice, and keyboardist Jon Lord;
vocalist Ian Gillian and bassist Roger
Glover joined in 1969, and first
featured on the band's fourth album,
the ambitious rock-classical hybrid *Concerto For Group And Orchestra*
(1970). After making the U.K. hit albums *Deep Purple In Rock* and *Fireball*,
the group decided to record its seventh album using the Rolling Stones'
mobile studio. On December 7th 1971 the group arrived in Montreux,
Switzerland, and intended to set up camp in the casino. Before they could
do that, however, a fire broke out at a Frank Zappa concert in the theater
connected to the casino, destroying the entire complex. Deep Purple moved
to the Grand Hotel across town, and quickly set to work on a song, 'Smoke
On The Water,' inspired by the fire. Other songs recorded at the Grand Hotel
for *Machine Head* include 'Highway Star,' 'Lazy,' and 'Pictures Of Home.'

Issued on the band's own Purple label in the U.K., *Machine Head* was their
first bona fide international hit album. It topped the U.K. chart and reached
Number Seven in the U.S.A., and helped to establish Deep Purple –
alongside Led Zeppelin and Black Sabbath – as one of the most important
British heavy-rock acts of the 1970s.

The Quadraphonic Debacle

**Stereo records and compact cassette were two
examples where the music and electronic industries
rationally adopted a single standard to everyone's
benefit, especially that of the consumer. That was
not always the case. The worst example must be the
quadraphonic fiasco of the early 1970s.**

Quadraphonic – or surround – sound came about because of a sense among mainly classical listeners that standard two-channel stereo was flat and could not recreate the ambience that you hear in a concert hall. But, even at that time, such listeners did not constitute a huge market. In due course it would become clear that a more impressive effect could be provided by mixing records so that instruments could be heard right around the listener. Sometimes they even moved.

With eight, 16, or 24 individual audio tracks to play with, it was a relatively simple matter to mix pop material down to four channels. Creating a system for getting those channels into the home, however, was a different matter. First, in 1969, came a four-channel open-reel tape deck that simply took all four tracks of a standard quarter-inch tape and played them simultaneously rather than using them for two lots of stereo material. Pre-recorded tapes were soon available. Then, in 1970, the Quad-8 8-track format was introduced, along with players and a selection of recordings. To compensate for the halved playing time, thinner tape was used, which did not help their already doubtful reliability. Initial offerings were enhanced versions of old recordings, including the 1965 soundtrack of *The Sound of Music*. Later, albums would be specially mixed for quad, including directional effects. But Quad-8 was dead before the end of the decade, with the final release apparently being Tomita's *Kosmos* in 1978.

Neither reel-to-reel nor 8-track presented any serious technical problems. Putting four channels of information on to the two sides of a vinyl groove, however, was a different matter. There were two main approaches. The first of these, matrixing, which was adopted by CBS for its SQ system and Sansui for its rival QS, meant mathematically combining four channels of recorded sound into two channels to be cut into a normal stereo groove on the disk. They were then decoded at the playback end and turned back into four channels to be amplified and reproduced over four loudspeakers. Stereo listeners would hear a combination of all four channels.

The CD-4 system, however, was much more ambitious as well as being fiendishly complicated. Devised in Japan by JVC, then a subsidiary of RCA, it required different groove dimensions and, eventually, a different stylus and reformulated vinyl. Each side of the groove now carried the sum of front and back channels on that side, but also an extra signal at an inaudibly high frequency. This was used to carry an encoded version of the difference between front and rear channels. At playback, the difference signal was used to separate out front and back sounds. Because the main audible groove carried combined front and back signals, stereo compatibility was achieved.

All this was a considerable engineering challenge, which made the equipment expensive and JVC late into the market. The first disks, marketed in Japan, were simply not durable enough. The improved disks did not appear in the U.S.A. until 1973, some time after the matrix systems. But it did work, producing a high degree of channel separation, which is more than can be said for the early matrix systems, which were inclined to leave the public wondering what the fuss was about. Few members of the public were as interested in quadraphony as the manufacturers and record companies, and by 1977 it was effectively dead, though matrixing did re-emerge later in the Dolby Surround system for home video.

1972

Talking Book Stevie Wonder

Motown TS319 (U.S.A.) / STMA 8007 (U.K.)
Released October 1972 (U.S.A.) / January 1973 (U.K.)

Talking Book belongs to the third flowering of Wonder's career. His breakthrough had been as 'Little' Stevie Wonder, the '12-year-old genius' of 1963's 'Fingertips'.

After his voice broke in 1966 he had given Motown hits such as 'My Cherie Amour' and 'Signed, Sealed, Delivered.' In 1971 the 21-year-old signed a new contract that gave him more creative freedom. He hooked up with Bob Margouleff and Malcolm Cecil of Tonto's Expanding Headband, pioneers of early synthesizers and programming. Vast sums were spent as the three labored in Electric Lady Studios in New York, finishing about 75 songs and leaving several hundred others in sketched forms. The first release from this material was *Music Of My Mind* (1972), which features the minor U.S. hit 'Keep On Running' and 'Superwoman (Where Were You When I Needed You).' Partly recorded during the same sessions, *Talking Book* followed, the critical and commercial success of which made Wonder one of the most influential black musicians of the early 1970s.

A multi-instrumentalist himself, Wonder was less reliant on having a team of session players around him, and the development of multitrack recording was making it easier for a musician of his ilk to make albums on a DIY basis, and instruments such as the clavinet and electric piano came to the fore. Perhaps surprisingly, however, the first voice heard on *Talking Book* belongs to Jim Gilstrap, who trades a couple of lines with fellow Wonderlove backing singer Gloria Barley on the opening 'You Are The Sunshine Of My Life' before Wonder himself joins in.

The album includes 'You Are The Sunshine Of My Life' and 'Superstition' – the latter written for Jeff Beck, who also played on 'Looking For Another Pure Love.' However, when Wonder heard Beck's version he withdrew permission, deciding the song was too good to give to someone else. Motown agreed, and the rush-released single was a big hit. It was his first U.S. Number One hit since 'Fingertips (Part 2),' which had topped the U.S. singles chart nine years earlier. There was also a timely black-consciousness significance to *Talking Book*'s cover, which depicts Wonder sitting on the ground looking distinctly African.

Wonder's run of classic 1970s recordings continued the following year with the release of *Innervisions*, which features the international hit singles 'Higher Ground' and 'Living For The City.'

■ *Right: Stevie Wonder working on* **Talking Book** *at Electric Lady Studios, New York, on February 22 1972. Electric Lady had been founded in the late 1960s by Jimi Hendrix.*

School's Out Alice Cooper

Warner Brothers 2623 (U.S.A.) / K56007 (U.K.)
Released July 1972

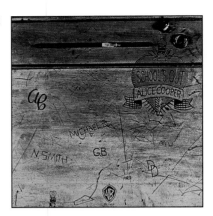

Along with The New York Dolls, it was Alice Cooper and *School's Out* that epitomized the U.S. version of glam rock.

The title track was a huge hit single on both sides of the Atlantic and the LP had a run of 32 weeks on the U.S. albums chart. The early versions of the semi-gatefold sleeve featured a pair of paper knickers wrapped around a school desk.

The Alice Cooper Band was originally on Frank Zappa's Straight label, and played the clubs of Los Angeles. Heavily in debt, they moved to Detroit, eventually signing with Warner Brothers. Their music was part Stones, part trashy adaptation of the garage rock of the likes of The MC5, and, like The Stones, they were a five-piece, with Glen Buxton and Michael Bruce on guitars. Their third album, *Love It To Death*, yielded a hit in 'I'm Eighteen,' and their fourth, *Killer*, opens with the live favorite 'Under My Wheels.' Cooper developed a highly theatrical act, with props that included a live snake, chopped up dolls, electric chair, and guillotine, and the singer plastered in mascara. This soon made them a top live draw.

School's Out is a concept album only insofar as it evokes a *West Side Story* world of teen delinquency. Many of the songs have above-average arrangements, but the title track was the standout moment, a classic school-day blues song that belonged to a tradition that went back to Chuck Berry's 'Ring Ring Goes The Bell.' It has a great riff and a memorable word play on the word "principles." Cooper's influence can be felt in later acts such as Guns N'Roses, Mötley Crüe, and Marilyn Manson.

I'm Still In Love With You Al Green

Hi Records 32074 (US) / London SHU 8443 (UK)
Released October 1972

I'm Still In Love With You is the centerpiece of a trio of classic Al Green albums that also includes Let's Stay Together (1972) and Call Me (1973).

Considered by many to be the greatest soul singer of the 1970s, Green was the primary beneficiary of the Hi Records house band, which included the exemplary five-piece Memphis Horns.

From the age of nine, in the late 1950s, Al Green had toured with his siblings as the gospel quartet The Green Brothers before scoring a Number Five hit on the U.S. R&B charts with 'Back Up Train' (1968), recorded with The Soul Mates. Green signed with bandleader and Hi Records executive Willie Mitchell in 1969, and recorded the albums *Green Is Blues* and *Al Green Gets Next To You* (1971). Neither was a commercial success, but Green's fortunes changed when the classic title track to *Let's Stay Together* (1972) topped the U.S. singles chart.

Green followed that album six months later with his masterpiece, *I'm Still In Love With You*. His fourth album to be recorded with the Hi Records band, it was co-produced by Green and Mitchell, and features the singer's first explorations into country and rock material. Most of the songs are Green originals, but he finds room for impressive renditions of Roy Orbison's 'Pretty Woman' and 'For All The Good Times' by Kris Kristofferson. The album failed to chart in the U.K. but reached Number Four in the U.S.A., where the title track was also a hit when issued as a single.

Exile On Main Street
The Rolling Stones

Rolling Stones 2900 (U.S.A.) / 69100 (U.K.)
Released June 1972

Here is an example of a rock band really taking advantage of the space offered by the double-vinyl format.

Exile On Main Street occupies a special position in The Rolling Stones' catalog, often acclaimed as the definitive expression of their 1970s-era music. It was the follow-up to *Sticky Fingers* (1971) and made Number One on both sides of the Atlantic. It is also an example of a band recording in unusual circumstances, breaking the rule that records are supposed to be made in recording studios.

Part of the album's legend is the situation in which it was recorded. Using The Rolling Stones' 16-track mobile unit, the band wrote and recorded the 18 songs in the greatest amount of disarray and informality that could be imagined, living in Richards's house, Château Nellcote, at Villefranche-sur-Mer in the South of France, between May and September 1971. The building had allegedly been used as the local Gestapo headquarters in World War II, which gained The Stones another brownie point in the decadence stakes. The decision was partly a result of tax exile, partly the desire to avoid the sterilities of being in a studio, and have the chance to blur the work-party boundary. Keith Richards said: "Suddenly for *Exile* we all left England and went to France and recorded in my house – and after that slowly everybody dispersed to different parts of the globe, so the lull in that period was more to do with just the geographical difficulties of getting it together."

The house was cold and damp, and overdubs were done in the kitchen while people were eating or talking. Band members came and went unpredictably with lovers and wives. Mick Jagger was often absent, leaving Richards as the prime architect of the material. The air of dishevelment runs right through to the sleeve's hand-written notes and raggedly assembled assortment of black and white photos by Robert Frank. The romanticizing of this *mise-en-scène* is evident when one critic invites us to listen to 'Loving Cup' and "imagine condensation streaming down the cellar walls, rattling chandeliers, and the ever-present mood-music of the mistral, the French summer wind that reportedly takes on a deeply ghostly aspect."

It did mean The Stones could record whenever inspiration struck. Of 'Happy,' on which Richards sang lead, he said: "The basic track was Bobby Keys on baritone sax, myself on guitar, and Jimmy Miller on drums. 'Happy' was cut one afternoon because the whole record was cut in the basement of my villa with The Stones' mobile truck parked in the driveway. So sometimes I would be ready to play and some of the guys would come over early. It was really like a warm-up, but had this idea for a song."

Exile drew on a blend of country blues, Chuck Berry, and Stax/Volt R&B, and is characterized by a murky production in which the lead vocals are pulled back – though the mix sounds clearer on the 66-minute CD reissue. The core of the music is the guitar interplay between Richards and Mick Taylor. There are up-tempo rockers ('Rip This Joint,' 'Happy,' and 'All Down The Line'), country rock songs ('Sweet Virginia'), as well as blues material such as the cover of Slim Harpo's 'Hip Shake' and 'Stop Breaking Down' (the latter recently revived by The White Stripes). Guest musicians included Bobby Keys (saxophone), Jim Price (trumpet and trombone), Nicky Hopkins (piano), and Al Perkins (slide guitar). The extra time allowed by having four sides to play with was exploited by arranging the 18 songs into four sections: Side One was full of rockers, Side Two was acoustic in emphasis, Side Three had some gospel touches, and Side Four had four upbeat soul-influenced songs.

Stones fans claim that this devil-may-care approach inspired some of the band's best music; the less committed may find that the LP's material is remarkably uninspiring for an album about which such big claims are made, and that *Sticky Fingers* is far more focused. The standout track is 'Tumbling Dice,' the epitome of The Stones' distinctive groove and a hit single. Richards himself conceded that double albums are problematic: "Double albums have a lot going against them. You know there's gonna be a certain amount of confusion, with so much material . . . in the beginning we didn't want to make a double album, but it all just poured out." Contrary to the legend, not all the songs came out in the South of France. 'Shake Your Hips,' 'Shine A Light,' and the basic track of 'Stop Breaking Down' were first recorded in October 1970 in London, 'All Down The Line' was put down in October 1969 in Los Angeles, and 'Loving Cup' went all the way back to the spring of 1969.

Producer Jimmy Miller commented: "Basically, *Exile on Main Street* was an idea to try and get back to good old rock'n'roll. Looking back over the recent albums, we felt there was a need to re-establish the rock thing." Not positively received at the time, *Exile* over the years has come to be influential as an example of how a rock album might be made as much as for its music.

1972

1972

Foxtrot Genesis

Charisma CAS1058 (U.S.A. & U.K.)
Released October 1972

One of the most enduring rock bands from the 1970s to the 1990s, Genesis had an impressive run of success across three decades on both sides of the Atlantic. *Foxtrot* finds the group at the start of its creative peak, and was the first Genesis album to chart in the U.K.

Vocalist and songwriter Peter Gabriel formed Genesis in 1967 with fellow pupils at the private school he attended, Tony Banks (keyboards) and Mike Rutherford (bass). The group released the albums *From Genesis To Revelation* (1968) and *Trespass* (1970), but didn't begin to reach its full potential until guitarist Anthony Phillips and drummer Chris Stewart were replaced by Steve Hackett and Phil Collins. This new-look Genesis, now signed to manager Tony Stratton-Smith's Charisma label, recorded *Nursery Cryme* in 1971, which began to show signs of the expansive, theatrical progressive rock the group would soon make its own. The follow-up, *Foxtrot*, is where the five members of Genesis finally reach their potential.

Working much faster than many of their prog rock contemporaries – who would take months to finish each album – Genesis recorded *Foxtrot* at Island Studios in Basing Street, London, between August 6th and 11th 1972. The album sessions were produced by David Hitchcock and engineered by John Burns. The band performed at the *Reading Festival* and then completed a short tour of Italy before mixing *Foxtrot* on the 25th, 26th, and 27th of the same month. The album's sleeve credits give an indication of how far the group had grown as musicians: Gabriel plays flute and oboe on some songs, while Rutherford provides flourishes of cello on others.

> ## "WE WORKED ON A PIECE THAT WAS 30 MINUTES LONG. I FELT WE'D OUTSTAYED OUR WELCOME BY THE TIME WE WERE FIVE MINUTES INTO IT."
>
> *GENESIS GUITARIST STEVE HACKETT*

Foxtrot opens with one of the band's best-loved songs, 'Watcher Of The Skies,' a powerful distillation of the group's sound, drenched in Mellotron strings. 'Time Table' evokes the more theatrical moments of David Bowie's recent *Hunky Dory* (1971) and *Ziggy Stardust* (1972), while 'Get 'Em Out By Friday' is a more sustained psychedelic piece. The 23-minute, seven-part epic 'Supper's Ready' dominates *Foxtrot*'s second side, leaping backward and forward from acoustic guitar-led whimsy to all-out rock. Peter Gabriel's lyrics and vocal performances are complex and extravagant throughout, giving some indication of the multilayered concept albums he would conceive shortly after *Foxtrot*.

Foxtrot peaked at Number 12 in the U.K., but Genesis didn't reach the U.S. albums chart until the release of the following year's *Selling England By The Pound*. That album was succeeded in late 1974 by the two-disk set *The Lamb Lies Down On Broadway*, after which Peter Gabriel left the group to pursue a solo career. Phil Collins then took over as the chief creative figure in Genesis, leading the band in a more pop direction.

■ *Genesis frontman Peter Gabriel on tour in support of* **Foxtrot** *at the City Hall in Newcastle, England.*

Something/Anything? Todd Rundgren

Bearsville 2BX 2066 (U.S.A.) / K65501 (U.K.)
Released February 1972

With its numerous false starts, breakdowns, and other charming imperfections, Todd Rundgren's one-man, double-disk *Something/Anything?* proved to an entire generation of do-it-yourselfers that the hits really could come from the home.

By the start of the 1970s portable multitrack technology had enabled multitalented types – Paul McCartney with *McCartney* and Pete Townshend with *Who Came First?*, for instance – to create an entire album's worth of material unassisted. Rundgren, a budding producer whose credits included The Band's *Stage Fright* (1970) and Badfinger's *Straight Up* (1971), was not to be outdone. Late in 1971 Rundgren set up shop inside ID Sound, a small Los Angeles studio, and began work on his first full-fledged solo effort. Manning the controls was James Lowe, a Los Angeles-based engineer and frontman for 1960s rockers The Electric Prunes. "ID was one of the first independents in Los Angeles," recalls Lowe, "the kind of place where you could go and really get hands-on and no one would bother you. Plus, it had the full compliment of Sennheiser and Neumann mikes, and really nice homemade effects as well."

Rundgren arrived at the studio with a large parcel of ideas – "a bouquet of ear-grabbing melodies," as he'd later call them – few of them fully formed. "The album was the demo – it all went down right there," says Lowe. "A lot of times Todd only had a rough sketch of a song, and it would just develop through the recording. It's a great way to work – things are happening spontaneously and that's when the real magic can happen."

Rundgren began each song by situating himself inside ID's closet of a drum-room. "I was never sure exactly where the song was going until we'd laid down about four or five tracks," says Lowe. "He'd leave these blank spaces all over the place – there would be like eight or 12 bars of nothing – and then he'd just go back afterward and pop in a piano or guitar in that spot." One thing was certain, Rundgren wanted the new work to have a muscular, uncompromising veneer. When it came time to track the pop rave-up 'Couldn't I Just Tell You,' Rundgren's acoustic guitar was sent through a compressor set to high gain. "That sucking limiter thing just worked great on that song," says Lowe. "Most of the tracks were right on the edge like that – we were really trying for something with a little more bite."

Guitar and vocal parts were later added up at Rundgren's place in Nichols Canyon, using a borrowed Scully 8-track machine. During one such living-room session, Lowe snapped a photograph of the artist striking a mock-Nixon pose from atop a makeshift platform, with wires and crumpled paper strewn across the floor and a vocal microphone taped unceremoniously to the handle of a floor mop. "I had a wide-angle lens," recalls Lowe, whose shot was later used for the album's gatefold, "in order to take in the full scope of the mess!"

With finishing touches applied at New York's Record Plant and Bearsville Studios, *Something/Anything?*, released in early 1972, spawned a pair of smash singles in 'I Saw The Light' and, more than a year later, 'Hello It's Me,' a remake of Rundgren's Nazz-era cut – and Rundgren's first and last trip to the Top Ten, though he had other lower-placed chart singles under his own name as well as many hits produced by him. The album consolidated Rundgren's reputation as a hit-making wunderkind – a label he promptly refuted with the formation of the left-of-center Utopia a short time later.

1973

Dark Side Of The Moon
Pink Floyd

Harvest 11163 (U.S.A.) / SHVL 804 (U.K.)
Released March 1973

"No," says Roger Waters, **"it's not our best album.** *The Wall* **is deeper and more musically powerful."**

Having composed the bulk of both albums, the estimable Mr Waters is more than entitled to his opinion, but the international record-buying public begs to differ. Over the past three decades we've shelled out for a mere 23 million copies of *The Wall*, while lapping up 34 million copies of *Dark Side Of The Moon*, which isn't bad for an album with somewhat humble beginnings.

"It began in a little rehearsal room in London," remembers Floyd guitar supremo Dave Gilmour. "We had quite a few pieces of music, some of which were left over from previous things." During the closing weeks of 1971, that room in Broadhurst Gardens, West Hampstead, saw the gestation of an epochal album, rich in sonic experimentation, powerful melodies, and startling lyrical concepts, which would elevate Pink Floyd from major-league cult status into the world's biggest rock band.

"At some point during the proceedings," Gilmour has said, "Roger came up with the idea of making it a piece about madness." Mental illness was something about which Pink Floyd knew a great deal, having watched their first leader, Syd Barrett, reduced from brilliantly inventive songwriter to

incoherent babbler through the onset of schizophrenia exacerbated by the frequent ingestion of LSD. Understanding that the 'madman' in *Dark Side Of The Moon* is Syd Barrett is essential to grasping why Waters's concept galvanized the band, sparking them to new creative heights.

Having spent the previous five years in a wilderness of pleasantly inconsequential electronic noodling, Pink Floyd now surged forward to create a genuinely ground-breaking album that charted one man's retreat into paranoid insanity via the medium of impeccably languid rock songs linked by beautifully realized electronic sound collages.

Dave Gilmour has asserted that another major reason why *Dark Side* differed from previous Pink Floyd albums was that "we'd played it live before we recorded it." He's absolutely right, and not only did the Floyd play it live, they developed it from gig to gig.

They emerged from West Hampstead on January 20th 1972 to give their first live performance of a musical suite entitled *Eclipse: A Piece For Assorted Lunatics*, at The Dome, Brighton, U.K., but it was very much a work in progress. Waters confirms, for example, that: "The actual song, 'Eclipse,' wasn't performed live until Bristol, Colston Hall, on February 5th. I can remember one afternoon rolling up and saying, 'Hey chaps, listen, I've written an ending.' So when we started performing the piece called 'Eclipse,' it probably did have 'Brain Damage,' but it didn't have, 'All that you touch, all that you see, all that you taste.'"

Critic Derek Jewell of the London *Sunday Times* saw the piece, now entitled *The Dark Side Of The Moon*, at London's Rainbow Theatre on the 17th, by which time it had been hammered into a shape that more closely resembled how the finished album would turn out. "In their own terms," wrote Jewell, "Floyd strikingly succeed. They are dramatists supreme."

Tours of the Far East, North America, and Europe enabled the band to fashion the material still further so that, according to Gilmour, when recording finally began at EMI's legendary Abbey Road Studios on June 1st 1972, "we all knew the material. The playing was very good. It had a natural feel."

Intriguingly, the first track they worked on was 'Us And Them,' which keyboardist Rick Wright had originally composed for the film *Zabriskie Point* in 1969. It failed to make the film's final cut so now, with additional input from Waters, it was pressed into service for the new album. A week later

1973

recalls as having been composed very quickly, in a mere 24 hours. "I knew there had to be a song about money in the piece," explains Waters, "and I thought that the tune could be a song about money, and having decided that, it was extremely easy to make up a seven-beat intro that went well with it. I often think that the best ideas are the most obvious ones."

The following day they laid down the basic track for 'Time,' the music of which is credited to the whole band but with lyrics by Waters. "For me it was the first time we'd had great lyrics," reckons Gilmour. "The others were satisfactory, or perfunctory, or just plain bad. On *Dark Side*, Roger decided he didn't want anyone else writing lyrics."

Before the month was out they'd also set to work on the basic track for 'The Great Gig In The Sky,' a wordless Rick Wright composition evoking Waters's fear of dying in a plane crash, and notable for session singer Clare Torry's astonishing gospel-blues wailing, intended to represent the pain and ecstasy of life and death.

Work on *Dark Side* was inconveniently derailed by further tours of the U.S.A. and Europe, not to mention the recording of a soundtrack, *Obscured By Clouds*, for the film *La Vallée*, plus work on a ballet score for French choreographer Roland Petit.

During October 1972 they returned to Abbey Road and, among other things, decided to bring in an outside musician to add sax solos to 'Money' and 'Us And Them.' "There were several big names we could have gone to," points out Gilmour, "but it can be tedious bringing in these brisk, professional session men. A bit intimidating." Instead, they called up their old Cambridge mate Dick Parry, who did them proud.

The final burst of studio sessions did not begin until January 18th 1973. During the last two weeks of the month they completed the spooky instrumental 'On The Run,' which had been recorded earlier as a guitar and keyboard piece. Now they added synthesizer sequences courtesy of a newly arrived EMS VCS Synthi-AK, then overlaid them with synthesized airplane sounds and running footsteps recorded in an echoey tunnel near London's Science Museum.

One of the most distinctive and, at the time, avant-garde aspects of the album was its ingenious use of spoken-voice samples, another innovation that Gilmour attributes to Waters. "He wanted to use things in the songs to get responses from people. We wrote a series of questions on cards and put them on a music stand, one question on each card, and got people into the studio and told them to read the first question and answer it. Then they could remove that card and see the next question and answer that, but they couldn't look through the cards so they didn't really know what the thread of the questions was going to be until they got into it."

Interviewees included roadies and their girlfriends, Jerry the Irish doorman at Abbey Road, and Paul and Linda McCartney, who turned out to be "much too good at being evasive for their answers to be usable."

The unseen questions included: When did you last hit someone? Were you in the right? Would you do it again? And, most crucially, What does the dark side of the moon mean to you? It was Jerry the doorman who responded with the astonishingly appropriate: "There is no dark side of the moon, really. It's all dark." Placed in the context of the closing track, 'Eclipse,' this spontaneous response resonates with as much power as if it had been written by a playwright.

It's worth noting that, though Waters was undoubtedly the primary architect of *Dark Side*, the album was made at a time when he and Dave Gilmour were working in harmony, with each contributing a unique set of attributes to the project. "I think I tend to bring musicality and melodies," is how Gilmour explains it. "Roger was certainly a very good motivator and obviously a great lyricist. He was much more ruthless about musical ideas, where he'd be

happy to lose something if it was for the greater good of making the whole album work. So, you know, Roger'd be happy to make a lovely sounding piece of music disappear into radio sound if it was benefiting the whole piece. Whereas I would tend to want to retain the beauty of that music."

The final studio session was held on February 1st 1973. "We'd finished mixing all the tracks," remembers Gilmour, "but until the very last day we'd never heard them as the continuous piece we'd been imagining for more than a year. We had to literally snip bits of tape, cut in the linking passages and stick the ends back together. Finally, you sit back and listen all the way through at enormous volume. I can remember it. It was really exciting."

The tone of the album is set from the opening seconds, when an ominous overture employs a heartbeat to underscore ticking clocks, cash registers, manic laughter, and screams, before giving way to the liquid slide guitar intro of 'Breathe.' Waters's stark lyrics tie the tracks together as much as the music, dealing in turn with the big issues of birth, time, death, and money before introducing the theme of madness with 'Us And Them,' and developing that idea to its logical but shattering conclusion on 'Brain Damage.' Looking back at that particular song, Roger Waters has said that the title line was: "Me, speaking to the listener, saying, 'I know you have these bad feelings and impulses, because I do, too, and one of the ways I can make contact with you is to share the fact that I feel bad sometimes.'"

Though many of the ideas – tape-loops, voice samples, sound effects, etc. – were not new, even in a pop context, the use of them on *Dark Side* to sustain a mood that permeates the entire work was startlingly innovative. And that's where Nick Mason deserves a hearty pat on the back. While the contributions of Waters, Gilmour, and Wright are self-evident, it's all too easy to see Mason as Floyd's Ringo, contributing not much more than a solid thump as and when required. *Dark Side* engineer Alan Parsons has pointed out that this view could hardly be more misguided: "He was always the guiding light in matters to do with the overall atmosphere," says Parsons, "and he was very good on sound effects and psychedelia and mind-expanding experiences."

It would be heartening to conclude that the album went on to massive success simply on its sublime musical merit, but no one in Pink Floyd is sufficiently self-delusional to believe that's the case. "It wasn't only the music that made it such a success," says Mason. "EMI/Capitol had cleaned up their act in America. They put money behind promoting us for the first time. And that changed everything."

Gilmour, too, has stated that, rather than the cerebral complexities of 'Brain Damage' or 'Eclipse,' it was the rootsy funk of 'Money' that reached out and grabbed the band a new audience. "It started from the first show in America. People at the front shouting at us to play 'Money!' and to give them something they could shake their asses to!"

Whatever the reasons, after its release on March 24th 1973 *Dark Side* went on to achieve astronomical worldwide sales. though, astonishingly, it has never topped the U.K. chart, and spent only one week at Number One in the U.S.A.

Perhaps unsurprisingly, Roger Waters never had any problem seeing the sow's ear behind the silk purse of Pink Floyd's greatest moment. "We'd cracked it. We'd won the pools. What are you supposed to do after that? *Dark Side Of The Moon* was the last willing collaboration. After that, everything with the band was like drawing teeth; ten years of hanging on to the married name and not having the courage to get divorced, to let go; ten years of bloody hell. It was all just terrible. Awful. Terrible." Certainly Pink Floyd's internal wrangles seem to have intensified after *Dark Side*, even though it finally put paid to the notion that the band could never creatively equal the work they had done on their first album when Syd Barrett was in the driving seat.

When all's said and done, *Dark Side Of The Moon* is a prime example of the progressive-rock concept album at its very best, one that survived the Year Zero of punk and subsequent movements to be rediscovered by new generations – as well as by those who liked it first time round but, having assigned it once to the trashcan of 'dinosaur rock,' now find that they probably always rather liked it after all.

1973

The Faust Tapes **Faust**

Not issued in the U.S.A. / Virgin VC501 (U.K.)
Released 1973

A hyperactive patchwork of song fragments, *The Faust Tapes* afforded the cult German band a brief window of commercial success when the recently formed Virgin Records decided to sell it for the price of a single.

Faust was the brainchild of Uwe Nettelback, a journalist-turned-producer who, despite not playing on any of their records, is the band's key figure. The group began rehearsing and then recording in his converted schoolhouse studio; their chaotic, sound-collage debut, *Faust*, was issued in 1971 by Virgin on clear vinyl housed in an eye-catching transparent sleeve. The follow-up, *Faust So Far*, is more song based but retains the first album's fiercely individual, experimental streak. Neither sold more than a couple of thousand copies.

The material that became *The Faust Tapes* was not originally intended for commercial release, but Virgin hit upon the idea of issuing it at a cost of just 49 pence – less than a dollar at the time. Taken from recordings made between 1971 and 1973, the album was a disorientating collection of 26 mostly untitled pieces of music, ranging from full songs to 30-second snapshots of ideas, several of which would turn up in more coherent form on *Faust IV*. The songs ranged from free jazz to psychedelic pop, but Virgin's marketing gimmick worked: all 60,000 copies of the original pressing sold within a couple of months, making *The Faust Tapes* the most mythical of the various Krautrock albums released around the same time – including Can's *Tago Mago* and Neu!'s *75*, both of which, along with *The Faust Tapes*, are often cited as seminal influences by such musical luminaries as David Bowie and Radiohead.

Paris 1919 **John Cale**

Reprise MS 2131 / K44239 (U.K.)
Released March 1973

Clasically trained and inclined toward the avant-garde, Cale's first three solo albums after leaving The Velvet Underground explored the territory of angry rock and minimalism.

But this fourth offering, with its heavily orchestrated introspective musings on religion, ghosts, and the British class system, came as a bolt from the blue.

Recorded in Los Angeles, largely at Sunset Sound, with the members of Little Feat acting as his backing band, *Paris 1919* was the first time Cale had used a producer other than himself, the duties here undertaken by Chris Thomas. It was a smart decision because, though Cale wearied of endless retakes of each song, Thomas had the patience to spend long nights in the studio choosing the best takes and enhancing the sound.

Cale's subtle arrangements for The University College Of Los Angeles Orchestra, often adding layers of harmony rather than melodies, give the likes of 'Hanky Panky Nohow' a sympathetically textured ambience that simply doesn't exist in any other rock album of the era. 'The Endless Plain Of Fortune,' for example, though pinned down by solid drums, seem to drift on currents of sound.

Cale's voice is, as always, an uncertain instrument, but reservations about his singing are swept away in the face of such inscrutable lines as: "If the sacheting of gentlemen gives you grievance now and then, what's needed is the memory of planning lakes." Listeners may never work out exactly what that means but, unlike most willfully contrived and obscure lyrics, there's a feeling that they definitely do mean something.

■ *Roxy Music on stage in Los Angeles in December 1972, in the midst of the group's only tour of the U.S.A. with keyboardist Brian Eno (left). Eno left Roxy Music shortly after the release of* **For Your Pleasure**. *He went on to record a number of acclaimed solo albums and to become one of the most important producers of recent times, helming albums by artists including David Bowie, Talking Heads, and U2.*

Warner Brothers 2696 (U.S.A.) / Island ILPS 9232 (U.K.)
Released July 1973

Along with David Bowie, Roxy Music were the intelligent art-rock end of glam, drawing on cultural references hitherto regarded in rock circles as hopelessly Establishment and unhip.

Bryan Ferry's donning of a tuxedo was almost as rebellious a gesture in 1973 as safety-pins were in 1976, except it was a revolt into style. Rock convention stated that 'proper' music – that is, music that annoyed your parents – had its Year Zero in 1956. This meant crooners such as Sinatra *et al.* and the songs they sang were out, as was anyone

male rock fan forgave them Eno all tarted up because they had drummer Paul Thompson, who looked like a regular guy and laid down a muscular beat, the bug-eyed Phil Manzanera on guitar, and a *femme fatale* on the record sleeve.

And Roxy Music didn't just look different, they sounded different from the average rock band. Eno supplied on-tap synthesizer weirdness and Andy Mackay's saxophone conjured visions of space-age rock'n'roll on songs such as the stomping 'Editions Of You' and the witty 'dance' single 'Do The Strand.' Manzanera played expressive lead in 'Strictly Confidential,' and a brilliant freak-out solo through a blizzard of phasing in the dramatic 'In Every Dream Home A Heartache,' a song that showcased the band's imagination. As for Ferry, his robot crooner vibrato and echo-laden electric piano brought an unforgettable brooding power and regret to such art deco nocturnes as 'Beauty Queen' and 'For Your Pleasure.'

1973

Goodbye Yellow Brick Road Elton John

MCA 10003 (U.S.A.) / DJM DJLP 1001 (U.K.)
Released November 1973

This 17-song double album cemented Elton John's international standing.

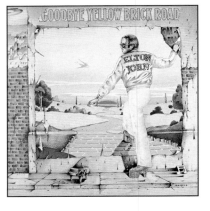

The former Reginald Dwight embarked on his career under the name of Elton John as a piano-playing singer-songwriter, composing music for Bernie Taupin's Wild West-infatuated lyrics. Once glam rock took off in Britain, Elton had license to dress up, wear outrageous spectacles and platform boots, and come on like a 1970s Little Richard.

Goodbye Yellow Brick Road was cut at the popular Château d'Hérouville studios in France in not much over two weeks. The original intention had been to record in Jamaica, but sessions were quickly aborted because of problems with the studio and a heavy atmosphere.

The album opens in somber mood with 'Funeral For A Friend' and the Marilyn Monroe-elegy 'Candle In The Wind,' one of the album's four single hits. 'Bennie And The Jets' was a nod in the direction of Bowie's Ziggy, complete with dubbed audience noise and the evocative couplet "You're gonna hear electric music / Solid walls of sound." It gave Elton his first R&B hit and a U.S. Number One. The album had up-tempo rockers – the fairground jive of 'Your Sister Can't Twist' and the Stonesy rocker 'Saturday Night's Alright For Fighting,' for example – which Taupin gave an English flavor, and the stately 'Goodbye Yellow Brick Road.' The likes of 'This Song Has No Title' and 'Grey Seal' had gospel-tinged melodies and progressions that could have come from the earlier Elton John of *Tumbleweed Connection*. *Goodbye Yellow Brick Road* reached Number One across the world and spent two years on the U.S. and U.K. albums charts.

The Singles 1969–1973 **The Carpenters**

A&M 3601 (U.S.A.) / AMLH/CAM 63601 (U.K.)
Released November 1973

The biggest-selling musical act of the 1970s, brother-and-sister duo Richard and Karen Carpenter had their greatest success with *The Singles 1969–1973*. Issued at the height of their fame, it spent 115 weeks on the *Billboard* albums chart.

Keyboardist-arranger Richard and drummer-singer Karen recorded an unreleased album for the RCA label in 1966 before signing to A&M Records in 1969. The Carpenters scored an impressive run of light and breezy Top 20 hit singles in the early 1970s, including the chart toppers 'Close To You' and 'Top Of The World.' They were the most successful of a number of wholesome, MOR performers to dominate the charts in the 1970s, the ranks of which also included Barbra Streisand and Bread. *The Singles 1969–1973* contains all of their hits, from their first release, a cover of The Beatles' 'Ticket To Ride,' to 'Yesterday Once More,' which reached Number Two in the U.K. and the U.S.A. in June 1973.

The Carpenters' career began to decline within a year of the release of *The Singles* album, as their light, harmonic pop had fallen from fashion by the latter half of the decade, while both siblings were beset by ill-health. Karen died tragically in 1983 as a direct result of the anorexia from which she had suffered throughout most of her adult life, bringing worldwide recognition to the condition for the first time. The Carpenters' music has continued to sell strongly since her death, in particular this collection, which has sold seven million copies in the U.S.A. alone.

Tales From Topographic Oceans Yes

Atlantic 18122 (U.S.A.) / K/K4 80001 (U.K.)
Released December 1973

The pinnacle of prog ambition in the 1970s, *Tales From Topographic Oceans* is an album that continues to divide not just critics and fans but also the group itself: keyboardist Rick Wakeman left shortly after the album's completion, unhappy with the direction Yes was taking.

After scoring four consecutive U.K. Top Ten albums – including *Close To The Edge* (1972) and the triple-vinyl live set *Yessongs* (1973) – Yes spent the latter half of 1973 attempting to fashion a record that would top all of the group's previous releases. Public anticipation for *Tales* was so high that the album, a double, achieved gold status in the U.K. on the strength of pre-sale orders alone. The LP's subject matter is rooted in the spiritual text *Autobiography Of A Yogi* by Paramhansa Yogananda, and is divided into four distinct sections, sporting names like 'The Revealing Science Of God,' each of which fills one side of vinyl.

Tales From Topographic Oceans is a sprawling, richly orchestrated work, awash with sudden changes in tempo and time signature, searing guitar solos, synthesizer flourishes, and impenetrable lyrics about Eastern mysticism – the kind of album that would today be derided as being hopelessly overblown and pretentious. Many critics at the time shared this view, but there was clearly a market for the band's prog excesses in its day: *Tales From Topographic Oceans* was the group's biggest commercial success to date, topping the U.K. albums chart and peaking at Number Six in the U.S.A.

Blackboard Jungle Dub
Lee Perry And The Upsetters

No Catalog Number
Released 1973

One of the key figures in the development and popularization of reggae, the eccentric Lee 'Scratch' Perry has produced hundreds of records in a career spanning five decades.

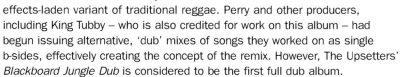

In the late 1960s and early 1970s he worked closely with The Wailers (featuring Bob Marley), whose backing band contained several members of Perry's own band, The Upsetters. Perry was also one of the earliest innovators of dub, a bass-and-drum-heavy, effects-laden variant of traditional reggae. Perry and other producers, including King Tubby – who is also credited for work on this album – had begun issuing alternative, 'dub' mixes of songs they worked on as single b-sides, effectively creating the concept of the remix. However, The Upsetters' *Blackboard Jungle Dub* is considered to be the first full dub album.

Perry's rich, spacious productions are all the more impressive given his primitive working methods. Perry's recording set-up in the 1970s consisted of a basic Teac 4-track recorder, a small mixing desk, and a few early effects units, including an Echoplex delay unit, which he would use to achieve his distinctive, echoing snare drum sound. In 1973 Perry built his Black Ark Studio in his own back yard, which allowed him to work full time on developing his sound. Perry continued to release dub albums and singles at a prodigious rate, his recordings proving inspirational to other reggae producers as well as the likes of The Clash.

In 1977 Perry brought an end to the Black Ark phase of his career, burning down his studio after claiming it had been beset by evil spirits. Black Ark

was just one of a number of famous studios to be destroyed by fire. The Caribou Ranch studio in Nederland, Colorado, burned down in 1985 after previously playing host to artists including Steely Dan, Neil Young, and Chicago. Easley McCain Studios in Memphis suffered a similar fate in 2005. Wilco, Jeff Buckley, and The White Stripes had all recorded there.

Countdown To Ecstacy Steely Dan

ABC 779 (U.S.A.) / PROBE SPB 1079 (U.K.)
Released July 1973

A flawless marriage of Brill Building pop suss, jazz elegance, and rock attitude makes this the most consistently satisfying Steely Dan artifact.

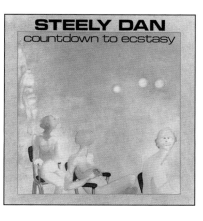

Founders Walter Becker and Donald Fagen had honed their skills working as staff songwriters at ABC Records, but forming their own band gave them a free hand to let their musical imaginations run riot. Their debut, *Can't Buy A Thrill*, included two major hit singles, 'Do It Again' and 'Reelin' In The Years,' but what *Countdown* lacks in hits is more than compensated for in sophistication. On *Thrill* the band was relatively inexperienced, but by *Countdown* they'd toured together, so, as Becker explains: "The musicians got to hear the songs and participate in developing the arrangements at an earlier stage. Because we knew what the band sounded like, we had a more developed conception of it, and it became a more integrated framework."

By this time the band had lost its original vocalist, David Palmer, so Fagen's intellectual sneer moved front and center, proving to be a better vehicle for the band's scathingly acerbic critiques of the U.S.A.'s foibles. The Stax

saxophone and stuttering guitar battle in the middle of 'My Old School,' the swing-meets-heavy-metal groove of 'Bodhisattva,' and the strutting cynicism of 'Showbiz Kids' make this perhaps the high-water mark of studio-perfect rock because the passion remains intact throughout.

Unfortunately, however, the album proved too cerebral for the MCA executives charged with marketing it. Promotion was minimal and sales were poor, but the passage of time has accorded *Countdown To Ecstacy* the status it always merited.

1973

Tubular Bells
Mike Oldfield

Virgin 13135 (U.S.A.) / V2001 (U.K.)
Released May 1973

Tubular Bells was a music-industry ground-breaker of epic proportions, cobbled together, as it was, by a teenage guitar geek.

Mike Oldfield would be the first to admit that he was something of a social misfit, a prodigiously talented young musician whose guitar was his life. He didn't set out to create an album that would expand the horizons of electric guitar as none had done since Hendrix, or an album that would break every rule about how to make hit records, or even an album that would make it possible for rock composers to be spoken of with the same respect as classical composers, but he achieved all three just by doing what came naturally to him.

The seed of *Tubular Bells* was sown on July 10th 1971, when Kevin Ayers And The Whole World played their final gig together in London, leaving Mike Oldfield, their 16-year-old guitarist, out of a job. Ayers, however, had also given the lad his key to fame and fortune, an old Bang & Olufsen tape recorder. "By soldering a few wires together and blocking off the tape with cigarette packets and things," recalls Oldfield, "I was able to multitrack on it. I took the insides out and did all kinds of strange things with tape loops and decided that I'd better have one of these Terry Riley things in there to start my very first demo. And that was the opening theme for *Tubular Bells*, which I played on a Farfisa organ."

Oldfield lugged his lo-fi, warts'n'all demo round to the smart offices of several top record company A&R men, only to find that "they all looked at me as if I was mad. They all said, because there was no vocals, no words, no drums or anything, that it was not marketable" – and, in a year when the British charts were dominated by the likes of Donny Osmond, David Cassidy, and Gilbert O'Sullivan, who could blame them?

Indeed, it might all have ended right there if Oldfield's next group, The Arthur Lewis Band, hadn't been chosen by chance to make some test recordings at Virgin's soon-to-be-opened Manor Studios in Oxfordshire. During some downtime at The Manor, Oldfield played his demo for studio boss Tom Newman. "He was just a funny little hippie," recalls Newman, but he was sufficiently impressed to allocate some recording time.

So, in late 1972 Oldfield squirreled himself away in the bowels of The Manor and set to work in earnest, piecing *Tubular Bells* together from what Newman had first heard as "half a dozen little unconnected pieces," and playing virtually all the instruments himself. As Oldfield remembers it: "I made up a list for Virgin of all the instruments I would need, and they ordered everything up for me. I had seen a set of tubular bells when I did some recording in Abbey Road, so I thought I may as well have some tubular bells, they might come in handy."

Though The Manor was being built from scratch as a state-of-the-art recording facility, it was still a time when editing of tracks was done by cutting up the tapes with a razor blade. From the start Oldfield pushed the existing technology to its limits. "I remember, on the second day of actual recording, explaining to Tom that I had this organ chord which I wanted to slowly slide into another chord," he says. "It would be simplicity itself with modern synths, but the only way we could do it then was to get the maintenance engineer to come in and record the first organ chord on a tape

loop, which he then put on to this great big machine with a huge dial on it and, as he turned the dial, the machine sped up which caused the chord to go up in pitch."

Tom Newman has vivid memories of some of the Heath Robinson/Rube Goldberg-like contraptions Oldfield used to achieve his guitar effects. "He had this awful home-made electronics box full of horrid transistors, covered in faders and knobs, which he called his Glorfindel. It was a piece of plywood filled with junk that he could plug his guitar into and sometimes a sound would come out. Most of the time it was terrible. It would go 'Eeeeoww, Arrrk!' It was like tuning a radio set. Then he would kick it and all of a sudden this glorious, amazing guitar sound would come out."

Much of the actual recording was carried out late at night, after the imbibing of far too much Guinness at a local hostelry. As a result, entire days of recording were sometimes wiped by accident and, as Oldfield readily admits, the tubular bells themselves were somewhat the worse for wear by the time they were put on tape. "Instead of using the little mallet provided, I hit the bell using a proper metal hammer," he explains, "because I wanted it to sound much bigger. I really wanted a huge cathedral bell, but all we had was these little bells. Anyway, I hit it so hard that I cracked it and there was so much gain wound up on the microphone channel that there's noticeable distortion."

On hearing the completed masterwork, Virgin supremo Richard Branson was far from convinced. According to Newman, getting his boss to release the record "was like dragging stuff uphill through treacle." In due course, however, Newman won Branson over and *Tubular Bells* entered the U.K. album chart on July 14th 1973. It wasn't exactly an overnight smash, but persistent marketing kept it moving up, peaking at Number Three in the U.S.A. in March 1974 and finally reaching the top of the

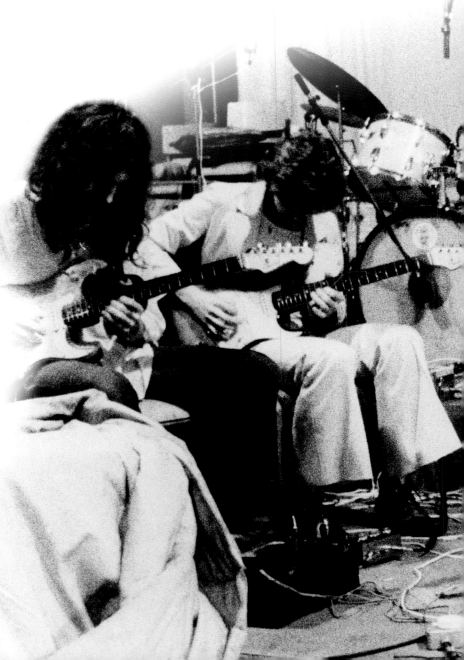

U.K. chart on October 5th 1974, one week after its follow-up, *Hergest Ridge*, had hit the top spot.

Ultimately, it became the second bestselling album in the U.K of the 1970s, outsold only by Simon & Garfunkel's *Bridge Over Troubled Water*. And, as if to prove all those doubting A&R men wrong, after *Tubular Bells* appeared on the soundtrack of the movie *The Exorcist* an edited excerpt became a U.S. Top Ten single.

■ *Main picture: Mike Oldfield (center) in rehearsals for a live performance of* Tubular Bells *at the Queen Elizabeth Hall, London, in June 1973. Among the guest musicians were Gong's Steve Hillage (left) and Mick Taylor of The Rolling Stones (second left).*

The Origins Of Virgin Records

Quite apart from the innovative characteristics of the music, *Tubular Bells* has a second claim to rock'n'roll greatness. Being the first record released by Virgin Records, it was also the start of the Richard Branson empire, which has since blossomed into a global conglomerate built on megastores, airlines, railways, telecommunications, and much, much more.

Branson, having left his private school with minimal formal qualifications, founded Virgin as a cut-price mail-order record store, but it was unquestionably the massive sales generated by *Tubular Bells* that transformed the toothy-grinned charmer into a business mogul, who went on to sell Virgin Records to EMI in March 1992 for £560 million (about $1,033 million at the time).

Branson's canny business instincts remain his empire's greatest asset, though his clever manipulation of his own image runs it a close second. He knows that to be seen abseiling down the side of a skyscraper or ballooning across the world's oceans brings the kind of advertising money can't buy. Pegged early on as "the hip capitalist," he is famous for apparently knowing nothing about music. "It was a bit beyond him," says Mike Oldfield, who points out that Branson's real gift was for employing people who did know what they doing. Those people signed Phil Collins, Culture Club, The Sex Pistols, and countless other acts that probably made Branson richer than any of them.

1973

Raw Power **Iggy Pop**

Columbia KC 3211 (U.S.A.) / CBS 65586 (U.K.)
Released May 1973

Among the most aptly named albums ever recorded, *Raw Power* captures the violent, proto-punk energy of Iggy And The Stooges right before the group imploded.

Born James Jewel Osterberg, Iggy Pop began his musical career as drummer in The Iguanas before forming The Stooges with bassist Dave Alexander and siblings Ron and Scott Asheton on guitar and drums respectively. The Stooges' eponymous debut, produced by John Cale, sounded like a more visceral Velvet Underground – and at the time Iggy was dating that group's sometime chanteuse Nico. Neither *The Stooges* (1968) nor *Fun House* (1970) sold more than a couple of thousand copies at the time, leading to the end of The Stooges' relationship with their label, Elektra. In 1972 the group split temporarily. Later that year, by chance, Iggy ran into David Bowie – a big fan of The Stooges – and Tony DeFries of Bowie's MainMan management team. Bowie would, over the course of the next year, become a crucial figure in resuscitating the careers of not just Iggy but also The Velvet Underground's Lou Reed, whose album *Transformer* (1972) he produced.

Bowie and MainMan brought Iggy to Britain with a slightly reconfigured line-up of The Stooges: Alexander was no longer in the group, while Ron Asheton had switched to bass to make way for new guitarist James Williamson. Somewhat surprisingly, given The Stooges' chaotic recent past and penchant for drink and drugs, MainMan allowed Iggy to produce himself what would become *Raw Power* at CBS Studios in London. Iggy's main aim was to capture the raw energy of what he still considers, 30 years after the fact, to be the finest and most powerful rock group of the time. To that end, everything on the record is bursting with distortion; the songs sound as though they could explode at any moment.

There are some touches, though, that distinguish The Stooges from other pre-punk garage-rock groups of the time: 'Penetration' makes use of a celeste – a keyboard instrument containing tuned bells, used in Tchaikovsky's 'Dance Of The Sugar Plum Fairy,' from *The Nutcracker Suite* – while 'Search And Destroy' contains the sound of sword fighting. According to Iggy, the latter sound is authentic: "We got some old sabers from an antique store. That was maybe a little unnecessary production touch which we took out of these new mixes." The "new mixes" to which Iggy is referring feature on a 25th anniversary edition of *Raw Power* issued in 1997 on the Legacy division of Columbia Records. When Iggy had handed in what he thought was the finished version of *Raw Power* to MainMan in early 1973 Tony DeFries hated the sound of the album and enlisted Bowie to remix the songs at Western Sound in Hollywood. While Iggy was reasonably happy with Bowie's mix, it didn't exactly stick to his original aim for the album, which was to show off the "rip-snortin' super-heavy, nitro-burnin', fuel-injected rock band that nobody in this world could touch at that time." Some of Bowie's changes and additions to the album were in too much of an eccentric, quintessentially English vein for Iggy's liking, hence his decision to return to the album two and a half decades later.

Like its predecessors, *Raw Power* was not a commercial success, though the Bowie connection helped boost its sales slightly. The album was, however, highly influential on most of the punk groups that followed, on either side of the Atlantic, from The Ramones to The Sex Pistols.

The Stooges backstage at the Whiskey A-Go-Go, Los Angeles, on October 30th 1973: Iggy Pop (seated, left), Scott Asheton (seated, right), Scott Thurston (standing, left), Ron Asheton (center), and James Williamson (right).

1974

Autobahn Kraftwerk

Vertigo 2003 (U.S.A.) / 6360 (U.K.)
Released November 1974

Though Kraftwerk perfected their sinisterly synthetic pop on later albums, it was *Autobahn* that woke the world up to the potential of electronic sounds.

Kraftwerk's earlier albums consisted largely of ambient instrumental noodlings, similar to their German contemporaries Tangerine Dream and Ash Ra Tempel, but with *Autobahn* they created a template for much of the cutting-edge pop and rock that was to follow. Florian Schneider recalls that *Autobahn* emerged when they returned to their whimsically named Düsseldorf studio, Kling Klang, after a long motorway drive. "When we came in to play, we had this speed in our music. Our hearts were still beating fast, so the whole rhythm became very fast."

Taking a revolutionary departure from their usual entirely instrumental approach, they decided to add some lyrics about driving on the Autobahn. Then, as lyric collaborator Emil Schult explains: "Ralf [Hutter, of Kraftwerk] specifically asked me to write some lyrics, and it took me one day. Ralf went over them and corrected them a little bit, and it was singable, so it became a song."

To capture sounds of passing traffic, several *Autobahn* journeys were undertaken in Hutter's Volkswagen – what else? – with the microphone of a portable tape recorder dangled out of the window. Despite its engine noises, evocative Doppler shifts, and rhythmic precision provided by their newly acquired custom-built 16-step analog sequencer, *Autobahn* wasn't intended as a map of the future: Kraftwerk themselves saw it as being similar in many ways to The Beach Boys' 'Fun, Fun, Fun.' Hutter and Schneider were fascinated by how Beach Boys songs, crammed with references to woodies, perfect waves, and beach bunnies, conjured instant mental pictures of West Coast teen society.

"A hundred years from now," explained Hutter, "when people want to know what California was like in the 60s, they only have to listen to a single by The Beach Boys." *Autobahn* was Kraftwerk's first attempt to do the same thing for their homeland, but 1970s Germany was radically different from 1960s California. "Walk in the street and you have a concert – cars playing symphonies," pointed out Hutter. "Even engines are tuned, they play free harmonics. Music is always there – you just have to learn to recognize it."

The 22-minute long 'Autobahn' is the album's centerpiece, and though other tracks are clearly descended from their earlier ambient output, Hutter's unlikely Beach Boys analogy is borne out by the unmistakable surf-rock drum patterns and chugging rhythms in 'Kometenmelodie 2.'

An edited version of 'Autobahn' reached Number 25 on the U.S. singles chart, but, just as the crooners of the mid 1950s couldn't grasp the significance of Elvis Presley, the music critics of the 1970s were so steeped in the traditional verities of the 12-bar and the blustering machismo of rock that many saw it as little more than a bizarre electronic novelty, a lifeless Teutonic descendant of 'Route 66.' It was, however, just a matter of time before nothing would ever be the same again, and Kraftwerk's influence was soon celebrated in the work of artists as diverse as Afrika Bambaataa, David Bowie, Depeche Mode, New Order, Orbital, The Chemical Brothers, and Michael Jackson.

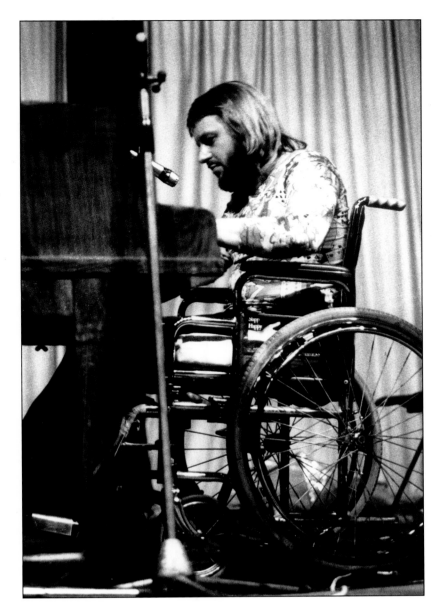

Head Hunters **Herbie Hancock**

Columbia 32731 (U.S.A.) / CBS CBS/40 65582 (U.K.)
Released January 1974

One of the most influential figures in jazz of the later 20th century, Hancock made perhaps the definitive jazz-funk album, *Head Hunters*, an early example of the potential of the synthesizer.

A prodigiously talented pianist, Herbie Hancock had a huge influence on the changing direction of The Miles Davis Quintet of the mid 1960s before forming his own sextet in 1968. Hancock's band made four albums in the early 1970s, experimenting with funk and cutting-edge synthesizers, but split because of financial difficulties. His next act was to form a stripped down funk group to record *Head Hunters*. Clearly inspired by James Brown and Sly Stone, Hancock's rich synthesizer playing on the album is more rhythmic in feel than the piano flourishes that made his name in the previous decade. Hancock also makes use of an early sequencer, which allowed him to program synthetic bass parts over which his band could perform.

Perhaps surprisingly, for a record so groundbreaking, *Head Hunters* was an instant commercial hit, becoming the first jazz album to achieve platinum status. Hancock remained popular throughout the 1970s, playing to stadium-sized audiences across the U.S.A. and releasing a series of albums that developed on themes introduced on *Head Hunters*. Hancock later had a pop hit with the robotic funk single 'Rockit' in 1983, while also making frequent returns to the acoustic jazz of his roots.

Rock Bottom **Robert Wyatt**

Virgin13112 (U.S.A.) / V/TCV 2017 (U.K.)
Released July 1974

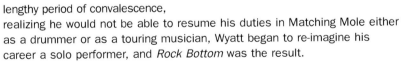

During the late 1960s Robert Wyatt was the drummer in the art-rock collective Soft Machine. After playing on their first four albums he began to tire of the role, so in 1971 he left to form Matching Mole, in which he sang as well as drummed.

Two albums later, Wyatt fell from a third-storey window at a party, suffering a spinal fracture that has left him wheelchair bound ever since. During a lengthy period of convalescence, realizing he would not be able to resume his duties in Matching Mole either as a drummer or as a touring musician, Wyatt began to re-imagine his career a solo performer, and *Rock Bottom* was the result.

Though Wyatt had written most of the material for *Rock Bottom* before his accident, the album clearly reflects his difficultly in dealing with his paralysis. Recorded by Pink Floyd's Nick Mason, the six stately songs are given time and space to develop by an impressive array of guest musicians, chief among them Mike Oldfield. Most deal with the insular life that Wyatt and his soon-to-be wife Alfie had adopted, notably the heartbreaking opener 'Sea Song,' on which he declares, in his trademark wistful falsetto, "When you're drunk, you're terrific." Though not a particular commercial success, *Rock Bottom* is rightly regarded as one of the real high points in progressive rock. Two months later, in a typical example of his idiosyncratic career, Wyatt had a U.K. hit with a cover of The Monkees' 'I'm A Believer,' and he continues to make the occasional, often highly political, album into the 21st century.

Court And Spark **Joni Mitchell**

Asylum 7E1001 (U.S.A.) / SYLA 8756 (U.K.)
Released March 1974

***Court And Spark* is a high point both in Joni Mitchell's career and for the 'sophisticated' end of the singer-songwriter genre.**

In contrast to the stark *Blue*, *Court And Spark* had a band sound, courtesy of Tom Scott's jazz-rock LA Express. Guitarists Larry Carlton, José Feliciano, and Robbie Robertson also assisted, while David Crosby and Graham Nash did some backing vocals. Elements of light rock and jazz dovetailed in a fine batch of songs about life and love. It went gold and had three hit singles: the ecstatic 'Help Me,' the playful 'Raised On Robbery,' and the breezy 'Free Man In Paris.'

Mitchell tells a salutary tale about sharing a house with David Geffen, head of Asylum Records, who at this time was hoping to release Dylan's new album, *Planet Waves*. When Mitchell had finished *Court And Spark* she took it home to play to Geffen. "I was so excited the night I finished it I brought it back to the house to play it. There were a bunch of people there, including Dylan [who] . . . fell asleep and snored all the way through it. When the record came to the end, the people went, 'Huh?' Then they played *Planet Waves* and everybody jumped up and down. There was so much enthusiasm . . . for the first time in my career I felt this sibling rivalry. It was an ordinary record for Bobby, a transitional piece, and yet everybody was cheering. Finally, one of the women took me aside and said, 'Don't pay them any attention. Those boys have no ears.'"

1975

Horses **Patti Smith**

Arista 4066 (U.S.A.) / ARTY 122 (U.K.)
Released December 1975

Patti Smith was one of the foremost poets of the punk era, while *Horses*, her debut album, remains one of the best-loved records to come out of New York in the 1970s, ranking alongside albums by The Ramones, Talking Heads, and Television.

Horses was produced by John Cale, formerly of The Velvet Underground, whose influence is clear on a number of its songs. Another key contributor was guitarist Lenny Kaye, who had regularly backed Smith on the New York performance-poetry circuit in the early 1970s and who had, in 1973, compiled the influential *Nuggets* album of 1960s garage rock. The album also features pianist Richard Sohl, bassist Ivan Kral, and drummer Jay Dee Daugherty.

Horses opens with a brief spoken-word passage that segues neatly into an energetic rendition of Van Morrison's 'Gloria.' There are also suggestions of reggae (on 'Redondo Beach') and several reflective, piano-led epics. 'Break It Up' was co-written by Television frontman Tom Verlaine, who also plays guitar on the track.

Smith recorded three more albums in the late 1970s before retiring to concentrate on married life with her husband, ex-MC5 guitarist Fred 'Sonic' Smith, and only returned to her musical career after his death in 1995. She marked the 30th anniversary of *Horses* with a live recreation of the album at the 2005 *Meltdown* festival in London.

■ *Patti Smith on stage in early 1976 with bassist Ivan Kral.*

Natty Dread **Bob Marley**

Island ILPS 9281 (U.S.A. & U.K.)
Released May 1975

Live! **Bob Marley**

Island ILPS 9376 (U.S.A. & U.K)
Released December 1975

The most iconic reggae performer of all time, Bob Marley made his international commercial breakthrough in 1975 with these two albums.

Both contain versions of his classic 'No Woman No Cry,' and the live set also features a rendition of his 'I Shot The Sheriff,' a major hit for Eric Clapton the previous year. With these songs, Marley brought reggae to a truly global audience for the first time.

Before Marley's arrival on the international music scene as a solo star, The Wailers – Marley, Peter Tosh, and Bunny Livingston (aka Bunny Wailer) – had established themselves as huge stars in their native Jamaica. During the 1960s and early 1970s the group worked with two of the most influential and pioneering figures in Jamaican music, 'Sir' Coxsone Dodd and Lee 'Scratch' Perry, producing numerous domestic hits. Among them, 'Trench Town Rock,' issued on The Wailers' own Tuff Gong label, topped the Jamaican singles chart for five months in 1971.

The Wailers signed with Chris Blackwell's Island Records in 1972, shortly after the release of a one-off single on CBS, 'Reggae On Broadway,' the group's first international release. Blackwell was at the helm of much of Marley's material from this point on, including *Catch A Fire* (1973), one of the first full reggae albums and the first to reach a wider, more rock audience. By the time *Natty Dread* was recorded, Bob Marley And The Wailers – as they were now called, Tosh and Wailer having left – had built up a strong live following, but had yet to achieve any hit records outside Jamaica.

Natty Dread was colored by the presence of a number of additional musicians, including American guitarist Al Anderson – who, along with Blackwell, introduced a more pronounced rock edge to Marley's music – and the African drummer Remi Kabaka. The album is also the first of Marley's to feature The I-Threes, three female backing singers – one of whom was Marley's wife Rita – who had replaced his former partners on vocal duties. *Natty Dread* contains some of Marley's strongest songs, including 'Rebel Music' and 'Revolution.' The album's key moment is the soulful ballad 'No Woman No Cry,' a live version of which provided Marley with his first U.K. hit single shortly after the album's release. *Natty Dread* itself peaked at Number 43 in the U.K., and edged into the lower reaches of the Top 100 in the U.S.A.

Shortly after the release of *Natty Dread*, Marley embarked on a sold-out tour of the U.K. that culminated in an appearance at the Lyceum Ballroom in London. *Live!* captures that performance, from July 18th 1975, and was recorded with the same band that features on *Natty Dread*. Marley is at the peak of his powers here, successfully recasting his traditional Jamaican music for a rock audience. The material is split equally between selections from *Natty Dread* and older songs, including 'Burnin' And Lootin'' and 'I Shot The Sheriff.' The musicians are barely audible on 'No Woman No Cry,' as they are overtaken by an ecstatic crowd singing every word in full voice. Later reissued with the more informative title *Live At The Lyceum*, the album improved slightly on *Natty Dread*'s chart placing, reaching Number 38 in the U.K. and Number 90 in the U.S.A. Marley achieved further commercial success the following year with *Rastaman Vibration*, which entered the U.S. Top Ten.

1975

Born To Run
Bruce Springsteen

Columbia 33795 (U.S.A.) / CBS CBS69170 (U.K.)
Released November 1975

Born To Run, Bruce Springsteen's breakthrough album, is one of the definitive rock albums inspired by life in the city.

It dramatizes the romantic longings of urban life, offering snapshots of tenements, streets, and highways, where radios blare through summer windows, bikers pose with their machines, and lovers make out on the beach. At the album's heart are the car and the open road, and the idea of driving away together and escaping.
This is most clearly caught in the famous title track, but it informs each of the record's eight songs, right from the opener 'Thunder Road,' a tale of broken-hearted boys crying over graduation gowns. No matter how desperate the characters, in Springsteen's mini-*West Side Story* there is always a better place at the freeway's end. Much of his career since has questioned that, but *Born To Run* is a city to visit when you need the strength to dream.

Springsteen made a long journey to find the music of his third album. In the late 1960s he was a long-haired guitarist playing heavy blues rock on a Les Paul in bands such as Earth, Child, Clearwater Swim Club, and Steel Mill. Then he appeared in a series of short-lived outfits, including Dr Zoom And The Sonic Boom and The Bruce Springsteen Band, all the while gaining vital experience as a live performer. Springsteem collaborator 'Miami' Steve Van Zandt commented: "He was into songwriting very early on and was always quite good at it. There weren't that many people writing back then; it was still the era of the old Brill Building thing."

By 1971 Springsteen knew it was time for a musical change: "I moved from hard rock to rhythm-and-blues-influenced music and I began to write differently." He played solo for noted A&R man John Hammond at CBS in May 1972. Hammond saw Springsteen as a new folk singer in the Dylan mold and signed him on that basis, but when recording for the first album started in June 1972 Springsteen insisted on using a band. By this point he had seven years of songwriting behind him, in a number of different styles. His lyrics were wordy and the impressionistic songs had cinematic qualities, and he was also experimenting with longer forms that would work well live. He later called the resulting album – *Greetings From Asbury Park, NJ* – "an acoustic record with a rhythm section."

In 1973 many critics dismissed Springsteen as a mix of Dylan and Van Morrison. His own personality and musical strengths were obscured. The first version of The E Street Band toured with Chicago to promote *Greetings*. For the second album, *The Wild, The Innocent And The E Street Shuffle* (1974), Springsteen wanted to inject a dose of bar-band sparkle'n'clatter into the new songs to up the energy of the band's live show, and 'Rosalita' quickly established itself as one of the highlights of the set. In May 1974 journalist – and later Springsteen producer as well as manager – Jon Landau wrote the famous review that featured the quote: "I saw rock'n'roll future and its name is Bruce Springsteen."

His first two albums had sold moderately, and Springsteen was building a reputation as a live act, but even as his profile grew, the band was almost broke and nearly dropped by CBS. His third album had to be

a killer. Roy Bittan replaced David Sancious on piano and Max Weinberg came in on drums.

After protracted and psychologically bruising sessions at 914 Sound Studio, Blauvelt, New York, and the Record Plant, New York City – with Springsteen, Jon Landau, and Mike Appel on production duties – *Born To Run* was released in August 1975, and it was the album that put him on the road to stardom. Springsteen said in 1978: "When I did *Born To Run*, I thought, 'I'm going to make the greatest rock'n'roll record ever made.' The only concept that was around *Born To Run* was that I wanted to make a big record, you know, that sounds like these words. Just like a car, zoom, straight ahead, that when the sucker comes on it's like wide open. No holds barred!"

Not for nothing did Springsteen name-check Roy Orbison in 'Thunder Road.' Roy Bittan confirmed: "He said he wanted a record where the singing sounded like Roy Orbison." Reaching past hard rock, Springsteen's musical landmarks were to be found in the late 1950s and early 1960s: Orbison, Presley, The Righteous Brothers, The Ronettes, The Beach Boys, Bo Diddley, Duane Eddy, Phil Spector. Critic Greil Marcus once described 'Born To Run' as a "'57 Chevy running on melted-down Crystals records." Springsteen himself said in 1987: "I wanted to make a record that would sound like Phil Spector. I wanted to write words like Dylan. I wanted my guitar to sound like Duane Eddy." The album, according to Springsteen, spoke "the traditional language of rock'n'roll." He never had forgotten the magical immediacy of mid-1960s pop and rock. One Springsteen biographer, Chris Humphries, describes him in concert as "a one-man history of rock'n'roll, a human jukebox," while another, Dave Marsh, calls him "the living culmination of 20 years of rock'n'roll tradition."

In 1980 Springsteen commented: "I've been influenced by a lot of people. Elvis was one of the first. Otis Redding, Sam Cooke, Wilson Pickett, The Beatles, Fats Domino, Benny Goodman, a lot of jazz guys. You can hear them all in there if you want to." Bo Diddley is the main rhythm reference for 'She's The One,' a cool jazz influence breathes through the wistful 'Meeting Across The River,' 'Tenth Avenue Freeze-Out' is updated Stax soul, while 'Jungleland' and 'Backstreets' closed each side of the vinyl record with an epic long-form song. The instrumentation is suitably impressive. Piano and glockenspiel glitter on the tracks like tarmac strewn with diamonds, and electric guitars and saxophone blend together in droning power-chords.

Born To Run simplified Springsteen's musical vision. He lost some of the funk and the street-dandy poetry but gained power and a bigger audience. The title track, with its Duane Eddy riff and unpredictable twisting and turning bridge, duly took its place in the pantheon of 'greatest-ever rock songs.' Live, it never failed to reduce artist and audience to one quivering mass of defiance and longing, growing more poignant as the years have passed. In October 1975 both *Time* and *Newsweek* put him on their covers – he was Rock's New Sensation.

■ *Below: Springseen with guitarist 'Miami' Steve Van Zandt (right).*

1975

Discreet Music **Brian Eno**

Antilles 7030 (U.S.A.) / Obscure OBS 3 (U.K.)
Released December 1975

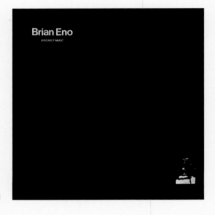

This extraordinary album took a slew of avant-garde ideas and seeded them into the heart of popular music culture where, amazingly, they took root and flourished.

In the early 1970s Eno was the flamboyant keyboard player of Roxy Music, an eccentric muso clad in peacock feathers and makeup, who coaxed weird electronic bleeps out of primitive synthesizers. He quit Roxy in 1973 to pursue a solo career, which took a radical turn on January 18th 1975 when Eno walked in front of a London taxi. Confined to a hospital bed for weeks, virtually immobile, he found himself listening one day to an album of harp music with the volume turned down too low to hear properly. Unable to move to turn it up, he found himself hearing the music as an aspect of the ambience of the room – like the changing qualities of the light or the sounds of the weather outside – and, to his surprise, he found that he enjoyed it that way.

On his release from hospital he decided to create a piece of music designed to be listened to at a low volume. He also decided that, rather than being composed, it should be generated. To achieve this he played a couple of simple melody lines on a synthesizer, which were harmonically compatible but of different lengths. He then fed both pieces through an echo unit and a delay system that looped them so that they would play simultaneously and repeatedly. Being of unequal length they would inevitably drift out of sync, creating a potentially endless pattern of variations.

Unusual as this was in a pop–rock context, *Discreet Music* was not a revolutionary work per se. Indeed, most of Eno's innovations had clear precedents in the avant-garde fields of minimalism and electronic composition. There had even been earlier electronic albums that found some acceptance with the rock audience, notably Terry Riley's *Rainbow In Curved Air* (1969), and two German works, Kluster's *Klopfzeichen* (1970) and Tangerine Dream's *Electronic Meditation* (1970). Eno himself, in collaboration with King Crimson guitarist Robert Fripp, had helped pioneer the use of ambient music loops on their 1973 album *No Pussyfooting*, and the original intention for *Discreet Music* was that it would become a musical background on top of which Fripp would improvise.

Many experimental composers set out to shock the musical establishment, but Eno took pains in the album's sleeve note to point out that his concepts owed more to the spirit of the early 20th century composer Erik Satie, "who wanted to make music that could 'mingle with the sound of the knives and forks at dinner.'" For some, this reduced Eno's composition to the same level as the despised Muzak systems, but others perceived it as a refreshing contrast to the self-aggrandizing high-volume bluster of rock music. Yet, without Eno's standing in the rock world, *Discreet Music* would have been confined to a much smaller audience, and it was his work with rock giants such as U2 and Talking Heads that would ultimately introduce many of Eno's ideas to vast mainstream audiences.

Blow By Blow **Jeff Beck**

Epic PE33409 (U.S.A.) / EPC69117 (U.K.)
Released March 1975

***Blow By Blow* was the nearest the mercurial Jeff Beck ever came to making an album consistently worthy of his undoubted guitar talents, and it stands as a good example of the jazz rock fusion style that was a minor thread in music during the first half of the 1970s.**

Beck came to fame in The Yardbirds in the mid 1960s, contributing idiosyncratic lead to some of their best material – and for a short time having as guitar partner Jimmy Page before Beck left to form his own band and Page went on to form Led Zeppelin out of the ashes of The Yardbirds. In 1968–9 Beck released *Truth* and *Beck-Ola* with a line-up that included Rod Stewart and Ronnie Wood before they re-emerged as The Faces. After further recordings with The Jeff Beck Group and the heavy-rock Beck, Bogert & Appice, Beck, with producer George Martin at the helm, made the all-instrumental *Blow By Blow*. The music put aside heavy riffs and three-chord blues for more complex progressions while still retaining some commercial appeal. Beck multiplied the lead parts by overdubbing and Jan Hammer played keyboards. Martin gave Beck's playing the backdrop of attractive strings and rhythm arrangements, and their partnership was kept for a second album, *Wired* (1976).

''Cause We've Ended As Lovers' is possibly the standout track here. However, Beck seemed fated never to find the right context or compromise by which his guitar skills could reach a wider public. He was also a stern critic of himself, once saying: "Emotion rules everything I do . . . I can switch on automatic and play, but it sounds terrible. I've got to be wound-up, in the right mood."

■ *Below: Brian Eno in his home studio during the mid 1970s.*

Gratitude Earth, Wind & Fire

Columbia 33694 (U.S.A.) CBS S80995 (U.K.)
Released December 1975

The year 1975 was a turning point for Chicago-based Earth, Wind & Fire. With the smash 'Shining Star' propelling parent album *That's The Way Of The World* to the top of the albums chart, EWF suddenly found themselves playing arenas to capacity crowds.

At Christmas they returned with *Gratitude*, a double-disk set of mainly live material, culled from the group's summer 1975 North American tour. It also included four new studio tracks: the single 'Sing A Song,' 'Can't Hide Love,' 'Celebrate,' and 'Gratitude,' all recorded the previous June at Colorado's Caribou Ranch. "We didn't have time to do a whole new studio album," explained Maurice White, "so we just started taping all our shows."

In concert, the phenomenal vocalizing of Philip Bailey breathed new life into the ballad 'Reasons,' while EW&F's impossibly funky horn section took 'Shining Star' up yet another notch – listening to Don Myrick's lyrical sax work during 'Reasons,' an awe-struck Bailey gushes to the audience: "He plays so beautiful. Don't you agree?"

Like its predecessor, *Gratitude* also climbed to the Number One spot, selling over a million copies in the process. Sadly, the joy surrounding EWF's newfound success was tempered by the loss of Charles Stepney – co-writer of 'Reasons' and 'That's The Way Of The World' – who died suddenly from a heart attack while the hit 'Sing A Song" was still in rotation.

As the first platinum-selling black R&B group, EWF became a major source of inspiration for scores of next-generation artists, among them multi-instrumentalist Lenny Kravitz, whose 1991 hit 'It Ain't Over 'Til It's Over' sounded strikingly similar to EW&F's 'That's The Way Of The World.'

CBS 33235 (U.S.A.) / CBS 69097 (U.K.)
Released January 1975

The Basement Tapes **Bob Dylan**

Columbia 32235 (U.S.A.) / CBS CBS/40 88147 (U.K.)
Released July 1975

Creatively, the early 1970s were a quiet time for Bob Dylan. The release of the much-maligned double album of covers and half-finished scraps, _Self Portrait_ (1970), was followed by the pleasant but modest _New Morning_, after which there was no new material at all until 1973, when the soundtrack to _Pat Garrett And Billy The Kid_ – a Sam Peckinpah movie in which Dylan appears – was released.

Early the following year saw the release of Dylan's and The Band's last studio collaboration, _Planet Waves_. Both albums had flashes of the old genius, but hard-line disciples of the one-time spokesman for a generation feared that their guru's creative fire had been all but extinguished by years of family life with wife Sara, the subject of _Blonde On Blonde_'s 'Sad-Eyed Lady Of The Lowlands.'

But by 1974 Dylan's life of apparent domestic bliss was crumbling. His marriage was in ruins, destroyed by the stress of enduring constant harassment from adoring fans and Dylan's alleged infidelities during a 1974 tour. It was from this sorry situation that Dylan drew inspiration for an artistic revival, writing a set of songs that detailed his pain, anger, frustration, and longing with an artistry that eclipsed even his greatest work from a decade earlier.

Sessions for _Blood On The Tracks_ were unusually protracted, at least by Dylan's usually spontaneous – and somewhat slapdash – standards. Recording started in New York during September 1974 when he booked studio time without even deciding who was going to accompany him. Producer Phil Ramone roped in ace session players Deliverance at the last moment, and a few songs were recorded. Dylan quickly dispatched Deliverance, however, and regrouped with a trio comprised of pedal-steel guitarist Buddy Cage, bassist Tony Braun, and organist Paul Griffin. With this stripped-down line-up Dylan recorded more songs, and a ten-song version of the album was completed, slated for release on Christmas Day 1974.

Promotional copies were pressed and sent out to radio stations, while Dylan took a copy back to the Minnesota farmhouse he was sharing with his brother David. There, listening through the songs, he persuaded himself that the mood was too mellow and, perhaps that the lyrics were just a little too obviously autobiographical. On Christmas Eve, the day before the album was due to be released, Dylan gave the order to stop production, stating that he wanted to re-record some songs.

A few days later he was in a studio in Minnesota with the cream of the local scene's musicians, where he re-cut the songs. Lyrics were edited and rewritten, tempos changed, and additional arrangement touches added. The album's two pivotal songs, 'Idiot Wind' and 'Tangled Up In Blue,' were among those reworked, becoming tougher, more energized, more caustic, and closer in spirit to classic Dylan from the mid 1960s in the process.

The revised version of the album was finally released in January 1975, to immediate critical acclaim and huge sales, eventually peaking at Number One in the U.S.A. and Number Four in the U.K. Bootleg versions of the earlier, scrapped version of the album – a much slower, more maudlin affair than the official release – have been circulating widely ever since.

Released later the same year, the songs on *The Basement Tapes* had been recorded by Dylan with The Band in 1966 and 1967 while the singer was apparently recuperating after a mysterious motorcycle accident. When the material was eventually released, it was during one of the busiest, most artistically rewarding periods of Dylan's career. The album appeared six months after *Blood On The Tracks* and six months before *Desire* (1976), at a time when he was touring with a revolving cast of singers and poets – including Joan Baez and Allen Ginsberg – on the 'Rolling Thunder Revue.'

The music Dylan and The Band had recorded was sent out as publishers' demo tapes in the late 1960s, resulting in hits for other artists, including 'Mighty Quinn,' a U.K. Number One for Manfred Mann. These recordings were among the first by any artist to be widely bootlegged, appearing from 1968 onward under various titles.

According to Dylan's recent autobiographical tome, *Chronicles: Volume One* (2004), the motorcycle incident was not quite as serious as he had claimed at the time: "I'd been hurt, but I recovered. Truth was that I wanted to get out of the rat race." Dylan spent several months with his wife Sara and newborn son Jesse at his home in Woodstock, New York, before inviting The Band to join him to work over some of his new songs. The musicians worked in near seclusion in the relaxed atmosphere of The Band's Big Pink recording base. In contrast to Dylan's output of the time, the frantic *Highway 61 Revisited* and *Blonde On Blonde*, much of the material on *The Basement Tapes* has an exuberant, playful feel, closer in spirit to the material recorded not long afterward for *John Wesley Harding* (1968).

Among the many highlights of the eventual 24-track, double-album issue of *The Basement Tapes* is his own version of 'This Wheel's On Fire,' already a U.K. hit for Julie Driscoll with Brian Auger And The Trinity, and the humorous 'Tears Of Rage,' on which Dylan sings: "I can drink like a fish / I can crawl like a snake / I can bite like a turkey / I can slam like a drake." The songs reveal Dylan and The Band at their most carefree, leading *Village Voice* critic Robert Christgau to remark: "What is most lovable about the album is simply the way it unites public and private, revealing a Dylan armed in the mystery of his songs but divested of the mystique of celebrity with which he has surrounded his recording career for almost a decade."

On its official release in July 1975 *The Basement Tapes* peaked at Number Seven in the U.S.A. and Number Eight in the U.K. For the previous seven years, however, most of the songs had been available in bootleg form, housed inside a plain white cover, decorated only with the title *The Great White Wonder*. While the practice of bootlegging music was not new, the success of *The Great White Wonder* was unprecedented: the album is claimed to have sold over 350,000 copies, though more conservative estimates place the figure closer to half of that. Whatever the actual sales, the popularity of *The Great White Wonder* gave a clear indication that music fans were willing to buy often poor-quality recordings of private tapes and live performances by the artists they admired.

The practice of bootlegging soon developed into a whole underground industry of its own. Among the notable pirate versions to follow *The Great White Wonder* into record shops were *Stampede* by The Who (a recording – in rather bad taste – of a performance at which twelve audience members were crushed to death), numerous live recordings of The Grateful Dead (which the group, unusually, encouraged), and the multipart series of Beatles rarities, *Unsurpassed Masters*.

1976

Desire **Bob Dylan**

Columbia 33893 (U.S.A.) / CBS CBS/40 86003 (U.K.)
Released January 1976

***Desire* and its predecessor, *Blood On The Tracks*, represent Dylan at the top of his second peak, his mid-1970s renaissance. They also confirmed the suspicion, long held by the cognoscenti, that no matter how far down he might go, Dylan could never be counted out.**

Anyone who had labored through *Self Portrait* in 1970 or *Planet Waves* in 1974 had every reason to believe that Dylan was a spent force. *Blood On The Tracks* was an assured return to form, but if anyone had any lingering doubts, just a few bars of *Desire*'s opening track, 'Hurricane,' was enough to sweep away the memories of half a decade of sub-standard material.

Sessions for the album had begun on July 28th 1975 at Columbia Studios in New York City. Emmylou Harris was on harmony vocals, Scarlett Rivera, a busker plucked from the streets of Greenwich Village, was on violin, and Eric Clapton was playing guitar. "It ended up with something like 24 musicians in the studio, all playing these incredibly incongruous instruments – accordion, violin . . ." recalled Clapton later. "It really didn't work. He was after a large sound, but the songs were so personal that he wasn't comfortable with all the people around. It was very hard to keep up with him. He wasn't sure what he wanted. He was really looking, racing from song to song. The songs were amazing." In consequence, from that first session, only 'Romance In Durango' made it to the finished album.

A few days later Dylan returned to the studio with no producer and an almost entirely different band, though Scarlett Rivera was still aboard. "The sessions were outrageous," she revealed subsequently. "There was just a rundown of the songs and, once the structure was understood, the red light went on." In this mood of unrehearsed spontaneity, they knocked off 'One More Cup Of Coffee,' 'Mozambique,' 'Hurricane,' and several others.

Clapton's assessment proved accurate, because the songs, mostly co-written with off-Broadway songwriter Jacques Levy, were extraordinary, particularly 'Sara,' an uncharacteristically transparent proclamation of undying love for his wife, from whom he was soon to part. 'Hurricane,' a powerful plea for the release of convicted murderer Ruben 'Hurricane' Carter, reasserted Dylan's role as a fighter for justice, a man of the people standing up against the system. And 'One More Cup Of Coffee' pulls off the classic Dylan trick of creating a startling contrast by interspersing seemingly mystical verses with a prosaic but evocative chorus.

If the band was somewhat loose, Rivera's soaring violin lines were more than enough to maintain the musical interest and, for his part, Dylan's vocals sounded more passionate than they had for years. "He wanted very unpolished and unaffected performances," explained Rivera. "He was really looking for lots of heart and genuine expression, as opposed to precision playing and a flawless performance."

The critics were divided on the merits of *Desire*, some clearly unable to hear the quality of the songs because of the slackness of the music, but the public had no such qualms, and the album reached Number One on the U.S. albums chart on February 7th 1976, staying there for five solid weeks.

1976

Stupidity **Dr Feelgood**

Not issued in the U.S.A. / United Artists UAS 29990 (U.K.)
Released September 1976

The quintessential English pub-rock band, Dr Feelgood hit the top of the U.K. chart with *Stupidity*, recorded at two 1975 live performances.

Dr Feelgood emerged from Essex, England, in the early 1970s, their frantic rock'n'roll soon earning a devoted local following. The band at the time was focused around twin frontmen Lee Brilleaux (vocals and harmonica) and hyperactive guitarist Wilko Johnson. On the strength of

their impressive live performances Dr Feelgood signed a multialbum deal with United Artists. Their first, *Down By The Jetty*, was recorded, unfashionably, in mono; the follow-up, *Malpractice*, was a minor U.K. hit, as was the single 'Back In The Night.'

Given that Dr Feelgood spent so much time on the road, leaving few opportunities for studio recording, the decision was made by United Artists to capture the band in their favorite environment, live on stage. The two sides of *Stupidity* were recorded at separate live shows, the first at Sheffield's City Hall, the second right in the band's backyard, at the Kursaal in Southend, Essex. The album includes definitive versions of many of the band's best-loved songs, including Johnson originals 'She Does It Right' and 'Roxette.' Its success briefly put Dr Feelgood's corner of Essex on the musical map, as other local acts including Eddie And The Hot Rods and The Kursaal Flyers had U.K. chart hits.

The band never really recovered, and was never able to repeat its early commercial success, after the departure of maniacal guitarist Johnson in 1977, though they continue to tour to the present day, albeit with a completely changed line-up. Brilleaux had remained in the band, but by the time of his untimely death from cancer in 1994 he was the only remaining original member.

■ *Above: Wilko Johnson (left) and Lee Brilleaux of Dr Feelgood, on stage in 1976. Dr Feelgood was one of the leading lights of pub rock, a pre-punk style that emerged from North London and Essex, England, during the mid 1970s as a reaction to the excesses of progressive rock.*

This was a band whose first gig, in early 1974, was so bad that many of their friends stopped speaking to them afterward. Vocalist Joey Ramone, however, was undaunted, believing firmly that by that time "rock'n'roll had got so bloated and lost its spirit. We stripped it down and re-assembled it under the influence of The MC5, The Beatles and The Stones, Alice Cooper and T. Rex."

So The Ramones persevered, tightened up, and won a sizeable live following. Even so, Hilly Kristal, owner of legendary New York venue CBGB's, vividly remembers the night when MOR queen Linda Ronstadt and her entourage pitched up at the club to see what the fuss was about. "They lasted less than five minutes. She literally flew out the door holding her ears."

The buzz was enough, however, to get them a low-budget deal with Sire Records, who put them into Plaza Sound Studios at Radio City Music Hall, New York City, to start recording the album on February 2nd 1976. Production on the album was in the hands of Sire's in-house A&R man Craig Leon with some assistance from Tom Erdelyi, aka Tommy Ramone, the band's drummer. Leon recalls: "A lot of people didn't even think they could make a record. There were weeks of pre-production on a very basic level, like when the songs started and when they ended."

Once the band was fully rehearsed it became a matter of deciding on a sound. Leon's point of reference for the guitars was the rasping din on 'Silver Machine,' the only hit single by British acid-rock warriors Hawkwind – bassist Lemmy, who sang lead on 'Silver Machine,' went on to form Motörhead. To achieve the huge yet dry overall ambience of the album he put each musician's amps into separate rehearsal halls so that "you could crank it up and still get isolation."

To the uninitiated, every Ramones song sounds identical to every other Ramones song, but, as with dub reggae or blues, the subtle differences emerge with repeated listens. Each compact capsule is crammed with minimalist hooks, hints of Phil Spector, almost buried Byrds-like guitars, and much more.

When it was finished, on February 19th, it had cost a mere $6,400 at a time when superstars could easily eat up – or snort up – half a million dollars in the studio, and all 14 tracks take up a mere 29 minutes. Punk rock, as we know it today, was born.

The Ramones The Ramones

Sire 7520 (U.S.A.) / 9103 253 (U.K.)
Released May 1976

The Ramones is the album that invented the 1970s incarnation of punk rock.

The term 'punk' had been used in the 1960s, usually applied to what were more commonly called garage bands, such as The Standells, ? And The Mysterians, and The Sonics. There's no denying that The Ramones shared with these bands not just a certain brazen attitude but a slavish devotion to the notion that a great song never lasted more than three minutes and never employed more than three chords. The slogan on The Sonics' first album – "Four great guys, three great chords" – would have been equally valid for The Ramones a decade later.

1976

Arrival **Abba**

Atlantic 18207 (U.S.A.) / Epic EPC/40 86018 (U.K.)
Released January 1977 (U.S.A.) / November 1976 (U.K.)

One of the most successful pop acts of all time, Abba achieved so much commercial success during the mid 1970s that the group was listed on the Swedish stock exchange as one of the nation's biggest exports.

They had seven Number One albums and nine chart-topping singles in the U.K., and achieved the kind of pan-European success that others could only dream of. While Abba was not quite so universally popular in the U.S.A., the group did top the *Billboard* singles chart with the disco classic 'Dancing Queen,' included on *Arrival*.

Songwriting duo Benny Andersson and Björn Ulvaeus formed Abba in 1971 with their partners, vocalists Anni-Frid Lyngstad-Fredriksson and Agnetha Fältskog-Ulvaeus. All four had achieved fame independently in Sweden, but Abba's wider breakthrough came when the group won the 1974 Eurovision Song Contest with 'Waterloo,' which subsequently topped the U.K. chart and reached Number Six in the U.S.A. Abba consolidated this success with the albums *Waterloo* (1974) and *Abba* (1975), a first *Greatest Hits* compilation (1976), and a string of international hit singles, among them 'SOS,' 'Mamma Mia,' and 'Fernando.'

As with previous Abba albums all songwriting and production duties on *Arrival* were handled by Andersson and Ulvaeus. The duo wrote in a very methodical way, reminiscent of the conveyor-belt-like practices of Tin Pan Alley. They would turn up at their shared office in the morning, pull out their acoustic guitars, and churn out hits day after day. *Arrival* was recorded at various points between the summers of 1975 and 1976 at Metronome, Glen, and KMH studios in Stockholm, Sweden, the sessions broken up by the group's hectic promotional schedule in support of *Abba* and *Greatest Hits*. Abba started work on the basic backing track to 'Dancing Queen' in August 1975, adding string parts and vocals the following month. 'Knowing Me, Knowing You,' and 'That's Me' were cut in March 1976, with the rest of the album completed in the summer of the same year.

Musically, *Arrival* has a much more synthesized sheen than previous Abba recordings, which tended to be based around the traditional pop instrumentation of piano and guitar. The songs stick mostly to the template of *Waterloo* and *Abba*, but add elements of the disco sounds that were beginning to dominate the singles charts in Europe and the U.S.A., and occasionally feature more adult lyrical themes than on earlier hits. 'Money Money Money' has a cabaret feel, while the power ballad 'Knowing Me, Knowing You' describes the decline of a marriage, presaging the split between Björn and Agnetha Ulvaeus, who had married shortly after the group's formation in 1971. Both songs were huge international hits. 'Knowing Me, Knowing You' topped the U.K. singles chart, as did 'Dancing Queen,' which was also the group's sole U.S. chart topper.

The first Abba record sleeve to feature the group's distinctive mirror-image logo, with the first 'B' reversed, *Arrival* topped albums charts across Europe on its release in late 1976 and reached Number 20 in the U.S.A. when it was issued there early the following year. *Arrival* has sold over ten million copies worldwide, just edging past *The Album* (1978) and *Voulez-Vous* (1980) as the band's biggest-selling studio album. Its sales have since been eclipsed by the definitive hits collection *Abba Gold*, which prompted revival in the band's fortunes during the 1990s and has sold in excess of 25 million copies.

■ **Main picture: Abba on stage at the 1974 Eurovision Song Contest, an annual televised event in which various European nations each performs a song, with the winner decided by a public phone vote. The event was inaugurated in 1956 in a spirit of European unity, and over the years has enlarged to include former Eastern-bloc countries, as well as Israel and Turkey. Left to right: Benny Anderson, Anni-Frid Lyngstad-Fredriksson, Björn Ulvaeus, and Agnetha Fältskog-Ulvaeus. Above: Anderson and Ulvaeus contemplate the mix of another pop hit later in the 1970s.**

The Rock Radio Revolution

In an effort to provide a refuge from the commerciality of AM pop radio, during the late 1960s a group of upstart U.S. broadcasters launched a succession of 'alternative' rock radio stations on the FM band, a frequency normally reserved for classical music and public-affairs programming.

Instead of the usual parade of Top 40 hits, stations such as Boston's WBCN, New York's WNEW, and San Francisco's KSAN aired obscure album cuts and works by lesser-known artists and gave equal time to lyrical content deemed unsuitable for mainstream radio. WBCN's Charles Laquidara, WNEW's Pete Fornatale, and KSAN's Tom Donahue weren't just DJs but bona fide heroes of the underground, who frequently aired their views on subjects ranging from the war in Vietnam to the presidency of Richard Nixon. Playlists were non-existent, and the improvisatory nature of the broadcasts was infectious. By the start of the 1970s the massive popularity of FM began to have a direct impact on the recording arts. One of the first bands to capitalize on the format was Led Zeppelin, whose music was specifically tailored to the burgeoning FM movement, defying the conventional wisdom that hit singles sold albums.

But, as the popularity of FM rock radio grew, stations found themselves in direct competition with one another and, eventually, began awarding air space to big-money advertisers such as McDonald's and Coca-Cola. By the mid 1970s the subversive nature of early FM had all but disappeared, replaced by the increasingly structured AOR format, as FM jocks became largely indistinguishable from the AM broadcasters they'd once rebelled against. By then rock'n'roll, for years the voice of the young and disenfranchised, was rapidly becoming the domain of the corporate consultant, who studied the demographics and installed rigid playlists that favored laidback acts along the lines of Fleetwood Mac and The Eagles. As the business of making rock became bigger, recording artists demanded and received fatter contracts and increasingly indulgent terms and conditions.

1970s Studio Excess

With cash – and cocaine – flowing freely during the early 1970s, major recording studios were given a plush facelift. Expensive lighting, fancy decor, fully equipped kitchens, and top-notch recreational facilities replaced the humble interiors of yesteryear. At the same time, studio owners began to rethink the layout of the recording space, the result of the latest innovation in tape technology: with 16-track – and soon to be 24-track – engineers could have a dedicated track for each band member for the first time. At the time, however, some of the industry's best studios still utilized large, open tracking-rooms that in many instances pre-dated the era of the multitrack. With all the instruments blending together as a result of the live environment, it didn't matter if there were 16 tracks or 160 tracks. Studio heads quickly realized that without addressing the issue their investment would be wasted.

"So, in a further attempt to really isolate the instruments, in order to take full advantage of the 16-track technology, they started to deaden the studios," recalls Chris Huston, studio designer and noted producer-engineer for Van Morrison, James Brown, The Who, and many others. "The idea was that, with that many tracks, you could really control things, you could create something by having the ability to isolate and replace entire sections of a song. That immediately became apparent to those in the recording industry. And in order to pull it off, you had to also re-think the way the studio was constructed, because up until that point you didn't have the wherewithal to really hone those parts individually. So, in turn, they began this new studio prototype: one where leakage could be maintained, if not completely eliminated. It was a tremendous change in the method of modern recording up to that point. And it turned everything on its tail."

Unfortunately, the redesign had the unintended affect of stripping away any innate room sound – an element that had played such a large part of the recording process for so many years. "When we were doing 4- and 8-track, I could listen to a record that was made in New York and tell you which studio it came from," says engineer Shelly Yakus.

Continued on page 183

1976

Frampton Comes Alive! **Peter Frampton**

A&M 3703 (U.S.A.) / A&M AMLM 63703 (U.K.)
Released January 1976

As 1975 unfolded, Peter Frampton, a British export based in the U.S.A., was a moderately successful 24-year-old solo artist in need of a commercial breakthrough.

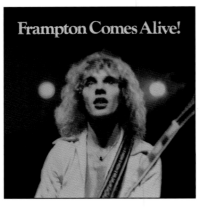

A skilled songwriter whose winsome good looks belied an extraordinary lead-guitar talent, the ex-Humble Pie member arrived at San Francisco's Winterland Ballroom on the night of June 14th backed by a tight new band and sporting an assortment of road-tested songs from his back catalog. At showtime, engineer Chris Kimsey – who had worked with The Rolling Stones and Ten Years After – snapped on a multitrack tape machine backstage and hoped for a few good takes.

The resulting work, issued the following January as *Frampton Comes Alive!*, made the industry reassess the power of live recordings and made Frampton an icon overnight. Sporting superior versions of studio tracks 'Show Me The Way,' 'Somethin's Happening,' and 'Lines on My Face' – and showcasing Frampton's acoustic side as well – the double-disk *Frampton Comes Alive!* spent ten weeks at the top of *Billboard*'s album chart, spawned three hit singles, and sold eight million copies in its first year alone. The album's trump card was, and still is, the stadium-sized 'Do You Feel Like We Do?' an extract from 1973's *Frampton's Camel* that somehow blossomed into a rocker of epic proportions, aided in no small part by Frampton's powerful solo breaks and expert timing.

In hindsight it's not too difficult to understand why *Frampton Comes Alive!* became the single-biggest live album in history – or, in the estimation of Wayne Campbell from *Wayne's World*, an album so popular "it was delivered in the mail along with samples of Tide." To his credit, Frampton understood the potential impact that a house full of unabashed – and uncoached – fans might have on the world at large if properly recorded. Of course, one can't create pandemonium in a vacuum – and to that end Frampton did his part by delivering some of the most melodic guitar work ever cut live. Eventually, the sound of 4,500 ecstatic Winterland fans was enough to convince 16 million record buyers that they were missing out on something huge.

It was a formula much too good to be ignored, and in the years that followed artists ranging from Bob Seger to Cheap Trick would follow the *Frampton Comes Alive!* blueprint all the way to the bank, even as Frampton himself was quickly unraveling from the experience. He eventually regained his composure in the 1980s and 1990s. Today, it's hard to get past Frampton's cheesecake cover photo, gimmicky talkbox work, and bizarre lyrics – "I have itchy fingers / And butterflies are strange" – yet, 30 years later *Frampton Comes Alive!*, which was repackaged in 2001 as a 'deluxe' CD set featuring four bonus tracks and an informative John McDermott essay, still sounds better than almost anything else that came out of that schizoid summer of 1976 and serves as a reminder of the magical possibilities that will always exist within the context of live performance.

Boston **Boston**

Epic BL34118 (U.S.A.) / EPC 81611 (U.K.)
Released February 1976

This is the story of how one man's musical obsession, a multitrack tape machine, and a home studio resulted in a multiplatinum record.

When the rock establishment in the U.K. was overthrown by punk in the mid-to-late 1970s, no such sweeping change took place in the U.S.A. There, the counter-culture rock of the late 1960s slowly mutated into AOR as its audience left their youth behind. A generation of musicians who'd grown up listening to blues-influenced hard rock, all riffs and solos, turned from revolution to rock's megawatt onslaught. One such was Tom Scholz, who had gained a Masters Degree in engineering at Massachusetts

and in his spare time put together a 12-track home studio. This background in electronics would eventually lead him into the field of inventing guitar effects-units such as the highly successful Rockman headphone amplifier.

A perfectionist and multi-instrumentalist, Scholz labored away, overdubbing parts until he reached a layered sound that was to influence profoundly the U.S. rock mainstream. In this process he was assisted by Barry Goudreau (guitar), Fran Sheehan (bass), Sib Hashian (drums), and Brad Delp (guitar and vocals). Scholz shaped heavy guitar riffs, amped-up old-time rock'n'roll, and short lead breaks with a pop sensibility, focusing on four-minute, verse-chorus songs that would appeal to a wide listenership with their straightforward lyrics. Scholz enthusiastically stacked vocal harmonies like The Eagles and created guitar choirs reminiscent of Queen. Legend has it that some of the home recordings ended up as the finished album.

The elegant punch of 'More Than A Feeling' is where everything cohered perfectly. A track best appreciated in its edited single form, it dusts off a few familiar chord progressions, adding for spice the lovely E-flat to E minor chord change heard between the chorus and guitar break. The melodic lead-guitar solo sounds as if it had escaped the mind of The Shadows' Hank Marvin in the early 1960s, lingering in the ether until Scholz made it the jewel in a more hi-tech musical crown. The rest of the album has a breezy, down-the-freeway vibe, though nothing matches the melodic strength of 'More Than A Feeling.'

For many years *Boston* was the biggest-selling debut album by a rock band in the U.S.A. Boston had created a radio-friendly, well-crafted sound that established certain rules for U.S. commercial rock. It persisted, in ever-more stifling form, for a decade until indie bands such as R.E.M. and the grunge explosion challenged and overthrew it – and, despite the persistence of a certain rumor, 'Smells Like Teen Spirit' does not have the same chords as 'More Than A Feeling,' though there is a rhythmic similarity which might be intentional irony on Kurt Cobain's part.

Scholz's perfectionism and periods of litigation combined to stretch out Boston's lifespan. *Don't Look Back* came out in 1978, *Third Stage* in 1986, and *Walk On* in 1994.

■ *Left: Peter Frampton on stage in 1976, using a talkbox to achieve the unusual vocal sound heard on* **Frampton Comes Alive!**

Continued from page 181

"When we went to 16-track, it was tougher, and when we went to 24 I couldn't tell anymore. The studios in New York all had distinctive sounds, a combination of the rooms, the equipment, and the main engineers. . . . I learned the sound of Bell, of A&R, of Mediasound, of Mira Sound. You could hear it on the radio. But it all went out the window with 24-track; 16 tracks on two-inch tape was as far as you could go and still maintain the personality of a room. The 24-track machines started to eat up the clarity of the instruments."

Once again, the ramp-up in recording technology helped shape the method of music making. Taking full advantage of the sophisticated multitrack machinery, in the U.K. art-rock groups such as Emerson, Lake & Palmer, Yes, and King Crimson issued lengthy, complex works built around layers of guitar, synthesizer, and carefully overdubbed vocals. The extended nature of albums such as Yes's double-disk opus *Tales From Topographic Oceans* (1974) was a far cry from the two-hits-eight-covers format of 1960s pop.

Funky Drumming And The Disco Explosion

During the 1960s the likes of Stevie Wonder and Marvin Gaye achieved stardom by creating pop music that easily crossed racial barriers. With the start of the 1970s, however, the sound of black America began to change rapidly. In early 1970 James Brown – the 'Godfather Of Soul' – released back-to-back singles, 'Funky Drummer' and 'Brother Rapp,' both built around long, repeating drum grooves that became the basis for funk, a highly rhythmic brand of soul music that would dominate the charts through the early part of the decade. Because most funk hits used the same tempo, dance-club DJs could segue from one song to the next without interruption, keeping the dance floor filled in the process. The phenomenon was not lost on record producers of the time, who began substituting an electronic-drum program in place of a real drummer. The machine-made drum track had an unpredictable – and explosive – side-affect. Unlike a real drummer – whose tempo may vary ever so slightly – a programmed drum track could keep the beat and hold it indefinitely, making it possible to assign an exact number of beats per minute for any given song. Before long, DJs were provided with special extended remixes of hit songs on 12-inch vinyl, each one bearing a 'BPM' designation. By matching songs according to their BPM, DJs could guarantee a virtually endless stream of dance music.

As it turns out, the dominant BPM of the decade – 120 – belonged to disco, a big, brassy synthesis of white pop and black rhythm popularized by mega-artists such as The Bee Gees and Donna Summer. Through to the end of the decade nearly every aspect of popular culture, from fashion trends to dance steps, were dictated by disco's unrelenting beat. Meanwhile, programmed drums and synthesizers were forming the basis for techno pop, spearheaded by Germany's Kraftwerk – whose hit 'Autobahn' became the first Top 40 record comprised entirely of electronic rhythms and instrumentation. Within a few years, the likes of The Human League, Soft Cell, and Yazoo (known as Yaz in the U.S.A.) were reaching the charts without the aid of a human drummer.

The Birth Of The Breakbeat

Not everyone was as enamored of the mechanized rhythms dominating the airwaves of the late 1970s, however. Just across the East River from Manhattan, a whole new sub-genre was brewing. Many Jamaicans had relocated to the Bronx during the early 1970s, and the neighborhoods were filled with the sounds of dub reggae, with improvised 'raps' over Jamaican recordings that poured forth from large, mobile sound systems. One such immigrant was a 22-year-old Bronx DJ named Kool Herc, who worked clubs and local parties using a pair of turntables, one microphone, a monstrous sound system, and a revolutionary new approach to spinning records. Herc discovered that dancers loved the long drum breaks on James Brown records. Using two copies of 'Funky Drummer,' Herc figured out a way to extend the drum passage indefinitely by 'cutting' back and forth between each disk. Herc's invention – which he called the 'breakbeat' – set in motion the events which would form the basis for rap.

Like Herc, young Joseph Saddler began his own career in the mid 1970s spinning records at block parties and dance clubs around the Bronx. But Saddler – aka Grandmaster Flash – wasn't your average kid with two turntables and a microphone. Manipulating the disks with a free hand, the teenage DJ devised a method for 'performing' the mixes, using cutting and other techniques that added a rhythmic flair to the non-stop stream of dance grooves. Additionally, Flash's stage show included a team of poetic 'MCs' – whom he later dubbed the 'Furious Five' – including soon-to-be rap stars Melle Mel and Kid Creole. The MCs introduced a completely new approach

Continued on page 185

1976

Hotel California **The Eagles**

Asylum 1084 (U.S.A.) / K/K4 53051 (U.K.)
Released December 1976

The Eagles were one of the most popular U.S. groups of the 1970s. *Their Greatest Hits*, released in early 1976, is one of the biggest-selling albums of all time in the U.S.A., having sold over 25 million copies, and set the stage perfectly for *Hotel California*.

The Eagles came together in 1971, having previously served as part of Linda Ronstadt's backing group. Indeed, all of the founding members of The Eagles were experienced country-rock session musicians before achieving fame in their own right. Vocalist and guitarist Bernie Leadon had been a member of former Byrd Gene Clark's group Dillard And Clark and one of Gram Parson's Flying Burrito Brothers, while bassist Randy Meisner had served in Rick Nelson's band; drummer-backing vocalist Don Henley had issued one album with his group Shiloh, and guitarists Glenn Frey and Don Felder had performed with Bob Seger and Stephen Stills respectively.

The musicians were encouraged to form The Eagles by Ronstadt's manager, John Boylan, who then found the group a deal with David Geffen's recently formed Asylum label. An eponymous debut established The Eagles' sound in 1972, a highly polished update of the country-and-folk-tinged rock that had begun to emerge from the West Coast of the U.S.A. in the late 1960s.

After making the concept album *Desperado* in 1973 The Eagles topped the U.S. pop singles chart with 'The Best Of My Love,' taken from the group's third full-length release, *On The Border* (1974). That single's success set the stage for their mainstream breakthrough, which they achieved with the following year's *One Of These Nights*, the group's first U.S. chart-topping album.

> ## "['HOTEL CALIFORNIA'] SORT OF CAPTURED THE ZEITGEIST OF THE TIME, WHICH WAS A TIME OF GREAT EXCESS IN THIS COUNTRY, AND IN THE MUSIC BUSINESS IN PARTICULAR."
>
> ### *DON HENLEY, LOOKING BACK ON THE SONG IN 1995*

By the time The Eagles released the phenomenally successful retrospective set *Their Greatest Hits*, Bernie Leadon, the chief country influence in the group, had quit. He was replaced by Joe Walsh, a heavy rock guitarist, known at the time both as a solo artist and member of The James Gang. While Walsh brought a more commercial rock edge to the group, it was drummer Don Henley who took over as the chief creative figure and lead vocalist from 1975 onward.

Henley wrote six of the nine songs that feature on *Hotel California*, including the famous title track. As on that song, most of his compositions paint California – and the U.S.A. in general – as a troubled, nihilistic land, on the verge of collapse under the weight of its own decadence. The album details, but also makes pains to disapprove of, the various excesses to which a popular rock group in the 1970s might succumb.

The Eagles spent the bulk of the time between the releases of *Their Greatest Hits* and *Hotel California* in the studio, perfecting the songs that would be included on the latter album. This lengthy gestation can be attributed both to the fact that they were conscious of how great a

launching pad the success of *Their Greatest Hits* was – and so wanted to ensure they made the most of that opportunity – and the knowledge that they had to formulate new working methods in the wake of Leadon's departure.

The Eagles maintained their trademark vocal-harmony style, but where some of the group's earlier work tended toward a pastoral, folksy feel, they now, with the addition of Walsh, had a solid, powerful sound more in tune with the commercial rock of the era.

Hotel California was recorded between March and October 1976 at Criteria Studios in Miami, Florida, and The Record Plant in Los Angeles. The album was produced by Bill Szymczyk, who had previously worked with artists including B.B. King and The J. Geils Band as well as recording all of The Eagles' albums since *Desperado*.

Sessions for *Hotel California* were strained and drawn out at times, particularly when it came to recording the title song. They had spent several months working in vain on 'Hotel California' until Felder, who came up with the song's distinctive 12-string guitar intro, decided that the group should try to recapture the spirit of an earlier demo recording. Remembering that the demo in question was at his home, Felder telephoned his cleaner, asking her to play the recording down the line to the group so that they could reacquaint themselves with their earlier performance.

Hotel California achieved gold status in the U.S.A. after its first week on sale in December 1976, selling over 500,000 copies. It rose to Number One on the U.S. *Billboard* albums chart the following month and peaked at Number Two in the U.K. The album has since sold over 20 million copies worldwide, 16 million in the U.S.A. alone. At the 1977 Grammy Awards it was named Album Of The Year, with Szymczyk winning the producers' award.

The first single to be drawn from the album was 'New Kid In Town,' which topped the U.S. chart and reached Number 20 in the U.K. This was followed by *Hotel California*'s six-and-a-half minute title track, now regarded as an all-time classic rock single. 'Hotel California' is built around a slightly reggae-tinged drum rhythm – likely inspired by Bob Marley's *Rastaman Vibration*, which had in 1976 become the first hit reggae album in the U.S.A. – and the dueling lead-guitar parts, played by Walsh and Felder.

For such a commercially successful song Henley's lyrics are strangely opaque, describing a hotel that "could be heaven or . . . hell," and from which guests can never escape. Like 'New Kid In Town,' 'Hotel California' topped the U.S. singles chart, giving The Eagles the fourth of five career Number One hits – the others being 'Best Of My Love,' 'One Of These Nights,' 'New Kid In Town,' and 'Heartache Tonight.'

In the wake of the vast success of *Their Greatest Hits* and *Hotel California*, bassist Randy Meisner left to embark on a solo career, but The Eagles maintained their popularity with *The Long Run* (1979) and *Eagles Live* (1980) before deciding to disband in 1981.

All five members of the group continued to make records throughout the 1980s and 1990s before reuniting in 1994 for the live album *Hell Freezes Over*. The group's high standing in popular music was confirmed in 1998 when The Eagles were inducted into the Rock'n'Roll Hall Of Fame.

■ *The Eagles perform in London, England, in April 1977, in support of their bestselling album* Hotel California. *Left to right: Rick Meisner, Don Felder, Glenn Frey, and Joe Walsh.*

Continued from page 183

to rapping by trading verses at will and working out meticulously coordinated routines. They were an immediate sensation in the dance clubs of New York. At a time when both rock- and disco-album production had become bloated and unimaginative, rap was unique, a homemade art form comprised almost entirely of 'borrowed' ingredients. More important, rap became a forum for urban musicians who were unable to afford major-label studio time or expensive instruments. Kurtis Blow's 1980 hit 'The Breaks' underscored rap's street appeal: though it barely cracked the pop charts, the legendary track still sold a million copies in New York City alone. Within a few years, rap had become a mainstream phenomenon, thanks in large part to the worldwide acceptance of hip-hop artists such as Run-DMC and Public Enemy.

The automated rhythms and instruments that were the lifeblood of rap, techno, and other genres of the late 1970s, however, further reduced the element of live studio performance. Combined with the industry's insatiable demand for track space, over the next several years the recording business continued its rapid transformation. Albums such as Steely Dan's *Aja* (1977) typified the changed environment. As Brian Wilson had done with The Beach Boys recordings a decade earlier, Steely Dan leaders Donald Fagen and Walter Becker cut tracks using a small army of virtuoso session players, among them guitarist Larry Carlton and drummer Bernard Purdie. Unlike Wilson, however, tunes such as 'Deacon Blues' and 'Josie' were assembled block by block, with an obsessive attention to detail – the finished work was apparently remixed at least a dozen times before the duo authorized its release. Though smartly packaged and brimming with top-flight jazz rock, to many listeners – and more than a few critics – the perfectionism that was at the core of *Aja* was somewhat off-putting.

1977

David Bowie Low

RCA 2030 (U.S.A.) / PL/PK 12030 (U.K.)
Released January 1977

At the height of punk in the U.K., David Bowie was one of the few acceptable faces of the old guard, and the first two albums in his so-called 'Berlin trilogy,' Low and "Heroes," had a huge impact on much of the synthesizer pop that would follow them.

Though David Bowie had reached his mid-1970s peak with the international hit albums *Young Americans* and *Station To Station*, his personal life was in turmoil, brought on by the collapse of his marriage and a growing drug dependency. With that in mind Bowie moved to Berlin with his friend Iggy Pop in 1976, purportedly to clean up. There he immersed himself in Germany's burgeoning music scene, taking a particular liking to Neu! and Kraftwerk, who had already started to impact on the Bowie sound on *Station To Station*'s epic title track.

Having worked during the summer on Iggy's *The Idiot*, Bowie decamped, on September 1st, to Château d'Hérouville Studios just outside Paris to begin work on *Low* with producer Tony Visconti. Also present at the sessions was art rock pioneer Brian Eno, formerly of Roxy Music, whose 1975 solo album *Another Green World* was another big influence on *Low*. Making use of numerous new synthesizers, including the Mini-Moog, Bowie and Eno soon instituted some curious recording methods. For example, they would enter the studio separately, turn down all but the rhythm tracks of the song they were working on, and build up layers of sound without knowing what the other had added. This threw up some highly original and impressive results, including the spacious instrumental 'Warszawa.' *Low*'s most striking element is the harsh, mechanical drum sound, achieved by Visconti using his new Harmonizer effects box, which allowed the user to shift the pitch of any sound without altering its speed.

Bowie's label RCA was, by all accounts, horrified when presented with *Low*; the label's head is said to have offered Bowie a house in Philadelphia if only he would, please, record another album in the vein of *Young Americans*. While *Low* was clearly the most experimental release of his career thus far, the first side of the album is made up of fairly conventional songs, and provided Bowie with another international hit single, 'Sound And Vision.' More problematic to the record company was the almost entirely instrumental second side, then highly unusual on a pop record by an established star. Perhaps symbolically, this farewell to the first commercial phase of his career was issued the week after Bowie's 30th birthday, its striking cover image – the artist in profile, taken from the movie *The Man Who Fell To Earth*, in which he had starred – a marked contrast to the extravagant sleeves of his earlier albums. *Low* has become the most admired recording in the Bowie catalog, and has influenced numerous musicians since, from the electro-pop stars of the early 1980s to Trent Reznor of Nine Inch Nails. The success of *Low* has also inspired other acts to take similar stylistic sidesteps at the height of their commercial appeal, including Talk Talk and Radiohead.

Several months after the release of *Low*, which peaked at Number Two in the U.K. and reached the U.S. Top Ten, Bowie was back in the studio, this time at Hansa Studios, situated right next to the Berlin Wall, to record *"Heroes."* Again working alongside Eno and Visconti, Bowie also recruited King Crimson's Robert Fripp, who provides the searing lead-guitar part on the title track, one of the most memorable of all Bowie's recordings. *"Heroes"* is both a refinement and a more extreme version of *Low*: the first, song-based side is snappier, while the second-half's instrumental material is more obtuse than anything on its predecessor. Bowie completed his Berlin trilogy with the less successful *Lodger* in 1979.

■ *Below: rather than promote* Low, *David Bowie chose to go out on tour, incognito, as the keyboardist in Iggy Pop's band.*

My Aim Is True **Elvis Costello**

Columbia JC 35037 (U.S.A.) / Stiff SEEZ/ZSEEZ 3 (U.K.)
Released August 1977

Issued at the height of punk, *My Aim Is True* established Costello as one of the enduring talents of the era.

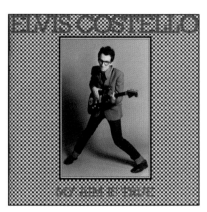

Born Declan McManus, Elvis Costello signed to the independent label Stiff Records in 1977 and promptly started work on his debut album, ditching his country-rock backing group in the process. Stiff paired him with producer Nick Lowe and the U.S. rock quintet Clover – here called Shamrock – two of whom would go on to found Huey Lewis And The News. Lowe was, at the time, the in-house producer at Stiff, having helmed numerous albums since the label's inception – of particular note is The Damned's *Damned Damned Damned*, the first British punk album.

However, *My Aim Is True* is not a punk album. While Costello's vitriolic lyrics and sneering vocal drew comparisons with punk acts, his music demonstrated an awareness and acceptance of rock history. There is a hint of the folksy singer-songwriter in the album's ballads, including the single 'Alison,' while 'Watching The Detectives' has a reggae beat. *My Aim Is True* was released in an eye-catching sleeve, designed by Barney Bubbles, with a photograph of a pigeon-toed, bespectacled Costello, looking more like the computer programmer McManus had once been than the rock star Costello was to become.

Aja **Steely Dan**

A.B.C. 1006 (U.S.A.) / ABCL/+C 5225 (U.K.)
Released September 1977

Steely Dan is not your typical rock band. For a start, there are only two permanent members of the group, the songwriting duo of Donald Fagen and Walter Becker, who formed Steely Dan as a reaction against the huge-selling soft-rock groups of the era.

Aesthetically, Becker and Fagen's albums stood apart from most of their contemporaries, particularly in 1977, in that they were always immaculately produced and full of musical complexity. *Aja* captures the group at its critical and commercial peak. Becker and Fagen did initially operate within the confines of the traditional rock band, recording and touring the albums *Can't Buy A Thrill* (1972) and *Countdown To Ecstasy* (1973) with a permanent drummer, guitarist, and vocalist. However, the duo became disillusioned with that line-up and with life on the road, which led to the break up of the original five-piece, leaving Becker and Fagen to concentrate exclusively on studio work.

Somewhat surprisingly, given that they refused to tour it, *Pretzel Logic* (1974) was the duo's greatest success to date, thanks in no small part to

the inclusion of the biggest hit single of their career, 'Rikki Don't Lose Than Number,' which peaked at Number Four in the U.S.A. *Pretzel Logic* introduced a more pronounced jazz edge to Steely Dan's music, which became more apparent on *Katy Lied* (1975) and *The Royal Scam* (1976). On these albums Becker and Fagen had begun to draw on a pool of impressive session musicians in their attempts to produce the slickest, most densely layered recordings possible.

Work started on *Aja* in the latter part of 1976 at Village Recorders in Los Angeles and a number of other studios in and around Hollywood. Writing about the album retrospectively, *Rolling Stone* magazine called *Aja* "music so technically demanding its creators had to call in a-list session players to realize the sounds they heard in their heads but could not play." Where Steely Dan's earlier works had been mostly guitar based, on *Aja* the songs are led by swathes of keyboards and saxophone. The sessioneers in question included Wayne Shorter, best known as the saxophonist in the second great Miles Davis quintet during the mid-to-late 1960s.

Aja is a rich, textured album, and one that was often used in electrical stores to demonstrate the capabilities of new hi-fi systems. Though the performances are full of complex musical flourishes, the songs on *Aja* are simpler and more immediate than on previous Steely Dan albums. The net result of this was that *Aja* is the most successful album of the group's career, reaching Number Three in the U.S.A. – where it was among the first albums to be awarded the newly founded platinum status – and Number Five in the U.K. It spawned a trio of U.S. hit singles, 'Peg,' 'Deacon Blues,' and 'Josie,' and even earned the respect of the jazz world, resulting in an album of covers of Becker and Fagen songs by Woody Herman. Legal wrangling between the label ABC and its new parent company MCA stalled the release of a follow-up. Becker and Fagen took a 20-year break from recording together after *Gaucho* (1980), but made a successful return in 2000 with the multiple Grammy Award-winning *Two Against Nature*.

Heavy Weather **Weather Report**

Columbia 34418 (U.S.A.) / CBS 81775 (U.K.)
Released March 1977

The definitive jazz supergroup of the 1970s, Weather Report played a concise, melodic form of the jazz-rock fusion that had emerged in the late 1960s.

The group was formed in 1971 by the composer and keyboardist Joe Zawinul and saxophonist Wayne Shorter, fresh from their work on Miles Davis's epochal albums *In A Silent Way* (1969) and *Bitches Brew* (1970). At the time of *Heavy Weather*, the group's seventh album, Weather Report also featured bassist Jaco Pastorius, drummer Alex Acuna, and percussionist Manolo Badrena.

By this stage, Zawinul had begun to experiment with cutting-edge synthesizer technologies. Moving away from the more traditional Fender Rhodes electric piano, Zawinul worked with an ARP 2600 – originally conceived as an entry-level keyboard for synthesizer novices – and a more complex Oberheim Polyphonic synthesizer, which also has the capacity for creating and storing eight-note sequences that could be repeated at the user's will.

Buoyed by Zawinul's synthesizer playing, the eight short songs – short at least by the standards of jazz fusion – have a warm, smooth feel that helped propel *Heavy Weather* up the U.S. pop charts, where the album peaked at Number 30. Recorded at Devonshire Sound Studios in North Hollywood, California, *Heavy Weather* opens with Zawinul's 'Birdland,' which has since become a jazz standard, and has been covered by numerous other artists, including the vocal quartet Manhattan Transfer. Another highlight is Shorter's frantic 'Palladium.' Demonstrating that Weather Report was not just about Shorter and Zawinul, *Heavy Weather* also includes compositions by the group's other members, among them Pastorius's 'Teen Town,' with its infectious disco beat.

1977

Never Mind The Bollocks Sex Pistols

Warner Brothers 3142 (U.S.A.) / Virgin V2086 (U.K.)
Released November 1977

This is *the* seminal punk album, where British rock rediscovered its energy. On its much-anticipated release it seemed a blast of untrammeled anarchy, setting fire to a music scene that, by 1976, was a dank mixture of chart bubblegum, the dregs of glam rock, and the lofty dinosaur bands of prog.

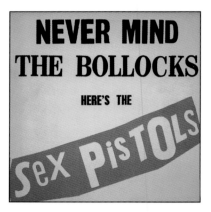

The Pistols, with help from manager Malcolm McLaren, were the most dramatic expression of punk's do-it-yourself ethic, and represented a genuine youth rebellion in contrast to the plastic version offered by supposed teen acts such as The Bay City Rollers. The first paradox is that musically The Sex Pistols were not new but grounded in 1950s rock'n'roll and 1960s garage rock; the second is that, for all its snarling nihilism, *Never Mind The Bollocks* is riotous fun.

It came suitably attired in a lurid pink and yellow sleeve unlike anything else in the racks. The prominent use of 'bollocks' led to shops refusing to display it, nor could it be advertised on television. It contains four Pistols hits: 'Anarchy In The U.K.' (the first significant punk single, at least as far as the wider public was concerned, though The Damned's 'New Rose' got there first), 'Pretty Vacant,' 'Holidays In The Sun' (with its goose-stepping intro), and 'God Save The Queen.' An incendiary rock single, 'God Save The Queen' was released to coincide with Queen Elizabeth II's silver jubilee – an occasion of great pomp and circumstance – and it made a big noise on

a small island, cementing The Pistols' reputation as Public Enemies Numbers One To Four. The single was originally to be put out on A&M but withdrawn, then issued by Virgin after the band had been signed by Richard Branson. The problems with A&M and an earlier bust-up with EMI were immortalized on the album's closing track, 'EMI.' Other cuts include the incoherent abortion horror-show 'Bodies,' the sinister 'Submission,' the sarcastic 'Liar,' and the hilariously knuckle-headed 'Seventeen,' with its refrain, "I'm a lazy sod."

The Pistols' sound had two main ingredients. The first was Johnny Rotten's vocal style, one of the most recognizable in rock history. Like Dylan, his refusal to pitch conventionally expressed rebellion, and the off-key sneering comes across powerfully, displaying a knack for forcing a note that doesn't fit against the underlying chord, as with the era-defining phrase "we mean it, maann" from 'God Save The Queen.' The lyrics are given further force by sarcastic touches such as the rolled 'r' in 'moron' and the pseudo-exultant exclamation of 'money,' touches that fitted Rotten's spiky-haired Artful Dodger persona. The second ingredient was Steve Jones's multitracked guitar onslaught. The semitone shifts for many of the riffs stem from such rock'n'roll influences as Eddie Cochran, and Jones recycled Chuck Berry lead breaks on a Les Paul played through an overdriven Vox AC30 amplifier with only one speaker working. By way of example, the lead solo on 'God Save The Queen' is not far removed from Brian May's Berry homage on Queen's 'Now I'm Here' (1974) – but the intent is entirely different.

It was a long time since a band had played with such ferocity, The Pistols' attitude giving what was left of the legacy of the 1960s a good kicking. This band wasn't interested in peace and love; it wasn't even interested in longevity or taking their rebellion any farther, and *Never Mind The Bollocks* is the only proper studio album The Sex Pistols completed, the band's fate sealed after Rotten left in January 1978 at the end of their one and only U.S. tour.

After Rotten's departure Sid Vicious – who, despite being perhaps the best-remembered and most iconic bandmember today, even though he played on almost no recordings – became the focus of what was left of the group until they finally fell apart.

■ *Below (left to right): Glen Matlock, Johnny Rotten, and Steve Jones.*

Talking Heads 77 Talking Heads

Sire 9103 328 (U.S.A.) / 9103 328 (U.K.)
Released October 1977

Marquee Moon Television

Elektra 7E-1098 (U.S.A.) / K52046 (U.K.)
Released February 1977

The New York new wave was a markedly different beast from its British offspring, punk rock. Punk focused heavily on just two elements of the New York scene, specifically the simplistic energy of The Ramones and the fashion sense of Richard Hell, using the former as a musical manifesto and the latter as a style template.

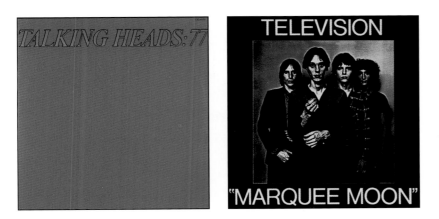

Meanwhile, back in the Big Apple, bands falling under the new-wave umbrella were about as musically diverse as it was possible to be, sharing little other than their emergence in the same time and place. The romantic Hispanic rock of Mink De Ville bore little resemblance to, for example, the trashy pop ethic of Blondie, and the two bands who formed the vanguard, Television and Talking Heads, were both different again.

The Lower East Side art rock of Talking Heads, with its staggered rhythms and sudden tempo changes, seemed a deliberate rejection of earlier rock

structures. The guitars were tuned oddly, David Byrne's singing was self-consciously strained, the lyrics didn't always rhyme and often sounded like the incoherent babble of asylum inmates. Byrne has explained his oblique approach to the lyric of *Talking Heads 77*'s signature song, 'Psycho Killer,' by saying that he intended it "to be like Randy Newman doing Alice Cooper. One way of telling the story would be to describe everything that happens – 'He walks across the room, he takes so many steps, he's wearing such-and-such.' That tells you everything that's going on, on one level, but it really doesn't involve you emotionally. The other extreme is to describe everything as a series of sensations. I think that sometimes has more power, and affects people a little stronger."

Television wrote punchy, concise lyrics that sounded as if they might have come from a Mike Hammer pulp detective novel, and conjured up dark, sinister atmospheres through the interplay of the guitars of Richard Lloyd and Tom Verlaine. By all accounts their early gigs were appallingly bad, but they persevered. "Television rehearsed for six to seven days a week for four to six hours a day," says Lloyd. "We were both really roughshod musicians on one hand, and desperadoes on the other, with the will to become good." By the time of Marquee Moon, their rhythms were tight and choppy and their coruscating, mercurial lead lines frequently recalled the heyday of San Francisco acid rock, as did the extended lengths of their improvisations.

Producer Andy Johns, who'd previously worked on *Goat's Head Soup* for The Rolling Stones, remembers Television as a hard band to fathom. "My first impression was that they couldn't play and couldn't sing and the music was very bizarre. But after we finished mixing, we went to some rehearsal place and played it on these large speakers, and I was bowled over." The centerpiece of *Marquee Moon* is the epic title track, a U.K. hit single despite its ten-minute running time. It was Talking Heads, however, who proved themselves able to change and adapt with the times, becoming one of the most successful bands of the 1980s, while Television, who initially looked a much safer bet for long-term stardom, rapidly crashed and burned amid serious ego clashes.

■ *Above: Talking Heads on stage in London, England in late 1976, just prior to the release of their debut album.*

1977

Bat Out Of Hell
Meat Loaf

Epic 34974 (U.S.A.) / EPC/40 82419 (U.K.)
Released October 1977 (U.S.A.) / January 1978 (U.K.)

**One of the biggest selling
albums of the 1970s, *Bat Out Of
Hell*, contains some of the most
extravagant, operatic rock music
ever recorded.**

Born Marvin Lee Aday in Dallas,
Texas, in 1947, the powerful singer
Meat Loaf acquired his nickname at a
young age on account of his sizeable
figure. In the late 1960s he moved to
Los Angeles and fronted the
psychedelic rock group Popcorn

Blizzard, who opened for the likes of The Who and Ted Nugent in 1967 and
1968. Meat Loaf quit the group in 1969, and for much of the next decade
concentrated his energies on appearing in a number of high-profile musical
roles in Los Angeles and on Broadway, though he did find time to record the
album *Stoney & Meat Loaf* (1971) with the female soul singer Stoney, for
Motown Records' Rare Earth subsidiary. This period of Meat Loaf's career is
best known for his performance as Eddy – on stage and screen – in the
Rocky Horror Picture Show (1975).

While working in musicals Meat Loaf began an association with the
songwriter and producer Jim Steinman. A classically trained pianist,
Steinman wrote the musical *More Than You Deserve*, in which Meat Loaf
starred, before the pair began touring the U.S.A. as part of the *National
Lampoon Show* in 1976. That year Meat Loaf made his first serious foray
into the rock'n'roll world, lending his immense vocal presence to half of the
songs on his old friend Ted Nugent's *Free For All*.

In 1977 Meat Loaf and Steinman started work on an ambitious musical
album project, *Neverland*, based on the story of *Peter Pan*, for which the duo
signed a development deal with the label RCA. When they objected to
Steinman's choice of Todd Rundgren as producer, he and Meat Loaf left the
label and signed instead with Epic. By this stage the *Neverland* songs had
mutated into a new project, *Bat Out Of Hell*.

Meat Loaf, Steinman, and Rundgren recorded *Bat Out Of Hell* in the summer
of 1977 with a group of accomplished session players, most notably

drummer Max Weinberg, a member of Bruce Springsteen's E Street Band. There is a suggestion of Springsteen's music in both the piano playing and the narrative songwriting style of *Bat Out Of Hell*, particularly in titles such as 'All Revved Up With No Place To Go.' The album also draws on the pomp and circumstance of Richard Wagner, and includes lavish arrangements conducted by The New York Philharmonic Orchestra's Gene Orloff.

Befitting an album of such ostentatious ambition, *Bat Out Of Hell* was recorded at a number of studios on the East Coast. Most of the songs were cut at Bearsville Sound and The Hit Factory, both in New York, with some additional tracking at Rundgren's own Utopia Sound, also in New York, and House Of Music in West Orange, New Jersey. No stranger to epic, overblown productions on his own solo works, the multi-instrumentalist Rundgren colors Steinman's already vast compositions with a widescreen sonic backdrop that jumps effortlessly from ferocious, apocalyptic hard rock to extravagant show tunes.

There are only seven songs on *Bat Out Of Hell*, but any fears that the listener is being short-changed are allayed by the fact that three of them are close to ten minutes long. *Bat Out Of Hell* threatens to collapse under the weight of its own bombast at times, particularly on the album's most infamous moment, midway through the three-part 'Paradise By The Dashboard Light,' when baseball announcer Phil Rizzuto is called in to provide a brief interlude of commentary that serves as a hilarious extended sexual metaphor.

The most striking elements of *Bat Out Of Hell*, however, are the vocals. Meat Loaf possesses a voice that could match Steinman's grandiose, theatrical compositions. Drawing on his stage experience, Meat Loaf is simply as close as rock music gets to opera. His voice isn't to everybody's taste, however: the *Rolling Stone* review of *Bat Out Of Hell* concluded that "his phrasing is way too stage-struck to make the album's pretensions to comic-book street life real. He needs a little less *West Side Story* and a little more Bruce Springsteen." This was a commonly held view among many critics, who thought *Bat Out Of Hell* was simply too overblown.

Given the album's enormous sales to date, initial chart placings were relatively modest – it entered the U.S. albums chart at Number 14 on its release and reached Number 9 in the U.K. early the following year – but began seriously to pick up momentum over the course of 1978. (In the U.K., the defining moment in Meat Loaf's rise to stardom was a show-stopping performance of the nine-minute title track on the influential television music program *The Old Grey Whistle Test*, which proved so popular that it was shown again the following week, despite its length.) The album's popularity grew on the strength of a series of epic singles, including the title track and 'Paradise By The Dashboard Light.' By 2004 *Bat Out Of Hell* had sold over 34 million copies worldwide, with sales of 16 million in the U.S.A. alone, placing it among the five bestselling albums of all time. It also spent 474 weeks on the U.K. charts, just 3 weeks short of the record of 477, held by Fleetwood Mac's *Rumours*. Until the release of Alanis Morissette's *Jagged Little Pill* in 1995, it was the bestselling U.S. debut of all time.

Bat Out Of Hell continues to shift an average of 200,000 copies per year, and as such is perennially one of the strongest-selling back-catalog albums by any artist. This can partly be attributed to the various different editions that have been released over time. The album sold strongly when it was first issued on CD in 1983, and was given a new lease on life when the singer recorded *Bat Out Of Hell II: Back Into Hell* in 1993. While this second volume of collaborations between Steinman and Meat Loaf – who had not worked together since falling out while making *Dead Ringer* (1981) – sat at Number One around the world, the original *Bat Out Of Hell* re-entered the U.K. chart at Number 19. In 2002 Epic issued a remastered edition in the high quality SACD format, while two years later Meat Loaf recorded *Bat Out Of Hell Live: With The Melbourne Symphony Orchestra*, which is exactly what its title suggests, the original album performed in its entirety, live on stage with a full orchestra.

■ *Meatloaf (left) and his songwriting partner Jim Steinman, pictured around the time of the release of* **Bat Out Of Hell**. *The duo fell out a few years later, and didn't work together again for two decades.*

Saturday Night Fever **(Original Soundtrack)**

R.S.O. 4001 (U.S.A.) / 2658 123 (U.K.)
Released November 1977

One of the biggest movies of the 1970s, *Saturday Night Fever* **introduced disco to the mainstream and made John Travolta a superstar. The accompanying soundtrack album was even more successful, spending 24 weeks at Number One in the U.S.A.**

The movie was based on a 1975 *New York* magazine article about the New York disco scene, 'Tribal Rites Of The New Saturday Night,' by the British rock writer Nik Cohn. (Two decades later it emerged that Cohn had invented most of the details in his article – including the character of Vincent, who was the inspiration for Tony Manero, the Travolta character in the movie – after spending a dull, uneventful weekend hanging around in New York clubs.)

The album was dominated by The Bee Gees, and marked the peak of the second and most memorable phase of the group's career across four decades. British-born brothers Barry, Maurice, and Robin Gibb began their musical journey as The Bee Gees in their adopted homeland of Australia in the early 1960s, but returned to the U.K. by the time their 'Spicks And Specks' topped the Australian singles chart in 1967. The Bee Gees had ten more Beatles-inspired hits in Britain and the U.S.A. over the next two years, but the brothers' careers began to slip in the 1970s. The group's fortunes began to improve when they issued the disco-inspired *Children Of The World* (1976), which led to them being asked to contribute to the *Saturday Night Fever* soundtrack. While it does contain songs by other artists, notably Kool And The Gang and KC And The Sunshine Band, *Saturday Night Fever* is generally considered to be a Bee Gees album. The group performs half of the album's songs, while several others – 'If I Can't Have You,' recorded by Yvonne Elliman, and the classic 'More Than A Woman,' sung by Tavares – were written by the Gibbs. In that respect, *Saturday Night Fever* demonstrates that, as well as being a phenomenally successful act in their own right, The Bee Gees were also among the dominant pop songwriters of the era.

Both album and movie open with a Bee Gees' song that has come to encapsulate the entire disco era, 'Stayin' Alive,' which already sat atop the U.S. singles chart when *Saturday Night Fever* opened at movie houses across the U.S.A. (The track showcases the falsetto vocals that have subsequently become the group's trademark style and which were used on this album for the first time.) The soundtrack album spawned two further Number One hits for them, 'Night Fever' and 'How Deep Is Your Love?'

Most of The Bee Gees' songs included on *Saturday Night Fever* had been written before the brothers had been approached to contribute to the movie soundtrack, and they had been intended for the follow-up to *Children Of The World*. They were recorded with the Turkish producer Arif Mardin, who had played a key role in establishing Atlantic Records, producing many of the label's biggest acts in the 1960s and 1970s. Mardin had previously worked on The Bee Gees' *Mr Natural* (1974), and had been largely responsible for shifting the group's sound away from 1960s pop toward soul and disco.

Saturday Night Fever topped the charts on its release in both the U.S.A. and the U.K., and has since shifted over 25 million copies worldwide, making it the most successful movie-soundtrack album of all time and re-establishing The Bee Gees among the pre-eminent stars of the pop scene. In 1999 *Saturday Night Fever* was recast as a stage musical in London to great success.

1977

Fleetwood Mac
Rumours

Warner Bros 3010 (U.S.A.) / K56344 (U.K.)
Released February 1977

Rumours went platinum within a month of release and is now approaching 20-times platinum – but these staggering sales figures reveal only a small part of the album's significance in rock history.

Technically, this classic album pushed production standards up to new levels, and, musically, it raised the stakes in terms of song quality, performance, and meticulous attention to detail. It was also the album where the artists' real lives became virtually indistinguishable from the songs they were singing. This had happened before, with The Mamas & The Papas, and it would happen again with Abba, but *Rumours* was the moment when the phenomenon of confessional pop-song writing really captured the imagination of the record-buying public.

Fleetwood Mac had started life in the mid-1960s as a British blues quartet, later becoming a quintet, and had the competition beaten hollow until their brilliant songwriter-guitarist, Peter Green, went off the rails. After other personnel hiccups – including the religious conversion of guitarist Jeremy Spencer and the declining mental health of another guitarist, Danny Kirwan – they relocated to California, where they noodled around for several years until drummer Mick Fleetwood heard the album *Buckingham-Nicks* by

aspiring songwriters Lindsay Buckingham and Stevie Nicks. Fleetwood invited them to join the band, and the first album with this new line-up, *Fleetwood Mac*, took off like a rocket. On February 15th 1976 they began recording the follow-up, *Rumours*, at the Record Plant, Sausalito, California.

"The Record Plant was this amazing hippy place," recalls Stevie Nicks. "We like to say we were all hippies but, in the beginning, we really weren't. But we went up to this incredible studio, which was all decorated with Indian saris and beautiful colors, there were little hippy girls everywhere making cookies. It was such a beautiful thing. You walked in and you were like, 'Aaaaah! I love this place.'"

Regrettably, however, the band had brought their own snakes into this hippy garden of paradise, because the two romantic relationships in the band, Buckingham and Nicks and John and Christine McVie, were rapidly disintegrating. The first thing they had to do was work out how to continue functioning as professionals when their personal lives had become seething cauldrons of disappointment, mistrust, and anger. "There was pain, there was confusion," says Buckingham, "and it all added up to make *Rumours* a soap opera on vinyl."

The bandage they used to cover their open sores was work. "We had two alternatives," explains Christine McVie. "Go our own ways and see the band collapse, or grit our teeth and carry on playing with each other. Normally, when couples split they don't have to see each other again. We were forced to get over those differences." This need to maintain the band trapped them in an environment where they were precluded from expressing publicly, or even privately, their true feelings. Almost inevitably, their emotional turmoil found its way into the songs.

Bassist John McVie was not a songwriter, so Christine's eloquently regretful reflections on their crumbling marriage, 'Don't Stop,' 'Songbird,' and 'Oh Daddy,' have no response from him. "I'd be sitting there in the studio while they were mixing 'Don't Stop,'" he reflects, "and I'd listen to

■ *Main picture: Christine McVie. Above right: Mick Fleetwood. Below right: Stevie Nicks.*

the words, which were mostly about me, and I'd get a lump in my throat. I'd turn around and the writer's sitting right there."

Buckingham and Nicks, however, were both songwriters, and their compositions effectively became substitutes for conversations they should have been having. "When we were writing and recording these songs," says Nicks, "I don't think we really thought about what the lyrics were saying. It was only later down the line that Lindsey did come to question the lyric of my song 'Dreams,' and my answer was that it was my counterpart to 'Go Your Own Way.'"

"The spark for that song," admits Buckingham, "was that Stevie and I were crumbling. It was totally autobiographical."

Mick Fleetwood remembers Stevie being particularly upset by the words "crackin' up, shackin' up" being directed at her by Lindsey through his song. For her part, Nicks felt that 'Dreams' was much more empathetic than 'Go Your Own Way.' "In my heart," she told him, "'Dreams' was open and hopeful, but in 'Go Your Own Way,' your heart was closed."

As well as their personal problems, they soon found that the Record Plant was a strange place in which to work. There was a sunken pit in one of the studios, known as Sly Stone's Pit, which Fleetwood remembers as being, "usually occupied by people we didn't know, tapping razors on mirrors." Cris Morris, the engineer who had helped build the studio, points out that "a lot of other musicians dropped by. Van Morrison hung out a lot. Rufus and Chaka Khan, Rick James."

It wasn't long, though, before Fleetwood Mac, who were now reaping the huge financial benefits of the success of their previous album, found themselves indulging in narcotic recreational pursuits. "It was the craziest period of our lives," says Fleetwood. "We went four or five weeks without sleep, doing a lot of drugs. I'm talking about cocaine in such quantities that, at one point, I thought I was really going insane."

Somehow, however, ground-breaking work continued to get done. In the powerfully driving 'Don't Stop,' for example, the voices of Buckingham and McVie were deliberately equalized and compressed to such an extent that they sounded almost identical. "We were trying to get unique sounds on every instrument," remembers Morris. "We spent ten solid hours on a kick-drum sound in Studio B. Eventually we moved into Studio A and built a special platform for the drums, which got them sounding the way we wanted."

Though the basic tracks were completed in Sausalito, there was a period of several months in Los Angeles, largely given over to the mixing process as well as vocal, guitar, and percussion overdubs.

"Looking back at it from 56 years old," said Nicks in 2004, "all I can think is, 'Thank God it wasn't worse.' Thank God we didn't get into heroin. We were lucky that we were always able to get ourselves together to make the music. Maybe it was the music that saved all of us."

1978

Blue Valentine **Tom Waits**

Elektra 6E 162 (U.S.A.) / Asylum K 53088 (U.K.)
Released October 1978

Blue Valentine was Waits's penultimate album for Elektra, before he signed to Island and moved into more experimental territory, and is the culmination of the first phase of the singer's career.

Waits signed to Elektra in 1973 after being spotted performing at the Troubadour in Los Angeles by Frank Zappa's manager Herb Cohen. His early albums – including *Closing Time* (1973) and *Nighthawks At The Diner* (1975) – showed Waits to be a talented writer who could, apparently, effortlessly, get into the mindset of the low-life, Bourbon-soaked characters that populated his songs.

By the late 1970s, however, Waits's hobo act had begun to grow stale. Realizing this, he expanded his repertoire beyond his usual first-person tales of life in the gutter, balancing them with aching romantic balladry. Waits also widens his musical pallet here, shifting the emphasis away from his own piano playing on some tracks and instead making use of guitarists Roland Bautista and Ray Crawford, who give 'Twenty-Nine Dollars' and 'Whistlin' Past The Graveyard' more of an R&B feel. The influence of swinging 1950s jazz still looms large, though, particularly on 'Romeo Is Bleeding,' while 'Somewhere' and 'Kentucky Avenue' stand apart from the rest of the album with their rich, orchestral arrangements.

Blue Valentine didn't chart on its release in 1978, but is now considered among the strongest works in the career of one of the greatest songwriters to emerge in the 1970s.

Some Girls **The Rolling Stones**

Rolling Stones COC 39108 (U.S.A. & U.K.)
Released June 1978

Though still routinely described as 'The Greatest Rock'n'Roll Band In The World,' by 1978 The Rolling Stones were looking like they would be swept away by the new generation of faster, tougher punk bands.

The band's recent studio albums had sounded tired and pedestrian, with just one or two songs reminding everyone what they were capable of. Coming a year after 1977's routine live set, *Love You Live*, *Some Girls*, the first Stones studio album of the punk era, came at a crucial juncture in the band's career. British critics in particular were gleefully anticipating the dismissal of the record as yet more evidence that the old guard had finally been displaced.

Grudgingly, even the hardest-bitten of hacks had to admit that *Some Girls* was a good album. A disco-influenced hit single, 'Miss You,' was just one highlight among the best set of Stones songs since the classic double, *Exile On Main Street*, six years earlier. The fast three-chord rocker 'Respectable' matched the young punks for energy, while guitarist Keith Richards's one lead-vocal contribution, 'Before They Make Me Run,' was a simultaneously vulnerable and defiant riposte to the drug-related legal troubles he had recently been experiencing.

The Rolling Stones continue to tour and record to this day. Though there have been hit singles and chart albums aplenty since *Some Girls*, many hail it as the last great Stones album.

Outlandos D'Amour The Police

A&M 4753 (U.S.A.) / AMLH 68502 (U.K.)
Released November 1978

A strange *ménage à trois*, The Police set out on their path to becoming the biggest band of the 1980s with this unusually eclectic album.

Prior to forming the band in 1977, Sting was a free-improvising jazz bassist from Newcastle, Andy Summers was a journeyman London-based rock guitarist, whose career stretched back into the early 1960s, and American drummer Stewart Copeland was a refugee from early 1970s prog outfit Curved Air. They came together on a largely pragmatic basis, because the mid-1970s punk-rock explosion led to a huge demand for new live acts. Dying their hair blond and masquerading as punks, they hitched a ride on the bandwagon and attracted enough attention to enable them, on January 19th 1978, to start recording their debut album in Surrey Sound Studios, Leatherhead, U.K. The sessions, in the £10-an-hour studio – which Sting remembers as "a cruddy, funky place with egg cartons on the wall" – were financed by £1,500 (about $3,000 at the time) borrowed from Copeland's rock-entrepreneur brother, Miles.

The album was somewhat musically diverse for a band hoping to pass itself off as punks. 'Next To You,' 'Peanuts,' and 'Truth Hits Everybody' certainly had enough reckless energy to pull off the deception, but beautifully crafted and executed songs such as 'Can't Stand Losing You' and 'So Lonely' can now clearly be seen as the work of musicians infinitely more sophisticated than the average punk hopeful.

Among the songs they recorded was one that Sting had knocked out in October of 1977 after an eye-popping walk through the red-light district of Paris. The song, named after Roxanne, the beloved of Cyrano de Bergerac in the play *Cyrano*, tells of a man's love for a prostitute whom he hopes to rescue from her seedy existence. "I was about to sing the first line," remembers Sting, "when I noticed a stand-up piano. I was tired, I'd been up all night, so I just sat down. I thought the piano lid was closed, but it was open, so I wound up playing this incredible chord with my arse. It was this sort of atonal cluster that went nicely against the G minor we were playing. We thought it was funny, so we left it in." The most distinctive aspect of the track, however, is the way in which it artfully combines rock attitude with reggae rhythms. "Bob Marley was the link," admitted Sting later. "'Roxanne' has a real Bob Marley feel. He's half white, so he's sort of a cultural go-between."

Even so, no one in The Police thought much of 'Roxanne.' Only Miles Copeland spotted it as a potential hit, and scored the band a deal with A&M Records on the strength of that one song. British radio wouldn't play it, deeming the subject matter unsavory, but a year later it broke out from a small station in Austin, Texas.

Though it never went higher than Number 32 in America, 'Roxanne' made The Police seem glamorous back in Britain and, by continuing to blend rock with reggae, they went on to conquer the world.

1978

Van Halen **Van Halen**

Warner Brothers 3075 (U.S.A.) / K56470 (U.K.)
Released February 1978

The air-brushed album cover looked silly, an over-the-top rendering of 'You Really Got Me' appalled many a Kinks fan, and yet, on their massive-sounding, exuberant Warner Brothers debut, Van Halen brought a touch of punk attitude to mainstream U.S. rock.

Southern California's Van Halen offered proof positive that they were no run-of-the-mill heavy-rock band, because behind the macho swagger lay four supremely talented individuals, who could play and write – and, apparently, drink, snort, and screw – rings around the competition.

It was immediately apparent that the driving force behind the band was 22-year-old guitar virtuoso Eddie Van Halen. Today, many can still recall first hearing Eddie's album-opening 'Eruption,' a spellbinding amalgam of hammer-ons, whammy-bar dives, and scorching volume, performed from start to finish in a single take. Mercurial, witty, impatient, and devil-may-care, Van Halen was the first guitarist since Hendrix to shake up rock guitar by opening a door to new sonic possibilities, notably in his use of 'tapping.' While he didn't invent the technique – whereby notes are produced by banging fretting fingers on the neck – he certainly popularized it. (A host of less talented rockers abused the technique through the 1980s until grunge rose up out of Seattle and cried 'Enough!')

The guitar pyrotechnics found a perfect complement in David Lee Roth's vocals. A vocal gymnast of the highest order, Roth's feral howl has the pheromone content of a sweaty football dressing-room, and he sings most of the album with a confident, gum-chewing insouciance. As a rhythm section, bassist Michael Anthony and drummer Alex Van Halen supply bottom end to spare.

The road to *Van Halen* began in mid 1977, when producer Ted Templeman accepted an invitation to check out the band – whose Gene Simmons-financed demo had already been rejected by scores of major companies – at Starwood, the venue where Van Halen had built a local audience. A contract was offered and demo sessions arranged. "As it turns out, we didn't need the extra studio time," recalls Templeman's longstanding engineer Donn Landee. "They cut 28 songs in about two hours. That's when we knew we had a band that could play."

On the first week of January 1978 Van Halen convened inside Sunset Sound's Studio 1. In order to capture the raw energy of the group's club work, Landee and Templeman decided on a no-overdubs approach. "There are only a couple of spots where we added anything afterward – on 'Runnin' With The Devil' and 'Jamie's Cryin'' – and those were done in one take," says Landee. "And we didn't use very many tracks at all. Alex's drums were probably cut using only four mikes total. You just don't need a lot of tracks to get a great sound."

To compensate for the live, one-guitar approach Landee placed Eddie's track slightly off-center in the mix, with a splash of delayed echo from Sunset Sound's extraordinary live echo-chamber filling up the opposite channel. "It made sense, because we didn't want to overdub guitars," he recalls. "If you put the guitar right down the middle with everything else, you'd wind up with the whole band in mono! So it seemed like a reasonable idea." That is, until a month later, when Eddie, vacationing in Italy, happened to get into a rental car that was short one channel, "at which point I got a panicked phone call from the other side of the world wondering why he couldn't hear his playing!"

Completed in less than three weeks, *Van Halen* – which settled at Number 19 on the *Billboard* albums chart – took just seven months to be certified platinum. All told, more than 10 million copies have been sold in the 27 years since its release.

The Last Waltz **The Band**

Warner Brothers 3WS-3146 9 (U.S.A.) / K66076 (U.K.)
Released April 1978

The final live gig by the definitive line-up of The Band set new standards for how a much-loved rock group should say goodbye.

Not only did they have the good grace to bow out while they were still at the top, they invited their pals along for the party and had the home movie shot by Martin Scorsese. This marketing-man's dream took place on November 25th 1976 at Winterland, San Francisco, with guest appearances from Bob Dylan, Neil Young, Joni Mitchell, Emmylou Harris, Muddy Waters, Stephen Stills, Dr John, Eric Clapton, Ronnie Hawkins, Van Morrison, Neil Diamond, and Ringo Starr.

Everything about the event was over the top. There was a 38-piece orchestra, three teams of ballroom dancers, and a food bill that came to $42,000, not including the 400 pounds of fresh salmon specially flown in by Dylan. There was even an all-white room, decorated with sheepskin rugs, Groucho Marx noses, and a glass-topped table complete with razor blades. Despite much behind-the-scenes grief – drummer Levon Helm didn't want to do the concert, Dylan made everyone jump through hoops, music director John Simon claims he never got paid – *The Last Waltz* remains a landmark

not just for its consistently superb music but for Warners' brilliantly manipulative marketing. Sold on the back of one event, we got the triple album, the movie, the home video, the double-CD reissue, the DVD, and the boxed-set four-CD reissue. As their fellow Canadian Leonard Cohen almost said: "Hey, that's the way to say goodbye."

■ *The Band and friends on stage at Winterland, San Francisco, on November 25th 1976. Above (left to right): Van Morrison, Bob Dylan, and Robbie Robertson. Below: Rick Danko with Robertson.*

1979

Rust Never Sleeps Neil Young And Crazy Horse

Reprise 2295 (U.S.A.) / K54105 (U.K.)
Released July 1979

The punk movement poured scorn on the reigning rock aristocracy as bloated, out of touch, and indulgent, so it was no surprise that most survivors of the 1960s viewed the new bands with something between suspicion and disdain.

Neil Young was one of the few members of the old guard to respond with enthusiasm to the likes of The Sex Pistols. Galvanized by the energy of the new wave, he recorded one of his great albums, *Rust Never Sleeps*. Throughout his career Young has bounced back and forth between country-folk acoustic ballads and raging, ragged rock. On *Rust Never Sleeps* he does both styles, performing Side One in acoustic-troubadour guise, then calling up long-serving backing band Crazy Horse for a second side of fierce electric rock. The result is a perfectly balanced set of consistently strong material. 'Thrasher' is one of Young's most affecting acoustic songs; while the electric 'Powderfinger' features one of the best recorded examples of his brink-of-collapse lead-guitar playing. The album's key song, 'My My, Hey Hey,' appears twice, in both acoustic and electric versions, the former subtitled 'Out Of The Blue,' the latter 'Into The Black.' In it Young name-checks The Sex Pistols' singer Johnny Rotten, having delivered one of rock music's most evocative slogans: "It's better to burn out than to fade away."

Off The Wall Michael Jackson

Epic 35745 (U.S.A.) / EPC/40 83458 (U.K.)
Released August 1979

After recording four albums as a teenager in the early 1970s and achieving countless hits as a member of The Jackson 5, Michael Jackson relaunched his solo career in 1979 with the more mature sounding *Off The Wall*.

The album marks the beginning of Jackson's association with studio wizard Quincy Jones, who would go on to produce Jackson's *Thriller* (1982), the biggest-selling album of all time.

Shortly after recording *Destiny* with fellow Jackson siblings Randy, LaToya, and Rebbie – as The Jacksons – Michael started work with Jones in Los Angeles on what would be his first solo release as an adult. Jones and Jackson had first worked together on *The Wiz*, a musical version of *The Wizard Of Oz* that also starred Diana Ross and Richard Pryor, for which Jones wrote the score. *Off The Wall* is best known for its lead track, one of Jackson's finest singles, 'Don't Stop 'Til You Get Enough,' which topped the U.S. chart in advance of the album's release. The album itself is a near-faultless collection of soulful funk and smooth balladry, which also spawned the hits 'Rock With You' and 'She's Out Of My Life.' *Off The Wall* peaked at Number Three in the U.S.A. and Number Five in the U.K., and has sold over eight million copies worldwide.

Off The Wall may stand a long way short of being Jackson's biggest commercial success but it remains his strongest artistic statement. Reviewing a reissued

edition of the album in 2001, *Rolling Stone* magazine decided that it "remains a perfect album . . . the rhythm never lets up, and neither does the quality," while two years earlier, *Q* magazine declared that *Off The Wall* contained "some of the best melodies in the history of pop."

Bop Till You Drop Ry Cooder

Warner Brothers WB 7599-27398-2 (U.S.A. & U.K.)
Released August 1979

A prominent member of Hollywood's studio-session scene during the 1960s and 1970s, Ry Cooder added his trademark slide licks for everyone from Paul Revere And The Raiders to The Rolling Stones – who had appropriated the open-G tuning method, favored by Cooder, for 'Honky Tonk Women.'

It was Cooder's second solo effort for Reprise, *Bop Till You Drop*, that gave the guitarist the dubious distinction of having the first popular-music album recorded entirely in the digital domain, utilizing a 3M 32-track recorder at Amigo Studios in North Hollywood. With support from drummer Jim Keltner, bassist Tim Drummond, and slide-guitar ace David Lindley, *Bop Till You Drop* featured competent updates of such old staples as 'Little Sister,' 'The Very Thing That Makes You Rich (Makes Me Poor),' and 'Go Home, Girl.' "He sends shivers down my spine," remarked no less an observer than the great Pops Staples of The Staples Singers. "He comes out with these old tunes your parents taught you, and it's like going back in time." Despite having engineering ace Lee Herschberg on board – whose previous clients had included Frank Sinatra and Rickie Lee Jones – Cooder, who would continue to serve as a sideman for the likes of Eric Clapton, Randy Newman, and John Hiatt, would later dismiss the technologically advanced *Bop* as a thin-sounding experiment. (Historical footnote: in early 1979 Stephen Stills had actually prepared his own all-digital effort, but it was never released, giving Cooder the non-analog accolade.)

Unknown Pleasures Joy Division

Not issued in the U.S.A. / Factory FACT10 (U.K.)
Released August 1979

One of the most revered bands of the post-punk era in the U.K., Joy Division's debut was also the first release of note on the influential independent Manchester-based Factory Records.

A local television presenter, Tony Wilson, formed the label in 1978, several months after he had started a popular alternative-music club night in Manchester, also called Factory. Joy Division was one of the first bands to play at the club, alongside other notable post-punk acts Cabaret Voltaire and The Durutti Column. All three were included on the label's inaugural EP release, *A Factory Sampler*.

Joy Division had already built up a fiercely devoted live following by the time they began recording their debut in July 1979 with Martin Hannett, producer of many early Factory releases. *Unknown Pleasures* is built around Peter Hook's droning bass lines and the abrasive guitar playing of Bernard Albrecht, with Stephen Morris's distinctive drum sound – which Hannett achieved by recording him on the roof of the studio – pinning it all down. The final and most important element of the band's sound was frontman Ian Curtis's despairing lyrics, sung in a low monotone, which has often been affected by later alternative-rock acts.

The album's £8,000 ($14,000) production costs came out of Tony Wilson's life savings; fortunately for him, *Unknown Pleasures* was greeted with overwhelming critical praise on its release in the U.K., and became a permanent fixture on the U.K. independent chart for several years. However, the album was not issued in the U.S.A. at the time – the group apparently having turned down a large distribution deal with Warner Brothers – and remained unreleased there until 1989.

On May 18th 1980, shortly before the release of the second Joy Division album, *Closer*, and on the eve of their first U.S. tour, Curtis hanged himself. The remaining trio, augmented by keyboardist Gillian Gilbert, went on to achieve considerable international success as New Order.

Metal Box [US title: Second Edition]
Public Image Ltd

Warner Brothers 3288 (U.S.A.) / Virgin METAL 1 (U.K.)
Released November 1979

The second release from former Sex Pistol John Lydon's second band of note, *Metal Box* was issued in the U.K. as three 45rpm 12-inch disks in a film canister embossed with their name.

Formed soon after Rotten – now reclaiming his family name of Lydon – left The Sex Pistols in 1978, Public Image Ltd were, from the outset, a much more musical outfit than his former band. The membership of PiL, as they are often known, was completed by guitarist Keith Levene, once of The Clash, and Lydon's old friend, bassist Jah Wobble, as well as a series of session drummers. Debut album *Public Image* had been recorded before the band had had much time to develop their sound; a year later, however, PiL had carved out a niche all of their own, as showcased on *Metal Box*.

Self-produced by the band at various studios in Oxford and London, *Metal Box* marks one of the first occasions of a rock band experimenting with elements of dub and world music as well as dance rhythms, over which Lydon rants about his dying mother and his general resentment toward the world. The album draws heavily on the trio's extensive record collections, notably Captain Beefheart, Lee 'Scratch' Perry, and German prog band Can. The eleven lengthy songs stick to an extreme tonal dynamic, all bass and treble with hardly any middle. In the U.S.A. *Metal Box* was issued in a more conventional sleeve in 1980 as *Second Edition*; the cost of the original packaging was so high that Virgin only produced 60,000 copies, and vetoed the band's plan to include a lyric sheet. The album includes the minor U.K. hit single 'Swan Lake' (aka 'Death Disco').

Journey Through The Secret Life Of Plants
Stevie Wonder

Tamla 371 (U.S.A.) / Tamla Motown TMSP 6009 (U.K.)
Released November 1979

In 1976 Stevie Wonder issued the sprawling, multiple Grammy Award-winning *Songs In The Key Of Life*, considered by many to be one of his strongest artistic statements.

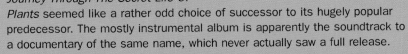

It took Wonder over three years to release a follow-up, an incredibly long time by 1970s standards, when most acts were set into a pattern of producing a new studio album every year. When it eventually arrived, *Journey Through The Secret Life Of Plants* seemed like a rather odd choice of successor to its hugely popular predecessor. The mostly instrumental album is apparently the soundtrack to a documentary of the same name, which never actually saw a full release.

Most of the tracks are wordless, heavily synthesized pieces that tend to sit closer to classical music than the soulful R&B Wonder is known for. When he does sing, however, his vocal performances are often unusual – on 'Venus Fly Trap And The Bug,' for example, his voice resembles that of Tom Waits.

Despite its unconventional musical content, *Journey Through The Secret Life Of Plants* reached Number Four in the U.S.A. on release and Number Eight in the U.K., demonstrating Wonder's undeniable popularity at the time, when even a quirky, pseudo-symphonic soundtrack album could become a huge hit. Two of the album's more traditional songs, 'Send One Your Love' and 'Outside My Window,' were minor hit singles on both sides of the Atlantic. *Journey Through The Secret Life Of Plants* remains an intriguing oddity in the canon of an unquestionably great artist.

The Wall Pink Floyd

Harvest 36183 (U.S.A.) / SHDW 411 (U.K.)
Released December 1979

The Wall* was Pink Floyd's most ambitious, sprawling concept album ever, a mammoth touring stage production, a full-length movie, and, some years later, a star-studded one-off concert in Berlin. It was also, as guitarist Dave Gilmour has pointed out, "the last embers of Roger's and my ability to work collaboratively together."

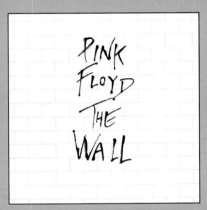

Roger Waters still rates *The Wall* as the best idea he ever had, and its songs of alienation, bitterness, and rage against the machines are generally viewed as the nearest he has come to an autobiography in music. The album's seed lies in an incident during a concert at Montreal's Olympic Stadium on July 6th 1977. It was the end of a lengthy tour, and Waters was increasingly disillusioned with his relationship with the audience. "There was a fan clawing his way up the storm netting to try and get to us," he remembers, "and I just snapped and spat at him. I was shocked, disgusted by myself as soon as I did it, but, after I'd thought about it, the idea of actually building a wall between us and the audience, it had wonderful theatrical possibilities."

The band was suffering tax problems, so the double album was recorded partly in France and partly in Los Angeles, but no expense was spared. "We got hand-built 16-track recorders from LA and carted them at great expense to France," remembers Gilmour. "They kept breaking down every two minutes. There was a whole range of new technology and all these new people we'd brought in to make this record a huge sonic advance."

In retrospect, Gilmour has reservations about the album. "I still think some of the music is incredibly naff," he says, "but *The Wall* is conceptually brilliant. At the time I thought it was Roger listing all the things that can turn a person into an isolated human being. I came to see it as one of the luckiest people in the world issuing a catalog of abuse and bile against people who'd never done anything to him."

The album included what would turn out to be Pink Floyd's first single for eleven years, the controversial 'Another Brick In The Wall.' The song, with its violently anti-education theme, was written by Waters, but the disco beat that helped propel it to Number One in the U.S.A. and the U.K. was suggested by producer Bob Ezrin, and the kids' choir was recorded in north London without any member of the band present. Other than 'Another Brick,' the album's most memorable track – and another source of friction between Waters and Gilmour – is probably 'Comfortably Numb.' "Roger was taking more and more of the credits," complains Gilmour. "In the songbook for this album against 'Comfortably Numb' it says 'Music by Gilmour and Waters.' It shouldn't. He did the lyrics. I did the music."

Though *The Wall* stalled at Number Three in the U.K., where the legacy of punk was still in full flow, the band must have taken some slight comfort when it topped the U.S. charts for 15 straight weeks.

1979

London Calling **The Clash**

CBS 36328 (U.S.A.) / CBS CLASH3 (U.K.)
Released December 1979

Though their early song '1977' had proclaimed "No Elvis, no Beatles or Stones," The Clash were always infatuated with classic rock images.

The sleeve of *London Calling* was a case in point, with an evocative photo of bassist Paul Simonon in a Who-like act of guitar destruction framed by graphics copied from Elvis Presley's 1956 debut album. It was a bold move, claiming for themselves some of rock's most potent myths, but it was easily matched by the quality of the music. Inside the sleeve was a double album of musical variety drawing on the full gamut of popular-music styles of the previous 25 years, a broad-minded approach that would have been unthinkable in the cultural revolution that had reached its peak little more than two years earlier.

From the start The Clash was the most musically adventurous of the first wave of British punk bands, grafting dub and reggae into their sound while still demonstrating only a rudimentary grasp of their instruments. By the time of *London Calling*, the band's third album, competence had caught up with ambition and The Clash had the guts to blend rockabilly, epic pop, jazz, and ska into the mix as well. That stylistic variety combined with a strong set of material, drawn mainly from the band's songwriting team of Joe Strummer and Mick Jones, made *London Calling* that rare rock phenomenon, a consistently good double album that maintains interest through all four sides of vinyl. Credit is due both to the band and producer Guy Stevens – who had previously worked with Jones's favorite band Mott The Hoople – that such a mixed bag ended up sounding like a unified statement rather than a collection of pastiches. It was good value, too, with the band insisting that it be sold for the price of a single disk.

London Calling marked a breakthrough in the U.S.A. The band's biggest American hit single, 'Train In Vain,' was an unlisted 'secret' track at the end of Side Four of the original vinyl release. The album was eventually voted by readers of *Rolling Stone* magazine as the best rock record of the 1980s – though it had first been released two weeks before the end of the previous decade. It did well at home, too, with the title track – featuring a backward guitar solo, the likes of which had not been heard on a rock record since the psychedelic age – becoming the band's biggest British hit single yet.

The Clash was a contradiction, both iconoclastic and traditionalist, and in Strummer and Jones there were two powerful musical voices that were often in conflict: Jones the melodic rock traditionalist, Strummer the sloganeering black-music evangelist. It was on *London Calling* that these opposing forces were most successfully balanced in creative tension. Though there was still great music to come, The Clash would never be this consistent or this good again.

1980

The Blues Brothers (Original Soundtrack)
The Blues Brothers

Atlantic 16017 (U.S.A.) / W50715 (U.K.)
Released June 1980

As The Blues Brothers, comedians John Belushi and Dan Aykroyd recorded several hit albums, wrote and starred in a hugely popular movie, and helped introduce soul and blues to a new audience in the early 1980s.

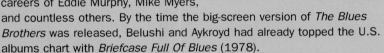

The duo's characters, Jake and Elwood Blues, started life as a sketch on *Saturday Night Live*, the U.S. variety show that also launched the careers of Eddie Murphy, Mike Myers, and countless others. By the time the big-screen version of *The Blues Brothers* was released, Belushi and Aykroyd had already topped the U.S. albums chart with *Briefcase Full Of Blues* (1978).

Though they sold strongly, The Blues Brothers' albums met with a mixed critical reception. While some were just happy to see the blues gain further exposure, others were angered by what they saw as the devaluing of a classic musical genre by a pair of greedy comics. While there may have been a hint of truth in these accusations, Aykroyd and Belushi did recruit a band of exemplary musicians to back them on screen and on record. Among them were two of Booker T.'s MGs – guitarist Steve Cropper and bassist Donald 'Duck' Dunn – and trumpet player Alan Rubin, who had previously worked with such musical luminaries as Frank Sinatra, Duke Ellington, and The Rolling Stones. As Jake and Elwood, Belushi's vocals and Aykroyd's harmonica playing are hardly flawless, but what does become clear throughout their recordings is that the duo have a genuine love for the music.

The Blues Brothers remains the most enduring of the duo's albums, mainly because, like the movie itself, it includes cameo appearances by a number of true stars of blues and soul: Ray Charles duets with Jake on 'Shake A Tail Feather,' while James Brown sings 'Old Landmark,' Cab Calloway powers through 'Minnie The Moocher,' and Aretha Franklin turns in a storming rendition of 'Think,' which she had first recorded at the peak of her powers in 1968. Any comparisons to this quartet of blues and soul legends would prove unfavorable to Belushi, but he handles the remaining six vocal tracks well, particularly the closing 'Jailhouse Rock.' The only unfortunate omission is John Lee Hooker, who has a guest role in the movie but didn't make the soundtrack album. *The Blues Brothers* was produced by Bob Tischler, with whom Aykroyd and Belushi had previously worked on a *Saturday Night Live* album, and who had recently produced another pair of comedy records for the *National Lampoon* team, *Gold Turkey* (1975) and *That's Not Funny, That's Sick* (1977).

Somewhat unwisely, MCA, the musical arm of Universal – who produced the movie – declined to release the accompanying album, leaving it instead to Atlantic Records to reap the financial rewards. *The Blues Brothers* reached Number 13 in the U.S.A. on its release and remains an international cult favorite. Aykroyd and Belushi capitalized on their success with a tour in the latter part of 1980 as well as a third album as Jake and Elwood, *Made In America*. After issuing a 'best-of' album in 1981, The Blues Brothers' career ended the following year when Belushi died of a drug overdose. In 1998 Aykroyd made a less successful follow-up movie, *Blues Brothers 2000*, in which James Belushi took on the role his brother had made famous.

Searching For The Young Soul Rebels
Dexy's Midnight Runners

Not issued in the U.S.A. / Parlophone 7213 (U.K.)
Released July 1980

Dexy's Midnight Runners had considerable success in the U.K. in the early 1980s, blending contemporary new-wave pop with 1960s-style brass arrangements.

The group was formed in 1978 by vocalist Kevin Rowland, whose backing musicians included a three-piece horn section. Dexy's were well on the way to becoming one of the iconic British pop acts of the era by the time the group issued its debut album, *Searching For The Young Soul Rebels*. 'Geno,' Rowland's enthusiastic tribute to the soul singer Geno Washington, had already topped the U.K. singles chart, while the group was just as well-known for its image – based at this point on the New York dockers' uniforms in Martin Scorcese's *Mean Streets* – as its music.

Searching For The Young Soul Rebels was produced by Pete Wingfield, who had in the 1970s worked as a session keyboardist for the likes of Van Morrison and Jimmy Witherspoon. The album's release was briefly held up when Rowland 'kidnapped' the master tapes, holding them hostage until Parlophone offered him a higher royalty rate. Despite the group's lack of cooperation with the music press – Rowland chose to communicate with fans via full-page magazine advertisements rather than speak to journalists – the album was hailed as a modern classic on its release. A relentless reimagining of Rowland's soul heroes, topped off by the singer's witty lyrics and theatrical vocal delivery, *Searching For The Young Soul Rebels* peaked at Number Six in the U.K. and spawned a further Top Ten hit single, 'There, There, My Dear.'

1980

Back In Black **AC/DC**

Atco CS-16018 (U.S.A. & U.K.)
Released July 1980

A quarter-century after its arrival, *Back In Black* remains, for many, the essential hard-rock record of the modern era.

Like many milestone efforts, *Back In Back* had little to do with pop trends of the time – which, in 1980, were all about skinny ties and Farfisa organs. Instead, with *Back In Black*, AC/DC – guitarists Angus and Malcolm Young, bassist Cliff Williams, drummer Phil Rudd, and singer Brian Johnson –

delivered a set of ironclad songs that are stripped to the bone, jacked up at the bottom, and outfitted with some of the most tastefully lean guitar accompaniment on record. Helping the band achieve its megaplatinum apex were producer Robert John 'Mutt' Lange – an unlikely ally, whose ear for slick pop nevertheless lent a subtle but essential mainstream sensibility to the proceedings – and Tony Platt, an engineer of impeccable taste, whose patience and mixing skills brought it all together on tape.

Back In Black marked a turning point in AC/DC's career. *Highway to Hell*, issued a year earlier, had finally pushed the group into platinum territory. But as the band was pulling together material for the all-important follow-up, in February 1980 original vocalist Bon Scott died an alcohol-related death, and the band's future seemed uncertain. Determined to push on in spite of the circumstances, in March the group hired Newcastle-based vocalist Brian Johnson to fill Scott's shoes, then immediately began rehearsing at London's E'Zee Hire Studios. As a diversion, that May the group repaired to the tropical surroundings of sunny Nassau and the newly constructed Compass Point Studios, where they prepared to cut tracks for their forthcoming Atco effort.

With AC/DC it had always been about the riff, and on *Back In Black* there are plenty of them: 'Hell's Bells,' 'Shoot To Thrill,' 'Have A Drink On Me,' and the unrelenting title track featured the dynamic interplay between Angus's right-channel Gibson SG lead guitar and brother Malcolm's left-channel Gretsch rhythm. From his control-room vantage point, Platt

realized the sound he was after was already coming through the monitors. Processing and other add-ons were purposely left off the rhythm tracks. "We all had a good idea of how we wanted it to sound right from the start," says Platt, "and so our goal was to get it on tape there, rather than leaving it for the final mix. Being restricted to 24 tracks meant that a lot of the decisions would be made early on, which also added to the feeling of immediacy. But most of all, they just played it like it is! There was hardly any patching required – we'd just cut takes until we had a nice balance of perfection and feel."

As so often happens, the makeup of the studio itself helped determine the recording dynamics. "The setup and approach was quite different from *Highway*," notes Platt, who'd come aboard during the mix phase of the previous album. "*Highway* had been recorded in a very dead studio, so much so that during mixing I'd fed various parts back through the speakers and into the studio, recording the result for extra ambience. So when it came time to do *Back In Black*, the idea was to get that ambience on tape right from the start. The room at Compass Point was fairly large but had a lowish ceiling, which concerned me a little as I didn't want the room to compress the sound. We spent some time choosing the right position for the drums by hitting a snare in various parts of the room. I discovered a 'sweet spot' where the snare suddenly sounded bigger, deeper, fuller, and – most important – snappier. I subsequently discovered that there was a void above this position that was obviously allowing the sound to rise without choking it!"

■ *Main picture (left to right): Cliff Williams, Malcolm Young, Simon Wright, Angus Young, and Brian Johnson, who joined AC/DC in 1980, a month after the death of original vocalist Bon Scott (pictured above).*

For Angus's solo tracks – which were overdubbed – Platt employed two amplifier stacks, one in the main room and another in a live chamber at the far end of the building. "We used Angus's radios to transmit to these amps," says Platt. "The radios actually proved to be quite an important part of the sound, as they added some mid bite. I used two Neumann U67s on each cabinet, so I could pan the result where I wanted. And absolutely no compression was used at all."

Despite the volume at hand, Platt encouraged leakage in order to maintain the ambient element. "We kept Cliff's bass in a separate booth so that Angus and Malcolm's guitars could really bleed into the room," says Platt. "There was some screening over the amps, but it was minimal. For Phil's drums, I kept several room mikes up at all times, which I would move around depending on the effect I wanted to achieve. But, really, it was mainly just tuning the drums carefully to get the sound as close to where we wanted it, with the overheads providing most of the texture."

For newcomer Johnson, cutting vocal parts worthy of his predecessor was only half the battle; crafting lyrics that fit the AC/DC sex/rock/mayhem mold turned out to be the most daunting task of the entire six-week affair. "Because the lyrics were written as we went along, all of Brian's vocals were overdubs," says Platt. "But that turned out to be for the best anyway, as one of Mutt's finest attributes as a producer is his ability to enable the singer to perform to the best of his abilities."

Mixing for the album took place at Electric Lady Studios in New York shortly after the sessions were completed. "The size of the sound is really a combination of things," says Platt. "The tuning is good, the arrangements are spacious, and the recording isn't heavily processed, aside from some subtle addition of delays and light reverb just for extra ambience. I remember we also monitored quietly so we could balance carefully."

Coming after years of synthesized disco and overproduced AOR, *Back In Black* proved once again the resilience of live, loud, and melodic rock, and listeners immediately responded. At 20 million and counting, today the AC/DC's seventh major-label release ranks as the sixth bestselling album of all time.

"Probably the biggest buzz I've ever had during my time in the business was walking into Madison Square Garden one evening and hearing *Back In Black* coming over the house PA," notes Platt. "The engineer told me he always used that album to run up a PA, because if it sounded good with *Back In Black* playing, then he knew he had it! I can't think of a better endorsement than that."

1980

The Game Queen

Elektra 513 (U.S.A.) / EMI EMA 795 (U.K.)
Released July 1980

Five years after the release of 'Bohemian Rhapsody' – and having survived the punk-rock boom that killed off many of their contemporaries in the late 1970s – Queen issued their most diverse studio album, *The Game*, which was also the only one of the group's 14 full-length efforts to top the U.S. albums chart.

After recording the modestly successful *Queen* (1973) and *Queen II* (1974), Queen issued a run of five studio albums throughout the remaining years of the 1970s that each entered the upper reaches of the charts on both sides of the Atlantic. The group ended the decade, and the first phase of its career, with the double-album set *Live Killers* (1979), recorded earlier that year on the huge arena tour in support of *Jazz* (1978). In the final months of the 1970s they issued the rockabilly-inflected single 'Crazy Little Thing Called Love.' The first of the group's singles to top the U.S. singles chart, the song peaked at Number Two in the U.K., and would also be included on *The Game*.

The Game was recorded in two stages at Musicland Studio in Munich, Germany, with producer-engineer Josh McRae. Initial sessions were booked for June and July 1979, but produced little more than 'Crazy Little Thing Called Love' and a clutch of rough versions of other songs. The bulk of the recording was completed between February and May of the following year. The opening 'Play The Game,' one of four hit singles drawn from the album, sets the tone. Beginning in the vein of a typical stomping Queen song from the 1970s, 'Play The Game' features an unexpected synthesizer solo midway through. During the 1970s Queen's album sleeves and promotional posters had been decorated with the phrase "no synthesizers were used on this record," a fairly transparent attempt by the group to align themselves with the serious hard rock of the likes of Led Zeppelin. By the time the group came to make *The Game*, however, Queen had succumbed to the power of the synthesizer. Guitarist Brian May provides most of the keyboard parts, and was largely responsible for the group's change in direction.

Issued in the summer of 1980, *The Game* quickly rose to the top of the albums charts in the U.S.A. and the U.K. as well as elsewhere in Europe. The album's success can partially be attributed to the trail of hit singles – 'Crazy Little Thing Called Love,' 'Save Me,' and 'Play The Game' – that preceded its release. *The Game* also spawned a fourth huge hit single, 'Another One Bites The Dust,' which has become one of Queen's best-known songs. The track is emblematic of the new musical direction Queen took in the 1980s: based around taut, funky bass and drums, and featuring occasional flourishes of warm synthesizer, the song is about as far as the group could get from their earlier, theatrical heavy rock.

After *The Game* Queen moved into ever more pop-orientated territory. The following year the group performed a duet with David Bowie on the single 'Under Pressure,' a song which features on both Queen's *Hot Space* (1982) and various hits compilations by both acts. While Queen's popularity began to dwindle in the later 1980s, particularly in the U.S.A., the group continued to record until Freddie Mercury's death in 1991.

Fresh Fruit For Rotting Vegetables
Dead Kennedys

Faulty-IRS SP 70014 (U.S.A.) / Cherry Red B-RED 10 (U.K.)
Released November 1980

Inspired by the British punk scene, The Dead Kennedys became one of the defining U.S. hardcore groups of the 1980s, mixing visceral rock with fiercely political lyrics.

Frontman Jello Biafra (born Eric Boucher) launched the famed underground rock label Alternative Tentacles in 1979, which issued the group's debut single, 'California Über Alles.' (In a busy year, the 21-year-old Biafra had also run, unsuccessfully, for mayor of San Francisco.) The band signed a distribution deal with another nascent independent label, Faulty, for the release of its full-length debut, *Fresh Fruit For Rotting Vegetables*. Faulty was a subsidiary of IRS, the label founded by Miles Copeland, a former record producer and manager of The Police, as well as being the brother of The Police's drummer Stewart.

Fresh Fruit For Rotting Vegetables was produced by the group's guitarist East Bay Ray and recorded at Moibus Music in San Francisco in the winter of 1980. The album is an unrelenting barrage of raw, guitar-led punk and left-wing, satirical lyrics, typified by song titles such as 'Let's Lynch The Landlord' and 'Chemical Warfare.' Though it failed to chart in the U.S.A., it reached Number 33 in the U.K. and spawned the memorable single 'Holiday In Cambodia.' The album is now considered to be one of the most important underground rock records of the early 1980s. The following year The Dead Kennedys issued the equally polemical *In God We Trust Inc.*, which included the single 'Nazi Punks Fuck Off.'

Peter Gabriel 3 Peter Gabriel

Mercury SRM13848 (U.S.A.) / Charisma CAS4019 (U.K.)
Released June 1980

Who would have guessed that the eccentric art rock of early Genesis would lead to two very different but successful careers for singer Peter Gabriel and drummer Phil Collins? Or that the two would collaborate so effectively on Gabriel's third solo album, a record on which the approach to arrangement and production would be so influential throughout the 1980s?

Peter Gabriel 3 showed that in rock music there were other types of song to sing, other themes about which to write, other beats to pound, and instruments other than guitars to be played. All this was contained on the chilling opener, 'Intruder.' Cymbals and hi-hats were put aside: the beat came from Phil Collins's stark snare and bass drum recorded with distant mikes in a large room but then subjected to compression and 'gating,' an electronic process that cuts off a signal before its sound naturally fades. The result was a drum sound that crackled with focused energy, and was much imitated.

Here Gabriel wrote more from rhythms than chord sequences or melodies, experimenting with the then state-of-the-art computer-controlled CMI Fairlight synthesizer. Several tracks feature marimba and the fretless bass sound popularized by Jaco Pastorius. The Jam's Paul Weller steps up to play the fiery guitar riff on 'And Through The Wire' and Kate Bush sings on the sardonic parody of international politics, 'Games Without Frontiers,' which was a hit single. An album whose themes were alienation and psychosis closes with an elegy for murdered South African civil-rights activist Steve

Biko, a track that includes African singing fading in and out of the mix. In a time when world music was not a recognized genre 'Biko' was both exotic and highly political.

Remain In Light Talking Heads

Sire SRK/SRC 6095 (U.S.A. & U.K.)
Released October 1980

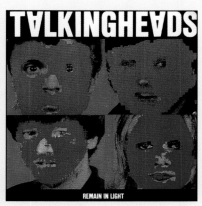

By adding African percussion, funk, and electronic production techniques to their art-rock repertoire, Talking Heads reached a creative peak, and the apex of their association with producer Brian Eno, with *Remain In Light*.

They had released an acclaimed debut, *Talking Heads 77*, on Sire before cutting the more experimental *More Songs About Buildings And Food* and *Fear Of Music* with Brian Eno, the producer fresh from making the critically lauded *Low* and *"Heroes"* with David Bowie. *Fear Of Music*'s opening track, 'I Zimbra,' was the first suggestion of the sound Talking Heads would arrive at on their next release, as the group began to draw on the polyrhythmic drumming of African music.

Eno and Talking Heads began recording *Remain In Light* at Compass Point Studios in the Bahamas in July 1980, with additional tracking and mixing taking place in New York and Los Angeles. As well as the original quartet of frontman David Byrne, guitarist Jerry Harrison, bassist Tina Weymouth, and drummer Chris Frantz, the recordings were augmented by Eno, two percussionists, backing vocalist Nona Hendryx, trumpeter Jon Hassell, and guitarist Adrian Belew, fresh from his work on Bowie's *Lodger*. Belew makes sublime use of wah-wah and delay effects on his guitar playing, while all four core members dabble with synthesizers. The album's eight tracks, all co-written by Eno, started life as lengthy, percussive, full-band jams; the tapes of these performances were manually sliced up and reconfigured as looped grooves and then padded out with additional instrumentation and Byrne's expansive vocal melodies.

> **"WE WANTED TO DEVELOP AN UNDERSTANDING OF THE AFRICAN MUSICAL CONCEPT OF INTERLOCKING, INTERDEPENDENT PARTS AND RHYTHMS THAT COMBINE TO MAKE A COHERENT WHOLE."**
> *TALKING HEADS FRONTMAN DAVID BYRNE*

Remain In Light begins with 'Born Under Punches,' a single looped funk groove that gradually grows as Byrne adds layers of vocals and the rest of the band make subtle changes to the rhythm. These hypnotic, multilayered beats are unrelenting throughout what is by far the most cohesive album in the Talking Heads catalog. The best known song here is 'Once In A Lifetime,' a flop on its original single release but now considered by many to be Talking Heads' greatest individual statement. *Remain In Light* became their biggest album hit to date, its commercial success only exceeded by the later, more pop-orientated *True Stories* (1986) and *Naked* (1988) at the end of the band's career. It remains one of the finest rock records of the decade.

A year after making *Remain In Light*, Byrne and Eno reconvened for the collaborative album *My Life In The Bush Of Ghosts*. The latter album develops many of the themes of the former, again merging world music with new studio technology. As on *Remain In Light* the pair built up their songs from tape loops and electronic percussion but also began to make innovative use of found-sound samples, including elements of Egyptian and Lebanese music as well as fragments of American talk radio stations and ambient static. The album – a minor hit in both the U.S.A. and Britain – has since become a signpost for the many musicians who have followed Byrne and Eno toward genre-bending, patchwork methods of working.

1981

Escape **Journey**

Columbia 37408 (U.S.A.) / CBS CBS/40 85138 (U.K.)
Released August 1981

Founded by Neal Schon, a former member of Santana, Journey started life as an instrumental trio before adding vocalist Steve Perry and becoming a huge-selling arena-rock act.

Formed in 1973, Journey was named by the winner of a San Francisco radio contest, and recorded three modestly successful jazz-rock albums before Perry joined the group in 1977. His smooth vocal delivery and

the group's arrival at a more concise, hard-rock sound immediately reaped dividends, with *Infinity* (1978) selling a million copies in the U.S.A. alone. By the end of the 1970s Journey had also become a hugely popular live act, regularly filling large venues across North America and Europe.

The group's fourth album with Perry, *Escape*, was Journey's mainstream breakthrough. Produced by Kevin Elson and Mike 'Clay' Stone and recorded at Fantasy Studios in Berkeley, California, *Escape* has a more polished, commercial sound than its predecessors.

The album spawned a trio of Top Ten hits in the U.S.A. – the ballads 'Don't Stop Believin',' 'Who's Crying Now,' and 'Open Arms' – and sold over nine million copies worldwide. *Escape* topped the U.S. albums chart and reached Number 32 in the U.K., and was followed by two more big sellers, *Frontiers* (1983) and *Raised On The Radio* (1986), after which the group split and Perry became a recluse.

Though Perry returned for the reunion album *Trial By Fire* a decade later, subsequent Journey albums have been made without his involvement and with Schon as the only original group member.

No Sleep 'Til Hammersmith **Motörhead**

Not issued in the U.S.A. / Bronze BRON/+G/C 535 (U.K.)
Released July 1981

Motörhead were fronted by one of the enduring figures of British heavy rock, bassist-vocalist Lemmy (born Ian Kilminster), and laid the foundations for thrash metal with a series of visceral albums in the late 1970s and early 1980s.

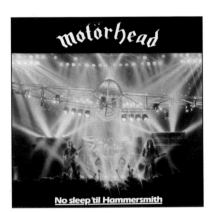

Originally a member of the progressive acid-rock group Hawkwind, Lemmy formed Motörhead in 1975 with guitarist 'Fast' Eddie Clarke and drummer Phil 'Philthy Animal' Taylor. The group built up a devoted following in the U.K. with the albums *Motörhead* (1977), *Overkill*, *Bomber* (both 1979), and *Ace Of Spades* (1980).

In March 1981 Motörhead scheduled a four-date U.K. tour specifically to record *No Sleep 'Til Hammersmith*, as nobody had ever thought to tape the group's live act before. The 'Short Sharp, Pain In The Neck Tour' took in performances at the West Runton Pavilion, Leeds Queen's Hall, and two dates at the Newcastle City Hall. The songs on *No Sleep 'Til Hammersmith* were recorded at the final three gigs by Vic Maile, who had previously recorded Dr Feelgood's live album *Stupidity* (1976). *No Sleep* takes in material from all four of Motörhead's studio album releases to date, including 'Iron Horse' and the classic 'Ace Of Spades.'

No Sleep 'Til Hammersmith reached Number One in the U.K. on its release, the only Motörhead album to do so, and remains the group's defining moment. Though Motörhead never rose beyond the level of cult act in the U.S., the group proved inspirational to many of the huge-selling heavy-metal acts that followed in the later 1980s.

■ *Above (left to right): Phil Taylor, Lemmy, and Eddie Clarke of Motörhead.*

Damaged **Black Flag**

S.S.T. SST 007 (U.S.A. & U.K.)
Released November 1981

Alongside The Dead Kennedys, Black Flag was one of the most important U.S. hardcore punk groups of the early 1980s.

Black Flag were formed in 1977 by guitarist Greg Ginn and bassist Chuck Dukowski, but the group didn't reach its full potential until vocalist Henry Rollins joined in 1980. By this stage the group also included rhythm guitarist Dez Cadena and drummer Robo.

The group recorded *Damaged* themselves in West Hollywood over three weeks during the summer of 1981, keeping to a budget of $8,500. The resulting album – 15 angry, disaffected songs crammed into a half-hour record – was clearly too much for MCA-Unicorn, the label to which the group had signed in 1980, who refused to issue it. Claiming that it was too outrageous, they particularly objected to such songs as 'Padded Cell' and 'Police Story,' which detailed the group's recent battles with the LAPD, who had assumed, incorrectly, that Black Flag was a cover for a drugs' ring.

Undeterred, Ginn released *Damaged* on his own SST label – later home to such influential bands as Hüsker Dü and The Minutemen – prompting legal action from MCA-Unicorn, who sued the group and succeeded in blocking them from recording as Black Flag for two years. The band eventually paid out a six-figure sum to free themselves from their contract and issued seven further albums between 1984 and 1986 before splitting up.

The muscular, tattooed Rollins has since become one of rock's unlikely renaissance men, recording several spoken-word albums and publishing volumes of poetry, short stories, and autobiography via his 2.13.62 imprint.

1981

Dare! The Human League

A&M 4892 (U.S.A.) / Virgin T/TP/TCV 2192 (U.K.)
Released October 1981

Non-Stop Erotic Cabaret Soft Cell

Sire 3647 (U.S.A.) / Some Bizarre BZ LP/MC 2 (U.K.)
Released December 1981

Hailing from the industrial English city of Sheffield, also home to contemporaries ABC, The Human League was the first synthesizer pop group to achieve widespread international fame.

Drawing on David Bowie's pioneering work with Brian Eno in the late 1970s on the albums *Low* and *Heroes* as well as his knack for capturing the cultural zeitgeist, The Human League peaked with *Dare!*, which spawned the Number One hit single on both sides of the Atlantic, 'Don't You Want Me.' The first, more avant-garde incarnation of The Human League was founded by former computer operators Martyn Ware and Ian Craig-Marsh alongside vocalist Phil Oakey. The trio soon recruited Adrian Wright, who became the group's visual technician, creating projections in front of which the other members performed. The Human League's line-up marked something of a sea change in popular music, as it was no longer necessary for a group to have a guitarist, bassist, or drummer when all of those sounds and more could be synthesized using keyboards and drum machines.

After several unsuccessful singles and an album, *Reproduction* (1979), Ware and Craig-Marsh left to form Heaven 17. They were replaced by Ian Burden on bass and synthesizers and a pair of backing vocalists, Jo Catherall and Susanne Sulley. This new Human League issued a trio of U.K. hit singles, of which 'Love Action (I Believe In Love)' reached Number Three, before commencing work on *Dare!*. The album was produced by the group and Martin Rushent, an engineer-cum-producer who had previously worked with T. Rex, The Stranglers, and Buzzcocks.

In contrast to The Human League's earlier experimental offerings, *Dare!* is a bright, polished collection of well-crafted love songs, underpinned by Rushent's sequencer-heavy style of production. The group's sound was bolstered by the addition of guitarist Jo Callis, who added melodic hooks to a predominantly synthesizer-based sound. Once again turning to Bowie's work – notably 'Sound And Vision' and 'Fashion' – as a template, the album also drew on the flamboyance of Roxy Music and the robotic groove of Kraftwerk. *Dare!* topped the U.K. albums chart in late 1981 and reached Number Three on its release early the following year in the U.S.A. As well as 'Don't You Want Me' and the previously issued 'Love Action'

and 'The Sound Of The Crowd,' *Dare!* featured a further U.K. hit single, 'Open Your Heart.'

Another important synth-pop act to emerge in 1981 was Soft Cell, whose 'Tainted Love' had already topped the U.K. singles chart by the time The Human League came to release *Dare!*. Though Soft Cell was ultimately overshadowed commercially by The Human League, the group issued the similarly innovative *Non-Step Erotic Cabaret*, which peaked at Number Five in the U.K. The album also contains two further U.K. hits, 'Bedsitter' and 'Say Hello, Wave Goodbye,' but failed to make as much of an impression in the U.S.A., where it peaked at Number 22.

■ *Above: Adam And The Ants. Below: Soft Cell. Left: The Human League.*

Prince Charming Adam And The Ants

Columbia 37615 (U.S.A.) / CBS CBS/40 85268 (U.K.)
Released November 1981

Adam And The Ants started life in the late 1970s as a fairly perfunctory, gloomy, post-punk act, whose debut, *Dirk Wears White Sox* (1979), failed to chart.

Former Sex Pistols manager Malcolm McLaren then hijacked the group's three backing musicians – rechristening them Bow Wow Wow and teaming them up with teenage singer Annabella Lwin – but not before he had encouraged frontman Adam Ant (born Stuart Goddard) to adopt a more theatrical image. Ant recruited a new band to record the Technicolor, rock'n'roll-influenced *Kings Of The Wild Frontier* (1980), which gave him a pair of U.K. hit singles, 'Ant Music' and 'Dog Eat Dog.'

Adam And The Ants' third album, *Prince Charming*, is an even more exuberant conceptual piece. Ant adopted the character – and costume – of an 18th-century highwayman on the record's sleeve and on the single 'Stand And Deliver,' which topped the U.K. singles chart, as did the follow-up 'Prince Charming.' A third single, 'Ant Rap,' peaked at Number Three in early 1982. The album was produced by Chris Hughes – who in another incarnation was the drummer in Tears For Fears – a highly sought-after producer and session musician. (Having produced all of Adam And The Ants' albums, Hughes went on to work with, among others, Paul McCartney, Enya, and Tori Amos.)

Despite a lukewarm critical response and few strong songs beyond the three hit singles, *Price Charming* entered the U.K. albums chart at Number Two, though it fared less well in the U.S.A., where it stalled at Number 94. Ant split the group in early 1982 to pursue a solo career.

1981

Face Value **Phil Collins**

Atlantic 16029 (U.S.A.) / Virgin V2185 (U.K.)
Released February 1981

Having achieved considerable international success during the 1970s as a member of Genesis, Phil Collins launched his solo career in 1981 with *Face Value*.

Originally the group's drummer, Collins emerged as the key figure in Genesis after the departure of Peter Gabriel in 1975, taking on the roles of chief songwriter and vocalist and steering the group toward a more adult contemporary pop sound. Collins started work on *Face Value* alone on an 8-track recorder before enlisting the help of Hugh Padgham, who had recently engineered Peter Gabriel's third solo album – on which Collins had guested – and produced *Ghost In The Machine* by The Police. Collins played all of the drum and synthesizer parts himself, while the guest musicians include Eric Clapton and the Earth Wind & Fire horn section. *Face Value* features eleven Collins originals that draw on recent changes in his personal life, from 'In The Air Tonight,' which details the collapse of his marriage, to 'This Must Be Love,' about the optimism of a new relationship.

Despite its sparse, somber arrangement and bitter lyrics, 'In The Air Tonight' reached Number Two in the U.K. singles chart and made the U.S. Top 20. *Face Value* itself peaked at Number Seven in the U.S.A. and topped the U.K. chart, outselling all of Collins's previous albums with Genesis.

Street Songs **Rick James**

Motown 12153 (U.S.A.) / MOT-5405 (U.K.)
Released November 1981

A blend of funk, rock, soul, and contemporary pop, Rick James's sound predated that which would propel Prince to superstardom, and helped revive the then-floundering Motown Records label.

Before signing to Motown, James had been a member of 1960s Toronto band The Mynah Birds with a pre-fame Neil Young, though the group never released a record. James signed to Motown in 1977 and hit the U.S. albums chart with his demo tape, issued as *Come Get It!*. By the time he began recording *Street Songs*, his fifth solo album, James was Motown's hottest property, and the label gave him free reign to write, produce, and perform most of the album himself. James worked on the album between December 1980 and July 1981 at a number of studios in and around Hollywood, employing an array of impressive guest musicians. Chief among them was Stevie Wonder, who guests on harmonica, while The Temptations provide backing vocals. On 'Fire And Ice' James performs a duet with the disco singer Teena Marie, whose own debut, *Wild And Peaceful*, he had produced in 1979.

Street Songs reached Number Three on the U.S. albums chart on its release in late 1981 and sold over a million copies, making it the biggest-selling album of James's career. Its success was due in no small part to the inclusion of his best known single, 'Super Freak (Part 1),' which reached the *Billboard* Top 20.

1982

■ *A still from the promo video for Michael Jackson's 'Thriller,' the title track from his landmark album. 'Thriller' was, at the time, the most expensive promo video ever made.*

Thriller Michael Jackson

Epic 38112 (U.S.A.) / EPC/40/CD 85930 (U.K.)
Released December 1982

The biggest-selling album of all time, *Thriller* has become a watershed in the history of popular music, selling in excess of 50 million copies worldwide. Incredibly, seven of the nine tracks also became huge hit singles.

Being an international star was nothing new to Michael Jackson, but his 1979 album *Off The Wall* had established him as a solo performer of astonishing ability and limitless mainstream potential. Produced by Quincy Jones, the album had given Jackson his first two U.S. Number One

hit singles in 'Don't Stop 'Til You Get Enough' and 'Rock With You,' and would eventually sell over seven million copies worldwide. Jackson remained loyal to his musical family, however, recording *Triumph* with the other Jacksons the following year. That album's high point is his 'This Place Hotel,' an early example of the horror-movie imagery he would develop further on *Thriller*.

Jackson began work on *Thriller* in March 1982 at Westlake Audio in Los Angeles, California. He was reunited on the album with Quincy Jones, a producer, composer, and record-company executive who had previously worked with artists including Miles Davis and Frank Sinatra. *Thriller* took its predecessor as a blueprint, perfecting its disco pop while adding heavy-rock elements to the funk tracks and making the soulful ballads even sweeter, giving the album a near-universal appeal.

Jones's production is one of the keys to the album's success, providing Jackson with a sparse but powerful backdrop over which to demonstrate his improved vocal abilities: gone for the most part is the adolescent falsetto of his earlier hits, replaced instead by a deeper, more determined delivery. The lyrical themes of *Thriller* are also more adult, as Jackson rails against press intrusion into his life on 'Wanna Be Startin''

Somethin'" and sounds almost paranoid on 'Billie Jean,' with its repeated refrain of "The kid is not my son." While the words seem downcast at times, the music remains vital throughout and – crucially to its enduring appeal – free of the schmaltzy over-production of much of the pop music of its era.

As well as containing some of the strongest hooks of Jackson's career, *Thriller* also featured several notable guest stars. The singer performed a duet with Paul McCartney on the album's first single, 'The Girl Is Mine' – the two would reconvene the following year for 'Say Say Say.' Of more historical importance is the guitar solo on 'Beat It,' provided by Eddie Van Halen at a time when a collaboration between a black pop star and a white heavy-metal musician was unprecedented. Many other black performers would follow Jackson's lead in subsequent years and work with rock musicians to boost their crossover appeal: Run DMC, for example, scored a Number Four hit in the U.S.A. in 1986 with 'Walk This Way' featuring Aerosmith. Jackson himself would repeat the feat a decade later, working with Guns N' Roses guitarist Slash on *Dangerous*.

Another contributor to *Thriller* was Vincent Price. Price had begun his acting career in the 1930s, starring in numerous darkly comic horror movies before switching tack in the 1970s and becoming a television chef. He returned to his earlier role on *Thriller*, providing a suitably spooky voice-over on the title track. The rest of the performers were Los Angeles session musicians, though one of the album's backing vocalists

would go on to have a hugely successful solo career in her own right: Jackson's sister Janet, already a sitcom star, would later record one of the decade's biggest selling albums, the hip-hop flavored *Control* (1986).

Jackson was adamant while making *Thriller* that it would vastly outsell *Off The Wall*, telling Jones that he intended it to be the most successful album of all time. He demonstrated his dedication to the project when he scrapped the album after the first official playback for label executives. Jackson and Jones returned to Westlake Audio to undertake a radical remix, so pushing the album several months behind schedule. On its eventual release in December 1982, however, *Thriller* entered the U.S. *Billboard* chart at Number One, where it would remain for an unrivalled 37 weeks of a two-year residency. The album also topped the U.K. chart and numerous others across Europe. Just as Jackson had planned during its lengthy gestation, *Thriller* would go on to become the bestselling album of all time, achieving worldwide sales of over 51 million copies.

Jackson helped maintain *Thriller*'s momentum by drawing an unprecedented seven hit singles from it. The first of these was the Paul McCartney collaboration 'The Girl Is Mine,' which was followed in early 1983 by 'Billie Jean' and 'Beat It.' Both releases topped the U.S. singles chart; the former was almost titled 'Not My Lover' after Quincy Jones opined that listeners might too readily associate the song with the tennis player Billie Jean King. ('Beat It' was successful enough that it inspired a

Weird Al Yankovich parody, 'Eat It,' itself a U.S. chart hit.) In May 1983 Jackson performed 'Billie Jean' on a television special commemorating 25 years of Motown Records. It was at this moment that Jackson became pop music's first megastar, inaugurating his moonwalk dance in front of an audience of 47 million.

Jackson released four more singles from *Thriller* during the remainder of the year; 'Wanna Be Startin' Somethin',' 'Human Nature,' 'PYT (Pretty Young Thing),' and the album's title track. All four reached the U.S. Top Ten and were hits in Britain. 'The Lady In My Life' proved to be the only song on *Thriller* not to be issued separately: an eighth song from the album, 'Baby Be Mine,' was also issued as the b-side to 'Human Nature.'

During 1983 Jackson also entered into a mutually beneficial relationship with MTV, becoming the first real star of the fledgling television station. 'Billie Jean' was the first video by a black artist to be playlisted by MTV, and also marked the first time a music video told a story while promoting a song. Jackson and director John Landis took the process a step further with the 'Thriller' promo. The extravagant piece, in which a werewolf

Above: Paul McCartney – who featured on the first single to be drawn from Thriller, *'The Girl Is Mine' – and his wife Linda pose with Jackson at the 1983 Brit Awards ceremony. Left: Jackson with his pet monkey, Bubbles, and an unnamed llama.*

Jackson dances with a troupe of other creatures of the night, ended up costing twice its already huge $600,000 budget. These costs were recouped in March 1984 with the VHS release of *The Making Of Michael Jackson's 'Thriller,'* which became the bestselling music video ever. By the time of its release, Jackson had won in a record eight categories at both the American Music Awards and the Grammys, bringing a fitting conclusion to a period of unparalleled success.

"ALL THE BRILLIANCE THAT HAD BEEN BUILDING INSIDE MICHAEL JACKSON FOR TWENTY-FIVE YEARS JUST ERUPTED."

QUINCY JONES, PRODUCER OF THRILLER

Michael Jackson's star showed no sign of falling during the rest of the 1980s. After a final tour with The Jacksons in 1984, Michael co-wrote the global hit single 'We Are The World' with Lionel Richie and bought the music publishing company ATV, which held the rights to much of the Lennon & McCartney songbook. His next solo release, *Bad* (1987), inevitably failed to reach the artistic and commercial heights of its predecessor, but still sold over 25 million copies and spawned four U.S. Number One hit singles. Though Jackson's career began to decline in the 1990s amid much negative publicity, *Thriller* remains one of the most important albums of all time.

The Digital Revolution

After the quadraphonic debacle, both industry and consumers were wary of new technology. Nonetheless, in the studio world things were changing all the time. Tom Stockham of the Massachusetts Institute of Technology had devised a digital audio recorder, using a computer tape transport, as early as 1962.

In 1975 he started a company called Soundstream with loudspeaker-maker Malcolm Low and launched the first commercial digital recording service in the world. In 1976 he recorded The Santa Fe Opera and then, in 1978, recorded Frederick Fennell and The Cleveland Symphonic Winds for Telarc. This would be the first commercially released digital recording. The first digitally recorded pop or rock album to be released was Ry Cooder's *Bop Till You Drop*. Both those records were released on album and cassette, garnering considerable interest from audiophiles and enthusiasts, though Cooder was scathing about both the sound and the complexities involved in pioneering it. But while there was keen interest there was, as yet, no digital delivery system for the home.

That came with Compact Disc, introduced in 1982, but a playback-only medium for the first ten years of its life. The CD was first conceived in 1969 by Dutch physicist Klass Compaan, but ten years passed before the format was ready to be officially unveiled. The CD is an amalgam of several technologies introduced in the 1960s and 1970s, including the laser and digital recording systems. Philips and Sony were at the forefront of the new medium's development and were jointly responsible for setting a number of standards for the format in 1979. All CDs would be recorded in 16-bit audio, with a sampling rate of 44.1 kHz (44,100 samples per second). Produced from polycarbonate, the disks were intended to be four and a half inches (115mm) in diameter, but were expanded to nearly four and three-quarter inches (120mm) to allow for just over 74 minutes of audio. All involved were optimistic that CDs would revolutionize the way we listen to music.

The first commercial CD players went on sale in Japan in October 1982, alongside an initial catalog of 112 CD titles. Europe and the U.S.A. followed in February and June of 1983 respectively. Many of the first titles were classical and jazz recordings or, in Japan, karaoke collections; among the early rock and pop titles on offer were Billy Joel's *52nd Street* and Michael Jackson's *Off The Wall*. The general trend tended to be for major-label hits of the past few years. Aside from Japan, traditionally more receptive to new technology and where demand almost immediately outstretched supply, CD sales began slowly, with many consumers unsure whether the new format would take off, and neither willing nor able to meet the high cost of the first CD players. Early CD machines, such as the Sony CDP 101, sold for around $1,000, with the disks themselves priced between $15 and $20, limiting their mainstream appeal. Research commissioned by Sony Japan suggested that virtually all CDs were being sold to young men in their 20s and early 30s, whose primary interest was in the high sound-quality of the format. Some industry people began to worry that this might limit the CD market to audiophiles and never expand it to what Sony had predicted would be "a music revolution in the home." Regardless, major record labels continued to expand their catalogs. One of the first new albums to be issued on CD was Bruce Springsteen's *Born In The U.S.A.*, which went on to become one of the biggest-selling albums of all time.

Initially, all CDs were manufactured either by PolyGram in Germany or by Sony Japan; the first major U.S. pressing plant did not open until late 1984. Up to 1986, the majority of CDs sold in the U.S.A. were imported from abroad. CDs sold modestly for the first couple of years before a sudden upsurge around Christmas 1985 that left record shops completely out of stock and pushed yearly sales up to 22 million. The same year also saw the introduction of the DiscMan. While such portable CD players would not become commonplace for several years, they gave CDs a further advantage over 12-inch vinyl albums because music fans could now listen to them while on the move.

The size of the CD meant that a new packaging format had to be created. It was decided that CDs should be sold in 12-inch by six-inch cardboard 'long-boxes,' perhaps because they could be displayed in the same racks as vinyl records. It was also considered that these large rectangular packages would be more of a deterrent to retail theft than something of five inches in diameter. However, as complaints were made about the amount of cardboard wasted in the production of the long-boxes, they

Continued on page 215

1982

Rio **Duran Duran**

Capitol 12211 (U.S.A.) / E.M.I. 3411 (U.K.)
Released January 1983 (U.S.A.) / May 1982 (U.K.)

**Duran Duran was the most
enduring and successful of the
new-romantic groups to emerge
from the U.K. in the early 1980s.**

The group's second full-length effort –
and international breakthrough album
– *Rio* typifies the decade's pop, not
just musically but also visually,
particularly in the title track's famous
video, in which the group cavorts with
beautiful models on a yacht.

Duran Duran was formed in 1980 by
DJ-turned-keyboardist Nick Rhodes
and bassist John Taylor, who named the group after a character in the kitsch
sci-fi classic movie *Barbarella* (1967). The group was augmented by
drummer Roger Taylor, guitarist Andy Taylor, and vocalist Simon Le Bon. In
1981 they signed to EMI – which hoped to capitalize on the success of
fellow new romantics Culture Club and Spandau Ballet – and recorded an
eponymous debut, which peaked at Number Three in the U.K., remaining on
the chart for 118 weeks. The album was not initially successful in the U.S.A.,
but entered the *Billboard* Top Ten two years later, with 'Durandemonium' at
its peak following the release of *Rio*.

Central to Duran Duran's success was the group's image, carefully cultivated
in press shots and a series of videos directed by Russel Mulcahy. Having
previously directed the video to Buggles' novelty hit 'Video Killed The Radio
Star,' Mulcahy cast Duran Duran as hedonistic playboys in the promotional
movie that accompanied the group's debut single, 'Planet Earth.' The image
stuck, and Mulcahy continued to work with the group throughout the 1980s,
directing memorable videos for 'Girls On Film,' 'Rio,' and 'Wild Boys,' among
others. Also integral to Duran Duran's visual appeal were the high-fashion
record sleeves, designed by Malcolm Garrett, in particular *Rio*'s iconic cover.

Having already conquered the U.K. and much of Western Europe with their
eponymous debut album, the group began to set its sights on the U.S.
market while making *Rio*. Like its predecessor, *Rio* was produced by Colin
Thurston, who had earned his spurs engineering David Bowie's *"Heroes"*
and Iggy Pop's *Lust For Life* in Berlin in 1977 before working on albums by
The Human League and Magazine. Thurston lends *Rio* a lush, exuberant feel
throughout, whether on the upbeat synth-pop of 'Hungry Like The Wolf' and
the title track or on more subtle ballads, such as 'Lonely In Your Nightmare.'
While the album is often dominated by dayglo synthesizer flourishes and
electronic drum-machine rhythms, *Rio* also reveals Duran Duran as a group
of talented musicians, particularly in the case of bassist John Taylor and
drummer Roger Taylor.

Rio reached Number Two in the U.K. on its release in 1982, while three
singles from the album – 'Hungry Like The Wolf,' 'Save A Prayer,' and the
title track – entered the Top Ten. In the U.S.A. the album's release was held
over until early 1983, at which point it reached Number Six, while 'Rio'
peaked at Number Two several months later. In the remaining months of
1983 Duran Duran reached the top of the singles and albums charts in the
U.K. for the first time, with 'Is There Something I Should Know' and *Seven
And The Ragged Tiger* respectively.

The Lexicon Of Love **ABC**

Mercury SRM-1-4059 (U.S.A.), Neutron NTRS1 (U.K.)
Released September 1982 (U.S.A.) / July 1982 (U.K.)

**With their dramatic, synthesized
pop, ABC became an instant
international success with their
first single, 'Tears Are Not
Enough,' and the album *The
Lexicon Of Love*.**

Based in Sheffield, England, ABC
earned considerable critical acclaim
from the outset for their classic pop
songwriting as well as former fanzine
editor Martin Fry's crooning vocal
delivery, which was often likened to
that of Bryan Ferry and David Bowie.
Though signed to Phonogram in the U.K., the group was allowed to issue
their debut through their own Neutron imprint.

What lifted *The Lexicon Of Love* above the often throwaway fare of ABC's
early-1980s contemporaries was the innovative production style of Trevor
Horn. His warm, dense arrangements, augmented by Anne Dudley's
sweeping orchestrations, proved the perfect foil for Martin Fry's theatrical
vocals. Horn, who had scored an international hit with 'Video Killed The
Radio Star' as a member of Buggles two years previously, would become
one of the most successful producers of the 1980s, working with Yes, Pet
Shop Boys, Frankie Goes To Hollywood, and Tina Turner, among others. He
also later formed techno-pop group Art Of Noise with Dudley and music
journalist Paul Morley.

The Lexicon Of Love quickly rose to the top of the U.K. albums chart on its
release and made the Top 30 in the U.S.A. The album spawned four hit
singles, including 'The Look Of Love' and 'Poison Arrow,' both of which
reached the *Billboard* Top 40. Though the band would never repeat the critical
and commercial success of their debut – in part because of Martin Fry's ill
health, which limited their activity in the mid 1980s – ABC did achieve an
isolated international hit in 1987 with the nostalgic 'When Smokey Sings.'
They continued to tour and record sporadically through the 1990s.

Nebraska **Bruce Springsteen**

Columbia 38358 (U.S.A.), CBS 40 25100 (U.K.)
Released September 1982

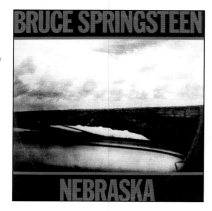

**In stark contrast to the glossy
production techniques employed
on most early-1980s albums,
Nebraska marks the first instance
of an artist issuing a collection of
songs recorded in demo form.**

In late 1981, following a lengthy
world tour in support of *The River*
(1980), Springsteen enlisted his
guitar technician, Mike Batlan, to find
him "a little tape machine – nothing
too sophisticated, just something I
can do overdubs on." Batlan duly
purchased a Teac 144 Portastudio – a basic 4-track tape recorder that had
been on the market since 1979 – and set it up in Springsteen's home in
Long Branch, New Jersey.

Springsteen originally intended to cut rough demos of his new songs
before recording them properly with The E Street Band. To this end, he
worked through the songs quickly, mostly in one or two takes, with just
acoustic or electric guitar, harmonica, and vocals. It soon became clear
that these demos fell into two distinct categories: half were typical
Springsteen rockers – these would later form the basis of *Born In The
U.S.A.* (1984) – while the rest had a sparse fragility at odds with his
earlier work.

> ## "I GOT THIS LITTLE CASSETTE RECORDER, PLUGGED IT IN, TURNED IT ON, AND THE FIRST SONG I DID WAS 'NEBRASKA.' I ONLY HAD FOUR TRACKS, SO I COULD PLAY THE GUITAR, SING, THEN DO TWO OTHER THINGS. THAT WAS IT."
>
> ### BRUCE SPRINGSTEEN

Some attempts were made to rework this set of songs with subtle instrumentation from the full band, but recordings repeatedly stalled as Bruce felt unable to match the feel of his original tapes.

When it was eventually decided to issue the demos as the follow-up to *The River*, Columbia insisted attempts be made to clean up the original tapes, though little could be done about the sound of a record that had been mastered on an old Panasonic boom box. While the primitive nature of the recordings is often exaggerated – Springsteen still used high-quality Shure microphones and a Gibson Echoplex unit – *Nebraska* remains one of the most rough-sounding releases of a major-label star. The album includes some of the strongest songs in the Springsteen canon, from the title track, a first-person retelling of the Charlie Starkweather killings – also the subject of Terrence Mallick's 1973 movie *Badlands* – to the epic 'Highway Patrolman.'

The Nightfly **Donald Fagen**

Warners 23696 (U.S.A.) / 923696 1/-4 (U.K.)
Released October 1982

After making a series of albums as Steely Dan between 1972 and 1980 alongside Walter Becker, Donald Fagen launched his solo career with the acclaimed conceptual set *The Nightfly*.

While it doesn't deviate far from the Steely Dan sound, *The Nightfly* is a stronger, more cohesive collection of songs than anything Fagen had recorded with Becker since the duo's defining work, *Aja* (1977).

Fagen had made his first tentative steps toward working apart from Steely Dan shortly after the release of the group's *Gaucho* in 1980, when he contributed to the score of Martin Scorsese's *King Of Comedy*. Stepping away from the biting cynicism of Steely Dan, Fagen conceived *The Nightfly* as an evocation of his teenage years, and to that end the songs succeed as snapshots of the period of post-war optimism of the years before the assassination of John F. Kennedy. Produced, like all of Steely Dan's work, by Gary Katz, *The Nightfly* is faultlessly performed by a revolving cast of over 30 session players, who give the album a lavish, smoky, jazz feel. Alongside seven Fagen compositions – held together by the conceit of a hip DJ speaking across the airwaves to Fagen's disaffected youth – is a rendition of the Leiber & Stoller song 'Ruby Baby.' Of the originals, 'IGY (International Geophysical Year)' and the Cold War drama 'New Frontier' were both minor hit singles in the U.S.A. *The Nighfly* itself reached Number 11 in the U.S. albums chart on its release, peaking at Number 44 in the U.K.

Continued from page 213

were eventually replaced by the hastily conceived and now familiar jewel-box.

A major limitation of the vinyl LP had been its maximum playing time of a little over 40 minutes. Artists were quick to exploit the capacity of the CD, which effectively doubled the prospective length of the albums they made. Albums in the 1960s and 1970s typically ran to around 35 minutes, but in the CD era were more likely to hit 50 or 60 minutes. The dynamic of the album also changed; traditionally conceived as two – or more – sides of vinyl, on CD it became a single body of work. These technical advances were not without drawbacks: many artists were overeager to use up all the available space, often resulting in bloated, unfocused albums. The potential length of CDs also had an effect on reissues of older titles. Earlier double-albums, such as Bob Dylan's *Blonde On Blonde*, could be re-pressed on a single disk, while for the first time lengthy classical pieces could be heard in one sitting. Back-catalog sales rose significantly in the latter half of the 1980s as consumers were encouraged to replace their vinyl with remastered CD editions. Past favorites, such as Simon & Garfunkel's *Bridge Over Troubled Water* and Pink Floyd's *Dark Side Of The Moon*, were given a new lease on life by the prospect of hearing them in an enhanced digital format for the first time.

In 1986 three million CD players were sold across the U.S.A. as sales of the traditional LP began to decline. For a brief period in the mid 1980s the cassette led the soundcarrier market, but it would soon be usurped by the CD. Worldwide CD sales reached one billion in 1990, by which time vinyl was increasingly perceived as a niche market. By 1995, 70 percent of all soundcarriers sold worldwide were CDs.

Tape did not give up that easily, however. In the early 1980s the Japanese giants Sony and Matsushita separately developed digital recording systems intended for home use. In 1983 they and some 80 other manufacturers agreed a common system – known as R-DAT or DAT – using the revolving-head recording technology familiar from video recorders. Unfortunately, the new technology terrified the record companies because of its capacity for making perfect copies of CDs, which they were just beginning to sell in large volumes as replacements for people's vinyl record collections. Consequently, they sought a modification of the DAT standard so it would not record CDs, followed by a more general system to stop DAT making digital copies of digital copies – copies of copies tend to proliferate much faster than copies of originals. At the same time they lobbied to prevent the import of DAT recorders without these limitations. In the end, Sony and Phillips agreed not to introduce DAT until the incorporation of SCMS – serial copy management system, the copy-protection system required by the record companies.

In the U.S.A., DAT machines without anti-copying systems were banned in 1987, and lobbying against the machines continued even beyond their eventual introduction in 1990, eight years after their original launch. The issue was not resolved until the Audio Home Recording Act of 1992, which applied to all digital recording devices though not, fatefully, to home computers, which were at the time considered unlikely ever to have the storage capacity to record CDs. SCMS was now mandatory, and manufacturers of machines and tapes also had to pay a levy to copyright owners. Interestingly, in 1988 Sony had taken over CBS Records and now began to see the copyright question from the other side of the fence. Besides, without machines reaching homes, record companies had no interest in producing pre-recorded tapes, essential if DAT was to replace the cassette. In the end, it settled down as an expensive, high-quality medium for studio mastering use and, later, for computer backup.

While Sony was embroiled in copyright wars over DAT, Phillips in Holland had another idea. Its Digital Compact Cassette, introduced in 1992, was a stationary-head digital recording medium using a cassette sufficiently similar to the existing compact cassette to allow old analog cassettes to be played in the same machines. However, the system did not record as much data as DAT, so the audio had to be compressed to fit. It was launched with "a huge selection of prerecorded titles," taking in everyone from The Cure to Ella Fitzgerald. In-car and portable players were made available. It was a success – but only in The Netherlands, where it seized a good share of the market – and it lasted until 1996, when production was halted. Elsewhere, it fought a grim and eventually losing battle with Sony's next invention, the MiniDisc, introduced the same year.

MiniDisc (MD) was intended by Sony to be a replacement for cassette and had several advantages: it offered the instant accessibility that people were getting used to with CD, and it also looked new and exciting compared with the Phillips machine, which was still identifiably a cassette recorder. It also lent itself to portability and came accompanied with a initial flurry of prerecorded music. But MiniDisc initially used a slightly more aggressive version of audio compression than DCC, and some claimed it was audible. MD never captured the American market, and the dream of a mass market for prerecorded disks soon faded. It lives on in a kind of limbo, assailed on one side by recordable CD and on the other by portable MP3 players such as the iPod. Sony, however, has not given up. In 2004 it introduced HiMD, using a 1GB disk that will hold 45 hours of music and can also be used for computer storage.

1982

1983

The Kids From Fame Kids From Fame

RCA 4249 (U.S.A.) / MGM KIDLP004 (U.K.)
Released October 1982

The Kids From Fame was a spin-off from the early 1980s NBC television series Fame.

The television show, which ran for six years between 1982 and 1987, was itself a by-product of the 1980 movie of the same name about a New York school for performing-arts students. Both the movie and television versions gave the 'students' regular opportunities to sing, and, given the popularity of both, an album of songs by them was inevitable.

The Kids From Fame features ten songs, some sung by the entire Fame ensemble, others performed by individual members of the cast,. All are in the standard pop vein of the time, taking in saccharine ballads and disco pop, all decorated by then cutting-edge synthesizer sounds. The album was only a minor hit in the U.S.A., particularly when compared with the success of the television series. Nonetheless, it was followed in 1983 by a second album, Songs, and the concert recording The Kids From Fame Live, which captured the group on stage at the Royal Albert Hall in London, performing 'Don't Stop 'Til You Get Enough,' 'We Got The Power,' and other pop hits. In the early 2000s Fame became an internationally successful musical, at a time when nostalgia for the music and styles of the 1980s was at its highest.

Hex Enduction Hour The Fall

Not issued in the U.S.A. / Kamera KAM 005 (U.K.)
Released March 1982

Hex Enduction Hour is arguably the best-loved of countless album releases by The Fall, the cult British group fronted by the eccentric Mark E. Smith.

Smith founded The Fall in Manchester, England, in 1977, and remains the only constant in an ever-changing membership. The group inaugurated its scratchy post-punk sound on two albums from 1979, Live At The Witch Trials (actually a studio album) and Dragnet. Then came Totale's Turns, Grotesque (both 1980), and the mini-LP Slates (1981).

The Fall started work on Hex Enduction Hour in late December 1981 at the disused Regal Cinema in Hitchin, England, before decamping – improbably enough – to a cave in Iceland to finish the album in early 1982. The eleven songs on Hex are dominated by Smith's freeform vocal rants, the scattershot attack of the group's two drummers, Paul Hanley and Karl Burns, and the spiky guitar interplay between Marc Riley and Craig Scanlon. The other musicians on the album are bassist Steve Hanley and percusssionist-vocalist Kay Carroll.

Hex opens with 'The Classical' – essentially The Fall's mission statement – and closes with 'And This Day,' an epic onslaught of relentless dissonance. In between, the songs' violence and cynicism is born out in titles like 'Hip Priest' and 'Who Makes The Nazis?' The album barely scraped into the U.K. chart, and was not issued in the U.S.A. until 1989, but remains a landmark of early 1980s art rock.

Let's Dance David Bowie

EMI America 17093 (U.S.A.) / AML 3029 (U.K.)
Released April 1983

Having recorded a run of innovative albums between 1970 and 1980, from the glam rock Ziggy Stardust (1972) to the electronic explorations of Low (1977), on Let's Dance Bowie changed direction again, opting for a contemporary pop sound, which brought him the biggest commercial success of his career.

Having retreated from the limelight to make his 'Berlin trilogy' of albums – Low, "Heroes" (both 1977), and Lodger (1979) – Bowie began to make more decisive inroads into the mainstream market again with Scary Monsters And Super Creeps (1980). That album featured collaborations with Pete Townshend and Robert Fripp and gave Bowie four U.K. hit singles, 'Ashes To Ashes,' 'Fashion,' 'Up The Hill Backwards,' and the title track. Despite its chart success, Scary Monsters was still a fairly abrasive, experimental record in places. The following year Bowie issued his second volume of greatest hits, Changestwobowie. This release marks a turning point in his career. Throughout the 1970s Bowie was renowned for setting trends and inspiring whole new musical genres. From *Let's Dance* onward his records tended to draw more explicitly on the sound of the times rather than leading them.

Let's Dance is notable for the fact that none of Bowie's regular musical collaborators from the 1970s appears on it. Dispensing with Tony Visconti, Bowie recruited the disco producer Nile Rodgers, who had achieved enormous success in the late 1970s as the key creative figure in Chic and had since made records with Diana Ross and Debbie Harry. Rodgers looms large over the sound of *Let's Dance*, which, though clearly still a David Bowie record, has a distinctly polished, dance-pop feel. The album has a bright synthesizer sheen throughout, and is laced with disco guitar hooks, played by Rodgers himself. In place of Carlos Alomar, who had featured on every Bowie album since *Young Americans* (1975), is Stevie Ray Vaughan, the guitarist who went on to lead the blues revival of the 1980s. (Vaughan's appearance on *Let's Dance* predates his own solo debut, *Texas Flood*, by three months, demonstrating that Bowie still had a knack for spotting fresh talent.)

Let's Dance was recorded at Mountain Studios in Switzerland, where Bowie was living as a tax exile. Side One of the vinyl opens with a trio of international single hits, each of them primed for the mainstream but retaining enough individuality to keep them apart from standard pop fare. The first track, 'Modern Love,' is followed by a cover of Iggy Pop's 'China Girl,' which Bowie had produced for Pop's 1977 album *The Idiot*. Bowie covered the song to help his friend – who was languishing in a period of diminishing success – by way of the huge royalty payments that started to go Pop's way as the song raced into the Top Ten of the U.S. and U.K. singles charts. The third song in

this opening salvo is the title track, one of Bowie's best-known songs and the only one of his singles to top the charts on both sides of the Atlantic. Though the rest of *Let's Dance* doesn't quite maintain the momentum of these three, there are few weak moments, resulting in the most aurally satisfying Bowie album of the 1980s. *Let's Dance* topped the U.K. albums chart on its release, and reached Number Four in the U.S.A.

Let's Dance was just one of a number of big-selling albums of the 1980s produced by Nile Rodgers. Rodgers had previously been best known as a member of Chic, the most influential disco group of the late 1970s. The band scored several huge international hits between 1977–9, most notably 'Le Freak' and 'Good Times,' but the group's popularity fell in the early 1980s.

Undeterred, Rodgers turned his hand to writing for and producing other artists, including Sister Sledge and Diana Ross. *Let's Dance* was the first of a run of hugely successful albums produced by him. He followed it with work on Madonna's *Like A Virgin* (1984), Duran Duran's *Arena* (1984), and Mick Jagger's solo debut, *She's The Boss* (1985). Most of Rodgers's 1980s productions were recorded at The Power Station in New York (now known as Avatar Studios), where he made regular use of his former Chic bandmates Bernard Edwards and Tony Thompson, on bass and drums respectively. The Power Station also lent its name to the pop supergroup formed in 1985 by the British soul singer Robert Palmer alongside Thompson and several members of Duran Duran, whose work Rogers produced.

■ *Below: Nile Rodgers (left) and Bernard Edwards (center) pose with David Bowie at the 1983 Frankie Crocker Awards in New York.*

1983

Synchronicity **The Police**

A&M 3735 (U.S.A.) / AMLX63735 (U.K.)
Released June 1983

As well as being the multiplatinum tombstone on the grave of The Police's career, *Synchronicity* illustrates how, by the mid 1980s, recording technology had advanced to such a degree that it was possible for a feuding band to record an album in the same studio without actually having to see each other.

Sting, in the process of breaking up with his actress wife Frances Tomelty, had written several songs, including 'Every Breath You Take,' at Golden Eye, the house formerly owned by James Bond author Ian Fleming in Jamaica. Armed with this material, The Police started work on *Synchronicity* on December 5th 1982 at Air Studios on the Caribbean island of Montserrat. Producer Hugh Padgham recalls: "Though the island is a kind of tropical paradise, making the album turned into a nightmare." This was because, as well as Sting's split from Frances, guitarist Andy Summers's marriage was disintegrating. To compound their misery, the always edgy relationship between Sting and drummer Stewart Copeland had deteriorated

to the point where the pair could not bear to be together. "For acoustic reasons, all of the band members played in different rooms," says Padgham tactfully, "but I'd have to admit that it was also a very convenient way of keeping them all apart." One specific bone of contention at this time was Sting's insistence that Stewart should drum in a more conventional rock mode, rather than his trademark reggae style.

After two weeks nothing had been completed, Padgham wanted to go home, and manager Miles Copeland had to fly in to force them back to work. Even so, Summers recalls "six weeks" being spent trying to record the bass and snare drum for 'Every Breath You Take,' which Copeland still regards as a wonderful song blighted by "an utter lack of groove. It's a totally wasted opportunity." At the start of 1983 recording moved to Le Studio, located in a ski resort near Montreal. "Sting would go skiing in the mornings," says Padgham. "Stewart would come in and lay down some complex drum track, then Sting would come back while Stewart was skiing, and say, 'What the fuck's that? Take it off.'"

Caught in the middle, Summers assumed the role of peacemaker. "Whenever Sting and I had our fists around each others' throats," remembers Copeland, "Andy would hold a two-inch tape – the ring of good vibes – over our heads, chanting 'I am nothing' until we stopped." Eventually, however, *Synchronicity* was completed and, as Padgham observes: "Ultimately, out of all that tension, came a quite wonderful album." The record-buying public certainly agreed, because on July 23rd 1983 it topped the U.S. albums chart for the first of 17 weeks, and had gone four-times platinum before the end of 1984.

Sting has since described *Synchronicity* as virtually a solo album. "Songs like 'Every Breath You Take' and 'Wrapped Around Your Finger' were all about my life," he points out. "I couldn't involve this kind of personal work in a democratic process, at least not about the issues. So it was very clear to me during the making of this record that this was the end of The Police."

Murmur **R.E.M.**

IRS 70604 (U.S.A. & U.K.)
Released May 1983

R.E.M.'s full-length debut, *Murmur*, introduced the sound that would dominate much of the alternative rock of the next decade.

Having already developed a cult following on the strength of the mini-album *Chronic Town*, R.E.M. started work on *Murmur* on January 6th 1983 at Reflection Sound Studios in Charlotte, North Carolina. The album sessions were produced by Don Dixon and Mitch Easter, who had recorded *Chronic Town* at his own Drive-In Studio, also in North Carolina. The band spent the best part of the next six weeks recording, adding multiple layers of arpeggiated guitar to a quiet, subtle backbeat. Still painfully shy at this point, Michael Stipe insisted on performing all his vocal parts alone in the dark.

The sound of *Murmur* is a darker, more obtuse version of the jangly, folk-tinged rock R.E.M. would perfect on the multiplatinum albums *Out Of Time* and *Automatic For The People* in the early 1990s. Stipe's trademark oblique lyrics are already in place, and are lent a further air of mystery on

Murmur by his suitably mumbled delivery. The focal point is often Peter Buck's distinctive guitar playing, which drew equally on The Byrds and the more contemporary sound of post-punk, while drummer Bill Berry and bassist Mike Mills provide a steady backdrop. *Murmur* reached the U.S. Top 40 on its release, and includes several fan favorites, notably a re-recorded version of the band's debut single 'Radio Free Europe' and 'Perfect Circle,' the latter still a staple of R.E.M.'s live performances 20 years after its release.

Under A Blood Red Sky **U2**

Island 414-818008-1 (U.S.A.) / IMA 3 (U.K.)
Released December 1983

This 8-track mini-album recorded the spirit and fire of U2's shows around the time of the *War* tour.

Formed in Ireland in the late 1970s, U2 had by 1983 released three albums. *Boy* and *October* had been moody, fragmented experiments in guitar rock, dominated by The Edge's heavily echoed riffs and guitar phrases; their third album, *War*, showed a considerable focusing of the band's music, with producer Steve Lillywhite creating a viciously compressed, explosive drum sound. The Cold War tension and barely restrained anger of the songs had a theatrical directness that was bound to electrify audiences. It was as if U2 had arrived to be to the 1980s what The Who had been to the 1960s: a counter-cultural rock band and a fantastic live act.

It made perfect sense, therefore, to get this stage act down on vinyl. Very wisely, U2 side-stepped the temptation of the live double album, and instead *Under A Blood Red Sky* came out as a mini-album at a reduced price – possibly, in part, to tempt those who had bought the video of the same name (of a show at Red Rocks, Arizona) that had been released earlier that year, though of the songs here, only 'Gloria' and 'Party Girl' are actually from the Arizona show. Other tracks, including '11 O'Clock Tick Tock' and 'New Year's Day,' showed that The Edge had discovered an echo-drenched guitar style that was neither riff nor lead but somewhere in between. The album features a passionate rendition of 'Sunday Bloody Sunday' and touching renditions of 'Party Girl' and the Biblical '40.' Unfortunately, a snippet from Stephen Sondheim's 'Send In The Clowns' sung by Bono during one of the songs required a five-figure sum in copyright settlement.

■ ***Below: U2 frontman Bono patrols the stage on the group's 1982 U.S. tour.***

1983

Eliminator ZZ Top

Warners 23774 (U.S.A.) / W3774/+4 (U.K.)
Released June 1983

occasional co-songwriter. In 1970 Gibbons and Ham recruited bassist Dusty Hill and drummer Frank Beard – curiously the only member of the trio without a full set of facial hair. ZZ Top produced five blues-based albums for London Records in the 1970s before signing to Warners in 1978. The group's Warners debut, *Deguello* (1979), demonstrated with a series of wry, surreal songs, that ZZ Top were not the simple, rustic trio most people had taken them for in the past, but musically the group was still mining 1960s-style blues rock. *El Loco* (1981) continued in a similar vein, adding a smutty sense of humor to songs such as 'Pearl Necklace' and 'Tube Snake Boogie,' before the group – or perhaps Ham – decided a change of sound was needed in order to achieve true international stardom.

Few would have expected ZZ Top to adopt the synth-pop stylings that dominated the singles charts in the early 1980s, but that is exactly the route the group took. *Eliminator* retains the driving blues guitars of previous ZZ Top albums, but adds a layer of synth hooks that immediately brought mainstream acceptance to the trio of two bearded and one mustachioed Texans. Produced, like all of ZZ Top's recorded output, by Ham, the album also sticks to the lyrical themes of its predecessors. Even if the group didn't quite look the part, ZZ Top's songs about fast cars and faster women were suddenly in vogue, dovetailing neatly with the international playboy image of the likes of Duran Duran. ZZ Top also adopted a similar promotional angle to Duran Duran, filling their music videos with scantily clad beauties as well as the obligatory red coupe. ZZ Top's videos – for 'Sharp-Dressed Man,' 'Gimme All Your Lovin,'' and 'Legs' – were rivaled only by Michael Jackson when it came to heavy MTV rotation in 1983.

Having achieved modest success in the U.S.A. during the 1970s with a traditional, guitar-based sound, bearded blues-rock trio ZZ Top began working with synthesizers on *Eliminator*, achieving widespread international fame in the process.

Eliminator also established a strong visual image for the band. The record's sleeve – an airbrushed image

of a red Ford coupe – stands among the most iconic album covers of the 1980s, while the videos for 'Gimme All Your Lovin'' and 'Legs' were MTV staples during the cable music channel's formative years.

ZZ Top was first conceived in the late 1960s by guitarist Billy Gibbons and Bill Ham, who, throughout the group's career, has been an unofficial fourth member, serving as manager, producer, and

Eliminator reached Number Nine in the U.S.A., and was ZZ Top's first hit album in the U.K., where it peaked at Number Three. Of the three singles to be drawn from *Eliminator*, 'Legs' was the most successful, charting at Number Eight in the U.S.A. and Number 16 in the U.K. ZZ Top followed the album with the equally successful – but less artistically rewarding – *Afterburner* (1985), which was essentially 'Eliminator II'.

Swordfishtrombones Tom Waits

Island 90095 (U.S.A.) / ILPS/ICM 9762 (U.K.)
Released September 1983

Tom Waits first emerged in the early 1970s under the guidance of Frank Zappa's manager Herb Cohen, recording seven albums of woebegone, after-hours balladry for Elektra in the U.S.A. and Asylum Records in the U.K. between 1973 and 1980.

After fulfilling his Elektra-Asylum contract with *Heart Attack And Vine*, Waits began to experiment with a wholly new sound, a melting pot of blues, jazz, and ragtime combined with more avant-garde influences such as the work of composer Harry Partch. The first fruits of this were issued as *Swordfishtrombones*.

Recorded at Sunset Sound in Los Angeles in August 1982 with producer Biff Dawes, *Swordfishtrombones* ditches the traditional arrangements and rich orchestral flourishes of Waits's earlier work in favor of a more idiosyncratic palette of weird instruments. Waits himself switches from piano to harmonium, while an impressive array of guest musicians, including Larry Taylor and Victor Feldman, conjures up a vaudeville opera with marimbas, African talking drums, and the sound of a chair being dragged across the studio floor. The songs are pitched somewhere between Kurt Weill and Howlin' Wolf, and Waits's lyrics, delivered in his trademark raw-throated voice, are as obscure as the musical settings behind them, as he sings of eggs that "chase the bacon from the fryin' pan" and "a hummingbird trapped in a closed-down shoe store."

Waits evidently had some trouble persuading a record label to take a chance on *Swordfishtrombones*, as it didn't see release until 13 months after its completion. Eventually issued by Island Records, with whom Waits would remain until the late 1990s, the album became an instant cult favorite, and is now regarded by many as one of the finest albums of the 1980s.

Can't Slow Down Lionel Richie

Motown 8051 (U.S.A.) / MOT-6059 (U.K.)
Released December 1983

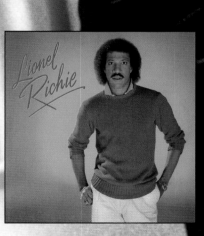

A former member of The Commodores, Lionel Richie as a solo performer was one of the most successful male vocalists of the 1980s. As well as being a hugely popular ballad singer, he also wrote and produced hits for other artists, including 'Lady,' a U.S. Number One hit for Kenny Rodgers.

Formed in 1968, The Commodores' early output was dominated by hard funk, but Richie's lush ballads gradually came to the fore in the 1970s. Richie left the group to pursue a solo career in 1982, releasing a self-titled debut album that spawned three U.S. Top Ten hits; his second solo album, however, elevated him to the ranks of superstardom. Using Michael Jackson's recent *Thriller* (1982) as a blueprint, *Can't Slow Down* aimed to cover all bases of the mainstream pop market, adding funky dance pop and watered-down elements of hard rock to the expected ballads. Richie co-wrote and produced all eight songs on the album, and spent six months honing the sound of the album at a variety of studios across the U.S.A.

On its release in late 1983 *Can't Slow Down* quickly rose to the top of the U.S. albums chart, eventually selling ten million copies in the U.S.A. and over 15 million worldwide. The album also gave him five U.S. Top Ten singles and won the 1984 Grammy Award for Album Of The Year. Of the singles, 'Hello' and 'All Night Long (All Night)' both topped the U.S. chart, selling a million copies each.

1984

Diamond Life **Sade**

Portrait 39581 (U.S.A.) / Epic 26044 (U.K.)
Released February 1985 (U.S.A.) / July 1984 (U.K.)

Among the most striking female singers to emerge in the 1980s, Sade achieved widespread international fame with the jazz-inflected *Diamond Life*, one of the biggest-selling debuts of the decade.

Born Helen Folasade Adu to an English mother and African father in the Nigerian city of Lagos in 1959, Sade grew up in London. In the early 1980s, while studying fashion at St Martin's College and occasionally modeling, she began to draw record-company interest as vocalist in the funk-rock collective Pride. Initially reticent to leave the eight-piece group behind and sign a major label deal as a solo performer, Sade stalled for a year before inking a contract with Epic in 1983, but only after she had been assured that the label would also take on guitarist-keyboardist Stuart Mathewman and bassist Paul Denman.

Sade started work on her debut album shortly thereafter, adding keyboardist Andrew Hale and drummer Paul Cooke to the band. Also featuring on *Diamond Life* are Mathewman's trumpet-playing sibling Gordon and percussionist Martin Ditcham, who would later work extensively with Talk Talk. *Diamond Life* was produced by Robin Millar, who lends the album a slick, light-jazz feel despite a lack of prior experience as producer. (Following the worldwide success of *Diamond Life*, Millar produced albums for Everything But The Girl, Fine Young Cannibals, and Big Country, among others.) The songs have an elegant cool, their precise guitar and keyboard licks offset by Sade's effortless vocal delivery, reminiscent at times of her childhood idols Billie Holiday and Nina Simone. There are suggestions of Afrobeat rhythms beneath the songs' sophisticated jazz-club stylings, but they are rarely allowed to spill over to the surface. Very few of the nine songs edge beyond mid-tempo, but then they were not intended to – *Diamond Life* is the perfect coffee-table or dinner-party album.

Diamond Life gradually climbed up the U.K. albums chart during the latter part of 1984, peaking at Number Two on the strength of the singles 'Your Love Is King' and 'Smooth Operator,' a collaboration between Sade and former bandmate Ray St John. Sade signed to the CBS subsidiary label Portrait for the U.S. release of the album in early 1985, where it reached Number Five and earned platinum status soon after 'Hang On To Your Love' and 'Smooth Operator' entered the Top Ten.

Sade kept up the momentum with a cameo role in the movie *Absolute Beginners*, which also starred David Bowie, in which she sang 'Killer Blow.' In late 1985 she issued a quick follow-up album, *Promise*, which proved even more popular than *Diamond Life* and gave her the international hit 'The Sweetest Taboo.' After winning a Grammy Award for Best New Artist, Sade's popularity was such that even her album tracks were being heavily rotated on U.S. radio stations. She continues to record and tour in the 21st century, and has to date sold over 40 million albums worldwide.

Like A Virgin **Madonna**

Sire 9251571 (U.S.A. & U.K.)
Released November 1984

Signed to Leo Stein's Sire Records in 1983, Madonna Louise Veronica Ciccone quickly broke into the mainstream with a pair of 1984 singles, 'Lucky Star' and 'Borderline,' and by year's end, her self-titled debut had gone platinum.

Nothing, however, could have prepared listeners for the singer's next move. In November came a single, 'Like A Virgin,' written by pop tunesmith Billy Steinberg, the title track from Madonna's forthcoming second album that revealed a tougher, hard-pop Madonna, a sound so irresistible that even rock radio took notice.

Manning the controls inside New York's Power Station Studio C for the making of *Like A Virgin* was Chic producer Nile Rodgers, who surrounded the singer with an economical rhythm section consisting of Chic bassist Bernard Edwards and drummer Tony Thompson, with Rodgers himself handling guitar duties. "Tony's got such a great way with drums – he plays so hard and so loud he just fills up the room up with sound," notes Rodgers's engineer Jason Corsaro. "I realized that it was something that had to be captured. I mean, if you've got a drummer who sounds so beautiful in the room, why would you want to take that away?" Initially, Corsaro's attempts at beefing up the backing were met with resistance. "The folks at Power Station were always telling me, 'You can't put R&B drums in the big room, they have to go in the dead room!' But that didn't make any sense to me – I knew there had to be a way to capture the power of the drums and keep the rhythm intact at the same time."

Corsaro eventually figured out a unique method that involved equal parts mike placement and just plain technical creativity. "By being too close, I knew I was going to miss a lot of those dynamics. By the same token, that music demanded a strong groove. So I started cutting the room tracks in time with the drums. Everyone thinks it was gated, but I actually wrote the parts into the computer as we were mixing! When I added Tony's drums on top of that, the sound was incredibly powerful. It was just what I wanted – a rock, room sound, but also very R&B." As a result of the minimalist mix, Thompson's drum kit became the featured instrument on 'Like a Virgin.' "That's one of the things that made the song so special," says Corsaro. "Because there was nothing but guitar and bass, the drums had so much space to fill. You could hear what Tony was doing so clearly."

Corsaro still had some selling to do during the initial playbacks. "To tell you the truth, Nile wasn't that into it in the beginning of the record," recalls Corsaro. "It really went against the grain of the early-'80s dance sound – I think he was looking for something a bit more 'normal.' But Madonna and her manager absolutely loved it. And that was all he needed to hear."

Corsaro's sound innovation was instrumental in helping to cross Madonna into the rock mainstream – an almost unheard-of feat at the time. "I was thrilled when they picked 'Like a Virgin' for the first single," says Corsaro. "It became the first dance-pop record to have a real rock drum sound. Of course, since then Madonna's proved herself quite capable at keeping up with new ideas – it's really one of her finer attributes."

Reaching Number One on December 22nd 1984, the title track to *Like A Virgin* remained at the top of the charts for the first five weeks of 1985, becoming Madonna's biggest career single. The album – which itself hit Number One in February – provided three additional smash hits in 'Material Girl,' 'Angel,' and 'Dress You Up.' Madonna never looked back, dominating the pop charts with ten straight Top Five singles and massive album sales through the remainder of the decade.

Island 90232 (U.S.A.) / ZTT-Island ZTT1Q (U.K.)
Released November 1984

Columbia 39595 (U.S.A.) / Epic EPC/40 86311 (U.K.)
Released November 1984

Frankie Goes To Hollywood was one of the biggest British pop phenomena of the mid 1980s, thanks in no small part to the slickly orchestrated campaign of controlled controversy that propelled the group's records to the top of the U.K. charts.

Having formed in Liverpool in 1980, Frankie Goes To Hollywood teamed up with producer Trevor Horn, who signed the group to his ZTT label in 1983. At this time Horn was best known as a performer on Buggles' novelty hit 'Video Killed The Radio Star,' though his production credits did by now include ABC's *Lexicon Of Love*.) The group's first single, the high-octane 'Relax,' sold a million copies in the U.K. after it was banned by the BBC because of its sexually suggestive lyrics. The accompanying homoerotic promo video was also banned, serving only to boost the group's popularity. In the meantime, Paul Morley, the music writer and promotional director of ZTT, began cleverly to insinuate the group into the national consciousness, largely by way of a series of hugely popular Frankie Says . . .' T-shirt slogans.

Welcome To The Pleasuredome, the group's double-album debut, arrived in late 1984, with Frankiemania continuing to rise in the U.K. following the release of 'Two Tribes,' which had spent nine weeks at Number One – 'Relax' taking the Number Two spot for some of that time – during the summer. Horn's disco-pop production is exemplary throughout, but few of the album tracks are as memorable as the singles, and covers of Gerry And The Pacemaker's 'Ferry 'Cross The Mersey' and Bruce Springsteen's 'Born To Run' are unnecessary filler. 'The Power Of Love' provided Frankie with a third consecutive U.K. Number One hit, while the album itself also topped the British charts.

Frankie was far less popular in the U.S.A., but did manage a Number Ten placing when 'Relax' was reissued in early 1985.

Wham! was one of the most internationally successful British pop acts of the 1980s. The duo's popularity peaked with *Make It Big*, which topped the charts in the U.S.A. and the U.K., as did three of the singles drawn from it.

George Michael, who wrote all of the duo's hits and produced the album, was clearly the dominant member of the pair, and few were surprised when he disbanded the group to embark on a solo career in 1986.

Wham!'s debut album *Fantastic!* shows few signs of the songwriting talents Michael would harness on *Make It Big* and in his solo work, and failed to make much of an impact outside the U.K. He and partner Andrew Ridgeley started work on a more mature follow-up in July 1984 with engineer Chris Porter, who had recently worked with Elaine Paige and The Alarm. Like many pop albums of the time, *Make It Big* contains a lot of filler between the songs earmarked as singles, but the singles themselves are near faultless. 'Wake Me Up Before You Go-Go' and the ballad 'Careless Whisper' – written when Michael was just 17 – had already topped the singles charts on both sides of the Atlantic and across Europe by the time *Make It Big* was released in late 1984. 'Everything She Wants' provided Wham! with a third U.S. chart topper, while 'Freedom' reached Number One in the U.K. *Make It Big* has sold over five million copies in the U.S.A. alone, while in 1985 Michael became the youngest ever winner of Britain's Ivor Novello Songwriter Of The Year award.

1984

Born In The U.S.A.
Bruce Springsteen

CBS 38653 (U.S.A.) / CBS86304 (U.K.)
Released June 1984

The commercial peak of Springsteen's career, *Born In The U.S.A.* sold more than ten million copies in the U.S.A. alone and gave him several hits, including the passionate 'Cover Me' and the poppy 'Dancing In The Dark.'

That many see Springsteen as the acme of American 'blue-collar' rock, a guy who sings about cars, girls, and not much else, is largely down to this album's international success. For many it fixed him for ever in their minds as a crude, sweaty stadium rocker, a Rambo of the six-string, populist and simplisitic.

Recording the acoustic demos of *Nebraska* made Springsteen go for a leaner band sound and more straightforward song structures when he returned to electric rock. The band played together in the studio and recorded as directly as possible. Guitarist Steve Van Zandt noted: "That was literally live, at least the eight or nine things we did before I left. If Bruce wanted to sing it again, we'd play it again; that's how live it was."

The title track was crucial, seemingly inescapable in 1984. Festival crowds sang it with gusto when it boomed out through PA systems, whether they were American or not. Springsteen said: "I had written a catchy song . . . probably one of my best since 'Born To Run.' I knew it was going to catch people – but I didn't know it was going to catch them like *that*, or that it was going to be what it was." 'Born In The U.S.A.' started life as a two-chord acoustic song during the *Nebraska* sessions, but was amped-up by The E Street Band with unparalleled ferocity and single-mindedness. Drummer Max Weinberg recalled: "Bruce started playing this droning guitar sound. He threw that lick out to [keyboardists] Roy [Bittan] and Danny [Frederici], and the thing just fell together. It absolutely grabbed us. We played it again and got an even better groove on it. At the end as we were stopping, Bruce gave me the high sign to do all these wild fills, and we went back into the song and jammed for about ten minutes, which was edited out. I remember that night as the greatest single experience I've ever had recording, and it set the tone for the whole record."

From celebrating the mythical romance of the American Dream earlier in his career, Springsteen was now exposing the plight of those who crawl at its margins and under its shadow. But this focus was often blurred by the radio-friendly bounce of 'Glory Days,' the perceived nostalgia of 'My Home Town,' and the apparent flag-waving of the chorus of 'Born In The U.S.A.' Despite the fact that the verses of that song painted a bleak picture of life in the U.S.A., they could be overlooked in the light of the seemingly patriotic refrain, as happened when President Ronald Reagan and others ignored Springsteen's ambivalence and co-opted the song for simplistic jingoism.

Its composer has reservations about the album that made him a global star. In 1987 he said: "I wasn't satisfied with the *Born In The U.S.A.* record. I did not think I made all the connections I wanted to make on it." It was his last studio album with The E Street Band for over a decade.

1984

The Smiths **The Smiths**

Warner Brothers 25065 (U.S.A.) / Rough Trade RTD25 (U.K.)
Released February 1984

One of the most original of bands of the 1980s, The Smiths were reminiscent of early R.E.M.: they were arty, they appealed to students, had unusual lyrics, plenty of Rickenbacker jangle, an unconventional vocalist, and a healthy contempt for chart formulas.

Guitarist Johnny Marr – whose work with The Smiths made him one of the most important British guitarists of the decade – summed up the group's spirit when he said: "We were against synthesizers, the Conservative government, groups with names like Orchestral Maneouvres In The Dark, the English Monarchy, cock-rock guitar solos, and the American music scene at the time. We stood for the Englishness of The Kinks, T. Rex and Roxy Music . . . We were into The Rolling Stones, The MC5, The Patti Smith Group, Oscar Wilde, [playwright] Sheleagh Delaney, and certain actors."

Recording the debut LP was a trial. The Smiths junked a whole batch of songs and had to start over. When they performed on television their first hit single 'This Charming Man' – not included on the album – they looked like nothing else on the U.K. music scene. Singer Morrissey was the anti-rock star, with a bunch of gladioli hanging out of the back pocket of his jeans

and sporting a pair of National Health Service glasses. His lyrics were allusive, anguished, and droll. He said: "It was always important to me to use lines that hadn't been said before, because it wasn't enough to use the usual pop terminology." His melodies were free of blues inflections, one reason why the music sounds so English. While 'What Difference Does It Make' and 'Hand In Glove' were hits, the album also features the sad dignity of 'Still Ill' and the creepy beauty of the controversial 'Suffer Little Children,' a song about the infamous 'Moors Murders' that took place in and around the band's home town of Manchester during the mid 1960s.

A Walk Across The Rooftops **The Blue Nile**

A&M 5087 (U.S.A.) / Linn Records LinnLP LKH 1 (U.K.)
Released April 1984

This most retiring of bands has made a career out of eschewing the promotional treadmill of record/video/tour/record, instead choosing to spend years fashioning infrequent albums that are adored by the cognoscenti.

The Blue Nile was formed in 1981 by three Glaswegian university graduates, Paul Buchanan, Robert Bell, and Paul Joseph Moore. That same year an early demo found its way to Robert Stigwood's RSO Records, resulting in a single, 'I Love This Life,' being released in 1981, just weeks before the company went out of business. After this false start the band came to the attention of Linn, a Scottish company known for its upmarket record turntables. Sensing a marketing opportunity for its hi-fi products, Linn formed a label, signed The Blue Nile, and released *A Walk Across The Rooftops*, the band's debut album.

Sales were initially slow, but the album's humane, meticulously crafted electronic white soul gradually drew in a coterie of fanatical admirers. Eventually it quietly slipped into the U.K. album charts and got a release in the U.S.A. on the A&M label. Most bands would have grabbed the moment and toured non-stop for a year on the back of this breakthrough, then quickly recorded a follow-up. Not The Blue Nile. They refused to play live, instead retreating from view to agonize over their next record for five years. *Hats*, as the follow-up was called when it finally appeared in 1989, was felt by many to be even better than *Rooftops*. This time, the band deigned to tour.

1985

Songs From The Big Chair **Tears For Fears**

Mercury 824300 (U.S.A.) / MERH 58 (U.K.)
Released March 1985

Tears For Fears – duo Roland Orzabal (vocals, guitar, keyboards) and Curt Smith (vocals, bass) – emerged during the new-romantic, synth-pop period of the early 1980s, taking their name from psychotherapist Arthur Janov's book *Prisoners Of Pain*.

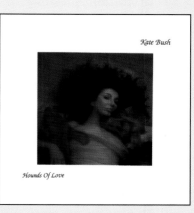

Their debut album, *The Hurting*, contained the hit 'Mad World,' and was followed by *Songs From The Big Chair*, the fifth-bestselling album of 1985. It had three big hits in 'Shout,' 'Head Over Heels,' and 'Everybody Wants To Rule The World.' 'Everybody' was a melody of Beatles-like catchiness, sung and played with such conviction it sounds like they were polishing the platinum disk even as the tape rolled.

The album had structural twists and turns, sculpted melodies, freaky guitar solos, bold singing, and imaginative textures. It was lyrically unified by the theme of psychological exploration and catharsis. Side Two of the vinyl best illustrates the record's dramatic ebb and flow. After the deep blue of the smoky night-club 'I Believe,' 'Broken' kicks in and takes rock somewhere you didn't know was on the map. Its anguish lightens into the walking-on-air 'Head Over Heels,' its Bowie-esque la-la-and-handclaps coda segueing into a cooking live reprise of 'Broken.' A measure of peace comes with the bewitching 'Listen,' with its haunting chords, fluid female vocal, and mysterious mantra-like chant. Time has not been kind to pop music from this period with its tinny, artificial beats and one-finger synth playing, but *Songs From The Big Chair* is an exception, leaving an impression greater than the sum of its parts.

Rum, Sodomy And The Lash **The Pogues**

Not issued in the U.S.A. / Stiff SEEZ 58 (U.K.)
Released August 1985

Blending a punk-rock sensibility with traditional Irish folk music, The Pogues built up a devoted cult following in Europe and the U.S.A. in the 1980s.

Shane McGowan formed the group in 1982, adding several folk musicians to the more conventional punk core of his previous group, The Nipple Erectors. The group soon built a reputation on the strength of McGowan's shambolic, drunken stage act and the battered elegance of 1984's debut album *Red Roses For Me*. The following spring The Pogues recruited Elvis Costello – whose own work had begun to betray more rootsy influences by the mid 1980s – to produce what became *Rum, Sodomy And The Lash*.

'The Sick Bed Of Cúchulaínn' set the tone for the album, erupting midway through from whiskey-soaked ballad to rousing, accordion-led punk folk. *Rum, Sodomy And The Lash* continues in this vein, mixing traditional Irish songs with McGowan originals. The album's centerpiece, 'A Pair Of Brown Eyes,' was a minor U.K. hit single. The Pogues would never again quite match the aching beauty of the songs on here. This was partly a result of the departure of bassist and backing vocalist Cate O'Riordan, who left the

group after marrying Costello in 1986, while McGowan began to descend into drug and alcohol abuse, his unpredictable behavior resulting in him being sacked in 1991. The Pogues did, however, manage an unlikely festive hit in 1987, when 'Fairytale Of New York' – a duet with Kirsty MacColl, featuring the line "Merry Christmas, my arse / I pray God it's our last" – reached Number Two in the U.K.

Hounds Of Love **Kate Bush**

EMI ST17171 (U.S.A.) / KAB 1 (U.K.)
Released September 1985

After the artistically successful but under-selling *The Dreaming* **(1982),** *Hounds Of Love* **– recorded at Windmill Lane Studios and Abbey Road between spring 1984 and summer 1985 – brought Kate Bush back from the commercial wilderness and won her new fans in the U.S.A.**

Album-opener 'Running Up That Hill,' a powerfully melancholic tale of communication failure between lovers, was the first of several singles. It was originally titled 'A Deal With God,' but Bush bowed to record-company advice that having the word God in the title would limit airplay in certain countries. The bold, galloping drum rhythm of 'Running Up That Hill' never lets up, with thunderous fills that punctuate the closing section. (Minus hi-hats and cymbals, Bush first encountered this stripped-back drum style when she sang on Peter Gabriel's third album.) 'Cloudbusting' features another innovative approach to percussion with its march-like rhythm track.

Side One of the vinyl offered five individual songs, whereas Side Two was a suite of inter-connected pieces, 'The Ninth Wave,' based on the memories and hallucinations of someone floating in the sea. Her most ambitious piece, it gave ample opportunity to make use of the exotic sounds of her brother Paddy's collection of unusual instruments, as well as Pink Floyd-inspired sound effects. Bush also made pioneering use of the Fairlight synthesizer system.

> **"I WANTED TO TRY AND GET ACROSS A SENSE OF POWER, AND THE WAY I RELATED TO THAT WAS VERY MUCH WHAT I CONSIDER VERY GOOD MALE MUSIC – THE KIND OF POWER I FOUND THERE WAS NOT WHAT I FOUND IN A LOT OF FEMALES' MUSIC."**
>
> *KATE BUSH, SPEAKING IN 1989*

In almost every way the distance between *Hounds Of Love* and her 1978 breakthrough hit 'Wuthering Heights' is enormous. The degree of progression in her music is remarkable, and not driven by fashion or style-hopping. It is always in an integral relationship with her music's emotional core.

After *Hounds*, Bush recorded *The Sensual World* (1989), which expressed a more feminine energy. Using The Trio Bulgarka to add plangent East European folk harmonies to several songs, as well as draw on the musical skills of violinist Nigel Kennedy, The Chieftains, and the Breton harp player Alan Stivell were inspired choices. Both albums show Bush's depth as a songwriter, whether in singing about love failing or lost, or reaching back to forgotten regions of childhood. She has a fine ear for melody and an ability to invent new arrangements for her songs, and she does all this without recourse to blues-inspired vocal clichés.

Bush is unquestionably one of the greatest female singer-songwriters to emerge from the U.K. Without her example things might have been very different for all the rebellious women who came through in the 1990s, such as Björk, Alanis Morissette, and Tori Amos.

1985

Biograph **Bob Dylan**

Columbia 38830 (U.S.A.) / CBS 66509 (U.K.)
Released November 1985

A career-spanning collection of hits, misses, and previously unissued recordings, the five-LP/three-CD set *Biograph* was the first widely successful boxed set by a rock artist.

While other acts had issued two- or three-volume packages of vinyl in the past, *Biograph* started a trend for lavishly packaged, multidisk sets of a single artist, intended as *the* definitive representation of a performer's work.

Compiled by Columbia to commemorate 24 years of Bob Dylan on record, *Biograph* was conceived as a comprehensive assessment of his career to date. The original ten sides of vinyl are arranged thematically rather than chronologically, making their way through the various aspects of Dylan's music. Side One of the first disk is, perhaps surprisingly, devoted to his love songs, while the rest of *Biograph* works its way through other areas, including Dylan's early protest songs, his first experiments with an electric band, and his most overtly Christian period. This arrangement allows key moments in the Dylan songbook – 'Like A Rolling Stone' or 'Blowin' In The Wind,' for example – to sit comfortably alongside lesser-known or never-before-heard recordings, which include 'Percy's Song' and 'Lay Down Your Weary Tune.' The downside of this scattershot approach is that the listener is left unaware at times of the many patterns, changes, and reinventions of Dylan's career. Perhaps heeding this, the compilers of the majority of the box sets that followed *Biograph* – including Dylan's later all-rarities set, *The Bootleg Series* (1991) – have tended to stick to a more rigid, year-on-year sequence.

Biograph also established another key ingredient of the box set: accompanying the music is an extensive booklet, which features notes by Dylan himself on each of the songs and several biographical pieces, aimed at reminding the listener just how important is the man and his music. As a further selling point these sleevenotes include a number of previously unpublished photographs.

Following the success of *Biograph*, other artists and their respective labels were quick to put together box sets of their own. The subjects of these sets tend almost without exception to be heavyweights of the worlds of rock and, to a lesser extent, jazz, weighted so as to appeal to fans old and new, with a selection of classic material for the uninitiated and an assortment of unreleased cuts for the devoted completist.

A year after *Biograph*'s release, Bruce Springsteen assembled a five-disk volume of concert recordings, *Live 1975–85*. By far the most commercially successful box set ever produced, *Live 1975–85* was one of the first albums to be given diamond status at the inauguration in 1999 of the award for sales of over ten million copies in the U.S.A. That a multivolume collection of live recordings could stand alongside *Sgt Pepper's Lonely Hearts Club Band* or *Dark Side Of The Moon* in sales terms is quite an astonishing achievement, considering the fact that most box sets are aimed at a small section of the record-buying public.

Of the countless other box sets issued over the course of the next two decades, several deserve a brief mention. A number of these contain their respective acts' entire discography, including The Velvet Underground's *Peel Slowly And See* and Led Zeppelin's *Complete Studio Recordings* (both 1993); all 13 U.K. Beatles albums were made available in 1988, housed inside an expensively priced mock bread bin. Sony has to date issued seven deluxe sets compiling the complete sessions from various periods in Miles

Davis's career, several of them with engraved metal spines. The Beach Boys' *Good Vibrations* collection neatly sums up 30 years of the band and includes half an hour of previously unheard material from the then incomplete *Smile* album. Beyond rock and jazz, box sets are less common. One notable exception, however, is *Tommy Boy's Greatest Hits* collection, five CDs of music from the pioneering rap label packaged within an eye-catching, scaled-down reproduction of a crate full of vinyl.

Riptide **Robert Palmer**

Island 90471 (U.S.A.) / ILPS 9801 (U.K.)
Released November 1985

In a career spanning five decades, Robert Palmer sang with The Alan Bown Set and Vinegar Joe before launching a solo career in the 1970s.

Establishing himself as a versatile white soul singer, Palmer had a number of minor hits in the U.S.A. and Britain in the late 1970s and early 1980s. In 1985 he found a wider mainstream audience as a member of the pop supergroup The Power Station, alongside members of Chic and Duran Duran. 'Some Like It Hot' and a cover of the T. Rex classic 'Get It On' both featured on *The Power Station* and both reached the U.S. Top 20.

The stage was therefore set for Palmer's solo career to move up a gear. *Riptide* was recorded in the Bahamas with several of the musicians Palmer had worked with earlier in the year with The Power Station, including Duran Duran's Andy Taylor. Producer Bernard Edwards lends *Riptide* a polished, 1980s pop sheen that stands some way apart from Palmer's previous blues- and soul-influenced work. It was his first to enter the Top Ten in the U.K. and the U.S.A., but is best remembered for the huge U.S. Number One hit it spawned, 'Addicted To Love.' The memorable promo video had Palmer performing with a 'band' of guitar-wielding models in mini-skirts and became an MTV staple. *Riptide* also featured 'I Didn't Mean To Turn You On,' which peaked at Number Two in the U.S.A. in the summer of 1986.

Brothers In Arms **Dire Straits**

Warner Brothers 2-25264 (U.S.A.) / Vertigo VERH 25 (U.K.)
Released May 1985

A classic record of the 1980s, *Brothers In Arms* is one of the biggest-selling albums of all time, reaching Number One in at least 25 countries, with worldwide sales in excess of 20 million, and many of the tracks becoming hit singles.

Dire Straits were fortunate enough to be the right band at the right time with the right product to benefit from a new music medium: *Brothers* was one of the first rock albums released on CD. Philips, who were making CD hardware, claimed later that this was "the key album in transforming CD from a new-fangled curiosity into a mass-market music carrier." Hi-fi stores liked its pristine production for demoing CD players and systems. (It was estimated that at one point, when CD players were still luxury items, everyone who had a player had a copy of the album.)

After their first two albums in 1978–9 and the wiry Fender-guitar licks of 'Sultans of Swing,' Dire Straits got more ambitious. By their fourth LP, *Love Over Gold*, they had left their pub-band origins far behind, stretching songs such as 'Telegraph Road' to 14 minutes. But, after the double-live *Alchemy*, Knopfler decided to trim back to more focused, hooky songs.

Brothers captured the mood of the time. It rocks – but not too much – and it doesn't scream at you, so millions who would normally never buy a rock album bought it. Knopfler's subdued gravelly voice seems reassuringly grounded – worse things happen at sea, it implies. He comes across as an unpretentious Man Of The People, like a commercial version of J.J. Cale. The gleaming steel guitar on the cover promises the illusion of rootsy authenticity delivered in a high-gloss digital package. The lyrics are straightforward. It has radio-friendly breezy tunes like the gentle regret of 'So Far Away,' 'Why Worry,' 'Your Latest Trick,' and 'Walk Of Life.' There is even an anti-war song in 'Brothers in Arms.' The sound combines guitars with ear-candy synth-pads and post-Phil Collins drum rolls.

Knopfler changed his trademark Fender guitar tone for an overdriven Les Paul on 'Money For Nothing,' the album's liveliest track, a harmonic-popping distant relative of 'Jumping Jack Flash,' with a guest vocal by Sting. The story goes that Knopfler wanted to emulate ZZ Top's guitar sound but they wouldn't tell him how, so he approximated it by wedging a wah-wah pedal half-open. 'Money For Nothing' might have been intended as a satire on the consumerism of the decade, but was all-too-quickly assimilated as an anthem for it, especially with its innovative video all over MTV. *Rolling Stone* called it "Led Zep for yuppies."

Whatever the quality of the record as a whole, its title track was genuinely impressive. The real vocalist with Dire Straits is the lead guitar, and 'Brothers In Arms' is one of Knopfler's greatest moments. Refusing to show off, he wrests from the Les Paul something magisterial. Rarely has the electric guitar possessed such dignity.

Studios Out Of Cities

From the jazz age through the 1960s the majority of recording sessions took place in the heart of the world's great cities – New York, Los Angeles, Philadelphia, London, and other metropolitan areas. But, beginning in the 1970s, the forces that fueled the flight from the cities to the suburbs – traffic, neighbors, crime – led many studio owners to open shop in outlying areas.

Built by artist manager Albert B. Grossman in 1970, Bearsville Studios in upstate New York offered all the amenities of a big-city studio in a relaxing, rural environment, and quickly gained favor among artists looking for an escape from the congestion of midtown Manhattan. The following year producer James Guercio opened the full-service Caribou Ranch Studio in the foothills of the Rocky Mountains near Boulder, Colorado. The studio featured upmarket accommodation that included cabins with brass beds and fieldstone fireplaces, as well as a full-time kitchen staff who served up sumptuous meals around the clock. Similarly, Longview Farms, located midway between Boston and New York in rural western Massachusetts, provided a peaceful respite from the noisy distractions of the city. Those who wished to lie in the sand while laying down tracks could head to a 'destination' studio such as Compass Point in the Bahamas, or George Martin's AIR Studios on the tiny Caribbean island of Montserrat. Albums recorded at AIR include *Synchronicity* (1983) by The Police, *Brothers In Arms* (1985) by Dire Straits, and Sting's *Nothing Like The Sun* (1987). Compass Point, meanwhile, was the recording location of The Rolling Stones' *Emotional Rescue* (1980) and several of Robert Palmer's albums, including *Secrets* (1979) and *Riptide* (1985).

The rise of the destination studio proved to be the final nail in the coffin for the older, no-frills recording establishments. Though the rock era had all but displaced the large jazz orchestras of yesteryear, during the 1970s many of the mammoth studios originally constructed to hold such ensembles were still in place. For years the big, reverberant live rooms of such facilities as Abbey Road in London and 30th Street Studio in New York had helped define the sound of pop radio. "Those studios had what you'd call a 'fingerprint' sound," remarked Jimmy Johnson, producer for Wilson Pickett, Aretha Franklin, and many others. "The kind of places where you hear a record on the radio today and know immediately where it was cut. And *that's* what made them so special."

At the start of the 1980s a major economic recession in U.S. album sales helped trigger the music industry's first major revenue falloff in nearly three decades. After years of rampant excess, record-company bosses frantically sought to cut loose all the extra baggage. Accountants crunched the numbers and then called for the removal of some of the biggest studios. Their rationale: smaller bands – and even smaller digital recording equipment – required considerably less space than was needed from a studio designed before the multitrack era. A few larger rooms survived the changeover, such as Capitol Studios in Los Angeles and Abbey Road, but in the city of New York, where soaring real-estate values put a premium on midtown property, one by one stately old facilities – including RCA, Mediasound, the Pythian Temple, Webster Hall, and 30th Street Studio – were sold and transformed into offices, apartments, and nightclubs.

Audio experts bemoaned the passing of the big-studio era, claiming that records produced within a smaller, more controlled environment were not nearly as vital sounding. "It really represented the changing of the guard," remarked one producer. "When you had that kind of room, you're moving air – and it made such a difference in the sound of the recording."

1986

Graceland **Paul Simon**

Warner Bros 25447 (U.S.A.) / 925447 (U.K.)
Released October 1986

Paul Simon's second Grammy-winner focused international attention on apartheid and energized the emerging world music scene.

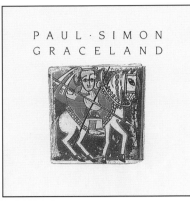

Graceland may not have contributed directly to the downfall of apartheid, but, in retrospect, it's hard to understand the barrage of criticism Simon attracted from anti-apartheid groups for working with the South African musicians on this genre-busting album. "*Graceland*'s instincts were right," he insists, "and it called into question a lot of thinking, which is good."

On March 29th 1985, largely because he had heard the track 'Gumboota' on the South African compilation *Gumboots Accordion Jive Hits Volume II*, Simon started two weeks of work with local musicians in Johannesburg. But the big change on *Graceland* was not that Simon was working with non-white musicians – his previous solo albums were peppered with exotic international sounds, and even in the days of Simon & Garfunkel he had championed world music long before it became a cause célèbre, introducing

South American instrumentation on 'El Condor Pasa.' What made this album different was that, in the past, Simon had tended to write songs and then create music tracks for them in the studio. Simon explained: "I thought, I have enough songwriting technique that I can reverse this process and write this song after the tracks are made."

This set him off on a journey of discovery in which he learned a great deal simply from observing the – to Western eyes – unusual techniques of his South African collaborators. "African guitarists and the bass players were altering what they were playing from verse to verse," he explains. "Choruses didn't have to always be the same. They could repeat, they could use material from a verse, they could introduce some new lyric idea and retain elements from one chorus to the next, like in that song 'Graceland.' None of the choruses are exactly symmetrical."

Happily, the resulting fusion of Western folk rock with township jive, kwela, and mbaqanga styles on *Graceland* seems to have prompted the revitalizing of Simon as a songwriter. Tracks such as 'Diamonds On The Soles Of Her Shoes' or 'The Boy In The Bubble' demonstrated a vigor and imagination that had been lacking in his work for some while. The first flash of Ladysmith Black Mambazo's vocal harmonies in 'Homeless' is a heart-stopper, as are Baghiti Khumalo's mercurially slithering basslines in 'You Can Call Me Al,' but it was Simon's determination to make the best album he possibly could that elevated it into the highest reaches of the pantheon of classic rock albums.

"When I was working on *Graceland*," he has said, "I was thinking, 'If I don't make this interesting, I will never get my generation to pay attention.' They are not paying attention any more to records. They were, at a certain point, certainly around the time of *Bridge Over Troubled Water*, but they no longer look to records to have their lives illuminated. They look to movies or literature."

Graceland certainly made music relevant again, not just for Simon's old audience but for a whole new generation.

Elektra 9-60439-1 (U.S.A.) / Music For Nations MFN60 (U.K.)
Released March 1986

In the U.S.A. in the late 1970s and early 1980s a new movement in heavy metal was beginning to emerge.

Drawing on the heritage of the original exponents of the genre – Led Zeppelin, Deep Purple, and, most importantly, Black Sabbath – as well as the so-called New Wave Of British Heavy Metal of the late 1970s, which included Iron Maiden, Saxon, and Tygers Of Pan Tang, this new incarnation was defined by detuned riffing played at lightning speed that owed little to the blues-based hard rock of the late 1960s and early 1970s. Anthrax, Slayer, and Megadeth were just three of the big names purveying this new sound. When the dust settled, however, Metallica emerged as kings of the pack.

Formed in Los Angeles in 1981, Metallica went through several personnel changes before settling on the four-piece line-up of James Hetfield (guitar and vocals), Kirk Hammett (lead guitar), Cliff Burton (bass), and Lars Ulrich on drums. After issuing *Kill 'Em All* (1983) on the independent label Megaforce, the group signed to Elektra for *Ride The Lightning* (1984), which

Neither album stands out particularly from the thrash metal of the time and both betray the usual hard-rock influences – Motörhead and Ted Nugent, for example – but there are suggestions of the force that Metallica would soon become. Another band might have been content, with their fan base rapidly growing and the rock press heaping praise upon their albums, to continue in the same vein and become bona fide rock stars in the Def Leppard mold. Metallica, however, had a different agenda, and decided it was time to reinvent the thrash-metal genre.

In September 1985 the group returned to Sweet Silence Studios in Copenhagen, Denmark, where they had recorded *Ride The Lightning*, to begin work on the third Metallica album. As with its predecessor, *Master Of Puppets* was produced by Flemming Rasmussen who, prior to working with Metallica, had engineered albums by the singer-songwriters Cat Stevens and Bert Jansch in the 1970s. Rasmussen's only previous heavy-metal production experience lay with Rainbow's *Difficult To Cure* (1981), but his uncluttered style is perfect for the visceral assault of Metallica. The group spent the last four months of 1985 in Copenhagen perfecting the eight songs on *Master Of Puppets*, but there is little evidence of over-elaboration. Though often musically complex, few songs sound as if they are comprised of any more than the four members of Metallica playing together.

'Battery' opens the album with ominous, intertwining flamenco guitar figures before the more familiar heavy guitar chords thunder in and out of conventional time signatures. The title track rides in on stop-start guitar and cymbal crashes, building to a frenetic crescendo then switching to an expansive mid-section closer to Queen than Aerosmith. The album has the feel of a horror-movie soundtrack throughout, particularly on 'Welcome Home (Sanitarium).' *Master Of Puppets* reached Number 29 in the U.S.A. and Number 42 in the U.K., making it Metallica's most successful album to date. Tragically, however, it was the last the group recorded with bassist Burton, who died in a road accident while the group was on tour in Scandinavia.

Slippery When Wet Bon Jovi

Mercury 830 264-2 (U.S.A.) / Vertigo VERH/+C 38 (U.K.)
Released September 1986

The biggest U.S. hard-rock group of the 1980s, Bon Jovi had a latent pop sensibility that helped elevate them above their peers in the world of heavy metal.

The group had a minor U.S. hit with debut single 'Runaway' (1984) shortly after settling on a line-up of vocalist Jon Bon Jovi (born John Bongiovi), guitarist Richie Sambora, keyboardist David Bryan, bassist Alec Such, and drummer Tico Torres. After releasing an eponymous debut and *7800 Degrees Fahrenheit* (1985) Bon Jovi enlisted the help of producer Bruce Fairbairn for what they hoped would be their breakthrough third album. (Fairbairn was best known at that point for his work with Blue Öyster Cult, but would later become one of the biggest rock producers of the late 1980s, producing albums by, among others, Aerosmith and AC/DC.) The group also turned to songwriter Desmond Child, who co-wrote *Slippery When Wet*'s two U.S. Number One hit singles, 'You Give Love A Bad Name' and 'Livin' On A Prayer.'

Bon Jovi recorded 30 songs for possible inclusion on the album and then played the rough mixes to several groups of New York and New Jersey youths, basing the tracklisting on their opinions. While Bon Jovi's earlier material drew most obviously on 1970s heavy metal, *Slippery When Wet* betrays the influence of Bruce Springsteen, who, like Jon Bon Jovi, hails from New Jersey. On its release in the fall of 1986, *Slippery When Wet* far exceeded the group's expectations, topping the U.S. albums chart and reaching Number Six in the U.K. It has since sold over 12 million copies in the U.S.A. alone.

■ *Clockwise from top: Cliff Burton, James Hetfield, Lars Ulrich, and Kirk*

1986

Guitars, Cadillacs, Etc., Etc. Dwight Yoakam

Reprise 2-25372 (U.S.A.) / Warner Brothers 925372 (U.K.)
Released March 1986

With his major-label debut, Kentucky-born, Ohio-bred Dwight Yoakam joined roots-based newcomers such as Randy Travis and Steve Earle in helping to establish the formidable new-country trend of the mid 1980s.

A singer-songwriter with a cowboy hat slung deviously over one eye and a throaty voice to match, Yoakam had spent his formative years with one ear on The Rolling Stones and the other on Buck Owens, and the convergence of styles would set the tone for Yoakam's solo career, which began at the age of 21 with an exploratory visit to Nashville in the fall of 1977.

Nashville at the time, however, had little use for a traditionalist with a rock sensibility. Frustrated, Yoakam charted a course for downtown Los Angeles, the polar opposite of Music City. Performing in the same clubs that housed regional punk acts – the likes of X and The Dead Kennedys – Yoakam began to establish himself as the hip alternative to contemporary country, even garnering a loyal fan base around Hollywood known as 'cowpunks.'

Enter guitarist-producer Pete Anderson, who, like Yoakam, had been weaned on a steady diet of C&W and rock'n'roll. In Yoakam, Anderson heard the direction Nashville needed to take and insisted that the singer immediately commit a handful of his originals to tape. Financial backing came in the form of a $5,000 credit-card advance from Tulsa drummer Richard Coffey, a friend of Yoakam's, who received a portion of the publishing for his trouble. In early 1984 Yoakam, Anderson, and a hastily assembled backing crew entered Excalibur Studio, an independent 24-track facility conveniently located behind a sewing-machine repair shop in nearby Studio City, and proceeded to hammer out six songs, including Yoakam originals 'It Won't Hurt' and 'South Of Cincinnati,' along with a cover of the Johnny Cash classic 'Ring Of Fire.'

"Excalibur was the kind of kind of place where you could just walk in, hand them $200 and go to work for eight hours or so and get as much done as possible," recalls Anderson. "That's how we recorded most of the EP – just get a bit of money, grab Brian Levi the engineer, run over there, and get tracking."

With funds running dry, Yoakam, Anderson, and Levi repaired to another low-budget facility, Hit City West, and proceeded to mix the songs in a series of overnight cram sessions. "We'd arrive at 11.30, have the tapes up by midnight, and start mixing non-stop," says Anderson. "There was no automation, so there we are, the three of us on our knees in front of the board at four in the morning, holding down mutes, going, 'OK, ready? Un-mute the mandolin! Didja get it?! Ride it up! Pull it down!' All night long. We even wild-tracked a few parts, just flying 'em in from tape. That was a *job*."

That November, Oak Records – a Los Angeles independent known for its hardcore punk roster – printed up 5,000 copies of Yoakam's debut EP, entitled *Guitars, Cadillacs, Etc., Etc*. Then Yoakam and Anderson sat back and waited for the big fish to bite, at one point even turning down alt-rock specialists IRS Records. "We were thinking, 'We're gonna be patient and get ourselves a nice major-label deal and then make them do things our way,'" recalls Anderson. "You would've thought we were nuts."

When Warner/Reprise came calling in May of 1985 Yoakam and Anderson were ready. Their list of demands included the stipulation that all six songs previously issued on the *Guitars, Cadillacs* EP be used untouched on Yoakam's full-length debut. "That was all part of it. We told them, 'You get what you get – we're not touching these tracks.' We just didn't feel like they needed to be done over again."

After recording four additional tracks, including Johnny Horton's 'Honky Tonk Man' and Yoakam's own 'Guitars, Cadillacs' at Capitol's Studio B – birthplace to innumerable Buck Owens classics – the album was complete. Released the following March, the 'extended' *Guitars, Cadillacs, Etc., Etc.* quickly tore up the country charts, made impressive inroads on the pop side as well, and spawned a handful of hit singles in 'Honky Tonk Man' (which went to Number Three) 'Guitars, Cadillacs' (Number Four), and 'It Won't Hurt' (Number 31). By 1999 *Guitars, Cadillacs, Etc., Etc.* had reached double-platinum status, making Richard Coffey's original credit-card loan one seriously profitable investment.

Control Janet Jackson

A&M 5106 (U.S.A. & U.K.)
Released March 1986

Being the kid sister of 'The King Of Pop' was no picnic for Janet Jackson during the early part of the 1980s. After appearing as backing vocalist on brother Michael's *Off The Wall* album in 1979, the younger Jackson went solo, but her first two offerings – 1983's *Janet Jackson* and 1984's *Dream Street* – failed to find significant audiences.

In 1985 the 19-year-old Jackson teamed up with Jimmy Jam and Terry Lewis, the renegade production team from Minneapolis, who had got their start in the business after being unceremoniously dumped by Prince. Setting up shop in their modest but comfortable Flyte Tyme Productions facilities, Jam and Lewis constructed a set of spare but supple grooves around a handful of Jackson's autobiographical lyrics. When the dust had settled the trio had compiled an entire album's worth of material that included 'What Have You Done For Me Lately,' 'Control,' and 'Nasty.' In Jam and Lewis, Jackson had finally found a winning formula. And the rest, as they say, is history.

According to Jam, the looseness that marked the *Control* recording sessions was key to the album's success. "When you come right down to it, it's the element of spontaneity that gives a record like *Control* its energy," says Jam. "The kind of thing that happens naturally during a live recording. You just have to be ready for it and know how to properly bottle it. With Janet, I just wanted to let it happen, I didn't want to have to tell her what I was after. Still, I think there are times when the singer needs to be coached, and Janet is no exception. Sometimes I would get her to use hand gestures, or have her put her hand on her hip, just to throw a little body language into the song. Prince used to say, 'Records should always be visual.' Meaning that when you're hearing a recording, you should also get a sense of what was going on in that room. The difference might be subtle, but believe me, it works."

Within months of its spring 1986 release, *Control* had gone multiplatinum – on its way to selling over five million copies – while spinning off five Top Five hit singles, including the Number One smash 'When I Think Of You,' a first-ever trip to the top for both artist and production team. Over the next 15 years Jam and Lewis would produced an additional 15 chart toppers, good enough to tie them for second place alongside Elvis Presley producer Steve Sholes on the all-time list of producers of Number Ones – only The Beatles' George Martin has more.

"If you look at the careers of Steve Sholes and George Martin, the one thing they both have in common is that each one had a single artist who defined what they did," says Jam. "With us, obviously, it's Janet. That's really what makes it happen. When you pick great artists to work with, they can't help but make you look good."

Raising Hell **Run-DMC**

Profile 1217 (U.S.A.) / London LP/C 21 (U.K.)
Released June 1986

The first hip-hop act to produce cohesive, fully-realized albums, Run-DMC brought its pioneering rap-rock hybrid into the mainstream with *Raising Hell*.

Though Run-DMC would soon be overtaken by more radical, politicized groups such as Public Enemy, *Raising Hell* remains one of rap's most important early statements.

Run-DMC was formed by rappers Joseph 'Run' Simmons and Darryl 'DMC' McDaniels with turntablist Jason 'Jam Master Jay' Mizzell in 1982. *Run-DMC* (1983) and *Kings Of Rock* (1985) established the trio as the most popular rap act in the U.S.A. and showcased a new form of hip-hop: the lyrics and vocals were harsher and more direct and made use of the street slang of the time, while the musical backing utilized elements of heavy metal. The first rap act to be considered truly a band in the traditional sense, they also introduced a new image to the genre, replacing Grandmaster Flash's jumpsuits with Adidas sportswear.

Raising Hell expanded on the template of its predecessors, keeping the trio a step ahead of their contemporaries. The sound is much denser than on the first two full-length Run-DMC efforts, adding layer upon layer of sonic bells and whistles to their sparse backbeat of drum machine and record scratching. Where the guitar parts on both *Run-DMC* and *Kings Of Rock* sound as if added as afterthoughts, here they are fully integrated into the sound. On 'It's Tricky' Run-DMC even make use of the main riff from 'My Sharona' by new-wave band The Knack. The rhymes on *Raising Hell* are more forceful than before, and draw on a wider range of subjects – for instance, 'Peter Piper' takes its inspiration from a number of fairy tales, including the story of Mother Goose.

The most important element of *Raising Hell*, however, was the appearance of Steven Tyler and Joe Perry of Aerosmith on a cover of their 1977 hard-rock hit 'Walk This Way.' It was issued as a single shortly after the release of the album, and almost single-handedly brought about hip-hop's mainstream breakthrough. In the U.S.A. the single reached Number Four, while its parent album eventually climbed to Number Three and became the first hip-hop record to achieve platinum status, selling over a million copies. The memorable promo video for the single also established Run-DMC as the first rap act to be featured regularly on MTV. In it, Run-DMC and Aerosmith are seen rehearsing either side of a brick wall, before knocking it down and performing together. This simple but effective symbolism neatly summed up exactly what was beginning to happen to music in the late 1980s. Run-DMC further developed its appeal to a white audience when the trio toured with The Beastie Boys shortly after the release of *Raising Hell*.

The Queen Is Dead **The Smiths**

Sire 25426 (U.S.A.) / Rough Trade ROUGH96 (U.K.)
Released June 1986

The definitive British guitar band of the 1980s, The Smiths were at their commercial and creative peak when it came to the recording of *The Queen Is Dead*.

Their previous effort, *Meat Is Murder* (1985), had topped the U.K. albums chart and provided the anthemic single 'How Soon Is Now?' Consequently, the band was under intense pressure to match its success with their third album. Undeterred, frontman Morrissey conceived *The Queen Is Dead* as a lament for the declining standards of British society since the 1950s.

Recorded during the winter of 1985 at various studios around the U.K., *The Queen Is Dead* was produced, like its predecessor, by Morrissey and guitarist Johnny Marr with engineer Stephen Street. The album's songs range from such ironic snapshots of British life as 'Frankly, Mr Shankly,' whose title character is deemed "a flatulent pain in the arse," to the mournful 'I Know It's Over,' in which the narrator "can feel the soil falling over my head." The orchestrations on the latter and several other tracks on *The Queen Is Dead* are credited to The Hated Salford Ensemble.

The Queen Is Dead reached Number Two on its release in the U.K., and was a minor hit in the U.S.A. The Smiths' success brought about a resurgence of guitar-led pop in Britain after a period dominated by synthesizers. The Smiths split a year later, after recording *Strangeways Here We Come*, their biggest U.S. success. Two decades after its release *The Queen Is Dead* is regularly acclaimed as one of the finest British albums of all time.

◼ *Run-DMC and Aerosmith recording 'Walk This Way' at Magic Venture Studio, New York, on March 9th 1986. Standing (left to right): Joseph 'Run' Simmons, Darryl 'DMC' McDaniels, Jason 'Jam Master Jay' Mizzell, Run-DMC publicist Bill Adler, and Aerosmith guitarist Joe Perry. Seated: Steven Tyler, and producers Russel Simmons and Rick Rubin.*

1987

Permanent Vacation **Aerosmith**

Geffen 24162 (U.S.A.) / 924 162-2 (U.K.)
Released August 1987

Aerosmith was hugely popular in the U.S.A. in the 1970s as part of the country's first wave of hard-rock groups. The band took on the mantle of The Rolling Stones, who had started to become a little too ancient for younger audiences, churning out numerous blues-based rock hits throughout the 1970s.

By the end of the decade, however, Aerosmith appeared to be washed up, particularly when guitarist Joe Perry – the Keith Richards equivalent to vocalist Steven Tyler's Mick Jagger – quit the group in 1979. Aerosmith had begun to halt a slow and steady decline into obscurity and drug addiction by reforming and signing to Geffen in 1984, but it took the success of Run-DMC's rap-rock cover of 'Walk This Way' (1986) to revive completely the group's fortunes.

Buoyed by the success of the single – which was billed as a collaboration between Run-DMC and Aerosmith and promoted by a video featuring the two acts performing together – the group started work on its proper comeback album. They recruited the team responsible for the recent huge success of Bon Jovi's *Slippery When Wet* (1986) to help them make *Permanent Vacation*. Producer Bruce Fairbairn gives the album a rich, modern sheen, while songwriter Desmond Child took rough drafts of Perry's and Tyler's songs and turned them into hook-laden, pop-rock gems. These efforts paid off handsomely, resulting in Aerosmith's strongest and best-selling album since the mid 1970s and a pair of U.S. hit singles, 'Angel' and 'Dude (Looks Like A Lady).'

Kick **INXS**

Atlantic 81796 (U.S.A.) / Mercury 832 721-2 (U.K.)
Released November 1987

After forming in Sydney, Australia, in 1977, INXS gradually built up an international following through the 1980s.

The band eventually scored a U.S. Top Five hit with 'Sweet As Sin' (1986), a single drawn from the group's fifth album, *Listen Like Thieves*, which peaked at Number 11. Its success paved for the way for a mainstream breakthrough on

both sides of the Atlantic, but few could have anticipated *Kick*'s popularity.

INXS entered Rhinoceros Studios in Sydney in March 1987 with Chris Thomas, whose various credits as musician, producer, and mixer take in such landmark albums as *The Beatles* (aka *The White Album*, 1968), *Dark Side Of The Moon* (1973), and *Never Mind The Bollocks, Here's The Sex Pistols* (1977). The resulting album, completed in the early summer at Studio de la Grande Armee in Paris, is the most potent of the group's career, taking in hard rock, string-drenched balladry, and soulful horn arrangements, each song equipped with a powerful pop hook to drive it up the singles charts if necessary. 'Need You Tonight' topped the U.S. singles chart prior to the release of *Kick*, while 'New Sensation,' 'Devil Inside,' and 'Never Tear Us Apart' all entered the Top Ten. All four singles reached the U.K. Top 30, as did 'Mystify.'

INXS helped maintain the album's momentum with a year-long worldwide tour, dubbed 'Calling All Nations.' *Kick* has sold over ten million copies, and was certified six-times platinum in the U.S.A. shortly before the death of frontman Michael Hutchence in 1997.

Appetite For Destruction **Guns N' Roses**

Geffen 24148 (U.S.A.) / WX 125+C (U.K.)
Released July 1987

Guns N' Roses was the quintessential American heavy-rock act of the 1980s, a potent blend of the best elements of Aerosmith, The Sex Pistols, The Rolling Stones, industrial quantities of hairspray, and rock star bad behavior.

Despite the group's image – something akin to a late-1980s version of The Stones at their most debauched – Guns N' Roses was also one of the few bands of the era to think beyond sex, drugs, and rock'n'roll. Songs such as 'Welcome To The Jungle' and 'Paradise City' focus on crime and poverty in inner-city U.S.A., while 'Mr Brownstone' is a first-person tale of heroin addiction.

The group was formed in 1985 by vocalist Axl Rose and guitarist Izzy Stradlin, with bassist Duff McKagen, drummer Steven Adler, and lead guitarist Slash joining in time for the release of the self-financed EP *Live ?!*@ Like A Suicide* and a residency at the famous Troubadour club in Los Angeles. The Guns N' Roses live experience caught the attention of David Geffen, who signed the group in March 1986.

The following month the group started work on its debut album at Rumbo Studios, Los Angeles, but nothing from those sessions was deemed good enough for release. The poor quality of these recordings was attributed to Slash's growing drug dependency, prompting an ultimatum by Rose: clean up or leave the group.

The band resumed work on what would become *Appetite For Destruction* at Take One Studio in Burbank, California, with Mike Clink on production duties. Clink had previously engineered albums by UFO, Jefferson Starship, and Joe Cocker, but had little experience as producer prior to working on Guns N' Roses' debut. (He would later work with Metallica, Whitesnake, and Megadeth.) Guns N' Roses spent five months perfecting the sleazy, blues-based metal of *Appetite For Destruction*, after which Geffen sat on the record for the best part of a year, waiting for the hype around the group to reach fever pitch before unleashing the album. The album's cover – a painting of a woman being raped by a robot – caused a huge media storm and the first of many accusations that Rose was a bigoted misogynist. The group eventually responded to calls to change the artwork, replacing it with a stark image of a cross on a black background, augmented by caricatures of the five group members as skulls.

Appetite For Destruction grew in popularity over the next year as Guns N'

Roses became America's most notorious band, eventually reaching Number One in August 1988. Four months later, following the release of *GNR Lies*, Guns N' Roses became the only act to have two albums in the U.S. Top Five simultaneously during the 1980s. *Appetite For Destruction* peaked at Number Five in the U.K. and has sold over 20 million copies worldwide, establishing it as one of the biggest-selling debut albums of all time. Its most famous song, the melodic 'Sweet Child O' Mine,' topped the U.S. singles chart in the summer of 1988, while 'Welcome To The Jungle' was a hit on both sides of the Atlantic.

■ *Left to right: Slash, Duff McKagan, and Axl Rose of Guns N' Roses.*

Hysteria **Def Leppard**

Mercury 830675 (U.S.A.) / Vertigo 830675 (U.K.)
Released August 1987

The biggest British heavy-rock act of the 1980s, Def Leppard battled against adversity to produce their definitive work, the 12-million selling *Hysteria*.

The group's previous album, *Pyromania* (1983), had introduced a new form of highly polished, melodic heavy rock, and was an international bestseller, shifting ten million copies globally. The group began work on what it hoped would be a quick follow-up in late 1984, but these plans were suddenly derailed when drummer Rick Allen lost an arm in a car wreck on New Year's Eve. Consequently, Def Leppard was effectively on hiatus for most of 1985, as Allen first recovered in hospital and then began to adapt to a new way of drumming, which made use of a Fairlight drum machine and a specially arranged kit.

The group started work afresh with regular producer Robert 'Mutt' Lange in early 1986, slowly piecing together the meticulous, glossy songs that would feature on *Hysteria*. The sessions were interrupted by Def Leppard's participation in the 'Monsters Of Rock' tour across Europe, which marked Allen's first live performances since his accident.

Def Leppard completed work on *Hysteria* in the early months of 1987, eventually releasing it that summer after a three-year absence. The album sold modestly to begin with, but gradually rose to the top of the U.S. charts and Number Two in the U.K., remaining a permanent fixture in the upper reaches of both charts well into 1989, buoyed by the release of six singles from the album, notably the U.S. Number One hit 'Love Bites.'

1987

Sign 'O' The Times Prince

Paisley Park/Warners 25577 (U.S.A,) / WX 88/+C (U.K.)
Released March 1987

With *Sign 'O' The Times* Prince struck the perfect balance between his catchy, pop-oriented hits and his most forward-thinking, adventurous work.

In 1985 Prince had founded his Paisley Park label and studio complex, a move that afforded him even more creative freedom than before. He had also announced a break from live performance for the foreseeable future, allowing him to devote his time exclusively to making records. He had recorded most of his 1980s output with his backing group The Revolution, but opted to produce and perform virtually every note of *Sign 'O' The Times* himself, with the exception of the occasional horn part or female backing vocal. Musically, *Sign 'O' The Times* serves as both a culmination of everything Prince had recorded previously and an indication of the directions he would take in the future. The album takes in sparse electronic funk, gospel-tinged rock, psychedelic pop-soul, and more across its 18 tracks, giving it the sort of sprawling, kaleidoscopic feel common among double albums. Prince originally conceived *Sign 'O' The Times* as a triple, with the working title of *Crystal Ball*, but eventually relented to pressure from Warners and trimmed it down to a double.

Many critics saw *Sign 'O' The Times* as a late-1980s update of Sly And The Family Stone's *There's A Riot Goin' On* in terms of its socially aware lyrics and all-encompassing musical themes. Prince's album, however, takes a much more moralistic viewpoint than the cocaine psychosis of Stone's early 1970s masterpiece. 'Sign 'O' The Times' sets the tone as Prince warns of America's problems with AIDS and drug abuse against a stark bass and drum-machine backing. 'Play In The Sunshine' and 'Housequake' are more upbeat, euphoric affairs, while Prince shows his more soulful side on 'The Ballad Of Dorothy Parker.' The remaining tracks continue in a similar vein, jumping from genre to genre, issue to issue at the drop of a hat. Among the many highlights of the remainder of the album, 'If I Was Your Girlfriend' is Prince at his pop-soul best, while the nine-minute 'It's Gonna Be A Beautiful Night' provides a fitting climax.

Sign 'O' The Times reached Number Six in the U.S.A. and Number Four in the U.K. on its release, eventually selling over ten million copies and reconfirming Prince's commercial potential after the more experimental, less popular albums *Around The World In A Day* (1985) and *Parade* (1986). The title track, 'U Got The Look,' and 'I Could Never Take The Place Of Your Man' all reached the Top Ten of the U.S. singles chart, while 'If I Was Your Girlfriend' was a U.K. hit.

For most of the 1980s Prince recorded at such a rate that for every song that saw the light of day on record numerous others remained unheard in the vaults of Paisley Park. Within six months of the release of *Sign 'O' The Times* he had readied a follow-up, the so-called *Black Album*. Shortly before it was due to go on sale, however, Prince withdrew the album, claiming it to be too immoral for public consumption. The *Black Album* was eventually issued in 1994 in the midst of Prince's long-running dispute with Warners, during which he declared himself to be the label's slave, changing his written name to a symbol and being referred to as The Artist Formerly Known As Prince.

■ *Prince leaps through the air in Rotterdam, The Netherlands, on his 1987 European tour in support of* Sign 'O' The Times.

Whitney Whitney Houston

Arista 208141 (U.S.A.) / AL-8405 (U.K.)
Released June 1987

***Whitney* was the first album by a female performer to debut at Number One in the U.S.A., while the four singles drawn from it completed a record-breaking run of seven consecutive chart-topping singles.**

Born into a musical family – her mother is R&B singer Cissy Houston, while Dionne Warwick is a cousin – Houston started her pop career as a backing singer, performing with Lou Rawls and Chaka Khan among others. Her solo debut, *Whitney Houston*, sold 13 million copies, making it the biggest-selling female debut until it was eventually overtaken by Alanis Morissette's *Jagged Little Pill* in the late 1990s. *Whitney Houston* spawned a trio of U.S. Number One hit singles, including 'The Greatest Love Of All,' leading to impossibly high expectations for her sophomore offering.

The production on *Whitney* was shared between Michael Masser, who concentrated on the ballads, and John 'Jellybean' Benitez, who was largely responsible for the more upbeat, disco-pop tracks. *Whitney* was Houston's international breakthrough, and served as a template for much of the contemporary R&B that followed in the late 1980s and early 1990s. While sales of *Whitney* didn't quite match those of *Whitney Houston*, it did beat its predecessor in terms of the number of hit singles it contains. The Grammy-winning 'I Wanna Dance With Somebody Who Loves Me,' 'Didn't We Almost Have It All,' 'So Emotional,' and 'Where Do Broken Hearts Go' all reached Number One in the U.S.A., and were all hits across Europe.

Introducing The Hardline According To Terence Trent D'Arby Terence Trent D'Arby

Columbia 40964 (U.S.A.) / CBS 450911 (U.K.)
Released October 1987 (U.S.A.) / July 1987 (U.K.)

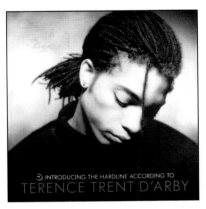

Terence Trent D'Arby is perhaps best remembered for announcing his emergence on the pop scene with the bold claim that his debut, *Introducing The Hardline According To Terence Trent D'Arby*, was the greatest and most important album since The Beatles' *Sgt Pepper*.

After serving in the U.S. Army, New York born D'Arby moved to London, England, where his demo tape caught the attention of CBS record executives. He was given an unusual amount of creative freedom when it came to recording his debut album, which he wrote and produced himself and on which he plays a variety of instruments, from piano and drums to clarinet and saxophone. This maverick spirit drew comparisons with Prince, whose genre-bending artistic leaps had clearly inspired D'Arby's attempts at assimilating elements of rock, pop, funk, and soul.

While not quite as good as D'Arby claimed it to be, *Introducing The Hardline* earned favorable reviews on its release across Europe in the summer of 1987. The album reached Number One in the U.K., where the singles 'If You Let Me Stay,' 'Wishing Well,' and 'Sign Your Name' all reached the Top Ten. The album took longer to catch on in the U.S.A., but eventually rose to Number Four and sold two million copies after 'Wishing Well' had topped the singles chart. D'Arby returned two years later with the conceptual *Neither Flesh Nor Fish*, but its self-consciously important themes put off many fans of his debut. After that D'Arby continued to achieve modest success in the U.K., but his career in the U.S.A. never recovered.

The Joshua Tree **U2**

Island 422-842298-1 (U.S.A.) / U26 (U.K.)
Released March 1987

***The Joshua Tree* was one of the biggest albums of the mid 1980s, shifting over 12 million copies, and the first platinum-selling CD in the U.S.A. The album took U2 on to the covers of *Rolling Stone* and *Time* as the world's premier rock band.**

Anton Corbijn's widescreen photograph on the dramatic black-and-gold cover has the band dressed like characters from a spaghetti Western, emphasizing the image of U2 as a pure, austere force of nature, something that could resist the materialism of the decade. The LP's title comes from a desert town in California associated with the death of singer-songwriter Gram Parsons as well as being home to a cactus capable of surviving terrible droughts. U2's

1987

international success came about partly because they were willing to take up the burden of being a rock band with seriousness of purpose. U2 were in a tiny minority of bands at the time who still played as though the music could change the world and whose lyrics expressed social, religious, and political themes. In this sense U2 are heirs to The Who, though without The Who's self-destructive streak of cynicism. For U2 the bitter wisdom of 'Won't Get Fooled Again' wasn't enough. You couldn't stop there. You had to hang on to an idealism that was ready to be fooled again, and again, for however long it took to get things done. There are other resemblances, too, notably that both are formidable live acts; Bono's voice has something of the power of Daltrey; and both bands have a guitarist with an immediately recognizable sound.

The Joshua Tree was released two years after their previous album, *The Unforgettable Fire*, had surprised many with its experimental approach. (This change in sound was due largely to the arrival of Brian Eno as the group's producer.) Realizing that they had gone as far as they could enthusing audiences with the naked aggression of the songs on *War* and *Under A Blood Red Sky*, U2 had decided to take a left turn and dismantle their rock machine. *The Unforgettable Fire* expanded their sound; *The Joshua Tree* is all the richer for that expansion, even though it was U2's most direct and disciplined set of songs to date.

Behind these songs was a widening of musical horizons as the band outgrew some of their teenage prejudices against older artists and Irish and American roots music. Touring the U.S.A. brought them into contact with genres of music that lay at the foundations of rock itself. Bono was inspired

by Coltrane's *A Love Supreme*, and The Edge looked back to Hendrix and blues rock to see what he could adapt. They were exposed to reactionary forms of Christianity, which led them to redefine their own faith. Bono in particular gained new insights into the relationship between social justice, poverty, and a radical Christianity that was far beyond that which the television evangelists were pushing. The group's political awareness grew with their involvements with Live Aid and Amnesty International. Bono's trip to Nicaragua led directly to the seething anger of 'Bullet The Blue Sky,' a song in which rock's sheer noise finds a commensurate theme. 'Mothers of The Disappeared' raised awareness of the plight of those kidnapped by the authorities in Argentina.

The writing of the music took a new direction. As they re-engaged with the notion of songs with verses and choruses, individual members started developing ideas in advance and presenting them to the others instead of getting material from jamming. They were now able to wear some of the styles of other bands while still sounding like U2. There is certainly no mistaking Bono's vocals and The Edge's echoed guitar patterns, heard to such brilliant effect on the opener 'Where The Streets Have No Name.'

U2's core sound arose the day The Edge got his hands on an echo device, which enabled him to side-step accepted notions of how rock guitar should sound – low overdriven riffs, barre chords, lead solos played on pentatonic scales. He once said: "Really I just started writing with the echo and it all happened . . . Parts that would have sounded at best bland without the echo suddenly sounded amazing." On 'Where The Streets Have No Name' the intro has The Edge playing a four-note figure on the higher strings. What makes this motif work is the echo; he plays it with a delay timed so that a rhythm is set up between the notes and their echoes, so it has rhythmic *and* melodic interest.

The new medium of CD really brought over the crisp high-end sparkle of

much of The Edge's guitar work. The opener, along with 'I Still Haven't Found What I'm Looking For,' 'With Or Without You,' and 'Bullet The Blue Sky' are immediately recognizable U2 classics. 'With Or Without You' demonstrates that even at the height of their stadium phase their sense of arrangement was far ahead of most rock bands. In 1987 The Edge said: "I now see that one of the great things is being able to do something original within a cliché." When it is not hovering on a D chord, 'With Or Without You' comprises a single four-bar, four-chord sequence that has been used on many hits, including Men At Work's 'Down Under,' The Police's 'So Lonely,' 'Since You've Been Gone' by Rainbow, and more recently by Busted.

U2's arrangement has two major differences. First, this progression is subjected to a dynamic in which the song starts quietly and slowly builds to a roaring climax, dies away, and then has a partial recovery. In other words it has an overarching form. In 'With Or Without You' everyone holds back until this dramatic climax is reached at around three minutes in. Second, at no time are the four chords fully articulated. Most bands would have had a couple of acoustic guitars merrily strumming their way through these changes, but U2 avoid this. Instead the chords are implied in the musical space between the bass root notes and The Edge's guitar parts – none of which are straightforward chords.

Aside from its most famous tracks, *The Joshua Tree* has the band venturing into unusual territory with the elegiac 'One Tree Hill,' the dark 'Exit,' and the anti-drug 'Running To Stand Still,' while 'In God's Country' is remarkable for its combination of power and wistfulness.

The Joshua Tree made U2 into international superstars, and marked a distinct turning point in the group's career. Four years later they returned with *Achtung Baby*, which showcased a harder-edged sound informed by dance music and a new image for the group, in particular Bono, who traded his cowboy shirt and hat for wraparound shades and leather trousers.

La Bamba (Original Soundtrack) **Various Artists**

Slash-Warners 25605 (U.S.A.) / Slash-London 828058 (U.K.)
Released August 1987

Gipsy Kings **The Gipsy Kings**

Elektra 60845 (U.S.A.) / Telstar 2355 (U.K.)
Released February 1988

With *La Bamba*, the soundtrack to a biopic of Mexican rock'n'roll singer Richie Valens, Los Lobos became the first act of Mexican extraction to enjoy widespread chart success in the U.S.A. since Valens himself in the 1950s.

Prior to recording *La Bamba*, Los Lobos had begun to enjoy modest success with a sound that mixed rock, country, and blues with traditional Spanish and Mexican music. After forming in Los Angeles in 1973, the group inked a deal with the Warners subsidiary Slash in 1983 and issued the acclaimed *How Will The Wolf Survive?* the following year. The album didn't make huge inroads into the charts, stalling at Number 47 in the U.S.A. and Number 77 in the U.K., but it did attract the attention of writer-director Luis Valdez, at the time in the early stages of making a movie about the life of Valens, who had died in the airplane crash in 1959 that also killed Buddy Holly and The Big Bopper. In 1986 Valdez invited Los Lobos to contribute to the soundtrack to the movie, a collection of re-recordings of Valens's hits. Eight out of the 12 songs on the album are by the band.

Valens's shimmering, upbeat rock'n'roll worked well in the context of the five-piece, acoustic-based Los Lobos. The band race through the first half-dozen songs, including the memorable title track – a Number One hit single in Britain and the U.S.A. – before a quartet of guest performers arrive for the more eclectic second half of the album. Former Klique vocalist Howard Huntsberry sings 'Lonely Teardrops,' while singer-songwriter Marshall Crenshaw offers a reading of Buddy Holly's 'Crying, Waiting, Hoping.' Bo Diddley's classic 'Who Do You Love' follows The Stray Cats' 'Summertime Blues' before Los Lobos finish with two more Valens songs.

The success of *La Bamba*, on screen and on record, catapulted Los Lobos into the mainstream in the summer of 1987, leaving the group in a difficult position. *La Bamba* – which sold two million copies in the U.S.A. on its route to the top of the albums chart, and was also a hit across Europe – was not particularly representative of the band's sound. Spurning the chance to consolidate its popular appeal, the group decided to return to the more idiosyncratic Tex-Mex sound of its earlier albums and never again came close to matching the success of *La Bamba*.

The following year The Gipsy Kings achieved international success with a similarly Spanish-edged sound. Hailing from Arles in the south of France, The Gipsy Kings brought flamenco-guitar-led pop to the mainstream for the first time. They group had already had a number of hits in France before *Gipsy Kings* entered the U.K. Top Ten in the summer of 1988. The single 'Bamboleo' was also a hit in the U.K., while the album reached Number 57 in the U.S.A. In 1989 The Gipsy Kings recorded *Mosaïque*, which added modern production techniques to the group's traditional sound, consolidating its popular appeal.

1988

Pontiac **Lyle Lovett**

MCA/Curb 42028 (U.S.A. & U.K.)
Released January 1988

Lyle Lovett was associated with the burgeoning alternative-country scene when he emerged in the mid 1980s, but in truth his music had more in common with the singer-songwriters of the 1970s, from Randy Newman to James Taylor.

Released in 1986, Lovett's self-titled debut album may have had a country sheen but it also drew on elements of rock, jazz, and soul. Five singles from *Lyle Lovett* reached the U.S. Country Top 40, but the singer was deemed a sell-out by Nashville traditionalists. Regardless of this, Lovett had begun to develop a more mainstream following after the release of his debut, setting the stage for the follow-up to be a bona fide crossover hit.

Pontiac was recorded using a newly installed digital 32-track system at Soundstage Studios in Nashville, with Tony Brown, previously the keyboardist in Emmylou Harris's group, on production duties. Harris herself provides backing vocals on *Pontiac*, as does Vince Gill, while the cutting-edge nature of the album's gestation is illustrated by a logo on the front cover that declares it to be a 'Digital Recording.' The album contains 11 Lovett originals that veer from the stark, surrealist opener 'If I Had A Boat' ("If I were Roy Rogers . . . we'd go riding through the movies") to the breezy 'LA County.' *Pontiac* was well received by rock critics, leading to strong sales of over 500,000 in the U.S.A. Lovett continues to record ever-more idiosyncratic albums into the 21st century and has also carved out a second career as an actor, earning widespread acclaim for his role in Robert Altman's *Short Cuts* (1993).

Surfer Rosa **The Pixies**

Electra 61295 (U.S.A.) / 4AD CAD803 (U.K.)
Released March 1988

Among the most important alternative-rock albums of the 1980s, The Pixies' debut played a large part in giving birth to the music that became known as grunge.

The Pixies' sound had already been established on 1987's mini-album *Come On Pilgrim* – which included a clutch of fan favorites, 'Caribou,' 'The Holiday Song,' and 'Nimrod's Son.' The follow-up was the band's first full-length effort, recorded in the fall of the same year at Q-Division in their native Boston, Massachusetts, alongside Steve Albini, who would become the most sought-after producer around when grunge broke in the 1990s. They worked quickly, laying down the instrumental tracks in two weeks and adding the vocals in another two days. Albini's production style is sparse and economical, which is well suited to the band's abrasive sound.

The album is driven by the twin-guitar assault of frontman Black Francis (born Charles Thompson IV) and lead player Joey Santiago, showcasing the quiet-verse-loud-chorus aesthetic that would so influence Nirvana and

others. Equally distinct is Francis's manic, Latin-inflected vocal delivery, which was apparently inspired by a Thai rock-star friend who told him to "scream it like you hate that bitch!" The album also has a powerful melodic edge, particularly when Francis's voice is twinned with the less abrasive tones of bassist Kim Deal.

Despite unanimous critical praise, *Surfer Rosa* failed to chart on its release. The album's key moment is the epic 'Where Is My Mind?' The track was given wider exposure a decade later when used memorably over the end credits of the movie *Fight Club*, which brought about a long-deserved commercial acceptance of The Pixies, and *Surfer Rosa* in particular. In 2005 the band reunited for a triumphant world tour.

Tracy Chapman **Tracy Chapman**

Elektra 60774-2 (U.S.A. & U.K.)
Released April 1988

The spirit of the folk era resurfaced in the late 1980s, thanks in part to the appearance of Boston-based newcomer Tracy Chapman, whose self-titled Elektra debut reintroduced audiences to the simple pleasures of unplugged music.

The highlight of the set was the lead-off single 'Fast Car,' the story of a working-class couple struggling to escape the ravages of urban poverty. (Chapman's stunning solo performance of the song at the 1989 Grammy presentation – where she received the award for Best Female Pop Vocal – remains a memorable moment in pop music.)

By 1984 Chapman, then a 20-year-old sophomore student at Tufts University, had begun performing her own tunes at clubs around the Boston area. Through a friend, Chapman was introduced to producer David Kershenbaum, who was immediately struck by Chapman's plaintive songs and vocal range, which bore a strong resemblance to Joan Armatrading with whom Chapman has often been compared. By the end of 1986 Chapman had inked a deal with Paul Rothschild's reputable label, Elektra Records, and prepared to cut a debut album at Kershenbaum's Los Angeles studio. Kershenbaum, who'd recorded Joe Jackson's *Look Sharp!* album using minimal overdubs for less than $10,000, employed a similar approach for Chapman, whose vocals and acoustic guitar were recorded live over a spare rhythm section consisting of drummer Denny Fongheiser and bassist Larry Klein.

"The difference between 'Fast Car' and some of the other songs on the album was when it hit the chorus, Denny really opened up with those big toms," Kershenbaum told writer Robyn Flans. "That was a wonderful exercise in dynamics, because it was so vulnerable in both the message and presentation. It was Tracy and her acoustic guitar, Larry and a little rhythm from Denny. And it took a while to get to the chorus, which worried some people. It broke rules of great song construction, and I wouldn't advise people to try it, but for some reason, it milked it so much that when it hit the release of the large chorus, it blew you over."

In the spring of 1988 *Tracy Chapman* made its debut on *Billboard*'s album chart and quickly pushed its way through a sea of hair bands and hip-hop acts on its way to the Number One position, while the single 'Fast Car' eventually topped out at Number Six. "What happened was something that none of us had dreamed – the album was gold before the single ever really got on the radio," remembers Kershenbaum. "It was one of those records where people still walk up to me and tell me exactly where they were and what they were doing when they first heard 'Fast Car.'"

Spirit Of Eden **Talk Talk**

EMI America 46977 (U.S.A.) / Parlophone 746977 (U.K.)
Released September 1988

At their commercial peak after *The Colour Of Spring* (1986), Talk Talk abruptly changed direction for the avant-garde, jazz-inflected ambience of *Spirit Of Eden*.

The group had initially ridden in on the back of the new romantics, in the wake of the likes of Duran Duran, and scored international hits with 'Talk Talk' and 'It's My Life.' After the critical and commercial success of *The Colour Of Spring*, the group's label, Parlophone, gave Talk Talk free rein to produce the follow-up themselves, anticipating more of the same thoughtful pop rock. Instead, guided by frontman Mark Hollis and multi-instrumentalist Tim Friese-Green, Talk Talk decamped to an old church in Suffolk, England, where the group spent a year perfecting the six otherworldly songs on *Spirit Of Eden*.

"THE MOST IMPORTANT THING WITH THIS ALBUM WAS JUST TO HAVE THE RIGHT FEEL – FOR IT TO HAVE AN ABSOLUTE CALM, BUT FOR IT TO HAVE AN ABSOLUTE INTENSITY INSIDE OF THAT."

TALK TALK FRONTMAN MARK HOLLIS

Unlike the three previous Talk Talk albums, which were recorded as a four-piece, *Spirit Of Eden* features a dozen guest players, including the classical-crossover violinist Nigel Kennedy and various brass instrumentalists. These 16 musicians, augmented in places by the choir of Chelmsford Cathedral, conspired to produce a work of hushed complexity. The album's delicate ambience was achieved using distant miking techniques.

Though Hollis and engineer Phill Brown used only pre-1967 analog equipment for the initial, semi-improvised recordings, they made pioneering use of digital technology in the second phase of creating *Spirit Of Eden*. The songs were pieced together and refined using a digital tape machine, in a manner that recalled the way Teo Macero shaped Miles Davis's late-1960s albums out of snippets of live and studio performances. The resulting music, unlike any rock album before or since, sits somewhere between Davis's *In A Silent Way* (1969), Brian Eno's early ambient work, and Erik Satie's sparest piano pieces. Needless to say, the album sold poorly. Dropped by Parlophone, Talk Talk made one more album, the majestic *Laughing Stock* (Polydor, 1991), before disbanding.

Nothing's Shocking **Jane's Addiction**

Warners 25727 (U.S.A.) / WX 216 (U.K.)
Released September 1988

Los Angeles-based Jane's Addiction stood apart from the often histrionic, over-egged heavy metal of the city's other rock groups of the time, typified by Guns N' Roses.

Instead, Jane's Addiction fused elements of folk, funk, and metal, creating a sound that, while nowhere near as commercially successful, stands up better to historical reassessment than the work of the group's peers.

Jane's Addiction formed in 1984, earning a deal with Warners three years later on the strength of a self-released, eponymous live album. The group recorded its debut album proper in early 1988 at Eldorado Studios in Los Angeles with producer Dave Jerden – who had previously worked with Talking Heads, The Rolling Stones, and Red Hot Chili Peppersduties.

Nothing's Shocking is an eclectic, challenging album, with songs ranging from visceral hard rock to instrumental jazz noodling. There is a lyrical intensity to most of the songs, be it the bleak 'Jane Says,' a tale of heroin addiction, to 'Ted, Just Admit It . . .' written about the serial killer Ted Bundy. The album's most striking element is Perry Farrell's unique vocal style, an eerie, siren-like wail that somehow stands out from but sits perfectly with the music beneath it.

Nothing's Shocking failed to chart on its release on either side of the Atlantic, but has since come to be recognized as an alternative-rock classic. The band achieved greater commercial success with the more streamlined *Ritual De Lo Habitual* (1990), which spawned a minor U.K. hit, 'Been Caught Stealing.'

1988

It Takes A Nation Of Millions To Hold Us Back
Public Enemy

Def Jam 4303 (U.S.A.) / 462415 (U.K.)
Released July 1988

Generally considered to be the greatest hip-hop album of all time, Public Enemy's second release was one of the landmark successes of the seminal hip-hop label Def Jam.

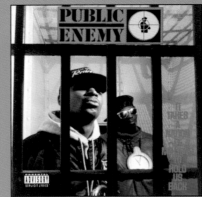

Def Jam Records was formed in 1984 by New York University students Rick Rubin and Russell Simmons, whose younger brother Joseph had already begun to have considerable success as one third of Run-DMC. Though Run-DMC was already signed to Profile Records, Rubin, and to a lesser extent Simmons, were responsible for producing much of the trio's early output, including the albums *Kings Of Rock* and *Raising Hell*. Rubin also produced LL Cool J's *Radio* (1985) and The Beastie Boys' debut, *Licensed To Ill* (1986), both of which were issued on Def Jam and helped establish the label as

the home of the bulk of the most important – and bestselling – hip-hop releases of the late 1980s.

In 1987 Def Jam signed the upcoming hip-hop group Public Enemy, whose first release, *Yo! Bum Rush The Show*, was released in the fall of that year. While Run-DMC had begun to move rap toward a more hardcore sound, Public Enemy took this process a step further, with rappers Chuck D and Flavor Flav advocating social revolution in their lyrics while production duo The Bomb Squad created a fierce collage of sound unlike anything heard previously. The group's setup was also highly unusual: while most hip-hop acts were in the Run-DMC mold of two or three rappers and a DJ, Public Enemy resembled something closer to a political organization. Alongside Chuck D, Flavor Flav, DJ Terminator X, and in-house production team The Bomb Squad, at the core of the group was publicist Bill Stephney and 'Minister of Information'/choreographer Professor Griff.

Yo! Bum Rush The Show was a minor success, failing to ignite the interest of many outside the hip-hop underground, but its follow-up, *It Takes A Nation Of Millions To Hold Us Back*, would prove impossible to ignore. Recorded

shortly after the first album at a number of studios around New York, *Nation Of Millions* is a refinement of the ideas and ideals of its predecessor. Chuck D had by this stage arrived at a more direct, focused lyrical style, and delivers his compelling rhetoric in a deep, authoritative voice while the more flamboyant Flavor Flav provides the lighter entertainment with a series of short, comical asides. D's raps covered a variety of subjects, from white supremacy and black nationalism to the manipulative nature of the record industry.

Equally radical here is the layered sonic backdrop provided by The Bomb Squad, led by producer Hank Shocklee. In the late 1970s and early 1980s most hip-hop records involved a rapper performing over the top of another record spun by a DJ, the most famous example being The Sugarhill Gang's 'Rapper's Delight,' which utilized a repeated break from Chic's 'Good Times.' By the mid 1980s, however, hip-hop producers had begun to make use of the new technology of the sampler, a digital recording device that allows the user to capture a short element of an existing recording and then repeat it to create something new.

Public Enemy's Shocklee took this process several steps further than his predecessors, who had tended to use samplers simply to loop a bar or two of an old funk or soul song. One of the major limitations of the earliest samplers was that they could only store a couple of seconds of music in their memory; Shocklee used this to his advantage, weaving together complex, claustrophobic rhythm tracks out of the tiniest fragments of other songs, utilizing literally hundreds of sonic fragments of other people's music to create something wholly original.

Where Run-DMC and others had taken samples from heavy-rock records, the sound sources on Public Enemy's album were more disparate: *Nation Of Millions* contains pieces of free jazz and avant-garde compositions, as well as the obligatory funk drum breaks. Occasionally The Bomb Squad throws in a recognizable sample – such as the guitar break from David Bowie's 'Fame' used in 'The Night Of The Living Baseheads' – but they have usually passed before the listener catches on. Most striking is the repeated use throughout the album of tiny snatches of squawking saxophones and sirens, which give the beats an unrelenting, uneasy feel. After The Bomb Squad had pieced together the basic rhythmic structure of each song, Chuck D and Flavor Flav would add their vocal parts. Shocklee would then finish the potent sonic brew by adding more sound effects and samples, including a number of well-chosen snatches of spoken social commentary.

At the time there were no laws in place to regulate the plundering of past recordings by Public Enemy and others. With the success of *Nation Of Millions* and other artists' albums – notably The Beastie Boys' *Paul's Boutique*, which used The Bomb Squad's production style as a template – the original performers started to become antagonized by hip-hop acts' unsanctioned recycling of their back catalogs. Record labels and industry lawyers moved quickly to put a system in place whereby the creators of the original music would be compensated financially for any samples used, and by the early 1990s artists would have to pay to clear each individual sample or risk being sued for a large chunk of their songs' royalties. Such an arrangement would be unmanageable for a outfit such as Public Enemy, who would sometimes use more than a dozen samples in a single song, and indeed the group had to change its sound in the 1990s to incorporate live instrumentation.

It Takes A Nation Of Millions To Hold Us Back was released in the summer of 1988 to high praise from rock and rap critics alike. It charted at Number 42 in the U.S.A. and reached the Top Ten in the U.K., where it also spawned two hit singles, 'Don't Believe The Hype' and 'Bring The Noise.' In 1995 the *New Musical Express* (U.K.) declared *Nation Of Millions* the greatest hip-hop album ever – an opinion later shared by numerous other publications – stating: "This wasn't merely a sonic triumph. This was also where Chuck D wrote a fistful of lyrics that promoted him to the position of foremost commentator/documenter of life in the underbelly of the U.S.A."

Public Enemy continued to rise in popularity after the album's release, scoring an international hit with the classic 1989 single 'Fight The Power,' which was given prominence on the soundtrack to Spike Lee's movie *Do The Right Thing*.

■ *Left to right: Professor Griff, Chuck D, Flavor Flav, and Terminator X.*

1988

Daydream Nation Sonic Youth

Torso 2602339 (U.S.A.) / Blast First BFFP 34 (U.K.)
Released October 1988

Daydream Nation was one of the more unusual successes of U.S. alternative rock of the 1980s.

While most of their contemporaries, including R.E.M. and The Pixies, were fairly reliant on conventional song structures, Sonic Youth took as their blueprint The Velvet Underground at their most freeform and eccentric. The group was founded in 1981 by guitarist-vocalist Thurston Moore and bassist Kim Gordon (the pair later married). Guitarist Lee Ranaldo joined in 1982, while drummer Steve Shelley arrived shortly after the release of *Bad Moon Rising* (1985), the first Sonic Youth album to gain international exposure.

Sonic Youth continued to hone their sound on the well-received *Evol* (1986) and *Sister* (1987) before recording an ironic tribute to Madonna and other pop stars of the time, *The Whitey Album* (1988), as Ciccone Youth. Returning to their day jobs, the group recorded what has come to be known as their defining work in July and August 1988 at Greene Street Recording, New York. *Daydream Nation* was produced by the group and Nick Sansano, who would later work with Public Enemy and The Manic Street Preachers among others. It veers – often without warning – from hypnotic psychedelia to balls-out art rock, and takes in such fan favorites as 'Teenage Riot' and 'Eric's Trip.' Although the album failed to chart, its word-of-mouth success earned Sonic Youth an unlikely major-label deal with David Geffen's DGC, for whom the group continues to record today.

■ *Left to right: Thurston Moore, Steve Shelley, Kim Gordon, and Lee Ranaldo of Sonic Youth.*

1989

The Lion Youssou N'Dour

Atlantic 91253 (U.S.A.) Virgin 91253 (U.K.)
Released August 1989

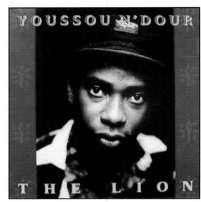

Following the success of Paul Simon's *Graceland* (1986) African music started to find a wider audience among Western listeners in the later 1980s. Youssou N'Dour was the biggest star of this burgeoning world-music market, and *The Lion* was his first internationally released album.

N'Dour started performing in his native Senegal as a teenager in the mid 1970s. By the age of 21 he had assumed control of the group Super Etoile De Dakar, which became hugely popular across Africa and developed a cult following in Europe and the U.S.A. In the mid 1980s N'Dour's expressive, five-octave voice featured prominently on both *Graceland* and Peter Gabriel's *So* (1985), which introduced him to a wider, more mainstream Western audience for the first time. Gabriel later invited N'Dour to record an album of his own at the former Genesis frontman's newly built Real World Studios. The resulting album, *The Lion*, consists mostly of re-recorded versions of older material, but did also include a handful of songs sung in English. Musically, the album is built on the

mbalax style N'Dour had helped pioneer with Super Etoile De Dakar, which blends elements of African, Cuban, and Western pop music. The single 'Shakin' The Tree,' a duet with Gabriel, was a minor U.K. hit single.

N'Dour had his biggest chart hit five years later when '7 Seconds,' recorded in collaboration with Neneh Cherry, reached Number Two in the U.K. Other African performers to find success in the post-*Graceland* music world include Baaba Maal and Orchestra Baobab.

■ *Real World Studios (pictured above and below) was founded by Peter Gabriel in 1988 on the outskirts of the English village of Box, Wiltshire. The main recording-room is surrounded on three sides by a river that runs around the grounds of the studio. As well as Youssou N'Dour, the many bands and musicians to have recorded at Real World since the late 1980s include Kylie Minogue, James, and The Super Furry Animals. Left: N'Dour at the North Sea Jazz Festival in The Hague, Denmark, in July 1989.*

1989

The Stone Roses *The Stone Roses*

Silvertone 1184 (U.S.A.) / ORE 502 (U.K.)
Released April 1989

The Stone Roses is regularly touted as one of the greatest albums of all time in the U.K., where it cast a long shadow over much of the guitar-based music of the 1990s. In the U.S.A., however, The Stone Roses never rose beyond the level of a cult act.

The band was formed in Manchester, England, by vocalist Ian Brown, guitarist John Squire, and drummer Alan 'Reni' Wren in 1984, but they didn't really get going until bassist Gary 'Mani' Mounfield joined three years later. The singles 'Elephant Stone' (1988) and 'Made Of Stone' (1989) failed to chart, but generated high

expectations among British tastemakers and trendsetters. *The Stone Roses* didn't disappoint; only The Smith's *The Queen Is Dead* comes close in terms of importance and influence among British guitar-based music. Produced by John Leckie, the album welded subtle dance rhythms to melodic, 1960s-style psychedelic guitar pop, each song topped by Brown's shamanic vocal delivery. The album's highlights include the slow-burning 'I Wanna Be Adored,' 'She Bangs The Drum,' and the eight-minute closing track 'I Am The Resurrection.'

> "WHEN I'VE HEARD ONE OF OUR SONGS ON THE RADIO, WHEN IT'S JUST BEEN BASS, DRUMS, AND ONE GUITAR LINE, I'D SAY THEY'RE AS DANCEABLE AS ANY HOUSE RECORD I'VE EVER DANCED TO. IT'S JUST ABOUT CREATING A GROOVE WITH SPACE AROUND IT."
>
> *STONE ROSES FRONTMAN IAN BROWN*

The Stone Roses was not a huge success initially, stalling at Number 19 on the U.K. chart, but seems to grow in stature with every passing year. In the wake of its success, countless other British groups – from The Charlatans and Happy Mondays through to Blur, Oasis, and The Verve – have scored U.K. hits owing a debt to The Stone Roses' sound. The Stone Roses themselves never really capitalized on this, however. After one more terrific single, 'Fools' Gold,' the group disappeared, eventually returning in 1994 with the disappointing *Second Coming* before splitting in acrimony.

■ *The Stone Roses make their U.K. television debut on* **The Late Show** *on November 21st 1989. Forty seconds into their rendition of 'Elephant Stone,' the group exceeded the BBC volume regulations, causing a power cut.*

Club Classics – Volume One **Soul II Soul**

Virgin 91267 (U.S.A.) / 10-Virgin DIX 82 (U.K.)
Released April 1989

Soul II Soul was the most influential U.K. dance act of the late 1980s and early 1990s, and launched the career of the producer Nellee Hooper, who later worked with U2, Madonna, and numerous others.

In 1988 Hooper, vocalist-keyboardist Jazzie B, and multi-instrumentalist Phil 'Daddae' Harvey issued a pair of singles, 'Fairplay' and 'Feel Free,' that made only minor dents in the U.K. charts but were big club hits. They gave little indication, however, of the artistic and commercial success that would follow with *Club Classics*, an album that actually lives up to its boastful title.

Preceded by the international hit single 'Keep On Movin',' *Club Classics* is a slick blend of R&B, soul, disco, and world-music influences. The album's smooth hip-hop beats, lush string arrangements, and dub reggae bass were a key influence on much of the British dance music of the 1990s. Alongside the group's core trio, an important presence on *Club Classics* is Caron Wheeler, who sang on and co-wrote 'Back To Life,' which topped the U.K. singles chart and reached Number Four in the U.S.A. The album itself also reached Number One in the U.K., peaking at Number 14 in the U.S.A., where it quickly sold two million copies. In the wake of the success of *Club Classics* Nellee Hooper became one of the hottest producers of the early 1990s, working with Sinead O'Connor ('Nothing Compares 2 U'), Massive Attack (*Blue Lines*), Björk (*Debut*), and Madonna (*Bedtime Stories*).

Disintegration **The Cure**

Elektra 60855 (U.S.A.) / Fiction FIXH14 (U.K.)
Released May 1989

One of the most enduring bands to emerge in the aftermath of punk in the U.K., The Cure were one of the principal acts responsible for laying the foundations of Gothic rock in the early 1980s.

The group looked to have peaked with the album *Pornography* in 1982, but gradually reestablished themselves later in the decade with a more pop-orientated sound. *Disintegration* was The Cure's biggest critical and commercial success. Already adored across Europe, the band had begun to make inroads into the U.S. market with the retrospective singles collection *Staring At The Sea* (1986) and the album *Kiss Me Kiss Me Kiss Me* (1987), which displayed a harder-rock sound than the group's earlier efforts.

Disintegration was recorded alongside David Allen, who had worked on synthesizer-pop group The Human League's breakthrough album *Dare!* before producing all of The Cure's albums between 1983 and 1996. *Disintegration* is essentially a refinement of everything that preceded it. Retaining the gloomy lyricism that had made The Cure one of the best-loved cult bands of the 1980s, the album adds a heightened pop sensibility to the arena-ready rock of *Kiss Me Kiss Me Kiss Me*. Key to *Disintegration*'s success was the upbeat single 'Lovesong,' which provided the group with a Number Two entry on the U.S. pop charts. The album itself reached Number 12 in the U.S.A. and Number Three in the U.K., and provided further chart hits on both sides of the Atlantic with 'Pictures Of You' and a remixed version of the song 'Lullaby.' Though frontman Robert Smith would claim in interviews around the release of the album that the group would soon

disband, The Cure have continued to tour and record into the 21st century, though never with the commercial success of *Disintegration* and its follow-up *Wish* (1992).

The Healer **John Lee Hooker**

Chameleon 74808 (U.S.A.) / Silvertone ORE 508 (U.K.)
Released October 1989

The Complete Recordings **Robert Johnson**

Columbia 46222 (U.S.A.) / 467246 (U.K.)
Released November 1990

One of the most important blues guitarists of all time, John Lee Hooker enjoyed a career that spanned over 50 years, from 1948 until his death in 2001. Hooker recorded little of note during the 1980s, however, until *The Healer*, which prompted a resurgence of interest in both his work and the blues generally.

In 1988 Hooker and slide guitarist-producer Roy Rogers set upon the idea of recording an album of collaborations with other musicians, in a similar vein to the series of LPs Hooker cut with Canned Heat, Van Morrison, and others in the early 1970s. Recorded at Russian Hill Recording Studios in San Francisco, The Plant in Sausalito, California, and Leon Haywood Studios in Los Angeles, *The Healer* features contributions from, among others, Keith Richards, Carlos Santana, Bonnie Raitt, Los Lobos, Charlie Musselwhite, and Canned Heat. None of them was able to outshine Hooker himself on the album, however, which contained his most vital performances in two decades, and the single 'I'm In The Mood' won a Grammy for Best Traditional Blues Recording.

The impressive guest list caught the attention of the mainstream press for the first time since Hooker's brief appearance in *The Blues Brothers* (1980), resulting in his strongest ever album sales. The album's popularity also prompted the release of countless CDs of material from Hooker's back catalog, as well as that of other Delta Bluesmen, notably *The Complete Robert Johnson* (1990).

Perhaps the best-loved of all the Delta blues singers, Johnson began writing and performing his own material as a teenager in the late 1920s. Legend states that he sold his soul to the devil in exchange for his peerless guitar skills. He made a number of recordings in the 1930s, which were issued in the U.S.A. on the Vocalian-Arc label. Johnson died in 1938, at the age of 27, having been poisoned by a jealous barman. His recorded output was first compiled in the midst of the mid-1960s blues revival as *King Of The Delta Blues Singers* (1966). *The Complete Recordings* builds on that set, and contains each of the 37 songs Johnson recorded in his lifetime.

Meanwhile, the John Lee Hooker revival continued into the early 1990s with *Mr Lucky* (1991), which peaked at Number Three in Britain, and the U.K. Top 20 hit, a re-recording of his 1962 hit 'Boom Boom' (1992), though neither had any serious impact in the U.S.A.

1989

Paul's Boutique Beastie Boys

Capitol 91743 (U.S.A.) / EST 2102 (U.K.)
Released July 1989

Somewhat under-appreciated on release in favor of the harder, gangsta rap typified by NWA, The Beastie Boys' second album has since been recognized as one of the high points of late-1980s hip-hop.

In 1986 The Beastie Boys issued what would become the biggest-selling rap record of the 1980s, *Licensed To Ill*. The album was sonically similar to the rap-rock hybrid of Run DMC's *Raising Hell* but has a jovial, frat-party feel quite apart from many of the band's hip-hop contemporaries. Most of the success of *Licensed To Ill* was down to the crossover appeal of the guitar-led single 'Fight For Your Right (To Party)' and the controversy that arose from the trio's apparently sexist lyrics.

Paul's Boutique is a completely different animal. Though some songs, such as 'Shake Your Rump,' wouldn't have been out of place on The Beastie Boys' debut, much of the album is a showcase for the deft production style of The Dust Brothers, Mike Simpson and John King. The duo was among the first to use a digital sampler, which allowed them to produce a much more precise, cohesive sonic backdrop than on the often primitive recordings of their peers. Following the lead of Public Enemy's production team The Bomb Squad, The Dust Brothers looked beyond the obvious guitar and drum samples used by most hip-hop record makers, instead taking elements from songs by the likes of Pink Floyd, Curtis Mayfield, Sly Stone, and The Ramones; one track, 'The Sounds Of Silence,' uses as its hook a couple of chords from 'The End' by The Beatles. The result is a psychedelic sound collage, often drowned in reverb that sounds nothing like anything that came before. In addition, the three Beastie Boys' vocal contributions take in a wider variety of subjects than on *Licensed To Ill*, and showcase a markedly improved delivery style.

Paul's Boutique reached Number 14 on its release in the U.S.A., but failed to match the success of its predecessor by some way. Many critics had already labeled The Beastie Boys as one-hit-wonder chancers who could never make another *Licensed To Ill*, and in many ways they were right: *Paul's Boutique* is a far more musically impressive statement than the group's debut, and one that would inspire a host of other artists and producers, in hip-hop and beyond. The Beastie Boys followed it with the more commercially successful albums *Check Your Head* (1992) and *Ill Communication* (1994), on which the group's members started to play their own instruments for the first time.

Straight Outta Compton NWA

Ruthless 57102 (U.S.A.) / 4th & Broadway 534 (U.K.)
Released August 1989

The first widely successful gangsta rap album, *Straight Outta Compton* established NWA as the first West Coast alternative to the New York-based hip-hop scene.

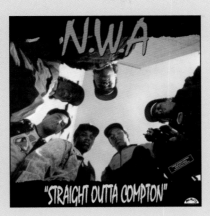

Niggaz With Attitude was formed in the mid 1980s by rappers Ice Cube, MC Ren, and Eazy-E, turntablist DJ Yella, and Dr Dre, who would go on to become perhaps the most important hip-hop producer of the next two decades. The group played a key role in the compilation album *NWA And The Posse* (1987), before Eazy-E formed his own Ruthless Records to issue *Straight Outta Compton*, the label allegedly funded by illegal activity.

Containing the infamous single 'Fuck The Police,' which drew a written warning from the FBI, *Straight Outta Compton* is a continuous stream of visceral, violent raps set against a backing of harsh drum-machine programming and occasional stabs of funk guitars and horns. Dr Dre had yet to arrive at the richer production style that would bring him so much commercial success in the 1990s, but the musical backing he provides here is the perfect accompaniment to the album's vocal focus.

Straight Outta Compton reached Number 37 in the U.S. albums chart on release, and immediately stirred up controversy as debate raged over whether the members of NWA were violent misogynists or simply seeking to document urban life. Such arguments have continued long since the band split in 1992, as a succession of artists from 2Pac to Eminem have kept up the gangsta-rap tradition.

As Nasty As They Wanna Be 2 Live Crew

Luke XR-107 (U.S.A.) / Atlantic 91651 (U.K.)
Released June 1989

Their third and most successful album, 2 Live Crew's *As Nasty As They Wanna Be* was one of the first albums to be labeled with a 'Parental Advisory' sticker to warn against its explicit content and also to be legally branded obscene.

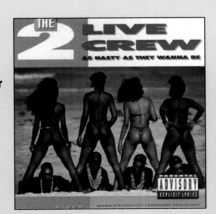

In 1985 two high-ranking U.S. politicians' wives, Tipper Gore and Susan Baker, formed the Parent's Music Resource Center, having been shocked at the lyrical content of some of the music their young daughters were listening to. There had been a long history of records being banned or censored, from Duke Ellington's so-called "devil's music" to the Frank Zappa single 'I Don't Wanna Get Drafted,' but never before had a system been set up to categorize "obscene" music. On the back of Gore's and Baker's campaigning, a growing number of albums – which tended to be by rap and hard-rock artists – were displayed with a warning in the late 1980s.

Not only was *As Nasty As They Wanna Be* one of the first to fall into this category, it was eventually banned outright in Florida. Taking the sexually charged, violent content of NWA's recently issued *Straight Outta Compton* several steps farther, the album's lyrical content borders on the pornographic. The majority of the album's 18 tracks, which include 'Me So Horny' and 'Bad Ass Bitch,' are frank, voyeuristic accounts of casual sex; equally offensive to many was the cover art, which depicted the group's

four members peering up from a beach at a quartet of scantily clad women.

The Parental Advisory sticker has since become an industry standard. In 1991 Wal-Mart, the largest music retailer in the U.S.A., announced it would no longer stock albums with "Explicit Content," prompting many artists to issue two versions of their albums, one of them cleaned up.

3 Feet High And Rising De La Soul

Tommy Boy TB1019 (U.S.A.) / DLS1 (U.K.)
Released March 1989

De La Soul's debut, *3 Feet High And Rising*, introduced an optimistic, 'daisy age' alternative to the gritty, political hip-hop of many of the group's peers.

De La Soul was formed in 1987 by a trio of rappers, David 'Trugoy The Dove' Jolicoeur, Kelvin 'Posdnuos' Mercer, and Vincent 'Pacemaster Mase' Mason, in Long Island, New York. In late 1988 the group started work on their first album with producer 'Prince Paul' Huston, a founder member of early-1980s rap crew Stetsasonic, at Calliope studio in New York.

Taking a similar approach to The Beastie Boys' *Paul's Boutique*, *3 Feet High And Rising* was built out of elements of a wide variety of music, from Johnny Cash to Steely Dan. The best-known song on the album, 'The Magic Number,' features elements of 'You Showed Me' by The Turtles, which prompted legal action from the cult 1960s group. The implications of The Turtles' eventual court victory affected not just De La Soul but hip-hop production methods in general. From the early 1990s onward all samples had to be cleared and paid for before an album could be released, leading many hip-hop acts to switch to using more live instrumentation.

Reaching Number 24 in the U.S.A. and number 13 in the U.K., *3 Feet High And Rising* opened the doors for a wave of other rap acts with a similarly positive outlook, including A Tribe Called Quest and The Jungle Brothers. De La Soul's debut is also notable for the spoof game-show segments interspersed between the album's songs; comic interludes between tracks would soon become a regular ingredient of hip-hop albums.

■ *Posdnuos (left) and Pacemaster Mace of De La Soul.*

1990

The Immaculate Collection **Madonna**

Sire 7599 26440 (U.S.A. & U.K.)
Released November 1990

The pre-eminent female performer of the 1980s, Madonna ended the first phase of her career with an unusual retrospective set, the biggest-selling best-of album of all time by a female artist.

The Immaculate Collection contains most of Madonna's hits from 1983 to 1990, but presents many of them in remixed form, with some sped up or shortened from their original length. The album was also the first to make use of QSound, a newly developed mixing technique that purported to simulate quadraphonic, three-dimensional sound using only two speakers. The year 1990 proved to be one of the busiest and most controversial years of Madonna's career. Prior to the release of *The Immaculate Collection* she issued *I'm Breathless*, a selection of songs "inspired by the film *Dick Tracy*," in which she also starred.

She also embarked on the Blonde Ambition Tour, which tied in with the greatest-hits theme of *The Immaculate Collection*. The notorious tour introduced Madonna's conical, Jean Paul Gaultier-designed bra to the world and drew protests from religious and conservative groups, who objected to the lewd dance routines, which included simulated sex with hermaphrodites. The singer was captured during the tour in the documentary feature *Truth Or Dare* – originally titled *In Bed With Madonna*, under which name it was released in the U.K. and elsewhere, but the name was changed for U.S. release.

The Immaculate Collection features 16 of Madonna's biggest hits to date – arranged in chronological order, from 'Holiday' and 'Material Girl' to 'Like A Prayer' and 'Vogue' – and two previously unheard cuts, both of which also became international hit singles, which makes for a highly impressive tracklisting. Of the new songs, the hypnotic, hip-hop-influenced 'Justify My Love' stands as one of Madonna's most controversial releases, largely because of the media storm surrounding the raunchy video, which was banned in Britain and the U.S.A. Despite this – or perhaps because of it – 'Justify My Love' was Madonna's seventh U.S. Number One hit single and marked the start of the most overtly sexual period of her recording career. Subsequent years saw the release of her soft-porn book, *Sex*, and the albums *Erotica* (1992) and *Bedtime Stories* (1994). The other exclusive track on *The Immaculate Collection*, 'Rescue Me,' reached Number Nine in the U.S.A. and Number Three in the U.K. The album itself surprisingly failed to top the U.S. albums chart, but soon became Madonna's biggest-selling album to date, selling over 23 million copies worldwide.

Some of the songs suffer from the exaggerated panning and separation of the QSound mixes, resulting occasionally in a strange, displaced sound. Once heralded as a revolution in audio technology, QSound was briefly popular in the early 1990s but failed to achieve the sort of music-industry dominance its creators had hoped for. While Sting and Luther Vandross both recorded Grammy Award-winning albums in the format in 1991, QSound has since only really been used on video-game soundtracks.

I Do Not Want What I Haven't Got
Sinead O'Connor

Ensign 21759 (U.S.A.) / CHEN 14 (U.K.)
Released March 1990

Though often better known for her controversial statements and actions, Sinead O'Connor was one of the most striking pop vocalists and performers of the early 1990s.

After issuing a debut album, *The Lion And The Cobra*, in 1987, O'Connor's career stalled briefly as she and drummer John Reynolds had a son and then divorced, events which would inform the mood of her second full-length album. O'Connor recorded *I Do Not Want What I Haven't Got* at STS Studios in her native Dublin, Ireland, during the summer of 1989. Among her collaborators here were former Smiths bassist Andy Rourke, ex-Public Image Ltd bassist Jah Wobble, and Nellee Hooper of Soul II Soul. Hooper was responsible for the stark arrangement of the Prince composition, 'Nothing Compares 2 U,' which topped the singles charts on both sides of the Atlantic. The striking, confessional nature of 'Nothing Compares 2 U' was a good indication of what else lay on *I Do Not Want What I Haven't Got*. The album jumps from string-drenched balladry and traditional Celtic folk to slick pop and the arresting a cappella title track, the common link throughout being O'Connor's impassioned vocal delivery.

I Do Not Want What I Haven't Got reached Number One in the U.S.A. and the U.K., but O'Connor's musical career soon began to take a back seat to the various controversies she got caught up in – be it refusing to sing 'The Star-Spangled Banner,' turning down Grammy Awards, or ripping up a photograph of the Pope on *Saturday Night Live*.

Violator Depeche Mode

Sire 26081 (U.S.A.) / Mute STUMM 64 (U.K.)
Released March 1990

Depeche Mode was one of only a handful of British acts to achieve true stardom in the U.S.A. in the 1990s.

The group was originally part of the early-1980s new-romantic scene, but soon moved toward a darker, more claustrophobic sound. *Music For The Masses* (1987) cemented a strong international following for the group, but what Depeche Mode really lacked – particularly in the U.S.A. – was a bona fide hit that would take them to the next stage. Issued in late 1989, 'Personal Jesus' was the group's most striking single yet. Built on a robotic blues stomp, with an insistent, echoing vocal, it reached the Top 30 in Britain and the U.S.A. The follow-up, an apocalyptic disco ballad by the name of 'Enjoy The Silence,' was even better, and became the group's biggest ever U.S. hit, peaking at Number Eight. That set the stage perfectly for *Violator*, recorded throughout the latter half of 1989 with Flood, producer and engineer of albums by U2, Nick Cave & The Bad Seeds, and Erasure. While nothing else on the album quite matches the power of the two singles that preceded its release, *Violator* is remarkably consistent both in the sound and the quality of the songs. Among the other highlights are the staccato funk of the opening 'World In My Eyes' and the bleak 'Waiting For The Night.'

Violator was a trans-Atlantic Top Ten hit, and has sold six million copies worldwide. The follow-up, *Songs Of Faith And Devotion* (1993), fared even better, topping the U.S. and U.K. charts, but *Violator* remains the group's defining work.

Soundtrack From Twin Peaks Angelo Badalamenti

Warner Brothers 26316 (U.S.A. & U.K.)
Released September 1990

Opening with one of the most memorable and evocative pieces of music ever written for television, *Soundtrack From Twin Peaks* was as much of a surprise hit as the much-heralded series, which first aired in 1990.

Twin Peaks was the brainchild of Mark Frost and the cinematic auteur David Lynch, best known for the cult-classic movies *Eraserhead* (1977) and *Blue Velvet* (1986). *Twin Peaks* marked Lynch's first foray into television.

Angelo Badalamenti, who had previously scored *Blue Velvet* and worked as an arranger for Pet Shop Boys and Liza Minnelli, was employed to write the main theme and incidental music for the series. 'Twin Peaks Theme' opens the album, riding in on delicate electric piano and strings, softly brushed drums and a distinctive, dreamy lead line, played on a six-string bass. Elsewhere, Badalamenti's smoky jazz on 'Freshly Squeezed' and 'Dance Of The Dream Man' is perfectly suited to the otherworldly atmospheres of *Twin Peaks*, and the stark, piano-led 'Laura Palmer's Theme' neatly encapsulates the double life of the title character, whose death provides the story around which the series is based. The three vocal tracks on *Soundtrack From Twin Peaks* are sung by Julee Cruise, and had all previously featured on her Lynch- and Badalamenti-produced album *Floating Into The Night* (1989). Cruise became something of a pet project for Lynch, and was given further exposure when she appeared in *Twin Peaks* as a nightclub singer. *Soundtrack From Twin Peaks* unexpectedly reached Number 16 on the U.S. albums chart, while 'Twin Peaks Theme' won a Grammy Award for Best Instrumental Pop Performance.

1991

Nevermind Nirvana

DGC 24425 (U.S.A. & U.K.)
Released September 1991

Ten Pearl Jam

Epic 47857 (U.S.A.) / 468884-2 (U.K.)
Released August 1991

**Without question the most influential rock album of the 1990s,
Nevermind signaled the arrival of the decade's most enduring white
youth-culture movement: grunge.**

Like many revolutionary albums before it, *Nevermind* came out of left field
and was roundly dismissed by many U.S. critics who heard it only as a
dirtier, simpler form of heavy metal. It took interest from the U.K. to launch
the album on its way to achieving ten-times platinum status before the start
of the new millennium.

Nirvana's debut album, *Bleach*, had much of the same raw-yet-melodic
sound as *Nevermind*, and a couple of great Kurt Cobain compositions,
'About A Girl' and 'Negative Creep,' that should have alerted critics to the
fact that something fresh was happening. What *Bleach* lacked, however, was
Dave Grohl's drumming. When Grohl replaced Chad Channing, producer
Butch Vig immediately noticed how "Dave was incredibly powerful and dead
on the groove. I could tell from the way Kurt and Chris were playing with him
that they had definitely kicked their music up another notch in terms of
intensity." Now they had the sound that Cobain once described as "The Bay
City Rollers getting molested by Black Flag," and all they had to do was get
it on tape.

Cobain described the process of creating songs for *Nevermind* by saying:
"We downed a lot of cough syrup and Jack Daniels and just lounged on the
couch in the recreation area of the studio for days on end, just writing down
a few lyrics here and there." In stark contrast, Vig recalls that Cobain was in
good spirits during the making of *Nevermind*, and worked long days,
beginning around noon and ending after midnight. "I think it took five or six
days in all," says Vig. "Dave was set up in the middle of the room. We built
a big drum tunnel on the front of his bass drum, so we could mike it from a
distance and still isolate it from all the bleed in the rest of the room. Chris
had his SVT bass rig off to the side, but he could play in the room. His
headphones were set up next to the drums. Kurt's amps were in a little
isolation area, but he was also in the room and he could sing into a mike."
Most tracks, he reckons, required only two or three takes.

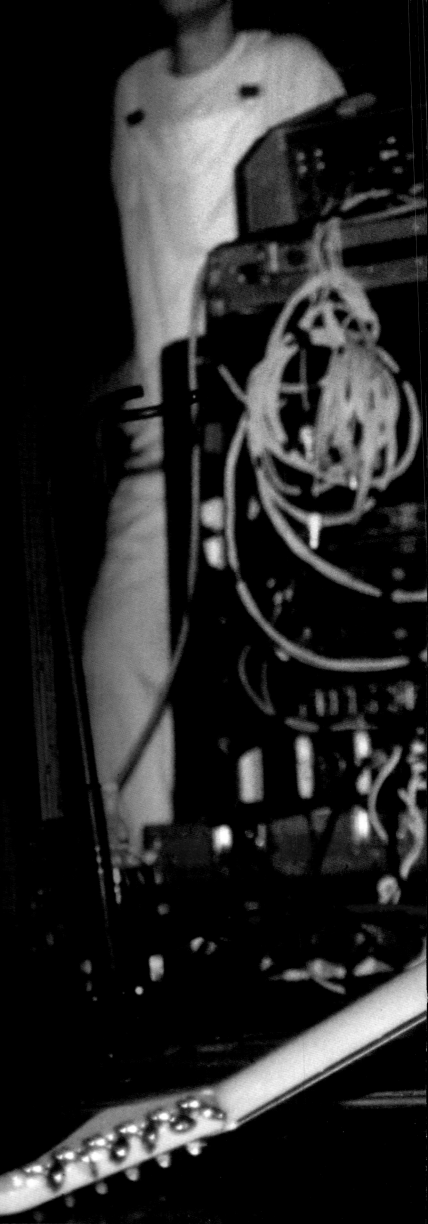

1991

teen spirit.' And earlier on, we were having this discussion on teen revolution and stuff like that, and I took that as a compliment. I thought she was saying I was a person who could inspire. I just thought that was a nice little title. And it turns out she just meant that I smelled like the deodorant, I didn't even know that deodorant existed until after the song was written."

Surprisingly, given the elemental passion on 'Teen Spirit,' Cobain's musical inspiration for the track is said to have been Boston's bombastic pomp-rock classic, 'More Than A Feeling.' Vig was immediately impressed by 'Teen Spirit,' and insisted that they play it over and over again. "There wasn't much that needed to be done with the song," he points out. "I think we did a little arranging. At the end of each chorus, there's a little ad-lib thing Kurt did with the guitar. Originally that only happened at the end of the song; he did it a whole bunch of times. I suggested moving that up into each chorus and cutting the choruses down a little bit."

The album's other really well-known cut, the chilly but compelling 'Come As You Are,' is much harder to get a handle on. Is it, as some Nirvana-watchers have suggested, an open invitation to the band's fans to join in their fun, or is it something much more sinister? "The lines in the song are really contradictory," said Cobain. "Y'know, one after another, they're kind of a rebuttal, to each line, and they're just kinda confusing I guess. It's just about people, and uh, what they're expected to act like." He has also claimed that: "At the time I was writing those songs, I really didn't know what I was trying to say. There's no point in my even trying to analyze or explain it." Given that the songs, though oblique, seem to be the work of an intelligent lyricist, it's hard to know how serious Cobain was being when he made these kinds of comments. There's so much variety on the album – from the punky thrash of 'Territorial Pissings' to the richly melodic 'Lithium,' or the acoustic strum of the nightmarish 'Polly,' detailing a horrific rape he'd

■ *Above and below: Nirvana record a live session for the Dutch radio stations VARA and VRPO on November 25th 1991, two months after the release of the group's groundbreaking* Nevermind *album. Opposite: Stone Gossard and Eddie Vedder of Pearl Jam on stage on the New York leg of the* Lollapallooza *festival in 1992.*

read about in a newspaper – that it's hard to accept *Nevermind* as anything other than the work of a rational, self-aware songwriter.

Like Bob Dylan, Cobain saw no merit creating a perfect take, preferring instead to leave each song fresh and vital, mistakes and all. "He really wanted to do everything on the first or second take," says Vig. "He'd do a couple of takes and say, 'That's it. I'm not gonna do it any more.' The tricky part was trying to figure out how to motivate him to give really good performances." The resourceful Vig, however, would record every word Cobain sang, including warm-ups, and would then piece a final take together from the best-sung lines from three or four versions.

Recording In The 1990s

After a decade of arena rock, hip-hop, and hair bands, the change that swept over the recording industry at the start of the 1990s was swift and dramatic.

It began with the re-emergence of 45-year-old Neil Young – whose full-tilt performance of 'Rockin' In The Free World' on *Saturday Night Live* served as a prelude to his landmark *Ragged Glory* – and continued with the arrival of a new crop of young bands, many of whom hailed from the rain-soaked metropolis of Seattle, Washington. Joining the likes of Nirvana, Pearl Jam, and Mudhoney were a contingent of upstart producers and engineers, whose use of old-school techniques and technology helped put some of the dynamics back into the recording environment.

One of the best of the behind-the-board bunch was Butch Vig, producer of Nirvana's *Nevermind*, Smashing Pumpkins' *Gish* and *Siamese Dream*, and many others. During the 1990s Vig worked much of his magic from his own hand-built recording facility, Smart Studios, located in downtown Madison, Wisconsin. It was there that, in 1995, Vig teamed with guitar buddies Duke Erikson and Steve Marker, plus Scottish vocalist Shirley Manson, to form Garbage. With Garbage, Vig found the perfect outlet for his old-school-rules-new-school-tools production style, which involved recording spontaneous song fragments live then cobbling together the disparate elements in a manner reminiscent of Vig's hero Brian Wilson. "Most of our songs come from simply improvising while we're running our 48-track Pro Tools," says Vig. "We compile bits and pieces, cut them up, and edit them together, and keep working on them until eventually it sounds like a song that was written on an acoustic guitar!"

Recording *Dookie*, the major-label debut from Bay Area's Green Day, in 1994 was UK-born, San Francisco-based engineer Neill King, who'd cut his teeth with the likes of Elvis Costello, Madness, and The Smiths and knew a little something about harnessing studio energy. Rather than try to contain Tre Cool's voluminous drum sound, King had the band set up in the expansive, wood-laden Fantasy Studio A, then proceeded to make the most of the enormous ambience. "There are huge ceilings in there, so I just put up a bunch of room mikes and tried to capture the sound of Tre's kit that way," says King. "If you can get it sounding really good in the room, it's going to come across so much better on record than just close-miking everything."

Meanwhile, up at Boston's Q Division Studios, singer–songwriter Aimee Mann was capping a masterful year in music with her second effort, *I'm With Stupid*, an album recorded during 1994 but not issued until early 1996, owing to record-company shenanigans. Its distinctive edge was the product of co-writer, producer, and multi-instrumentalist Jon Brion, who learned the art of creative dabbling from old heroes such as The Beatles and The Zombies. Brion's quest for unique guitar tones often led him down some fairly unusual paths. "On 'Long Shot' I had Aimee record consecutive rhythm-guitar tracks, each one played the same but with different colorations each time," says Brion. "For the first track, I'd say, 'OK, let's go with all red things – this guitar is red, that fuzz box is red, that amp's got a little red on it, fine, go . . .' For the second part, I had her play a Tele through a Matchless amp with a Vox Tonebender; on the next track, she's playing the worst guitar in the building through the cheapest fuzz pedal we could find into a Kustom head. I know it sounds crazy, but eventually you get that cool juxtaposition. It always seems to pan out in the end."

The leaner, meaner production style of the 1990s was just the ticket for veteran songwriter–guitarist Tom Petty. After a fruitful four-year stint with producer Jeff Lynne, Petty handed the control-room keys to Def Jam's Rick Rubin and Rubin's trusted engineer Jeff Scott. In late summer 1993, Petty and Rubin checked into Sound City in Van Nuys, a mammoth structure with several decades-worth of California pop lore behind it (and birthplace to Petty's 1979 commercial breakout *Damn The Torpedoes*).

Released in the fall of 1994, the resulting album, *Wildflowers*, left the impression of a middle-aged tug-of-war, an effect made all the more pronounced by the immediacy of Rubin's production work. Says Joe Baresi, assistant engineer on the album: "*Wildflowers* is a great example of the kind of sound you can get out of a great studio with the right people running it."

Sweetened with some remixing by Andy Wallace, Vig's production was undeniably a major factor in the success of the album. Though he would no doubt have preferred Cobain's vocals to be higher in the mix, he was able to create a sound that was balanced beautifully between grunge distortion and pop clarity. It was a combination that worked equally well for hi-fi quality FM stereo radio and for lo-fi student or underground stations, and it appealed to pop fans and metalheads alike. Just about the only person in the U.S.A. who didn't like it was Kurt Cobain: "Our music, especially on this album, is so slick-sounding," he grumbled. "A few years ago, I would have hated our band, to tell you the truth."

> **"A LOT OF THE TIME I WRITE A SONG AND WHEN SOMEONE ASKS ME ABOUT IT I'LL MAKE UP AN EXPLANATION ON THE SPOT, BECAUSE I WRITE LYRICS IN THE STUDIO, AND I HAVE NO IDEA WHAT I'M TALKING ABOUT HALF THE TIME."**
>
> *KURT COBAIN*

From the outside, however, everything looked fine, and when the little band from Aberdeen, Washington, reached Number One in the U.S. albums chart on January 11th 1992 it sparked an explosion of interest in the so-called 'Seattle Sound' that would change the lives of dozens of local musicians, not least among them being the five members of Pearl Jam.

The core of Pearl Jam lay in 1980s Seattle favorites Mother Love Bone, whose promising career ended with the heroin-related death of singer Andrew Wood. While guitarist Stone Gossard and bassist Jeff Ament were struggling to regroup, Jack Irons, former drummer of The Red Hot Chili Peppers, suggested they should consider recruiting a young San Diego surfer, Eddie Vedder, who also wrote songs. As Vedder recalls it: "Jeff sent me a tape of three songs, and I sent him back a mini-opera." The tape he received consisted of instrumental backing tracks, which he transformed into complete songs with the addition of lyrics and vocal melodies. Among them were 'Once' and 'Alive,' both of which wound up on *Ten*. It was clear that Vedder worked well with Gossard and Ament, so they played a few gigs and recorded a bunch of demos as Mookie Blaylock, a name borrowed from a favorite basketball player, which they soon realized was too much of a joke to be taken seriously.

So, on May 11th 1991, when the now renamed Pearl Jam began recording their Epic Records debut album at London Bridge Studios, Seattle, Washington, with producer Rick Parashar. The old Mookie demos were rerecorded without too much alteration, because the band had been playing them live for months and knew exactly how they should be done.

Musically, Pearl Jam and Nirvana had very little in common, beyond a raw, raging power that had been missing from rock for too long. Where Nirvana kept things deliberately simple and grungy, Pearl Jam sounded more like a souped-up, socially-aware, essence of Led Zeppelin with a hint of Southern rock thrown in for good measure, all topped off with Vedder's heart-stoppingly powerful vocals. The first track they completed was 'Alive,' the

1991

stirring twin-guitar-powered rocker that would become their first single. The cut that would put them on the map, however, was 'Jeremy,' based on the true story of Jeremy Wade Delle, a seriously disturbed 16-year-old student at Richardson High School in Dallas, Texas, who had shot himself dead in front of his class on January 8th 1991. Vedder combined Delle's story with his own recollection of a fellow-student in junior high school, in San Diego, California, who had taken a gun to his class and gone on a shooting spree, though with less disastrous results. He and Pearl Jam guitarist Jeff Ament then put music to the words and, though it was never a huge hit, the accompanying video walked off with no less than four MTV Video Music Awards, including Video Of The Year, Best Group Video, Best Metal/Hard Rock Video, and Best Direction.

Parashar's contribution to the album extended beyond faithfully recording the band's music into helping them actually make it. "Rick's a super talented engineer-musician," notes Jeff Ament, and he adds that, on a day when guitarist Stone Gossard was sick: "Ed, Rick, and I conjured up the art piece that opens and closes the record. That was so fun, I wanted to make a whole record of that kind of stuff."

When the album was released on August 27th 1991, insiders realized that Mookie Blaylock might be gone but it wasn't forgotten, because *Ten* had been the number on his New Jersey Mets shirt. "I think we all felt pretty good about the record," remembers Gossard, "but we didn't feel like it was the end-all recording, by any means. And I think we kind of felt like, wow, we set the deal up the way we wanted, people seem to be into hearing us play, and at that point Mother Love Bone was helping us get some attention. So we were feeling positive."

Epic Records secured an attention-grabbing promotion for 'Alive,' by having it pre-released via a Coca-Cola promotion. But Vedder soon found himself dismayed by the machinations of the industry, hating the endless round of hand-shaking, back-slapping company functions the band had to attend. It must have stung him badly when Kurt Cobain dismissed Pearl Jam as "corporate" rockers.

A slow-burner, *Ten* didn't peak until almost a year later, when it hit Number Two on the *Billboard* chart in the week of August 22nd 1992 and went on to eclipse *Nevermind* with its rapid progression to five-times platinum status, making Pearl Jam, briefly, more popular than Nirvana.

Tragically, one curious side-effect of the popularity of Seattle's grunge-era bands was the, presumably unintended, glamorization of self-loathing. Cobain seemed to feel he had betrayed his own integrity by finding fame and fortune, and Vedder clearly felt tainted by the embracing tentacles of the business without which he would never have become a superstar. Other Seattle bands, notably Alice In Chains, expressed similarly negative feelings about themselves, and when significant numbers of high-profile icons all seem to share the same philosophy, some of it will inevitably rub off on their fans.

The horrific circumstances of Kurt Cobain's death sent shock waves around the world, but the media glamorization of that waste of an enormous talent simply shored up the impression that such behavior was, somehow, the epitome of cool.

Metallica **Metallica**

Elektra 61113 (U.S.A.) / Vertigo 5100221 (U.K.)
Released August 1991

Metallica are to heavy metal what the stealth bomber is to aviation: darker and meaner than anything else.

With their seminal 1986 album *Master Of Puppets* they had jettisoned the more cartoonish aspects of earlier versions of heavy metal and played up the existential despair. They had popularized a new harmonic vocabulary for the genre, using unusual scales for their riffs and solos. In came the 'scalloped' power-chord with its thumping top and bottom-boosted EQ. Along with the extreme riffing they also had a maniacal sense of arrangement.

In 1991 the eponymous fifth album, in its blacker-than-black sleeve, took head-banging to new levels of precision and went to Number One on both sides of the Atlantic. It was composed with a desire to match riffs to more commercial songs and reduce the length of instrumental passages. 'Enter Sandman' is the standout track and an obvious hit single, and quickly established itself as one of those licks that every aspiring heavy-metal guitarist had to learn to play. Drummer Lars Ulrich commented: "I always find that the first song that you write for an album has a certain magic to it, and that was 'Enter Sandman.' This song just has such a feel to it that we felt it should be the first new thing people heard." They made dramatic use of strings on 'Nothing Else Matters,' with vocalist James Hetfield singing a love song that manages to sound like a curse at the same time.

The whole pantomime of heavy metal has little to do with any recognizable world of ordinary human experience. But it's a vicarious thrill to ride the back of this particular beast. Earlier Metallica albums are more thrashy and frenetic, with epic convoluted songs. With this album they cut the waffle and perfected their style. Ever since, they've been trying to escape the black-hole event horizon of their own darkness.

Blood Sugar Sex Magik **Red Hot Chili Peppers**

Warners 26681 (U.S.A.) / WX 441 (U.K.)
Released September 1991

***Blood Sugar Sex Magik*, The Red Hot Chili Peppers' fifth album, arrived just as Nirvana had begun to open the doors for alternative rock in the mainstream, and was the group's commercial breakthrough.**

RHCP had made four albums of funky punk in the 1980s before inking a deal with Warners in 1990. The group recruited Rick Rubin, co-founder of Def Jam Records, to produce *Blood Sugar Sex Magik*. Though best known for his pioneering work with Run-DMC and Public Enemy, Rubin had plenty of experience with rock bands, too, having produced albums by The Cult and Slayer among others. Rubin helped refine the RHCP sound, which had previously tended at times to drift into jam-band territory. *Blood Sugar Sex Magik* is dominated by the bruising, sexual funk of 'Give It Away' and 'Suck My Kiss,' while the mournful 'Under The Bridge' narrowly missed out on the top spot of the U.S. singles chart.

Blood Sugar Sex Magik was a big hit in the U.S.A. and across Europe, eventually selling more than seven million copies worldwide. The group took four years to follow it with the half-baked *One Hit Minute* (1995), before returning to form with *Californication* (1999).

1991

Screamadelica Primal Scream

Sire 26714 (U.S.A.) / Creation CRE076 (U.K.)
Released September 1991

Loveless My Bloody Valentine

Sire 26759 (U.S.A.) / Creation CRE060 (U.K.)
Released November 1991

In the fall of 1991 independent label Creation Records released two of the most innovative British albums of the 1990s: Primal Scream's dance-rock hybrid *Screamadelica* and the pioneering noise-pop of *Loveless* by My Bloody Valentine.

Having recorded a pair of albums of guitar-led rock in the late 1980s, Primal Scream was drawn to the growing acid-house scene and its upbeat, euphoric dance music. Inspired by these new, cutting-edge sounds, frontman Bobby Gillespie asked DJ Andrew Weatherall to remix 'I'm Losing More Than I'll Ever Have' from the group's eponymous second album. Weatherall removed the drums, bass, guitars, and vocals from the original, a mid-tempo rocker reminiscent of The Rolling Stones, keeping only the piano and horn parts from the song's outro. Adding a new drum beat, dub bass, a soulful vocal sample, and some fresh guitar lines, Weatherall created 'Loaded' (1990), a single that would not only earn Primal Scream its first U.K. hit, but also bridge the gap between rock and dance audiences.

Inspired by the success of 'Loaded,' Primal Scream set about recording an album with the same crossover appeal. The group again worked with Weatherall on eight of the album's 11 tracks – though this time the producer worked with the band from the outset rather than remixing finished tracks – including the epic single 'Come Together' and a version of The 13th Floor Elevators' 'Slip Inside This House.' *Screamadelica* also features a contribution from Jimmy Miller – famous for his work with The Rolling Stones – on soulful opener 'Movin' On Up,' and techno act The Orb assist on the electronic psychedelia of 'Higher Than The Sun.' The resulting album still stands as a unique, genre-bending statement, and was Creation Records' most successful release to date, reaching Number Eight in the U.K. albums chart.

After making a series of fairly lightweight EPs in the mid 1980s, My Bloody Valentine recorded the acclaimed *Isn't Anything* in 1988. The album's droning, layered guitars and dreamy vocals inspired a host of imitators and raised expectations for My Bloody Valentine's second full-length album, particularly after the group issued the *Glider* EP, a richly textured work that made *Isn't Anything* sound like a rough sonic template.

My Bloody Valentine started work on the follow-up to *Isn't Anything* in mid 1989, but it soon became apparent that, given guitarist-songwriter Kevin Shields's growing perfectionism, the group would not be issuing any new material soon. The recording of *Loveless* eventually spanned more than two years, 16 engineers, and countless studios across the U.K., almost bankrupting Creation, who are rumored to have invested over $500,000 in its gestation, a huge sum for a small independent label.

The resulting album was undoubtedly worth the wait in terms of artistic merit, but failed to recoup its production costs, leaving Creation in a fragile

state until its huge worldwide success with Oasis later in the 1990s. *Loveless* is a near-perfect work, founded on an impenetrable wall of dense, searing guitars and deftly programmed rhythms, which mark My Bloody Valentine as one of the first rock bands to utilize digital sampling. Despite the album's moderate commercial success it casts a long shadow over much of the experimental rock that followed it. My Bloody Valentine disbanded in the mid 1990s after Shields decided there was no way the group could top *Loveless*. In 2000 he joined Primal Scream as additional guitarist and occasional producer.

Spiderland **Slint**

Touch & Go T&Glp*64 (U.S.A. & U.K.)
Released March 1991

Though never commercially successful, *Spiderland* was a defining, pioneering influence on post-rock, one of the dominant forms of experimental music in the 1990s and early 2000s.

While it has since become an umbrella term for any group that dares reach beyond the boundaries of conventional rock music, post-rock was originally typified by droning, hypnotic soundscapes with abrupt dynamic shifts and long, complex song structures.

Spiderland was Slint's second and final album. The group was formed in 1988 by Louisville, Kentucky, schoolfriends Brian McMahan on guitar and vocals and Britt Walford on drums, with guitarist David Pajo and bassist Ethan Buckler (replaced by the time *Spiderland* was cut by Todd Brasher). The album was recorded in the fall of 1990 by Steve Albini – one of the key record producers of the 1990s – and Brian Paulson, an engineer who would later work with Beck and Wilco. Its central track, 'Good Morning, Captain,' is emblematic of the whole album in its shifts from quiet, foreboding verses to loud, distorted choruses. The long list of bands inspired by Slint – and this album in particular – includes Mogwai, Tortoise, and Godspeed You Black Emperor!

After Slint disbanded, Pajo joined the equally influential Tortoise, appearing on their highly regarded *Millions Now Living Will Never Die* (1996) before forming his own groups Aerial M and Papa M. McMahan founded The For Carnation, and both he and Pajo have featured on albums by the otherworldly singer-songwriter Will Oldham – aka Palace Music and Bonnie 'Prince' Billy, among other pseudonyms – who took *Spiderland*'s enigmatic cover photograph.

Seal **Seal**

Sire 26627 (U.S.A.) / ZTT ZTT9 (U.K.)
Released May 1991

The London-born soul singer Seal topped the U.K. singles chart in 1990 with his first release, 'Killer,' a collaboration with the techno producer Adamski. Shortly thereafter he started work on his full-length debut with producer Trevor Horn, who also signed Seal to his ZTT label.

Seal was preceded by a huge international hit single, 'Crazy,' which reached Number Two in the U.K. in late 1990 and Number Seven in the U.S.A. the following spring. The light, funky house production of 'Crazy' gave a good indication of the sound of half of the songs on the album; the rest of the tracks on *Seal* are guitar- and piano-led ballads, typified by 'Whirlpool,' which serve mainly to show off Seal's striking vocal ability. The sweeping string parts on the album were arranged by Anne Dudley, a member of Trevor Horn's Art Of Noise group, who would later go on to compose movie soundtracks.

Seal sold three million copies worldwide and spawned two further U.K. hit singles, 'Future Love Paradise' and a remixed version of 'Killer.' The album also earned the artist a prestigious Ivor Novello Award for songwriting in 1992.

Seal issued a second eponymous album three years after the release of his debut. Again produced by Horn, *Seal* (1994) featured contributions from Joni Mitchell and Jeff Beck and included the U.S. Number One hit single 'Kiss From A Rose,' which was featured on the soundtrack to *Batman Forever* (1995) and cemented his reputation as the pre-eminent British soul singer of the 1990s.

1991

Ropin' The Wind Garth Brooks

Capitol 96330 (U.S.A.) / ESTU 2162 (U.K.)
Released September 1991

Garth Brooks was the first country artist to achieve multiplatinum sales figures in the U.S.A. *Ropin' The Wind* was the first country album to debut at Number One on the *Billboard* Top 200, where it remained for 18 weeks.

After issuing an eponymous debut in 1989, Brooks began to gain attention outside the country-music world with the following year's *No Fences*, which reached Number Three on the pop albums chart. *Ropin' The Wind* was Brooks's third album in 22 months. Like its predecessors, the album was produced by Allen Reynolds, who had previously worked with Don Williams, Patsy Cline, and Emmylou Harris. It is built on a solid country foundation but also draws on the arena rock of The Eagles and Journey. It was also the first of his albums to blend traditional country elements with 1970s-style rock – most notably on a version of Billy Joel's 'Shameless' – which angered some C&W purists. Despite this, Brooks did more than anybody else to bring country music into the mainstream in the 1990s, while retaining a country audience – 'What She's Doing Now,' 'Shameless,' and 'The River' all reached the Number One spot on the country singles chart.

No Fences and *Ropin' The Wind* both sold over ten million copies, and Brooks issued eight more hit albums in the 1990s, while his run of multiplatinum successes was broken only by *The Life Of Chris Gaines* (1999). That album – for which the singer took off his stetson, grew a goatee, and dabbled in pop rock – remains something of an oddity in the Brooks catalog. He returned to what he does best – and the top of the U.S. albums chart – on *Scarecrow* (2001).

Unplugged **Eric Clapton**

Reprise 45024 (U.S.A.) / Duck-Warners 480 (U.K.)
Released August 1992

Unplugged EP **Mariah Carey**

Columbia 52758 (U.S.A. & U.K.)
Released March 1992

Uptown MTV Unplugged **Various Artists**

MCA 10858 (U.S.A. & U.K)
Released June 1993

Unplugged **Neil Young**

Reprise 45310 (U.S.A.) / 9362 45310 (U.K.)
Released June 1993

MTV Unplugged In New York **Nirvana**

DGC 24727 (U.S.A.) / GED24727 (U.K.)
Released November 1994

In the early 1990s there was no greater signifier of the importance or musical worth of a group or singer than being invited to tape a set for MTV's *Unplugged* series. After airing on MTV, many of these performances were also issued on record. Some – the sets by Eric Clapton and Nirvana, for example – have become significant albums in their own right.

MTV hit upon the idea of *Unplugged* after watching the overwhelming response to an acoustic rendition of 'Wanted Dead Or Alive' at the cable television station's 1989 Music Awards by Jon Bon Jovi and Richie Sambora. At first *Unplugged* tended to group together two or three complementary acts, but by mid 1990 had settled into putting the spotlight on one established performer per show. The Eagles' Don Henley was the first artist to be given a whole *Unplugged* of his own, while other early successes were Elton John and Aerosmith.

Not many of the earliest *Unplugged* performances were issued on record, and those that did become available in album format – including Paul McCartney's set – tended to be seen as novelty items and were not particularly successful. That began to change with the release of two big-selling sets in 1992. The first of these was the three-million-plus selling *Unplugged* EP by Mariah Carey, which compiled the seven songs from her March 16th performance at the Kaufman Astoria Studios in Queens, New York. Carey was backed by harpsichord, celeste, a string quartet, an eight-member vocal workshop, and the horn section from *Saturday Night Live*.

Released later in 1992, Eric Clapton's performance remains the biggest-selling *Unplugged* album of all. It has sold more than seven million copies in the U.S.A. alone, where it reached Number One, and achieved the Number Two slot in the U.K. Clapton's set was taped at Bray Film Studios in Windsor, England. It was Clapton's first performance since the tragic death of his young son Conor, and marked the first public airing of his heartfelt tribute to his son, 'Tears In Heaven.' Clapton also worked through a number of his best-known songs, and a series of blues classics, including Muddy Waters's 'Rollin' And Tumblin'' and Robert Johnson's 'Malted Milk.'

The idea behind the series had originally been to show popular groups and their music in a different light. Too often, though, it became simply an uninspiring

acoustic set of the artist in question's greatest hits performed in a way that barely deviated from the recorded versions. To that end, *Unplugged* was often at its most interesting when it showcased artists from outside the guitar-based rock world. One of the more unusual sets was a showcase for Uptown Records taped on February 6th 1993 at Universal Studios, Los Angeles. It featured performances by Mary J. Blige, Father MC – later better known as Puff Daddy – and others, backed by The Swing Mob. Blige was surprisingly outshone by Jodeci, particularly on a version of Stevie Wonder's 'Lately,' which reached Number Four on the U.S. singles chart.

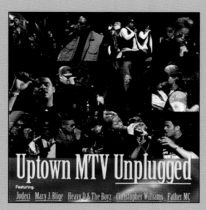

However, some rock artists did go to greater lengths to give their fans – and MTV – something different. One such performer was Neil Young. Though a short acoustic set had been a staple of his live performances for years, Young made an effort to present some of his songs in new and unusual settings at the taping, recorded the day after the Uptown Records set at the same venue. Most striking was his version of 'Like A Hurricane,' previously a harsh guitar-rock track, here reset for pump organ and harmonica. While other songs – particularly 'Needle And The Damage Done' and selections from his recent 'comeback' album *Harvest Moon* (1992) – hardly differed from the studio versions, Young had at least offered a bit of variety and the sense that this was a one-off performance. Both Young's *Unplugged* and the Uptown Records stable's set were issued in album form in June 1993. Young's was the more successful, reaching Number 23 in the U.S.A. and Number Four in the U.K.

For many, the most memorable *Unplugged* was recorded at Sony Music Studios in New York City on November 18th 1993. Right up until the taping there was some concern as to whether Nirvana, and frontman Kurt Cobain in particular, would be fit to perform. In the event, Cobain and his group gave one of the most striking live television performances ever witnessed. Ignoring 'Smells Like Teen Spirit,' the group concentrated on subtle renditions of lesser-known songs, including 'About A Girl' and 'On A Plain,' and made use of non-rock instrumentation such as accordion and cello. The performance also revealed Cobain as a superb interpreter of other people's songs, breathing new life into David Bowie's 'The Man Who Sold The World' – embellished by a hint of cheekily distorted guitar – and the stark blues of a version of Leadbelly's 'Where Did You Sleep Last Night.'

Nirvana's *Unplugged* took on greater significance by virtue of being the final live taping of the group before Cobain's suicide in April of the following year. Issued six months after his death, *MTV Unplugged In New York* serves as a fitting epitaph for the career of perhaps the most important rock singer and songwriter of his generation. It topped the charts on both sides of the Atlantic and has since sold nearly four and a half million copies in the U.S.A. alone. Inevitably, no subsequent *Unplugged* set could come close to the emotional resonance and iconic status of Nirvana's performance or the record sales of Eric Clapton's set. With the exception of the occasional, isolated highlight, such as Bob Dylan's 1994 performance, the series began to dwindle in the later 1990s, when it was dominated by middling alternative-rock acts. MTV tried to relaunch the show as *Unplugged 2.0* in 2001, at which point R.E.M. became the first group to feature on the program twice. *Unplugged 2.0* never reached the heights of the early-1990s tapings, however, and was canceled in 2002.

1992

Automatic For The People **R.E.M.**

Warner Bros 45505 (U.S.A.) / 9362450552 (U.K.)
Released October 1992

After five albums with the IRS label, R.E.M. signed to Warner Brothers, and in the process moved away from being a college-radio rock outfit toward a more mature, commercial sound.

Their 'second' career commenced with *Green*, but it was their seventh album, *Out Of Time*, that made them a huge international act on the back of the popularity of 'Losing My Religion.' These circumstances turned *Automatic For The People* –
the title is the motto of a restaurant called Weaver D's Delicious Fine Foods, in Clarke County, Georgia, where the staff acknowledge any order with the word 'automatic' – into something of a challenge as a follow-up record.

Sessions took place in studios right across the U.S.A. As the band jammed ideas, it seemed to Buck that "a lot of the songs are kind of like old folk or blues songs." 'Drive' makes an unusual album opener and was the first single. 'Try Not To Breathe,' 'The Sidewinder Sleeps Tonite,' and 'Man On The Moon' are infectious, upbeat R.E.M. songs. (The maddeningly indecipherable hook-line on 'Sidewinder' is apparently "Call me when you try to wake her.") Several tracks – notably 'Sidewinder' – benefit from the production and arrangement skills of Led Zeppelin's John Paul Jones. Buck praised Jones for being able to write string parts that were "nonsweet." These, along with the bold 'Ignoreland,' are counter-balanced by quieter material, such as the piano-led 'Nightswimming' and the plangent, hymn-like 'Find Me A River.'

'Everybody Hurts' shows R.E.M.'s preparedness to side-step expensive technology and make music with whatever came to hand – in this case a cheap drum machine, acoustic guitar, and keyboard. 'Monty Got A Raw Deal,' which alludes to the life of 1950s movie star Montgomery Clift, was written by Buck on a Greek bazouki and given additional color with a cello. Knowing their rock music recording history also helped some of the tracks: 'Star Me Kitten' has the band using a similar vocal texture to 10cc's 'I'm Not In Love.'

The subject-matter is often dark. Themes of mortality, suicide, AIDS, and memory make the songs somber but not so bleak as to make the record a depressing listen. The lyric of 'Find Me A River,' for example, is genuinely poetic and beautiful in its regret, while 'Everybody Hurts' features one of Stipe's most clearly focused lyrics. He explained: "That was written for teenagers, basically, saying don't kill yourself . . . My sister is a teacher and someone she knows, who is 15, tried to kill himself, and it led to this song. The idea was to write something that would appeal to someone who is having trouble."

Automatic For The People was both a commercial high-point for R.E.M. – around the time of this album's release they were bigger than U2 – as well as a critical one. The album has been praised for its cohesiveness, for its ability to be positive while dealing with some dark themes, even as it gave R.E.M. a brace of hit singles. Fulfilling such different criteria is no mean feat.

Ingénue kd lang

Sire 7599 26840 (U.S.A. & U.K.)
Released March 1992

kd lang – she insists on the lower-case letters – became one of the most controversial figures in country music when she emerged in the late 1980s.

Like Garth Brooks, she mixed traditional C&W elements with other rock-based styles. What caused more of a stir, however – at least among Nashville's elder statesmen – was the fact that lang is an out lesbian, though by the time of *Ingénue* she was more of a pop star than a country singer.

A real-life Canadian cowgirl, lang released four albums of rockabilly-tinged country in the 1980s. *Absolute Torch And Twang* (1989) was the first to make a dent on the U.S. pop chart. As its title suggests, the album marked the beginnings of lang's move away from country toward adult contemporary ballads. Issued in the immediate aftermath of her first public admission of her homosexuality, *Ingénue* has a pronounced pop edge, though it does betray slightly the influence of Patsy Cline. Produced by lang and the multi-instrumentalist Ben Mink, the album was lang's first since her debut to be recorded without her backing group The Reclines. They are replaced by Mink's programmed rhythms and an assortment of session musicians playing everything from marimbas to tamboura. Mink also co-wrote the lion's share of the songs with lang, including the U.K. Top 20 hit single 'Constant Craving,' which won a Grammy for Best Female Pop Vocal Performance. The album itself reached Number Three in the U.K. and Number 18 in the U.S.A., and sold 1.6 million copies worldwide.

Connected Stereo MC's

Gee Street 514061 (U.S.A.) / 4th & Broadway BR 589 (U.K.)
Released October 1992

Stereo MC's was the first widely successful British hip-hop group. The group was formed by rapper Rob Birch and producer-DJ Nick 'The Head' Hallam in 1985.

The duo set up their own Gee Street label using the £7,000 (about $14,000) they were paid to vacate their flat by property developers before recruiting vocalist Cath Coffey and drummer Owen If. Their first offering *33-45-78* (1989) and follow-up *Supernatural* (1990) failed to chart, but the group scored an unexpected U.S. hit in the summer of 1991 with 'Elevate My Mind.'

Connected was Stereo MC's breakthrough album. The album was a huge success in the U.K., where it peaked at Number Two, buoyed by the popularity of its title track, a Top 20 hit on both sides of the Atlantic. With its shuffling drums, funky horn sample, and Birch's laconic vocal delivery, 'Connected' was typical of the Stereo MC's sound.

The album is more laidback and melodic than a lot of U.S. hip-hop of the time, but retains the kind of cool, urban sound required for success in the rap market. Despite the high chart placing for 'Connected,' the album stalled at Number 92 in the U.S.A. Back in the group's homeland, *Connected* spawned three further Top 20 hit singles, 'Step It Up,' 'Ground Level,' and 'Creation.'

Poised for further mainstream success, Stereo MC's effectively retired for the remainder of the 1990s. When the group returned nine years later, it was with the lukewarm *Deep Down & Dirty* (2001), which quickly fell off the radar.

Rage Against The Machine
Rage Against The Machine

Epic 52959 (U.S.A.) / 472224 (U.K.)
Released November 1992

Rage Against The Machine was one of the first groups to find a viable common ground between rock and hip-hop in the 1990s.

The group's sound prefigured that of Korn, Limp Bizkit, and other so-called rap-metal acts. RATM was also highly politicized, and regularly lent its support to various left-wing causes. Unsurprisingly, then, the songs on *Rage Against The Machine* are doggedly polemical, a sequence of revolutionary tracts about the state of the U.S.A. in the late 20th century.

RATM started work on its debut in early 1992 with producer Garth Richardson, who had previously worked with Red Hot Chili Peppers. While that group's punk-funk influence can be detected on the album, RATM has a much harder, angrier sound. 'Bombtrack' opens the album with a supercharged Led Zeppelin riff, while vocalist Zack de la Rocha seems to delight in yelling the mantra "Fuck you, I won't do what they tell me" over 'Killing In The Name.' Song titles 'Take The Power Back' and 'Bullet In The Head' speak for themselves; the aggression never lets up. While much has been made of de la Rocha's impassioned raps over the alternative-metal backing and the influence this had on subsequent groups, what is most striking about *Rage Against The Machine* is Tom Morello's guitar playing. Only Radiohead's Jonny Greenwood could claim to have coaxed so many otherworldly sounds out of a guitar in the 1990s. *Rage Against The Machine* has sold three million copies worldwide, while 'Bullet In The Head' was a U.K. Top 20 hit.

The Bodyguard (Original Soundtrack)
Whitney Houston / Various Artists

Arista 18699 (U.S.A.) / 7822-18699 (U.K.)
Released November 1992

One of the most successful female vocalists of the 1980s and 1990s, Whitney Houston made her big-screen debut in the romantic thriller *The Bodyguard* (1992).

The movie was a box-office success, but was outshone by its soundtrack, which is dominated by Houston. Its success was due in no small part to the inclusion of her rendition of Dolly Parton's 'I Will Always Love You,' which spent a then-record 14 weeks at Number One in the U.S.A.

For such a successful album *The Bodyguard* is an uneven affair. It opens with 'I Will Always Love You' and five more Houston songs that wouldn't have seemed out place on 1990's *I'm Your Baby Tonight*. The rest of the material is in the typical big-budget soundtrack vein: Lisa Stansfied, Joe Cocker, and Curtis Stigers each provide a song, and Kenny G offers up a couple of slices of his mellow jazz. The album is rounded off by an extract from the movie's orchestral score and lengthy versions of 'I'm Every Woman' and 'Queen Of The Night' by Houston. Nothing unpleasant, then, but not what you would expect to find at the top end of a list of all-time big-selling albums. Needless to say, *The Bodyguard* did sell by the truckload – it is one of the biggest-selling albums of all time, having sold 17 million copies in the U.S.A. alone – topping albums charts across the globe and winning Houston a pair of Grammy Awards.

1993

Siamese Dream Smashing Pumpkins

Caroline 88267 (U.S.A.) / Hut HUT011 (U.K.)
Released July 1993

While most of their grunge contemporaries were inspired by 1970s punk and 1980s metal, Smashing Pumpkins drew more heavily on earlier psychedelic and progressive-rock groups as well as the recent dreamy, wall-of-sound productions of My Bloody Valentine.

The group's sophomore effort, *Siamese Dream*, is one of the best alternative-rock albums of its time. Debut album *Gish* (1991) had marked Smashing Pumpkins as a band of immense potential, but the group was in a state of crisis as the tour in support of the album ended the following summer. Frontman Billy Corgan was battling depression and writer's block, guitarist James Iha and bassist D'Arcy Wretsky were in the midst of a turbulent romantic break-up, and drummer Jimmy Chamberlain was struggling with heroin and alcohol addiction. Chamberlain spent a month in rehab before the group decamped to Atlanta, Georgia, hoping the drummer would find it less easy to maintain his drug habit away from The Pumpkins' home city of Chicago.

Smashing Pumpkins started work on *Siamese Dream* in December 1992 at Triclops Sound alongside Butch Vig, who had produced *Gish* as well as Nirvana's recent breakthrough album *Nevermind*. The group opted to record the album's basic tracks in a live setting, despite Chamberlain's erratic appearances at the sessions as his drug problems continued. Already something of a perfectionist when it came to recording, Corgan then built up numerous layers of guitar and keyboards, giving the songs an impressive, widescreen feel. Corgan brought in a violinist and cellist to embellish the album's quieter moments, while R.E.M.'s Mike Mills plays piano on closing track 'Luna.'

Siamese Dream is an accomplished, diverse work, both heavier and more melodic than much of the alternative rock of the early 1990s. Despite Corgan's apparent writer's block, it includes some of the strongest songs of his career, either as chief Smashing Pumpkin or later as the key figure in alternative-rock supergroup Zwan. The album's rich production stands apart from the rawness of other grunge bands, evoking early Pink Floyd, Queen, and The Cure in places. Opening track 'Cherub Rock' is a powerful statement of intent, riding in on insistent, multitracked guitar and drums, with the rest of the album divided between spacious atmospherics and unrelenting heavy rock.

Siamese Dream reached the Top Ten in both the U.S.A. and the U.K., where it spawned two hit singles, 'Disarm' and the ironic 'Today,' which was promoted by a music video in which Corgan drove an ice cream van. 'Disarm' is among the album's high points, an arresting blend of fiercely strummed acoustic guitar, bells, strings, and Corgan's pleading vocal. Though the group would make three more albums – including the commercially and critically successful *Mellon Collie And The Infinite Sadness* – *Siamese Dream* remains the most complete statement of Smashing Pumpkins' career.

■ *Left to right: D'Arcy Wretsky, Jimmy Chamberlain, Billy Corgan, and James Iha.*

Tuesday Night Music Club Sheryl Crow

A&M 0126 (U.S.A.) / 540 126 (U.K.)
Released October 1993

Sheryl Crow scored a huge international hit with the rootsy, countrified rock of her debut. A highly collaborative affair, the album was conceived and recorded, as the title implies, at a regular Tuesday-night jam session attended by Crow and her musical friends.

Prior to launching her solo career, Crow worked as a teacher in her native Missouri before moving to Los Angeles in search of work as a backing singer. Her most memorable singing job was on Michael Jackson's *Bad* tour. She has since claimed that she was not allowed to make eye contact with Jackson off stage, and that he insisted she change her name to Shirley. In 1990, after further session work, she signed a deal with A&M Records and readied a debut album for the following year. It was withdrawn shortly before its release, however, as Crow grew tired of its slick pop sound. Surprisingly, A&M allowed Crow to scrap the album and begin work afresh in a more relaxed setting.

In 1992 Crow was introduced to a group of Los Angeles-based session players by her then-boyfriend Kevin Gilbert, who had made an ill-fated attempt at remixing the tapes of her scrapped work from the previous year. This loose collective of musicians had been meeting once a week at producer Bill Bottrell's Toad Hall studio for the 'Tuesday Night Music Club.' Crow was invited to join them and, as the only member of the club with a record deal, became the focus of the weekly songwriting and jam sessions. Over the course of the year the musicians assembled the laidback, bluesy songs that feature on her second attempt.

Tuesday Night Music Club was not particularly successful on its initial release in 1993, but eventually climbed into the U.S. Top Five on the strength of the international hit single 'All I Wanna Do.' Ironically the only song on *Tuesday Night Music Club* that Crow didn't have a hand in writing, its sound was emblematic of the album as a whole. While 'All I Wanna Do' initially seems quite loose, with its rambling pedal steel and Crow's laidback vocal delivery, the song is in fact underpinned by a slick, lightly funky backing.

Producer Bottrell laid similarly polished foundations beneath the other songs, from the opening 'Run, Baby, Run' – which borrows a riff from The Beatles' 'I Want You' – to the smoky jazz of 'We Do What We Can.' Lyrically, the album is split between typical post-breakup fare – 'Can't Cry Anymore,' 'Nobody Said It Would Be Easy' – and the more upbeat self-encouragement of 'Strong Enough' and 'Solidify.'

On subsequent albums Crow's songs became more political, addressing such issues as abortion and nuclear war. For *Tuesday Night Music Club*, however, she keeps to the tried and tested themes of classic romantic rock. The album eventually shifted ten million copies worldwide, while the singer consolidated her success through the 1990s with the Grammy-winning albums *Sheryl Crow* (1996) and *The Globe Sessions* (1998).

1993

The Chronic **Dr Dre**

Death Row 57128 (U.S.A.) / Interscope 7567 92233 (U.K.)
Released February 1993

Behold, the birth of G-funk: *The Chronic* introduced the sound that would dominate hip-hop for the rest of the 1990s.

After leaving NWA, the group with whom he had revolutionized West Coast rap, Dre formed Death Row Records with Marion 'Suge' Knight in 1992. His first release was a single, 'Deep Cover,' a collaboration with the then-unknown rapper Snoop Doggy Dogg. As well as being one of the finest hip-hop producers of all time,

Dre also had a knack for finding and launching new talent. Dogg became Dre's protégé in the same way Eminem did in the late 1990s.

'Deep Cover' and *The Chronic*, issued nine months later, marked an important change in the way hip-hop records were made. Before, they had tended to be built around a frenetic, James Brown-style drum loop. As suggested by its marijuana-referencing title, *The Chronic* pioneered a more laidback sound that drew on George Clinton's work with Funkadelic and Parliament. Dre had also begun to make more use of live instrumentation than had previously been heard on rap records. His liquid basslines and synthesizer squeals would soon become ubiquitous. Dogg featured on half of the songs on *The Chronic*, including the Number Two U.S. chart entry 'Nuthin' But A "G" Thang.' It was no surprise, therefore, that by the end of 1993 Dre had produced Snoop's own debut, *Doggystyle*. *The Chronic* peaked at Number Two in the U.S.A., while *Doggystyle* went one better, topping the charts in December 1993.

Republic **New Order**

Qwest 45250 (U.S.A.) / Centredate 828413 (U.K.)
Released May 1993

***Republic* was New Order's sixth and bestselling album, but found the group in a state of flux.**

New Order had emerged from the ashes of the cult post-punk quartet Joy Division after the suicide of vocalist Ian Curtis in 1980. New Order adopted a more synthesized, beat-driven sound, and had numerous U.K. hits throughout the 1980s. True U.S. success proved elusive until the release of *Republic* – which, coincidentally, followed *Violator*, by

another British electronic group of the 1980s, Depeche Mode, into the upper reaches of the U.S. albums chart.

By this stage, however, New Order had begun to fragment. Rumors of internal conflict were rife and matters were not helped by the fact that all four members of the group had started working on side projects by 1989: Bernard Sumner collaborated with former Smiths guitarist Johnny Marr as Electronic, bassist Peter Hook fronted Revenge, and drummer Stephen Morris and keyboardist Gillian Gilbert formed The Other Two. To exacerbate matters, Morris and Gilbert were upset that the *Republic* sleeve design had originally been intended for their *The Other Two And You* (1993) album, until it was co-opted by the other members of New Order.

Given the tension within the group *Republic* sounds subdued and disjointed in places, but still contains flashes of New Order's best work, particularly on the aptly titled 'Regret.'.

Music Box **Mariah Carey**

Columbia 53205 (U.S.A.) / 474270 (U.K.)
Released September 1993

Mariah Carey was the most successful female performer of the 1990s, during which time she released nine huge albums and had 13 U.S. Number One hit singles, more than any other woman in history.

Unlike many of her contemporaries, Carey also writes or co-writes most of her material. She also had the advantage – until their 1997 divorce – of being married to Columbia Records boss Tommy Mottola. Her eponymous debut (1989) and second release *Emotions* (1991) were both multimillion sellers, but drew accusations that she over-used her much vaunted five-octave voice. Stung by these criticisms, she aimed to make her third album more subtle musically and less reliant on vocal gymnastics. Her two dozen collaborators on *Music Box* include the Brazilian pop maestro Walter Afanisieff, who co-authored half of the album, David Cole and Robert Clivilles of C&C Music Factory, and Babyface, who duets with Carey on the slick ballad 'Never Forget You.' *Music Box* spent a total of eight weeks atop the U.S. albums chart and was the first of Carey's albums to reach Number One in the U.K. The biggest-selling album of Carey's career, it has sold more than 27 million copies worldwide, and spawned her eighth and ninth U.S. chart-topping singles, 'Hero' and 'Dream Lover.' Subsequent albums could not quite match the sales of *Music Box*, but none of her albums during the 1990s shifted less than nine million copies, bringing her total sales for the decade to an incredible 140 million albums.

Enter The Wu-Tang (36 Chambers) Wu-Tang Clan

Loud-RCA 66336 (U.S.A.) / 74321 20367 (U.K.)
Released November 1993 (U.S.A.) / May 1994 (U.K.)

Wu-Tang Clan introduced a new modus operandi for hip-hop groups, using *Enter The Wu-Tang* to establish the Wu brand, before launching various solo projects, a clothing line, and even a Wu-Tang comic.

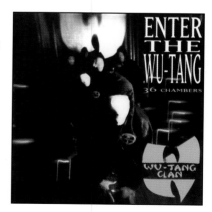

From the start, Wu-Tang Clan was not your typical rap group. Led by the production wizard RZA, the collective was influenced as much by chess and kung-fu movies as it was by other hip-hop acts. Unlike other more intellectual hip-hop groups, however, Wu-Tang Clan retained a hardcore edge to its music. The group signed an unusual deal with RCA in 1992, which allowed all of its members to pursue parallel solo careers. Work began shortly thereafter on *Enter The Wu-Tang* at Firehouse Studio in the group's native New York. The songs are raw and sparse and held together by samples from martial-arts movies. Lyrically, the album is intense and often violent, but more literate than any other hip-hop group: who else has rhymed "elephant tusk" with "Egyptian musk," or made reference to the Emancipation Proclamation in song?

Enter The Wu-Tang was a critical and commercial hit on its release in late 1993. Within the next couple of years it was followed by hit albums by group members including Method Man, Raekwon, and Ol' Dirty Bastard, confirming The Clan as one of the 1990s most important hip-hop empires.

1994

American Recordings **Johnny Cash**

American 45520 (U.S.A.) / 74321 23685 (U.K.)
Released May 1994 (U.S.A.) / October 1994 (U.K.)

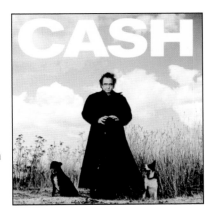

American Recordings was the first in what became a series of four albums of rock covers and Cash originals recorded by the legendary country singer during the latter part of his life. The albums were not a huge commercial success, but were unanimously adored by critics and introduced Cash's music to a younger generation.

In 1992 Cash's recording contract with Mercury Records expired. With his country audience dwindling, some assumed this would mean the end of his 40-year career, but Cash had other ideas. The following year he unexpectedly signed a new deal with Rick Rubin's American label. Rubin had been one of the most important producers of the previous decade, having worked with both rock and hip-hop artists, most notably on the Run-DMC album *Raising Hell* (1986), which brought those two disparate genres together for the first time. As producer of 'The American Series,' Rubin guided Cash toward a similar stylistic crossover – essentially, *American Recordings* is a set of rock songs performed by a country artist in a folk style.

The album was recorded in late 1993 at Rubin's Los Angeles home and at the Cash residence in Hendersonville, Tennessee. There were no other musicians present at the sessions: Rubin simply plugged in a microphone

and recorded Cash alone, backed only by his own acoustic-guitar playing. They taped over 70 songs in all, of which eleven feature on *American Recordings*. Two more songs were taken from a solo live performance at the Viper Room in Los Angeles.

American Recordings does contain a clutch of Cash originals, old and new, but – like the three albums that follow it – is dominated by his interpretations of other people's songs, and the way he manages, without fail, to make each one his own. The highlights include his rendition of Nick Lowe's 'The Beast In Me,' and readings of Leonard Cohen's 'Bird On A Wire' and 'Down There By The Train' by Tom Waits. The most important song, however, in terms of finding Cash a new audience, is the murder ballad 'Delia's Gone.' The accompanying video, in which Cash kills and buries the model Kate Moss, brought the singer to the attention of the MTV generation for the first time.

Shortly after the release of *American Recordings*, Cash enthused: "I'm more proud of it than anything I've ever done in my life. This is me. Whatever I've got to offer as an artist, it's here." Music critics lapped up the album, with *Rolling Stone* magazine declaring it to be "unquestionably one of his best albums" and remarking that "his voice is the best it has sounded in 30 years." Though it failed to chart in either the U.S.A. or the U.K., *American Recordings* sold solidly through the 1990s and early 2000s and won a Grammy Award for Best Contemporary Folk Album.

The three subsequent albums in the series are more collaborative affairs, while the more surprising song choices tended to be Rubin's suggestions. *Unchained* (1996) featured contributions from Tom Petty And The Heartbreakers, and a version of 'Rusty Cage' by the heavy-rock group Soundgarden. Cash's output slowed after he was diagnosed with Parkinson's Disease in 1997, but his ill-health did nothing to detract from the subtle beauty of his final pair of albums. *American III: Solitary Man* (2000) includes covers of songs by U2 and Nick Cave, while *American IV: The Man Comes Around* (2002) is best remembered for Cash's stark reading of Nine Inch Nails' claustrophobic 'Hurt.'

Interest in these albums inevitably peaked after Cash's death on September 13th 2003. The five-disk set *Unearthed* (2003) is made up mostly of previously unissued recordings from the previous ten years of American sessions.

Grace **Jeff Buckley**

Columbia 57528 (U.S.A.) / 475928 (U.K.)
Released August 1994

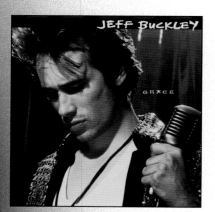

The only full-length album Jeff Buckley completed during his lifetime, *Grace* has become one of the best-loved albums of the 1990s.

Buckley struggled throughout his short career against the expectations of being the son of a father he barely knew, cult singer-songwriter Tim Buckley. The lives and careers of Jeff and Tim shared a number of parallels: both were among the outstanding vocalists of their respective generations, both made highly individual and expressive music, and both died too young.

Brought up by his mother, Buckley met his father only briefly, shortly before Tim's death from a drug overdose in 1975. His haunting performance of his father's 'Once I Was' sparked a major-label bidding war, eventually won by Columbia, who issued the *Live At Sin-E* EP the following year. He started work on his first full-length album in the fall of 1993 with his newly formed band, which comprised bassist Mick Grondahl, drummer Matt Johnson, and guitarist Michael Tighe. The album's sessions were produced and engineered by Andy Wallace, who had worked on Run-DMC's 'Walk This Way' before mixing Nirvana's *Nevermind*. An audacious debut, *Grace* draws on the sound and emotional power of Led Zeppelin and Van Morrison. The key ingredient is Buckley's voice, which resembles a somewhat more subtle Robert Plant in its five-octave range. He steps effortlessly from delicate crooning to a soaring falsetto on the album's ten songs, which include well-chosen covers of Leonard Cohen's 'Hallelujah,' Jim Shelton's 'Lilac Wine,' and Benjamin Britten's 'Corpus Christi Carol.'

Buckley's own songwriting contributions are equally as impressive as his vocal performances. The first two songs on *Grace* were co-written alongside Gary Lucas, guitarist in the final incarnation of Captain Beefheart's Magic Band. Of these, opening track 'Mojo Pin' had previously been issued in more skeletal form on the *Sin-E* EP, while the title track is classic epic rock. 'Last Goodbye,' meanwhile, grows into a deft Middle Eastern string arrangement, while 'Lover, You Should've Come Over' is underpinned by stately acoustic guitar and organ. The album closes with two of its most powerful songs: 'Eternal Life' is as close as Buckley gets to the sound of early-1990s alternative rock, while 'Dream Brother' evokes his father's 'Dream Letter,' gradually building to a cathartic crescendo after a tabla-laden intro.

The final line of 'Dream Brother' – "Asleep in the sand, with the ocean washing over" – would prove eerily prophetic. On May 29th 1997, during the recording of what would have been his second album, provisionally titled *My Sweetheart, The Drunk*, Buckley took a swim in a treacherous part of the Mississippi, and was sucked under the water as a steamboat passed. He was 30 years old.

While *Grace* had only sold modestly on its initial release, reaching Number 50 on the U.K. albums chart, it has grown in stature and influence substantially since Buckley's passing. Numerous bands and artists, including Radiohead and Coldplay, have cited *Grace* as a key influence on their work. Since Buckley's death, his mother, Mary Guibert, has coordinated the release of a number of posthumous albums, most notably *Sketches For: My Sweetheart The Drunk*, a collection of demos and unfinished recordings from 1997.

Jeff Buckley was just one of a number of performers following in the footsteps of a famous musical parent to emerge in the 1980s and 1990s. John Lennon's first son, Julian, the subject of Paul McCartney's 'Hey Jude,' released his debut album *Valotte* in 1984, which also provided him with four hit singles. His later releases were less successful, however. Lennon's son with second wife Yoko Ono, Sean, recorded two albums in the late 1990s for The Beastie Boys' Grand Royal label. Carnie and Wendy Wilson, daughters of Beach Boy Brian, and Chynna Phillips, daughter of John and Michelle of The Mamas And The Papas, formed Wilson Phillips, selling four million copies worldwide of their eponymous debut in 1990. Dweezil Zappa, son of Frank, has made four albums of experimental metal; while Loudon Wainwright III's son Rufus has carved out a career of his own, making extravagant, orchestral pop since the late 1990s.

Definitely Maybe **Oasis**

Epic 66431 (U.S.A.) / Creation CRECD 169 (U.K.)
Released February 1995 (U.S.A.) / September 1994 (U.K.)

Park Life Blur

SBK-Food 29194 (U.S.A.) / EMI-Food FOOD10 (U.K.)
Released April 1994

Different Class **Pulp**

Polygram 524165 (U.S.A.) / Island 8041 (U.K.)
Released October 1995

Suede Suede

Columbia 53792 (U.S.A.) / Nude NUDE1 (U.K.)
Released April 1993

Brit-pop emerged in the mid 1990s in Britain. It started as an anti-grunge movement around 1992 and developed into a collective desire to relive the 1960s and make Britain swing again.

The rehabilitation of The Beatles' reputation with the release of the *Anthology* and *Live At The BBC* CDs fueled an interest in the 1960s. Suddenly the Union Flag was hip again and on the cover of magazines, and the key bands included Oasis, Blur, Pulp, Suede, Supergrass, Elastica, and Sleeper. The Beatles connection was worked most strongly by Mancunian band Oasis. Their debut, *Definitely Maybe* (1994), brims with no-nonsense, WYSIWYG swagger. It has 'Rock'n'Roll Star,' the powerful 'Live Forever,' and the T. Rex-Chuck Berry-inspired 'Cigarettes And Alcohol.' Oasis offer juggernauts of layered guitars turned up to 11, and Liam Gallagher sings in a voice part-Johnny Rotten and part-John Lennon – taking as his cue Lennon's vocalization of the word 'shine' on 'Rain.'

The Beatles influence also shaped the 1995 follow-up *What's The Story (Morning Glory)?*, with the Lennonesque ballad 'Don't Look Back In Anger,' while 'Roll With It' sounds like a 1990s 'Hard Day's Night.' 'Cast No Shadow' has slide guitar and strings eerily evocative of *All Things Must Pass*. After that, arrogance, drugs, and fame sent Oasis into a creative tailspin, despite sell-out megagigs.

In contrast to Oasis, Blur were based in London, and their influences were at the time more along The Kinks-Small Faces axis of 1960s pop than The Beatles so beloved of their rivals. *Park Life* offers more eccentricity and more focused evocations of everyday life than Oasis's work. The press attempted to fan inter-band antagonism between the two groups, emphasizing

the polar opposites of northern working-class Oasis versus southern art-school Blur. Eventually Blur withdrew from the Brit-pop scene and had deconstructed their sound by the time they recorded the grungy 'Song 2' with its memorable "woo-hoo" catchphrase.

In some ways Pulp resembled a Human League reborn for the 1990s, with a Morrisseyesque figure penning the words. The admirably unpretentious Jarvis Cocker wrote sensitively and wittily about a whole range of subjects on *Different Class* (1995), which included a clutch of timely U.K. hit singles, among them 'Common People' and 'Sorted For Es and Whizz.' And who else but Cocker could have put a song like 'Help The Aged' on an album like *This Is Hardcore* (1997), with its magnificently sleazy title track, in which the spirit of lounge MOR gets hijacked by a John Barry orchestration and a Led Zeppelin drumbeat?

Brit-pop wasn't just about evoking the 1960s, however – at times Oasis could sound as though they wanted to be Slade. While no one stepped up to be the 1990s T. Rex or Roxy Music, Suede emerged in 1993 to play at being Bowie – their third single, 'Animal Nitrate,' sounds like an outtake from *Ziggy Stardust*. Their debut album went to Number One in the U.K. and won the 1993 Mercury Music Prize. Suede – and in particular singer Brett Anderson – made the right glam moves in terms of the bisexual, are they/aren't they game – witness the two people kissing on the cover of their debut album and the naked figure on the cover of the second, *Dog Man Star* (1994). Resident guitar star Bernard Butler, who did a mean line in Mick Ronson-

style riffs, left in 1994 and has since pursued a solo career – though in 2005 Butler and Anderson returned as The Tears.

The high point of Brit-pop coincided with the election of a Labour government in May 1997 after 18 years of Conservative rule. The new administration actively and publicly courted the aristocracy of British culture, both popular and more rarified, in an attempt to ride a wave of credibility in the new world order of 'Cool Britannia.' The 'movement,' however, didn't last.

1994

The Downward Spiral Nine Inch Nails

Nothing/TVT 92346 (U.S.A.) / Island ILPSD 8012 (U.K.)
Released March 1994

The most successful industrial-rock act of the 1990s, Nine Inch Nails is the recording pseudonym of Trent Reznor, also the producer of much of Marilyn Manson's early material.

A classically trained pianist, Reznor wrote and played the entirety of the first two Nine Inch Nails releases, *Pretty Hate Machine* (1989) and *Broken* (1992), the latter a Top 20 hit in the U.S.A. and U.K. For *The Downward Spiral* Reznor recruited a number of session musicians, including drummers Chris Vrenna and guitarist Adrian Belew, most famous for his work with David Bowie and Talking Heads in the late 1970s and early 1980s. Belew's appearance offers a clue to the sound of *The Downward Spiral*, which in places feels like an updated, heavier take on Bowie's *Low* (1977) and *Scary Monsters* (1980), as well as earlier industrial-rock acts such as Ministry and Skinny Puppy. The album's session drummers also make a big impact, particularly on the oppressive, multilayered rhythms of 'Piggy.'

The Downward Spiral was met with much public disapproval on release for

its recording location. In 1993 Reznor had begun renting the Los Angeles house where The Manson Family had murdered actress Sharon Tate in 1969. Deciding his new home would provide a suitable recording environment, Reznor built a studio in the basement. Despite this controversy the album remains Reznor's greatest artistic success and also the biggest-selling Nine Inch Nails album. The single 'Closer' was a hit on both sides of the Atlantic, and was followed a year later by the remix collection *Further Down The Spiral*.

Dummy Portishead

Polygram 828552 (U.S.A.) / Go Beat 828552 (U.K.)
Released August 1994

A number of trip-hop acts – so called because they merged slowed-down hip-hop beats with jazzy, psychedelic instrumentation – emerged in the early 1990s from the English city of Bristol. Portishead's debut, *Dummy*, was the short-lived genre's most successful album.

In 1991 Massive Attack issued what is generally considered to be the first trip-hop album, *Blue Lines*, a mix of soulful vocals, stoned raps, and edgy dub and hip-hop samples. One of the engineers on the album was Geoff Barrow, from the nearby sleepy coastal town of Portishead. Two years after the release of *Blue Lines* Barrow formed a group of his own with vocalist Beth Gibbons and guitarist Adrian Utley. Taking the name of Barrow's hometown, the trio recorded *Dummy* at State Of The Art and Coach House Studios in Bristol with engineer Dave McDonald during the latter part of 1993 and the early months of 1994.

Building on the rather more sparse sound of Massive Attack's debut, Barrow and Utley created a claustrophobic, cinematic backdrop for Gibbons's haunting, melancholic vocals. Half-speed drum-fills and eerie, droning organs vie for space with a few well-chosen samples from recordings by artists including Weather Report, Isaac Hayes, and Johnny Ray. Preceded by the singles 'Numb' and 'Glory Box,' a minor hit in the U.S.A., *Dummy* was released to widespread critical praise on both sides of the Atlantic. The album reached Number Two in the U.K., where it was awarded the Mercury Music Prize for Album Of The Year.

A month after the release of *Dummy* came Massive Attack's excellent sophomore album *Protection*. The latter group's former rapper, Tricky, released his similarly acclaimed debut, *Maxinequaye* (1995), a gritty, harder-edged take on the Portishead sound. All three acts distanced themselves from the trip-hop tag, however, particularly as a number of watered-down imitators began to hit the U.K. charts in 1996 and 1997.

Weezer **Weezer**

Geffen 24629 (U.S.A. & U.K.)
Released August 1994 (U.S.A.) / February 1995 (U.K.)

When grunge began to implode following the death of Kurt Cobain, Weezer was one of the first groups to fill the void. The group's awkward, nerdy, hook-laden rock also helped lay the foundations for 'emo' (emotional hardcore), as typified by Jimmy Eat World and The Get Up Kids, in the late 1990s.

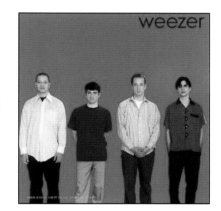

Weezer was formed in 1993 in Los Angeles by guitarist-vocalist Rivers Cuomo, bassist Matt Sharp, and drummer Patrick Wilson, and within a year had earned a deal with Geffen. The group quickly started work on a debut album with producer Ric Ocasek, former frontman of the late-1970s new-wave group The Cars.

On the album's release, most reviewers recognized that Weezer sounded like a cross between The Pixies and The Beach Boys. Brian Bell, who joined Weezer just three days before the recording sessions began, provides most of the angular lead-guitar parts reminiscent of the former group. He is also responsible, alongside Sharp, for the breezy Californian harmonies that neatly offset Cuomo's melodies. This blend of wiry alternative rock and pop hooks was crucial to making *Weezer* one of the biggest albums of 1994. Just as important, however, was the Spike Jonze-directed video to the single 'Buddy Holly,' still regarded as one of the finest of all time. In it, through clever editing, Jonze slotted the group into an episode of *Happy Days*. 'Buddy Holly' was an international hit, as was *Weezer*, which peaked at Number 16 in the U.S.A. and Number 23 in the U.K.

CrazySexyCool **TLC**

LaFace 26009 (U.S.A.) / Arista 26009 (U.K.)
Released November 1994

TLC had a huge international hit with their second album, *CrazySexyCool*, just as the personal lives of the trio started to resemble some kind of warped soap opera.

The group had made their recording debut in 1992 with *Oooooooohhh . . . On The TLC Tip*, an album of youthful exuberance rooted in the softer side of early-1990s hip-hop and urban pop. TLC opted to aim for a more

mature, soulful sound with the follow-up, which was recorded in the summer of 1994 with producers Dallas Austin and L.A. Reid, head of the group's label LaFace. *CrazySexyCool* resembles Prince in places, most obviously when the group cover his 'If I Was Your Girlfriend,' while there are also suggestions of *Very Necessary*, the album on which TLC's predecessors Salt 'N' Pepa attempted a similar transition from raucous rap to a more mature R&B sound.

CrazySexyCool was preceded by a single, 'Creep,' a U.S. Number One hit. The album's worldwide exposure was further enhanced by the release of 'Waterfalls,' one of the defining R&B pop hits of the mid 1990s, which spent seven weeks at the top of the U.S. chart and was also hugely successful across Europe. Shortly before the release of *CrazySexyCool*, the group's Lisa 'Left Eye' Lopes burned down the mansion of her NFL wide-receiver boyfriend Andre Rison in a fit of rage. She was eventually sentenced to five years probation after admitting an alcohol problem. In early 1995, as *CrazySexyCool* sat in the upper reaches of albums charts across the globe, TLC filed for bankruptcy, claiming to be $3.5 million in debt. The situation was not helped by the huge insurance payments Lopes faced after the arson incident or by the group's claims that they were not being paid adequate royalties for their hugely successful second album. In 1996 Tionne 'T-Boz' Watkins announced she was suffering from sickle cell anemia, while Rozonda 'Chilli' Thomas was going through a messy public breakup with producer Austin, with whom she had recently had a son. Despite these personal setbacks, TLC remain one of the biggest-selling female R&B groups of all time, while *CrazySexyCool* contains some of the finest urban pop of the decade. Tragically, Lopes was killed in a car crash in 2002.

1995

The Bends **Radiohead**

Capitol 29626 (U.S.A.) / Parlaphone PCS 7372 (U.K.)
Released March 1995

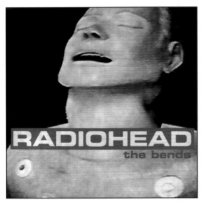

Radiohead shook off the one-hit-wonder tag with *The Bends*, which built on the epic rock of early U2 and R.E.M. to often startling effect. The album in turn inspired a wave of new British bands, notably Travis and Coldplay.

Radiohead scored an unexpected international hit in 1993 with the single 'Creep,' but many critics considered its parent album, *Pablo Honey*, to be a lightweight attempt at jumping on the grunge bandwagon. Stung by these criticisms, the group felt under intense pressure to record a worthy follow-up, resulting in several months of strained recording sessions in mid 1994, during which numerous songs were scrapped or repeatedly reworked.

The band eventually completed the album early the following year, re-recording its twelve songs in two weeks after a confidence-boosting U.S. tour. *The Bends* was produced by John Leckie, a former Abbey Road engineer, who had worked on Pink Floyd's *Dark Side Of The Moon* and John Lennon's *Plastic Ono Band*. Radiohead's three guitarists dominate *The Bends*, though the most striking element is Thom Yorke's vocal delivery. Apparently, Yorke found the confidence to let loose his emotive falsetto after witnessing a live performance by Jeff Buckley. The album also contains a much wider range of material than *Pablo Honey*, particularly on the opening 'Planet Telex,' with its delayed piano-chords and staccato drum loop.

The Bends reached Number Six in the U.K. albums chart, where its profile grew with the success of the singles 'High And Dry,' 'Fake Plastic Trees,' and 'Street Spirit,' a Number Five U.K. chart entry. The album peaked at Number 88 in the U.S.A., where Radiohead toured in support of R.E.M. and Alanis Morissette in an attempt to broaden their appeal.

A Live One **Phish**

Absolute A-Go-Go 61772 (U.S.A.) / Not issued in the U.K.
Released July 1995

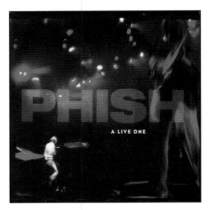

Taken from a series of performances recorded in late 1994, the two-disk set *A Live One* was intended as the definitive representation of the Phish concert experience.

Phish was formed in 1983 by Vermont University friends Trey Anastasio (guitar and vocals), Jon Fishman (drums), and Jeff Holdsworth (guitar); bassist Mike Gordon joined the following year. The group self-released their debut album, *Junita*, in 1988, before signing to Absolute A-Go-Go and starting to develop a strong live following across the U.S.A., particularly on the college circuit.

Like The Grateful Dead before them, Phish are well known for vastly expanding their recorded works on stage; studio versions of their songs are often seen as templates to be developed further in a live setting. In its original form on *A Picture Of Nectar* (1992), 'Tweezer' runs to just under nine minutes – here the song is stretched out to more than half an hour. Some of the songs on *A Live One* are also given a new musical lick of paint and taken off into the uncharted waters of jazz, funk, and psychedelia. The album also includes seven songs previously unheard on record, some of which would later see release in studio form on subsequent Phish albums.

Fittingly, *A Live One* was the first of the group's albums to reach the U.S. Top 20, and it was the first of numerous live releases from the group. A six-CD set, *Hampton Comes Alive*, followed in 1996, and in 2001 the group started the 'Live Phish' series, which within a couple of years numbered 20 double-disk concert recordings. Even that isn't enough for many Phish fans, who continue to trade bootlegs of Phish gigs on tape and over the internet with the band's blessing. Phish fandom is apparently a uniquely North American experience, however; outside the U.S.A., the group – and similar acts such as The Spin Doctors – is virtually unheard of.

■ ***Below: Radiohead perform on the U.K. TV music show* Later With Jools Holland *in 1995. Left to right: Ed O'Brien, Phil Selway, Thom Yorke, and brothers Colin and Jonny Greenwood. Opposite: Alanis Morissette.***

Jagged Little Pill **Alanis Morissette**

Maverick 9362-45901 (U.S.A. & U.K.)
Released August 1995

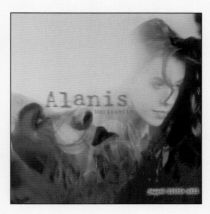

**Jagged Little Pill is the 12th
biggest-selling album of all time
and has shifted 16 million copies
in the U.S.A. alone.**

Morissette's success helped sell
alternative rock to a more adult
audience for the first time and also
opened the doors for a number of
other rock-orientated female performers
in the mid-to-late 1990s, notably Joan
Osborne, Jewel, and Fiona Apple.

Though *Jagged Little Pill* is generally
considered to be Morissette's debut, her musical career began a decade
earlier. She first came to prominence in her native Canada after joining
the cast of children's variety show *You Can't Do That On Television* at the
age of ten. Using the money made from her television career, the
precocious starlet pressed 2,000 copies of her self-penned debut single,
'Fate Stay With Me,' on her own Lamor Records label. Her next move was
to sign to MCA Records, which issued the pop-dance *Alanis* in 1991.
Both the album and its single 'Too Hot' made the Top Ten in Canada but
failed to make an impact elsewhere, despite a tour in support of Vanilla
Ice. Her second album, *Now Is The Time* (1992), failed to match the
success of the debut and resulted in the end of her association with
MCA, which opted not to renew her contract.

In 1993 Morissette moved to Los Angeles where she met producer and
songwriter Glen Ballard. He had made his name as a member of Quincy
Jones's studio team and previously worked on Barbra Streisand's *Till I Loved
You* and Paula Abdul's *Forever Your Girl* (both 1988) as well as the Wilson
Philips self-titled debut, which had earned him several Grammy Awards. He
had also played keyboards on Michael Jackson's *Bad* (1987).

Though Morissette and Ballard were both best known for their work in the
pop sphere, they made a conscious effort to move toward an edgier,
alternative-rock sound in their work together. Ballard provided the perfect
musical backdrop for the vituperative lyrics that Morissette had begun
writing, which dealt with failing relationships and her attitude toward the
Catholic Church, as well as her quest for self-improvement and personal
reinvention. By this stage, Morissette's image had mutated as far as her
music: no longer the teen-pop princess, she now looked the part of a rock
star, complete with the obligatory leather pants.

The duo's demo tape sparked a bidding war among the major labels,
eventually won by Madonna's fledgling Maverick Recordings, a Warner

Brothers subsidiary. After inking the deal, Morissette headed straight for
Westlake Studios in Hollywood, where she and Ballard began the task of
fleshing out the material on her demo into a full album. Flea and Dave
Navarro of Red Hot Chili Peppers added bass and guitar to several tracks,
which were largely built around Ballard's thick power chords and driving
rhythms. While a few of the songs sound too polished, given the angst-
ridden nature of the vocals, most of the album successfully combines an
alternative-rock edge with a pop sensibility, which is what its two creators
set out to achieve.

Back in Canada *Jagged Little Pill* was met with a degree of skepticism, with
many considering Morissette's change of sound and image to be a
transparent attempt to jump on the alternative-rock bandwagon. This was
less of a problem in the rest of the world, however, where hardly anybody
had been aware of her previous career – and Alanis herself is even prone to
referring to it in interviews as "my debut."

Jagged Little Pill soon climbed to the top of the U.S. *Billboard* charts, which
it would dominate for much of the next 18 months. Key to the album's
success was the single 'You Oughta Know,' a bitter tirade aimed at a record
company executive who took advantage of a young Alanis. The song caused
a stir on its release for the explicit sexual content of the lyrics – the result
being that Morissette soon had an army of devoted, neo-feminist fans. The
album spawned several other international hit singles, including the more
jangly, acoustic-guitar-led 'Hand In My Pocket' and 'Ironic,' both of which
were hugely successful across Europe.

As well as its flurry of single releases, *Jagged Little Pill*'s momentum was
maintained by Morissette's incessant touring around the globe. Shortly
before the album's release she had put together an impressive live band
that included guitarist Jesse Tobias, formerly of the band Mother Tongue,
and drummer Taylor Hawkins, who would later join Foo Fighters. At the 1996
Grammys Morissette was nominated in six categories, of which she won
three, including Album Of The Year. *Jagged Little Pill* soon surpassed
Whitney Houston's *Whitney* as the biggest-selling U.S. debut album of all
time, and worldwide sales have passed the 33 million mark.

The French Album [U.K. title: D'Eux] **Celine Dion**

550 Music / Epic 67101 (U.S.A.) / Sony International 80219 (U.K.)
Released October 1995 (U.S.A.) / September 1998 (U.K.)

**At her peak in the mid 1990s,
Celine Dion worked at a
prodigious rate, issuing new
albums regularly in both French
and English, which helped make
her one of the decade's dominant
pop figures.**

Dion had achieved considerable
success since the early 1980s,
particularly in France and her native
Canada. Toward the end of the
decade she was advised by manager
– and future husband – Rene Angelil
to remake her image in order to match that success in the U.S.A. This soon
achieved the desired result, and Dion sang the title track to the 1992
Disney movie *Beauty And The Beast*, following it with her biggest-selling solo
album to date, *The Color Of My Love* (1993). In the meantime, albums such
as *Dion Chante Plamondon* (1994) and *Des Mots Qui Sonnent* (1995)
helped maintain her profile in French-speaking territories.

The French Album was Dion's first attempt to bridge her two separate fan
bases. Written in the main by Jean-Jacques Goldman – a singer and
songwriter who had achieved fame in his own right in France – the album
kept to the sugary, adult-contemporary-pop formula of her recent U.S. hits
but with French lyrics. The ploy worked, and the album sold well across the
globe. In 1998 it was reissued as *D'Eux* and reached the U.K. Top Ten. By
then Dion had sold 25 million copies each of *Falling Into You* (1996) and
Let's Talk About Love (1997), making her one of the best-selling female pop
artists of all time.

1995

Post **Björk**

Elektra 612740 (U.S.A.) / One Little Indian TPLP51 (U.K.)
Released June 1995

A child star in her native Iceland, Björk fronted post-punk groups Kukl and The Sugarcubes before moving to London in the early 1990s and recording the euphoric dance-pop album *Debut* (1993), which sold three million copies worldwide and provided her with the U.K. hits 'Venus As A Boy' and 'Big Time Sensuality.'

Where Soul II Soul producer Nellee Hooper dominated the sound of *Debut*, the eclectic *Post* is a much clearer representation of Björk herself. The album is built on collaborations with some of the most highly regarded electronic musicians of the time, including 808 State's Graham Massey, Howie B, and Tricky, who duets with Björk on the edgy closing track 'Headphones.' *Post* opens with one of the most striking of Björk's songs, the punishing programmed bass-and-drum assault of 'Army Of Me.' The remainder of the album takes in melodic drum & bass and richly orchestrated electronic torch song, while a quirky cover of the jazz standard 'It's Oh So Quiet' provided Björk with an unlikely pan-European hit single. Though the song is musically unrepresentative of the overall sound of *Post*, it does hint at the many idiosyncratic moves of Björk's career.

Post is also the album where Björk comes into her own as a singer, though hers is a voice that continues to divide opinion. To some Björk is one of the finest and most individualistic vocalists of recent times; to others she sounds like a malfunctioning firework. *Post* reached Number 32 in the U.S.A. and Number Four in the U.K., where it provided her with five hit singles.

To Bring You My Love **PJ Harvey**

Island 524085 (U.S.A.) / 8053 (U.K.)
Released February 1995

After two albums of angst-ridden alternative rock, PJ Harvey developed a richer, blues-based sound on *To Bring You My Love*.

Harvey split up her original power trio shortly after touring in support of her second album, *Rid Of Me* (1993), a ferociously sexual record produced by grunge stalwart Steve Albini. She then started work on *To Bring You My Love* in September 1994 at Townhouse Three in London, gathering together an impressive avant-rock supporting cast, including multi-instrumentalists John Parish and Mick Harvey — no relation, but a member of Nick Cave's Bad Seeds — Tom Waits's guitarist Joe Gore, and Eric Drew Feldman, once of Pere Ubu.

To Bring You My Love remains the most consistent body of work of Harvey's career, and was hailed as a masterpiece by many critics on its release. The title track, which opens the album, quotes a line from Captain Beefheart's 'Sure 'Nuff 'N Yes I Do' from *Safe As Milk*, a key influence on some of *To Bring You My Love*'s guitar-led material. Other songs are driven by trippy, downbeat drum loops and mournful organ, reminiscent at times of Portishead's recent *Dummy*, while the vituperative relationship dramas of Harvey's earlier songs are replaced by dark, uneasy meditations on lost children and the slow inevitability of death. *To Bring You My Love* is Harvey's most successful album to date in the U.S.A., where it entered the charts at Number 40 and won a Grammy for Best Alternative Rock Album. In the U.K. the album spawned three minor hit singles, 'Down By The Water,' 'C'Mon Billy,' and 'Send His Love To Me.'

Garbage **Garbage**

Almo Sounds 80004 (U.S.A.) / Mushroom 31450 (U.K.)
Released August 1995 (U.S.A.) / October 1995 (U.K.)

Garbage's eponymous first album added a pop sensibility to the dreamy soundscapes of My Bloody Valentine's *Loveless*.

Unusually, the group was founded by a trio of record producers: Butch Vig, Steve Marker, and Duke Erikson. Of the three, Vig had been the most successful by far, having produced such landmark albums as Nirvana's *Nevermind* (1991) and Smashing Pumpkins' *Siamese Dream* (1993). Rather than continue in his role as the most sought-after producer of the decade, however, Vig started playing with Erikson and Marker in the latter's basement studio in Madison, Wisconsin. In 1994 the trio recruited the Scottish-born singer Shirley Manson after seeing her singing with her group Angelfish on MTV. Manson gave Garbage a powerful, sexy focus, and in the early days of the group she was often likened to The Pretenders' Chrissie Hynde.

As might have been expected, given the pedigree of its creators, *Garbage* is immaculately produced. The album is built on a bedrock of stuttering drum loops, heavily processed guitars, and shimmering keyboards, over which Manson weaves a web of smooth, sultry vocals. *Garbage* was a Top 20 hit on both sides of the Atlantic, and in the U.K. the album also provided four hit singles, including 'Only Happy When It Rains,' 'Queer,' and 'Stupid Girl.' As well as the usual CD issue, the album was released as a double LP – which ran at 45rpm – and as a boxed set of six seven-inch records.

Tragic Kingdom **No Doubt**

Trauma/Interscope 92580 (U.S.A.) / 90003 (U.K.)
Released October 1995 (U.S.A.) / June 1996 (.U.K)

No Doubt provided a welcome antidote to the relentless misery of most 1990s alternative rock. Drawing on new wave and ska, the group's upbeat guitar-pop brought them widespread international success late in the decade. *Tragic Kingdom* was the group's breakthrough, eventually selling 15 million copies worldwide.

The band formed in Orange County, California, in 1987, but their early momentum was halted by the suicide of original vocalist John Spence in 1990. Now with Gwen Stefani on vocal duties, the albums *No Doubt* (1992) and *The Beacon Street Collection* (1995) sold poorly, but did just enough to resume an interrupted relationship with Interscope, who gave 1980s singer Matthew Wilder –   best known for his 1983 smash 'Break My Stride' – the job of producing the group's major-label debut.

While *Tragic Kingdom* evokes the sound of Madness and The Specials in places, as big an influence during the album's gestation was the end of the seven-year relationship between No Doubt vocalist Gwen Stefani and the band's bassist Tony Kanal. Fortunately, though, the album isn't all doom and gloom, as the singles 'Just A Girl' and 'Spiderwebs' testify. Both were big hits on U.S. radio in 1996 as *Tragic Kingdom* made its slow climb to the top of the *Billboard* chart. In the U.K. the album wasn't a particular success until the release, in early 1997, of the ballad 'Don't Speak,' a Number One hit.

The key element of No Doubt's appeal was Stefani's über-cool, Madonna-light image, the antithesis of her intense, angsty mid-1990s peers. After two more No Doubt albums she launched the inevitable solo career with *Love Angel Music Baby* in 2004.

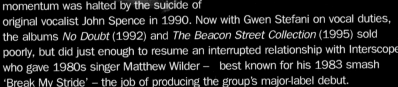

1996

Odelay **Beck**

DGC 24823 (U.S.A.) / Geffen 24908 (U.K.)
Released June 1996

An eclectic, multitalented singer-songwriter, Beck drew on everything from hip-hop to folk rock to create *Odelay*, a landmark of 1990s genre-bending.

Beck first came to prominence in 1994 with the single release of 'Loser,' which became the alternative-rock anthem of the summer. 'Loser' announced the arrival of not just a major new talent but also a whole new genre, christened lo-fi by the music press. Lo-fi had its roots in U.S. underground rock of the 1980s, from R.E.M. to Beat Happening, and describes music recorded cheaply, often on a 4-track at home. Beck was one of several important artists to emerge in the mid 1990s who stuck to this lo-fi aesthetic; others include Pavement and Liz Phair.

Though most of his key albums were released by DGC, Beck had an unusual clause in his contract that allowed him to issue some of his more experimental offerings through smaller independent labels. In 1994, as well as his DGC debut *Mellow Gold*, which sold well on the strength of 'Loser,' Beck put out the albums *Stereopathic Soul Manure* (on Flipside) and *One Foot In The Grave* (on K Records, generally considered to be the original lo-fi label). Beck spent much of 1995 on tour before starting work on the 'official' follow-up to *Mellow Gold* with highly regarded production duo The Dust Brothers.

The Dust Brothers' role in the making of *Odelay* is significant because Beck's album has a number of ideological similarities to its producers' earlier work with The Beastie Boys on their groundbreaking *Paul's Boutique* (1989). Like The Beastie Boys, Beck drew on any number of disparate artists and genres; *Odelay* is an eclectic melting pot of ideas, on which Beck and The Dust Brothers take elements of folk, rock, hip-hop, psychedelia, jazz, blues, movie soundtracks, and the avant-garde to create a dense, original collage of sound. Beck's music has the playfulness of The Beastie Boys but is closer thematically to the sardonic, slacker-generation attitude of movies like *Reality Bites* (1992) than the latter group's frat-party humor.

Odelay was issued to unanimous critical plaudits in the summer of 1996. The album's release was followed by the single 'Where It's At,' a sparse blend of hip-hop beats, a single distorted guitar, and off-hand vocals

that became a minor hit in the U.S.A. and U.K. *Odelay* itself reached the Top 20 in both countries as well as numerous others across Europe. The album spawned three further singles, including the wiry blues of 'Devil's Haircut' and a more upbeat, psychedelic piece, 'The New Pollution.' Each of the single releases from *Odelay* arrived backed with various remixes by eye-catching artists, including Aphex Twin and Oasis guitarist Noel Gallagher, demonstrating the respect Beck already commanded among his peers.

Since *Odelay* Beck has continued to jump from genre to genre in the manner of David Bowie in the 1970s. The low-key, Brazilian-tinged *Mutations* (1998) was originally intended to be released on the tiny independent label Bong Load before DGC realized the record's potential and snatched up the rights to it. *Midnite Vultures* (1999) was clearly inspired by Prince's erotic funk, while on *Sea Change* (2002) Beck veered toward richly orchestrated folk rock before touring with The Flaming Lips as his backing band.

The Score **The Fugees**

Ruffhouse/Columbia 67147 (U.S.A.) / 483549 (U.K.)
Released February 1996

The Fugees' second album and mainstream breakthrough, *The Score*, provided a much-needed alternative to the trend for aggressive gangsta rap in the mid 1990s.

The Fugees formed in 1992 in New York City when rapper Lauryn Hill began to work with MCs Prakazrel 'Pras' Michel and Wyclef Jean, first cousins of Haitian decent who had grown up in New Jersey. The group's name was a reference to the cousins' refugee status.

The Fugees' debut, *Blunted On Reality* (1994), did little on its release to distinguish the group from their rap contemporaries, but a closer inspection reveals a love of reggae and jazz beneath the album's hard hip-hop exterior. These influences became more apparent on *The Score*. Much of the album was recorded at the group's Booga Basement Studio in East Orange, New Jersey, and The Crib in New York. A number of other songs were cut at

Anchor Studios in Kingston, Jamaica. Pras and Hill were responsible for creating most of the album's beats, as well as providing vocals, while Wyclef and another cousin, Jerry Duplessis, assisted with general production.

Shortly after the album's release Hill described it as an "audio film . . . it's almost like a hip-hop version of *Tommy*, like what The Who did for rock'n'roll." While her claims may be slightly exaggerated, *The Score* has a distinctly cinematic feel, and there is a definite thread running through it. Hill's vocals shine throughout, and she sounds equally at home rapping or singing in a sweet, soulful voice reminiscent at times of Nina Simone.

The Score's key track is 'Killing Me Softly.' Based on Roberta Flack's 'Killing Me Softly With His Song,' it provided The Fugees with a huge worldwide hit single, proving to mainstream audiences that hip-hop didn't always have to be about the dark side of life. 'Ready Or Not,' built around an uncleared sample of Enya's 'Song For Boadecia,' was another big international success. Enya's label, Island Records, threatened legal action against The Fugees before the Irish new-age singer intervened, deciding she was happy for the group to use her song after all – for a hefty fee – particularly after discovering that they were not "pro-crime" gangstas. The core trio's love of reggae is represented most directly with a version of Bob Marley's 'No Woman No Cry,' which featured a guest vocal by his son Ziggy and would eventually be the fourth international hit single to be taken from the album, after 'Fu-gee-la.'

Though the group never officially disbanded, there have to date been no further Fugees albums. All three members have since gone on to successful solo careers. Wyclef Jean recorded the Afro-Caribbean-styled *The Carnival* in 1997 and had a hit on both sides of the Atlantic with the single 'Gone Till November,' while Pras released the more hip-hop orientated *Ghetto Supastar*. After several years out of the public eye, Hill eclipsed both her former bandmates with *The Miseducation Of Lauryn Hill* (1998), for which she earned five Grammy Awards. The album topped the U.S. charts, as did her debut solo single, 'Doo Wop (That Thing).'

Spice Spice Girls

Virgin 42174 (U.S.A.) / 2812 (U.K.)
Released February 1997 (U.S.A.) / October 1996 (U.K.)

One of the biggest-selling girl groups of all time, Spice Girls exploded on to the pop scene in the summer of 1996 with debut single 'Wannabe' and the album *Spice*.

Spice Girls had been assembled by father-and-son management team Chris and Bob Herbert in 1994, but the monster outgrew its creator after a year and signed with Simon Fuller's more powerful 19 Management, who also handled Annie Lennox. After honing their talents for a further year, the five girls unleashed 'Wannabe,' which topped the charts in 23 countries. As important as Spice Girls' music, however, was their quasi-feminist 'Girl Power' philosophy, which helped the group become a cultural phenomenon, just as likely to be discussed in broadsheet newspapers as teen magazines. Each girl cultivated a distinct personality, be it 'Scary Spice' Melanie Brown or 'Baby Spice' Emma Bunton.

Spice was put together by a host of highly regarded figures in British pop, including production team Absolute, with string arrangements by Craig Armstrong and mixing by Mark 'Spike' Stent. While there was nothing particularly original about the music on *Spice*, its tight, catchy dance-pop sold in extraordinary numbers across the globe, providing three more huge hit singles, 'Say You'll Be There,' '2 Become 1,' and the double a-side 'Mama' / 'Who Do You Think You Are?' The group followed *Spice* with the album and movie *Spiceworld* (both 1997) before becoming a four-piece – after Geri 'Ginger Spice' Halliwell left – and then drifting into solo careers of varying success.

Antichrist Superstar Marilyn Manson

Nothing-Interscope 90006 (U.S.A. & U.K)
Released October 1996

Marilyn Manson was the latest in a long line of shock rockers, from Alice Cooper to G.G. Allin, and quickly became the most controversial rock performer of the 1990s.

Former music journalist Brian Warner renamed himself Marilyn Manson in 1989, when he began to recruit like-minded musicians in the Florida area. (Like Manson, each of the group members was given the first name of a doomed actress and the surname of a serial killer.) Manson soon became associated with Trent Reznor of Nine Inch Nails, to whose Nothing label he signed. *Portrait Of An American Family* (1994) and *Smells Like Children* (1995) had more shock value than musical worth, but a cover of The Eurythmics' 'Sweet Dreams (Are Made Of This)' started to generate interest outside the industrial-rock underground.

Antichrist Superstar was Manson's first serious attempt at commercial success. Produced by Reznor and Skinny Puppy's Dave Ogilvie, the album was still intended, first and foremost, to stir up controversy, particularly among right-wing and Christian groups. Unlike its predecessors, however, it has a solid musical backing, driven by doomy guitar, synthesizer lines, and harsh, programmed percussion. The album reached Number Three in the U.S.A. in late 1996, shifting two million copies. In the U.K. it grew in popularity after 'The Beautiful People' and 'Tourniquet' both made the Top 30 when issued as singles in the summer of 1997. Manson's follow-up, *Mechanical Animals*, was a bigger commercial success, but by that stage the singer's work had begun to slip into self-parody.

Richard D. James Album Aphex Twin

Elektra 62010 (U.S.A.) / Warp WARP 43 (U.K.)
Released November 1996

Aphex Twin is one of the most important and innovative electronic musicians of all time, and the best-known act on the roster of the pioneering Warp Records label. Though he is perhaps better known for his Brian Eno-style ambient experiments, his defining work is the *Richard D. James Album*.

Aphex Twin started making music as an escape from the boredom of life in rural Cornwall, England. His early work alternated between the hard techno of 'Digeridoo' (1991) and the subtle soundscapes of *Selected Ambient Works Volume II* (1994). The *Richard D. James Album* takes elements of both strands of his previous work. *New Musical Express* (U.K.) called the album "drill'n'bass," but that only tells half the story: the stark, compressed beats are overlaid with melodic synthesizer flourishes and lush string arrangements. In the fast-moving world of electronic music, many records once deemed cutting edge soon sound tired and dated. A decade after its release, *Richard D. James Album* still holds up and still sounds like a blast from the future.

Ever the eccentric – he claims to live in a bank vault and drive a tank – Aphex Twin chose not to release another album for five years, limiting his output to two groundbreaking singles, the industrial nightmare 'Come To Daddy' (1997) and the mutant breakbeats of 'Windowlicker.' Shortly thereafter various rock groups, including Radiohead and Linkin Park, began to cite Aphex Twin as a key influence on their work.

1996

All Eyez On Me 2Pac

Death Row Records 52404 (U.S.A.) / 524249 (U.K.)
Released March 1996

Life After Death The Notorious B.I.G.

Bad Boy / Arista 78612 73011 (U.S.A. & U.K.)
Released March 1997

No Way Out Puff Daddy And The Family

Bad Boy / Arista 8612 73012 (U.S.A. & U.K.)
Released July 1997

In the mid 1990s gangsta rap was the dominant force across the charts and airwaves of the U.S.A. At the time, two of the genre's biggest stars, 2Pac and The Notorious B.I.G., were involved in a high-profile feud. In the space of six months, between September 1996 and March 1997, both were shot dead; neither's killer has, to date, been apprehended.

The most notorious of all rap labels, Death Row Records was formed in 1991 by Marion 'Suge' Knight, whose aim was to create the Motown Records of the 1990s. The Los Angeles-based label dealt exclusively in the gangsta rap that had been introduced to the mainstream by the likes of NWA several years previously. Death Row became an immediate success with the release of *The Chronic*, the debut solo album by Dr Dre, formerly of NWA, which would eventually sell over ten million copies. Its next big success was Snoop Doggy Dogg's debut, *Doggystyle* (1993), also a U.S. Number One. The biggest star to emerge from the Death Row stable, however, was Tupac '2Pac' Shakur. 2Pac's earliest solo recordings, which include *Strictly 4 My NIGGAZ* (1993) and *Thug Life Volume 1* (1994), were issued on Interscope Records and failed to sell beyond the hip-hop underground, but he made his mainstream breakthrough in 1995 with *Me Against The World* and the U.S. hit single 'Dear Mama,' which demonstrated an affinity for sentimental balladry as well as hard-hitting raps.

Unlike many of his contemporaries, 2Pac really did come from the background of bleak, inner-city violence he rapped about. He had already faced charges, which were subsequently dropped, of shooting two off-duty police officers and attacking Allen Hughes, the director of the movie *Menace II Society* (in which he was to have appeared). 2Pac was then jailed in 1995 for sexual assault, just as *Me Against The World* was climbing to the top spot on the U.S. albums chart. By this stage, 2Pac and Knight had begun a bitter feud with various associates of the New York-based label Bad Boy, in particular its founder Sean 'Puff Daddy' Combs and his biggest star, Christopher 'The Notorious B.I.G.' Wallace.

While the exact origins of the hostilities between these two rap labels from opposite sides of the U.S.A. are unclear, the tension was raised significantly with 2Pac's claims, in interviews and on record, that he had slept with B.I.G.'s wife Faith Evans, an up-and-coming R&B singer; 2Pac also suspected B.I.G. of being behind a 1994 incident in which he was shot

several times in the lobby of a New York recording studio. The conflict between these two stars then became entangled with a separate disagreement between Combs and Knight, which again centered on one's infidelities with the other's wife. Knight publicly insulted Combs at the 1995 Soul Train Music Awards before posting a $1.4 million bail bond that saw the release of 2Pac from prison after the rapper had served only eight months of a four-and-a-half year sentence.

In return 2Pac started work on his debut album for Death Row, released the following year as *All Eyez On Me*. This two-disk set gave 2Pac his second U.S. Number One album and spawned his first chart-topping single, 'California Love,' a smooth piece of Dre-produced rap-funk and one of the biggest hits of the summer of 1996. The single's b-side, 'Hit 'Em Up,' summed up 2Pac's feelings toward the Bad Boy family, when he asks: "Who shot me? You punks didn't finish. Now you're about to feel the wrath of a menace, nigga."

The song was, to all intents and purposes, a declaration of war between the presiding rap labels of the East and West coasts, and this war would have its first casualty on September 13th 1996, when 2pac Shakur died in a Nevada hospital. Six days earlier, he had been shot repeatedly while riding away in Suge Knight's limo from a Mike Tyson-Bruce Seldon boxing match. Shortly before the shooting, 2Pac and Knight had been involved in the assault of a member of the powerful Crips gang; Knight is claimed to have deep affiliations with their arch-rivals, The Mob Piru Bloods. Numerous allegations have since been made – against B.I.G., Combs, Knight himself, and The Bloods organization – but no arrests have ever been made. Knight was subsequently arrested for parole violation after the assault incident, and would spend five years in prison, during which time Death Row's influence and popularity fell.

Bad Boy Records, which had recently become part of Arista, enjoyed better fortunes in the wake of 2Pac's death. The label's biggest release to date, The Notorious B.I.G.'s sophomore album *Life After Death* was issued in March 1997. It was the follow-up to his multiplatinum debut *Ready To Die* (1994), which had made him the U.S.A.'s biggest-selling male artist of 1995 and reinvigorated East Coast hip-hop. Several days before *Life After Death* hit the stores, its title became strangely prescient as, like his great rival 2Pac, The Notorious B.I.G. was shot dead in a drive-by shooting in Los Angeles. As with 2Pac's murder, the killer is still at large. *Life After Death* was hugely successful in the wake of The Notorious B.I.G.'s death, topping the U.S. albums chart and spawning a pair of Number One singles, 'Hypnotize' and 'Mo Money, Mo Problems.'

Three months after B.I.G.'s death, his former employer Puff Daddy and his widow Faith Evans released a single in tribute to him. 'I'll Be Missing You,' which utilized the chords and chorus melody of 'Every Breath You Take' by The Police, topped the singles charts in the U.S.A. and the U.K. Stepping away from his roles as producer and label executive, Puff Daddy issued his full-length solo debut, *No Way Out*, shortly after. Puff Daddy – later rechristened P Diddy – has since gone on to become the acceptable face of rap, scoring numerous hits on both sides of the Atlantic, introducing his own clothing line, and dating the actress and singer Jennifer Lopez.

Two of rap's biggest and most talented stars, however, were long gone as the genre they helped popularize grew into a period of mainstream respectability. Both 2Pac and The Notorious B.I.G. have become increasingly popular since their deaths, due in no small part to the regular posthumous releases of half-finished and reworked material. In 2002 noted British documentary-maker Nick Broomfield made *Biggie And Tupac*, an ultimately inconclusive investigation into the rappers' lives and deaths, which serves as a stark warning of what can happen when life too closely imitates art.

■ *Main picture: Notorious B.I.G. on stage in 1996. Inset: Tupac Shakur*

1997

Buena Vista Social Club **Buena Vista Social Club**

Nonesuch 79478 (U.S.A.) / World Circuit WCD050 (U.K.)
Released June 1997

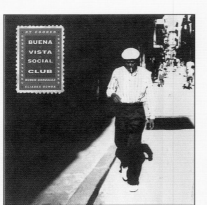

The Buena Vista Social Club is a group of musicians who have been meeting to sing and play together in Cuba since before Fidel Castro's rise to power in 1959.

In March 1996 the U.S. guitarist Ry Cooder traveled to Cuba to jam with them and record some songs, even though most of them were then in their late 70s or early 80s.

One of the constants of Cooder's varied career as solo performer, session musician, and movie-soundtrack composer has been his desire to explore new styles, from Tex-Mex to Dixieland jazz. Having all but exhausted the musical heritage of North America, Cooder chose Cuba as the destination for his next project. Cuban music had been popular in the U.S.A. in the early part of the 20th century but had fallen into obscurity after the 1959 Revolution and subsequent U.S. blockade. Cooder sought to rekindle interest in Cuban song by working with veteran musicians from the island, including the vocalist Ibrahim Ferrer, the pianist Ruben Gonzalez, and the guitarist Compay Segundo. Most of these men were by now in semi-retirement, living in dilapidated apartments in Havana – Ferrer had even turned to shining shoes to earn some much-needed cash.

The performances on *Buena Vista Social Club* have a relaxed atmosphere, evoking a time long before Cuba became, at least in the eyes of the U.S. Government, an ideological pariah state just off the coast of Florida. The songs themselves often date back to the 1950s and beyond and take in a variety of styles. There are piano instrumentals and acoustic folk ballads, joyous traditional dance tunes, and a bolero sung by Segundo and his former lover Omara Portuondo. They were captured with warmth and intimacy by Cooder using analog recording techniques; any digital embellishments would have sounded incongruous alongside such evocative music. The two-week sessions at EGREM Studios in Havana also resulted in the albums *Introducing Ruben Gonzales* and The Afro-Cuban All Stars' *A Toda Cuba Le Gusta*.

Buena Vista Social Club was met with unanimous critical praise on its release the following summer. The album was a minor chart hit in the U.S.A. and across Europe, but gradually sold over a million copies, so making it the biggest success of Cooder's career and bringing unparalleled mainstream exposure to Cuban music.

Not everybody was happy to see the album's release, however. Cooder was fined $100,000 by the U.S. State Department for breaching the embargo with Castro's "evil" communist empire. That didn't stop Cooder from returning to Cuba the following year to make another album with Ibrahim Ferrer. This time he took with him the movie director Wim Wenders, who

caught the recording sessions and a pair of live performances in a heart-warming documentary, also called *Buena Vista Social Club*. (Cooder had previously provided the seminal, evocative solo-guitar soundtrack to Wenders's 1984 movie *Paris, Texas*.) Issued in 1999, the film was also very well received, topping numerous critics' polls and gaining an Academy Award nomination for Best Documentary.

Time Out Of Mind Bob Dylan

Columbia 68556 (U.S.A.) / 486936 (U.K.)
Released October 1997

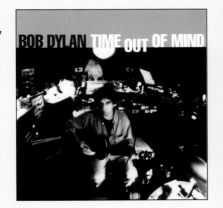

Bob Dylan's 31st studio album was recorded with Daniel Lanois, producer of Dylan's *Oh Mercy* (1989) and U2's *Joshua Tree* (1987).

Lanois had given Dylan's sound a subtle modern update on *Oh Mercy*, an album hailed as a major comeback – it had come at the end of a decade Dylan himself admits "left me pretty whitewashed and wasted out professionally." The albums he made in the intervening period – the sub-standard *Under The Red Sky* (1990) and the traditional-folk sets *Good As I Been To You* (1992) and *World Gone Wrong* (1993) – suggested that Dylan wasn't quite out of his slump yet. At the very least, they implied a lack of solid new material.

Time Out Of Mind redressed that balance in some style with Dylan's strongest set of songs since the mid 1970s. The production is gentle, allowing the songs to shine, though sometimes the ethereal background textures that Lanois creates are at odds with the stark bitterness of Dylan's lyrics. Dylan is unrelentingly downcast throughout, from the opening lines of 'Love Sick' – "I'm walking through streets that are dead . . . my feet are so tired . . . the clouds are weeping" – to the 17-minute closer 'Highlands.' The latter song is reminiscent of 'Desolation Row,' the lengthy final track on *Highway 61 Revisited* (1965), in the way the narrative unfolds, never rambling, despite its length and monotonous structure.

Time Out Of Mind reached Number Ten in the U.S.A. and the U.K. and won Dylan three (more) Grammys, including Album Of The Year.

Come On Over Shania Twain

Mercury 536003 (U.S.A.) / 558000 (U.K.)
Released November 1997 (U.S.A.) / March 1998 (U.K.)

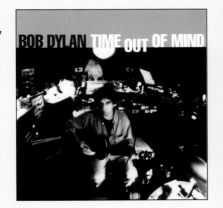

The biggest-selling album of the 1990s, *Come On Over* by the country-pop crossover singer Shania Twain has sold over 35 million copies worldwide.

Taking a leaf out of Michael Jackson's book, Twain drew eight singles from the album, of which three reached the U.S. Top Ten. She was also the first country-based performer truly to engage with MTV audiences.

Canadian-born Twain had recorded an eponymous debut in 1993, but her career didn't take off until she met – and eventually married – the rock producer Robert 'Mutt' Lange. He guided her second album, *The Woman In Me* (1995), toward a more rock-orientated sound, propelling Twain to mainstream pop stardom.

Come On Over was essentially more of the same, but with even more hooks and a more polished, commercial sound. There are still country

elements, such as the fiddles on 'Man! I Feel Like A Woman,' but even they have been processed to fit with the record's modern pop sheen. Twain updated her image accordingly, and now looked less like a country singer and more like she'd just walked out of the pages of *Vogue*. This immediately boosted her appeal internationally. Twain had previously never charted in the U.K., but *Come On Over* climbed to Number One and gave her six Top Ten hit singles, including 'That Don't Impress Me Much,' 'From This Moment On,' and 'Don't Be Stupid.' The latter song charted three full years after the album's release, highlighting the incredible longevity of – and colossal marketing push behind – *Come On Over*.

1997

OK Computer **Radiohead**

Capitol 55229 (U.S.A.) / Parlophone NODATA02 (U.K.)
Released June 1997

With *The Bends*, released in 1995, Radiohead had demonstrated that there was still an audience for intelligent, serious rock at a time when the often throwaway conviviality of Brit-pop dominated guitar-based music in the U.K.

Another group might have been happy with having produced one of the most acclaimed albums of the decade, but Radiohead clearly had plans for a more ambitious follow-up even as *The Bends* was climbing up the U.K. albums chart. The group recorded one of the songs that would feature on *OK Computer*, 'Lucky,' for the *Help* compilation album in September 1995. A number of the biggest British groups of the time were asked to contribute a song to the album – which aimed to raise money for and focus attention on the children caught up in the war in the former Yugoslavia – with all of them having to be recorded during a 24-hour period. Most bands donated a cover or a reworking of an older song; Radiohead's offering was not only a brand new composition but also one of the group's most striking recordings to date.

Around the same time Radiohead also cut a handful of songs to be issued as b-sides to single releases from *The Bends*. One of these, 'Talk Show Host,' gives an indication of the kind of sound Radiohead would soon be aiming for. As impressive as *The Bends* is, it is clearly in debt to the likes of R.E.M. and U2. Built on sparse electric piano and a hypnotic, Krautrock rhythm, 'Talk Show Host' is the sound of a band preparing to head into uncharted waters.

Radiohead's September 1995 recordings were produced by Nigel Godrich, a relatively inexperienced studio engineer who had got his break on *The Bends*. Impressed at how well they worked together, the group asked Godrich to seek out the necessary equipment to record their third full-length album. After touring in support of *The Bends*, Radiohead started work with Godrich on *OK Computer* in a remote English mansion owned by the actress Jane Seymour. The group spent most of the latter half of 1996 working on the album, cutting most of the basic tracks live in the house's large dining-room late at night.

The resulting album is a staggering leap forward from the arena rock of its predecessor, totally redefining what a rock band could achieve. *OK Computer*'s songs shift in time signature and dynamics at the drop of a hat, taking in elements of recordings by artists as wide-ranging as Ennio Morricone, Miles Davis, DJ Shadow, and Pink Floyd. Lyrically, the album is also a huge improvement on its predecessors. Before, Thom Yorke's songs tended toward miserable introspection, but on *OK Computer* his scope widens to include urban decay and alienation in a world overrun by technology, neatly capturing the tense, pre-millennial zeitgeist and dovetailing effectively with the futuristic-sounding musical backdrop.

OK Computer was preceded by the release of the six-minute single 'Paranoid Android,' memorably described at the time as "the 'Bohemian Rhapsody' of the 1990s." This multipart epic opens with descending acoustic-guitar chords, brushed percussion, and chiming lead guitar before erupting abruptly into an electrified section reminiscent of The Pixies at their most aggressive; a mournful choral part follows before Jonny Greenwood ends the song with another deft, economical guitar solo. One of the most ambitious singles of recent times, 'Paranoid Android' is essentially *OK Computer* in microcosm. The album's remaining 11 tracks span the cut-up hip-hop drum loops of the opening 'Airbag,' the claustrophobic, dissonant string arrangements of 'Climbing Up The Walls,' and the glockenspiel-led lament 'No Surprises.'

OK Computer was immediately hailed as a modern classic, topping the U.K. albums chart and reaching Number 21 in the U.S.A. A mere six months after its release, the album was chosen as the greatest of all time by readers of *Q* magazine. In addition to 'Paranoid Android,' *OK Computer* spawned the U.K. hit singles 'Karma Police' – which borrows a chord progression from The Beatles' 'Sexy Sadie' – and 'No Surprises.' With worldwide sales of over six million, *OK Computer* has proven inspirational to a host of other guitar bands, most notably Travis and Coldplay.

The Fat Of The Land **The Prodigy**

Geffen 46606 (U.S.A.) / XL XLS80 (U.K.)
Released July 1997

The biggest-selling electronica album of the 1990s, *The Fat Of The Land* is also one of a select few British albums to enter the U.S. chart at Number One.

Arriving at the height of early-1990s rave culture, The Prodigy established themselves as one the most commercially viable electronic acts in the U.K. with the albums *Experience* (1992) and *Music For The Jilted Generation* (1995) and a stream of Top 20 chart singles. Much of The Prodigy's early recordings – which merged hardcore breakbeats with euphoric dance-music samples – were made in producer Keith Howlett's bedroom studio. In 1996 the group topped the U.K. chart with the controversial 'Firestarter,' a frantic, visceral single built on a nagging guitar riff and the demonic, chanted vocal of Keith Flint, formerly one of The Prodigy's on-stage dancers.

The success of 'Firestarter' and its follow-up, 'Breathe,' considerably raised expectations for The Prodigy's third full-length album, which was delayed several times as the perfectionist Howlett tinkered with the final mix. Both singles were eventually included on *The Fat Of The Land*, which also features vocal contributions from highly regarded rapper Kool Keith and Crispian Mills of the short-lived psychedelia-revival group Kula Shaker. The album was successful enough that Howlett received invitations to work with Madonna, U2, and David Bowie. He turned them all down.

Urban Hymns **The Verve**

Virgin / Hut 44913 (U.S.A. & U.K.)
Released September 1997

Ladies And Gentlemen We Are Floating In Space **Spiritualized**

Arista 18974 (U.S.A.) / Dedicated DED034 (U.K.)
Released June 1997

Two of the finest British guitar-based albums of the later 1990s emerged within two months of each other in 1997, each of them inspired by the same woman.

The upbeat, euphoric songs on The Verve's *Urban Hymns* were informed by frontman Richard Ashcroft's new marriage to Kate Radley, the former musical and romantic partner of Spiritualized leader Jason Pierce, whose *Ladies And Gentlemen* drew on quite the opposite set of emotions.

Urban Hymns was The Verve's third album, and was recorded after a year-long split instigated by the tempestuous relationship between Ashcroft and guitarist Nick McCabe. It was preceded by the majestic, orchestral single 'Bittersweet Symphony,' which reached Number Two in the U.K. in the week that Radiohead's *OK Computer* topped the albums chart, effectively bringing to an end the

waning Brit-pop era and replacing it with something more serious and substantial. The single did, however, cause legal problems for the group, as it contained a small sample from an orchestral reworking of The Rolling Stones' 'The Last Time' by their former manager Andrew Loog Oldham. The Verve had to surrender 100 per cent of the royalties on the song to The Stones' publishing company, ABKCO, while 'Bittersweet Symphony' was rather bizarrely re-credited to Jagger & Richards. Despite this setback, the single's success propelled *Urban Hymns*, released two months later, to the top of the U.K. chart and widened the group's exposure in the U.S.A., where the album reached Number 23. The Verve had split again within a year, however, and this time for good.

Ladies And Gentlemen, meanwhile, was the third full-length effort from Spiritualized, the group formed for the ashes of the cult garage-rock group Spacemen 3. Housed in an elaborate, CD-sized reproduction of a prescription pill packet, the album was an expansive, psychedelic meditation on love, religion, and chemical dependency, and a minor U.K. hit.

Zaireeka **The Flaming Lips**

Warners 9362 46804 (U.S.A. & U.K.)
Released October 1997

A set of four CDs designed to be played simultaneously, The Flaming Lips' *Zaireeka* might have been written off as an eccentric oddity had it not also contained some of the best psychedelic rock recorded in years.

Bandleader Wayne Coyne had started to toy with the idea of music for multiple stereo systems in 1995, when he held his first 'boom box experiment.' He called together groups of his friends and gave each of them one of a set of tapes to play, on cue, on either their car stereos or on portable tape machines. *Zaireeka* is a similarly interactive experience, requiring four CD players to gain the full effect of the music. Each of the four disks contains different mixes of the same eight songs. Depending on the song, Disk One might highlight the rhythm section, Disk Two a choral part, Disk Three guitars and strings, Disk Four piano and vocals. Part of the fun of listening to the album is the different combinations of sounds that form if disks are out of sync with each other.

Given its unusual format, *Zaireeka* didn't sell well, but The Flaming Lips did begin to edge toward mainstream success two years later with *The Soft Bulletin*, the group's tenth album. A critical smash, it shared many stylistic similarities – widescreen, string-drenched arrangements; frail, Neil Young-style vocals – and a producer, Dave Fridmann, with the equally acclaimed *Deserter's Songs* by Mercury Rev, the band led by one-time Lips guitarist Jonathan Donahue.

■ *Below: Wayne Coyne (center) conducts a 'boom box experiment' at the Forum, London, on May 16th 1998.*

1998

Moon Safari **Air**

Caroline CAR6644 (U.S.A.) / Source-Virgin V2848 (U.K.)
Released January 1998

In the late 1990s Air was one of several French groups to achieve unexpected international success.

Historically, French music has been largely ignored – at least by sneering Anglophone critics – outside its homeland and Francophone Canada, aside from a few notable exceptions such as the enduring lothario Serge Gainsbourg and child star Vanessa Paradis. This can be attributed as much to snooty post-war attitudes toward France as to the quality of the nation's music. The first rumblings of a French pop renaissance came with the release of the compilation album *Super Discount*, which featured Air among other less well-known French acts. Techno-pop duo Daft Punk then topped the U.K. chart with the single 'Da Funk' and had a minor U.S. hit with 'Around The World.' Both singles were included on Daft Punk's debut album *Homework* (1997).

With worldwide audiences suddenly able to accept that French music could be cool, the stage was perfectly set for Air's full-length debut *Moon Safari*. The duo of Nicolas Godin and Jean-Benoit Dunckel recorded the album in their own home studio on the outskirts of Paris, making pronounced use of vintage synthesizers, particularly the Mini Moog. *Moon Safari* has an easy, seductive sound, full of soft, hypnotic drum machines, rich synthesizer strings, and echoing electric pianos. The album draws on artists as diverse as Claude Debussy, The Beach Boys, and ELO, which somehow combine toward an impossibly cool end product. *Moon Safari* reached Number Six in the U.K., where it provided Air with the memorable hit singles 'Sexy Boy' and 'Kelly Watch The Stars.'

You've Come A Long Way, Baby **Fatboy Slim**

Astralwerks ASW 66247 (U.S.A.) / Skint BRASSIC 11 (U.K.)
Released October 1998

Fatboy Slim – aka Norman Cook, under which name he had recorded with The Housemartins – was the key figure in British dance music in the late 1990s.

He had scored numerous hits throughout the decade under a variety of pseudonyms, including topping the U.K. singles chart with 'Dub Be Good To Me' (1990) as Beats International. After working as both Freak Power and Pizzaman in the mid 1990s, he settled on the name Fatboy Slim in 1996 and made the critically acclaimed *Better Living Through Chemistry*. Alongside The Chemical Brothers, Fatboy Slim typified the 'Big Beat' style that had begun to dominate the U.K. club scene. Big Beat essentially meant hard, rocky beats served with deep bass lines and catchy, repetitive vocal samples.

You've Come A Long Way, Baby is a more refined, hook-laden update of its predecessor, and was the album that made Fatboy Slim a star. It's not hard to see why. Cook's energy and enthusiasm never lets up, and each of the 11 songs sounds like a ready-made hit. In the end, four songs from the album

reached the Top Ten of the U.K. singles chart, including the relentless 'Right Here, Right Now' and the gospel-tinged 'Praise You,' while the album itself debuted at Number One. Significantly, it was also a hit in the U.S.A. Following The Prodigy's recent success there with *The Fat Of The Land*, electronica seemed finally to have broken out of the underground club scene and into the pop charts, but the genre's popularity ultimately proved to be fleeting.

Ray Of Light **Madonna**

Maverick-Sire 9362 46847 (U.S.A.) / Maverick-Warners 9362 46847 (U.K.)
Released March 1998

Ray Of Light re-established Madonna as the most important female solo performer of the late 20th century.

Up to that point, her work in the 1990s had been inconsistent: the forced sexuality of *Erotica* (1992) and *Bedtime Stories* (1994) had seemed pale in comparison with her best work and both were relatively poor sellers.

In 1996 Madonna revived her fortunes with a star turn in the movie adaptation of the musical *Evita*. Later the same year she gave birth to her first daughter, Lourdes. This led to a creative rebirth for Madonna, who sought out the dance producer William Orbit as her main collaborator on *Ray Of Light*. Orbit's productions draw on the best elements of 1990s electronica, taking in low-key, ambient ballads, unfussy trip-hop rhythms, and euphoric dance pop. Madonna turns in the strongest and most assured vocal performances of her career, the result of singing lessons taken prior to the filming of *Evita*.

Ray Of Light quickly became Madonna's most successful album since *Like A Prayer* (1989), selling 15 million copies. The gothic ballad 'Frozen,' 'The Power Of Goodbye,' and the title track were all huge international hit singles. No longer in thrall to controversy, she became a universal, pan-generational megastar. 'Ray Of Light' did land Madonna in a spot of legal hot water, however, when it was found that the song was based on an early-1970s composition, 'Sepheryn,' by Curtis Muldoon and Dave Curtis. Both were granted a significant portion of the song's royalties.

Painted From Memory
Elvis Costello And Burt Bacharach

Mercury 538002 (U.S.A. & U.K.)
Released September 1998

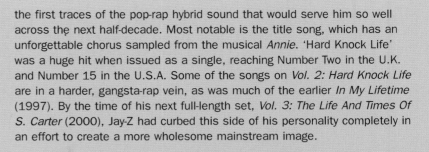

Elvis Costello began his career in the midst of the U.K. punk explosion of 1977 as a cynical new-wave singer-songwriter and continued to record hit albums through the 1980s.

By the start of the 1990s, however, Costello was fast approaching his 40s and could no longer play the angry-young-man role, so he began to turn to more challenging, 'mature' projects. The highest-profile of these was *Painted From Memory*, a collaboration with the legendary popular composer Burt Bacharach, writer of countless hits since the 1960s for artists including Aretha Franklin, Dionne Warwick, Tom Jones, and Dusty Springfield.

Costello and Bacharach first worked together in 1996 on 'God Give Me Strength,' written for the soundtrack to *Grace Of My Heart*. The song won a Grammy Award, prompting its composers to commence work on a full album together the following year. The result was the best work from either party for some time. There is none of the cloying schmaltziness of Bacharach's lesser work, while Costello manages to avoid the wordiness and over-complex song structures that marred some of his 1990s output. Many of the songs are arranged for full orchestra, giving them a timeless feel, to which Costello responds with some of his strongest ever vocal performances.

Painted From Memory was heaped with critical praise in Britain and the U.S.A., and became a minor chart hit in both countries. One of the album's standout tracks, 'I Still Have That Other Girl,' earned the pair a second Grammy, this time for Best Pop Collaboration.

Vol. 2: Hard Knock Life Jay-Z

Roc-a-fella 558902 (U.S.A.) / Northwest-Arista 74321 63533 (U.K.)
Released October 1998 (U.S.A.) / January 1999 (U.K.)

In the late 1990s and early 2000s, Jay-Z – real name Shawn Carter – was like a hip-hop barometer. He worked with the coolest producers – Timbaland, The Neptunes, Kanye West – and the hottest rappers, including DMX, Ja Rule, and Missy Elliott.

He also founded the Roc-A-Fella record label, which later expanded to take in a clothing line and movie production company, and even found time to date Beyoncé Knowles, the sometime Destiny's Child vocalist and solo performer.

Despite all his extra-curricular activities, Jay-Z worked at a prodigious rate, recording ten albums between 1996 and 2003. *Vol. 2: Hard Knock Life* – actually his third album – was his commercial breakthrough and contains

the first traces of the pop-rap hybrid sound that would serve him so well across the next half-decade. Most notable is the title song, which has an unforgettable chorus sampled from the musical *Annie*. 'Hard Knock Life' was a huge hit when issued as a single, reaching Number Two in the U.K. and Number 15 in the U.S.A. Some of the songs on *Vol. 2: Hard Knock Life* are in a harder, gangsta-rap vein, as was much of the earlier *In My Lifetime* (1997). By the time of his next full-length set, *Vol. 3: The Life And Times Of S. Carter* (2000), Jay-Z had curbed this side of his personality completely in an effort to create a more wholesome mainstream image.

Jay-Z's profile continued to rise in the early 21st century with the release of albums including *The Blueprint* (2001), *The Black Album* (2003), and an MTV *Unplugged* set.

Follow The Leader Korn

Immortal/Epic 69001 (U.S.A. & U.K.)
Released August 1998

On its third outing, Southern California alt-metal outfit Korn made it very big with *Follow The Leader*.

The album became the band's biggest-selling record to date – eventually reaching the five-million mark – as well as "one of the most essential alternative albums of the '90s," according to *Rolling Stone*.

In many ways *Follow The Leader* was the ultimate expression of alt-metal as a genre during the late 1990s, which, unlike grunge, was less about song form than song sound. In the hands of lesser artists – and there were plenty of them – the droning guitars, scratching bass, and unrelenting psychobabble could get tedious in a very sort time, but somehow Korn made it work on a commercial level, no doubt owing to the tenacity of its lead singer, Jonathan Davis, as well as the instrumental prowess of guitarists James 'Munky' Shaffer and Brian 'Head' Welch.

While the band's two previous efforts – *Korn* (1994) and *Life Is Peachy* (1996) – had offered glimmers of studio craft, on *Follow The Leader* the sound is completely focused throughout, Davis's visceral gibberish notwithstanding, and the controlled sonic attack presented within served as a blueprint for up-and-coming metal artists in the years that followed. Not that this makes for easy listening by any stretch: on *Follow The Leader* Davis's decidedly dark lyrical content includes grisly tales of childhood ('Dead Bodies Everywhere'), and suicide ('BBK'), capped by a particularly gruesome 'love song' to his girlfriend ('My Gift To You').

While lite raps by guests Fred Durst and Ice Cube and the presence of veteran cut-ups Cheech & Chong – heard on a cover of the 1970s send-up 'Earache My Eye' – offer some comic relief, Davis's resentment looms large throughout. That the hit 'Freak On A Leash,' which reached the Top Ten and still receives regular airplay, was both radio friendly and supremely unnerving is testament to Korn's underlying talent.

A large degree of credit should go to 1990s studio wunderkind Brendan O'Brien – producer for Stone Temple Pilots, Rage Against The Machine, Michael Penn, and others – whose supreme effort in mixing *Follow The Leader* helped bring out the best in Korn's capable rhythm section. An obviously impressed Korn retained O'Brien as producer for the follow-up, 1999's *Issues*, as O'Brien expanded his nu-metal and rap-rock credentials to include the likes of Limp Bizkit and Papa Roach.

Wide Open Spaces Dixie Chicks

Monument 68195 (U.S.A.) / Epic 489482 (U.K.)
Released January 1998 (U.S.A.) / September 1998 (U.K.)

Blending bluegrass, rockabilly, and country rock with infectious pop hooks, The Dixie Chicks' major label debut, *Wide Open Spaces*, was an unexpected international hit, selling 12 million copies worldwide.

Dixie Chicks was formed by sisters Martie Seidel (fiddle) and Emily Erwin (banjo) in 1989. The group issued three albums of fairly traditional country on independent labels between 1990 and 1993, after which the sisters ousted vocalist Laura Lynch, allegedly because she didn't fit the youthful image they wanted. Her replacement, Natalie Maines, was younger and more glamorous and the daughter of noted pedal-steel guitarist Lloyd Maines. The trio signed to the Sony subsidiary Monument in 1995 and began working the following year on a new album, one that would have a much more contemporary sound, ripe for an assault on the mainstream.

Wide Open Spaces does, however, keep a firm footing in country music. Unlike Shania Twain, then in the midst of a similar transformation from country performer to pop star, the group sticks to its musical heritage, albeit with the addition of more pop savvy than before. The fiddles, dobro guitar, and pedal steel remain an integral part of the trio's sound rather than just being a gimmick for the pop charts. The songs are light and breezy unchallenging country, and on that basis – given the perceived political stance of the world of C&W – it may surprise some that, a few years later, Dixie Chicks would be one of the first U.S. groups to date to criticize the second Iraq war. They were encouraged to apologize.

Car Wheels On A Gravel Road Lucinda Williams

Mercury 558338 (U.S.A. & U.K.)
Released July 1998

Lucinda Williams is one of the most feted female singer-songwriters of recent times, whose work blends country, blues, and rustic folk. Always a critical favorite, she found a wider audience at a time of growing enthusiasm for Americana in the late 1990s.

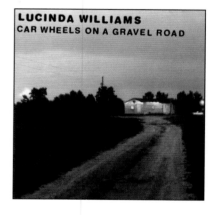

Car Wheels On A Gravel Road had a troubled gestation. Interest in Williams's work had begun to rise following the widespread acclaim for her *Sweet Old World* (1992) and covers of her songs by artists including Emmylou Harris and Tom Petty. In 1994 she signed to Rick Rubin's American label and started work on her fifth album. The initial sessions were produced by Gurf Morlix, with whom Williams had worked since the late 1980s. Deciding that these recordings didn't do justice to her songs, she moved to Nashville the following year and started recording afresh with Steve Earle, but this time she felt the results were too polished and upped sticks again. Now in Los Angeles, she worked with tireless perfectionism on overdubbing the Nashville sessions with former E Street Band member Roy Bittan. Eventually, in 1997, she handed over the tapes for mixing to Rubin, who was in the process of selling American Recordings to Mercury, meaning Williams had to renegotiate her deal with a new label.

Car Wheels On A Gravel Road was finally issued in 1998 to pretty much unanimous critical praise. It topped many an albums-of-the-year poll and was named Best Contemporary Folk Album at the Grammys. Williams followed it in 2001 with her most commercially successful album, *Essence*.

1999

Play Moby

V2 27049 (U.S.A.) / Mute STUMM172 (U.K.)
Released May 1999

A staggering example of how a home-recorded album could become a huge international hit, *Play* sold over ten million copies worldwide after its creator allowed over 200 companies to license its songs for use in television advertisements.

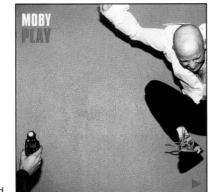

Taking his name from his ancestor Herman Melville's classic novel *Moby Dick*, Moby had an early U.K. hit with the single 'Go' in 1991, which melded a memorable piano sample from the soundtrack to *Twin Peaks* with an unrelenting techno beat. While much of his subsequent work failed to chart, Moby continued to work at quite a pace throughout the 1990s. After two albums of hard techno, Moby issued 'Thousand,' which is notable for being, at 1,000 bpm, the fastest single ever released. The first phase of Moby's career, which included remix work for the likes of Michael Jackson and Depeche Mode, ended with the release, in 1993, of three collections of his early recordings.

In 1994 he signed to Elektra in the U.S.A. and Mute in the U.K., where he had two minor hit singles, 'Hymn' and 'Feeling So Real.' *Everything Is Wrong* (1995) was the first Moby album to gain any kind of exposure in the U.S.A.,

but still failed to chart. Many expected his commercial breakthrough to follow, but Moby confounded all but his most devoted listeners with the political, hardcore guitar rock of *Animal Rights* (1996), which made explicit the singer's militant vegan attitudes. In late 1997 Moby scored a U.K. Top Ten hit with the James Bond theme 'Tomorrow Never Dies,' but the instrumental album *I Like To Score* was a commercial failure.

Animal Rights aside, an important thread throughout Moby's work is that he has always worked alone in a small home studio. One of the prevailing trends to develop during the 1990s and into the early 21st century is the galloping progress in computer-based music production. An earlier revolution in music production had occurred in the 1970s with the introduction of the first budget 4-track cassette recorders for home use, but they still required a full band to be present and often gave poor-quality sound recordings. With the arrival in the mid 1980s of the first samplers and cheap synthesizer modules and then the widespread availability of computer-based recording methods in the 1990s, musicians could make high quality recordings alone and on a fairly small budget. Software programs such as Pro Tools and Cubase allow amateur and professional musicians alike to put together songs in a virtual multitrack environment that requires no bulky, expensive mixing boards. In the late 1990s it also became possible to record CD-quality sound direct on to the hard drive of a computer, eliminating the need for tape machines in home studios. This way of working soon became so widespread that by 2004 all Apple Mac computers were packaged with GarageBand, a basic music-production program.

An early advocate of these new technologies, Moby wrote, recorded, produced, and mixed *Play* in its entirety on his own in a small bedroom studio in his New York apartment in 1997 and 1998. The album's 18 tracks were whittled down from around 200 recorded over the period. Overall, the album has a more restrained, downbeat feel when compared with his earlier, abrasive techno, though some songs – the meaty, beaty 'Bodyrock,' for example – still had the potential to be dance-club hits. The key ingredient of *Play*, however, is Moby's clever use of vocal samples from early blues recordings, all old enough to be out of copyright, and therefore royalty free. On almost half of the album's songs he lays these spare, soulful vocal tracks over fragmented, melancholy beats, light synth strings and the

1999

occasional flourish of piano. He also provides vocals of his own on some of the album. While not a technically strong singer, Moby is aware of the limitations of his voice, so doesn't overuse it, instead adding subtle, touching melodies to a number of songs, including 'Porcelain.'

Play was not greeted with particular interest or enthusiasm on its release. If anything, many earlier Moby supporters considered it to be a transparent attempt at a more commercial sound. The album and the first two singles to be taken from it, 'Run On' and 'Bodyrock,' entered the lower reaches of the U.K. charts but made little or no impact in the U.S.A. Gradually, however, advertising executives became aware of the album and began to use the songs from *Play* as the sonic backdrop to numerous television commercials. Unlike a lot of other indie acts, Moby had few reservations about licensing his music for commercials, though he did draw the line at anything involving animal cruelty, cosmetics, or petrochemicals – but not, strangely, cars. Moby's songs also became a regular fixture on movie soundtracks, including *The Next Best Thing*, *The Beach*, and *Any Given Sunday*.

During the course of 1999 and 2000, every single track from *Play* was used as background music for something, many of them repeatedly. It has been claimed that Moby has earned over ten million dollars from licensing tracks from the album, which led to much criticism of him and his principles from some of his peers and various sections of the media. He has since informed his detractors that he has donated a chunk of the proceeds to humanitarian and animal charities. Many are still suspicious of his motives, however, and the ubiquity of the songs from *Play* in advertisements has blurred the line between whether, in such cases, the song is selling the product, or the product is selling the song.

What is undeniable is that this wide-ranging, often subliminal exposure of *Play* is what eventually propelled sales of the album toward the ten million mark after its slow start. In 2000 *Play* gradually rose to the top of the U.K. chart – providing Moby with three U.K. hit singles in 2000, 'Why Does My Heart Feel So Bad,' 'Porcelain,' and 'Natural Blues' along he way – and reached Number 38 in the U.S.A., where none of his releases, albums or singles, had ever charted before. The album *Play* was still selling strongly in 2001, when Moby had his first U.S. hit single with a reworked version of the track 'Southside,' featuring guest vocals by No Doubt's Gwen Stefani. By this stage the German record label Wrasse had capitalized on the success of *Play* by releasing *Natural Blues Vol. 1*, a compilation album that included the original recordings of a number of the songs Moby had sampled on *Play* alongside other early blues recordings.

. . . Baby One More Time Britney Spears

Jive 42545 (U.S.A.) / 052169-4 (U.K.)
Released March 1999

Britney Spears emerged with this, her debut album, at the tail end of the 20th century, and has since become the most recognizable pop starlet of the new millennium.

In 1993, at the age of 11, Spears was a regular performer on *The New Mickey Mouse Club* alongside a number of other future pop stars, including boyfriend-to-be Justin Timberlake and Christina Aguilera. In 1997 she signed a deal with the large independent label Jive and began work the following year on her debut album with a host of big-name writers and producers. These included Eric Foster White – best known for his work with Whitney Houston – and Swedish pop supremo Max Martin, who had already produced big records for Ace Of Base and The Backstreet Boys, and would, between 1999 and 2000, write huge global hits for Celine Dion, Bryan Adams, Bon Jovi, and *Nsync as well as Spears herself.

Spears's debut single, '. . . Baby One More Time,' topped the U.S. chart in November 1998 and rose to Number One across Europe in early 1999. A key part of the single's success was Spear's image: despite making it known that she intended to remain a virgin until she married, the 17-year-old cultivated a coy, Lolita-like sexuality by way of her ambiguously suggestive lyrics and the skimpy school uniform she wore in her debut video. The album capitalized on the success of the title track in the singles market, topping the charts in over 20 countries and selling over 25 million copies worldwide, and shifting many more records than any of the other U.S. teen-pop acts that flooded the charts in the late 1990s and early 2000s.

Several months after the release of . . . *Baby One More Time*, Spears's former *Mickey Mouse Club* co-star Aguilera topped the charts at home and abroad with the single 'Genie In A Bottle' and her eponymous debut album, which sold eight million copies in the U.S.A. alone.

Supernatural Santana

Arista 07822 19080 (U.S.A. & U.K.)
Released June 1999

One of the leading jazz-rock fusion guitarists of the late 1960s and 1970s, Carlos Santana scored a huge international hit with *Supernatural* in the late 1990s after years of relative obscurity.

The album is notable for the number of high-profile guest performers it features, among them Eric Clapton, Lauryn Hill, and Rob Thomas of the group Matchbox Twenty. *Supernatural* also equaled the record held by Michael Jackson's *Thriller* by winning eight Grammy Awards, and sold over ten million copies, making it far and away the biggest commercial success of Santana's career.

Until the release of *Supernatural*, Santana was probably best known for his hit cover of Fleetwood Mac's 'Black Magic Woman,' as featured on the classic album *Abraxas* (1970). In the ensuing decades his most notable releases were *Illuminations* (1974), a collaboration with Alice Coltrane, *The Swing Of Delight* (1980), recorded with the 1960s line-up of The Miles Davis Quintet (minus Davis himself), and the U.S. hit album *Zebop!* (1981).

Santana hadn't recorded much of note during the remaining years of the 1980s or the 1990s, but was offered a new deal by Clive Davis of Arista Records in 1997. Davis had been responsible for signing Santana to his very first recording contract in 1969 in his capacity as an A&R man for Columbia. He hoped Santana could make a similar comeback to those made by other rock veterans in the late 1990s, including Bob Dylan, who had recently issued *Time Out Of Mind* (1997), his best work since the mid 1970s.

> ## "*SUPERNATURAL* IS A BEAUTIFUL EXAMPLE OF SYNCHRONICITY. EVERYONE WHO PARTICIPATED WAS ON THE SAME WAVELENGTH AND ARTISTIC ENERGY AS I WAS."
>
> *CARLOS SANTANA*

Davis and Santana hatched the idea of an album that would allow the guitarist to work with a number of younger stars, in the hope that this would introduce Santana to a new generation of fans while also appealing to older fans nostalgic for rock's golden age. To that end, most of the songs on *Supernatural* feature the vocal talents of a modern pop or rock singer, but also afford Santana space to showcase his silky-smooth guitar playing. Eric Clapton was the only guest on the album from the 1960s or 1970s, aside from some of the session musicians in the band. 'Do You Like The Way' was sung by former Fugees vocalist Lauryn Hill, and 'Love Of My Life' featured Dave Matthews, who had recently achieved huge popularity in the U.S.A. with the albums *Crash* (1996) and *Before These Crowded Streets* (1998).

The most successful collaboration, however, was 'Smooth,' fronted by Rob Thomas. His group Matchbox Twenty were not particularly well known outside the U.S.A., but had scored a big U.S. hit in 1997 with the album *Yourself Or Someone Like You.* 'Smooth' topped the U.S. singles chart, as did 'Maria Maria,' which featured another former member of The Fugees, Wyclef Jean. Both were Top Ten hits in the U.K., while *Supernatural* itself was a Number One entry there and in the U.S.A. The album's biggest success, though, was at the 1999 Grammy Awards, where it won in eight of 11 categories in which it was nominated, including Record Of The Year and Album Of The Year.

Enema Of The State Blink-182

MCA 111950 (U.S.A.) / 11950 (U.K.)
Released June 1999

Blink-182 was the latest in a long line of groups to take the three-chord exuberance and anti-social attitudes of classic punk and turn it into something much more commercially viable.

The likes of Blink-182 – and similar acts from earlier in the 1990s, Green Day and The Offspring – were able to achieve far more fame and fortune than The Sex Pistols or The Ramones despite paling somewhat in comparison with their 1970s forebears. The band was formed in 1993 by guitarist-singer Tom Delonge and bassist Mark Hoppus. Drummer Travis Barker didn't arrive until after the albums *Buddha* (1994), *Cheshire Cat* (1996), and *Dude Ranch* (1997), joining just before the group signed a deal with MCA in 1998. Despite graduating to a major label, the group saw no reason to deviate from the childish humor of its first three albums on *Enema Of The State.*

The album's content is summed up by the cover image – a porn starlet dressed in nurse's uniform preparing to administer said enema – and the song titles, which include 'Dysentery Gary' and 'Dumpweed.' The songs themselves rarely depart from neat, upbeat two-minute punk anthems, albeit punk that has been expertly crafted by producer Jerry Finn. (Finn had previously worked with a host of other punk revivalists in the 1990s, including Pennywise and Rancid.) *Enema Of The State* was hugely popular in the U.S.A. and across Europe, shifting seven million copies worldwide, and spawned a U.S. and British Top Ten hit single, 'All The Small Things.'

Human Clay Creed

Wind Up-Epic 13053 (U.S.A.) / 495027 (U.K.)
Released September 1999

Human Clay was a huge success in the U.S.A. at a time when most grunge-influenced groups there were being supplanted by the rock-rap crossovers of Limp Bizkit, Korn, and their ilk.

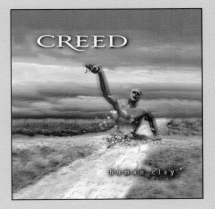

Creed was initially labeled a Christian rock band on the basis of the religious themes of the many of the group's songs. If anything, however, Creed was an act of rebellion for vocalist Scott Stapp against his Pentecostal minister father rather than an attempt to follow in his footsteps as a rock'n'roll preacher.

Creed's debut, *My Own Prison* (1996), sold five million copies despite little interest from the mainstream media and provided the first four of a record-breaking run of seven Number One entries on *Billboard*'s rock-radio charts. In the late 1990s many alternative rock groups tended to disappear after one hit album. *Human Clay* did more than just buck that trend, it topped the U.S. albums chart and sold ten million copies in the U.S.A.

Like its predecessor, *Human Clay* was produced by John Kurzweg, and features a sound highly reminiscent of Pearl Jam. 'Higher,' 'What If,' and 'With Arms Wide Open' dominated U.S. rock radio for the next year, while the latter cut was named Best Rock Song at the 2000 Grammy Awards. Creed's third album, *Weathered* (2001), was equally successful, and holds the record for most consecutive weeks spent at Number One by an album that debuted at the top of the chart. During those eight weeks alone it sold five million copies.

Hours . . . David Bowie

Virgin 48157 (U.S.A.) / V2900 (U.K.)
Released October 1999

Still innovating in his 50s, David Bowie made pioneering use of the internet as a promotional device with Hours . . .

As with every album Bowie recorded in the 1990s, *Hours . . .* was greeted as his best work since *Scary Monsters* (1980). While the album contains a clutch of strong songs, in particular the singles 'Thursday's Child' and 'Seven,' it is not one of Bowie's most sonically interesting recordings. It is notable, however, for the way he made use of the internet in both its conception and promotion. Apparently stuck when it came to writing the lyrics to 'What's Really Happening,' Bowie set up a contest via his Bowienet website in which entrants could listen online to an instrumental version of the song and then had to come up with a suitable set of lyrics. The winner received a $5,000 publishing contract and the honor of being part of Bowie's new album.

As the release of *Hours . . .* neared, Bowie announced that internet users would be able to preview the album in its entirety in the weeks leading up to its on-sale date. Such a move was unprecedented and came at a time when most musical acts were in a state of panic about how internet downloads could harm their earnings. The move clearly helped Bowie, however, as *Hours . . .* became his strongest-selling album in a decade, reaching Number 47 in the U.S.A. and Number Five in the U.K.

2000

The Marshall Mathers LP
Eminem

Interscope 490629 (U.S.A. & U.K.)
Released May 2000

The best-selling and most controversial rapper of the new millennium, Eminem made his mainstream breakthrough with *The Marshall Mathers LP*.

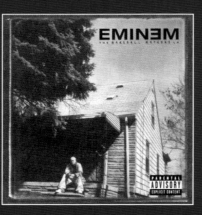

As with its predecessor, *The Slim Shady LP*, the album's lyrical content provoked accusations of homophobia and misogyny, but didn't stop *The Marshall Mathers LP* becoming the fastest-selling rap album of all time, selling two million copies in its first week.

Eminem had made his recording debut with the independently issued *Infinite* in 1996 before finishing in second place at the 1997 Rap Olympics in Los Angeles. This drew the interest of Interscope Records boss Jimmy Iovine, who paired Eminem – born Marshall Bruce Mathers III in 1972 – with the highly regarded hip-hop producer Dr Dre, a former member of NWA who had also worked with the likes of Snoop Doggy Dogg and 2Pac Shakur. Legend states that Eminem and Dre had created the basic elements of 'My Name Is' – soon to become the rapper's first hit single – within an hour of their first meeting. *The Slim Shady LP* followed shortly thereafter, reaching Number Two on the U.S. charts. Eminem's raps, delivered in his scattershot, nasal style, brought him instant notoriety in the U.S.A. He rails against a litany of targets on *The Slim Shady LP*, most famously his mother – dismissed as a bad parent and drug addict – and his new wife Kim, whom he gleefully imagines murdering on ''97 Bonnie And Clyde.'

At the outset of his career, Eminem made repeated claims that his skin color made it difficult for him to gain any respect in the rap world, given that his most famous white predecessor, Vanilla Ice, was seen by many as a lame caricature, a white performer attempting to capitalize on a predominantly black style of music. While that may be true, once he earned a record deal, Eminem's Caucasian skin tone helped him burst through so many more doors than had previously been opened to black rappers. He became a regular fixture on daytime MTV, on popular alternative-rock radio stations, and on the covers of such magazines as *Rolling Stone* and *Entertainment Weekly*. Eminem provided a voice that young, white, suburban hip-hop fans could relate to, further boosting both his mainstream appeal and the controversy surrounding his bad-tempered, foul-mouthed records. With the emergence of Eminem, out-of-touch critics could no longer ghettoize rap as the music of a black underclass. For his part, despite attacking virtually all other minority groups – in what he claims is the voice of an exaggerated character, and one who does not always represent his own views – Eminem appears to be very careful not to say anything in his songs that could lead to him being branded a racist. He is also keenly aware of his debt to his predecessors in the rap world. On the single 'Without Me' (2002) he describes himself as ". . . the worst thing since Elvis Presley / To use black music so selfishly."

Some critics expected Eminem's anger to subside on his second album – after all, much of the dissatisfaction on *The Slim Shady LP* seemed to stem from his poverty-stricken upbringing in a run-down part of Detroit, and he could hardly continue on that track now that he had become a big international star. If anything, however, *The Marshall Mathers LP* ups the ante further. Recorded in late 1999 and early 2000, again with Dr Dre at the helm, this is an even darker journey through Eminem's twisted psyche, full once again of profanity-ridden tales of rape, murder, and drug abuse.

Though the focus of interest and debate with Eminem is inevitably the album's lyrical content, *The Marshall Mathers LP* is highly accomplished musically. The songs are set on a foundation of sparse, staccato drum loops and smooth, liquid bass lines, with additional instrumental flourishes where necessary, be it the synthesized guitar on 'Kill You' or the foreboding bells on 'The Way I Am.'

The Marshall Mathers LP easily surpassed the success of its predecessor, chalking up two million sales in its first week in the U.S.A. alone and topping the charts there and in the U.K. The album was trailed by the single 'The Real Slim Shady,' on which Eminem decries the sudden surge of white rappers to have emerged in the wake of his success before suggesting that he caught a venereal disease from pop singer Christina Aguilera. She is just one of a number of pop and rock stars at whom Eminem takes aim on *The Marshall Mathers LP*: others include Britney Spears, Limp Bizkit's Fred Durst, and one of his white rap forebears, Marky Mark.

As on his first record, Eminem treats all comers with a violent disdain, particularly women and homosexuals. His insult of choice on *The Marshall Mathers LP* is "faggot," regardless of the sexual orientation of his victim. On one of the album's most infamous cuts, 'Criminal,' Eminem announces "my words are like a dagger with a jagged edge that'll stab you in the heart whether you're a fag or a les." This, as well as many other examples of apparently homophobic lyrics, provoked a strong reaction from The Gay And Lesbian Alliance Against Defamation (GLAAD), who began to picket Eminem's concerts and organized a protest outside the 2000 MTV Music Awards, at which the rapper performed and won in several categories. Eminem took some of the wind out of their criticisms at the 2001 Grammy Awards, where he dueted with Elton John on an impressive rendition of the U.K. Number One hit single 'Stan.'

'Stan' was the song that elevated *The Marshall Mathers LP* beyond being merely a huge-selling rap album toward its status as one of the biggest and most important albums of the early 21st century. The track makes use of the melodic chorus from the then unknown British soft-rock singer Dido's 'Thank You,' before Eminem embarks on an epic, cinematic lyric about the title character, a devoted fan who takes his own life after being shunned by the rapper. The single shows off a thoughtful, sensitive side of Eminem rarely seen on his early albums. Just as importantly, however, it provides a pop hook that even non-rap fans could grab hold of. ('Stan' also helped launch the career of Dido, whose 1999 debut album, *No Angel*, became a big international hit.)

The Marshall Mathers LP arrived in by far the most turbulent year of Eminem's life to date. He faced legal action from his mother, suing for defamation of character, and a Detroit clubber, allegedly beaten by Eminem after kissing the rapper's wife. Kim Mathers attempted suicide after hearing the songs 'Kim' and 'Kill You,' in which Eminem again fantasizes about the violent murder of his wife. They divorced in 2002. The net result of all this controversy, however, was more publicity for Eminem and more sales for *The Marshall Mathers LP*, which has to date sold over 15 million copies. Eminem's next release was another global chart topper, *The Eminem Show*, after which he starred in the autobiographical movie *8 Mile*. His success has inspired a host of other white rappers, but none has come close to his talent or staying power.

Metallica vs. Napster

At the turn of the 21st century a technological revolution began that changed the way we listen to and acquire music.

It began with the peer-to-peer file-trading software program Napster, which allowed registered users to swap songs stored in the digital MP3 format on each other's computers. Inevitably, the recording industry was furious that its products were being shared for free online, and reacted with a fervor reminiscent of the 1980s, when it had decided that "home taping is killing music."

Some commentators were calmer in their assessments of the effects of Napster, however, and saw file-sharing as a way for music fans to hear new bands and artists, whose albums they would invariably then buy on CD. They pointed to the fact that, as downloading grew in popularity in 2000, Eminem's *The Marshall Mathers LP* was regularly swapped on file-sharing programs before its release, but still sold two million copies in its first week on sale.

The attitudes of bands and musicians were equally diverse. Some – Radiohead and David Bowie, for example, and more recently U2 – embraced the new technology and looked for ways to integrate themselves and their music with it. Others made pseudo-liberal pronouncements that they made their music "for the people man," and didn't mind if their fans were no longer paying for it. However, many musicians were justifiably worried about the effect that illegal file sharing could have on them and their earning power. The most vocal opponent of Napster and its users was the hard-rock act Metallica, and in particular the group's drummer, Lars Ulrich. The group was incensed when, in 1999, it found that its entire discography was being shared online, for free, without any consideration for the records' copyright and the group's intellectual property.

By early 2000 the Recording Industry Association Of America (RIAA) had instigated legal action against Napster and various U.S. colleges, who, the organization claimed, did nothing to stop their students using the file-sharing program. Metallica made the battle personal when, on May 3rd 2000, Ulrich handed over a list of 300,000 Napster users who, he claimed, were using the software to share illegally the group's music. All 300,000 were banned from using Napster, as were a similar number of culprits named on another list offered up by Ulrich later the same month.

A backlash soon started against Metallica and Ulrich, who was painted in many sections of the media as a poster boy for greedy, corporate rock stars. Many of the Metallica fans now banned from Napster claimed to own most or all of the music they were sharing through the program on CD or vinyl, so were not doing anything to affect the group's financial viability; others maintained that they only traded live recordings of the group, and pointed to the fact that Metallica had always allowed – and encouraged – fans to tape its concerts. It also didn't help Ulrich's cause that, regardless of the legalities involved, he was one quarter of one of the biggest-selling rock groups of all time, so hardly needed the money.

By mid 2001 the RIAA had succeeded in shutting Napster down. Numerous other file-sharing programs soon sprung up in its place, however, including Soulseek, Kazaa, and Gnutella. Many had the advantage – for the file sharers – over Napster that they were completely anonymous and that it was no longer possible to trace who was downloading what.

Ironically, for a program that was once the scourge of the music industry, Napster was relaunched as a legal download site, with the full co-operation of countless international record labels in 2004. To date, however, no Metallica material is for sale on the site.

2000

Kid A **Radiohead**

Capitol 2435 27753 (U.S.A.) / Parlophone 2435 27753 (U.K.)
Released October 2000

After reinvigorating rock music with *The Bends* and *OK Computer*, Radiohead made their 'difficult' fourth album, *Kid A*, notable for the unorthodox promotional campaign that trailed it.

Radiohead found themselves at a creative impasse after *OK Computer*, with frontman Thom Yorke adamant that the group could not continue with the guitar-based sound that had brought so much fame and acclaim – in part because he felt it had been devalued by the emergence of similar groups such as Coldplay, Muse, and Travis. Following fruitless recording sessions in Paris and Copenhagen in early 1999, Radiohead started work afresh in September at their own newly built studio complex just outside Oxford, England, with *OK Computer* producer Nigel Godrich, where they remained until midway through the following year.

Kid A leaves behind the guitar heroics of *OK Computer*, replacing them with an uncompromising computer-manipulated sound, drawing on influences as diverse as Aphex Twin and Charles Mingus. The album's ten songs span the moody electric piano and cut-up vocals of 'Everything In Its Right Place,' the breakbeat-driven 'Idioteque,' and the free-jazz cacophony of 'The National Anthem.'

Refusing to issue any singles or videos from the album, and giving few interviews, Radiohead instead created a number of 30-second blips – short animated clips that were broadcast over the internet. Prior to the album's release, Radiohead had kept their internet-savvy fan base informed of their progress with several webcasts from their studio, during which they debuted songs from *Kid A* and its successor *Amnesiac*.

Despite the group's unusual methods of production and the album's unconventional sound, *Kid A* topped the charts in both the U.S.A. and the U.K.

■ *Radiohead premiered material from* **Kid A** *on their summer 2000 tour of outdoor European venues. Bootleg recordings appeared on the internet mere hours after each performance; the band was bemused to find that large sections of the audience knew the words to the new, unreleased songs within a few dates of the the tour.*

Hybrid Theory **Linkin Park**

Warner Bros 9362 47755 (U.S.A. & U.K.)
Released April 2000 (U.S.A.) / October 2000 (U.K.)

Often lumped together with the numerous rap-metal and nu-metal acts of the late 1990s and early 2000s, Linkin Park is, in fact, a more musically inventive group than many of its peers.

As well as the stock influences of Korn and Rage Against The Machine, the sextet draws on The Roots' hip-hop polyrhythms and Aphex Twin's nightmarish electronica.

Formed by a group of early 20-somethings in 1999, Linkin Park had earned a recording contract with Warner Bros within a year. The group has two vocalists: Chester Bennington is the more traditional alternative-rock singer, while Mike Shinoda is a hip-hop style MC. As well as the usual drums, bass, and guitar, Linkin Park has a permanent turntablist in its ranks. Most members of the multitalented group also dabbled with electronic production techniques during the making of *Hybrid Theory*.

The album was recorded at NRG Recordings in North Hollywood, California, and produced by Don Gilmore, engineer of Pearl Jam's landmark *Ten* (1991). The title *Hybrid Theory*, of course, refers to the fusion of rap and metal contained within, but the album is a subtle work in places, even if, lyrically, it tends toward alt-rock clichés – "Crawling in my skin / These wounds, they will not heal." 'One Step Closer,' 'Crawling,' and 'In The End' were hit singles both in the U.S.A. and the U.K., while *Hybrid Theory* itself has sold in excess of 15 million copies worldwide, making it one of the biggest successes of the early 21st century.

Rated R **Queens Of The Stone Age**

Interscope Records 10007 (U.S.A.) / 490683-2 (U.K.)
Released June 2000

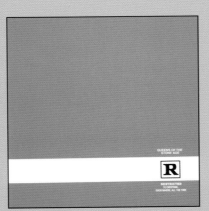

After 45 years of guitars and drums, can anyone make a great rock record? Queens Of The Stone Age proved you could, with the right blend of humor, aggression, lyricism, and mania, channeled into a hook-ridden collection of songs.

Rated R is, by turns, loud, hip, poetic, funny, trashy, dignified, and unexpected. It is 42 minutes of the most varied rock imaginable that comes roaring in with the jump-around-the-room buzz of the ironically titled 'Feel Good Hit Of The Summer,' whose lyric consists mostly of the names of six drugs sung over a backing that resembles a head-on collision between Nirvana and The MC5. It segues straight into the bells'n'riff combination of 'The Lost Art Of Keeping A Secret' with its gently sung vocal over an ultra-grunge chorus. 'Leg Of Lamb' is as quirky as early Roxy Music, 'Auto Pilot' is a 21st-century fuzz-guitar minor blues, 'Monsters In The Parasol' is a hipper ZZ Top boogie, and the 1:42 of 'Quick And To The Pointless' puts a manically hormonal vocal over a neo-T. Rex riff, handclaps, and the "yeah, yeah, yeah, yeahs" of the female backing singers.

The masterpiece of arrangement is 'Better Living Through Chemistry,' where the band pull the amazing stunt of stopping the song at just over 90 seconds, letting a chord drift in low-level feedback for almost 40 seconds, and resuming with a guitar solo, which in turn is pushed aside at the three-minute mark by vocal harmonies, as though CSN&Y had gate-crashed a Soundgarden session.

Parachutes **Coldplay**

Capitol 30162 (U.S.A.) / Parlophone 527783 (U.K.)
Released December 2000 (U.S.A.) / July 2000 (U.K.)

Coldplay became the most successful of a number of British groups that emerged around the turn of the millennium with a sound reminiscent of the anthemic, melancholic guitar rock of Radiohead, The Verve, and Jeff Buckley.

Coldplay was formed in 1998 by pianist-guitarist-vocalist Chris Martin and Phil Harvey – who stepped back from performing and recording to become the group's manager – with the addition of guitarist Jon Buckland, bassist Guy Berryman, and drummer Will Champion. The group issued the independent 'The Safety EP' (1998) and 'Brothers And Sisters' (1999) before signing to Parlophone. After issuing another EP, 'Blue Room,' the group started work on its full-length debut with producer Ken Thomas in November 1999 at Parr Street in Liverpool and Rockfield Studios in Wales.

These sporadic sessions lasted until May 2000, at which point Coldplay emerged with a well-rounded debut that took in wistful acoustic ballads, dissonant – but never tuneless – rock, and the occasional subtle hint of psychedelia. Coldplay cleverly positioned themselves in the middle ground between Radiohead (too arty) and Oasis (too arrogant), the two most feted British groups of the 1990s. *Parachutes* became the biggest album of the year in the U.K. on the strength of two exemplary singles – 'Yellow' and the soulful, piano-led 'Trouble' – and was a minor U.S. hit when released there in late 2000. The group rose to bona fide superstar status with *A Rush Of Blood To The Head* (2002), which has a more epic feel that draws on U2 and Echo And The Bunnymen.

Sing When You're Winning **Robbie Williams**

Capitol 29024 (U.S.A.) / Chrysalis 528125 (U.K.)
Released August 2000

Robbie Williams was the cheeky, chirpy face of British pop in the 1990s and early 2000s, first as a member of Take That, and then as a solo performer.

When Take That, the most popular British teen group since the 1960s, split in 1996, songwriters Gary Barlow and Mark Owen were deemed most likely to achieve solo success. After a shaky start, however, it was Williams who went on to become the defining face of British pop at the turn of the millennium.

His first few solo singles were fairly lightweight, but Williams stamped himself on the national consciousness with the heartfelt ballad 'Angels' and the Kiss-aping rock showmanship of 'Let Me Entertain You.' Williams's third full-length effort, *Sing When You're Winning*, doesn't deviate far from the pattern set by its predecessors, *Life Thru A Lens* (1997) and *I've Been Expecting You* (1998). The album was co-written and produced by his regular collaborator Guy Chambers, who again offers Williams the perfect backdrop to showcase both the roguish bad-boy and the sensitive new man in him. Williams's third consecutive chart topper in the U.K., the album provided four Top Ten hit singles, including the 1980s pop of 'Rock DJ' and a duet with Kylie Minogue on 'Kids.' Try as he might, transatlantic success has continued to elude Williams, even though his next album, *Swing When You're Winning* (2001), was a tribute to The Rat Pack. It did, however, give him a fourth solo U.K. Number One hit single, a duet with Nicole Kidman on the Frank and Nancy Sinatra classic 'Somethin' Stupid.'

Beyond CD

The big question in audio today is what will replace CD. The aging digital format has always had its critics among audio enthusiasts, though the bulk of the population appears happy with it. Indeed, it is a very real question whether there is a long-term future for any physical delivery system for home music.

For many, especially the young, music involves collecting digital music from legal or illegal sources and then storing it on portable devices. With the iPod and similar players now beginning to take on the role of providing music in the home, through players with built-in speakers or simply plugging one into a stereo system, the future of the plastic disk is possibly in the balance.

That has not stopped the electronics giants from conjuring up new hi-tech paths for us all to follow, promising improved sound – even though CDs' promise of "perfect sound forever" still lingers in the memory of many consumers – and, once again, they have managed to introduce competing and incompatible formats. Two systems are currently being promoted: Super Audio CD (SACD) and DVD-Audio. Both use the same plastic disk as DVD video, but there the similarities end.

SACD, introduced by Sony and Philips in 1999 as a replacement for CD, boasts a greatly improved system for digitizing sound – known as Direct Stream Digital or DSD – the capacity for six-channel 5.1 sound, and an inbuilt CD track that gives it total compatibility with the older system: you can play SACD disks on your old system as well as old disks on your new SACD player, without, of course, getting any of the benefits. But SACD remains strictly an audio product, without on-screen graphics or video.

When DVD video was introduced in 1996 it had to cope with carrying two hours of moving pictures and a 5.1 soundtrack on a single disk. That meant compromises, with sound being compressed to the point that its quality fell below that of standard CD. That didn't much matter, since DVD customers were watching television rather than concentrating on the sound, but it did mean that a new format needed to be devised and negotiated if DVD was to be used as a high-quality sound medium. The answer was DVD-Audio, and it arrived in 1999. This provides for the usual 5.1 channels of high-quality sound, though these do not have the theoretical advantages of SACD's DSD system, being effectively an update of the CD system. Where DVD-Audio scores is in having the ability to carry visual program material – namely lyrics, photographs, and short videos – as well as sound. Where it falls down, however, is in being entirely incompatible with CD, though it will play on DVD-Video players.

This incompatibility has become a cause of great concern for DVD-Audio makers, and recently considerable efforts have gone into making a format in which a standard CD is placed on the reverse side of the DVD-Audio disk. The current front-runner is called DVDPlus, but its CD side is not technically compatible with the Philips standard, and some equipment manufacturers have warned that their players won't play it. Nonetheless, as things stand at the time of writing, many of the major labels showed signs of adopting it.

While both formats have their fans, there is a general admission that the improvements in quality are not significant enough to persuade ordinary music-lovers to shell out either on new equipment or premium-priced disks. The multichannel aspect may appeal more to some, especially as increasing numbers of people use home cinema equipment, but for portable or car use the improvements would hardly seem to represent great value for money. And, as things stand, even six years after the announcement of the new systems, there is little music available to encourage buyers to invest. SACD seems to be slightly ahead, but neither system appears to be gaining much in the way of momentum.

What little enthusiasm the record companies can muster for these formats, however, has more to do with their continued battle against copying. Most CDs can be copied easily on any modern computer. In consequence, record companies have recently started introducing locked CDs. Both SACD and DVD-Audio are designed with copy-protection built in – an example of the manufacturers trying to bolt the stable door

Continued on page 300

2001

Celebrity *Nsync

Jive 41758 (U.S.A. & U.K.)
Released July 2001

***Celebrity* marks the culmination of a period of teen-pop dominance on the U.S. charts – which also included Britney Spears, Christina Aguilera, and Destiny's Child.**

The album sold over two million copies in its first week in the U.S.A., falling just short of the sales record of 2.4 million *Nsync had set with the previous year's *No Strings Attached*. The group split shortly after the release of *Celebrity*, however, leaving frontman Justin Timberlake to pursue a career as a more mature solo artist.

One distinct change in pop music in the early 21st century, as online downloads began to rip the heart out of the singles market, is that the likes of *Nsync began to make more of an effort to create stronger, more cohesive albums than the traditional two-good-singles-and-a-load-of-filler variety. Recruiting the cream of contemporary writers and producers was nothing new, but *Nsync took the idea to its logical conclusion, deploying a different team on almost every song on *Celebrity*. The net result is a diverse, kinetic collection of cutting-edge pop. British dance producer BT provides a skittering electronic backdrop for the opening song and lead single 'Pop,' while the slick title track is the work of R&B hitmaker Rodney Jerkins, best known for his collaborations with Whitney Houston and Jennifer Lopez. *Celebrity*'s finest cut is the sultry, smooth single 'Girlfriend,' produced by The Neptunes and featuring a guest vocal from rising rap star Nelly. Timberlake himself also co-produced several songs, while other contributors to the project include Max Martin, writer of Britney Spears's breakout hit '. . . Baby One More Time.'

In Search Of . . . NERD

Virgin Records 11521 (U.S.A.) / 8100972 (U.K.)
Released March 2002 (U.S.A.) / August 2001 (U.K.)

Better known as The Neptunes, Pharrell Williams and Chad Hugo became the hottest producers in commercial rap and R&B around the end of the century, working their magic on hits by the likes of Ol' Dirty Bastard, LL Cool J, Jay-Z, and Britney Spears.

The duo issued their debut, *In Search Of . . .*, across Europe in the summer of 2001, under the name NERD (an acronym for No one Ever Really Dies), just as the single 'Lapdance' had begun climbing up the U.S. chart. The album met with a lukewarm critical response, however, prompting NERD to delay its U.S. release.

Deciding they were unhappy with the sound of the album, as well as taking note of the way it had been received in Europe, Williams and Hugo returned to The Record Plant in Los Angeles to make alterations. The duo removed much of the electronic, programmed rhythm sections, replacing them with taut live guitar and drum parts that at times resemble the nu-metal of Linkin Park or Limp Bizkit. Despite these surface changes, the songs themselves remain much the same, and are in keeping with the vibrant, funky, modern-pop hybrids with which The Neptunes had made their name. The album also reveals Williams as a talented vocalist, with his smooth falsetto providing the focus of most of the songs.

The re-recorded *In Search Of . . .* earned much more positive reviews than the original version, but fell well short of the commercial success of many of the duo's productions as The Neptunes, stalling at Number 56 on the U.S. chart.

Miss E . . . So Addictive
Missy 'Misdemeanor' Elliott

East West 7559 62639 (U.S.A.) / Elektra 7559 62639 (U.K.)
Released May 2001

Alongside her mentor and regular co-producer Timbaland, Missy Elliott was one of the most influential and respected figures in hip-hop in the late 1990s and early 21st century.

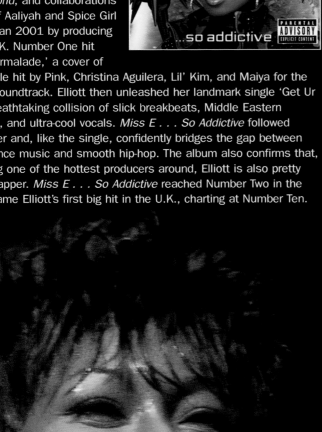

Elliott's early work includes two U.S. Top Ten solo albums, *Supa Dupa Fly* and *Da Real World*, and collaborations with the likes of Aaliyah and Spice Girl Mel B. She began 2001 by producing the U.S. and U.K. Number One hit single 'Lady Marmalade,' a cover of the 1975 LaBelle hit by Pink, Christina Aguilera, Lil' Kim, and Maiya for the *Moulin Rouge* soundtrack. Elliott then unleashed her landmark single 'Get Ur Freak On,' a breathtaking collision of slick breakbeats, Middle Eastern instrumentation, and ultra-cool vocals. *Miss E . . . So Addictive* followed shortly thereafter and, like the single, confidently bridges the gap between cutting-edge dance music and smooth hip-hop. The album also confirms that, as well as being one of the hottest producers around, Elliott is also pretty faultless as a rapper. *Miss E . . . So Addictive* reached Number Two in the U.S.A. and became Elliott's first big hit in the U.K., charting at Number Ten.

Elliott scored further international hits with the album tracks '4 My People' and 'One Minute Man,' which features a cameo from the rapper Ludacris.

The sly line "I'm copywritten, so don't copy me," from 'Get Ur Freak On,' anticipated a rash of rap and hip-hop releases over the next year that were highly derivative of Elliott's and Timbaland's work. Not content to rest on her laurels, Elliott issued the equally impressive *Under Construction* barely a year later.

Songs In A Minor Alicia Keys

J Records / Arista 80813 20002 (U.S.A. & U.K.)
Released June 2001

A prodigiously talented vocalist and pianist, Keys studied briefly at Columbia University before signing a deal with Clive Davis at Arista.

So sure was Davis that Keys was a major new talent that, when Davis formed his own J Records in 1999, he insisted she follow him as one of the new label's flagship artists. Keys began work on her debut album early the following year in her native New York with producer Kerry 'Krucial' Brothers. The album was recorded with a host of talented session players as well as a handful of established stars, most impressively Isaac Hayes, who adds an electric piano part to 'Rock Wit U,' which was also included on the soundtrack to the remake of the movie *Shaft* (2000).

Songs In A Minor is a highly accomplished debut for a 19 year old, drawing equally on smooth 1970s soul, Prince's funky erotica, and the mid-1990s hip-hop of 2Pac Shakur and The Notorious B.I.G. Keys is clearly a talented singer, and manages to rein in the kind of vocal excesses that blight the recordings of so many of her contemporaries. She was immediately tagged as an important new star, the latest in a line of classic singer-songwriters. *Rolling Stone* magazine concluded that "many young female artists court the tweenie market by exaggerating their girlish charms, but Alicia Keys sings for adults . . . we're only beginning to see the depth of her talent." *Songs In A Minor* has since sold over ten million copies worldwide, winning Keys three Grammy Awards and providing her with the international hit single 'Fallin'.'

■ *Main picture: Missy Elliott. Below: her regular co-producer, Timbaland.*

Continued from page 298

long after the file-sharing horse has bolted. It may be that they eventually persuade record buyers to move to the new medium, but the whole back catalog of recorded music history will still be readily available to anyone with a portable MP3 player.

The name MP3 is now applied generically to any compressed digital music file or system, but it really belongs to the original 'codec' – compression-decompression system – developed by Karlheinz Brandenburg and others at the Frauenhofer Institute in Germany. In 1977 Brandenburg joined a project that was looking at ways of compressing sound so that high-quality music could be sent down a telephone line. Their solution was to remove portions of the sound that are inaudible. (Brandenburg used quiet tracks, such as Suzanne Vega's 'Tom's Diner,' as test material, because flaws would be more apparent.) In 1989 Brandenburg was awarded a German patent for MP3 – the U.S. patent followed in 1996 – and set about developing playback software, though with no great success.

That came in 1997 when Tomislav Uzelac of Advanced Multimedia Products developed the AMP MP3 Playback Engine. Two university students, Justin Frankel and Dmitry Boldyrev, then ported AMP to Windows and created Winamp, which soon became widely available free over the internet. The business of 'ripping' and swapping tracks had begun, though it took the arrival of file-sharing software such as Napster before it really took off and the record industry belatedly woke up to what they saw as the threat of their own extinction.

Today, other compression systems are in use, including AAC/MP4 – The Frauenhofer Institute's own replacement for MP3 and Apple's choice for the iPod – and WMA, Microsoft's format intended for use with its Windows Media Player. What these new formats have in common – at the insistence, once again, of the record companies – is 'Digital Rights Management,' allowing the copyright owners to control how the files are used. Files downloaded from Apple's legal iTunes Music Store, for instance, have a built-in limit on the number of times they can be copied, and can only be used on five computers registered with Apple. Despite this, Apple had sold over 500 million songs by July 2005 – just 27 months after opening the first iTunes Music Store.

Much ink has been wasted on the change from physical music delivery to electronic delivery. The change is already being felt in two ways. In the first place, packaging ceases to be of consequence, but then many felt that the jacket died as an art form when the LP gave way to the nasty CD jewel-box. The second result is that artists can no longer lay down a default running order for their music and expect listeners to follow it. Though the iPod and other players will play music in the correct album order, they also shuffle and randomize playback at the touch of a button. Many listeners to digital files enjoy the serendipity that comes when your music is randomly selected from several thousand tracks you know you already like.

Perhaps this method of delivering music has a lot of advantages for pop. It throws attention back to the individual song, the individual track, for the first time since the 1960s. And that may be no bad thing, with Brian Wilson's stated ambition with *Pet Sounds* to create "an album with all good tracks" remaining an elusive goal for many artists.

2001

Gorillaz **Gorillaz**

Virgin 33748 (U.S.A.) / Parlophone 531138 (U.K.)
Released June 2001 (U.S.A.) / March 2001 (U.K.)

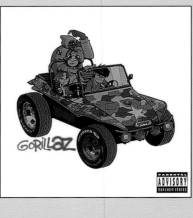

The brainchild of Blur's Damon Albarn, Gorillaz was the world's first cartoon hip-hop pop group.

After recording four U.K. Number One hit albums with Blur in the 1990s, Albarn conceived the idea of Gorillaz in 1999 with cartoonist Jamie Hewitt, best known for the cult comic-book series *Tank Girl*. While Hewitt created the four-piece animated group, Albarn sought out a team of musical collaborators, the nucleus of which consisted of producer Dan 'The Automator' Nakamura, DJ Kid Koala, and rapper Del Tha Funky Homosapien, who had all previously worked together – with Albarn – as Deltron 3030. The album also features contributions from former Talking Heads Tina Weymouth and Chris Frantz.

Sonically, *Gorillaz* builds on the futuristic hip-hop of Deltron 3030's eponymous debut (2000), adding elements of dub, 2-Tone, and Albarn's knack for a catchy pop hook. The album reached the Top 20 on both sides of the Atlantic – giving Albarn his first true taste of mainstream success in the U.S.A. – while 'Clint Eastwood,' '19-2000,' and 'Rock The House' were all U.K. hit singles.

The musicians involved originally attempted to keep their identities a secret, but the music press soon got wind of who was involved. That didn't stop the group performing live behind a large screen, on to which their animated alter egos were projected. Albarn next refocused his energies on Blur – who issued their strongest album to date, *Think Tank*, in 2003 – before recording a second Gorillaz album, *Demon Days*, in 2005.

■ *Gorillaz perform live at the 2002 Brit Awards at Earls Court, in London, England. The musicians played behind screens, on to which images of the cartoon band were projected.*

White Blood Cells The White Stripes

Sympathy For The Record Industry SFTRI 660 (U.S.A. & U.K.)
Released July 2001

The White Stripes were at the forefront of a new wave of pared-down, retro rock groups charged with reinvigorating guitar-based music in the early 2000s.

The group, unusually, is a blues-based, bass-less duo, made up of guitarist-vocalist Jack White and drummer Meg White, both of whom stick to a strict dress code of red, white, and black. Adding to their quirky appeal was the pair's initial claim to be siblings, though the *Detroit Free Press* soon discovered that they are, in fact, a divorced couple, and that Jack had taken Meg's surname. (Despite this, he still introduces his ex-wife on stage as "my big sister.")

The White Stripes' sound is an electrified update of the early blues of Blind Willie McTell or Robert Johnson, with a hint of late-1960s psychedelia. *White Blood Cells* was the group's third album, and was cut in the winter of 2001 at Easley-McCain Recording in Memphis. With its ancient tube amplifiers, vintage microphones, and clunky, analog tape machines, Easley-McCain was the perfect venue for Jack to indulge his love of pre-digital recording equipment. While a White Stripes on-stage performance is the picture of minimalism, *White Blood Cells* does make some concessions to modern, multitrack recording, as several songs are underpinned by Hammond organ, while others are embellished by piano and over-dubbed vocal harmonies. Though never a huge chart hit, *White Blood Cells* caused quite a stir on its release in the U.K., with some critics going so far as to say that Jack White was the greatest guitarist since Jimi Hendrix. A single, 'Hotel Yorba,' reached the U.K. Top 30.

Is This It The Strokes

RCA 68101 (U.S.A.) / Rough Trade RTRADE CD/LP 30 (U.K.)
Released September 2001

The Strokes were the most successful of a new wave of garage-rock groups to emerge during the early 2000s.

Vocalist and songwriter Julian Casablancas – son of the Elite modeling agency CEO John Casablancas – guitarist Nick Valensi, and drummer Fab Moretti started playing together in 1998 after meeting at the exclusive Dwight School in Manhattan. Bassist Nikolai Fraiture and guitarist Albert Hammond Jr – whose singer-songwriter father, also named Albert, penned the hits 'It Never Rains In Southern California' and 'The Air That I Breathe' – joined in 1999.

In 2001 the *New Musical Express* (U.K.) placed The Strokes at the head of its "new rock revolution," alongside a number of other New York groups and Detroit duo The White Stripes. While they did succeed in making their home city the epicenter of cool guitar-based music for the next few years, The Strokes lacked the musical innovations of their forebears, notably The Velvet Underground and Television, to whom their sound was so indebted. Given a spacious, uncluttered sheen by producer Gordon Raphael, *Is This It* reached Number Two in the U.K. – where The Strokes became the most hyped new band since Oasis in the mid 1990s – and spawned a pair of British hit singles, 'Hard To Explain' and 'Last Nite.' The album was less successful in the U.S.A., where it stalled at Number 74. Issued in the aftermath of the World Trade Center terrorist attacks, the U.S. edition of *Is This It* omits the scathing 'New York City Cops,' and opts for an abstract, psychedelic cover instead of the mildly controversial gloved-hand-on-naked-buttock U.K. edition.

2002

Original Pirate Material The Streets

Atlantic 93181 (U.S.A.) / Locked On 0927 43568 (U.K.)
Released October 2002 (U.S.A.) / March 2002 (U.K.)

Boy In Da Corner Dizzee Rascal

Matador Records OLE600 (U.S.A.) / XL Recordings XL150 (U.K.)
Released July 2003

While U.S. rap and hip-hop has sold strongly in Britain since the late 1980s, there was no viable homegrown response until the emergence of the U.K. garage scene in the early 2000s.

U.K. garage is a loose term to describe sped-up drum & bass rhythms overlaid with spoken or sung vocals. After a clutch of hit singles by other artists, The Streets' *Original Pirate Material* became the genre's first big critical and commercial success in the albums market.

The Streets is the recording pseudonym of Mike Skinner, a native of Birmingham, England, a city not particularly well known for its hip-hop stars. Recorded, like all of his music, on a home computer, *Original Pirate Material* builds on the musical template of fast, stuttering U.K.-garage beats by adding elements of the likes The Specials and Blur.

Where his predecessors So Solid Crew's gritty, inner-city caricatures suggested they had listened to too much mid-1990s gangsta rap, *Original Pirate Material* provides a more realistic snapshot of urban British life in the early 21st century. Skinner's half-spoken, half-rapped lyrics reveal all manner of seemingly mundane but captivating details, from drunkenly playing computer games to going out for Indian takeout food, while on 'The Irony Of It All' Skinner and a friend debate the relative merits of alcohol over cannabis. The Streets earned a mainstream following in the U.K. with the successful singles 'Let's Push Things Forward' and 'Don't Mug Yourself,' while the album was a cult hit in the U.S.A.

Several months after the release of *Original Pirate Material* came 'I Luv U,' the debut single by the 17-year-old Dizzee Rascal (aka Dylan Mills). Like Skinner, the London-born MC and producer recorded the single and the following year's full-length album *Boy In Da Corner* on his home computer, utilizing skills picked up at a community music project. *Boy In Da Corner* is a much more volatile, moody album than The Streets' debut, and has a sparser, grittier production highly evocative of its gestation. Dizzee's vocal style has more in common with traditional rap than Skinner's, but still has a distinct Britishness to it.

Dizzee Rascal had a U.K. chart hit with the single 'Fix Up Look Sharp' from the album, which won the 2003 Mercury Music Prize. Not only is he far and away the youngest recipient of the award to date, his is also the most outré, cutting-edge album to win it, making his victory all the more impressive. In 2004 *Boy In Da Corner* was licensed by Matador Records for release in the U.S.A., where it has received positive reviews but failed to make any great waves commercially.

2002

Come Away With Me **Norah Jones**

Blue Note 32088 (U.S.A.) / Parlophone 5386092 (U.K.)
Released February 2002

Norah Jones was one of the most startling breakout successes of the early 2000s, scoring a huge international hit and countless Grammys with her debut.

Come Away With Me is an effortless blend of folk, jazz, and blues, accentuated by Jones's cool vocal delivery – which drew comparisons with Nina Simone and Billie Holiday – and a flair for concise, catchy melodies.

Jones is the daughter of the world's most famous sitar player, Ravi Shankar, but was brought up by her mother in Texas. She studied jazz piano at the University Of North Texas for two years before moving to New York in 1999 at the age of 20. She originally intended only to stay for the summer, but soon got hooked on the city's musical nightlife, playing in folksy coffee houses and jazz clubs. A demo tape of songs written with guitarist Jesse Harris and bassist Lee Alexander caught the attention of the famous jazz label Blue Note, who signed Jones in early 2001. She spent the first half of the year honing her songwriting and performing talents before commencing work on her debut album at Sorcerer Sound and Allaire Studios in New York. Production duties were split between Craig Street and the legendary Arif Mardin, who had previously worked with a galaxy of stars, including Dusty Springfield and Aretha Franklin. There are also a number of impressive guest musicians – particularly given that the album is Jones's debut – including jazz guitarist Bill Frisell and drummer Brian Blade.

Come Away With Me is a remarkably assured first effort. Though the overall feel is one of gentle, acoustic-guitar pop, there are elements of jazz, folk, soul, blues, and country within the songs. Unlike the equally prodigious Alicia Keys, Jones eschews contemporary pop production in favor of a self-contained, timeless sound. The songs are split between covers – notably an arresting rendition of Hank Williams's 'Cold Cold Heart' – and original material written by Jones with Harris and Alexander. These include the moody, subtle title track and the lighter, languid 'Don't Know Why,' a Top 30 hit in the U.S.A. and Britain.

Audiences took to Jones's album almost immediately, confounding all expectations of what was assumed might be a modest crossover success, not a worldwide smash hit. *Come Away With Me* topped the charts across Europe and in the U.S.A., and has sold over 18 million copies. Jones cleaned up at the 2002 Grammy Awards, taking home six trophies including Record, Song, and Album Of The Year.

Jones's success opened the doors for a number of other performers with a similar cross-genre sound. Perhaps surprisingly, they have tended mostly to hail from Britain. Most notable of this new breed of jazz-based youngsters is Jamie Cullum, who rose to fame in 2003 on the back of his *Twentysomething* debut. Among the others were Katie Melua, Amy Winehouse, and Joss Stone, the latter of whom emerged at the age of 16 in 2004 with an astoundingly mature voice and an acclaimed album, *Mind, Body And Soul*.

Yankee Hotel Foxtrot *Wilco*

Nonesuch 7559-79669 (U.S.A. & U.K.)
Released April 2002

The fourth Wilco album was much more than just a triumph over the difficult circumstances surrounding its creation and release: it was the metamorphosis of the rootsy Americana alt.country genre from caterpillar into butterfly.

Wilco's lynchpin, Jeff Tweedy, first attracted attention as a member of Uncle Tupelo, a Belleville, Illinois, high-school band dedicated to the notion of blending their love of punk rock with their equal affection for traditional American roots music. After four acclaimed but financially unrewarding albums, Uncle Tupelo splintered, with various other members going on to become guiding lights in such bands as Son Volt, Bottle Rockets, and The Gourds, while Tweedy formed Wilco. Wilco's 1995 debut, *AM*, was unimpressive but, by the time of 1999's *Summer Teeth*, they had quantum-leaped to an album that skillfully combined elements of classic country with the worlds of avant-garde, ambient, and psychedelic music.

> "THE RECORD NAMED ITSELF. ONE THING THAT INTRIGUED ME ABOUT THE STATIONS THAT BROADCAST IN CODE WAS THE RANDOMNESS OF COMMUNICATION, THE SAME THING THAT ALWAYS INTRIGUED ME ABOUT MUSIC AND PUTTING OUT RECORDS."
>
> *JEFF TWEEDY*

Work on *Yankee Hotel Foxtrot* started optimistically in Chicago, on a Reprise Records budget of $85,000, but Tweedy's ongoing search for new avenues of musical expression led to conflicts with multi-instrumentalist Jay Bennet and drummer Ken Coomer, both of whom quit during recording. The kind of ideas that disturbed the more traditionally inclined Bennet would probably have been the decision, during the recording of 'Poor Places,' to set up instruments that could play themselves – including a drum machine, a keyboard with several keys taped down, and a guitar strummed by an electric fan – and then just let them roll. The song ends with a disembodied sample from a short-wave radio transmission of a woman reciting the phonetic code-words "yankee hotel foxtrot," which gave the album its title.

Tweedy has revealed that another technique involved recording songs with standard band arrangements and then, "just to see how sturdy the melody was," breaking them down and rebuilding them, sometimes adding totally random noises. "We worked along film-editing lines," he explains, "trying to think about pacing and the overall shape, trying to make something that started one place and ended in another."

The album was scheduled for release during September of 2001, and an excited media buzz was already building when suddenly everything changed. "Initially there seemed to be some excitement about the songs we were sending in," remembers Tweedy, "but once we got serious about making the record and shaping it into what it became, one of the comments from them was, 'It keeps getting worse and worse.'" Essentially, the record company couldn't hear any hits and demanded changes. Instead, the band stuck to its guns and negotiated a release from the Reprise contract, which included buying the rights to the album. Shortly afterward it became available on Wilco's website, and rapidly notched up 30,000 hits.

Several companies, Reprise among them, were now clamoring to sign the band. The eventual winners were Nonesuch, and on release the album drew rave reviews and debuted at Number 13 with an immediate sale of 56,000 copies. Since then it has earned two Grammies, much to the chagrin of Reprise, which is, like Nonesuch, a division of the Time-Warner group. Tweedy takes understandable delight in pointing out to interviewers that this means Time-Warner has paid for *Yankee Hotel Foxtrot* twice.

Best Of Both Worlds *R Kelly And Jay-Z*

Universal 586783 (U.S.A.) / Jive 9223512 (U.K.)
Released March 2002

Expectations were high for *Best Of Both Worlds*, a collaboration between two of the most successful urban-music performers of recent times.

The two stars first collaborated in 2000, when Jay-Z guested on a remix of Kelly's 'Fiesta.' It was a hit, and prompted them to start work on a full album together the following year. *Best Of Both Worlds* finds a pretty formulaic middle ground between both artists' work: Jay-Z raps the verses, Kelly sings the choruses. Though at times the performances sound half-hearted, where the album works Jay-Z and Kelly are a perfect match, particularly on the single 'Get This Money.' Both had hopes that it might end up as the biggest-selling hip-hop album ever made. In the event, *Best Of Both Worlds* didn't reach its potential and falls well short of either Kelly's or Jay-Z's best work.

The release of the album was overshadowed by a string of allegations about Kelly's sexual relationships with a number of underage girls. Radio stations banned his songs and some former fans organized protests against him, which did little to help the album's commercial performance. It debuted at Number Two in the U.S.A., but quickly fell out of the charts. Undeterred by its poor performance, which in no way equals the multiplatinum successes of either artist's solo work, Jay-Z and Kelly reconvened for *Unfinished Business* in 2004. That, too, failed both critically and commercially, while Kelly left a co-headlining tour amid rumors of bad blood between the duo.

■ *Below: a still from* I Am Trying To Break Your Heart, *Sam Jones's documentary movie about the making of Wilco's* Yankee Hotel Foxtrot. *Inset: the cover of the DVD edition.*

2002

Justified Justin Timberlake

Jive 41823 (U.S.A.) / 9224632 (U.K.)
Released November 2002

After recording the two fastest-selling albums ever in the U.S.A. as a member of *Nsync, there was perhaps little left for Justin Timberlake to prove. Nonetheless, 18 months after the release of *Celebrity* he launched his solo career with a more mature sound and image.

Justified was recorded in the main with production wizards The Neptunes. It is, essentially, a 21st-century update of Michael Jackson's *Off The Wall* and *Thriller*: not only is the music clearly indebted to Jackson but so was Timberlake's new image and moonwalk-style dance routine.

Thematically, the album has a 'before and after the breakup' air, which most commentators assumed must surely allude to the end of Timberlake's romantic relationship with fellow pop starlet Britney Spears, with whom he had starred in *The New Mickey Mouse Club* a decade earlier. Such suspicions were confirmed when the promo video for the single 'Cry Me A River' featured Timberlake singing to a Britney look-alike.

Regardless, this was the album that made Timberlake a star in his own right rather than just being Britney's ex or the guy from *Nsync. *Justified* peaked at Number Two on the U.S. chart and provided three further hit singles: 'Like I Love You,' 'Rock Your Body,' and 'Senorita.' It also won a Grammy for Best Pop Vocal Album.

Timberlake's former bandmates fared less well as solo performers. JC Chasez's *Schizophrenic* was a U.S. hit, but paled in comparison with *Justified* both in terms of sales and artistic merit.

2003

Dangerously In Love Beyoncé

Sony 86386 (U.S.A.) / Columbia 5093952 (U.K.)
Released May 2003

Like Justin Timberlake the year before, in 2003 Beyoncé Knowles, formerly of Destiny's Child, made the successful transition from teen-pop group member to solo star.

Destiny's Child had been one of the most commercially successful female pop acts of the late 1990s and early 2000s. *The Writing's On The Wall* (1999) and *Survivor* (2001) both sold in extraordinary quantities, while the group had a string of international hit singles including 'Bills, Bills, Bills,' 'Independent Women Part 1,' and 'Bootylicious.' In 2002 the three group members announced a desire to pursue solo careers. Always the focal point of the band, Beyoncé's has been by far the most successful.

Dangerously In Love keeps to pretty much the same formula as *Survivor*, but the songs sound less throwaway. Smooth soul ballads vie for space with 1970s-style disco-inflected dance tracks, provided by an impressive think tank of contemporary producers, including Missy Elliott and OutKast's Big Boi. The album topped the charts in the U.S.A. and the U.K. and provided a huge international hit single, 'Crazy In Love,' on which Beyoncé duets with her beau, the rapper Jay-Z. (The pair had previously collaborated on his ''03 Bonnie and Clyde.') A year later Beyoncé reunited with Destiny's Child for what is presumably the group's swansong, *Destiny Fulfilled*. It has been alleged that the group's other two members drafted an agreement to ensure that Beyoncé didn't stand centerstage in any press photographs during the promotion of the album, suggesting that this might not have been the most amicable of reunions.

Speakerboxxx / The Love Below OutKast

La Face 53022 (U.S.A.) / Arista 82976 52905 2 (U.K.)
Released September 2003

Essentially a pair of solo albums by the group's two members, *Speakerboxxx / The Love Below* contains some of the most innovative and forward-thinking hip-hop of recent years.

Big Boi's *Speakerboxxx* pushes out the boundaries of contemporary rap with hard-edged techno production, while Andre 3000's *The Love Below* is in a melting pot of soul, funk, rock, jazz, and hip-hop.

After recording a trio of acclaimed albums in the 1990s, OutKast became a bona fide pop phenomenon with the release of *Stankonia* (2000) and its resplendent singles 'BOB' and 'Ms Jackson,' a U.S. Number One hit. (The Ms Jackson in question is actually the mother of the singer Erykah Badu, with whom Andre 3000 had a child in 1997.) The retrospective compilation album *Big Boi And Dre Present . . . OutKast* (2001) effectively drew a line under the first phase of the group's career, as it was subsequently announced that the duo was working separately on what were perceived to be solo albums.

In fact, the pair decided to issue these two very different albums in one package, under the unifying OutKast banner. Big Boi's *Speakerboxxx* is the more conventional of the two, but is still leaps and bounds ahead of most of his rap contemporaries. Musically, the album is built around a blend of retro drum-machine sounds and cutting-edge electronic rhythms, overlaid with deep bass pulses and funky guitar flourishes. For the most part, the songs retain an upbeat, post-disco feel, though in 'War' the album does contain a rare criticism from an American artist of the Bush administration's War On Terror: "Operation Anaconda: ask yourself, was it full of bleeps and blunders? / Did they ever find Osama? And why the fuck did Daniel Pearl have to pay the price of his life?" *Speakerboxxx* also contains the only direct collaboration between Big Boi and Andre 3000, 'Ghetto Musick.'

The album's other disk is a completely different animal, and one that makes a mockery of genre categorization. *The Love Below* begins with a sweeping orchestral title track, before 'Love Hater' somehow bridges the gap between psychedelic funk and swinging 1950s jazz. Unusually for a supposed hip-hop album, *The Love Below* is laced with acoustic guitars and warm, vintage synthesizer parts. The rest of the album takes in soulful electro-pop ('She Lives In My Lap'), a touching, piano-led tribute to Andre's mother ('She's Alive'), a fuzz bass-led duet with the equally eccentric Kelis ('Dracula's Wedding'), and a restrained collaboration with Norah Jones ('Take Off Your Cool'). *The Love Below* also featured one of the best and most recognizable singles of 2003, 'Hey Ya!'

Speakerboxxx / The Love Below was the first OutKast album to top the U.S. albums chart – the group's three previous efforts all stalled at Number Two – and reached the Top Ten in the U.K. The album provided four international hit singles, the aforementioned 'Ghetto Musick' and 'Hey Ya!' plus Big Boi's 'The Way You Move' and Andre's 'Roses.' The album also won the duo three Grammys, including Album Of The Year.

■ *Main picture: Beyoncé struts her stuff on stage in 2003. Inset: Big Boi (left) and Andre 3000 of OutKast.*

2003

Permission To Land The Darkness

Atlantic 60817 (U.S.A.) / Must Destory 5046 67452 (U.K.)
Released July 2003

Out of nowhere, The Darkness made the oft-derided sound and image of late-1970s hard rock fashionable again.

Written off at first as a novelty act, The Darkness began to look more and more like the real thing as *Permission To Land* climbed to the top of the British charts and became a cult hit in the U.S.A.

The Darkness formed on New Year's Eve 1999 in Lowestoft, England – a small coastal town not exactly known for its musical heritage – by vocalist-guitarist Justin Hawkins and his guitar-playing younger brother Dan. Adding bassist Frankie Poullain and drummer Ed Graham, the group built up a

reputation as a highly entertaining live act. The Darkness drew unapologetically on the big hair, spandex, falsetto vocals, and wild guitar soloing of Queen and Aerosmith, and soon signed a deal with the independent label Must Destroy. The group was often pilloried by a picky music press, but won over huge swathes of the British public with the singles 'I Believe In A Thing Called Love' and 'Get Your Hands Off My Woman.'

After a triumphant, televised performance at the *Glastonbury Festival*, *Permission To Land* topped the U.K. albums chart and stayed in its upper reaches for much of the next year. While some elements might have been included self-consciously for entertainment purposes, the album is underpinned by fine musicianship and catchy songwriting. *Permission To Land* became harder to write off as a joke when it entered the U.S. Top 40 in early 2004.

Elephant The White Stripes

V2 27184 (U.S.A. & U.K.)
Released April 2003

Rock history is littered with bands who disappeared into 48-track high-tech studios for years of overdubbing, only to end up with a record that couldn't match its predecessor cut in a fortnight on 16-track.

The White Stripes didn't fall into that trap, however. Instead the duo recorded the follow-up to their breakthrough album *White Blood Cells* in ten days in the sparse, retro environment of Toe Rag Studios in east London, England. As Jack White put it: "Having a huge budget or unlimited time or tracks to make an album, all that opportunity robs you of a lot of creativity, because you're not focused or confined. We purposefully confined ourselves to help us be more focused."

Elephant doesn't deviate much from the template of *White Blood Cells*, but then it doesn't need to. Each of the 14 songs is dispatched in The White Stripes' trademark economical garage-blues style. The only surprise element is the multitracked vocal part on 'There's No Home For You Here,' which brings to mind Queen's 'Bohemian Rhapsody.' 'Seven Nation Army' opens the set with what sounds like a bass, but is actually just Jack White's guitar played through an octave pedal. The album also includes the primal, staccato 'Hardest Button To Button' and 'It's True That We Love One Another,' a duet with cult British singer Holly Golightly on which Jack mocks the endless media speculation about the group.

Elephant topped the U.K. albums chart and provided The White Stripes with their first widespread success in the U.S.A., where it peaked at Number Six. It was named Best Alternative Music Album at the 2003 Grammy Awards, while 'Seven Nation Army' was chosen as the year's Best Rock Song.

2004

Smile Brian Wilson

Nonesuch 79846 (U.S.A. & U.K.)
Released September 2004

Brian Wilson's *Smile* – a "teenage symphony to God" conceived in 1966, but not completed or issued until 2004 – had by far the longest gestation of any popular-music album.

For decades it was *the* great lost work of the rock era, a supposed masterpiece that might have surpassed even The Beatles' *Sgt Pepper* had Wilson's group, The Beach Boys, released it on schedule in 1967.

Wilson sought out a lyricist to collaborate with him and help him realize his ideas for *Smile*, as he had done for *Pet Sounds* in 1966. He chose Van Dyke Parks, a songwriter and producer who, like Wilson, was considered to be something of a musical prodigy. He and Parks started to write together in May 1966 at the piano Wilson had situated in an indoor sandbox at his Los Angeles home – installed to evoke the feeling of being at the beach. The songs they wrote were intended to represent a journey through the history and musical heritage of the U.S.A.

The prototype for *Smile* was 'Good Vibrations,' Wilson's first "pocket symphony" – as he called it – recorded during the late spring and summer of 1966. Wilson had pioneered his 'modular' recording technique on 'Good Vibrations,' taping the different parts of the song separately before piecing the various sections together into a seamless whole. He intended to take this methodology a step further with *Smile*, and create an entire album out of repeated musical themes and song fragments, in a manner that often evoked his favorite piece of music, Gershwin's 'Rhapsody In Blue.'

After completing 'Good Vibrations' Wilson started work on *Smile* in July at Gold Star Studios and Sunset Sound in Los Angeles. He spent the rest of the year and the first few months of 1967 working through such songs as 'Wind Chimes,' 'Our Prayer,' and 'Wonderful' with a cast of talented session players and, occasionally, the other Beach Boys.

The wider world got its first taste of *Smile* on April 25th 1967 when a staggering solo piano performance of 'Surf's Up' by Wilson aired as part of the CBS documentary *Inside Pop: The Rock Revolution*. By this stage, however, *Smile* had begun to fall apart at the seams. Obsessed with the idea of creating the perfect pop album before The Beatles got there, Wilson scrapped and restarted songs repeatedly. Deadlines came and went. Much of the album had been recorded, but still lay in the form of isolated fragments.

On May 19th, after ten months of sessions, Wilson stopped working on *Smile*. Rock historians have long since discussed his reasons. What is clear is that Wilson suffered some kind of mental breakdown, likely aggravated by his intake of hallucinogenic drugs. Notoriously thin-skinned, he was also wounded by the reluctance of the other Beach Boys, in particular Mike Love, to engage fully with a project they found too weird and avant-garde. A major sticking point was the 'Fire' section of 'Mrs O'Leary's Cow.' Recording that wonderfully evocative piece, Wilson insisted the musicians wear firemen's helmets as they played. Such was his mental state at the time that, on hearing that fires had broken out nearby, he scrapped the tapes, fearing that his music had the power to burn down buildings.

On June 1st The Beatles issued the epochal *Sgt Pepper*, and Brian was defeated. He would never again attempt to record music of such complexity or magnitude as *Smile* with The Beach Boys. Instead, the group released *Smiley Smile* in September, a hastily re-recorded, watered-down version of the album. Beset by manic depression and substance abuse, Wilson began to withdraw from The Beach Boys and led a life of semi-seclusion for much of the next three decades.

Over the years, several more *Smile*-era songs found release on The Beach Boys albums *20/20* (1969) and *Surf's Up* (1971), and bootleg recordings of others began to surface, further fueling the mythology surrounding Wilson's lost masterpiece. The 1993 boxed set *Good Vibrations: Thirty Years Of The Beach Boys* included 30 minutes of previously unheard *Smile* recordings that offer tantalizing glimpses of what might have been.

In 1998, to the surprise of many, a rehabilitated Wilson embarked on his first regular live performances since 1965. His 2001 tour centered on a rapturously received live replication of *Pet Sounds*. Two years later he announced an even more surprising project: a live *Smile*. Few would have predicted that Wilson could ever revisit the unfinished album that, it seemed, had caused him so much emotional turmoil. For years he refused to speak about *Smile* and had often denied that any tapes of the sessions still existed. In the spring of 2003, however, he began to reassemble the songs into a cohesive whole with the help of Darian Sahanaja, keyboardist in his current band, and Van Dyke Parks, who provided new lyrics to the incomplete sections.

The live *Smile* premiered at the Royal Festival Hall in London in February 2004 and was met with unanimous awe. Two months later Wilson and his band finally recorded *Smile* at Sunset Sound, the studio he had used in the 1960s to create numerous Beach Boys classics. This time the songs were completed in five days, between April 13th and 17th. The album was recorded and mixed by Wilson, Sahanaja, and Mark Linett, who had previously been responsible for compiling the 1966–7 tapes for the *Good Vibrations* boxed set.

Above all else, the release of *Smile* marks a personal triumph for Wilson, after 38 years able to complete his masterwork. Inevitably it lacks the zeitgeist in which it was originally conceived, as the world is a very different place today than it was in that departed decade. However, if it is not quite the album it might have been – Wilson's voice, at 62, is not what it was at 24, and the other vocalists can't match the uncanny harmonic cohesion of The Beach Boys – it does contain note-perfect renditions of some of the finest compositions by the man many consider to be one of the greatest songwriters of the 20th century. For that alone, and given its rich history, *Smile* is an important entry into the canon of popular-music albums. It remains a flawed masterpiece, as it likely would have been had it seen release in 1967.

■ **Brian Wilson gives Smile *its first public airing at the Royal Festival Hall in London, England, on February 20th 2004.***

2004

How To Dismantle An Atomic Bomb U2

Interscope Records 000361302 (U.S.A.) / Island CIDU214 (U.K.)
Released November 2004

U2's 11th album, *How To Dismantle An Atomic Bomb*, was accompanied by more promotional gimmicks than any album before it.

Capitalizing on the growing popularity of MP3 technology, the group and Apple Computer, Inc. launched a special edition U2 iPod to coincide with the album's release. The record itself was also made available in a variety of formats, including a deluxe boxed-set edition.

Musically, *How To Dismantle An Atomic Bomb* shares the back-to-basics sound of its predecessor, the multiple Grammy Award-winning *All That You Can't Leave Behind* (2000). U2 had spent the 1990s experimenting with cutting-edge production techniques and dance-music rhythms, resulting in a sequence of uneven and less commercially viable albums. However, in 2000 the band returned to the stripped-down, guitar-led sound that had served the group so well during the 1980s, resulting in sales of more than 11 million copies of *All That You Can't Leave Behind*.

U2 consolidated its position as "biggest band in the world" with *How To Dismantle An Atomic Bomb*, a British and U.S. chart topper. The album is

U2's sparsest sounding since the early 1980s, but is given a sharp, polished sound by a mouthwatering assortment of producers, including Brian Eno, Flood, Nellee Hooper, Steve Lillywhite, Chris Thomas, and Daniel Lanois, who also plays pedal steel and mandolin. Given the presence of six very different producers, the album is never allowed to become repetitive, and just about manages to hang together as a cohesive unit. Its highlights include the raw, post-punk of lead-off single 'Vertigo' and 'Sometimes You Can't Make It On Your Own,' Bono's heartfelt tribute to his recently deceased father. On other songs, however, his well-meaning if somewhat glib political rhetoric can begin to grate, particularly on 'Love And Peace Or Else.'

On its release in November 2004 *How To Dismantle An Atomic Bomb* was made available in four different physical formats, in addition to the digital download. Alongside the standard CD and vinyl copies were a limited-edition CD plus DVD version and a special boxed set. The DVD – also included in the boxed set – features studio footage of the making of the album and live performances of four songs. For the U2 completist, the boxed set, which sold for three times the price of a normal CD, is packaged as a lavish, hardcover book, complete with drawings and paintings by the band members and illustrated lyrics.

U2 wasn't the first group to present an album in this format – notable antecedents include Pearl Jam's *Vitalogy* (1994), which included extracts from old medical texts, and Radiohead's *Amnesiac* (2001), made to look like an old library book – but was certainly the first, and, to date, only, group to have its own special-edition iPod. More expensive than a standard iPod, though with the same hard-disk capacity, the U2 model is housed in a distinctive black case with red controls, in striking contrast to the familiar all-white finish.

The group also made available its complete discography – 446 songs – as a digital boxed set through the iTunes Music Store.

Scissor Sisters Scissor Sisters

Universal 000277202 (U.S.A.) / Polydor 9866058 (U.K.)
Released February 2004

Something strange happened in the mid 2000s: modern groups began to achieve considerable success by mining music from the 1970s and 1980s in a way that would, a few years previously, have been met with derision.

First came the British group The Darkness, which drew on the flamboyance of late-1970s heavy rock. Then Scissor Sisters emerged from the other side of the Atlantic a year later, with an Elton John-inspired sound that wouldn't have been out of place in a 1970s New York gay club.

Fronted by vocalists Jake Shears and Ana Mantronic, the group's early live performances resembled drag shows. Aside from a cover of Pink Floyd's 'Comfortably Numb,' all of the songs on the group's self-produced eponymous debut are originals, though most sound as though they could have been released in the 1970s or early 1980s. Along the way Elton, The Bee Gees, Frankie Goes To Hollywood, and George Michael are referenced as *Scissor Sisters* veers from epic rock balladry to shimmering disco pop. Perhaps the album's strongest quality is its unstinting enthusiasm: the group's energy and total lack of cynicism shines through each of the 11 tracks. *Scissor Sisters* spent the best part of 2004 in the upper reaches of the U.K. albums chart, while 'Mary,' 'Take Your Mama,' and 'Filthy / Gorgeous' were all British hits.

Sweat Nelly

Universal 33140 (U.S.A.) / Mercury 9863935 (U.K.)
Released September 2004

Suit Nelly

Universal 33160 (U.S.A.) / Mercury 9863936 (U.K.)
Released September 2004

Abattoir Blues / The Lyre Of Orpheus
Nick Cave & The Bad Seeds

Anti 86729 (U.S.A.) / Mute STUMM233 (U.K.)
Released October 2004

In the fall of 2004 two very different artists released two-album sets that demonstrate different sides of their musical personalities.

Nick Cave's *Abattoir Blues* and *The Lyre Of Orpheus* were packaged together for the price of a single disk, while Nelly's *Sweat* and *Suit* were sold separately. Both are, in essence, an extension of the double album, which, in rock music, has traditionally symbolized a big artistic statement by an 'important' band. In the mid 2000s it became a similar signifier in hip-hop, with acts such as OutKast and R Kelly opting to release expansive, two-disk sets. Nelly took the process a step further, issuing a pair of albums on the same day in 2004. He had risen to prominence several years earlier with the albums *Country*

Dear Heather Leonard Cohen

Columbia 92891 (U.S.A.) / 5147682 (U.K.)
Released October 2004

When Leonard Cohen's debut album appeared in 1967 no one would have predicted that the soberly dressed 30-something would be in for the long haul.

Already an established poet and novelist, surely this was at best a flirtation with song, at worst a vanity project? Yet here he is, nearly 40 years later, one of the few performers of his generation still sufficiently vibrant artistically to attract new listeners.

On *Dear Heather* Cohen ruminates on his familiar themes of sex, mortality, and religion in a voice reduced to a husky bass growl by decades of red wine and cigarettes. Often he just speaks the lyrics, leaving the singing to the handful of women who co-wrote and produced the album with him. At times he rouses himself to a few grizzled notes, his sense of melody still sufficiently sharp that even with such limited vocal resources he is able to fashion some memorable tunes.

By the mid 1980s, on *I'm Your Man*, Cohen had set aside his familiar nylon-string guitar to embrace synthesizer technology. *Dear Heather* finds him integrating the two approaches into a warm, seasoned sound that makes an unobtrusive backdrop for what everyone who buys a Cohen album really wants to hear: that fathoms-deep voice gravely intoning some of the best lyrics in pop music.

The lazy stereotype of Cohen's music is that it's depressing, but that's simply not true. Serious, maybe, but it's seriousness with a glint in the eye, shot through with many a droll aside.

The College Dropout **Kanye West**

Roc-A-Fella 20300 (U.S.A.) / 9862061 (U.K.)
Released February 2004

Before launching his solo career as a rapper, Kanye West was – and remains – one of the most sought-after hip-hop producers of the early 2000s.

West has to date been responsible for hits by the likes of Jay-Z ('Izzo (HOVA)' and ''03 Bonnie And Clyde'), Ludacris ('Stand Up'), and Alicia Keys ('You Don't Know My Name'). Stylistically, West's production owes a debt to the likes of Run-DMC in the way that he creates new beats out of snatches of recognizable songs, from The Doors to The Jackson 5. West's own solo career was repeatedly stalled by the success of his work as a producer and by a near-fatal car accident in October 2002. West reflects on this incident on his first solo single, 'Through The Wire,' a big hit on U.S. radio in late 2003.

West finally unleashed his long-awaited, self-produced debut album early the following year. His productions had by this point become ubiquitous on the U.S. charts, which lent a useful familiarity to his solo work and helped send *The College Dropout* straight in at Number Two in the U.S. albums chart. Unlike many of his rap peers, West does not draw on – or, in the case of some, invent – a past of poverty and violence, instead imbuing his songs with an Everyman charm and a cheery sense of humor. (How many other hip-hop artists would wear a bear suit on the cover of their debut album?) Issued on Jay-Z's Roc-A-Fella label, the album includes the hits 'Jesus Walks' and 'All Fall Down.'

Grammar and *Nellyville*, with its huge international hit single 'Hot In Herre.' Unlike many of his more aggressive rap contemporaries, Nelly's vocal delivery is smooth and laidback, as, generally speaking, is his music, which helped him develop a strong mainstream pop following. Aware of his cross-genre appeal, Nelly opted to divide his new material into two themed albums in 2004. *Sweat* is the more up-tempo of the two, containing 13 songs ripe for club play. *Suit*, meanwhile, is a slowed down, sensual collection. Across both albums Nelly collaborates with some of the biggest stars of pop and rap, from Snoop Dogg and Missy Elliott to Christina Aguilera and The Neptunes. While from an artistic standpoint it could be argued that Nelly might have been better advised to put together one single, concise, yet more diverse set out of these two, the commercial sense of issuing simultaneous albums is hard to fault: *Suit* and *Sweat* entered the U.S. albums chart at Numbers One and Two respectively.

Nick Cave's *Abattoir Blues* and *The Lyre Of Orpheus*, recorded with his longtime backing group The Bad Seeds, are similarly split between two different musical styles. Both albums were recorded in 16 days in April 2004 with producer Nick Launay at Studio Ferber in Paris. The latter set is a more sedate affair, dominated by the piano balladry to which Cave had begun to turn in the mid 1990s on albums such as *The Boatman's Call* (1997). Its doomy elegance recalls Leonard Cohen in places, and it is embellished by subtle touches of flute, violin, and mandolin. By contrast, *Abattoir Blues* recalls the apocalyptic rock of the early part of Cave's career, from his work with The Birthday Party in the 1980s to

the acclaimed albums *The Good Son* (1990) and *Henry's Dream* (1992). From the opening 'Get Ready For Love' through to 'There She Goes, My Beautiful World' and the title track, *Abattoir Blues* sounds like it could self-destruct at any moment, while The London Community Gospel Choir feature on several of the songs. Taken together, *Abattoir Blues* and *The Lyre Of Orpheus* provide a fitting encapsulation of the two sides of Cave's musical career.

2004

Franz Ferdinand Franz Ferdinand

Sony 92441 (U.S.A.) / Domino WIG 136 (U.K.)
Released February 2004

Hot Fuss The Killers

Island 000246802 (U.S.A.) / Lizard King LIZARD011 (U.K.)
Released June 2004

Silent Alarm Bloc Party

V2 205 (U.S.A.) / Wichita WEBB075 (U.K.)
Released January 2005

In the early 2000s, guitar-based rock was revitalized first by The Strokes and The White Stripes and then by a slew of bands that drew on the post-punk and new-wave scenes of the late 1970s and early 1980s.

In the U.K., the charge was led by Franz Ferdinand, the group formed in Glasgow in 2001 by a trio of art students and a life-model-turned-drummer. The group signed to Domino in 2003 and became overnight sensations in their homeland with the release of their second single, 'Take Me Out,' which mixed wiry guitars with a disco backbeat and euphoric, chanted vocals. Issued later the same year, *Franz Ferdinand* kept to much the same template. It topped the U.K. albums chart and won the 2004 Mercury Music Prize.

Hailing from the Nevada desert, the Las Vegas quartet The Killers arrived fully formed in the summer of 2004 with a sound derived equally from the angular art rock of Television and the synthesized new-wave pop of early-1980s Duran Duran. The Killers' debut, *Hot Fuss*, was an instant hit in the U.K., where sales were buoyed by the success of the singles 'Mr Brightside' and 'Somebody Told Me,' but struggled to have the same impact back home.

Back in Britain, the London foursome Bloc Party first caught the attention of the U.K. music press with the singles 'She's Hearing Voices' and 'Banquet' (2004), which sounded like Gang Of Four by way of Sonic Youth. Released early the following

year, *Silent Alarm* was immediately hailed as one of the more promising debuts of recent years. The album makes use of a much wider sonic palette than most of the group's peers' work, taking in windswept ballads and politically aware pop as well as the de rigueur arty punk.

2005

Arular M.I.A.

XL 186 (U.S.A. & U.K.)
Released March 2005

An intoxicating mix of Eastern and Western musical influences, held together with cutting-edge beats and chart-friendly hooks, *Arular* is one the most forward-thinking pop records of recent times.

The album was preceded by the release of a 'mix-tape,' *Piracy Funds Terrorism*, which gave a strong indication of the multicultural mishmash of musical styles that would appear on M.I.A.'s debut album proper. Its title also hints at the revolutionary political aspect to the lyrics of many of her songs. These clearly bear the influence of the singer's upbringing: her Sri Lankan father was a prominent activist in the country's civil war.

Born Maya Arulpragasam, M.I.A. spent her childhood in Sri Lanka, before returning to London, England, the city of her birth, in her teens to study art. There she became acquainted with former Elastica vocalist Justine Frischmann, who co-wrote *Arular*'s closing track, 'Galang.' Issued as a single in 2004, the electro-dancehall-hip-hop hybrid of 'Galang' gave M.I.A. an instant U.K. club hit, and brought anticipation for her full-length debut to fever pitch.

She didn't disappoint: *Arular* – which leaked on to the internet months before its official release, serving only to increase the hype around it – is positively overflowing with memorable songs that recall Dizzee Rascal or Missy Elliott at their most euphoric. M.I.A.'s vocals are delivered in a mix of London street slang and Sri Lankan patois, while the non-standard musical elements – the steel drums on 'Bingo,' the Brazilian trumpets on 'Bucky Done Gun' – are integral to the songs rather than sounding like artificial afterthoughts. The album makes canny use of an intriguing assortment of producers and co-writers, from former Pulp bassist Steve Mackey to U.K. chart-pop mastermind Richard X.

Be Common

Geffen 004670 (U.S.A.) / Island 9882497 (U.K.)
Released May 2005

Hip-hop in the early 21st century had begun to resemble rock music in the 1970s, with too many acts opting to punish their listeners with bloated, unfocused double-disk concept albums. *Be* is a rare beast: a short, punchy masterpiece of modern rap, all killer and no filler.

Born Lonnie Rashied Lynn, Common produced some of the best underground hip-hop of the 1990s, on such albums as *Resurrection* (1994, under the name Common Sense) and *One Day It'll Make Sense* (1997). He began to attract wider mainstream attention with his first major-label effort, 2000's *Like Water For Chocolate*, but misfired on the sprawling, psychedelic *Electric Circus* (2002), intended as a hip-hop update of Jimi Hendrix's *Electric Ladyland*.

On *Be*, Common reined in his talents to produce a concise, 40-minute set of refined, thought-provoking songs. Some long-term fans were dubious about his decision to place pop-rap producer Kanye West behind the board for the bulk of *Be*'s 12 songs, fearing that Common was planning to move towards a slick, commercial sound. But *Be* is nothing of the sort. Instead, it draws on the effortless funk and murky textures of Sly & The Family Stone and Curtis Mayfield. The album was Common's most popular to date, peaking at Number Two in the U.S.A. and drawing near-unanimous critical plaudits.

In Your Honor **Foo Fighters**

Roswell/RCA 68038 (U.S.A.) / 82876701932 (U.K.)
Released June 2005

Foo Fighters' defining work, the two-disk set *In Your Honor* is split equally between electric and acoustic rock.

The bulk of the songs on *In Your Honor* were inspired by people who frontman Dave Grohl met on John Kerry's 2004 Presidential Election campaign trail. Kerry might have lost out to George W. Bush, but Grohl stuck with the songs, molding them into this sweeping double album.

Grohl was, of course, the drummer in Nirvana, until Kurt Cobain's suicide brought the band to a sudden end. By the end of the 1990s, however, he had established Foo Fighters as an important band in its own right, by way of a 1995 self-titled debut (much of which Grohl had recorded alone, at home, while still in Nirvana), *The Color And The Shape* (1997), and *There Is Nothing Left To Lose* (1999). The post-grunge formula had grown stale by the time of *One By One* (2002), leading Grohl and his current crop of bandmates – bassist Nate Mendel, drummer Taylor Hawkins, and guitarist Chris Shiflett – to try something new with *In Your Honor*.

The album devotes one whole disk to each of the two sides of Foo Fighters' musical personality, and in doing so affords the group room to diversify. Grohl sings through a wall of distortion on the punishing title track, and sounds angrier than ever before on the short sharp shock of 'Hell.' The second disk is much more reflective, however, and even finds room for an unexpectedly gentle duet with Norah Jones. Former Led Zeppelin bassist John Paul Jones appears on the acoustic disk, too, as does John Homme of Queens Of The Stone Age (Grohl had previously starred as guest drummer on the latter group's *Songs From The Deaf*). *In Your Honor* continued Foo Fighters' unbroken run of commercial success, peaking at Number Two in the U.S.A. and the U.K., while 'Best Of You' was a transatlantic hit single.

Recording The Future

Has the evolution of recording technology helped or hindered the art of music during the last 50 years?

Naturally there are many different opinions. One can only imagine what Duke Ellington would have thought about a device like Pitch 'n Time, a studio processor that automatically corrects an out-of-tune vocal, or how many choice expletives Buddy Rich would have used to describe Roland's V-Drums, an electronic percussion kit that comes complete with rubber cymbals. It's quite clear, however, that with the passing of time – and the advent of affordable, professional-grade home-studio equipment – that the business of recording has increasingly become a one-dimensional affair. By and large, popular genres such as hip-hop and techno have had little use for big-studio acoustics. Automation and sophisticated do-it-yourself recording machinery have all but taken the professional studio out of the equation. Today, what once took an army of trained musicians and a roomful of songwriters now only takes a single producer and a modest amount of gear.

Consequently, the recording business, like many other industries, now finds itself in a perpetual state of consolidation. In 2005 three of the most respected recording studios – New York's Hit Factory, Alabama's Muscle Shoals Sound Studio, and Cello Studios in Los Angeles (formerly the renowned Western Studios) – ceased operations within weeks of each other. Observers claim that the demise of these and other legendary facilities is due in large part to the DIY trend. "People can easily have a studio in their home if they want," remarked a Hit Factory employee. "This is an expensive building to run." Meanwhile automation, which helped seal the fate of studio house bands – the likes of Motown's Funk Brothers and Hollywood's Wrecking Crew – during the 1970s and 1980s, has made it increasingly difficult for those hoping to launch a brilliant career as a session player in today's music market.

And yet the proliferation of home-studio digital technology, combined with a growing internet-based independent music movement, has been a godsend for countless up-and-coming musicians looking for a way to bust into the business. Unlike their predecessors, who were forced to borrow large sums of cash to make a decent demo or make knee-marks on the rug of some record executive's office, for only a few hundred dollars today's musical wannabe can create a studio-quality multitrack production using little more than a guitar, an entry-level digital recorder, and a CD burner. Such functions as drag-and-drop editing and motorized faders have become standard issue on many digital audio workstations, and this kind of micro-ingenuity has given basement dwellers a fighting chance against the forces of evil in the big, bad world of music.

"In reality, maybe one-third of the hits I've done have originated in the home or home-type studio," says R&B engineer Dave 'Hard Drive' Pensado, who prepared Pink's 2001 multiplatinum effort *M!ssundaztood,* recorded mainly in the home studio of Pink's producer Linda Perry. "While there are definitely some sonic improvements to be made, in many ways there are a lot of things the home guys do that are in fact better than the recordings that come from a big facility. That's because, in general, the creativity that emerges from a home studio almost always surpasses that of an expensive studio. Never mind the sound quality; personally, I'd rather start with the kind of feeling, emotion, and creativity you get on a homemade record like Pink's. That's the main thing."

Hear Today, Gone Tomorrow

One thing's for certain: the tremendous technological wave that swept over the music business during the 1990s has irrevocably altered the way we receive our music. The recent popularity of downloadable music sites such as Apple's iTunes and Napster's subscription service is living proof that music is no longer the tactile commodity it once was. Of course, this is nothing new: the fragile plastic and cramped cover space of the Compact Disc long ago diminished the visual aspect of the vinyl LP, while the ability for listeners to compile, burn, and shuffle tracks at will has rendered the age-old art of Side-One-Side-Two song sequencing obsolete.

Still, there's no denying the many benefits of digital portability. In a world where laptops outnumber desktops and cell phones are fast replacing landlines, being able

Continued on page 313

2005

X&Y **Coldplay**

Capitol 74786 (U.S.A.) / Parlophone 72434747862 (U.K.)
Released June 2005

A transatlantic Number One hit, Coldplay's third album cemented the group's position as the biggest new band of the 2000s.

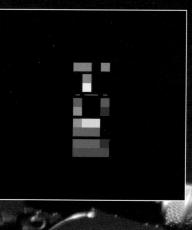

X&Y was one of the most eagerly anticipated album releases of recent times, to the extent that, when it was announced that Coldplay would be unable to deliver the album by March 2005 (and thus the end of the financial year), shares in EMI – the parent label of Capitol and Parlophone – fell by 18 percent.

Sessions for *X&Y* began in January 2004, and lasted into the early months of the following year. As on its predecessor, *A Rush Of Blood To The Head* (2002), production duties were split between Danton Supple, Ken Nelson, and Coldplay themselves. There had been much speculation prior to the release of *X&Y* that its long gestation was the result of the band's attempts to redefine its sound. Ultimately, though, the furthest they stray from the melodic, anthemic rock of their earlier work is on the lead-off track, 'Square One,' which begins with vocalist Chris Martin intoning 'You're in control / Is there anywhere you wanna go?' over soothing synthesizer chords and a funky backbeat from drummer Will Champion, but is reined back into familiar territory by Jonny Buckland's chiming guitar-playing.

The next three songs – 'What If,' 'White Shadows,' and 'Fix You' – stick to a template easily recognizable from earlier Coldplay albums. Each begins with Martin crouched over his piano or organ, before slowly building into an epic, string-laden chorus. It's a measure of their success that the group have already achieved such a distinctive signature sound; even the much talked-about 'Talk,' which appropriates a riff from 'Computer Love' by the pioneering electronic group Kraftwerk, sounds like nothing so much as it does Coldplay.

The second half of *X&Y* continues in much the same vein, alternating between epic, widescreen ballads and rock tracks that sound like a gentler U2. 'Low' features a guest appearance from Brian Eno, whose synthesizer parts are subtly reminiscent of his work in the late 1970s with David Bowie. Martin originally wrote the unlisted closing track, 'Til Kingdom Come,' for Johnny Cash, but the legendary country singer died before he could record it.

X&Y's centerpiece, 'Speed Of Sound,' was the first song by a British group to go straight into the Top Ten of the U.S. singles chart since The Beatles' 'Hey Jude' in 1968. The album itself was only the ninth in chart history to simultaneously debut at Number One in both the U.S.A. and the U.K. (the last was Radiohead's *Kid A* in 2000). It is also the second fastest-selling album of all time in the U.K., after *Be Here Now* (1997) by Oasis, having shifted close to 500,000 copies in its first week on sale.

Devils & Dust Bruce Springsteen

Sony 93900 (U.S.A.) / Columbia 5200002 (U.K.)
Released April 2005

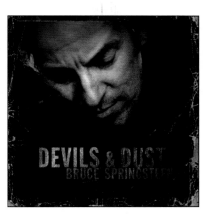

On *Devils & Dust*, his 13th studio album, Bruce Springsteen ditched the E Street Band (again) in favor of a sparse, intimate sound pitched somewhere between *Nebraska* (1982) and *The Ghost Of Tom Joad* (1995).

Springsteen's previous full-band set, the 9/11-themed *The Rising*, seemed almost obligatory in places, as though Springsteen – as one of the great American rock'n'roll heroes of the past three decades – felt compelled to reflect on a national tragedy. *Devils & Dust*, on the other hand, feels more like an album he wanted to make rather than one he felt he had to.

On the opening title track, Springsteen asks: "What would you do to survive? / Kill the things you love / Fear's a powerful thing." This theme of facing demons crops up time and again on the 12 narrative tales of *Devils & Dust*. Springsteen sings from the perspective of a range of troubled but essentially well-intentioned characters, from errant husbands to Nevada prostitutes. The already infamous lyrics to the song 'Reno' – "$200 straight in / Two-fifty up the ass" – earned Springsteen the first 'Parental Advisory' sticker of his career. Sonically, the album is brighter than either *Nebraska* or *The Ghost Of Tom Joad*, and in places producer Brendan O'Brien's overdubbed parts – be they strings, organ, or pedal steel – are a touch obtrusive. *Devils & Dust* works best at its starkest, such as on the closing 'Matamoras Banks.'

In the early 2000s no big album release was complete without a deluxe, audio-visual 'special edition,' and *Devils & Dust* is no exception. For a few dollars more you get the album itself plus a DVD of Springsteen performing solo-acoustic versions of five of the songs. *Devils & Dust* was well received by critics – *Rolling Stone* magazine concluded that it "sparkles in the right places like stars in a clear Plains sky" – and entered the U.S. *Billboard* chart at Number One.

Continued from page 311

to cart your entire record collection around on an MP3 player the size of your shirt pocket is enormously attractive. Above all, the transformation of music from a physical medium to a bunch of bits and bytes on your computer – as well as the seemingly infinite selection offered by most internet music libraries – has had the effect of making music increasingly disposable as listeners grow accustomed to downloading and listening, then quickly deleting and repeating.

"I've watched my kids buy a CD, and once they'd rip it, they could roller-skate over the original if they wanted to," says Napster's Chris Gorog. "It didn't matter, because at that point they didn't value it. What I believe is happening is an absolute paradigm shift in all media, but in music in particular, where people will clamor for instantaneous access to everything, any time, anywhere. That's what they'll pay for and that's what they'll really value. Let's face it, if you were a record collector, you spent years dragging around all those albums and CDs from place to place, listening to only a small percentage of them while all the rest gathered dust. But in this new environment, the idea of owning a CD, or a set of music files, or whatever, will become less essential. And, in time, the whole concept of how we value our music will change for good."

The question remains: are we better off today than we were 50 years ago when Frank Sinatra issued *In the Wee Small Hours*, proving once and for all the artistic merits of the long-playing album? Analog enthusiasts might argue that, even now, a mint-condition copy of the 1955 classic would still sound 'warmer' than its CD update; proponents of digital technology could counter that the luxury of downloading Ol' Blue Eyes' whole catalog in a matter of minutes is well worth any negligible loss of sound quality.

And yet rather than one medium proving its superiority over the other, within the past few years analog and digital have in many ways formed a mutually beneficial alliance. In the studio, recording artists seeking that 'classic' sound still cut their tracks using old-fashioned tape machines, then transfer the music on to digital equipment in order to edit and manipulate. At home, an array of user-friendly software packages make it possible for listeners to copy their favorite old vinyl selections on to the computer, removing crackles, pops and other annoyances along the way. In some respects, the merging of the two disparate cultures has helped bring the entire process full circle. Somewhere tonight, a traditionalist baby-boomer perusing Napster for the first time will stumble upon some long-lost classic album, download the tracks in seconds, and will be hooked instantly; while in the next room, his teenage offspring will carefully drop a needle on to his dad's pristine vinyl copy of *The White Album,* then sit transfixed at the sound of Paul McCartney's piano and the sight of that hypnotic rotating green apple.

INDEX

INDEX

ACKNOWLEDGEMENTS

Authors

The following key indicates who wrote which album entries: Johnny Black (JB), Mark Brend (MB), Michael Heatley (MH), Thomas Jerome (TJ), Rikky Rooksby (RR), David Simons (DS). The entries on recording technology and delivery systems were written by John Morrish and David Simons.

'S Wonderful MH; A Christmas Gift For You JB; All Eyez On Me TJ; All Summer Long TJ; A Love Supreme TJ; A Walk Across Rooftops MB; Abraxas TJ; After The Goldrush TJ/DS; Aftermath JB; Aja TJ; All Things Must Pass RR; American Recordings TJ; Antichrist Superstar TJ; Appetite For Destruction TJ; Around The World In 80 Days MH; Arrival TJ; Arular TJ; As Nasty As They Wanna Be TJ; Astral Weeks RR; At Folsom Prison DS; At Newport MH; At The Hollywood Bowl MH; Autobahn JB; Automatic For The People RR; Baby One More Time TJ; Back In Black DS; Bat Out Of Hell TJ; Be TJ; Biograph TJ; Bitches Brew TJ; Blackboard Jungle Dub TJ; Blonde On Blonde TJ; Blood On Blood Tracks MB; Blood Sugar Sex Magik TJ; Blow By Blow RR; Blue RR; Blue Valentine TJ; Blues Breakers With Eric Clapton RR; Blues Brothers TJ; Bop Till You Drop DS; Born In The USA RR; Born To Run TJ; Boston DS; Bridge Over Troubled Water DS; Bringing It All Back Home JB; Brothers In Arms RR; Buena Vista Social Club TJ; Call On Me / That's The Way Love Is MH; Calypso MH; Can't Slow Down TJ; Car Wheels On A Gravel Road TJ; Celebrity TJ; Cloud Nine RR; Club Classics Vol. 1 TJ; Come Away With Me TJ; Come On Over TJ; Connected TJ; Control DS; Countdown To Ecstacy JB; Court And Spark RR; CrazySexyCool TJ; Crosby, Stills & Nash RR; Curtis TJ; Damaged TJ; Dangerously In Love TJ; Dare! TJ; Dark Side Of The Moon JB; Daydream Nation TJ; Days Of Future Passed RR; Dear Heather MB; Definitely Maybe RR; Desire JB; Devils & Dust TJ; Diamond Life TJ; Discreet Music JB; Disintegration TJ; Disraeli Gears RR; Dummy TJ; Dusty In Memphis RR; Eddie Cochran Memorial Album MH; Electric Ladyland RR; Electric Warrior RR; Elephant RR; Eliminator TJ; Elvis MH; Elvis' Golden Records MH; Enema Of The State TJ; Enter The Wu-Tang (36 Chambers) TJ; Escape TJ; Exile On Main Street RR; Exotica MH; Face Value TJ; Film Encores MH; Finger-Style Guitar MH; Fire And Water RR; Follow The Leader DS; For Your Pleasure RR; Forever Changes JB; Foxtrot TJ; Frampton Comes Alive! DS; Franz Ferdinand TJ; Fresh Fruit For Rotting Vegetables TJ; Garbage TJ; Gilded Palace Of Sin JB; Goodbye Yellow Brick Road RR; Gorillaz TJ; Grace TJ; Graceland JB; Gratitude DS; Greatest Hits JB; Green Onions RR; Guitars, Cadillacs, Etc., Etc. DS; Hank Williams Memorial Album MH; Have 'Twangy' Guitar Will Travel RR; Headhunters TJ; Heavy Weather TJ; Here's Little Richard MH; Hey Let's Twist! MH; Hex Enduction Hour TJ; Horses TJ; Hot Hits MB; Hotel California TJ; Hounds Of Love RR; Hours TJ; How To Dismantle An Atomic Bomb TJ; Human Clay TJ; Hunky Dory TJ; Hybrid Theory TJ; Hysteria TJ; I Do Not Want What I Have Not Got TJ; I'm Still In Love With You TJ; I Never Loved A Man (The Way I Love You) DS; In Search Of TJ; In The Court Of The Crimson King RR; In The Wee Small Hours MH; In The Wind MH; In Your Honour TJ; Ingénue TJ; Introducing The Hardline TJ; Is This It TJ; It Takes A Nation Of Millions To Hold Us Back TJ; It's Everly Time RR; IV RR; Jagged Little Pill TJ; Jazz Samba MH; Jerry Lee Lewis MH; Joan Baez MH; John Barleycorn Must Die TJ; Johnny's Greatest Hits MH; Journey Through The Secret Life Of Plants TJ; Justified TJ; Kick TJ; Kid A TJ; Kind Of Blue RR; La Bamba TJ; Led Zeppelin RR; Let's Dance TJ; Like A Virgin DS; Live At The Apollo JB; Loaded JB; London Calling MB; Look At Us DS; Low TJ; Machine Head TJ; Make It Big! TJ; Master Of Puppets TJ; Metal Box TJ; Metallica RR; Miss E . . . So Addictive TJ; Modern Sounds in Country & Western Music MH; Moon Safari TJ; Muddy Waters: Folk Singer TJ; Murmur TJ; Music Box TJ; Music From Twin Peaks TJ; My Aim Is True TJ; Natty Dread TJ; NBC Special MB; Nebraska TJ; Nevermind JB; Never Mind The Bollocks RR; No Sleep 'Til Hammersmith TJ; Nothing's Shocking TJ; Nuggets MB; Odelay TJ; Off The Wall TJ; OK Computer TJ; On Her Majesty's Secret Service RR; One Dozen Berrys MH; Original Pirate Material TJ; Otis Blue RR; Outlandos d'Amour JB; Painted From Memory TJ; Parachutes TJ; Paranoid RR; Paris 1919 JB; Paul's Boutique TJ; Permanent Vacation TJ; Permission To Land TJ; Pet Sounds JB; Peter Gabriel 3 RR; Pictures At An Exhibition RR; Pink Moon TJ; Play TJ; Please Please Me DS; Pontiac TJ; Post TJ; Prince Charming TJ; Rage Against The Machine TJ; Raising Hell TJ; Rated R RR; Raw Power TJ; Ray Of Light TJ; Remain In Light TJ; Republic TJ; Revolver RR; Richard D James Album TJ; Rio TJ; Riptide TJ; Rock And Rollin' With Fats Domino MH; Rock Bottom TJ; Ropin' The Wind TJ; Rum, Sodomy & The Lash TJ; Rumours JB; Rust Never Sleeps MB; Sail Away TJ; Sam Cooke MH; Saturday Night Fever TJ; School's Out RR; Scissor Sisters TJ; Screamadelica TJ; Seal TJ; Searching For The Young Soul Rebels TJ; Sgt Pepper's Lonely Hearts Club Band JB; Siamese Dream TJ; Sign 'O' The Times TJ; Sing When You're Winning TJ; Sings The Rodgers & Hart Songbook MH; Slippery When Wet TJ; Smile TJ; Some Girls MB; Something/Anything DS; Songs From The Big Chair TJ; Songs In A Minor TJ; Sounds Of Silence JB; Speakerboxxx / The Love Below TJ; Spice TJ; Spirit Of Eden TJ; Sticky Fingers JB; Stoney End TJ; Straight Outta Compton TJ; Street Songs TJ; String Along MH; Stupidity TJ; Supernatural TJ; Surfer Rosa TJ; Surrealistic Pillow JB; Sweat TJ; Sweet Baby James TJ; Sweethearts Of The Rodeo JB; Swordfishtrombones TJ; Synchronicity JB; Tales From Topographic Oceans TJ; The Basement Tapes TJ; The Bends TJ; The Best Of Both Worlds TJ; The Bodyguard TJ; The Buddy Holly Story RR; The Chronic TJ; The Circle Game MB; The College Dropout TJ; The Downward Spiral TJ; The Fat Of The Land TJ; The Faust Tapes TJ; The Freewheelin' Bob Dylan JB; The French Album TJ; The Game TJ; The Girl Can't Help It MH; The Healer TJ; The Immaculate Collection TJ; The Joshua Tree RR; The Kids From Fame TJ; The Last Waltz TJ; The Lexicon Of Love TJ; The Lion TJ; The Marshall Mathers LP TJ; The Monkees JB; The Nightfly TJ; The Piper At The Gates Of Dawn JB; The Platters MH; The Queen Is Dead TJ; The Ramones JB; The Score TJ; The Shadows RR; The Singles 1969–73 TJ; The Smiths RR; The Songs Of Leonard Cohen JB; The Soul Of Ike And Tina Turner MH; The Sound Of Fury MH; The Sound Of Music TJ; The Stone Roses TJ; The Tommy Steele Story MH; The Velvet Underground And Nico JB; The Velvet Underground JB; The Ventures In Space RR; The Wall JB; Talking Book RR; Talking Heads 77 JB; Tamboo MB; Tap Root Manuscript JB; Tapestry JB; Tea For The Tillerman TJ; Their Satanic Majesties Request JB; There's A Riot Goin' On TJ; Things Are Swinging MH; 3 Feet High And Rising TJ; Thriller TJ; Time Out RR; Time Out Of Mind TJ; To Bring You My Love TJ; Tommy RR; Tracy Chapman DS; Tragic Kingdom TJ; Trout Mask Replica TJ; Tubular Bells JB; Tuesday Night Music Club TJ; 12 Year Old Genius MH; Under A Blood Red Sky RR; Unforgettable MH; Unknown Pleasures TJ; Unplugged TJ; Urban Hymns TJ; Van Halen DS; Violator TJ; Vol. 2 Hard Knock Life TJ; Weezer TJ; Welcome To The Pleasuredome TJ; West Side Story MH; What Now My Love? TJ; What's Going On TJ; White Blood Cells TJ; Whitney TJ; Who's Next RR; Wide Open Spaces TJ; Woodstock JB; Workingman's Dead DS; X&Y TJ; Yankee Hotel Foxtrot JB; You've Come A Long Way Baby TJ; Zaireeka TJ.

Picture Credits

The photographs in this book are reproduced with permission from the following copyright holders, and we are grateful for their help. Most of the images are supplied by Redfern's (indicated below by the initials RF), Michael Ochs Archives (MOA), Rex Features (RX), Pictorial Press (PP), and the Main Artery Collection (MAC). In the key below, the page number is followed by the artist name and details of the photographer and/or picture library. All efforts have been made to contact the original photographers or picture libraries where possible. We apologize for any omissions, and will correct them in any future editions.

Jacket front Elvis Presley MOA/RF; Bob Dylan MOA/RF; David Bowie Nicky J. Sims, RF; Kurt Cobain Michel Linssen, RF; 3 Simon & Garfunkel MOA/RF; 6–7 Gene Vincent MOA/RF; 8–9 Frank Sinatra Bob Willoughby, RF; 8 Frank Sinatra both by Bob Willoughby, RF; 10–11 Frank Sinatra MOA/RF; 11 Frank Sinatra both by Bob Willoughby, RF; 12 Frank Sinatra Bob Willoughby, RF; 13 Liberace MAC; Baxter MAC; 14 The Girl Can't Help It Balafon Image Bank; 16 Ella Fitzgerald MAC; Williams MAC; 17 Duke Ellington MAC; 18–19 Elvis Presley Frank Driggs; 19 Sun Records Glenn A. Baker, RF; 20 Chet Atkins MAC; 21 Beale Street Mike Rowe Blues Unlimited; 22 Tommy Steele MAC; Little Richard MAC; 23 Jerry Lee Lewis MOA/RF; Fats Domino MAC; 24–5 Capitol Tower Frank Driggs; 25 Peggy Lee MOA/RF; 26 South Pacific PP; 27 West Side Story MAC; 28 Johnny Mathis MAC; Chuck Berry Chuck Stewart; 29 Sam Cooke MAC; 30–3 Miles Davis All by Don Hunstein; 34–5 Elvis Presley MOA/RF; 37 Buddy Holly MOA/RF; Duane Eddy MAC; 38 Mantovani MAC; 39 Kingston Trio MOA/RF; 40 Dinah Washington MAC; Everly Brothers MAC; 41 Billy Fury MAC; Dave Brubeck MAC; 42 Eddie Cochran MAC; 42–3 The Shadows MAC; 43 Ike And Tina Turner MAC; 45 Steve Cropper MOA/RF; 46 Ray Charles MOA/RF; 47 Phil Spector

ACKNOWLEDGEMENTS

MAC; **48** *Bob Dylan* MOA/RF; **49** *Peter, Paul & Mary* MAC; **50** *James Brown (portrait)* MAC; *James Brown (live)* Chuck Stewart; **51** *Phil Spector* MOA/RF; **52** *Stevie Wonder* MAC; **53** *The Ventures* MAC; **54** *The Beatles* Terry O'Neill, RX; **55** *The Beach Boys* MOA/RF; **56** *Elvin Jones* Lee Tanner; **56–7** *John Coltrane* Lee Tanner; **58** *The Sound Of Music (still)* MAC; *The Sound Of Music (poster)* PP; **59** *Sonny & Cher* MAC; **60** *Bob Dylan* MAC; **60–1** *Bob Dylan* MOA/RF; **62–3** *Bob Dylan* both by Don Hunstein; **64** *Bob Dylan* Jan Persson, RF; **65** *Bob Dylan* MAC; **66** *Simon & Garfunkel* MAC; **67** *Monkees* three from private collection; *Monkees live* MAC; **68** *Cassette player* Nicky J. Sims, RF; **69** *The Beatles* Bill Orchard, RX; **70** *Otis Redding* Don Paulsen, RF; *Eric Clapton* Rick Richards, RF; **71** *John Mayall* both from MAC; **72–3** *The Rolling Stones* all by Gered Mankowitz; **74–5** *Andrew Loog Oldham* Gered Mankowitz, RF; **76–81** *The Beach Boys* all by MOA/RF; **82–3** *Aretha Franklin* both by Chuck Stewart; **83** *Jefferson Airplane* Lee Tanner; **84–5** *The Doors* MOA/RF; **87** *Love* MOA/RF; **88** *Cream* Chuck Stewart, RF; **89** *Cream* Robert Whitaker, Strange Things; **90** *The Velvet Underground* Glenn A. Baker, RF; **90–1** *The Velvet Underground* MOA/RF; **91** *Leonard Cohen* MOA/RF; **92–3** *Abbey Road* Phil Dent, RF; **94** *George Martin* David Magnus, RX; **94–5** *The Beatles* David Magnus, RX; **97** *Pink Floyd* both by Andrew Whittuck, RF; **98** *The Supremes* MOA/RF; **99** *The Four Tops* MAC; *The Hollies* MAC; **100** *Johnny Cash* Jan Olofsson, RF; **101** *The Byrds* MOA/RF; *Tom Rush* Phil Smee, Strange Things; **102** *The Moody Blues* MAC; *The Small Faces* MAC; *The Kinks* MAC; **103** *The Pretty Things* MAC; **104** *Elvis Presley* MAC; **104–5** *Elvis Presley* MOA/RF; **106–7** *Van Morrison* Elliott Landy, RF; **108** *Jimi Hendrix* MOA/RF; **109** *Jimi Hendrix* MOA/RF; **110** *King Crimson* MOA/RF; **111** *Captain Beefheart And His Magic Band* MOA/RF; **112** *Crosby, Stills & Nash* RB/RF; **113** *Crosby, Stills, Nash & Young* RB/RF; **114** *Dusty Springfield* BBC/RF; **115** *Flying Burrito Brothers* MOA/RF; **116** *Led Zeppelin* Chris Walter, Photofeatures; **118–19** *The Who* all by Baron Wolman; **120–1** *Quadrophenia* PP; **122** *On Her Majesty's Secret Service* PP; **126–7** *Miles Davis* David Redfern, RF; **127** *Santana* Richard Upper, RF; **128** *Woodstock* Elliott Landy, RF; **129** *Janis Joplin* Elliott Landy, RF; **130–1** *The Grateful Dead* Amalie R. Rothschild; **132–3** *Black Sabbath* all by Chris Walter, Photofeatures; **134** *George Harrison* Glenn A. Baker, RF; **136** *James Taylor and Joni Mitchell* Jim McCrary, RF; **137** *Carole King* Jim McCrary, RF; **138** *The Rolling Stones* MOA/RF; **139** *The Who* Ron Howard, RF; **140** *T. Rex* Keith Morris, RF; **142–3** *Marvin Gaye* both by GEMS/RF; **144** *Sly Stone* MAC; **145** *Funkadelic* MOA/RF; **146** *David Bowie* PP; **149** *Electric Prunes* MOA/RF; **151** *Stevie Wonder* MOA/RF; **152–3** *The Rolling Stones* Robert Knight, RF; **154** *Genesis* Ian Dickson, RF; **156–7** *Pink Floyd* Mick Gold, RF; **158–9** *Pink Floyd* MAC; **160–1** *Roxy Music* MOA/RF; **162** *The Carpenters* Chris Walter, Photofeatures; **163** *Steely Dan* MOA/RF; **164–5** *Mike Oldfield* both by Barry Plummer; **166–7** *The Stooges* MOA/RF; **168** *Kraftwerk* Glenn A. Baker, RF; **169** *Robert Wyatt* MAC; **170** *Patti Smith* Richard A. Aaron, RF; **170–1** *Bob Marley* Andrew Putler; **172** *Bruce Springsteen* Richard A. Aaron, RF; **173** *Bruce Springsteen* GEMS/RF; **174** *Brian Eno* Erica Echenberg, RF; **175** *Earth, Wind & Fire* David Redfern, RF; **176** *Bob Dylan* MOA/RF; **178–9** *Dr.*

Feelgood Ian Dickson, RF; **179** *The Ramones* MOA/RF; **180** *Abba* Glenn A. Baker, RF; **180–1** *Abba* David Redfern, RF; **182** *Peter Frampton* Richard E. Aaron, RF; **183** *Boston* MAC; **184–5** *The Eagles* PP; **186** *David Bowie* Ian Dickson, RF; **187** *Elvis Costello* Keith Morris, RF; **188** *Sex Pistols* Ian Dickson, RF; **189** *Talking Heads* Barry Plummer; **190** *Meatloaf* MAC; **192–3** *Fleetwood Mac* Fin Costello, RF; **194** *Tom Waits* Alain Dister, RF; **195** *The Police* Barry Plummer; **196** *Van Halen* Fin Costello, RF; **197** *The Band* both by MOA/RF; **200** *The Clash* Lex Van Rossen, RF; **201** *The Blues Brothers* PP; **202–3** *AC/DC* Glenn A. Baker, RF; **203** *AC/DC* Dick Barnatt, RF; **204** *Queen* Rob Verhorst, RF; **206** *Journey* MAC; **207** *Motörhead* Fin Costello, RF; **208** *The Human League* PP; **209** *Adam And The Ants* Peter Still, RF; *Soft Cell* BBC/RF; **210** *Michael Jackson* Skyline, RX; **211** *Michael Jackson* Sipa Press, RX; **212** *Michael Jackson* Richard Young, RX; **216** *David Bowie* Ebet Roberts, RF; **218** *The Police* PP; **219** *R.E.M.* Ebet Roberts, RF; *U2* Ebet Roberts, RF; **220** *ZZ Top* Charlyn Zlotnik, RF; **221** *Tom Waits* MAC; **223** *Frankie Goes To Hollywood* Virginia Turbett, RF; **224–5** *Bruce Springsteen* Paul Bergen, RF; **226** *The Smiths* Stephen Wright, RF; *The Blue Nile* Kerstin Rodgers, RF; **229** *Dire Straits* Ebet Roberts, RF; **230** *Paul Simon* David Redfern, RF; **231** *Metallica* Ebet Roberts, RF; **233** *Run DMC/Aerosmith* Lloyd Nelson; **234** *Aerosmith* Grant Davis, RF; **236** *Prince* Ilpo Musto, RX; **238–9** *U2* Lex Van Rossen, RF; **240–1** *U2* Ebet Roberts, RF; **242** *Tracy Chapman* All Action/RF; **243** *Jane's Addiction* Fredrich Cantor, RF; **244** *Public Enemy* Suzi Gibbons, RF; **246** *Sonic Youth* PP; **246–7** *Real World Studios* both by York Tillyer, Real World Holdings Ltd.; **247** *Youssou N'Dour* Paul Bergen, RF; **248** *The Stone Roses* Ian Tilton; **250** *Beastie Boys* Ricky Powell; **251** *De La Soul* Ebet Roberts, RF; **252** *Madonna* Rob Vernhorst, RF; **254–5** *Nirvana* George Chin, RF; **256** *Nirvana*, both by Michel Linssen, RF; **257** *Pearl Jam* Ebet Roberts, RF; **259** *Red Hot Chilli Peppers* Ebet Roberts, RF; **260** *Pearl Jam* Mick Hutson, RF; **261** *Seal* Mick Hutson, RF; **262–3** *Garth Brooks* both by PP; **264** *Eric Clapton* Ebet Roberts, RF; **266** *R.E.M.* Michel Linssen, RF; **268** *Smashing Pumpkins* Paul Bergen, RF; **269** *Sheryl Crow* PP; **271** *Johnny Cash* Beth Gwinn, RF; **272** *Jeff Buckley* Michel Linssen, RF; **274** *Nine Inch Nails* Mick Hutson, RF; **275** *TLC* Michel Linssen, RF; **276** *Radiohead* PP; **277** *Alanis Morissette* Mick Hutson, RF; **278–9** *Björk* Paul Bergen, RF; **280** *The Fugees* Mick Hutson, RF; **282** *Notorious B.I.G.* Des Willie; *2Pac* PP; **284** *Buena Vista Social Club* Paul Bergen, RF; **285** *Shania Twain* Ebet Roberts, RF; **286** *Radiohead* Ken Sharp; **287** *Flaming Lips* Brigitte Engl, RF; **288** *Fatboy Slim* PP; **290** *Dixie Chicks* Nicky J. Sims, RF; **291** *Moby* Ebet Roberts, RF; **292** *Moby* Brigitte Engl, RF; **295** *Eminem* PP; **296** *Radiohead* Mick Hutson, RF; **299** *Missy Elliott* Salifu Idriss, RF; *Timbaland* Michael Benabib; **300** *Gorillaz* JM International, RF; **302** *Norah Jones* Paul Bergen, RF; **303** *Wilco* Sam Jones, Plexifilm; **304** *Justin Timberlake* PP; **305** *Beyoncé* Tabatha Fireman, RF; *OutKast* Jon Super, RF; **306** *The White Stripes* Scarlet Page, Idols; **307** *Brian Wilson* Mick Hutson, RF; **309** *Nick Cave* Paul Bergen, RF; **311** *Foo Fighters* Martin Philbey, RF; **312** *Coldplay* Hayley Madden, RF; **313** *Bruce Springsteen* Carey Brandon, RF; **jacket back** *Brian Wilson* MOA/RF; *Frank Sinatra* MOA/RF; *Tracy Chapman* All Action/RF; *Pink Floyd* Andrew Whittuck.

Publisher's Thanks

Bill Adler, Stephen Atkinson (Rex Features), Jack Barnett, Paul Cooper, Tony Gale (Pictorial Press), Joel McIver, Nigel Osborne, Tamara Palmer, Barry Plummer, Ricky Powell, Julian Ridgway (Redfern's), Amalie R. Rothschild, John Ryall, Ken Sharp, Phil Smee, Peter Symes, York Tillyer, Chris Walter.

The publisher would also like to acknowledge the following sources, which have proved invaluable in the research and compilation of this book.

The AllMusic Guide; *Beat Instrumental*; *Before I Get Old: The Story Of The Who*, Dave Marsh; *Billboard*; *Chronicles, Volume 1*, Bob Dylan; *Down The Highway*, Howard Sounes; *The Encyclopaedia Of Pop, Rock, And Soul*, Irvin Stambler; *Entertainment Weekly*; *The Great Rock Discography*, Martin C. Strong; *Guitarist*; *Guitar World*; *History Of Rock*; *Kerrang!*; *Making Music*; *The Making Of Kind Of Blue*, Ashley Kahn; *Melody Maker*; *Mojo*; *Music Week*; *New Musical Express*; *Off The Record: An Oral History Of Popular Music*, Joe Smith; *Q*; *Q Rock Stars Encyclopaedia*, Dafydd Rees and Luke Crampton; *Record Collector*, *Rock Record*, Terry Hounsome; *Rolling Stone*; *Spin*; *Story Of Rock*; *Strange Days*; *Street Life*; *Trax*; *Village Voice*; *Where Did Our Love Go*, Nelson George

"A lot of people tell me they enjoy that album. It's hard for me to relate to people enjoying that type of pain . . ."
Bob Dylan on *Blood On The Tracks*.